MW00785799

AUTOCOURSE

Hazleton Publishing, Richmond, Surrey

Contents

Photographs in *Autocourse 1985-86* have been contributed by:
L'Agence de Presse Rougier, Bernard Asset/Agence Vandystadt, Diana Burnett, Paul-Henri Cahier, John Colley, Gary Gold, Lukas Gorys, Alan Henry, Michael Hewitt, David Hutson, International Press Agency, Michael Keppel, Charles Knight, Mike Levasheff, Lisa Newsome, Robert Newsome, Graham Smith, Nigel Snowdon, Keith Sutton, Steve Swope, John Townsend, Franco Villani, Paul Webb.

ACKNOWLEDGEMENTS

The Editor of *Autocourse* wishes to thank the following for their assistance in compiling the 1985-86 edition:
Canada: Canadian Automobile Sports Club. France: Automobiles Ligier, Renault Sport, Jean Sage. Germany: BMW GmbH, Dieter Stappert, Zakspeed Racing. Great Britain: Arrows Racing Team, John Barnard, Cosworth Engineering, Barry Griffin, Team Haas, Brian Hart, Patrick Head, Tony Jardine, Edgar Jessop, Brian Lisles, Team Lotus, McLaren International, Motor Racing Developments, Neil Oatley, RAM Automotive, Spirit Racing, Toleman Motorsport, Tyrrell Racing Organisation, Dave Wass, Williams Grand Prix Engineering, Peter Windsor. Italy: Euroracing, Ferrari SpA SEFAC, Minardi Team, Brenda Vernor. Switzerland: Kaspar Arnet, Agnes Carlier, Olivetti/Longines. United States of America: Championship Auto Racing Teams, Daytona International Speedway, International Motor Sports Association, NASCAR News Bureau, Sports Car Club of America, United States Auto Club.

PUBLISHER
Richard Poulter
EDITOR
Maurice Hamilton
EXECUTIVE PUBLISHER
Elizabeth Le Breton
PUBLISHING ASSISTANT
Jane Payton
HOUSE EDITOR
Stephen Spark
SECRETARY
Nicky Harrop
PRODUCTION ASSISTANT
Katie Fenner
RESULTS AND STATISTICS
John Taylor
LAP CHARTS
Angela Poulter
TECHNICAL CORRESPONDENT
Giorgio Piola
FRENCH EDITOR
José Rosinski
UNITED STATES EDITOR
Gordon Kirby
CHIEF PHOTOGRAPHER
Nigel Snowdon
ART EDITOR
Jim Bamber

AUTOCOURSE is published by Hazleton Publishing 3 Richmond Hill, Richmond, Surrey TW10 6RE
Printed in Holland by drukkerij de lange/van Leer bv, Deventer
Typesetting by C. Leggett & Son Ltd, Mitcham, Surrey, England.

© Hazleton Securities Ltd. 1985. No part of this publication may be reproduced, stored in a retrieval system, or transmitted, in any form or by any means, electronic, mechanical, photocopying, recording or otherwise, without prior permission in writing from Hazleton Securities Ltd.

ISBN: 0 905138 38 4

UK distribution by
Osprey Publishing Limited
12-14 Long Acre
London WC2E 9LP

United States distribution by
Motorbooks International
Publishers & Wholesalers Inc
Osceola, Wisconsin 54020
USA

The picture on the dust jacket was taken by Paul-Henri Cahier and depicts the 1985 World Champion, Alain Prost, at the wheel of his Marlboro McLaren MP4/2B.

Title page photograph:
The Champion weighs in. Alain Prost's Marlboro McLaren is checked on the scales during practice for the German Grand Prix at the new Nürburgring.
Photo: Paul-Henri Cahier

Supporting the Sport

Over the years Lucas equipped cars have been driven to more championship victories, simply because they have performed with total reliability throughout the season.

This illustrious record has been achieved by our technical support, monitoring and constant development of Lucas competition equipment which has attained a level of reliability unsurpassed in motor sport today. To pass this support on to the competitive motorist there is a nationwide network of dealers known as the "Lucas Special Section."

Racing and Competitions Department Lucas Electrical Limited
Great King Street, Birmingham B19 2XF England
Telephone: 021-554 5252

Lucas Special Section Lucas Electrical Limited
Great Hampton Street Birmingham B18 6AU
Telephone: 021-236 5050

Lucas Electrical

PARTS OF A WINNING FORMULA.

AP Racing Automotive Products plc, Leamington Spa, Warwickshire CV31 3ER. Telephone: 0926 312025. Telex: 311571 AP PLCG. Fax: 0926 35983.
Manufacturers of Lockheed brakes and Borg and Beck clutches for race cars and bikes.

Photo: Lukas Gorys

Foreword

by Alain Prost

For 35 long years, the French tried in vain to win the World Championship. In the past three years, first Didier Pironi was poised to take this hallowed title; then, on two occasions, I came close to achieving it. But still it eluded us ... At last, it is over; the curse has been beaten and I am happy to have the honour of writing the foreword which Autocourse *reserves each year for the new World Champion.*

These repeated failures eventually gave rise to doubts. Although a driver does not set out to win a championship in the same way as a Grand Prix, I am the type who always pushes himself to the limit. I have been criticised for it. So this year I decided to hold myself back. Then, to my surprise, some of those who had formerly reproached me for not being more restrained, started to criticise my lack of panache!

At the beginning of the season, some people also expressed doubts about the ability of my team to come to terms with their victory of the previous year; indeed, all the records show how difficult it is to win the World Championship more than once. But, personally, I have always felt confident. And, I was right. Nobody let up for a moment. Engineers, mechanics, engine builders, tyre technicians, have all worked with incredible motivation, at least equal to the 1984 effort.

Bear in mind that between the Brazilian Grand Prix at the opening of the season, and the Grand Prix of Europe where I secured the title, a run of 14 consecutive Grands Prix, my car did not once break down during the race! That is the true indication of the part which the team played in my victory.

Neither should I forget to mention those who set me on the road to success, particularly François Guiter of Elf. I am glad that Autocourse *gives me the opportunity of paying tribute to them.*

EXTRAO

The Eagle VR tyre has a performan

RDINARY

e level even beyond that of your car.

This is the exceptional tyre for the exceptional car.

The Eagle VR delivers control efficiency in the higher speed range ... water dispersal efficiency equal to 86% tread contact at 55 mph. The Eagle VR combines a unique uni-directional racing rain tread with exceptional mileage, steel belted toughness and an ultra smooth ride.

There is a sense of power in the control you feel when your high performance car is more than matched by the ultra high performing Eagle VR. That's Goodyear...

LEADING THE WORLD IN TYRE TECHNOLOGY

GOOD YEAR

Hello and Goodbye

As in any end of term report, the valedictory piece is the saddest and, frequently, the most difficult to write. It is even more poignant in 1985 since it has been an otherwise excellent season, the variety and competitiveness of which has made predicting the outcome of the 16 races an impossible task.

Yet, we must say farewell. The saddest sight of 1985 was the familiar figure of Niki Lauda, balaclava rolled onto his forehead, walking away from his McLaren at Adelaide. A win for The Rat would have provided a splendid finish to an excellent race and an equally remarkable career.

It would also have rounded off the season nicely. But, then, motor racing is not always that straightforward and the numbing nature of the sport froze the senses, not once, but twice in quick succession at the height of a hectic summer. To lose Manfred Winkelhock and Stefan Bellof was to be deprived of two great characters, both of whom had much to offer in different ways. Their deaths not only came as a shock to Formula 1 but the circumstances reverberated throughout Endurance Racing in a manner which highlighted several safety shortcomings.

Lauda, of course, was a great advocate of safety and the result of his work, combined with the unstinting efforts of others, has made Grand Prix racing a comparatively safe haven for drivers; so much so, that we tend to forget the standards which have been left behind and still exist in other Formulae.

Yet Formula 1 requires urgent attention, particularly in the increasingly fatuous business of qualifying, a procedure which bears no relation to the race. To allow teams to use engines of 1000 bhp and more and yet restrict power in the race illustrates the blind folly shown by Formula 1. It seems ludicrous that a great deal of fuss can be made over the dimension of brake ducts and yet nothing is done about the serious and potentially lethal situation presented by a driver running enormous boost on just two sets of qualifying tyres. Lauda was right. Form the starting grid on the result of the last race and be done with it. You win some, lose some but, at the end of the day, the well-organised and talented performers will win through.

Lauda's departure leaves a void in Formula 1 but, fortunately, the fast-moving and competitive nature of the sport brings forward replacements. And, in that respect, 1985 will be remembered for the emergence of Ayrton Senna as well as bringing the crowning achievement of Alain Prost's career.

To watch Senna claim pole position is to witness a deft performance which is on a different plane. Without doubt, Senna will be the star of the next decade and it is not a question of *whether* he will feature on the cover of this book, but, *when*.

In the meantime, we salute Alain Prost and McLaren International. To win the title two years in succession is something to be justifiably proud of – particularly in the face of such excellent competition. Prost, of course, had to fight his own battles as he fended off the attention of the home press, anxious to fête the first Frenchman to win the title.

The Formula 1 mechanics join the Renault team in a pit lane farewell in Adelaide.

Bellof and Winkelhock.

Never mind the spelling, it's the thought that counts. Australia's farewell to Niki Lauda.

Mass Media. Alain Prost survived the heavy pressure exerted by the jingoistic French Press. At Kyalami, once the Championship had been won, there was hardly a French journalist to be seen. . . .
Photo: Paul-Henri Cahier

That was at Brands Hatch. Two weeks later and there was hardly a Frenchman to be seen at Kyalami. Such hypocrisy is laughable in a sport which is quite happy to race in Brazil or behind the Iron Curtain. And as for Jean-Marie Balestre's astounding conceit when he claimed his presence in South Africa would have political overtones . . .

Away with politics. We have, inside the covers of this book, a record of one of the toughest seasons of Grand Prix racing. There are, as usual, detailed reports of each race and you may at first be alarmed by the apparent absence of Grand Prix statistics. Fear not. Limitations of space and the need to avoid wasting colour pages has prompted the grouping of the statistics at the end of the book rather than alongside each Grand Prix. We hope you find this more convenient when making seasonal comparisons.

Reviewing the season in words, Doug Nye and Russell Bulgin delve into the various technical and human aspects, each writer stamping his own opinions on the facts and figures which emerge. Lauda, of course, cared little about statistics although Jackie Stewart's record of 27 wins undoubtedly beckoned. A win in Australia would not have helped but it would have given the people of Adelaide an appropriate finish to what was, unquestionably, the Race of the Year.

Adelaide also marked the last race for Renault, the team which introduced turbocharging to contemporary Formula 1 but failed to make the most of their advantage while it lasted. During their brief stay in Grand Prix racing, the Renault team brought a typically French flavour to the pit lane. They may have been ridiculed at first, but the grudging acceptance of a major manufacturer in Formula 1 makes their rather unnecessary departure all the more unfortunate.

Maurice Hamilton
Ewhurst, Surrey
November 1985

MAKE MORE VROOO

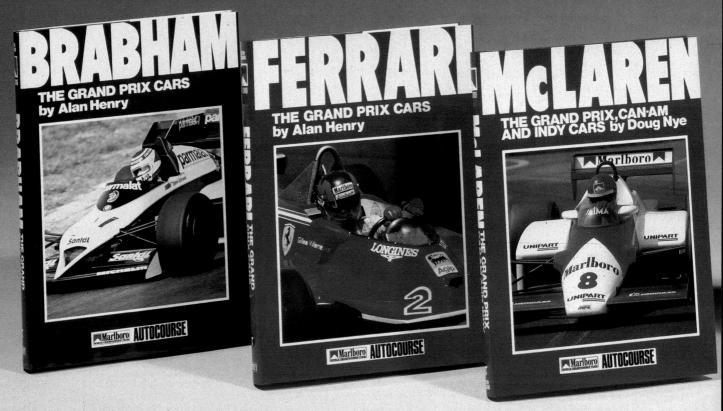

BRABHAM: The Grand Prix Cars by Alan Henry

The latest in the AUTOCOURSE marque history series, this book charts the story of the Brabham Grand Prix team from its early pioneering days in the Sixties through the takeover of the team by Bernie Ecclestone in 1972.

A succession of technically ambitious Formula 1 contenders emerged, including the cars which propelled Nelson Piquet to his World Championship titles in 1981 and 1983.

With personal reminiscences of designers and drivers the reader is given a unique insight into one of today's leading Formula 1 teams.

28 colour and 127 black & white photographs
288 pages 240mm × 170mm Hardback
ISBN: 0 905138 36 8
Price: £14.95

FERRARI: The Grand Prix Cars by Alan Henry

This volume takes the story of the most famous Italian racing marque of them all from its first hesitant steps on to the Grand Prix stage in the early post-war years through to its World Constructor's Championship winning status in the highly specialised and complicated world of turbocharged Grand Prix engines in the 1980s.

35 colour and over 100 black & white photographs
320 pages 240mm × 170mm Hardback
ISBN: 0 905138 30 9
Price: £14.95

McLAREN: The Grand Prix, Can-Am & Indy Cars by Doug Nye

Another of the AUTOCOURSE marque histories – this is the full story of McLaren cars from 1963 and of the subsequent McLaren International team carrying on the old traditions.

Emerson Fittipaldi won the first Grand Prix World Championship title for McLaren in 1974 and two years later James Hunt did it again, winning his historic season-long battle with Niki Lauda.

The cars, the races, the men behind the scenes – it's all here, supported by comprehensive appendices providing detailed race results and chassis numbers.

20 colour and over 90 black & white photographs
270 pages 240mm × 170mm Hardback
ISBN: 0 905138 28 7
Price: £12.95

MOTOR SPORT BOOKS FROM HAZLETON

M ON YOUR SHELVES

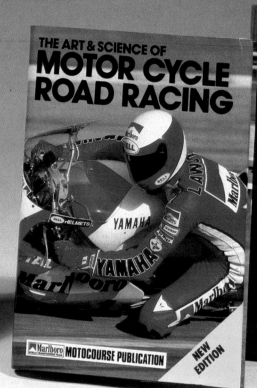

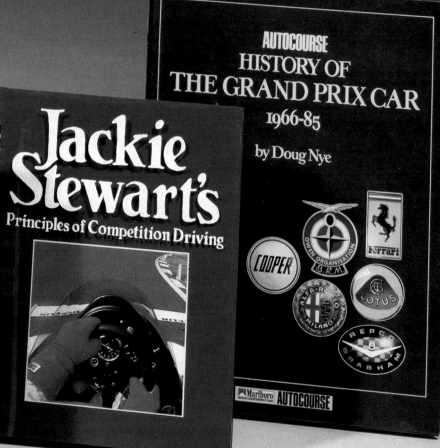

THE ART & SCIENCE OF MOTOR CYCLE ROAD RACING
by Peter Clifford

The second edition of this best-selling book which has been acclaimed as the most accurate and authoritative account of the skills and principles involved in motor cycle road racing.

Cornering, engines, steering, suspension, frames, tyres – all are explored in detail, with advice and explanations from the sport's most respected personalities – plus a completely new chapter covering the latest technical innovations and how these affect the rider.

20 colour and 80 black & white photographs
272 pages 240mm × 170mm Hardback
ISBN: 0 905138 35 X
Price: £12.95

JACKIE STEWART'S PRINCIPLES OF COMPETITION DRIVING

Jackie Stewart's name became a legend in Grand Prix racing when he retired in 1973 with three World Championships and a record number of Grand Prix wins to his credit.

Now, for the first time, he shares his own personal insights into the essential skills needed to become a champion driver and reveals his views on the many attributes needed both on and off the track to compete at peak performance.

This is not merely a 'how to race' book, instead it gives the reader a very personal look at what it takes to be a winner.

16 colour and 130 black & white photographs and illustrations
232 pages 244mm × 184mm Hardback
ISBN: 0 905138 43 0
Price: £15.95
Publication: Autumn 1986

THE AUTOCOURSE HISTORY OF THE GRAND PRIX CAR 1966–85
by Doug Nye

This detailed, illustrated history book spans the era from the 350 horsepower tube-framed cars to the nearly 800 horsepower turbocharged carbon-composite cars of 1985. The fortunes of the great teams and the not-so-great are described – combining the inside technical story of the cars with the human story of the men who devised, designed and developed them.

To be published in Spring 1986, this major production from the AUTOCOURSE stable will be essential reading for all Formula 1 enthusiasts and an important collector's item.

50 colour and 250 black & white photographs, plus factory blueprints
256 pages 313mm × 233mm Hardback
ISBN: 0 905138 37 6
Price: £19.95
Publication: Spring 1986

Published by Hazleton Publishing, 3 Richmond Hill, Richmond, Surrey TW10 6RE
Distributed by Osprey Publishing Ltd and available through your local or specialist bookshop.

The Editor's evaluation of the leading Grand Prix drivers in 1985

TOP TEN

Alain Prost

1 **Alain Prost**
2 **Ayrton Senna**
3 **Keke Rosberg**
4 **Nelson Piquet**
5 **Michele Alboreto**
6 **Nigel Mansell**
7 **Niki Lauda**
8 **Elio de Angelis**
9 **Stefan Johansson**
10 **Thierry Boutsen**

1 Alain Prost

Is Alain Prost better than Ayrton Senna? In the long run, probably not. But, in terms of getting the job done with the equipment available, Prost had no equal in 1985 and there are those who will argue strongly that he *is* the top driver. On the other hand, he has yet to convince one or two doubters of his all-round ability. They will point to his spins at Estoril and the Nürburgring. If that is the sum total of his errors then it is better to look at the beautifully controlled race at Rio, the tactical drive at Imola, the self-control at Monaco, the brave practice lap at Detroit, the daring overtaking move on Rosberg at Ricard, the flawless drive in Austria, the ability to accept second and let Rosberg go at Monza. The fact that he actually took nine points in Italy indicates that good fortune was on his side at times. But Prost's diligent work during testing and practice illustrated how a driver with the ability to drive quickly at any circuit can generate his own luck.

2 Ayrton Senna

A driver of such staggering potential that he is widely disliked in the pit lane. Rivals, frustrated by his innate skill, question his Formula 3 tactics under pressure but when it comes to using his car – controlling it with deceptive ease – Ayrton Senna has no peers. Despite his inexperience, he showed remarkable calm at Rio and Estoril and the manner in which he overcame an open dislike of Detroit to take pole gave some indication of a commitment to succeed which is frightening in its intensity. And succeed he will, judging by the ability to shake off a disastrous day of practice at Spa, claim a place on the front row and then lead with ice-cold confidence. It has been a character-building season for the man who led at Imola, Monaco, Detroit, Silverstone, the Nürburgring, Brands Hatch and Adelaide, only to be heavily criticised for the slightest indiscretion. He *knows* he is the best – but rivals who vaguely understand him say he will go to pieces if this belief is blown apart unexpectedly. Was his uncharacteristic performance at Adelaide a case in point?

3 Keke Rosberg

The list is endless; practice at Rio, Estoril and Imola, the race at Detroit, practice and the race in France, pole again at Silverstone, the race at Zandvoort, practice and the race at Monza, the charge at Brands Hatch and Kyalami, the race at Adelaide; take any one of the foregoing and you have a virtuoso performance from a driver who is a superb qualifier and a never-say-die racer. As far as Rosberg was concerned, the Williams FW10 was there to be *used*. His ability to amble across the pit lane, climb aboard and take the car to its limit – immediately – had about it a carefree and exuberant quality which cut a delightful swathe through the serious image of Formula 1. And, more important, there were few mistakes as a result of this on-the-limit brilliance. In 1986, Rosberg moves to McLaren to pit his raw ability against the cool precision of the reigning World Champion. Who will win? The decision could go either way. That says a lot for Keke Rosberg.

Keke Rosberg

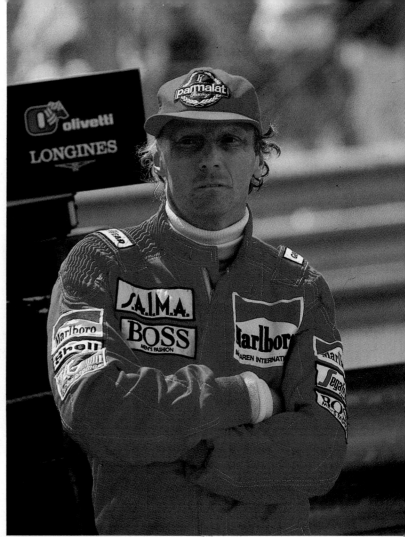

Bernard Asset

Alain Prost, Niki Lauda and Michele
Alboreto scored victories for the Marlboro
World Championship Team although the
Ferrari driver's win in Canada played a
small part in the overall picture of the 1985
season.

4 Nelson Piquet

The argument still stands; Nelson Piquet is considered by many to be better than Prost and Senna. A bitterly disappointing season in spite of a 100 per cent effort by Nelson to overcome the Pirelli shortcomings. The progress made by Brabham and Pirelli was due entirely to Piquet's dedication and willingness to churn out miles and miles of testing; the grid positions for Brabham number seven were thanks to his unbridled enthusiasm for controlling a difficult car propelled by prodigious qualifying power. And, when race day conditions were right (a regrettably rare occurrence) we saw the fluid style which will make Piquet the favourite for 1986. Two World Championships are not enough for Nelson Piquet; the Williams-Honda-Goodyear package will help him succeed where the Brabham-BMW-Pirelli combination failed.

5 Michele Alboreto

Ferrari wrecked his chances of winning the Championship and yet Alboreto did not throw a tantrum, nor did he throw his car into the wall in desperation. That, perhaps, was a failing as much as it was an attribute. The feeling persists that Michele will drop into a lower mental gear if the equipment is not perfect. But, when the car is competitive, as it was during the first half of the season, then we are treated to the precision and speed seen at Monaco and Montreal, drives which helped Alboreto lead the Championship. Luck did attend one or two performances but the fact remains that Ferrari failed to capitalise on this easly-season momentum – and Alboreto seemed incapable of helping the team extract themselves from the technical mire when the momentum ceased.

6 Nigel Mansell

The switch to Williams vindicated everything we said last year. A more sympathetic environment put Mansell at ease and he found his own level rather than desperately trying to emulate Rosberg. The result? Mansell out-qualified the Fastest Man in the World seven times and took two wins which were notable for a new-found assurance to match the basic skills which had been lurking beneath a previously troubled surface. The season started badly at Rio and seemed to plumb new depths of misfortune at Ricard. Mansell's comeback at Silverstone, when everything was at stake, ranks alongside his head-down performance at Monza, where there was little to achieve other than fastest lap and a great deal of personal satisfaction. The most-improved performer of the year, Mansell may not be in the Piquet mould but the comparison in 1986 will be an interesting one.

Marlboro WORLD CHAMPIONSHIP TEAM
AUTOCOURSE DIARY & CALENDAR 1986

KEEP TRACK IN 1986

AUTOCOURSE Grand Prix Calendar 1986 **Marlboro** WORLD CHAMPIONSHIP TEAM

Make 1986 a 'record' year with the latest AUTOCOURSE calendar and pocket diary.

The 96-page diary features: exclusive driver profiles, Formula 1 team information, race-by-race recording sections, detailed circuit diagrams, previous championship results, PLUS 16 pages of full-colour photographs and a page-per-week general diary section.

The large-format, 13-leaf calendar vividly recreates the action and atmosphere of the Formula One season in 37 sensational full colour photographs – every motor racing enthusiast should have one.

The Pocket Diary measures 172 x 81mm and costs £4.60. The Calendar measures 590 x 420mm and costs £7.00. Order your Calendar or Diary from the address given below – but order both together and take advantage of the special combined offer price of £10.60 – a saving of £1.

(All prices include VAT, postage and packing.)
Send your order today, making cheque or postal order payable to HAZLETON PUBLISHING. Note that cheques on orders from outside the U.K. must be drawn on a London bank in £ Sterling, no Eurocheques. Calendars/Diaries will be despatched separately. Order now! They go faster every year.

Marlboro Autocourse Diary Offer

Hazleton Publishing
3 Richmond Hill, Richmond, Surrey TW10 6RE

7 Niki Lauda

It was the usual story: practice would be average; the race, a perfect blend of tactics and just enough speed without sacrificing the car and tyres. We had one or two lacklustre performances but, from Silverstone on, there followed a string of drives which showed the importance of winning in Lauda's uncomplicated and practical lexicon of motor racing. The reliability of his car was appalling (by McLaren's standards) and Lauda was denied at least two wins as he shaped up to strike at the appropriate moment. But, at Zandvoort, he showed the value of his unrivalled experience by turning on a classic display of racecraft. The saddest aspect of 1985 was his retirement at Adelaide. This gentle drive, from 16th place to the front of the field, embodied everything we had come to expect – and, regrettably, will no longer enjoy.

8 Elio de Angelis

Very much the Number Two driver. The gradual assumption of control by his team-mate appeared to dull de Angelis' superb natural talent; whether that was self-inflicted or brought about by politics within the team depends on who you talk to. Paradoxically, Elio's ability to bring the car home paid dividends in the first half of the season. Then, the mechanical reliability disappeared under equally obscure circumstances. Was it the car? Was it the driver? The move to a new team will allow one of the quickest drivers around to answer that – assuming he is hungry enough.

9 Stefan Johansson

His most outstanding achievement has been to win a second term with Ferrari. That answers all the arguments about the quality of his car, his ability as a test driver, the problems during practice; Stefan did enough when it mattered most. He is a racer pure and simple. Johansson's uncomplicated approach allowed him to deal with the pressures and schedules which suddenly changed his life last April. He responded by driving with a seat-of-the-pants ability which skirted around, rather than cured, deficiencies in the car but, none the less, the ability to charge in the second half of the race brought a number of finishes in the points. And, when the car was good, Detroit and Montreal showed the true potential of a driver who puts the lie to the saying: 'There's no prizes for the nice guys'.

10 Thierry Boutsen

Thierry Boutsen is not underrated by the Formula 1 world despite a lack of results. He is the Arrows team's greatest asset. Quiet, unassuming, very talented, Boutsen's qualifying performance at Monaco with a less than nimble car underscored his delicate control. He deserved a better result after such a heroic effort and, conversely, seventh at Detroit was a timely reward for an impressive recovery from a terrible practice. Spa brought his ability into perspective but that was to be one of the few occasions when the mechanical problems would be severe enough to prevent Boutsen's sympathetic touch from nursing the car home. Put him in a Williams and we would be talking about championship potential in 1986.

Tenth place was a toss-up between Boutsen and Patrick Tambay, the Frenchman emerging from a difficult season in a manner which underlines his status as a thorough professional. The Renault RE60 was a lemon from the moment it first turned a wheel but Tambay persisted and continued to give gutsy performances – Rio, Estoril and Ricard – and he out-qualified Derek Warwick for five races in succession in the second half of the season. Warwick seemed to have the upper hand at the start of the year but, in total, 1985 was a complete disaster. Personal upheavals did not help and Warwick did not appear to cope as well as Tambay when the Renault's inconsistent performances continued to baffle the drivers, never mind the alleged technical brilliance of Gérard Toth. There were flashes of Warwick the Racer (the practice lap at Detroit, the determination to finish at Silverstone and a hard-charging drive at Spa) but, otherwise, Derek will be keen to forget a season which did its best to wreck his career. If anyone can survive, however, it's the guy who remains one of the sunniest and most unaffected drivers around.

Running through the remainder of entry list, it is appropriate that we should reach Martin Brundle first. Brundle may not have emerged with championship points (a fact which may haunt him needlessly over the winter) but he did very little to harm a growing reputation as a clean and eminently sensible racer. The manner in which he overcame the mental bogey of qualifying and racing at Monaco (in the light of his street-circuit shunts the previous year) cannot be understated. Indeed, Brundle poses the 'If only . .' question of the year. If only he had allowed Alliot the benefit of the doubt at Detroit then a classic drive would not have ended against the wall. Mind you, if he *had* been more circumspect, he would not have been running fourth at the time . . .

One of Brundle's assets is a realistic analysis of his talent and he was the first to appreciate that, on a lap for lap basis, he was not as quick as Stefan Bellof (although Monaco tended to disprove the theory). The loss of the affable German remains one of the season's great tragedies. His performance in the wet at Estoril and the ability to bring his car home at Detroit, despite a broken clutch, hinted at the consistency which, combined with his tingling car control, would have made Bellof one of the great drivers of the Eighties.

Tyrrell chose to replace Bellof with Ivan Capelli and Philippe Streiff, two drivers who can be judged to have great potential, even on their limited showings in 1985. Capelli, a perky and intelligent young Italian, was given the impossible task of making his debut at Brands Hatch. He was quick to learn and Adelaide showed that he has enough composure to stay the distance and bring the car home. Streiff, serious and outwardly more sure of himself than Capelli, has the speed (witness his Ligier drive at Brands Hatch) but his tactics at Adelaide (regardless of his genuine excuse) were mind-blowing in their stupidity.

There can have bee no more gratifying sight in 1985 than to watch Marc Surer's solid performance with the number two Brabham, a traditional Formula 1 backwater. No one can compare with Nelson Piquet in a Brabham yet Surer grabbed his opportunity and frequently qualified within a second of the Brazilian. He was often amazed by Nelson's speed and yet was realistic enough to accept it, all of which made him the perfect number two. François Hesnault had four races with Brabham but, in the light of Surer's performances, the Frenchman did little to develop a reasonable reputation forged with Ligier in 1984.

A drive with the Gustav Brunner-designed RAM promised much for Manfred Winkelhock but it was not to be, a series of quick and brave drives being confounded by an endless run of mechanical problems. Manfred may have been hard on the car, but he was an all-or-nothing racer who deserved greater success before his untimely and sad departure. John Macdonald chose Kenny Acheson as a replacement and, again, the drive should have polished a reputation revived by a successful season in Japan. Problems within the team did not allow Acheson the chance he deserved. Philippe Alliot, on the other hand, did have the opportunity to save RAM from an ignominious end but, unfortunately for the Frenchman, he will be remembered for throwing away a place in the points at Spa.

Gerhard Berger out-qualified Thierry Boutsen at Spa, which says much for his natural talent and startling *brio*. At Monaco and Detroit he was positively frightening during qualifying but the fact remains that he had fewer shunts than his flamboyant style suggests. Remember, Berger has just completed his fifth full season of racing – ever. It also pays to be reminded that four months before the start of the season, Berger was recovering from a broken neck sustained in a road accident. Here is a driver of great potential who needs Tyrrell-type control and moulding.

The award for the enigmatic driver of the year goes to Teo Fabi. The tendency is to forget about the diminutive and shy Italian but the quality of the Toleman chassis allowed him to speak loudly on the track. Let down by technical problems as the team attempted the impossible by joining in while the season was in full flight, Fabi nevertheless showed the potential is there. The switch to BMW power will propel Toleman into contention and a solid programme of testing should give Fabi that final boost to his confidence.

As soon as Toleman were able to run a second car, they chose Piercarlo Ghinzani, a logical move. In the event, the Italian has been slightly disappointing although it is difficult to judge fairly when the team have been struggling to keep pace

themselves. The unsettled mood did not help Ghinzani relax until the end of the season when he began to keep pace with Fabi. But, by then, it may have been too late . . .

Riccardo Patrese can ill-afford another season like 1985. His reputation did flourish – but in the wrong direction. There was the usual sprinkling of accusations about his apparent inability to use a rear-view mirror but the Monaco fiasco punted him into the headlines thanks to a piece of thoroughly irresponsible driving. The shame is that Patrese started out with good intentions. He was fit, he qualified well, tried hard but, somehow, the year brought very little to highlight his natural talent. With so many young chargers on the grid, Patrese's time may have passed him by. The same could be said for Eddie Cheever. But that would be equally unjust. The Alfa Romeos have been appalling but, in the rare moments when they remained assembled and competitive, Cheever has shown the flair which surfaces when conditions favour the driver rather than the car. It would be Formula 1's loss if Eddie were to be left out in the cold. The spectators would miss the hellfire and fury of his energetic driving; the pressmen would miss the wonderful quotes.

When Ghinzani left Osella for Toleman, he was replaced by Huub Rothengatter, a driver who wins the Resilience Prize for 1985. Quite how he persevered so cheerfully with such a dreadful car remains a mystery. In the light of Andrea de Cesaris's accident at the Österreichring, it is easy to understand why Ligier dismissed the Italian. And yet he continued to give deft performances which were not blemished by bouts of brain-fade. On the other hand, the incident when he spun at Montreal and collected the hapless Winkelhock, the silly manoeuvre at Rio and the shunt at Imola, tended to support Guy Ligier's decision.

So Jacques Laffite did not retire after all; thank goodness for that. The sunny Frenchman may have seen practice as an interruption to his golf and fishing but he never failed to give his best in the races. And the net result of a wealth of experience was three well-deserved visits to the rostrum and a gentle poke in the ribs for the more serious members of Formula 1.

Pierluigi Martini would have been better off in Formula 3000; there, at least, he might have qualified on the penultimate row rather than at the very back of the Formula 1 grid. If that sounds unfair, remember his hopeless attempt to qualify the Toleman at Monza in 1984, the car then at the peak of its form. Martini may have been up against it with a fledgling team and a capricious car but that merely added to the danger he imposed on other drivers. So much for the FISA Superlicence . . .

Any sympathy there may have been for the Minardi team was lost once the highly professional Zakspeed outfit arrived. And much of the credit must rest with Jonathan Palmer. If you doubted the value of the Englishman's enthusiastic and irrepressible input, you only had to look in the Zakspeed garage at Spa. While Palmer languished in hospital, the team appeared to lose their sense of direction, if not that extra spark of vitality. Qualifying and finishing at Monaco remains one of the outstanding achievements of the year. And they can only get better.

Much the same applies to the Beatrice team. With such a wealth of experience spreading from the management team to an accomplished band of mechanics, the thought of Alan Jones getting his hands on the Ford-Cosworth turbo must worry other teams. He may have had trouble completing more than a handful of laps at a time, but Jones did show that he has not been deserted by the determination and single-minded racing instincts which won him the Championship in 1980.

Jacques Laffite

Great performers

One of the world's great performers set numerous track records in the Sports Car Club of America's 1985 Trans Am and National racing series. Paul Newman and his partner Jim Fitzgerald enjoyed a successful season in the Bob Sharp Racing Team's Nissan 300ZX Turbos. One of the main reasons behind their great performances? A Bendix electronic engine control system and Bendix DEKA™ fuel injectors developed by Allied Automotive. Both are available to car and truck makers today.

The Bendix electronic fuel injection system used by Bob Sharp Racing provides improved programming flexibility, greater power over a broader speed range and better dynamic response than the system it replaced. Fiber optics are used to eliminate electromagnetic interference — one of the first such applications in an engine control system.

Bendix DEKA™ fuel injectors are critical links in the system. These high-performance injectors,

deserve great parts.

with exceptional dynamic range capability, allow a system design using only one injector per cylinder.

The Bob Sharp Racing Team uses other Allied Automotive high-performance components, including Autolite spark plugs, Prestolite ignition wires and Fram filters. And we're working with Bob Sharp Racing in developing and testing new Bendix friction materials for competition and commercial brake applications.

In the automotive business where performance is the name of the game, Allied Automotive plays a leading role in supplying the world's vehicle manufacturers and the aftermarket with great parts.

Allied Corporation, Automotive Sector, World Headquarters, P.O. Box 5029, Southfield, MI 48086.

© 1985 Allied Corporation

 Automotive

AT LAST A HO
NOISY, CRAMP
A FORTUN

ONDA THAT'S
ED AND COSTS
E TO RUN.

Honda. Our standards are higher.

HONDA (UK) LIMITED., POWER ROAD, CHISWICK, LONDON W4 5YT.

Is your team in a bad way? Are your results getting worse all the time? Is your status becoming doubtful? Don't waste a second . . . only one place to go – call in the Miracle Man! Present him with an impossible task, a dangerous bet, an insane challenge, and, if possible, a large cheque. This Zorro, Gérard Ducarouge, will come to your rescue . . .

'Murray, Barnard, Head, they are stable, well-established assets. As a result of this, they can, at a stretch, afford to make a mistake from time to time. But I can't. Ducarouge, as you say, is the Miracle Man of Formula 1. I'm called in to the hopeless cases. So, I can't afford to make a mistake.'

That would be too much of a risk, as much to the reputation of the doctor as to the health of the patient. It is true that technical chiefs are generally stable people. Murray is identified with Brabham in the same way as Barnard is with McLaren or Head with Williams. Once it was the same for Ducarouge at Ligier. Between 1976 and 1981 it would have been impossible to imagine the 'Blues' without him.

However, one fine day, right in the middle of the '81 season, the path of his destiny, which he thought was all planned out, took an abrupt turn. It was 'turned around' by Guy Ligier himself, the boss but also a friend, to end the association of two 'mates' thought to have been inseparable.

'It was a terrible wrench', recalls Gérard. 'I went through a bad time, without doubt the worst time of my life.' The divorce was brutal and took everyone by surprise, including Gérard himself. Now the wound has healed, the two men are once again on friendly terms and the press even suggest, from time to time, the return of the prodigal son to Vichy. 'Above all else Gérard is a tremendous worker, and is passionately involved in his work', says Guy Ligier. 'Bear in mind that the team at that time comprised only 27 people. He was everywhere, doing everything . . .'

Perhaps he even did too much? 'The tale of Ligier in Formula 1, is one of constant challenge', Ducarouge recounts. 'There was no structure or organisation and, above all, no money! I had to be in several places at once. For me, arriving from Matra, it was like the world turned up side down.'

Qualified by diploma as an Advanced Aeronautic Technician, Ducarouge does not hold a degree in engineering. He was not particularly interested in motor racing, but became bored with his routine job at Nord Aviation. This prompted him to reply one day to a small advertisement from Matra-Sports, where he started work on 1 January 1966. He was installed in the Sports-Prototype department because he had the rare ability among technicians to speak English, and he was given the job of liaison with BRM who at that time were supplying their engines for the Matra M620 endurance car.

'Endurance racing is fantastic because of the team work. From this point of view, I still miss it today, you feel much more involved than in Formula 1, and really get the feeling of taking part in the race, from start to finish.'

Paradoxically, in his nine seasons with Matra, Ducarouge never had anything to do with Formula 1, although in 1968, when the MS11 had its debut at Monaco in the hands of Beltoise, Gérard was already in charge of prototype development. 'I learned my trade on the shop-floor, watching and benefiting from the experience of others. To start with, as I was a good draughtsman, they put me in the drawing office.'

But I am really a rather down to earth man. Little by little I started suggesting small modifications, mainly of a practical nature, to make the mechanic's job easier or the cars more reliable.' Moreover, Gérard quickly established himself as an exceptional organiser with the title of 'Head of Operations'. He became the force behind the historic Matra triple championship in the Le Mans 24 Hours of 1972, 1973 and 1974 and of two World titles which the French team carried off in 1973 and 1974 at the expense of Ferrari and Alfa Romeo. But the epic story of Matra Sports came to an end.

'At that time I found myself with two alternatives before me: to be relocated within the group in their space division (that was the safe option) or to accept an offer from Ligier, who was getting together a Formula 1 Team. One of the marvellous things about Matra was that they always had funds available. Nothing was too expensive or too much of a luxury, as long as it was well justified and in those conditions a perfectionist like me is in seventh heaven. On the other hand I was only a small fish in a big pond – an important one perhaps but nothing more. Ligier gave me the chance to take control of everything.'

The Ligier JS5 was the first car designed by Gérard Ducarouge, and the first Formula 1 car with which he had been involved. It was technically similar to the Matra in every way, as he willingly admits. Likewise, he makes no bones about the fact that he is no 'visionary'.

'I am a man in a hurry. I am not used to working on long term projects. I like to be able to see the fruits of my labours in the shortest possible time – by a pole position in practice or by winning a race. That is why I put my faith more in a methodical approach rather than inspiration.' It is this characteristic which provides one of the greatest contradictions to mark Ducarouge's career – succeeding Colin Chapman, who represented exactly the opposite approach.

'During Colin's time the team progressed according to the pattern of his inspired ideas – in dramatic leaps', recalls Peter Warr. 'With Gérard it works quite differently. Far more time is devoted to researching the details and in checking calculations and innovations and to a gradual development programme. Also, Gérard likes everyone to work very fast, but we are quite used to that at Lotus, so it suits us very well. Perhaps we have even surprised him . . .'

Here Warr is referring to the incredible achievement of Ducarouge and JPS Team Lotus when they constructed the 94T in the record time of five weeks in June/July 1983. A challenge in the true Gérard style, who, rather than try and patch up the 93T, preferred to start almost from scratch, in spite of the almost impossibly tight schedule which Peter Warr had presented him with.

Ducarouge says reassuringly: 'In my opinion, it

The
Miracle Man

A profile of Gérard Ducarouge
by José Rosinski

AFTER THE CALM, THE SOUND

For 16 World Championship Formula I seasons, the Ford
Cosworth DFV engine has been the dominant force in
international motor sport. In addition to being the power
behind the winners of 155 World Championship Grands Prix,
12 FI Drivers' and 10 Constructors' World Championships, the
3.0 litre Ford V8 has provided the outstanding performance
and reliability necessary to win the Le Mans 24 hours
endurance race—twice as well as Division 2 of this year's
World Endurance Championship. In its turbocharged DFX
form, it has also powered the winning cars at Indianapolis for
the past eight years. With total production now well past
the 500 mark, this world-famous V8 has set a sales record
which is unlikely to be repeated.
Now Ford and Cosworth have joined forces again; dedicated
teams of engineers, scientists and electronics experts are
well advanced in the design, development and production
of a totally new family of race winning engines.
The turbocharged 1.5 litre V6 Ford FI engine will be
racing with the new Beatrice team early in 1986.

OF DISTANT THUNDER

Reliability and the art of the driver are as important as ever, but tyres, new materials and fuel economy have substantially changed the design requirements of the sport. And that is why Ford is bringing new thought to the Formula I engine.

Proposed design for cam covers.

Preaching the gospel of St Gérard. Ducarouge confers with de Angelis at Ricard.

'My most satisfying professional achievement, to date, is to have designed the JS19. At the beginning of the '79 season we were way ahead of the others. But they copied us after six months, they overtook us, because we had run out of money and could not continue with our development programme.'

'Of all the drivers I have worked with, Senna is the most outstanding. He is unbelievably clear-sighted; he is capable of mentally dividing a corner into four parts to enable him to describe to you how the car behaved during each stage, while he was actually recording a timed practice lap . . . It's magic!'

was, in fact, the least risky solution to the problem. On the one hand, I had no guarantee of succeeding with improvements to a car that I had not designed and which was very different from those I was familiar with. On the other hand, I had the conviction that with the tremendous support and potential which Team Lotus possessed we could construct a competitive Formula 1 car.'

There remained the time problem: a challenge. None the less, Elio de Angelis achieved the fastest time of the first practice session for the British Grand Prix, hardly six weeks after Ducarouge had accepted Peter Warr's proposition.

Gérard Crombac recounts the story that Ducarouge had earlier been contacted by Colin Chapman who had taken him to Norwich in his plane. At the end of the visit to Ketteringham Hall, Chapman showed him into a huge finely furnished room and said 'Gérard this is your office'.

'But I wasn't able to make up my mind', confesses Ducarouge. 'I was flattered, but I feared that living with a man endowed with such a forceful personality would be difficult. For the same reason, I cannot see myself at Ferrari . . .'

He did, in truth, suffer a bitter experience with Carlo Chiti when he joined Autodelta straight after his separation from Ligier. 'A terrible wasted opportunity', he recalls. 'However, everything started well. I came into action at Zandvoort, at the end of August, and Giacomelli, who hadn't scored a single point until then through the preceding 11 Grands Prix, came in third at Montreal and fourth at Las Vegas, only just saving the season for the team. But my relationship with Chiti went quickly downhill. At the beginning of 1982 at Long Beach, de Cesaris was taking pole position and leading the race, whereas in Milan I was organising the building of new workshops. Alas, they were never used. At the end of the season the President of Alfa Romeo called me in to tell me that Formula 1 effort had been handed to Euroracing for 1983. I went to join them and was devastated to discover that all I could do was to start all over again.'

Not so easily discouraged, Ducarouge then undertook the organisation of the building of a second workshop in the space of a few months. Unfortunately, and albeit for different reasons, things went no better with Pavanello than they had with Chiti: 'We were not on the same wavelength', he says with regret. 'I asked him to invest money in testing, in development and wind tunnel testing. He wanted to make cut-backs . . .'

At the time of practice for the French Grand Prix in 1983, de Cesaris was credited with fastest time in the first qualifying session. But in the scrutineering, it was discovered that he had been running with empty fire extinguishers . . . The driver was disqualified, and our hero, who carried the can, was fired by his team. For the second time in two years, Ducarouge found himself out of a job right in the middle of the season! But again, not for long. Five weeks later, he fastened his suitcase for Norwich.

Thus by chance and by necessity, Gérard Ducarouge has become a sort of mercenary, an exile for more than four years. Of course, a prophet is not recognised in his own country, but it is none the less ironic that the foremost French chassis specialist has never been invited to join the Renault-Elf team.

In fact, this almost happened in 1983, when at the end of the year Prost suggested to Bernard Hanon a reorganisation of Renault Sports, involving the transfer of the Chassis Department to the Paul Ricard Circuit with Gérard Ducarouge at the head. 'Renault had everything necessary to succeed in F1, on the condition that they distanced themselves from the tight hold of the hierarchy and worked in a much more autonomous way', Gerard confirms. But the project never took off. Prost left France, and Ducarouge never went back . . .

With his head in Norwich, and his heart in Paris where his wife Colette still lives and whose life he only shares at Grand Prix weekends, Gérard is not comfortable with this state of affairs. In addition, his flamboyant nature does not always fit in well with the natural reserve of the British. This becomes apparent on occasions when, to the horror of Peter Warr, 'Ducared' comes out with some spontaneous (and not always very diplomatic) remarks in front of the press . . . The man himself is subject to extremes of depression as well as of enthusiasm, and whatever he says or does is adjusted by people who know him well using the 'Ducarouge co-efficient'. But this behaviour is all part of his charm.

Nine years with Matra, seven with Ligier, two with Alfa and three with Lotus: Gérard Ducarouge alias Ducarosso, alias Ducared, has a wealth of experience.

And, for the future, there is no doubt that he dreams of being his own boss. He is sought after by several racing teams but his ambition in the long term is to set one up himself. The Ducarouge Dream? Why not? At 44 years old he still has his future ahead of him.

Elio de Angelis led the championship during the early part of the season in the Lotus 97T.

Alain Prost

John Townsend

Champion du Monde

by Nigel Roebuck, Grand Prix Editor, *Autosport*

'By this time tomorrow', Patrick Tambay said to me at Brands Hatch, 'Prost will be World Champion. And, you know, he is *still* underrated! I think it's incredible. People talk about "natural talent", a gift for driving race cars, and I suppose we must all have it in different degrees. But during my time in racing I would say there have been three with something extra – and maybe that "something extra" was different in each case. The three? Villeneuve, Senna, Prost.'

As usual Alain won more races than anyone else this year, but it was gratifying that in 1985 they brought him the World Championship. In the three seasons preceding this one, he had more victories than the man who took the title. It was an irony that he clinched it with a fourth place at Brands Hatch, having for once played no significant role in the race.

'I took the Championship lead back from Alboreto in Holland', he says, 'and then I looked at the situation. There were six races to go, and I had only three points' advantage. In 1983 I led by 14 points with only four races left – and I lost it! But still this year I felt more confident. There were circuits ahead where I knew the McLaren would be quicker than the Ferrari.'

Monza, Prost maintains, was the real turning point of the season. Unable to keep pace with Rosberg on this 'horsepower' circuit, he inherited the win when the Williams-Honda failed late in the race. 'A bonus', he calls it. 'I was thinking that six points were not too bad. I was lucky to get nine.'

The next couple of races, at Spa and Brands Hatch, he hated. Alain is not psychologically equipped to coast and collect, but finished third in Belgium with a car which could have won. John Barnard, for one, was less than thrilled with the outcome of that day.

'Listen', Prost says, 'I've won a lot of races with McLaren. I don't need to be told that Spa was disappointing – it was for me, too. I was fastest in all four practice sessions that weekend, and the car was maybe the best I've ever known. Nearly perfect. And if the weather had been good, I would have won. Later in the race, when the line dried, I got fastest lap. No problem.

'I wanted to go for the win, become Champion with style, but it was the kind of day when anything could have happened – I nearly hit Piquet when he spun at the first corner, for example. They told me on the radio that Michele was out early, so then I decided to be prudent. I didn't enjoy driving that way, but I don't regret it. Keke did exactly the same at Vegas in '82, and so did Piquet at Kyalami the year after.

'The point is, I would have been World Champion before if I had driven a *tactique* race occasionally, like Niki did last year.'

Surely, though, he is the man who has always maintained that races were more important than championships, that the title meant less by far than being competitive every time out?

'That's true, and I still believe it', Prost answered at once. 'When you win a race, the feeling you get is fantastic, something happening *now*! That's why I would love to have clinched the championship with a win. As it was, it happened after a race where we were not competitive. I knew I was World Champion, but that instant elation wasn't there. It sort of came over me during the following days.

'To be honest, I drove for points at Spa and Brands because I wanted to get the Championship settled and out of the way. In the previous two years I lost it at the last race, and I did *not* want that to happen again. Because I had been so close, it had become too important to me, both in my career and my life. Now it's finished, and I feel great relief.'

One title, he says, will be enough. If others follow, fine, but they come only once a year, and of more consequence is being on the pace every couple of weeks. He is a man, unlike Lauda, who needs targets. A World Championship was one, and can now be struck from the list. At Kyalami he broke the points record for a single season. The next goal is winning more Grands Prix than anyone in history.

'Le Professeur' was the nickname Alain acquired during his time with Renault, and in those days he was an introspective fellow, his face perpetually worried. I reminded him of a remark he made to me in 1983: 'There is so much deceit and hypocrisy in Formula 1 – I always wonder if that hand slapping me on the back has a dagger in it...' He admits that his years with the Régie made him cynical and wary. 'Every time I opened my mouth I seemed to upset someone. Impossible to work like that.'

Ron Dennis and John Barnard, he says, are not easy to work with either, but his admiration for their abilities is consummate. The achievements of the McLaren management, as Lauda observed more than once, almost measure up to its collective ego. Dennis's inclination is to play down the role of the driver, but he thinks highly of Prost: 'I don't know why they called him "The Professor". That sells him short. John Barnard will tell you what a good test driver he is, but in a Grand Prix I think he's a hard, instinctive racer.'

Barnard, indeed, appreciates Alain's qualities in helping to make his job easier: 'For one thing, his memory – for settings and stuff like that – is unbelievable. And when you've been testing somewhere with him, you know the car's been round that circuit at its limit. With Prost, that's always a constant factor, and you know exactly where you are.'

Alain's desire to play down the 'French' aspect of his World Championship has been quite striking. Indeed he was irritated after the race at Brands Hatch by the attitude of chauvinistic journalists from his own country. 'I'd won the Championship with an English car', he says, 'with a German engine, with American tyres and sponsor... All they talked about was how fantastic it was for France. I said, "Today I celebrate for *me*! Next week we can

think about France..."'

He is not, he stresses often, much of a nationalist. Nor a man who forgets. Who can doubt that much of his present attitude was shaped during the years with Renault? I well remember the inquest – it was nothing less – at Kyalami in 1983, when Alain and Gérard Larrousse faced the French press. 'All this way we've come to see you win the Championship for France, and you've let us down...' That was the tone of the occasion.

Momentarily Prost was tempted to quit: 'I was disgusted by the suggestion, in one or two places, that I'd retired from the race because Piquet was beating me and I didn't want to look bad...' However, within days he had signed for McLaren. At Rio, the opening race of 1984, he had both arms in the air as he took the flag. 'It was the most satisfying win of my life. And, yes, there was a bit of revenge involved, even if I don't like to admit it...' That day the Renault ghost was laid to rest.

Alain has markedly changed since then. 'I don't suppose I have ever been really relaxed for the last 30 years!' he said after Brands Hatch. 'But I am much better than I was. For sure, being around Niki has helped – in racing there is nothing he has not seen. But maybe the biggest influence on me has been Jacques (Laffite). We are very close friends, we both love all sports, and he has shown me you don't have to be at the circuit for hours, worrying about the car. Sometimes it's better to get away, have a swim or something...

'Detroit, for example, I hate. But this year I went back to my hotel room after the warm-up, and watched the golf for a couple of hours. I relaxed, forgot about the race; but I could never have done that a few years ago.'

Ironically the drive he rates as the best of his season, maybe his life, was the one taken away. 'I was proud of the job I did at Imola, although it was not truly a race because fuel economy played such a big part. But I fought with Senna as long as I could – until I knew that I had to back off, or run out. Maybe he could run the whole race at that speed, and finish – I didn't know. All I did know was that I couldn't.

'I calculated the fuel absolutely right, or so I thought, and ran out on my slowing down lap. Perfect. I had 200 miles to run, with 220 litres of fuel, and I think I drove that whole race as fast as it could have been done. It wasn't *racing*, but it was satisfying in a way...'

Dry of fuel, the car failed the post-race weigh-in. With a small bag of potatoes added, it would have passed. After receiving the trophy, waving to the crowds, Prost took the news hard. An Italian photographer, trying to freeze the moment, spun him round, and for a second I thought Alain was going to clobber him.

There was no sign of 'le Professeur' in that moment. This was an emotional racer who felt he'd been robbed. Prost can be very direct. When the British Grand Prix of 1984 was speciously stopped after an unimportant accident, he stormed up to Jean-Marie Balestre to tell him in words of one syllable (and four letters) what he thought.

He is a much warmer man than the Renault driver we used to know. In a couple of years with McLaren his English has improved to the point that sometimes he instinctively uses it for swearing. He has come to like this country very much.

'It amazes me how happy the English are when I win', he says. 'After Silverstone this year... incredible. I think they like me much more than in France. You know, since my problems with Renault, I never cared too much about popularity – I mean, I don't need it. But at Brands, when I won the Championship, I was very moved by the reaction of the crowd. Mansell had won his first race – an Englishman at home – but still they cheered like crazy for me. Something like that would never happen with a French crowd.

'Mind you', he says, thoughtfully, 'I am more popular at home than I was in my Renault days. How to explain that? It's the same with Michel Platini. The French like him much more since he left home to play for an Italian club...'

Perhaps, in 1985, the British public began to see Alain Prost for what he is, not only a brilliant racing driver (indisputably the greatest France has ever produced), but also an attractive character, with a quick mind and fine sense of dry humour.

Appearances on TV chat shows did him no harm at all. He likes to dress casually, but fashion-consciousness goes no further than regulation Timberland shoes.

'It was hard season, 1985, more competitive than any I have known – a good year to win the Championship. Aerodynamically, our car was still the best, I think, particularly on the quick circuits. But we needed that advantage to make up for the engine's power deficit. In qualifying I was sometimes 30 kph slower through the traps than the BMW and Honda.

'I had fantastic reliability, though, in the second half of the year, and I prefer Porsche to put their efforts into that than look for another 200 horsepower for qualifying, which has become just a stupid game.'

Perhaps the most important of his targets is the one which only he will ever recognise. From his first day in Formula 1 he has sought the elusive 'perfect lap', every line clean, every apex clipped, not an inch wasted. He came close, he says, with his qualifying lap at Paul Ricard in 1983, taking pole position by two clear seconds. Did he find it, finally, in 1985?

'No, not exactly... well, there was one lap in practice at Spa, my last one, which put me on the pole. I was proud of that, but I was maybe a little wide out of *Eau Rouge*...

'I don't think, though', he concludes, 'that I made too many mistakes in 1985'.

CURIOUSLY ENOUGH, IT'LL REMIND

Anyone who spends between £15,000 and £30,000 on a luxury

THE BMW 7 SERIES STARTS AT £15,950 FOR THE 728i. 728iSE: £17,610. 732i: £18,225. 732iSE: £20,175. 735i: £20,550. 735iSE: £25,995. SHOWN ABOVE WITH OPTIONAL LEATHER SEATS £27,501. PRICES. CORRECT AT TIME OF GOING TO PRESS. INCLUDE CAR TAX + VAT BUT NOT DELIVERY OR NUMBER PLATES. INCLUSIVE DELIVERY CHARGE. INCORPORATING

WCRS

OU OF YOUR TWO-SEATER DAYS.

r without trying the BMW 7 Series obviously doesn't like driving.

THE ULTIMATE DRIVING MACHINE

MERGENCY SERVICE AND INITIAL SERVICES £208 + VAT. FOR A BMW 7 SERIES INFORMATION FILE, PLEASE WRITE TO: BMW INFORMATION SERVICE, PO BOX 46, HOUNSLOW, MIDDLESEX OR TEL: 01 897 6665, 17 DAYS A WEEK, 9am-5.30pm. LITERATURE REQUESTS ONLY). FOR TAX FREE SALES, 56 PARK LANE, LONDON W1. TEL: 01 629 9277

1985 Formula 1 car specifications

THE CARS

McLaren won the Constructors' Championship for the second year running. They also won six races, two more than Williams and twice as many as Lotus. Yet it was left to Ferrari, who took just two victories, to provide McLaren with the closest competition, an indication that the British team was no longer the dominant force it had been in 1984.

Ferrari relied on constant point-scoring by two drivers; McLaren, by contrast, were carried by the remarkable record of Alain Prost. He retired on three occasions, was disqualified once, and for the remaining 12 races, finished in the top three – with the exception of Brands Hatch where he took fourth place. Had Lauda enjoyed similar reliability, McLaren would not have been fending off a team with a vastly inferior car: inferior to

Williams, who took time to develop the FW10 into a reliable and powerful package; inferior to Lotus who had the pace during practice but failed when it mattered most. Brabham took the remaining victory, a brief flicker in an otherwise dismal year for the leading Pirelli runner.

The Spirit team took part in the early races before leaving Formula 1, while Zakspeed, Beatrice and Minardi entered Grand Prix racing. Renault, after nine years in Formula 1, pulled out at the end of the season.

THE ENGINES

1985 marked the final appearance of the Ford Cosworth. Tyrrell raced with the DFY before switching mid-season to join Ligier and Lotus as customers for the Renault turbo V6, while Zakspeed designed and built their own four-cylinder turbo. Minardi used the Ford-Cosworth

before switching to the Motori Moderni, a new V6 engine designed by Carlo Chiti.

Once again the Porsche-designed TAG turbo won the most races, but significant development by Honda saw their V6 win mid-season and then dominate the final three races. Lotus carried the Renault flag in the face of falling competitiveness by the works team; Ferrari took two wins and BMW had their worst season since joining Formula 1 in 1981. Renault took eight pole positions and four fastest laps; TAG, two poles and five fastest laps; Honda, three poles and four fastest laps. Hart and Ferrari claimed one pole position each, with two fastest laps for the latter, while BMW, winner of nine pole positions in 1984, took just one.

Note: The above facts and figures were supplied by the respective teams and manufacturers.

	Alfa Romeo 890T	BMW M12/13 Turbo	Ferrari 126C Turbo	Ford Cosworth DFY	Hart 415T Turbo	Honda RA 163E Turbo
No. of cylinders	V8	4 in-line	V6	V8 (90°)	4 in-line	V6
Bore and stroke	74 mm × 43·5 mm	89·2 mm × 60 mm	81 mm × 48·4 mm	90 mm × 58·8 mm	88 m × 61·5 mm	–
Capacity	1497 cc	1500 cc	1500 cc	2994 cc	1496 cc	1500 cc
Compression ratio	7:1	7·5:1	–	12·3:1	7·0:1	–
Maximum power	700 bhp	850 bhp	–	510 bhp	750 bhp at 10,500	–
Maximum rpm	11,800	11,000	12,000	11,000	11,000	11,000
Valve sizes	–	35·8 mm - Inlet	–	–	35·0 mm - Inlet	–
		30·3 mm - Exhaust			30·0 mm - Exhaust	
Valve lift	–	–	–	–	10·5 mm	–
Valve timing	–	–	–	102°	–	–
Block material	Aluminium	Cast iron		Aluminium	Aluminium	Cast iron
Pistons and rings	Mahle	Mahle/Goetze	Mahle	Cosworth/Goetze	Mahle	Honda
Bearings	Clevite	Glyco	Clevite	Vandervell	Vandervell	Honda
Fuel injection	Spica	Bosch	Weber/Magneti Marelli	Lucas	Zytek/Hart	Honda/PGM-FI
Ignition system	Marelli	Bosch	Magneti Marelli	Lucas	Marelli	Honda
Turbocharger(s)	Avio/KKK	Garrett	2 × KKK	–	Holset	2 × IHI
Weight (less intercooler)	160 kg	160 kg		136 kg	290 lb	–

	Motori-Moderni Turbo	Renault EF4B	Renault EF15	TAG PO1 (TTE PO1) Turbo	Zakspeed
No. of cylinders	V6	V6	V6	V6	4
Bore and stroke	80 mm × 49·7 mm	86 mm × 42·8 mm	80·1 mm × 49·4 mm	82 mm × 47 mm	–
Capacity	1498·9 cc	1492 cc	1494 cc	–	1495 cc
Compression ratio	7:1	7:1	7:1	7·5:1	7:1
Maximum power	720 bhp	760 bhp	810 bhp	750 bhp (race boost)	700 bhp
Maximum rpm	11,300	11,500	11,500	12,000	11,500
Valve sizes	–	–	–	–	–
Valve lift					
Valve timing	–	–	–	–	–
Block material	Aluminium alloy	Aluminium alloy	Aluminium alloy	Aluminium alloy	Aluminium
Pistons and rings	Mahle	Mahle/Goetze	Mahle/Goetze	Mahle/Goetze	Mahle
Bearings	Vandervell	Glyco	Glyco	Glyco	SKF/Timken
Fuel injection	Lucas/Ferrari	Electronic Renix/	Electronic Renix/	Bosch Motronic MPI4	Kugelfischer
		Weber injectors	Weber injectors		
Ignition system	Marelli	Marelli	Marelli	Bosch Motronic MPI4	Zakspeed
Turbocharger(s)	2 × KKK	2 × Garrett	2 × Garrett	2 × KKK	KKK
Weight (less intercooler)	154 kg	–	–	145 kg	–

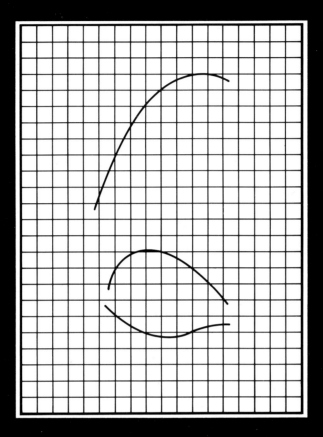

COSWORTH ENGINEERING

**The success of Cosworth engines in international
motor racing is legendary.
We're making legends too in -:
High performance engine designs and
specialist projects for Automotive, Marine
and Aero applications.
Prototype, pre production and series engine build.
High integrity precision Aluminium castings.**

COSWORTH ENGINEERING LTD.

ST. JAMES MILL ROAD, NORTAMPTON, NN5 5JJ U.K.
TEL : NORTHAMPTON (0604) 52444
TELEGRAMS : COSWORTH, NORTHAMPTON
TELEX : 31454

RENAULT recommend **elf** lubricants.

THE 182 bhp RENAULT 25 V6 TURBO.
(USE WITH DISCRETION.)

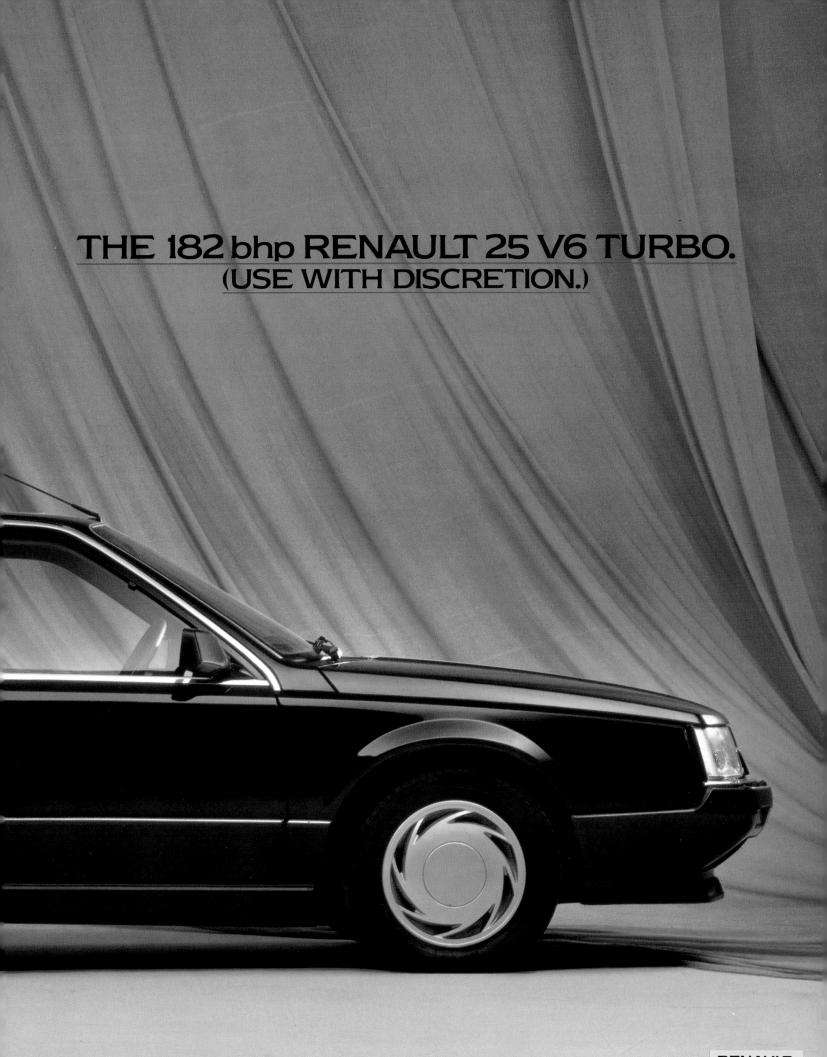

RENAULT
BUILD
A BETTER
CAR

	Alfa Romeo 185T	Arrows A8	Beatrice-Lola THL-1
Sponsor(s)	Benetton	Barclay/DeLonghi	Beatrice
Designer(s)	–	Dave Wass/Dave Nielson	Neil Oatley/Ross Brawn/John Baldwin
Team Manager(s)	Paolo Pavanello	Alan Rees	Teddy Mayer
			Tyler Alexander
Chief Mechanic(s)	–	Dave Luckett	Phil Sharp
No. of chassis built	4	6	2
ENGINE			
Type	Alfa Romeo 890T	BMW	Hart 415T
Fuel and oil	Agip	BMW/Castrol	Shell
Sparking plugs	Champion	Champion	Champion
TRANSMISSION			
Gearbox/speeds	Alfa (5)	Arrows	Force/Hewland (6)
Driveshafts	Alfa	Arrows	Force
Clutch	Borg & Beck	AP	AP
CHASSIS			
Front suspension	Pushrod (184T)	Top & bottom wishbones,	Double wishbone,
	Pullrod (185T)	pushrods	pushrod
Rear suspension	Pushrod	Top & bottom wishbones,	Double wishbone,
		pushrods	pushrod
Suspension dampers	Koni	Koni	Koni
Wheel diameter	front: 13 in. rear: 13 in.	front: 13 in. rear: 13 in.	front: 13 in. rear: 13 in.
Wheel rim widths	front: 12 in. rear: 16·3 in.	front: 11·75 in. rear: 16·375 in.	front: 12 in. rear: 16 in.
Tyres	Goodyear	Goodyear	Goodyear
Brakes	Brembo	AP	AP
Brake pads	Brembo	Ferodo	Ferodo
Steering	Alfa	Arrows	Force
Radiator(s)	IPRA/Secan	Behr/Unipart	Secan/Llanelli
Fuel tank	ATL	ATL	ATL
Battery	Yuasa	Varley	–
Instruments	BOI	VDO	VDO
DIMENSIONS			
Wheelbase	109 in./2780 mm	111 in./2819 mm	110 in./2794 mm
Track	front: 71·65 in./1820 mm (184T)	front: 70 in./1778 mm	front: 71 in./1803 mm
	70·47 in./1790 mm (185T)	rear: 65 in./1651 mm	rear: 64 in./1626 mm
	rear: 65·00 in./1660 mm		
Gearbox weight	132 lb/60 kg	105 lb/48 kg	–
Chassis weight (tub)	66 lb/30 kg	72 lb/32·65 kg	–
Formula weight	1223 lb/555 kg	1191 lb/540 kg	1191 lb/540 kg
Fuel capacity	48·3 gal./220 litres	48·3 gal./220 litres	48·3 gal./220 litres
Fuel consumption	–	4·3 mpg/65 litres/100 km	–

	Brabham BT54	Ferrari 156/85	Ligier JS25
Sponsor(s)	Olivetti	Agip/Fiat/Goodyear/Marlboro	Loto/Gitanes/Candy/Mase/Antar
Designer(s)	Gordon Murray/David North	Ferrari-Gestione Sportiva	Michel Tétu/M. Beaujon
Team Manager(s)	Herbie Blash	Enzo Ferrari	Guy Ligier
			Gérard Larrousse
Chief Mechanic(s)	Charlie Whiting	Bellentani/Scaramelli	J. P. Chatenay
No. of chassis built	9	9	5
ENGINE			
Type	BMW M12/13 Turbo	Ferrari 156/85	Renault EF15 & EF4
Fuel and oil	–/Castrol	Agip	Antar
Sparking plugs	Champion	Champion	Champion
TRANSMISSION			
Gearbox/speeds	Hewland/Brabham/Weismann/	Ferrari	Ligier/Hewland
	Getrag (5/6)		
Driveshafts	Brabham	Löbro/Ferrari	Löbro
Clutch	Borg & Beck	Borg & Beck	AP
CHASSIS			
Front suspension	Double wishbones,		Pushrods
	pushrods		
Rear suspension	Double wishbones,		Rocker arm
	pushrods		
Suspension dampers	Koni	Koni/Marzocchi	Koni
Wheel diameter	front: 13 in. rear: 13 in.	front: 13 in. rear: 13 in.	front: 13 in. rear: 13 in.
Wheel rim widths	front: 12 in. rear: 16·5 in.	front: 12 in. rear: 16 in.	front: 12 in. rear: 16·5 in.
Tyres	Pirelli	Goodyear	Pirelli
Brakes	SEP/Brabham/Girling	Ferrari/Brembo/SEP	Brembo/SEP
Brake pads	SEP	Ferrari/SEP	Ferodo/SEP
Steering	Brabham	Ferrari rack and pinion	Ligier
Radiator(s)	Unipart/Llanelli/Behr	Behr/Valeo/IPRA/Secan	IPRA/Secan
Fuel tank	ATL	Pirelli	ATL
Battery	Yuasa	Yuasa	Yuasa
Instruments	Bosch	Borletti/Magneti Marelli	Brion/Leroux
DIMENSIONS			
Wheelbase	119 in./3023 mm	102·4 in./2600 mm	112 in./2835 mm
Track	front: 69 in./1753 mm	front: 70·5 in./1790 mm	front: 70·5 in./1790 mm
	rear: 65 in./1651 mm	rear: 64·7 in./1644 mm rear	rear: 65·4 in./1662 mm
Gearbox weight	110 lb/50 kg	–	141 lb/64 kg
Chassis weight (tub)	93 lb/42 kg	–	75 lb/34 kg
Formula weight	1191 lb/540 kg	1191 lb/540 kg	1201 lb/545 kg
Fuel capacity	48·3 gal./220 litres	48 gal./218 litres	48·3 gal./220 litres
Fuel consumption	3·5-4·5 mpg/63-80 litres/100 km	–	4·3 mpg/65 litres/100 km

	Lotus 97T	McLaren MP4/2B	Minardi M/85
Sponsor(s)	Imperial Tobacco Co./	Marlboro/Saima/Goodyear/	Simod/Gilmar/Resolder/
	Olympus Cameras	Boss/Hercules/Unipart	Pool Romagna
Designer(s)	Gérard Ducarouge/Martin Ogilvie	John Barnard	Giacomo Caliri
Team Manager(s)	Peter Warr	Ron Dennis	Giancarlo Minardi
Chief Mechanic(s)	Bob Dance	Dave Ryan	Ermanno Cuoghi/Bruno Fagnocchi
No. of chassis built	4	6	–
ENGINE			
Type	Renault EF4B/EF15	TAG Turbo PO1 V6	Motori Moderni V6 Turbo
Fuel and oil	Elf	Shell	Agip
Sparking plugs	Champion	Champion	Champion
TRANSMISSION			
Gearbox/speeds	Lotus/Hewland (5)	McLaren (5)	Minardi
Driveshafts	Löbro/Lotus	McLaren	Minardi
Clutch	AP	AP	AP
CHASSIS			
Front suspension	Double wishbones,	Pushrod operating inboard auxiliary	Double wishbones,
	pullrods	rockers, upper & lower wishbones,	pullrods
		inboard springs	
Rear suspension	Double wishbones,	Pushrod operating inboard auxiliary	Double wishbones,
	pullrods	rockers, inboard springs, top &	pushrods
		bottom wishbones & rear	
		lower toe link	
Suspension dampers	Koni	Bilstein	Koni
Wheel diameter	front: 13 in. rear: 13 in.	front: 13 in. rear: 13 in.	front: 13 in. rear: 13 in.
Wheel rim widths	front: 11·5 in. rear: 16·25 in.	front: 11·75 in. rear: 16·3 in.	front: 12 in. rear: 16·5 in.
Tyres	Goodyear	Goodyear	Pirelli
Brakes	Brembo/SEP	McLaren/SEP discs	Brembo
Brake pads	SEP/Ferodo	SEP	Ferodo
Steering	Lotus/Knight	McLaren	Minardi rack and pinion
Radiator(s)	IPRA/Secan	McLaren/Unipart and Behr cores	Behr
Fuel tank	ATL	ATL	Pirelli
Battery	Yuasa	Yuasa	Yuasa
Instruments	Mors-Brion Leroux	Bosch/Contactless	–
DIMENSIONS			
Wheelbase	107 in./2720 mm	110 in./2794 mm	102·6 in./2607 mm
Track	front: 70·9 in./1800 mm	front: 71·5 in./1816 mm	front: 71·3 in./1813 mm
	rear: 63·7 in./1620 mm	rear: 66·0 in./1676 mm	rear: 65·39 in./1661 mm
Gearbox weight	99 lb/45 kg	125 lb/57 kg	–
Chassis weight (tub)	81·57 lb/37 kg	78 lb/35 kg	–
Formula weight	1191 lb/540 kg	1191 lb/540 kg	1212 lb/550 kg
Fuel capacity	48·4 gal./220 litres	48·4 gal./220 litres	48·3 gal./220 litres
Fuel consumption	4·3 mpg/65 litres/100 km	4 mpg/68 litres/100 km	–

	Osella FA1F	Osella FA1G	RAM 03
Sponsor(s)	Kelémata	Kelémata	Skoal Bandit/Radar Pigier/
			Rizla/Newsweek
Designer(s)	G. Petrotta	G. Petrotta	Gustav Brunner/Sergio Rinland/Tim Feast
Team Manager(s)	Enzo Osella	Enzo Osella	Mick Ralph
Chief Mechanic(s)	–	–	Ray Boulter
No. of chassis built	2	2	4
ENGINE			
Type	Alfa Romeo V8 Turbo 1984	Alfa Romeo V8 Turbo 1984	Hart 415T
Fuel and oil	Agip	Agip	Shell
Sparking plugs	Champion	Champion	Champion
TRANSMISSION			
Gearbox/speeds	Osella/Hewland FGB	Osella/Hewland FGB	RAM (6)
Driveshafts	Osella	Osella	RAM
Clutch	Borg & Beck/AP	Borg & Beck/AP	AP/Borg & Beck
CHASSIS			
Front suspension	Pushrods	Pushrods	Double wishbones,
			pullrods
Rear suspension	Pushrods	Pushrods	Double wishbones,
			pullrods
Suspension dampers	Koni	Koni	Koni
Wheel diameter	front: 13 in. rear: 13 in.	front: 13 in. rear: 13 in.	front: 13 in. rear: 13 in.
Wheel rim widths	front: 11·5 in. rear: 16·5 in.	front: 11·5 in. rear: 16·5 in.	front: 12 in. rear: 16·5 in.
Tyres	Pirelli	Pirelli	Pirelli
Brakes	Brembo	Brembo	AP/Lockheed
Brake pads	Ferodo	Ferodo	Ferodo
Steering	Osella	Osella	RAM/Knight
Radiator(s)	IPRA/Secan	IPRA/Secan	Behr
Fuel tank	Pirelli	Pirelli	ATL
Battery	Magneti Marelli	Magneti Marelli	Varley
Instruments	VDO	VDO	VDO
DIMENSIONS			
Wheelbase	108·46 in./2755 mm	111·42 in./2830 mm	109·6 in./2784 mm
Track	front: 68·11 in./1730 mm	front: 70·9 in./1800 mm	front: 71·38 in./1813 mm
	rear: 63 in./1600 mm	rear: 63 in./1600 mm	rear: 65 in./1651 mm
Gearbox weight	83·7 lb/38 kg	83·7 lb/38 kg	110 lb/50 kg
Chassis weight (tub)	81·57 lb/37 kg	81·57 lb/37 kg	70·5 lb/32 kg
Formula weight	1256 lb/570 kg	1267 lb/575 kg	1190 lb/540 kg
Fuel capacity	48·1 gal./219 litres	48·1 gal./219 litres	48·4 gal./220 litres
Fuel consumption	–	–	3·7–4·1 mpg/69–77 litres/100 km

	Renault RE60	Renault RE60B	Spirit 101D
Sponsor(s)	Elf	Elf	Various
Designer(s)	Michel Tétu/J. M. D'Adda	J. M. D'Adda/Renault Sport Design Office	Gordon Coppuck
Team Manager(s)	Jean Sage	Jean Sage	John Wickham
Chief Mechanic(s)	Daniel Champion	Daniel Champion	–
No. of chassis built	–	–	2
ENGINE			
Type	EF4B/EF15	EF15	Hart 415T
Fuel and oil	Elf	Elf	Elf/Shell
Sparking plugs	Champion	Champion	Champion
TRANSMISSION			
Gearbox/speeds	Renault/Hewland (6)	Renault/Hewland (5)	Hewland (5/6)
Driveshafts	Löbro	Löbro	Spirit
Clutch	AP	AP	Borg & Beck
CHASSIS			
Front suspension	Double wishbones, pushrods	Double wishbones, pushrods	Top rocker arms, lower wishbones, inboard springs
Rear suspension	Double wishbones, pushrods	Double wishbones, pushrods	Top rocker arms, lower wishbones, inboard springs
Suspension dampers	Tambay: De Carbon Warwick: De Carbon and Koni	Tambay: De Carbon Warwick: De Carbon and Koni	Koni
Wheel diameter	front: 13 in. rear: 13 in.	front: 13 in. rear: 13 in.	front: 13 in. rear: 13 in.
Wheel rim widths	front: 12 in. rear: 16·25 in.	front: 12 in. rear: 16·25 in.	front: 11·5 in. rear: 17 in.
Tyres	Goodyear	Goodyear	Pirelli
Brakes	SEP	SEP	Lockheed
Brake pads	SEP	SEP	Ferodo
Steering	Renault	Renault	Spirit
Radiator(s)	Secan	Secan	Serck
Fuel tank	Kleber	Kleber	Marston/Premier
Battery	Magneti Marelli	Magneti Marelli	–
Instruments	–	–	Smiths
DIMENSIONS			
Wheelbase	109·45 in./2780 mm	109·45 in./2780 mm	107 in./2718 mm
Track	front: 70·9 in./1800 mm	front: 70·9 in./1800 mm	front: 73 in./1854 mm
	rear: 65·07 in./1650 mm	rear: 64·96 in./1650 mm	rear: 65 in./1651 mm
Gearbox weight	–	–	110 lb/50 kg
Chassis weight (tub)	–	–	76 lb/34·5 kg
Formula weight	1267 lb/575 kg	1191 lb/540 kg	1232 lb/559 kg
Fuel capacity	48·3 gal./220 litres	48·3 gal./220 litres	48·4 gal./220 litres
Fuel consumption			4·2–4·5 mpg/63–67 litres/100 km

	Toleman TG185	Tyrrell 012	Tyrrell 014
Sponsor(s)	Benetton	Maredo	Maredo/Porchester Group
Designer(s)	Rory Byrne	Maurice Phillippe/Brian Lisles	Maurice Phillippe/Brian Lisles
Team Manager(s)	Peter Collins	Ken Tyrrell	Ken Tyrrell
Chief Mechanic(s)	John Mardle	Roger Hill	Roger Hill
No. of chassis built	5	6	3
ENGINE			
Type	Hart 415T	3-litre Cosworth DFY V8	Renault EF4/EF15
Fuel and oil	AGIP	Elf	Elf
Sparking plugs	Champion	Champion	Champion
TRANSMISSION			
Gearbox/speeds	Toleman (5/6)	Tyrrell/Hewland (5/6)	Tyrrell/Hewland (6)
Driveshafts	Toleman	Tyrrell	Tyrrell
Clutch	Borg & Beck	AP	AP
CHASSIS			
Front suspension	Upper and lower wishbones, tension link operated inboard spring/damper units	Pullrod, upper and lower wishbones	Pullrod, upper and lower wishbones
Rear suspension	Upper and lower wishbones, compression link/bellcrank-operated inboard spring/damper units	Pullrod, upper and lower wishbones	Pullrod, upper and lower wishbones
Suspension dampers	Koni	Koni – gas filled	Koni – gas filled
Wheel diameter	front: 13 in. rear: 13 in.	front: 13 in. rear: 13 in.	front: 13 in. rear: 13 in.
Wheel rim widths	front: 11·8 in. rear: 16·25 in.	front: 11·5 in. rear: 16·5 in.	front: 12·25 in. rear: 16·3 in.
Tyres	Pirelli	Goodyear	Goodyear
Brakes	Brembo/Lockheed	AP	AP
Brake pads	Ferodo	Ferodo	Ferodo
Steering	Toleman/Knight	Tyrrell	Tyrrell
Radiator(s)	Behr	Serck	Unipart/Secan
Fuel tank	Marston	ATL	ATL
Battery	National Panasonic	RS	RS
Instruments	VDO	Smiths/Contactless	Brion Leroux
DIMENSIONS			
Wheelbase	106 in./2692 mm	104 in./2642 mm	108·5 in./2756 mm
Track	front: 71·5 in./1816 mm	front: 65 in./1651 mm	front: 69·5 in./1765 mm
	rear: 66·25 in./1683 mm	rear: 58 in./1473 mm	rear: 64·5 in./1638 mm
Gearbox weight	120 lb/54·5 kg	112 lb/51 kg	112 lb/51 kg
Chassis weight (tub)	88 lb/40 kg	65 lb/29·5 kg	78 lb/35 kg
Formula weight	1195 lb/542 kg	1191 lb/540 kg	1191 lb/540 kg
Fuel capacity	48·3 gal./220 litres	39 gal./177 litres	48·3 gal./220 litres
Fuel consumption	3·8–4·2 mpg/67–74 litres/100 km	5·6 mpg/47·57 litres/100 km	4·0 mpg/70·6 litres/100 km

DONINGTON
THE HEART OF BRITISH MOTOR SPORT

EUROPE'S INTERNATIONAL MOTORSPORT CENTRE

onington Park Racing Ltd.,
astle Donington, Derby DE7 2RP.
elephone: Derby (0332) 810048. Telex: 377793

	Williams FW10	Zakspeed 841
Sponsor(s)	Canon/Mobil/ICI/Denim	Reemstma International
Designer(s)	Patrick Head	Paul Brown
Team Manager(s)	Frank Williams/David Stubbs	Helmut Barth
	Alan Challis	Peter Krumbein
Chief Mechanic(s)		
No. of chassis built	8	2
ENGINE		
Type	Honda RA163-E 80° V6 turbocharged	Zakspeed
Fuel and oil	Mobil	Shell
Sparking plugs	NGK	Champion
TRANSMISSION		
Gearbox/speeds	Williams/Hewland (6)	Hewland/Zakspeed (5/6)
Driveshafts	Williams	GWV
Clutch	AP	AP
CHASSIS		
Front suspension	Double wishbone,	Double wishbone,
	pushrod operated	inboard springs
	inboard spring damper	
Rear suspension	Lower wishbone, rocker operated	Pullrod
	inboard spring damper OR	
	Double wishbone, pullrod operated	
	inboard spring damper	
Suspension dampers	Penske	Koni
Wheel diameter	front: 13 in. rear: 13 in.	front: 13 in. rear: 13 in.
Wheel rim widths	front: 12 in. rear: 16·3 in.	front: 11·5 in. rear: 16·5 in.
Tyres	Goodyear	Goodyear
Brakes	SEP	AP
Brake pads	SEP	Ferodo
Steering	Rack & pinion	Zakspeed rack & pinion
Radiator(s)	Llanelli/Secan	Behr
Fuel tank	ATL	Marston
Battery	RS Components	Bosch
Instruments	VDO/Honda	Zakspeed
DIMENSIONS		
Wheelbase	110 in./2794 mm	111 in./2820 mm
Track	front: 71 in./1803 mm	front: 70·8 in./1800 mm
	rear 64 in./1626 mm	rear: 63 in./1600 mm
Gearbox weight	–	–
Chassis weight (tub)	–	61·73 lb/28 kg
Formula weight	1191 lb/540 kg	1245 lb/565 kg
Fuel capacity	48·3 gal./220 litres	48·3 gal./220 litres
Fuel consumption	–	–

Alfa Romeo 184T/185T

Arrows A8

Beatrice-Lola THL-1

Brabham BT54

Ferrari 156/85

Ligier JS25

Lotus 97T

McLaren MP4/2B

Minardi M/85

Osella FA1G

RAM 03

Renault RE60B

Spirit 101

Toleman TG185

Tyrrell 014

Williams FW10

Zakspeed 841

The wider the tyre, the greater the grip.

Ⓓ *DUNLOP SP LOW PROFILES.*

Car of the Year

For the first time, *Autocourse* draws up a Designer Top Ten. Considering the varied and complex factors which influence a car's performance (not to mention one or two of the egos pushing the pencils!), this has proved an infinitely more hazardous business than selecting the Top Ten drivers. None the less, for better or worse . . .

1 Lotus 97T: Gérard Ducarouge
Simple and straightforward. The best handling chassis of the season. Let down by engine-related problems. Senna's ability to show the car in a favourable light cannot be underestimated.

2 McLaren MP4/2B: John Barnard
True potential only apparent during race rather than qualifying. Barnard confounded all predictions by keeping a previous winner competitive thanks to subtle changes and diligent test work. The most complete package – for the full season.

3 Williams FW10: Patrick Head
A match for anyone in the final quarter of the season. Full credit must be given to the Williams design team for producing a chassis to match the remarkable Honda development work and power.

4 Toleman TG185: Rory Byrne
A chassis the equal of McLaren and Lotus, despite zero development work last winter. Hamstrung by tyre and engine problems. The prospect of an association with BMW should worry rivals.

5 Brabham BT54: Gordon Murray
Potential masked by tyre development programme. At times, the BT54 looked as bad as it was exceptional when the conditions were right for Pirelli.

6 Ferrari 156/85: Harvey Postlethwaite
The best looking car of the year. Could have won the Championship had early-season form been maintained. Engine department fell behind in horsepower stakes and subsequent chassis compensation caused steepest decline of the season.

7 Ligier JS25: Michel Tétu
Not pretty by any means but Tétu's work improved the JS25 into an extremely useful chassis. No more immune to Pirelli foibles than Brabham.

8 Tyrrell 012: Maurice Phillippe
The ultimate 3-litre car. Neat, straightforward, vice-free. A joy to watch in the tailor-made conditions at Detroit.

9 Arrows A8: Dave Wass
Workmanlike but kept the drivers busy. Additional cash and testing might have added the small but necessary refinements.

10 RAM 03: Gustav Brunner
A very effective chassis let down by engine problems which may or may not have been related to inadequate cooling and a lack of wind tunnel testing.

1 Nose support with deformable structure

2 Brake ducts

3 Computer for fuel consumption

4 Electronic box by Bosch

5 Shorter side pods for 1985 due to a new position of the radiators

6 Push rod suspension

7 Top wishbone

8 Lower link to adjust the toe-in

9 Frame to fix the rear suspension to the McLaren-made gearbox

10 Aerodynamic platform

11 Side fin around the rear tyres

12 Small piece of bodywork in the suspension area (new for 1985)

13 Rear wing with bigger side plates for 1985

14 The revised gearbox included a fixing point for the wing support

15 The bodywork in the back was narrower than last year's car

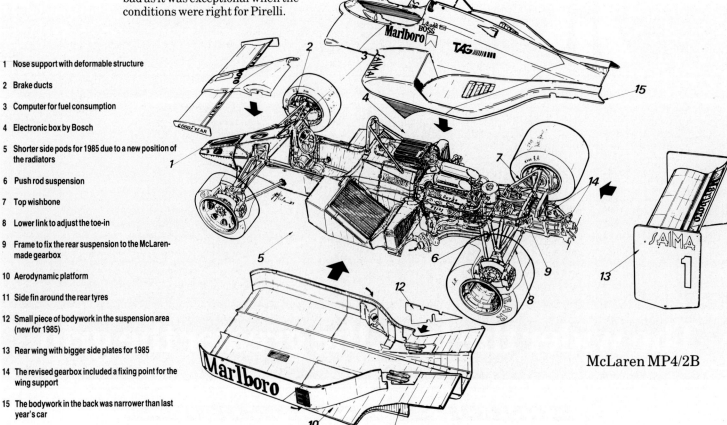

McLaren MP4/2B

The affair begins at first sight.

The MR2

You may be attracted to our new baby by its revolutionary 16 valve, 1600cc, twin-overhead-cam, fuel injected engine.

Or perhaps it is the mid-engine layout which will appeal.

Or Toyota engineering at its best (the engine will idle to red line in less than a second).

Or is it getting to 60 in 8.2 seconds that thrills you to bits?

Whatever makes you finally fall for our MR2, you only have to take one look to be seduced.

TOYOTA

That's motoring

The Hardest Season

by Doug Nye

Ferrari: 'the awful realisation that they were being blown-off in the horsepower race hit Maranello like an ice-cold shower'.
Photo: Bernard Asset/Agence Vandystadt

At the end of the 1984 season, every team in Formula 1 had a clear mental picture of what was required for '85. The McLaren-TAG Turbo cars had spreadeagled all opposition and simply steamrollered it into the ground. It was as if the old time Gulf-McLaren CanAm sports car programme had come to Formula 1, and that was just as depressing for McLaren International's Grand Prix racing rivals as it had been for the old team's victims in the North American sports car series at the turn of the Seventies.

Now for the new year McLaren knew that the easiest way to go was down. Their 12-win '84 season would be a difficult act to follow. For everyone else, the only way was up, to match and if possible improve upon what McLaren were doing. Neither proposition – McLaren doing better, the opposition somehow matching them – was going to be easy.

Everybody sought more power, more torque, better economy from their engines. In qualifying tune the horsepower of BMW's 'specials' ran well into four figures: some calculations on frontal area, maximum velocity and probable drag coefficient at Monza for example, where Piquet exceeded 208 mph past the pits, suggest it reached over 1290 bhp. That seems excessive but 1000 bhp is now a minimum requirement. Yes, that's 666 bhp per litre; achieved by rapidly improving electronic engine management and highly classified internal engineering to burn specially mixed legal-octane fuel under 2.8 ata boost or more, with ever increased efficiency.

Only four years ago an output of no more than 181 bhp per litre was able to dominate the Championship. In race-tune today 533 bhp per litre is accepted as standard, and the better heat-rejecting iron-block Bee-Ems and Hondas could be up to 600.

Everybody also hunted the Holy Grail of improved handling, better efficiency, *time* in their chassis. And then they tried to add reliability and serviceability, ploys which would save hours in the workshop. These are the practicalities of racing which are too often forgotten amongst the performance-generating technicalities but which can make all the difference between a team run ragged by job-sheet demands and one capable of giving itself breathing space to stand back and think properly between races.

Meanwhile, FISA amended the technical regulations to ban the sidestep winglets introduced by Ferrari late in 1983 and used by everyone through 1984 to enhance aerodynamic download. They also applied a new measured-standard crushable footbox extension safety measure which made good sense, especially after Cecotto's fearful Toleman accident at Brands Hatch the previous summer. Then their finalised calendar – admittedly revised courtesy of some brainless Walloon resurfacing in Belgium – eventually produced several races only one week apart and, for the first time since 1977, included events on four continents.

The upshot was what the teams seem unanimously to regard as the hardest season. . . .

McLaren

McLaren's 1984 waltz to Championship honours was a painful squib up the trouser leg for all their opposition. With considerable justification Gordon Murray of Brabham mused 'all they had to do to win was for us to retire . . .'

Through the winter months, McLaren's lead was eroded and for much of this past season all the leading marques were better matched than for several seasons past. This highlighted the relative merits of the drivers and, with Prost and Lauda, McLaren were in fine shape. But they were harder pressed all season, and though it was clear that they still possessed the most effective all-round package in Formula 1, its armour was being probed as never before, and some chinks became exposed.

John Barnard had improved his World Championship-dominating MP4/2 design and updated the existing moulded carbon-fibre chassis with new regulation footbox extensions, all-new B-spec bodywork, new pushrod rear suspension, new front uprights and a new hub package, plus a redesigned rear wing *sans* winglets, balanced by new flaps on the nose wings.

There was more under the skin as John explains. 'What I wanted was a car which would be totally predictable on the servicing side, so we could say this part does 500 miles and that part does 1000 miles; so we could accurately life all our components and then, apart from accidents, we could accurately predict how many parts we would need for the year's racing. I wanted a gearbox, engine and four suspension corners which we could completely ignore for two races at a time. With two pairs of races spaced only one week apart this was vital. I have nightmares about trying to race-prepare a car away from home in circuit lock-ups.'

Late in '84 McLaren had already completed a fourth MP4/2 monocoque, carbon-moulded by Hercules in Salt Lake City, and it was finalised as 'MP4/2B-4', and a fifth car was subsequently completed from new as 'MP4/2B-5'.

The joker in the pack was Michelin's withdrawal from Formula 1, which left McLaren hurriedly changing to Goodyear for the first time in Barnard's era. 'Perhaps us coming to Goodyear fresh from Michelin confirmed something they had suspected in '84 but couldn't prove. Initially the Goodyear rear was much less durable as a race tyre, which created problems of much less grip at the rear than in the front. Later, that reversed . . .'

The MP4/2Bs continued McLaren's winning ways straight out of the box. Prost won three of the first four GPs on the road, only to be

1985: the year of the brake duct.
Photo: Paul-Henri Cahier

disqualified from one at Imola where his car used up too much of its consumables like fuel, oil, brake pads and tyre tread, and finished underweight.

Judging the optimum startline weight of a racing car in a minimum-weight Formula with post-race topping up now *verboten* is virtually a matter of 'who dares wins'. If you load too much fuel, too many excess grammes just in case, performance will suffer and what might have been a narrow advantage could suddenly become a deficit. On the other hand, should you start too light you risk disqualification after a lucrative and hard-won result.

McLaren had dared to their usual degree at Imola. Their Bosch Motronic engine management system normally meters fuel consumption so accurately they can trim fuel load with incredible precision. But on that occasion the car devoured more of everything than normal and they suffered – just as they had with Lauda's car in Belgium '82 when it was 1.8 kg underweight at post-race scrutineering while Wattie's winning sister car just scraped through, by 1 kg.

After Imola there was much soul-searching about how light they dare prepare their cars, weighed absolutely dry, for Monaco. There, Prost won again but his car was barely 2 kg above the limit (just 5 lb), which McLaren accepted was splendid but far too close for comfort on that particular weekend.

How close they had come to a second consecutive disqualification didn't bear thinking about; imagine what the Continental press would have made of that! But, to repeat, startline-spec is always a finely-judged matter.

And at Monaco in any case, McLaren ran into deep trouble of another kind. John: 'Most of our year was dominated by incessant work upon the brakes . . . our blokes will probably remember 1985 as the "Year of the Brake Duct"! Throughout '84 we ran carbon brakes everywhere using our own aluminium twin calipers, no problems at all. At the end of that season I was happy with the brakes and felt that was one area at least which could continue unchanged for '85 . . . I was wrong.

'This year we have been running higher turbo boost in race trim and the cars have generated less aerodynamic drag from the new bodywork, so they have been a lot quicker at the end of the straights.

'The problem with brakes is that in effect they either work OK – or don't work at all. Until you reach their limit and run into trouble you have no way of knowing how close to that limit you are. Although we had no trouble with them in 1984 I suspect now that in places we were using 99 per cent of their capacity. This year, because we have been going quicker between the corners, by mid-season we just ran out of braking.

'We had a real struggle in Canada, we had been on the limit in Monaco even though we won, and suddenly those teams using their Brembo calipers bought off the shelf from your friendly dealer looked in better shape than we were with our specials . . . In Detroit we were a complete flop. We just ran out of brakes, simple as that, and at that

Duckhams has a history of looking after engines.

We developed Europe's first Multigrade.

We launched the world's first 20W/50.

Today, whatever the engine, there still isn't a better oil than Duckhams Hypergrade, with it's SF/CD specification.

Don't forget, your engine's faced with a lifetime of stopping and starting, of hot journeys and cold starts.

So if you have any doubts about which is the best oil you can buy, the answer's simple.

Listen to your engine.

HYPERGRADE IS A TRADE MARK OF ALEXANDER DUCKHAM AND CO. LIMITED, SUMMIT HOUSE, WEST WICKHAM, KENT BR4 0SJ.

time I got heavily into the braking side and looked at *everything* in the system.

'Ricard and Silverstone of course are no problem for brakes. Then we tested at the Nürburgring and were really in deep trouble but, by the time of the German GP, I'd found the problem and fixed it and that made it all come right again.'

After Ricard, Prost tested a front suspension mod at Silverstone and the following day Barnard told me he had a tweak up his sleeve: 'just watch Alain go in the British GP, I think we'll be in good shape' – and he went, and he won.

'Before we made the front suspension geometry change we were not really *plagued* by anything, no dreadful problems at all, but the drivers complained that the cars seemed to fall into an oversteer in/understeer out condition which was not very predictable and could be improved. They did not have total confidence in their cars' handling. So we just moved the suspension pick-ups and achieved a considerable improvement in feel.'

Subsequently the MP4/2Bs' rear suspension geometry was also modified to bring the cars into still better balance.

So what about the TAG Turbo engine which everybody was raving about in '84, but which suddenly seemed to be caught in the New Year? Certainly during the winter Barnard was alarmed at the apparent complacency within the project. It was smashed back into gear, a reviewed 1985 engine spec was ready for Rio after which few changes were made. The team still did not resort to the high-boost, lightweight car qualifying ploys used by some teams and when Prost suddenly popped his '4/2B onto pole at Spa some thought this marked a major TAG engine advance. It wasn't like that at all. The Spa lap is long, the McLarens have been notably light on their tyres and Prost's qualifiers survived more of his 'quick one' than anybody else's.

There's more to this game than horsepower and a quick driver.

But come race day and the TAG V6's race-tune output was always very competitive. Barnard credits this largely to Bosch's tailor-made all-electronic management system which MI commissioned and which caused intense grief in early TAG Turbo outings. John never offers praise without good reason and he blistered Bosch mercilessly early on. He now says their tiny team did '. . . a brilliant job of making that system perform really well . . . most races have seen us use all our fuel, and everywhere but Imola the system has enabled us to do that perfectly while other teams have to carry extra fuel weight just in case their management system doesn't quite get consumption right. The system is a marvellous piece of kit – it really has come good and people should be more aware that it's a Bosch development.' So now the Germans can really take a bow.

Their Motronic system emerged at a time when they still had not reached that level of complexity on a road car. It is very difficult indeed to match injection and ignition requirements to a turbocharged engine across such an immense range of airflow from idling on zero boost up to 11,500 rpm on full boost. 'Mapping' engine performance across such a wide range is a very complex business.

Overall TAG's Porsche-engineered V6 ended the season as still the most consistent combination of power, reliability and economy in Formula 1.

The most important change was the mid-season delivery of new mirror-image turbochargers tailor-made to TAG Turbo order, to replace the original interchangeable type which demanded a slightly different exhaust system either side of the engine. This slightly compromised efficiency of one cylinder bank, so the new mirror-image KKKs put this right. The persistent water loss of 1984 had been cured, while otherwise, beyond detail power improvement, there was little alteration to the TAG Turbo engine.

The big question which remained was why Lauda's car should be so unreliable?

'I'm afraid it's just been rotten luck. At Rio he had a problem with the engine cutting out, a Motronic box problem which took a while to solve. It hit him again at Imola, but in the races it was always on Niki's car, not Alain's. Monaco was a driver error, but the oil had been dumped right in his path so there was bad luck there too. The Ricard transmission failure was partly due to running too much boost, but in Austria we had two turbo failures of a type we'd never had before, and both on Niki's car. Now that is simply rotten luck . . .

'I think his problems early in the year made him a bit despondent, but lately he had a couple of good races and that really fired him up again. Look at the way he drove in Holland!'

Ferrari

For Maranello, 1985 was a season much like '83 with one exception: this time they lost the Constructors' Championship as well as the Drivers' title, as their form fell apart at year's end.

During 1984 they had wrestled with internal turmoil until the removal of Mauro Forghieri from the *Gestione Sportiva* coincided with improved 126C4 fortunes in the final races of that year. Dr Harvey Postlethwaite designed a new moulded composite chassis for 1985, while the engine section under *Ing.* Renzetti sought to match TAG Turbo power-plus-economy in what Mr Ferrari now decided would be called the Ferrari 156/85.

The much-heralded in-line four-cylinder F1 engine became Forghieri's stillborn last hurrah. It was a little jewel but its slant-four design made installation difficult, forcing the hefty turbocharger up high and when it proved mechanically suspect in *Ing.* Caruso's dyno test section it was set aside. In retrospect perhaps its significance is that a V6 replacement was considered necessary. Was the V6 near-obsolescent?

Ferrari built nine 156/85 chassis, numbered 079-087, every one a little different from its predecessor, but 079-082 were more similar to each other than to chassis 083-087. New low-mounted turbochargers were adopted instead of the earlier in-vee layout, and the smooth, long-tailed, low-slung 156s looked superb and went very well early in the year. A quad-turbo engine was tested at Fiorano with electronically controlled wastegates pre-Imola but not raced. For Monaco, rear suspension geometry was modified and the front was revised for the first fruitless visit to Spa, where electronic wastegate control was also featured. Still chassis balance was not quite right and new tubs at Ricard had revised front suspension but events suggested a team in increasing trouble. Intercooler, oil radiator and water radiator positions were all altered for Germany but it appears that was the last occasion on which Ferrari had competitive horsepower.

Balancing race-tune power against fuel consumption had always been a nice trick which Ferrari seemed to have well under control. McLaren certainly regarded the 156s as matching their TAG Turbo engine's race-tune economy, but the pressure of the new E-Type Honda engine and also BMW's latest-version M12 late in the year, as Pirelli produced Brabham tyres which allowed the Bee-Em its head, seemed simply to break Ferrari's heart.

The awful realisation that they were being blown-off in the horsepower race hit Maranello like an ice-cold shower. It was a difficult, *difficult*, thing to swallow; it was as if somebody had told the mechanics and Italian engineers there was no Father Christmas. Latterly, to match even Renault and TAG-Porsche race-tune development, Ferrari had to run a degree of boost under which they could no longer hold their alloy-block engine together. It had become thermodynamically unreliable.

From the American tour forward, the chassis seemed not to perform as well as previously. It appeared better suited to Fiorano-like circuits than to the Österreichring. It was very efficient but much too sensitive to different types of track; fine at the *ersatz* Nürburgring, in trouble at bumpy Zandvoort and Brands Hatch. Modern Formula 1 has outgrown the Ferrari test-track, Fiorano lacks very high-speed corners and apparently it will now be extended to include some.

The 156 chassis spec at Monza differed considerably from its predecessors, Harvey Postlethwaite's section having swopped downforce generated by ground effects for downforce generated by wings. They ran minimum download, minimum drag in qualifying but still they were roundly blown-off by BMW and Honda and they even struggled against Renault. That was the point – on the holy ground of Monza – at which the cold shower hit the engine section.

But until their end of season disasters, Ferrari

Qualifying sessions became divorced from the realities of race day, BMW turning up more than 1000 bhp at maximum boost for Nelson Piquet's use during some staggeringly powerful laps.
Photo: Paul-Henri Cahier

had led McLaren comfortably in the Constructors' Championship and were very happy with Alboreto and Johansson's efforts. The 'almost Nordic' former was rated an excellent race driver who looked after his car almost too well, never using up gearbox or brakes, while the perversely 'more Latin' Johansson was considered a better race driver than tester but one who was affected by the inadequacies in a car more than Alboreto (who just drove round them), so proving very useful in testing.

One possible escape from their late-1985 engine problems could be the adoption of a thinwall iron block like BMW's and Honda's for better heat absorption than their traditional aluminium-alloy. But, whatever may happen after the rebuffs of 1984-85, Maranello are not about to take defeat lying down.

Brabham

Gordon Murray admitted, 'For us it's been a strange season. In 1984 only McLaren and us were competitive, but we didn't finish at all well due to engines. For the New Year we swopped from Michelin to Pirelli and that change combined with working with BMW to put the engines right meant about 12,000 miles of testing! It was like finishing one race season then immediately doing another, only more concentrated, through the winter . . .

'We definitely emerged from that period with a more reliable engine but it wasn't reliable enough and gearboxes were also unreliable. Meanwhile we'd initially said to Pirelli we wanted to develop a competitive race tyre first – forget the qualifiers – then bring on a qualifier subsequently. Our winter testing in South Africa gave us a super hot-weather tyre for Rio where we were in excellent shape only for a gearbox failure to put us out.

'After that we had problems. The Pirellis were always very weather sensitive. If we had the appropriate tyres at the circuit for whatever ambient conditions happened to be, we were OK. It was like that at Ricard, with a new tyre good in very hot weather. That new tyre was a big change, and from half-way through the season we got a qualifying tyre that worked properly as well. Tyre testing has gone on continuously, and they weren't only good in hot weather – we were very quick in a cold test at Nürburgring and quickest in a freezing test at Zandvoort too. Then look how we went at Brands Hatch on a cool grey day . . .

'Generally speaking we weren't helped by the mid-season driver change, but Marc did well.'

Gordon's BT54 monocoque was the last in Formula 1 to retain an aluminium outer skin, stiffened by a complex moulded carbon-composite

inner-cum-scuttle-and-tank-top. Like the BT52s/53s, it featured modular construction with the entire front suspension hung on a machined-from-solid nose bulkhead plugged into the front of the tub structure, and a similar engine/gearbox/rear suspension module at the rear. Continuous torsional tests through the season monitored each chassis' health, weakening ones being retired. Just after Spa 'BT54/9' was about to enter service.

One disadvantage with the four-cylinder was that Brabham could only 'flow' one side of their car's undertail ground-effects diffuser section. Throughout 1983/84 it had become standard Brabham practice to produce a B-spec update mid-season, but after their intensive winter testing for '85 the BT54 layout remained broadly unaltered. Brabham had at last abandoned their American Hitco carbon brakes for French SEPs with modified Girling calipers, the SEPs testing well and their manufacturers offering a good deal.

While BMW tightened up quality control to retrieve engine reliability, Brabham asked them to lower its inlet level allowing a lower intake box and new body giving better flow to engine and rear wing. Their float of 25 engines was clearly amongst the most powerful around, at least 800 bhp being a fair estimate for 220-litres race consumption, 'when everybody', as Gordon says, 'tops up on the grid', and a minimum 200 bhp more for qualifying. In fact Brabham ran higher race horsepower at the beginning of the year than through mid-season in deference to their tyres. A computer failure at Imola saw them burn all their fuel while, at Silverstone, 'we cocked-up completely, and were just utterly uncompetitive and finished with a lot of fuel left over . . .'

They had their share of fires during the season, notably one in testing at the Nürburgring which wrote off a car, and Surer's cheery blaze ending his superb drive at Brands. Turbocharger bearings are fed pressurised engine oil. If the bearing disintegrates or its seals fail, that oil cascades through the incandescent 'charger and inevitably ignites. In the BT54s' case, it would flood the left side pod, hence the car burned to the waterline in Germany. But by the end of the season the Brabhams were hot stuff everywhere as Pirelli's tyres became truly competitive. The team could return to start-of-season race horsepower without compromising tyre life and optimism rose for '86.

Lotus

For the Ketteringham team, 1985 was satisfying only insofar as every year since Colin Chapman's untimely death has seen them do better. Four of Gérard Ducarouge's Renault-powered Type 97Ts were built for the new year, closely based upon the

promising 95T of 1984 (the Type 96 having been the stillborn Winkelmann Indy project). Duca-rouge adopted small winglets on the rear of each side pod to compensate for lost download from the new regulation rear wings, and also introduced vertical vanes within the front wheels to clean up turbulence and reduce drag. Others would copy him with varying degrees of comprehension and success.

Yet again Team's tiny car inventory was sufficient and although some tubs were damaged, none were written off. By season's end they had built 21 tubs over five seasons in their entire carbon-composite series and never lost a single one.

They used a mixture of Renault's old EF4 and revised new EF15 V6 engines, serviced for them by Renault's customer sub-contractor, Mecachrome in Bourges. The EF4s were in qualifying-boost tune, which the customer EF15s would not accept to the same degree. After qualifying, EF15s would be fitted for warm-up and the race, along with new drive-trains/rear ends to replace the assembly freshly-compromised by qualifying loads. Essentially the spare car was EF15-powered throughout, being used in practice to assess appropriate race-tune consumption. Through the year until Spa, Team had received and fitted fresh engines from 87 Mecachrome rebuilds, an average 270 miles going onto each unit before it was returned.

Renault engine designer Bernard Dudot used Lotus 'as the reference car to judge the engine. I think we were second to the Honda; a good compromise between power and fuel consumption'. Interestingly, he found there could be an 80 bhp spread between outputs (i.e. boost level) necessary at the same lap time on Lotus, Renault, Ligier and Tyrrell chassis. Renault Sport still tried new tweaks first but because they had so many other problems, results were often inconclusive. Garrett pursued relentless turbo development. The 137 kg EF15 V6 worked well.

Unlike 1984 when the 95T spec was set at the start of the year and changed hardly at all throughout the season, the 97T saw more change, partly due to Goodyear tyre development as they improved rear tyres, then fronts, to-and-fro but generally moving forward all the time.

Certainly Ayrton Senna was Team's not-so-secret weapon for '85, winning two races and having others in his pocket before technical failure. In between victory at Estoril and Spa and good placings elsewhere, Senna's first eight retirements effectively broke down as follows: two due to Team's chassis, five to Renault's engine and its ancillaries, and one driver error. The Rio electrical fuel pump was blocked by a blob of adhesive which caused the motor windings to burn out. Pumps had been in short supply so an old type using internal adhesive had been fitted, which was not used on the new pumps. Lotus also claimed the *ersatz* Nürburgring CV joint failure as their fault. The interesting thing about the engine problems was that the 1985 season saw less turbocharger trouble than ever before, the

Piquet, Pirelli and the Brabham BT54: 12,000 miles of testing.
Photo: Paul-Henri Cahier

Renault change from KKK to Garrett seeming a wise one.

While de Angelis did his usual reliable and unobtrusive job for the team and was there to take first place at Imola after Prost's disqualification, Senna impressed everyone with not only his natural talent but also his remarkable perception.

At Monaco he reported that he had over-revved in the morning warm-up. Elio's engine was already being changed in the pit lane but Senna believed this would be OK for the race. However, although he hadn't buzzed it badly, it did fail. At Silverstone he had remarked: 'There's something strange about the exhaust gas temperature' and the problem he suffered in the race proved him right again.

At Zandvoort he warned that the water temperature was a little bit high, and in the race his car lost all its water except 1.5 litres. Peter Warr admitted, 'We realise we've got to take notice of what he says now', while Renault's likeable chief engineer Bernard Dudot laughed, 'With him we don't need telemetry . . .'

They have been using onboard recording which can either monitor 10 functions for a limited period, or two functions for race duration. Normally it records boost pressure and revs throughout a race, and it has laid the rumour that Senna has been winding up boost at the expense of consumption in race situations. At Silverstone he didn't boost himself to a vainglorious dry tank in his battle with Prost; like Fangio, Moss, Clark or Stewart before him he found the quicker lap times within his own systems. Then, after the German GP, the read-out revealed how he had been using minimum boost and changing up at only 10,200-10,300 rpm while leading comfortably and controlling the race.

For Peter Warr one significant landmark was reached at Monza. 'There in 1970', he said, 'Team used a 200 mph final-drive for the first time, in a Lotus 72 running low-drag configuration. It's taken us 15 years, but this year at Monza we were back up to 200 mph again . . .' And in safety.

Progress lives.

Williams

Patrick Head's engineers at Didcot had some real problems throughout 1984 as they learned to combat the brutally powerful Honda V6 engine's wicked torque curve and the team's drivers discovered everything a bright lad should know about initial understeer, followed by instant, stunning, mind-blurring oversteer.

Late that season Patrick decided to abandon his favoured aluminium honeycomb monocoque construction in favour of moulded carbon composite, and the resultant FW10 was the first 'black Williams'. After one pilot-build prototype shell had been moulded eight more followed, seven being completed immediately, one written off at Detroit when Nigel Mansell front-ended a barrier (easier to replace than repair, and the torn tub may yet be recommissioned as a show car), then the tyre explosion at Ricard, and the ensuing accident destroying another. Finally, chassis

'FW10/4' went to Japan for Honda's engine development test programme, driven by Satoru Nakajima.

It has always taken time to build a relationship of mutual and open trust with the Japanese, but Williams-Honda's grew through fire in '84 and while the new chassis was prepared in Didcot, Nobuhiko Kawamoto's engine group at Honda R&D, Wako, near Tokyo, sought to build a more useable power curve, better mechanical reliability and improved structural rigidity into a new version of their iron-block engine.

In the early part of the year Williams ran modified D-Type engines, then from Montreal the revamped E-Type. The D engines had the improved engine mounts of the forthcoming Es to match the FW10 chassis, and were further modified to sidestep early IHI turbocharger problems. A new transmission, still six-speed to cope with the D engine's narrow rev band, had been adopted and throughout the year Patrick considered power had been good enough 'to break traction in second and third . . . [sigh, then a rather rueful chuckle] . . . and fourth and fifth as well . . .'

The new E engines emerged at Montreal where Rosberg ended up 25 seconds behind Alboreto despite two stops; one where he lost boost due to an electrical problem, then a puncture. Mansell had a boost problem and ended up running what was effectively a 185-litre race. Next time out at Detroit, Keke won.

The FW10-Honda Es were mechanically satisfactory at Ricard but the heat and speeds there aggravated their already rampant hunger for tyres. A spell of unreliability followed – the car at Silverstone, largely the engine subsequently – until Spa where it began to come good. Before Brands Hatch the rear of the body was lowered to improve airflow to the rear wing and the FW10 could handle the Honda's now-reliable power well enough for a convincing team 1-3 and Nigel Mansell's maiden win.

A redesigned transmission and new pullrod instead of rocker-arm rear suspension emerged late-season. Williams used French SEP carbon brakes everywhere except Detroit and Adelaide, where they reverted to iron, just to be sure.

Failures included a clutch, once; exhaust prob-

lems losing boost, twice; engines in Austria; a wrong tyre choice on Nigel's car at Zandvoort, and so on.

The Honda engine rebuild shop beside Williams's lavishly equipped factory at Didcot came into commission in June, and the team ended the season as the performance standard by which others were measured.

Patrick himself was confident of Honda power and, surveying the Formula 1 engine scene overall, he would talk freely of the better engines qualifying around 1000-1250 bhp, and at one point in race tune reaching 900 horsepower. He's a tough, logical engineer never given to exaggeration so perhaps it's significant that the figures which come naturally to him as a generalisation are higher than those of his rivals.

Of all the teams, Williams-Honda ended 1985 looking in the best position for the season to come, thanks to three commanding wins in succession.

The Rest

Of the non-winners, Toleman deserved special praise for their fine Rory Byrne-designed chassis, one of the best-handling in Formula 1 once the politics of tyre supply had been overcome. That early-season hiccup crippled both Toleman chassis and Hart engine development and Rory considers 'it took until Silverstone to catch up'. Often very quick in qualifying, with Fabi on their first-ever Formula 1 pole in Germany, Toleman's races were spoiled by unreliability, including some recurring engine failures. From May they had four cars all with the monocoque underside aerodynamic step which Byrne developed in exclusive use of the Royal Military College wind tunnel at Shrivenham. This device enhanced download without drag penalty and certainly showed its worth on some circuits. Pirelli did more for the team than their original commitment implied and Toleman ended the season with their reputation greatly enhanced. They *could* do it without Senna.

Ligier provided an even greater revelation as ex-Renault designer Michel Tétu – who had once been Ligier's GT car designer pre-*Régie* – dragged them back into serious contention by the end of the season, making their best-ever use of the Renault Mecachrome engines.

Renault themselves sank without trace after their retirement had been announced. It was sad to see, while their third customer, Tyrrell, gave the Cosworth V8 its last hurrah at the *ersatz* Nürburgring, then, thanks to Ron Dennis, non-started in Austria. Only seven of the ultimate true DFYs were built: 022-027 went to Tyrrell, 'DFY 001' was Cosworth's development unit also used by the team, and one of them was lunched in Germany, going out in a smother of smoke, steam, shrapnel . . . and glory. Some 382 serious Cosworth V8s had been built since 1967, including '40-ish' sports car engines. The Nürburgring marked the end of their long career and the true end of an era. Just consider that its successor is like replacing a Ford 10 with a Ferrari Testa Rossa! Then the magnitude of recent development becomes clear.

"Some 382 serious Cosworth V8s had been built since 1967. The Nürburgring marked the end of their long career and the true end of an era."

A heavy development programme by Honda helped the Williams team into a strong position for 1986.

KONI

Koni shock absorbers. Out of this world.

BANKS

Koni shock absorbers are distributed exclusively throughout the U.K. by
J W E Banks & Sons Ltd., Crowland, Peterborough PE6 0JP. Tel: 0733 210316. Telex 32533.

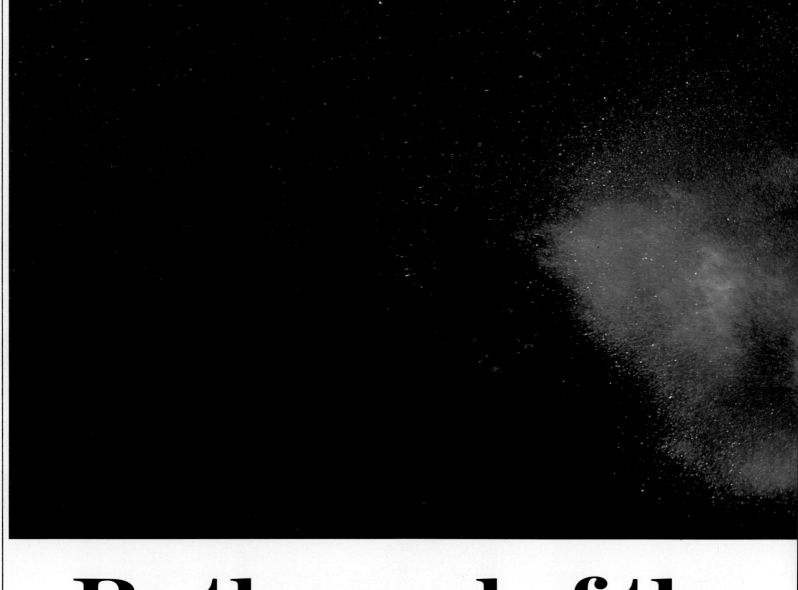

By the end of the championship it was champagne he was spraying.

As you can see, Russell Brookes caused quite a splash on the rally scene this year.

He won the Shell RAC British

Open Rally Championship.

We would like to congratulate him on his hard-earned title.

We would also like to take this

opportunity to claim a little of the credit for our Dealer Team.

It was their car that he drove to victory. An Opel Manta 400.

It's not the first time a Vauxhall or Opel has won the title.

It is, in fact, the fourth time we've won it in the last five years. (The hiccup was in 1983.)

Nevertheless, we're particularly pleased about this year's triumph.

The 4-wheel drive fraternity were out in greater force than ever. And the stages were particularly demanding.

No matter. Russell and the Manta were up to the task.

As were some of their stablemates.

Our Astra GTE took first place in the demanding Group N. And an impressive 1st, 2nd and 3rd, in the 1600 to 2000cc class of Group A.

It was heartwarming news to us, back at the ranch.

The good news for you is that all these machines have road-going brothers, waiting to be put through their paces, at your local Vauxhall-Opel dealership.

Clearly their top speed and road holding isn't of the same vintage as Russell Brookes' Manta 400.

But rest assured, compared to their rivals, their performance is just as sparkling.

BACKED BY THE WORLDWIDE RESOURCES OF GENERAL MOTORS

FOR 20 YEAR
A STRONG
THE GRAND P

Over the years 1965 to 1985, Goodyear have been involved in excess of 160 Grand Prix wins.

We have achieved this incredible record by following a simple rule. Tyre development is equally as important as car, team and driver improvement. Just look at our past

The 1968 McLaren-Ford on Goodyear.

record. We were the obvious choice to be used with the revolutionary Ford Cosworth engines back in 1968.

During the early seventies, we helped the Tyrrell team and Jackie Stewart down the road to two Formula One World Championships.

Tyrrell and Goodyear record-breaking success in the 70's.

The mid-seventies saw Goodyear totally dominate the Grand Prix circuit. Every Grand Prix during this period was won by a car using Goodyear tyres.

By 1977–78, Lotus had developed ground-effect aerodynamics. This added an extra 1½ tons download

S WE'VE HAD HOLD ON RIX CIRCUIT.

to the car, and although this meant they would go through corners quicker, immense stress was put on the tyres.

Goodyear were chosen and coped admirably with the pressure.

The Lotus 79 on Goodyear.

In 1982, the new turbo-charged Ferraris raced their way to the World Constructor's Championship. 1984 saw Goodyear introduce its new Eagle Tyres and it was these tyres

that Alain Prost and Marlboro-McLaren used to take the Drivers World Championship title in 1985.

The 1985 Marlboro-McLaren and Goodyear Eagles.

The amount of devotion we put into developing our Grand Prix tyres means you can be sure of one thing. Drivers on Goodyear will keep coming over the line first.

LEADING THE WORLD IN TYRE TECHNOLOGY

Paul-Henri Cahier

Like the iceberg that sank the *Titanic*, 90 per cent of racing tyre development goes on beneath the surface. The helter-skelter of Grand Prix activity where, on the day, tyre performance is either taken for granted (if all goes well) or roundly berated (if anything goes wrong), is merely the glamorous front to a multi-million dollar high technology operation for those who have chosen to prove their products in this most exalted international category of motorsport.

Tyre technology (and, indeed, supply) is something which too many people have taken for granted for too long. Over the past few years there have been one or two unpleasant hiccups in the smooth continuity of that supply, exposing Formula 1 paddocks to the chill wind of reality. Finally, last winter, a little bit of history was made. A tyre company actually declined to supply a Grand Prix team. Toleman, following the withdrawal of Michelin, had nowhere to turn but to Goodyear. And Akron said 'no'. Many people didn't believe what they were hearing, but Goodyear certainly meant what it was saying. Suddenly the racing world was up in arms.

Director of International Racing for the Goodyear Tyre and Rubber Company is 49-year old Leo Mehl, an old hand at the Formula 1 political party games who hides a wealth of shrewd experience behind a weatherbeaten face, creased through an excess of smiling over the years – although there have been times when it has been hard to understand what on earth he might have to smile about. Ever since he graduated from university in 1959, Mehl's entire working life has been spent with the Akron industrial giant (apart from an obligatory interruption for his national service with the US Air Force). He is a company man who delivers the corporate message in a sugar-coated pill. A conformist without appearing bland, a character wielding power and influence without being unduly obtrusive, Mehl has done a good job for Goodyear in particular and Formula 1 in general over the years, capitalising on solid experience and affection laid down originally in the late 1960s when company competition business brought him to Europe for the first time.

Mehl grew up with the current Formula 1 generation, overseeing Goodyear's Formula 1 operation between 1969 and 1971, so for most people in the paddocks, Mehl's benignly crinkled features represent the beaming corporate face of the giant American concern. But don't be fooled; Leo retains a hard-nosed awareness that Goodyear's racing involvement must show a worthwhile return, from the point of view of publicity and technical feedback.

Over the past couple of decades Goodyear has, at various times, faced up to Firestone, Pirelli and Michelin in a battle for Grand Prix tyre supremacy. Today Goodyear squares up to Pirelli alone on the Formula 1 front, but has been through a spell (1975-77) when it had a monopoly of tyre supply amongst World Championship contenders. And there is always the possibility that at sometime in the future Goodyear might find itself called upon to supply tyres to the field. Amongst the participating teams there is an optimistic assumption that, should the situation arise, Goodyear would be prepared to provide tyres for everybody. Did Mehl agree with this possible scenario? And does Goodyear prefer a monopoly, a 'one tyre formula', or feel happier in a fight against a rival?

His reply came without hesitation: 'We much prefer a fight because the benefits that accrue from this business are split pretty well 50/50 between the advertising benefit and the technical feedback. But you run the danger of losing both benefits to some extent if you don't have the stimulus of competition. If you've got a monopoly you find that development work starts to slow down. At the present time, for example, we do something in the nature of ten major Formula 1 tyre tests every year and every one is as competitive and demanding as a racing event. That would be one area in which we would

automatically cut back if we were on our own.

'From the publicity point of view if you're in a monopoly situation you also run the risk of bad publicity. The only real way to get your name in the paper when you've got a monopoly is to do something dumb. You read things like "he blew a tyre going into the first corner", or "the tyres were out of balance, so he stopped", or "it's too cold and the tyres won't work" – I mean, how many times have you heard that one?

'So you really expose yourself and suddenly find that you haven't simply got five teams telling you what's wrong, but 25. And you've got nothing else left in the truck to give them as an alternative. That's the problem!'

However, Mehl is quick to remind us that the technical challenge of F1 is so demanding that one couldn't just sit back in a monopoly position and deal out any old tyre. Goodyear currently has a monopoly in NASCAR and Indy car categories, but that doesn't stop them being every bit as demanding as the Formula 1 programme.

'For F1 racing you can't just make 15,000 hard tyres and say "drop by the local warehouse and pick them up" because if you do that the chances are that you'll be beaten by anybody – Avon, Pirelli, Bridgestone, M & H . . .

'You've got to tailor the tyre to suit the circuit, as much anything for your own self-protection. By self-protection I'm talking about the safety of

drivers at the same time as producing a tyre which is more than adequate for the race. You don't want to risk ruining a race, for example, by saying "here's a nice hard rain tyre, the set will last you all season" and then find, when it rains for the first time, they all crash! We have a lot of experience about the possible pitfalls of this sort of situation in NASCAR. We've had a NASCAR tyre supply monopoly for the past 10 years, but we still use some 15 different tyre compound/constructions for the 30 events. Like Indy car racing, certain tracks need a special left-front or right-rear. OK, so they are control tyre formulae in the sense that the competitors don't have any choice, but I can tell you I've been in some pretty unpleasant situations where a control tyre has been used, perhaps, into the following season, just to empty the warehouse sort-of-thing.

'It is important, if you're going to be in this business, to do as good a technical job as you possibly can. If you take an unacceptably hard tyre to certain sorts of circuit and you wind up by upsetting all your teams it's probably better not to be there at all if you're not going to do the job correctly. And doing the job correctly is not influenced by whether or not you're operating in a monopoly situation.'

Mehl agrees energetically with the proposition that the Formula 1 tail has been wagging the dog in some respects and that, certainly in the past, some Grand Prix teams have been attempting to dictate terms when they have simply not been in a position to do so.

'It's happened many times in the past', he grinned, 'but I think you can take it that things are different now. The company management is in a position now where they will support any programme I submit to them to prevent that sort of situation arising again. I think if we ever get to have a monopoly again, we will have a stronger programme to protect Goodyear's interests than we did in the past. I think we will always want to have several key teams with which there is a special relationship for testing and development work – and we'll have an obligation to those guys to give them anything.

'But we will not set ourselves up in a situation where we are obligated to 25 cars and then have a situation where a new tyre company comes in, takes two teams and leaves us with the balance. So what we would be saying is that we'll supply all the same tyres in a monopoly, but would have to review our approach once any opposition appears.

'I think Goodyear is a lot more confident than in the past over its ability to control our own destiny in Formula 1. Two major things have changed our attitude. Firstly, after starting very late in the radial tyre development race, we have caught up. It's absolutely essential that our programme is built around winning. We don't have to win everything, but we have to be associated with winners. And we had a rough F1 season in 1983. Mr. Mercer [Goodyear's President] has said that racing is a great programme, but you've got to win, and I've no qualms at all about that. There is no question in my mind that we're the number one tyre company and intend to stay that way. But we've got to win . . .'

The second development which has increased Goodyear's racing self-confidence is the vexed case of the Toleman team. At the end of the 1984 season Toleman suddenly found itself facing a new year with no firm source of tyre supply. Pirelli had

been upset by the clumsy manner in which the British team had changed to Michelin mid-season, and although Goodyear showed some initial interest in supplying them for '85, the whole complexion of Akron's problem changed dramatically when Michelin withdrew and Goodyear faced supplying Renault in addition to World Championship winning McLaren International squad.

Goodyear told Toleman quite firmly that it would not be able to supply tyres for 1985. Toleman waited in disbelieving limbo, then looked round for somebody to blame when no tyres materialised at the start of the year. Goodyear came in for some stick. It was difficult for the man in the street to grasp why the huge industrial giant was not in a position to help out this tiny underdog of the Formula 1 fraternity.

Mehl is very firm and very adamant about Goodyear's response. 'For the first time in the 20 years that I've been around this business, Goodyear actually said "no". And, in this, we had the support of all management at many levels in the company. We explained our capacity problem and our general economic position with regard to the Toleman situation.

'To service the Toleman team we would have been obliged to take between 80 and 100 additional tyres to each Grand Prix, all of which would have to be hauled across the Atlantic and then round Europe. As it was our truck was full to capacity, so that would have meant buying a new truck, finding more space in the paddocks, and so on. I just can't put a financial bottom line on what supplying Toleman would have cost us, but you must understand that we have other obligations for our radial equipment outside of Formula 1.

'One of those other categories is IMSA, where we're stepping up the pressure in the face of competition from Bridgestone. We're expanding our Indy involvement because we want to compete there on radials in 1986. We planned to run radials at all the remaining CART races this year with Indy following next season. These are all integral parts of our overall racing programme and all have to be taken into account when assessing how much of our resources we can apply to Formula 1.'

Focusing more closely on Goodyear's day-to-day involvement in the business of Grand Prix racing, the much-discussed question of qualifying rubber is something about which Mehl is acutely concerned. Some people in the Formula 1 business believe that the current situation, with two marked sets of qualifying tyres per official session, amounts to the worst of both worlds, believing that there should either be no qualifiers or that they should be supplied in unlimited quantities. Others want to see an Indy-style qualifying system evolved, perhaps requiring that cars start the race on the same tyres as they qualified on.

Mehl explains that he has given a great deal of consideration to this whole complicated business. 'A year or two ago, Michelin's Pierre Dupasquier and I jointly agreed on an Indy-type qualifying programme for F1 which we recommended to FISA as the only method by which one could completely eliminate qualifying tyres. You go out on Saturday, draw your number out of a hat and line up. It's the same for everybody and if it rains mid-way through the runs, that's your problem. If the wind comes up, if somebody puts down oil . . . bad luck. That is the only way of eliminating qualifying tyres and we couldn't find a *single* F1 team which would agree to it.

Steve Swope

John Townsend

'The problem does *not* lie with the tyre companies, you've got to remember. It lies with nobody being prepared, or willing, to alter the current system of qualifying. Everybody is frightened of traffic – yet they won't even divide the field in half to run in separate 30-minute sessions, a simple step which would halve the traffic problem at a stroke. Nobody would agree to that. So even if we turned up and said "OK, you're not getting anything softer than B compound so you'd better just get used to it", we would then still have to control the number of sets we supplied because, if we didn't, you'd find everybody wanting to use eight sets every session. So, as I keep saying, I can't see a way out of the current qualifying dilemma, but I think the situation we're in at the moment with two marked sets per session is as good a compromise as we tyre people can think of.

'If there was a situation where qualifiers were unlimited, we would find ourselves supporting fewer teams and I believe that would be a silly way of taking some good teams off some good tyres. It would be a waste of resources. What's more, I think that exposure to unlimited sets of qualifiers is extremely dangerous. It reminds me of the argument last year when it was suggested that there could perhaps be a 10-lap qualifying run with the best eight counting for the grid position. Keke said at the time that the system would mean him taking eight chances of crashing rather than the one or two he was taking under the current system – because if he didn't, then somebody else would. All in all, I think that for F1 – where you're basically dealing with ultimates, the best that money can buy in every area – the compromise we have at present is not bad at all.'

Like few other areas in the sport, racing improves the production breed in tyre technology in a quite dramatic fashion. When it came to tracing the path of direct racing development influencing road car tyres, Mehl had no difficulty in being very specific indeed.

'Take the "gator back" tread design which we used as our wet weather F1 tyre back in 1981. That tread pattern really worked. It was the initial biased rain tyre, running against Michelin radials, and it was very respectable indeed. Now you can see it as the most successful high-performance road tyre in America – the Eagle VR – fitted to quick cars like Corvettes and so on. That is a definite example of a racing development which is there for all to see.

'In the radial passenger and truck tyre areas there are a number of other developments with exciting new materials, although I'm not really at liberty to discuss them with you. But they have definitely contributed to the overall pool of technical knowledge within the company and, taken as a whole, I'd say the technical work done over the last year has been very exciting indeed. On this radial development we've been learning like a bunch of kids and the racing department is probably making a better technical contribution to the company than ever before. Technically, we have a better reputation at present than we have enjoyed for a long time.'

We asked Mehl whether he felt there was any area in tyre development where a major quantum leap forward could be realistically expected. He shook his head. 'No, I don't think things happen like that in tyre development. But I think the progress we have made has helped American car manufacturers to really appreciate what a tyre

John Colley

can do for their vehicle and our products are now so good that the average road car now comes out of the showroom on a set of radials and the owner will only need one replacement set, at perhaps 30,000-40,000 miles, to see out the life of his car.

'It used to be that the original equipment wouldn't last nearly as long, so perhaps he'd use five sets, rather than two, during the life of the car. This is one of the reasons that tyre business in the United States is contracting. The replacement market is reducing because the tyres are better now than they were five years ago. And racing programmes have contributed towards this.'

Mehl is happy to confirm that, notwithstanding minor hiccups – 'most of which have been, and probably will be, financial!' – Goodyear's long-term commitment to motor racing is fairly open-ended. For the Formula 1 team in today's Grand Prix paddock, the racing tyre is simply one of the specialist components which is blended into a winning recipe. Victory is the prime consideration. Goodyear, and its rival tyre companies, certainly relish the individual track successes, but it is the long-term technical lessons which change and improve the nature of the road product which is the ultimate payoff.

Leo puts the pace of improvement into sharp perspective by rounding off with an affectionate little tale involving Jochen Rindt back in the summer of 1968.

'It was the free day between final qualifying and the race, French Grand Prix weekend at Rouen. Jochen had planted the Brabham-Repco on pole but he wasn't very confident about it lasting more than a few laps on the Sunday, so he took me off into Paris to do the full tourist bit on the Saturday.

We came home pretty late in Jochen's Porsche 911, running absolutely flat-out on the road when I started to be worried about this clunking sound.

'I said to Jochen, "what on earth's wrong?" and he just shrugged, replying "it's those bloody tyres again, they're always chunking like that . . ." I looked over at the instruments and the speedometer was off the clock at what looked like 130 mph, then there was another big clunk and I shouted "Jochen, stop the car!" So we pulled over and got out and, would you believe, the whole inside shoulder had come away! I just said "good grief . . ." or something like that while Rindt simply stood there on the side of the road muttering "I've tried every tyre in the world and they're all junk". Needless to say, they were *not* Goodyears, incidentally! I suddenly realised that these guys drove like this as a matter of routine, so I went back and enquired whether we had anything up to that sort of job and we had nothing at the time which was really rated for more than 100 mph. Now there are any number of tyres rated at 125 mph!

'Take our partnership with Ferrari. It's not merely a racing obligation, it's a high performance tyre commitment to produce a tyre for whatever Maranello thinks up next. For a GTO which runs 210 mph on the streets which you still want to drive round your local neighbourhood, run it into kerbs, then go out again and do 210 mph after it's been sitting in your garage for a month. It has to have adequate ride qualities at 55 mph, yet be capable of being run at 185 mph at the other end of the scale . . .

'This is what racing enables us to find out about . . .'

WE WERE IN AT THE START...

No other spark plug in the world has a record of success in motorsport like Champion. And the technology we've developed in racing has helped us produce new Champion + spark plugs. With wider based longer nosed insulators, and copper cores, you can rely on them to stay cleaner, overcome misfiring and make starting easier. That's why they are used and recommended by leading car manufacturers and engine builders throughout the world.

So when you fit a set of Champion + plugs, you can be sure of one thing. You'll start as you mean to go on.

YOU CAN'T BEAT A CHAMPION

Niki Lauda:

Picture the scene: a small hotel in Albi, south-west France, in September 1971. I am in conversation with a slightly-built, buck-toothed Austrian, 22 years old and just completing his maiden season at the wheel of a Formula 2 March. He seemed, to me at least, to be facing a major dilemma. He is pledged to produce the sterling equivalent of around two million Austrian schillings (about £40,000 at the time) for credit to the account of March Engineering at Barclays Bank, Oxford. And he has got to find it within ten days. His existing sponsor has just withdrawn its support and he has no idea where he will obtain the necessary funds to back his move up the ladder into Formula 1. Meanwhile, Max Mosley is putting pressure onto him. If he does not produce the money on time, the drive will go to somebody else. The Austrian understands and stalls for time. Mosley, not exactly swamped with applications for the second March seat alongside Ronnie Peterson, is also playing for time – with the bank. March has made a trading loss of around £70,000 in its second full season so the company is relying on the Austrian's money to keep afloat. But the Austrian does not know that. After a few weeks of shadow boxing, the money eventually arrives. The Austrian has sweet-talked a new sponsor (another bank) into sponsoring his graduation into the sport's most exalted category.

From such small acorns . . . Andreas Nikolaus Lauda was to make the Grand Prix grade and within four years of this delicate financial shortfall, would stand poised on the verge of his first World Championship title. Another two such titles, interrupted by a temporary retirement from the Formula 1 scene, would punctuate his career before he finally called a halt at the end of the 1985 season. In the course of his career he stamped his identity on a decade of Grand Prix motorsport in a manner rivalled by only a handful of men in its entire history.

Max Mosley's abiding impression of the young Lauda was that he was an unusually *intelligent* racing driver. Of that there can be no doubt. Privately, Mosley also adds that he doubted whether Niki would be quick enough to achieve great success. In that, Mosley was wrong. But what was impossible to anticipate in those early years was just what an incredible mixture of pragmatism, restraint, speed and commitment this young man would apply to his chosen sport.

Lauda proved that he had the speed during his unsuccessful 1973 season driving for BRM. He also had the luck, a commodity without which a racing driver can never have a hope. Enzo Ferrari noticed his BRM P160 holding third place briefly at Monaco – ahead of Jacky Ickx's Ferrari. Clay Regazzoni also recommended Niki as a promising new lad and, hey presto, he moved across to Maranello at the end of the year. He had to extract himself from some legal entanglements with Louis Stanley, but he got off the hook quite lightly, considering he was now on his way to becoming a millionaire.

Ferrari and Lauda got together at precisely the right time for each other. Revelling in test and development work, Niki capitalised on the facilities available at the team's Fiorano test track to get miles under his belt and develop his knowledge of what makes a racing car tick. He developed an almost intuitive flair for coming up with the right technical answers, worked well with the engineers – notably Mauro Forghieri – and took the absolute minimum out of the cars in terms of wear and tear. In 1974 he won two Grands Prix; the following year he won five to take the World Championship.

The man in the street may have come to know Niki's name through newspaper banner headlines the following summer when he survived that fiery crash at the Nürburgring, but the remarkable aspect of that affair was the way in which he remained unscathed mentally by the ordeal. Much was made of his decision to withdraw from the rain-soaked 1976 Japanese Grand Prix, a decision which handed the Championship to James Hunt, but this was a classic example of Lauda being his own man. He had made *his* decision, and the rest of the world would have to live with it.

Confounding the naïve critics who believed him over the top, Niki came back to win the 1977 Championship for Ferrari before joining forces with Bernie Ecclestone to drive the Brabham-Alfa Romeo in 1978. The combination promised much, but never quite managed to deliver in terms of hard results. Things got worse in 1979 when the Alfa V12 engine appeared and Niki retired abruptly mid-way through first practice for the Canadian Grand Prix.

For over two years his world was his airline, Lauda Air, and he hardly ever bothered to 'look over the fence' into the motor racing field. He professed not to miss the challenge of Formula 1, but the notion of making a return, against the odds, was irresistibly tantalising. He eventually succumbed to the temptation and was back in the cockpit – this time of a Marlboro McLaren – for the start of the 1982 season.

The rest of the tale is recent history: that Championship in '84, won by the sensationally scant margin of half a point from team-mate Prost; the trough into which Niki slipped during the first half of 1985; the amazingly frank retirement announcement in Austria, followed by that stupendous victory at Zandvoort. Right up to the end, he could still drive like a 22-year old . . . when he wanted to.

His wry sense of humour, honed to a very English edge during those early days in Formula 2, will be missed. As he vanished into a world of Boeing 737s and Gates LearJets he will leave behind him a definite void in the Formula 1 ranks. He was unequalled in terms of personal candour during his glittering Grand Prix career; although he contrived to remain a very private person he nevertheless always had time for those he numbered amongst his friends.

And, on his day, he could be a quite remarkable racing driver.

The Last Goodbye?

by Alan Henry

Paul-Henri Cahier

Niki Lauda
A1 neg.

Diana Burnett

Niki Lauda produced marvellous displays of
race-craft and aggression in the Marlboro
McLaren MP4/2B, the former World
Champion keeping everyone guessing over
his future until the very end.
Photos: International Press Agency and Michael Hewitt

Formula 1 Review
Little Big Man

by Russell Bulgin, Sports Editor, *Motor*

In 1985, Alain Prost, Formula 1's biggest little man and most consistent race winner, finally clinched the World Championship.

I am going to go on holiday for three weeks, which is unusual for me. With my wife and with my son; relax, and play golf.

Alain Prost, Kyalami, October 1985

They whistlestopped through the winter, Alain Prost and Niki Lauda. Marlboro press conference to Marlboro press conference in a haze of high-altitude hype. Lauda-Air Lear Jet Model 36A, registration OE-GNL, tracked across Europe and around the periphery of South America. Same questions everywhere . . . looking back on the 12 wins of 1984: seven to Prost, five and the World Championship for Lauda. And what of the future?

Alain Prost would give that gentle half-smile once again. This was a good line, and he knew it. In 1985, he would try to become World Champion with only one win. Play the system as it seemed it was meant to be played. But, in the end, Prost did what he had done for the past two seasons by winning more races than any other Formula 1 driver. Only in 1985, he did take the Championship.

There was an air of cool inevitability about his success: more than ever, he was the man most likely to. It was not just the statistics of the year, but his temperament and his equipment. If Marlboro McLaren TAG was not the invincible high-tech steamroller which mashed the previous season into a dayglo orange blur, it was nevertheless the finest team in Formula 1 for the opening two-thirds of a long, grinding season which, from August through to mid-September, compacted five races into seven weekends. No, McLaren had real opposition this year, from John Player Special Team Lotus and Canon Williams Honda. Yet neither team could mount a season-long two-car challenge to McLaren. Consistency, as defined by Prost and Lauda in 1984, was elusive to all teams in 1985. But McLaren came closest, and Prost took the title.

So how many races did Prost win? Five said the scorecard, six claimed the television cameras. Prost lost the San Marino Grand Prix because the car was two kilogrammes underweight. That's equivalent to the amount of Shell racing fuel he burned – give or take a throttle blip or two – completing the victory lap. Then again, Imola was

Photo: Paul-Henri Cahier

the most insidiously scrappy of all Grands Prix, blighted by the fuel-consumption restrictions which downgraded Formula 1 in 1985. From the trackside, San Marino looked to reveal 57 of the finest laps in contemporary Grand Prix history. That was before Ayrton Senna, leading for Lotus, ran out of gas, and before the electrics of Stefan Johansson's Ferrari croaked after heading lap 58, giving the race to Prost. He crossed the line after 60 laps, only to be excluded. That, in turn, handed a win – of sorts – to Elio de Angelis in a low-boost, sticking-throttle Lotus 97T which ran out of brakes with two laps to go. After Imola, McLaren regrouped and Prost won. The Championship momentum had been regained. Those nine points from Imola would not have allowed Prost to stitch up the title any sooner, however, thereby providing an indication of how McLaren's opposition mounted as autumn approached.

So it was indisputably, decisively, Alain Prost's Championship, beginning with a win in Brazil that represented his third consecutive 1984-85 Formula 1 victory, irrespective of the opposition's winter testing round Circuit Paul Ricard and Rio and Kyalami as they tried to come to terms with the technical excellence of the McLaren, if not its TAG V6 engine. McLaren's design team under Technical Director John Barnard, may have produced a new car in the shape of the MP4/2B (which was essentially the 1984 Constructors' Champion with a revised aerodynamic shaping, particularly around the rear deck, and a new pushrod rear suspension to replace the original rocker design), but Porsche did not come up with a true qualifying-specification engine. There was no big turbo or blanked off wastegates for Prost to go pole-hunting with, nor was there any slimy-black cloud to trail Prost's efforts on his second set. No 5.2 bar boost pressure and 1270 bhp grenade-motors featured at McLaren, in contrast to Brabham, where, in qualifying, Nelson Piquet could hit 209 mph at the end of Paul Ricard's *Mistral* straight and ahead of the Österreichring's *Bosch-kurve,* and 211 mph before Crowthorne corner at Kyalami. Alain Prost's pole positions at Spa and in Austria speak volumes for him and the McLaren chassis balance rather than a trick programme in the single-unit Bosch Motronic engine management system cutting engine life back to just 35 miles. Right through to the end of the season, McLaren would not be drawn as to why there was no qualifying engine in a year when Ayrton Senna took seven Renault-Lotus poles, but, given McLaren's thoroughness in every other aspect of running a race team, then the shortcoming must belong to Porsche.

According to Niki Lauda, the MP4/2B only came good at the French Grand Prix in July, when John Barnard introduced a new front suspension upright. 'Now, for me, its a big improvement; it's

normal again', said the Rat, matter-of-factly. By that time, without the freshened-up front end, Prost had already won two (or should that be three?) races. He went on to take first place in Great Britain, Austria and Italy. Lauda's only win was in Holland, that was from Prost, in an all-out scrap. His year was, overall, as mediocre as his generally lacklustre qualifying technique which saw him start the Italian Grand Prix, for example, with a grid time 2.5 seconds down on Prost, yet Lauda was running a McLaren set-up which he admitted he could find no fault with.

Indeed, qualifying was one of the factors which not only shaped the year but also produced a superb sideshow of great pole laps. If 1985, was to be Prost's Championship, then it was also Ayrton Senna's year. Putting Senna's attributes into some kind of context is difficult without smothering his talent with hyperbole, but qualifying is a good place to start. Take, for example, the Grand Prix of Europe final timed session, Brands Hatch. Senna cuts a 1m 7.169s second flier and makes Brands a 140 mph circuit for him alone. On that same day, both John Watson, returning for a sad, languid stand-in race at McLaren, and 1980 World Champion Alan Jones, battling the new Beatrice Lola, admitted that they could not get the best from their Goodyear qualifying tyres. They failed to warm them up, either by driving so fast as to destroy the rears before the fronts heated up or by dawdling round to enter the first corner of the one-shot quick lap with cold, slippery rubber. Senna, as he had done all year, made it look easy.

As easy, say, as his first Grand Prix win in Portugal looked. From his first pole-position, he led from start to finish and picked up fastest lap on the way. That was in the worst washed-out conditions seen in Grand Prix racing since Monaco 1984 – where, in the rain and the scudding cloud, he had finished second for Toleman. This year, Senna led more laps than any other driver, winning in Belgium to back up Portugal. More significantly, he re-motivated JPS Lotus, stamping a fiercesome authority over his, and the team's, every move. He spent the time between practice sessions painstakingly decoding the computer squiggles of Bruno-the-engine-man's diagnostic equipment. His driving technique, visually smooth but aurally sloppy as the throttle of the Renault was stabbed repeatedly up to the apex of the corner, was ripped off wholesale by a number of rivals. For the late-comers it demanded a whole new technique: for Senna it was an extension of his karting days. And, when the clones had mastered the Senna-style, what did they discover? That pumping the accelerator, literally putting the boot in with balletic footwork, not only spooled up the turbochargers for a faster corner exit, but also, somehow, made the boost pressure overstep its

pre-set marker. So, by jabbing the revs, Senna could not only keep the engine revving in the peak of the torque-band but also (and for this there is, apparently, no wholly convincing technical explanation) eke out higher flash-boost readings through the bend. He could find horsepower, and thus speed, where it didn't exist for his rivals.

He used his Astaire tap-dancing technique everywhere, from Monaco's hairpins to Brands Hatch's Paddock Bend. Everywhere save Austria he was quick in qualifying. Broken turbos, low-boost, unduly short-lived qualifiers and no pre-race testing reduced him to 14th, but he hung on and finished that race. In terms of being a season-long threat, Gérard Ducarouge's Lotus 97T matched McLaren. But, just as Lauda's three points-scoring races meant that McLaren was often a one-car team, so was Lotus. Senna drove seven fallow races, from San Marino to Germany, putting in drives that were stunning but, literally, pointless. Team-mate Elio de Angelis, meanwhile, managed seven scores in the opening seven races. That much was a carbon-copy of his 1984 season; his only problem was his team-mate. Younger, supposedly greener in only his second year of Formula 1, just his fifth of driving single-seaters, was quicker and cleverer in both his driving and in making Lotus, collectively, push for him.

At Adelaide, the best new Grand Prix venue ever, Senna's smash-and-grab race was generally considered as enigmatic as his carefully-phrased conversation. There was a Senna backlash. Yes, Niki Lauda thought Senna deliberately baulked him on a quick lap in Monaco qualifying. Senna carefully pointed out that his 13th race-tyre lap all but equalled his pole time. Elio de Angelis told the world that in surviving a dive over the entry and exit of the first chicane at Monza immediately after the start, Senna was lucky. Maybe, but the clinical way Senna sliced low into Detroit's turn three – again on a cold-tyre first lap, from pole – to take the lead from Nigel Mansell, showed his uncanny sensitivity to perfection, as had his Estoril walkover. Michele Alboreto gave Senna a hard time passing at Zandvoort. 'These people are stupid', said Senna a couple of weeks afterwards. 'They don't think I will remember.' Senna never forgets anything about his racing. He could tell you every front wing setting Lotus ran this year without digging through engineer Steve Hallam's copious set-up data; he could describe a 1981 Formula Ford race in freeze-frame detail. At Brands Hatch, Senna leads and Keke Rosberg tries to hack up the inside of him at the off-camber Surtees bend. Lotus nudges Williams – or vice versa. A racing accident. Rosberg spins, is collected by Nelson Piquet's Brabham, heads off to the pits with a left-rear puncture and comes out ahead of Senna on the road, a lap down on the Longines-Olivetti timing computer.

Then Rosberg baulks Senna – blatantly. Williams team-mate Nigel Mansell passes Senna, under a yellow flag, and disappears to win. Afterwards, Rosberg spoke of needing to return to Formula 3 to brush up on his early-lap resistance to Senna. A cheap shot – for had Senna been as dourly hard-headed as Rosberg claimed, then he could have tangled wheels quite easily with Mansell in the dramatic passing manoeuvre instigated by Rosberg's singular bloody-mindedness. Senna, meanwhile, said nothing in public about Rosberg. They exchanged brief, Anglo-Saxon, critiques on the podium. Would Senna suggest to Lotus that they protest Mansell for overtaking under a yellow caution flag, a misdemeanour for which Formula Ford drivers' knuckles are rapped? He looked surprised. You don't protest a British driver on home ground, he commented coolly. By the end of the year he had grown in stature sufficiently to be the only top driver willing to go on record as being against apartheid when doubts were raised about staging the South African Grand Prix. Of those who would comment publicly, none would even mention politics: they talked blandly, keeping to safe abstractions. Senna, as in everything, was crisp and concise and straightforward. At 25, with a monastic devotion to his chosen job, life can be clear-cut for Ayrton Senna. His reward? Privacy

Ayrton Senna: uncanny sensitivity in the quest for perfection.

Bernard Asset/Agence Vandystadt.

in the paddock and an increasingly frequent assertion from a panoply of pundits that, at last, here was the true successor to the late Jim Clark.

Ayrton Senna could have joined Ferrari for this year. Instead, he wriggled away from Toleman and moved to Lotus, in what was judged, in August 1984, as a less clever switch. Hindsight has shown that it was the perfect prologue to his 1985 season, while the points table and the pit lane now reveal that he made the smart choice.

Ferrari made a number of canny moves for 1985, the best being the dumping of the erratic, wild-eyed René Arnoux and his replacement by buoyant, sane, underrated Stefan Johansson. But it was Johansson who made the most telling comment about Ferrari's summer. 'We had a little understeer when we tested at Silverstone', he explained at the French Grand Prix, 'but it was a windy day and we put most of it down to that.' Ferrari's difficulties ran way deeper than being misled by a cross-breeze. Simply, the 156/85 was an embarrassing flop.

True, Michele Alboreto won in Canada, heading home Johansson, and he defeated Prost's sick McLaren in Germany. But he should have won the World Championship. By December 1984, Ferrari had tested every major part of the 156/85 – engine, suspension, new gearbox with a flicked up underside to allow the attachment of bigger rear diffusers – on the older 126C4M2 chassis. It looked a masterpiece of logical development: try each of the new pieces on an older car, cut down the variables, mount them all in an exquisite new composite chassis and get set for title-sniping. Somewhere along the development route, wires got crossed and Ferrari sank into the mire. In France, a revised chassis with new front suspension geometry was debuted – and rolled back into the transporter, unloved, after the first day of practice. Then, at the same race, spasms of engine-breaking hit Ferrari. The 156/85 developed an aversion to bumps; then understeered in, oversteered out, as mediocre cars do. Even though the car often felt rather better on qualifiers rather than race rubber as the dramatically increased grip masked chassis shortcomings over a single lap, Michele Alboreto qualified 16th, behind the Tolemans, at both Zandvoort and Kyalami. All Ferrari drivers could hope for was that reliability would see them through. Johansson took fourth in South Africa in a typically lonely drive.

But why the decline? Ferrari, with its tradition of treating the media as petulant schoolboys, won't admit to any major shortcoming ... which leads to the following speculation. That some teams work better with a driver to act as a focus – Lotus with Senna, Brabham with Nelson Piquet – through which all decisions are rubber-stamped. At Ferrari, the system is all. Subsequently, Ferrari's attention was taken by Teo Fabi's comparatively underpowered Toleman on pole at the Nürburgring. So Ferrari copied the aerodynamic outline of Rory Byrne's glorious TG185 chassis. Seeking an instant solution, Ferrari mimicked the Toleman rear wing – not for nothing did Toleman shroud the multi-bladed foil in the pit lane – and plagiarised the soft compound curves of the Toleman hindquarters. But whereas aerodynamic grace was integral to the essential concept of the Toleman, complete with an ingenious vee-shaped 'snowplough' to deflect air from beneath the car (a neatly radical piece of flat-bottom lateral-think), Ferrari regarded the Toleman planform as a simple add-on refinement. The change was pretty, but ineffective.

And neither Michele Alboreto nor Stefan Johansson are – by popular repute – ranked with Prost, Piquet and Senna as the truly unwavering test drivers of the year. Ferrari's hiring of 1984 British Formula 3 Champion Johnny Dumfries to do the bulk of the donkey-work driving then seemed all the more illogical. That is not to decry Dumfries. He is obviously quick and talented, but two years of honing a 170 bhp Ralt RT3 is unlikely to provide the ideal background for cross-checking the technical developments of the oldest team in Grand Prix racing. For Dumfries, the Ferrari deal meant days of turbo-testing and

'He dropped his ever-present cigarette on the concrete, ground it to powder with the heel of his red racing boot and said, "OK, let's do it".'

Paul-Henri Cahier

instant credibility. For Ferrari, it ultimately meant nothing at all.

Ferrari, given time, should return. Just as Canon Williams Honda did this year. Patrick Head's FW10 chassis, his first in carbon-composite materials, was as good as the outgoing FW09B had been irksome. But Head has drawn World Championship-winning cars before. What characterised the Williams year were three factors: Honda, Rosberg and Mansell. For the Canadian Grand Prix, Honda introduced a revised engine, on schedule. Only its gruffer exhaust note hinted that the bore-and-stroke dimensions had been changed: lengthening the stroke saw the Honda change from an all-or-nothing-at-9000 rpm screamer to a pedigree race engine with a useable mid-range. It may not have been as torquey as the Renault V6, but it was impressive none the less. At Brands Hatch, a low-line motor derivative allowed the bodywork to hug closer to the engine inlets, cleaning up the rear wing airflow combined with new pullrod and wishbone rear suspension to cleave for grip. That was the second rear suspension change for Williams in 1985, which also demanded a new gearbox casing to hang the hardware from. Williams worked hard this year.

The rewards were impressive, too. Keke Rosberg drove better than ever with an insouciant spunkiness to his every on-track move. At the British Grand Prix he waited on the pit wall until his pole time looked threatened. In a move that was pure Hollywood, he dropped his ever-present cigarette on the concrete, ground it to a powder with the heel of his red racing boot and said 'OK, let's do it'. Rain was sprinkled between Stowe and Club corners. At Stowe, he ran wide and both left-side wheels flicked spray skywards. The result was a 1m 5.591s lap – an average speed of 160.925 mph. 'Of course I'm glad to be over 160 mph', he said afterwards with understatement as colossal as his bravery. 'That's really some sort of challenge ...' Holding off the McLarens along the straight at Paul Ricard, Rosberg, with no fuel mileage worries, wound the boost to the maximum every lap, just to try and outrun Prost. He couldn't stay with a fleet Nelson Piquet, but he could have fun none the less. His Detroit and Adelaide triumphs had that magical, flourished-finger tension which epitomises Rosberg on a street track. That electricity had also distinguished his previous road course wins in Monaco 1983 and Dallas '84.

Suddenly, towards the season's close, Nigel Mansell shook off the shackles of dogged persistence and matured into a race-dominator. Before Belgium his year had seemed almost parodic – albeit painfully parodic – an appearance which, in 1985 language, was positively *Ramboid.* A 201 mph crash in French Grand Prix qualifying

when a left-rear tyre exploded at the notorious *Signes* corner left him deeply concussed. In Italy, another rear tyre blow-up tore his chest muscles, and then at Spa a broken steering wheel spoke aggravated the injury which was subsequently discovered to include cracked ribs. But, in Belgium, he outran Rosberg, for both qualifying and race, and gained second place. At Brands, he won. But there was the underlying feeling that overtaking under a yellow had slightly devalued his maiden victory. So, at Kyalami, Mansell took the Grand Prix by the throat from pole, holding up magnificently under the toughest start-to-finish pressures doled out by Prost, Rosberg and Lauda singly and in combination, and proved to the world that there was nothing flukey about N. Mansell. At Williams, Mansell received all the respect, devotion and attention that was so patently lacking in his last year at Lotus, and he repaid in kind and in wins. Mansell's coming of age, for him and for Britain, was worth the wait.

Remember Parmalat? Remember Michelin? Remember Nelson Piquet getting nine 1984 Brabham-poles and never being less than a lead threat? 1985 was very different. Bernie Ecclestone made one of his best-ever moves by tying Pirelli down to a long-term tyre-and-megadollar deal before the Michelin pull-out was made public. In other words, before he needed Pirelli more than Pirelli needed him. Less than 12 months later, Ecclestone made what looked to be one of his worst-ever moves by letting Nelson Piquet slip away to Williams and the come-good Honda. For Brabham, as ever, revolved around the Piquet-Gordon Murray driver-designer axis. There was an enervating winter of Pirelli and BMW-testing involving 75 Grand Prix distances in three-week stints of running round Kyalami like a demented clockwork toy. Months of Southern Hemisphere running in South Africa and Brazil saw Pirelli come up with a selection of radials which worked best in very hot, fast conditions. Those conditions were matched at the French Grand Prix, where Piquet romped away in classic Brabham style, which means, as in Detroit 1984, he made a last-minute switch to the T-car and still cleaned up. But when it was wet or cold, and if the track was slow and twisty, the Pirellis were off the pace. Gordon Murray seemed, by mid-season, to take the slings and arrows of inconsistent rubberwear with his usual laid-back nonchalance. His head was deeply into the new 1986-model Brabham from April onwards. The accent, he said, would be on the radical.

Indeed, although Pirelli made progress the Italian company often served to remind how Goodyear made supplying competitive tyres, race in, race out, look so easy. From Goodyear's viewpoint, 1985 represented more of a tactical annihilation than an old-fashioned tyre war such

The sun sets on Equipe Renault-Elf. The team which introduced turbocharging to Formula 1 decided to pull out after a disastrous season.

as the battle with Michelin through 1983 and 1984. 1985, belonged, in all but one race, to Goodyear. Pirelli also featured in the year's oddest political saga: the Toleman affair. Toleman and Pirelli split acrimoniously at Imola in 1984, and for the rest of the season Toleman secured a low-key deal with Michelin, helped by Brabham boss Bernie Ecclestone. Then Michelin announced their withdrawal from Formula 1. Toleman couldn't go with Goodyear due to some longstanding disagreement neither party would talk about and had severed its links with Pirelli. Hence the problem. The new TG185 was quick in testing on a mix of loaned Pirellis and old Avon cross-plies but drivers Stefan Johansson (firm) and John Watson (not so) became unemployed. Johansson raced a Tyrrell in Brazil but was picked up by Ferrari and promptly deified by the Italian press. Watson took a back seat. Toleman lost their sponsorship, and the team was threatened with closure. Their purchase of the Pirelli contract from Spirit (remember Spirit?) for a reputed £500,000, put Toleman back in business. They picked up Benetton backing, Teo Fàbi, Piercarlo Ghinzani and pit lane praise for producing the only Formula 1 chassis in the same league as McLaren for road-car ride quality and impeccable balance. End of story.

Or it would be, except that Toleman still run Hart engines and thus fall victim to the same bouts of mechanical genocide which have stricken RAM and Beatrice. When Fabi put the Toleman on pole at the German Grand Prix, the quality of the chassis was clear to all. But repeated engine problems dogged the year, leading to a rotten, detonation-induced finishing record. With former Williams team manager Peter Collins running the show, Toleman came of age in all bar durability this year. In one sense, an impending Benetton buy-out meant Toleman was effectively a new team.

But the best of the newcomers – Beatrice Lola, Simod Minardi and West Zakspeed – was Zakspeed. Erich Zakowski made a reputation in Germany running Ford Capri sports cars which were either wonderful or very silly, depending on which way they were viewed. There was nothing frivolous about his new Grand Prix team.

The car, designed by Paul Brown was neat and well-finished, the all-new Zakspeed engine and gearbox being marred only by the inevitable teething troubles. It was often promising none the less, and Jonathan Palmer used all his considerable driving and testing ability to keep the whole show rolling. This was a low-key beginning, taking in just the European races, and suffered a lack of continuity when Formula 3000 Champion Christian Danner sat in for Palmer after JP was injured in a Group C shunt at Spa. But progress was made, and considering Zakspeed

had never before run a single-seater more sophisticated than the Reynard FF2000 used by the boss's son, the portents were good.

By contrast, the new Minardi was a semolina pudding of a racing car, and despite having a superficially interesting Motori Moderni turbo-motor produced in six months by ex-Alfa chief Carlo Chiti, it appeared to be nothing more than an anti-intellectual in-joke created by the Italian racing community.

When the Beatrice team finally arrived, dispensing turkeyburgers to journalists as the crew battled to dial out the early-race understeer, it could not be discounted. Difficult as the car may have looked, cynical as Alan Jones' putdowns were, once the new Ford engine is tied to the British-built design, it has to succeed. With Jones and Patrick Tambay driving for 1986, pre-judging the team by its mediocre 1985 Hart-broken performance is irrelevant.

Tambay left Renault after another disastrous year for the French team: the only difference between Renault in 1984 and Renault in 1985 was that this year Renault finally pulled the plug on its own racing team. Running the same Goodyear tyres and still-impressive V6 engines as power-customers Lotus, Renault were always outrun. Tambay and Derek Warwick battled hard, but a lack of confidence, both in and from the management saw the team crumble. In 1977, Renault introduced turbocharging to Formula 1; in 1985, having irrevocably changed the shape of racing, the company pulled out . . . marketing decisions both.

Of course, much of Formula 1 is now shaded by market forces. Yet there was a South African Grand Prix in a year when the mainstream Western media turned names such as Soweto and Mandela into the small change of casual conversation. And Kyalami was dominated by talk of tyre choice and turbo-boost rather than civil disturbances and human rights. FISA had no statutes covering what to do if a Grand Prix was to be staged in a country whose politics are intolerable to many. So there was a race, and a good one, though McLaren, Arrows and Beatrice raced cars lacking prime-site sponsorship logos. If racing in South Africa was considered so morally unpalatable to the moneymen, why did they compete there at all? Such limply 'political' gestures, in the end, compromise Formula 1's progression as a major international sport.

The same was true of the meanderings of Britain's RAC Motor Sports Association, rather than Formula 1's governing body, FISA. After managing to put behind them a succession of traumatic races in the Seventies, the RAC hung the chequered flag out prematurely, and ended the British Grand Prix a lap early. Cars ran out of fuel on what should have been the final lap.

Positions and points scores were changed. In 1985, the accent was on car efficiency, struggling to survive a Grand Prix on the mandated 220 litres of fuel so cutting a race short did more than screw up consumption calculations; it belittled the Grand Prix. Again, at the European Grand Prix, Nigel Mansell passed Ayrton Senna under a yellow flag. No, he should not have been denied his victory, but the RAC should at least have commented on the incident instead of collectively sticking their heads in the sand of bureaucracy. A Formula Ford driver would have been lucky to escape with a reprimand. The RAC, it should not be forgotten, refused to help licence-holder Ken Tyrrell in his lengthy fight for justice from FISA through the previous year.

FISA, meanwhile, tinkered with the regulations and reduced the size of brake ducts (teams were using them as additional downforce producers) but failed to obtain the necessary team unity on reducing the awesome qualifying speeds. Niki Lauda, predictably, suggested the simplest way out. Eliminate qualifying entirely: plot out race grids on the result of the previous Grand Prix. If you'd had a lousy race, tough luck. A win would put you on pole, automatically. This was, Lauda admitted, a radical suggestion, but he believed in it.

As in every year, it was the people who created the most enduring memories. That Stefan Bellof was never seen in a truly front running car is unspeakably sad: the thought of him, eyes alive, on opposite lock in a future Ferrari, for instance, is one that remains just a thwarted dream. Manfred Winkelhock, was one of the good guys in the pit lane, always waiting for the break, thinking of the future and driving hard. To have both men killed in Porsche sports cars darkened the summer. Then there was Marc Surer, who replaced François Hesnault at Brabham and finally got noticed as a solid, capable number two by everyone in the pit road bar Bernie Ecclestone.

Or observe Ron Dennis, emotionless epicentre of McLaren International, neglecting to thank Niki Lauda for winning the 1984 World Championship, while pointing out, with a precision that bordered on paranoia, designer John Barnard's contribution to the team. Lauda, at the same retirement press conference in the Österreichring press tent, was dignified in his praise for McLaren.

Thierry Boutsen and Gerhard Berger added considerable driving talent and mates-together straightforwardness in an Arrows team which impressed through reliability and preparation. Jacques Laffite occasionally quit the 18th green to put in punchy races in Britain, Germany and Australia, reminding the watchers that, for him at least, being 41 years old is nothing to worry about.

Recall John Macdonald watching his RAM team go down the tubes behind a soundtrack of broken turbos and shattered engines. Then there was Liz Brundle explaining to a television interviewer what a wet Grand Prix start was like, with husband Martin watching as she described it all in rev-perfect clarity: as a twosome, the Brundles were inseparable. As a driver, Brundle time and again served notice that he is a man to watch.

Alain Prost did likewise five years earlier – and virtually every year that followed. 1985 was just another chapter in his biography of Grand Prix success, the folios where he finally attained what should have been his at least once before. A good, professional job from a great, professional driver. Ahead there lay another winter of promotion, of cigarette-selling. And what of the future?

Alain Prost would give that faint half-smile once again. Yet another good line; and he knew it, too. In 1986, he would aim at the Championship, for sure. And he would also try to beat Jackie Stewart's all-time best of 27 Grands Prix wins. If motivation was required, snatching that statistic would be motivation enough.

'I just don't believe this year, you know. Every time we test, nothing happens to my car. Same in practice – and in the race, every time something silly happens. I just don't know why.'

Ayrton Senna: Paul Ricard, July 1985.

Bernard Asset/Agence Vandystadt

Protection above all.

No conventional oil can meet the demands of hard driving quite like Gemini. Above all, Gemini, the latest and most advanced formula from Shell, sets new standards in protection. Through high revs and fierce temperatures Gemini stays in grade. Mile after mile, day after day, protection beyond the capabilities of conventional oils.

Shell Oils

Technology you can trust

GEMINI

THE PERFORMANCE OIL THAT STAYS IN GRADE

GRANDS PRIX 1985

Photo: John Townsend

Grande Prêmio do Brasil

In the paddock at Rio, when Formula 1 people gathered in the shade for a chat and respite from the searing heat, there was a buzz of excitement – a sophisticated version of the prattle found in the school cloakroom at the start of a new term.

Talk was of this and that but, frequently, one theme would crop up; after a break of over five months, there was the fervent hope that someone – anyone – would beat Marlboro McLaren International. Not just beat them; really hammer them into the ground; remove the smug expressions from the faces of one or two of the men in red and white.

After practice, there appeared to be every chance of an end to the monopoly of 1984. Michele Alboreto's Ferrari was on pole, Keke Rosberg had flung his Canon-Williams onto the front row while behind them sat the impressive black-and-gold JPS Lotus team of Ayrton Senna and Elio de Angelis. Alain Prost was fifth fastest in his McLaren; Niki Lauda was ninth.

After the race, it was clear that nothing had changed. Prost, winner of three of the last four races of 1984, won the Brazilian Grand Prix more or less as he pleased. There had been a race for 18 laps, first Rosberg and then Alboreto leading. After that? McLaren monotony.

Alboreto, suffering understeer after banging wheels with Nigel Mansell's Williams-Honda at the first corner, could offer no resistance as Prost moved in for the kill. Indeed, it might have been a McLaren one-two had Lauda not been forced to retire with a problem with the electronic control box. As it was, with the exception of the Ferrari, Prost lapped the entire field and set fastest lap for good measure.

The Lotus-Renaults simply did not have the race speed but both de Angelis and Senna drove consistently, the Italian finishing third, Senna disappointing himself and the home crowd by retiring with a niggling electrical failure after a surprisingly circumspect performance from the Brazilian.

The only highlight of the second half was the charge into fourth place by René Arnoux, the Ferrari driver having lost ground earlier after tangling with another competitor and puncturing a rear tyre.

Patrick Tambay thoroughly deserved fifth place, the Frenchman working hard for two points after a miserable weekend spent struggling with a Renault RE60 which not only handled badly but also developed an alarming brake problem during practice. Making it four French drivers in the top six, Jacques Laffite took the final point after a useful performance with the Ligier-Renault.

As the colourful Brazilian crowd took part in their own Grand Prix on their way home, they rushed past vast hoardings urging their new hero, Ayrton Senna, to win races. The posters were, in fact, badly doctored pictures of Elio de Angelis in the previous year's car.

Elio's helmet had been painted yellow and the number changed to '12' but, in truth, there was to be no getting away from 1984 no matter which way you looked at the 1985 Brazilian Grand Prix.

ENTRY AND PRACTICE

Those responsible for the British American Tobacco account in Brazil certainly did their job. The black and gold colours dominated the landscape, the pits, the track, the hotels and restaurants. The Lotus team and, more precisely, Ayrton Senna, were under pressure from the moment practice commenced at 10 a.m. sharp on Friday, 5 April.

Lotus, in common with their well-heeled rivals, had spent the five-month lay-off cramming in test miles in South Africa and South America. More recently, they had run at Donington, where the new 97Ts appeared with additional vertical aerofoils mounted behind the front wheels.

The drivers were unable to detect a distinct performance advantage but, since the cars were quick from the outset, the aerodynamics remained unchanged, thus giving Peter Warr the opportunity for a splendid display of British amateur dramatics as he instructed the front and rear suspension to be covered every time a Lotus rolled to a halt.

Rival teams claimed they knew precisely what Gérard Ducarouge was up to but that did not detract from the fact that Lotus were to dominate the first timed session on Friday afternoon.

It was Elio de Angelis who eventually set the fastest lap despite the fact that his chassis had only covered 60 miles or so, the engine was misfiring very slightly at peak revs and the gear linkage was rather stiff. Ayrton Senna, recovered from a virus infection which he had picked up the previous November, was just over six-tenths in arrears after being held up by a slower car.

Senna was baulked again during the final session although he did manage to improve his time by half a second. De Angelis, however, was forced to abandon both his quick laps when first Ghinzani and then Johansson inadvertently blocked the Italian as he tried to answer a new challenge from Ferrari.

The Lotus 97T looked superbly balanced and its handling was matched by just one car – the Ferrari 156/85. Michele Alboreto had set the fastest time during testing, a sign of important changes within Ferrari following their disastrous season in 1984. Mauro Forghieri had been removed from the racing team and Harvey Postlethwaite, usually no more than an interested spectator at one or two races a year, was now plugged into the decision-making process at Rio.

Alboreto, fastest in the untimed session on Friday morning and third quickest in the afternoon, found a clear lap in the final session to set a time three-tenths faster than de Angelis. Still searching for further improvement, changes were made to the car for the second and final set of qualifiers but the handling was not as precise. René Arnoux was not as confident with his car and a change of springs on Saturday morning saw the unhappy Frenchman spin. To make matters worse, his engine was down on power in the afternoon and René switched to the T-car to set what would be seventh fastest time.

With luck running against de Angelis in the final session, Alboreto's challenge came, not from Senna, but from the irrepressible Keke Rosberg.

The Williams team did not have high expectations since the FW10 had completed the minimum of shake-down tests prior to shipment to Rio.

Nigel Snowdon

International Press Agency

Rosberg was four seconds off the pace on Friday afternoon, not because of a fundamental failing with the carbon-fibre chassis, but due to more mundane reasons such as an engine which felt flat and a turbo failure while running his second set of qualifiers.

Another turbo failure on Saturday morning meant Keke had to use the spare FW09 and it was immediately apparent that the engine in the 1984 car was more responsive, due, it was thought, to different ducting for the turbo. A similar side vent was cut in the side pod of FW10 and the effect was immediate. However, it was not to be that straightforward.

Half-way round his first lap, a hose blew off the engine and Rosberg coasted in for repairs. As he left the pits, still using the same set of qualifiers, the clutch began to slip but Keke pressed on without using the left-hand pedal and cut a breathtaking lap, just one-tenth slower than Alboreto.

Giving Williams two cars in the first six, Nigel Mansell set fifth fastest time while playing himself in with his new team and car. Apart from a brush with marshals after his engine had cut out due to an electrical failure on Saturday morning, Mansell had an uneventful practice.

Holding to their policy of producing their new car late in the day, McLaren brought the MP4/2B to Rio having completed a brief run in the rain at Brands Hatch. Prost and Lauda claimed the new car was a distinct improvement over the all-conquering MP4/2, particularly in the fast corners, although they did concede that development was needed to bring the handling up to scratch in the slower corners.

A more immediate problem was the refusal of the TAG turbo to take qualifying boost during practice, which explained Prost's sixth place and Lauda's almost customary position on the fifth row. Alain had also suffered from a slight misfire and a stiff gearchange between fourth and fifth while Lauda confined his complaints to excessive oversteer. Both drivers, however, felt confident for the race.

So, too, did Brabham even though Nelson Piquet was back in eighth place. This was expected since Brabham had spent most of their massive test programme working on race tyres with Pirelli rather than developing a qualifier. This seemed to be the sensible policy to take in the long term but the deficiency with the qualifier told during practice as Piquet recorded the fastest straightline speed and yet he was never higher than eighth in the timed sessions. Brabham produced three BT54s; Gordon Murray's immaculate and purposeful answer to a variety of configurations tried during winter's test mileage which exceeded 30 Grands Prix! Nelson spent most of his time in the spare car while his new team-mate, François Hesnault, simply became accustomed to his new surroundings.

There had been wholesale changes within the management structure at Renault and it

The spectacular coastline of Rio de Janeiro formed the backdrop to the opening race of the season *(far left)*.

An unfortunate start to the season for Nigel Mansell as the Williams driver tangled with Michele Alboreto's Ferrari while chasing Rosberg's Williams into the first corner. Mansell retired after damaging the exhausts when he spun off; Rosberg went out with a blown turbo and Alboreto led before being overhauled by Prost's McLaren

New uniform for the start of a new term. Michele Alboreto soaked the palms of his new driving gloves to make them more supple *(left)*.

The unacceptable face of McLaren. This was the view the McLaren team's rivals were forced to endure yet again *(below)*.

Paul Henri-Cahier

Paul Henri Cahier

remained to be seen whether the assured but inexperienced Gérard Toth could turn the team's fortunes around. The latest car, the RE60, did not give the new regime the best start.

Initial tests had shown a handling imbalance which kept Renault four seconds off the pace. By the time practice began in Rio, they were two seconds away from the required standard. Worse still, the RE60 had developed a worrying brake malady. Warwick spun on Friday and Saturday when the pedal went to the floor while Tambay went into the catch-fencing during the final session when he lost his front brakes and locked the rears. Patrick's time from Friday earned the Frenchman 11th place on the grid alongside his team-mate.

Renault brought along one of their new EF15 engines which Warwick ran during the untimed session on Saturday morning. It was intended that the Englishman would race this unit which meant a switch to the spare car for the final session.

Arrows had been highly encouraged when Thierry Boutsen set the fastest time with their latest car, the A8, during tests at Imola. However, the team lost their way during the first day's practice and it was some time before they discovered that the addition of a larger rear wing was the root cause of a handling problem. Added to that, Boutsen lost boost pressure during his qualifying run and the turbo finally gave out half-way through what would have been his fastest lap.

It was hard to believe that Gerhard Berger had been lying in hospital with a broken neck five months previously as he played himself in with the Arrows team. A sore neck was the painful legacy of the road accident and his only mechanical problem was a recalcitrant gearbox which forced the Austrian to use the spare car on Saturday afternoon.

With the arrival of Gérard Larrousse, Michel Tétu and Jacques Laffite at Ligier, the French team appeared to be top-heavy. Appropriately enough, the blue cars were among the heaviest during the qualifying session weigh-ins – Laffite's car tipping the scales at 605 kilos compared to the 559 kg for Lauda's McLaren. Jacques was half a second slower than Andrea de Cesaris, the Italian suffering clutch trouble on Friday and an engine drive belt failure on the Renault V6 which forced him to use the spare car for the final session.

The new Alfa Romeo may have looked the part but Eddie Cheever was close to despair at the end of practice. The handling was so bad that there was talk of revising the suspension pick-up points and the American managed only half a lap on his final set of qualifiers when the fuel pump broke forcing Eddie to switch the partly scrubbed tyres to the T-car. Cheever finished the day over a second slower than Patrese – which didn't help his mood either.

John Macdonald's RAM team faced the new season with optimism. At last they had a designer worthy of the name and Gustav Brunner's main

TECHNICAL FILE

McLAREN

Used the same chassis as 1984 but, otherwise, numerous improvements. Longer and stiffer nose section to conform with crash-test requirements brought into force in 1985. Dashboard-mounted computer readout to indicate number of laps left at the current boost setting with remaining amount of fuel in tank. Shorter side pods (8-10 cm); different weight distribution. One-piece electronic black box the outward indication of heavy development work by Bosch. Pushrod rear suspension replaced rocker arm. Reprofiled underbody which enclosed most of rear suspension. Exhaust closer to engine; rear bodywork 3-4 cm narrower with vertical 'fins' around rear tyres. Narrower gearbox (now 70 per cent McLaren made) which also carried fixing points for rear suspension and wing.

TYRRELL

Apart from deformable structure necessitating a longer nose cone, nothing new on 1984 012 chassis.

WILLIAMS

FW10 their first carbon-fibre composite monocoque. No spacer between engine and gearbox (standard practice elsewhere to allow cleaner airflow to rear wing) gave a more cluttered appearance. Wheelbase the same as FW09 but FW10 monocoque longer. Only two new FW10 chassis ready. Pushrod front suspension. The only team which used rear rocker arms. Underbody had vertical fin to separate airflow around exhausts. Used small wing below standard rear wing.

BRABHAM

Three new BT54s. Only chassis number 1 ran before shipment to Brazil. Major modifications to internals of BMW engine. New position for turbo; lower position for wastegate. Problems with dirt entering inlet duct on BT53 avoided by high entry for NACA duct to feed turbo on BT54. Side pods up to 10 in. longer than normal gave forward position for centre of pressure. Weight heavily biased to rear. Ran less wing at the front, therefore less drag and better cooling and airflow. The longest wheelbase (by 10 cm) of all the 1985 cars. Suspension basically the same as 1984. Monocoque new and car on weight limit. Tried Garrett turbo during testing; a political move to persuade KKK to make a new turbo.

RAM

Gustav Brunner-designed 03 ran revised positions for oil and water radiators. Spray for intercooler. Electronic black box mounted in rear platform of bodywork. Additional water radiator at rear tried and abandoned after Friday's practice. Underbody profiles cut for the race. Winkelhock ran large Holset.

LOTUS

Three 97Ts; totally new and logical progression from 95T. Small winglets mounted on rear of side pods to compensate for regulation change banning 'ears' from side plates of rear wing. Vertical front wings mounted behind front wheels (as seen by Ducarouge in CART racing) improved airflow into and around side pods. Also reduced drag at rear of tyres and generally made the side pod area more efficient. Additional benefit the deflection of rubber away from radiator and intercooler inlets. Black box mounted in left side pod (unlike Renault and Ligier) to reduce frontal area.

RENAULT

Completed fourth new RE60 chassis (designed by Michel Tétu before his departure to Ligier) in paddock at Rio. Almost vertical ducting

inside engine cover to turbo. Revised underbody hid rear suspension. Four exhausts (including one wastegate) on each side (similar to system first seen in Monaco 1983). New Renault caliper for carbon brakes. Brake problem during practice led to recall of calipers used in 1984. Modification to gearbox meant additional weight penalty (believed to have been 25 kilos). Warwick used EF15 engine (new block with revised bore and stroke) for practice on Saturday morning and for race.

ARROWS

A8 the first carbon-fibre chassis for Arrows. Three new cars in Rio with new wings to counteract lack of downforce during testing. The only car that had bodywork without ducting top and bottom. Pushrod front suspension; pullrod rear. AP brake caliper mounted underneath disc. Exhaust from Mader-prepared BMW engine rose up through rear suspension similar to Brabham.

SPIRIT

1984 car with major changes to aerodynamics. Different positions for radiators and intercooler required new side pods. Changed to pushrod front suspension; rear unchanged. Band from driveshaft ran alternator.

ALFA ROMEO

Brought two John Gentry-designed 1985-spec cars and one 184T as spare. Wastegates mounted parallel to the ground. Rear suspension links carried small wing profiles. Tried different rear wing configurations and revised exit to radiators in a bid to improve airflow to rear wing. Brought 11 engines, including five qualifying-spec V8s, to Brazil.

OSELLA

Apart from wider (5 cm) front suspension, nothing new on 1984 car. No testing whatsoever during winter.

LIGIER

Third new JS25 finished in Brazil. Exhausts originally exited in front of rear tyres but all three cars had new layouts following a fire after three laps of testing at Ricard. Apart from the Osella, the JS25 the heaviest car in the pit lane.

FERRARI

Arnoux given third of new 156/85 series, which had not run before practice began. Relocated turbos and ancillary equipment meant elegant, low-profile rear bodywork. Revised one-piece duct for inlet to turbo. Ran SEP carbon brakes with new Brembo caliper and titanium pads. Ran special turbo for qualifying. Revised bypass for wastegate. Intricate electronic fuel cut-off activated when driver lifted off throttle.

MINARDI

M85 chassis built to accept Alfa V8. Presented with Chiti-designed Motori Moderni V6 but appeared in Brazil with Ford-Cosworth which meant revised engine mounting points and spacer between engine and gearbox to keep wheelbase the same. Ran with horizontally mounted rear shock absorbers. Rear brake calipers mounted below discs.

GP

NEW FOR 1985

The sudden withdrawal by Michelin at the end of the 1984 season meant McLaren and Renault switched to Goodyear while Brabham and Ligier chose Pirelli. Toleman spent the winter months trying unsuccessfully to arrange a tyre deal with either company.

McLAREN

Very little change. Alan Jenkins, Prost's race engineer, moved to CART. Shell replaced Unipart.

TYRRELL

Plans to run Renault turbos later in the season the best kept secret of the winter. Resolved their differences with FISA.

WILLIAMS

Mansell replaced Laffite. Canon joined as principal sponsor.

BRABHAM

Hesnault replaced Teo Fabi; Olivetti in place of Parmalat.

RAM

Hired Gustav Brunner to design new car. Alliot stayed but Winkelhock replaced Palmer.

LOTUS

Mansell's contract not renewed. Senna joined as joint Number One with de Angelis. Olympus returned to Formula 1 sponsorship with Lotus.

RENAULT

Gérard Larrousse and Michel Tétu left; Gérard Toth appointed Director of Renault Sport.

ARROWS

Surer left Formula 1, replaced by Berger. De Longhi added sponsorship after ditching Tyrrell half-way through 1984.

TOLEMAN

Started the season with new car but no tyres and no sponsor. With Senna gone to Lotus, Watson finally nominated at the last minute to partner Johansson.

SPIRIT

No change.

ALFA ROMEO

Carlo Chiti left; otherwise, no change.

OSELLA

No change.

LIGIER

Signed Laffite and took on Larrousse and Tétu.

FERRARI

Mauro Forghieri moved off racing team and into road car division.

MINARDI

Moved up from Formula 2, starting with Cosworth engine while awaiting development of Carlo Chiti's Motori Moderni turbo.

ZAKSPEED

New to Formula 1. Running their own chassis and engine. Palmer joined from RAM.

worry during practice was a problem with the gearbox end plate on the Skoal cars. Philippe Alliot also had a wheel-bearing seize but, at the end of practice, the 03s were inside the top 20. RAM were earning qualifying money with both cars for the first time in over a year.

With the Toleman team absent because neither Pirelli nor Goodyear were interested in supplying tyres, Stefan Johansson did not expect to be employed at Rio. At nine o'clock on Friday morning he received a call from Ken Tyrrell, advising him that the British team was in dispute with their contracted driver, Stefan Bellof, and that the drive was available for the Swede.

Fortunately, Johansson had just taken delivery of a new set of overalls and, with a helmet borrowed from Rosberg, Stefan found himself in business. The differential between the turbos in qualifying trim and the normally aspirated Cosworths was embarrassing but that did not stop Johansson and Martin Brundle from flinging the cars around Jacarepaguá, driving flat-out all the way. Rio marked Brundle's return to Formula 1 for the first time since his shunt at Dallas the previous year and the fact that his time was slower than the grid position achieved during his Grand Prix debut 12 months previously was an indication of the turbo-biased tyre development by Goodyear rather than a sluggish performance by Brundle.

Splitting the Tyrrells, Piercarlo Ghinzani took 22nd place with the Osella after spending most of Saturday's practice switching back and forth to the spare car after problems with the Alfa turbo on his race chassis. Neither Mauro Baldi nor Pierluigi Martini recorded times on Saturday, the Spirit struggling with a misfire caused by a faulty fuel sensor while the Minardi team, rather out of their depth in Formula 1, struggled unsuccessfully to change a DFV in time. None the less, both drivers would qualify thanks to Toleman's absence and the fact that Jonathan Palmer's Zakspeed was not scheduled to appear until the next round in Portugal.

RACE

There were audible groans along the pit wall as the warm-up finished on race morning. After 30 of the most important minutes in the entire five-month period since the end of the previous season, Alain Prost's McLaren was fastest. And Niki Lauda was in third place. Forget the McLaren team's relatively poor showing in practice; they were competitive in race trim – just like 1984.

Alboreto split the McLarens with de Angelis taking fourth place, the Lotus-Renault having little hope of running with the TAG turbos without sacrificing fuel consumption. A spread of 2.4 seconds over the first ten cars painted an even more accurate picture of the disparity between the front runners – never mind those at the back, several seconds off the pace.

There was further despondency in the Renault pit when Warwick, running the new long-stroke EF15 engine, suffered a misfire and Tambay was forced to take the spare chassis since his car could not be repaired after the previous day's accident.

A fuel leak from a recently installed BMW

Lotus made a song and dance about hiding the relatively straightforward aerofoils mounted on the front suspension of the 97Ts. De Angelis and Senna set the fastest times during practice on Friday, the Italian finishing third after a steady drive on Sunday *(left)*.
Nodding acquaintance. Alain Prost and Michele Alboreto congratulate each other after finishing first and second *(below)*.

engine caused a fire to break out in the back of Berger's Arrows and the damage was such that the Austrian made a late switch to the T-car. Senna had fuel vapourisation problems while an oil leak on de Angelis's car meant a swift engine change during the lunch interval. The season had started with a vengeance.

As they formed on the grid, Alboreto knew he should have the measure of Rosberg, fifth fastest in the warm-up, but it was essential that the Ferrari should reach the first corner ahead of the Williams. Keke, of course, was not about to let a golden opportunity to head the field slip by and he duly made one of his storming starts as the lights turned green.

Alboreto was, in fact, to have trouble with a Williams as Mansell made a superb getaway from the third row and sliced through the Lotus team before lining up for the first right-hander.

He was passing the Ferrari as he turned into the corner and what happened next depends on which driver you spoke to. Mansell said he was ahead of Alboreto as he claimed second place and the Ferrari then bounced off a kerb, its left-front wheel striking the right-rear tyre of the Williams. Alboreto said Mansell simply tried to cut across the Ferrari when his rear wheel was level with the Italian's cockpit and photographs tend to prove this to be the case.

No matter how the blame was apportioned, the Williams rode into the air and then spun across the grass while Alboreto continued on his way. It was the worst possible start to the season for the Englishman – regardless of the circumstances.

Rosberg, meanwhile, was carrying the Williams flag in typically energetic style as he powered away from the rest of the field, the FW10 sliding and twitching in a manner which suggested neither the driver nor the Goodyears could maintain such a pace in temperatures of about 100°F. But, at the end of the first lap, Keke led by 2.5 seconds and it was an advantage which had been earned in glorious style . . .

Alboreto was second. And, more important, Prost was third with Lauda eighth, pressing Piquet's Brabham. In between sat the Lotus-Renaults (Senna leading) with Arnoux pulling away slightly from Piquet. Patrese had made a good start to take ninth ahead of de Cesaris, the Alfa and Ligier demoting Tambay to 11th after the Renault driver had made an excellent start only to be swallowed up when the V6 refused to pick up cleanly out of the slow corners.

Behind sat Laffite and Cheever, followed by Brundle, the Tyrrell driver having rocketed through from the ninth row of the grid but now paying the penalty for not having a turbocharged engine. Winkelhock was next and about to be passed by Warwick (a slow start) and Berger whose water bottle had come loose as the Arrows driver attempted to negotiate the first corner. Berger flung the bottle out of the cockpit – and scored a direct hit on Ghinzani's helmet!

The Osella was back in 20th place, behind Johansson's Tyrrell and Hesnault in the Brabham while, bringing up the rear, Alliot led Martini and Boutsen, the Arrows driver losing his fuel pressure on the grid before receiving a push start once the field had departed. Trundling along at the rear, Baldi was in trouble already, the Spirit having cut out briefly on the warm-up lap before ingesting dirt into the turbo and causing a pit stop for a replacement a few laps later. At the very back came Mansell, the Williams on the move again although the exhaust diffusers, damaged at the point where they passed through the undertray, would eventually cause his retirement.

Rosberg's Honda sounded as healthy as ever and, on lap four, he reduced his pace by a second a lap as he settled into a comfortable rhythm. Alboreto, at the same time, set the fastest lap of the race so far and closed on the Williams, the Ferrari having a serious look at the inside line as they barrelled off the 180-mph back straight. Rosberg's reaction was predictable enough to cause Michele to drop back and give the matter more thought. He could, of course, always wait and discover how the various tyre choices would pan out.

Given that the abrasive surface meant planned stops for tyres and that the anti-clockwise nature of the circuit called for a hard compound on the right-rear, the teams naturally chose conservatively. Rosberg had the most complex selection; the extra-hard 'AA' for the right-rear with a 'B' on the left-front and the rest 'A'. The McLaren drivers had chosen 'A' all round while the Ferraris

Ayrton Senna carried the hopes of Brazil, the Lotus driver responding to the pressure with exceptional calm as he held third place before retiring with electrical trouble.

ran on 'B' on the left and 'A' on the right. Lotus, on the other hand, chose 'A' with the exception of an 'AA' on the right-rear.

The one unknown quantity before the start had been the quality of the Pirelli race tyres. Brabham had spent their winter working on competitive rubber for the races rather than developing a qualifier and Piquet's progress was being watched with interest. It lasted until half-way round lap three. The Brabham transmission suddenly seized and the subsequent spin not only sent Nelson into retirement but the trip across a kerb (with, don't forget, a full load of fuel on board) seriously tweaked the monocoque.

Alboreto had his problems too, the incident with Mansell having rearranged the left-front geometry on the Ferrari to such an extent that Michele was grappling with understeer while watching Prost's McLaren grow ever larger in his mirrors. Rosberg, therefore, was untroubled but his moment of glory was to last only until lap nine when a sudden puff of smoke announced the failure of the left-hand turbo. The Williams coasted into the pits where it would be joined shortly by Mansell's sister car. None the less, an encouraging start to the season for the Williams team and its various sponsors.

The outcome of this race grew increasingly obvious. Prost was menacing Alboreto's Ferrari and, while the Italian had the measure of the Frenchman on the straights, the McLaren was climbing all over the Ferrari through the corners. And it was on just such an occasion on lap 18 when Michele missed a gear and hesitated momentarily. It was the break Prost had been waiting for and, once again, a McLaren was leading a Grand Prix. And there were 43 laps to run . . .

Alboreto backed off slightly and, in an instant, he had another McLaren glued to his gearbox. Lauda had taken five laps to catch and pass Arnoux; he dealt with the Lotus drivers thanks to superior speed on the straights and it was clear that Alboreto would not last long in second place.

Then, a light began flashing in the McLaren cockpit to indicate that all was not well with the electronic black box. Lauda did not need a light to tell him something was amiss when the TAG faltered on lap 23. The World Champion crept slowly into the pits, a desultory wave of his hand indicating that his race was over. (Lauda would return to the track much later, purely as a precautionary measure to see if the Bosch technicians had cured the problem.)

One of the best battles had been further down the field as Patrese kept Laffite out of eighth place. The Ligier was clearly a competitive proposition with its Pirellis (de Cesaris supporting this by running strongly in seventh place) but there was nothing Laffite could do about the wide Alfa. Then, on lap 20, the Ligier hit a rear wheel on the Alfa, causing Patrese to limp slowly towards the pits. Laffite also made a stop and, while he was there, Cheever came in for tyres.

The American's race had not been without its moments, Cheever rudely chopping Hesnault and damaging the front end of the Brabham to end an impressive climb from 19th to 13th place by the Frenchman.

That was on lap 10 and, 17 laps later, there was to be another controversial incident as the enthusiastic de Cesaris tried to tackle Arnoux for what had become fourth place. The Ligier rammed the back of the Ferrari and, unfortunately for Arnoux, he had just passed the entrance to the pit lane when he became aware that the left-rear tyre was deflating. There was nothing for it but a slow drive back to the pits and, by the time René had covered the 3.126 miles, the Ferrari was running on its rim. A new Goodyear was slammed into place and Arnoux was heading down the pit lane for another of his storming drives. De Cesaris, meanwhile, had walked back to the pits to explain how he had lost a certain place in the points.

The Lotus pit stops had not been notable for their speed but, once everyone had been in for fresh tyres, the order at the front remained the same: Prost, Alboreto, Senna and de Angelis. A lap behind came Tambay (having survived a trip across the grass as he avoided the hobbled Patrese), Alliot (fifth during the pit stops but about to drop down the order when fifth gear began to fail), Laffite and Boutsen (still charging after his delayed start).

Senna's drive was one of great maturity considering the intense pressure exerted by the expectations of the heaving grandstands. From an early stage, Ayrton had realised fuel consumption and a conservative tyre choice would keep him out of contention and he drove accordingly, pacing himself beautifully. Then, on lap 49, the engine cut out as he approached the pit lane and he rolled in to retire.

A contact breaker had popped out and an immediate cure could not be found. The Lotus mechanics felt bitterly disappointed for the man who, against all predictions, had made himself at ease with the team. (It was discovered later that a small pump buried deep in the fuel system was causing a short-circuit.)

Ayrton's retirement, a dozen laps from the finish, allowed his team-mate to assume a distant third place. Tambay was fourth but coming under pressure from the remarkable Arnoux. Laffite was running strongly in sixth while the Tyrrell drivers had swapped places as Johansson made up ground rapidly after stopping for tyres. Alliot continued to drop back, Boutsen experiencing a similar frustration as the fuel pressure problem returned. (Berger had since retired the second Arrows with broken suspension, thus ending an impressive mid-field drive on lap 52.) Winkelhock's RAM was 11th while Ghinzani was struggling along at the back of the field and about to be overhauled by Warwick's Renault.

The British driver was running strongly but that did little to compensate for what had been a thoroughly frustrating day. The EF15 engine had developed a misfire during the early laps and Warwick could stand it no longer when he found Brundle's Tyrrell-Cosworth snapping at his heels and looking for a way past! A change of spark plugs cured the problem but he lost more time by stopping for tyres – a job which could have been done during his first pit stop a few laps earlier!

Twelve months previously, Warwick had led the Brazilian Grand Prix. His retirement had handed victory to Prost and here was the Frenchman about to repeat the procedure. Such was his confidence that Alain eased off during the closing laps and allowed Alboreto to close the gap. But, at the end of the day, it was nine points for Marlboro McLaren and their eighth victory in succession. The official scales showed the MP4/2B to be right on the weight limit with plenty of fuel to spare in the tank. Nothing had changed. Agreed, there was a long way to go but, in Rio, it seemed certain that McLaren would be waiting at the end of the season for the rest to catch up. The only interest appeared to be which of the two drivers would carry off the Championship . . .

M.H.

Grande Premio de Portugal

'They all said that I made no mistakes, but that's not true. On one occasion I had all four wheels on the grass, totally out of control... but the car came back onto the circuit. "Fantastic car control", everybody said. No way! It was just luck that I got back on the tarmac...' Thus spoke Ayrton Senna as he reflected on his victory in the Portuguese Grand Prix at Estoril, an event which took place in such a torrential monsoon that standing water on the start/finish straight pitched wet-weather ace Alain Prost into a heart-stopping spin and out of the contest. Even the eventual winner came past the pits on several occasions gesticulating furiously that the race should be stopped.

In reality, perhaps the conditions were worse than at Monaco and the previous summer when Jacky Ickx took that controversial decision to put out the chequered flag mid-way through a thrilling chase. Of course, the supreme irony of the Portuguese situation was that it represented, in effect, a complete reversal of what had happened round the streets of the Mediterranean Principality almost 12 months earlier. There, circumstances had favoured Prost, with Senna a close second. This time Ayrton got his own back.

Starting from a comfortable pole position, he serenely speedboated his way to one of the most impressive wet-weather victories of the last decade. His unassuming assurance was so visually unobtrusive that it took the presence of his slipping, sliding, precarious-looking rivals to put his brilliance into true perspective. The only thing that matched his on-track flair was his even-tempered, balanced – almost muted – response to the success once the race was over. Yes, he was happy for the team because he'd proved that the Lotus 97T was not simply a qualifying special. No, he hadn't had any problems apart from lapping one or two of the slower cars.

Then came that comment about his autocrossing moment – and suddenly one realised the depth of Senna's quality. Here was a man who couldn't get over-emotional about his first Grand Prix win because his inner confidence had bred him to *expect* it from the moment he first drove a Formula 1 car. A man who matched flair behind the wheel with a generosity to those others who had contributed to his success, making his own contribution in the cockpit seem but a minor footnote to Team Lotus's triumph.

Michele Alboreto's Ferrari 156/85 was the only other competitor to survive on the same lap as Senna's victorious Lotus, but the genial Italian none the less might as well have been on another planet – along with all his colleagues. Bland statistics reveal that the top six finishing positions were also occupied by Patrick Tambay's Renault Elf RE60, Elio de Angelis in the second JPS Lotus 97T, Nigel Mansell's Canon Williams FW10 and the irrepressible Stefan Bellof's Cosworth DFY-engined Tyrrell 012.

But mere words on paper could hardly do justice to the day Ayrton Senna firmly arrived in the front-rank of a new generation of Grand Prix aces.

ENTRY AND PRACTICE

The previous October, Estoril had been the venue for that nail-biting World Championship finale when the title just dropped into the canny Niki Lauda's lap by a half a point. On that sunny autumn afternoon Ayrton Senna had driven brilliantly in his Michelin-shod Toleman TG184, following the McLarens across the line in third place to round off a splendid first season in Formula 1. The manner of his defection to Team Lotus represented an unpleasant blot on his otherwise exemplary record as Grand Prix racing's most promising new acquisition, but nobody can now argue that the decision to switch to Lotus was not completely correct from the point of view of winning races. The fact that Senna had made a clever decision, however, in no way minimised the feeling of brutal injustice felt by the Toleman team, now facing no future at all since neither Goodyear nor Pirelli seemed prepared to provide tyres on *any* realistic basis. Optimistically, the Toleman transporter lurked around Estoril for a few days but there was to be no sympathetic ear cocked in the English team's direction. Dis-appointed, the rig trailed off towards home...

Since the 1984 race, resurfacing of the bumpy start/finish straight had made Estoril a more comfortable ride for the competing drivers, but there was still a light covering of sand and dust on the track to catch out the unwary as unofficial practice got underway on the Friday morning. Fired up like seldom before in the days when he had what might best be described as a 'less worrying' team-mate, Elio de Angelis indicated that he wasn't about to be eclipsed by Senna and turned an impressive 1m 23.58s best in that opening 90-minute sprint. But things were destined to be somewhat different when the first hour-long scramble for grid positions got going at two o'clock.

Fuel system problems had caused Senna's retirement in the Brazilian Grand Prix at Rio two weeks before and, as the cars had been air-freighted direct from South American to Portugal, his race car displayed the same worrying symptoms when it was fired up for the first time. During the morning session he had been obliged to start work with the team's spare 97T, but when that suffered clutch failure he swapped to his still-troubled race car and tried to make the best of a decent lap grappling with the misfire. Only in the last few minutes of the session did the Lotus mechanics trace the fault to a blocked electric pump which had short-circuited. The offending component was replaced in time for him to show impeccable style during first qualifying.

Using an EF4B Renault V6 and the aerodynamic flaps first seen at Rio, Ayrton picked his moment on a damp, but drying, track surface and tore round in an assured 1m 21.7s, convincingly quickest of all. De Angelis, determined not to be left out of the frontline action, responded with everything he had but could only turn a 1m 23.06s for second spot ahead of Niki Lauda's McLaren MP4/2B.

Senna had not finished, of course, and the following afternoon he undercut his Friday best by a healthy fraction to button up pole with 1m 21.007s, thereby earning premier position on an F1 starting grid at only his 16th attempt. Ayrton allowed himself only a slight flicker of a grin: 'I think we had the car working very well indeed – well balanced and, more importantly, good on full tanks.' He followed up this masterpiece of under-

Happiness is . . . Peter Warr leads the bedraggled Lotus ensemble in an impromptu dance as they celebrate a well-earned win; their first since August 1982.

statement with the propitious words, 'tomorrow I would like to get away in the lead, settle down into a rhythm and pace myself carefully . . .' Meanwhile, back in the Lotus garage Ayrton's mechanics were shielding his 97T's rear wing from public gaze, but it was Brabham designer Gordon Murray's eagle eyes which noticed just how lucky the Brazilian had been on his final run. As Senna roared out onto the start/finish straight to begin his pole-position lap, the rear aerofoil tail flap started to collapse backwards and he did the whole of the lap with it slightly distorted. As he slowed, it popped back into shape and he slid unobtrusively into the pit lane garage almost before anybody had seen it.

Elio de Angelis's attempts to join his team-mate on the front row of the grid were spoiled when he found himself held up badly by a couple of cars on his first Saturday qualifying run, while turbo failure scotched his efforts on his second set of soft Goodyears. That left the way open for Rio victor Alain Prost to slide confidently into second place on the front row, the Frenchman using little more than race boost to produce a 1m 21.420s in his McLaren-TAG MP4/2B. On Friday, Alain had

been a little edgy after being obliged to use his spare car when his race machine developed a misfire, while team-mate Niki Lauda also found himself sampling the spare on Saturday when *his* race car ran into gear selection trouble. Niki didn't like this chassis's handling and consequently ended up a disappointed seventh on 1m 23.670s.

Over in the Williams camp progress seemed to be obstructed by a whole succession of minor problems, so it was an index of Keke Rosberg's dauntless determination that he persevered to reach third on 1m 21.904s – whereas the previous afternoon he had been easily the slowest of all.

The sudden power delivery of the still 'peaky' Honda V6 engine kicked the FW10s into sudden oversteering lurches out of the tight corners, so alarmingly that even Rosberg complained about it. 'A balanced chassis is extremely important here because there is so little grip', he explained thoughtfully, 'but this sudden delivery of power means we're losing out quite dramatically coming out of the tighter corners . . .'

With the Portuguese weather at its most unpredictable, making the most of the few dry patches within rain showers was of paramount

importance on Friday afternoon and the air of tension in the Williams pit was heightened when Rosberg's FW10 suffered a turbo failure as the Finn accelerated away down the pit lane to start his first run. The turbo was duly replaced, but Keke was in such a hurry to record a decent time before the rain returned that he spun as he attempted to dive inside Gerhard Berger's Arrows A8 on the tight uphill right-hander two corners beyond the pits.

'I thought I was going to get away with it, but I just tapped the guard rail with a nose fin just before I came to a halt', shrugged Keke. All that amounted to a fastest lap of just over 15 minutes by the time the Williams had been retrieved by its crew. It was just the sort of disappointment calculated to bring out the best in Keke, and the following afternoon he gathered everything together to nail home that third place on the grid with his customary flair.

Poor Nigel Mansell started out his Estoril weekend on a dejected note. Already pilloried by some sections of the press for his over-ambitious first-corner manoeuvre at Rio, the Englishman found his first qualifying run in the FW10 ending

Nigel Snowdon

firmly against the barrier through absolutely no fault of his own. Electing to conserve his first set of marked Goodyear qualifiers, Mansell backed off after a lurid slide as a rain shower began to douse the circuit and was cruising gently back to the pits when the warring Alfa Romeo 185Ts of Cheever and Patrese came bearing down on him.

Since the previous year's British Grand Prix, the Alfa Romeo drivers had not spoken to each other in anything approaching a civil fashion, and from then on their relationship had spiralled downhill, completely out of control – just like their cars, for most of the time! As Mansell moved off-line to let them through, Patrese failed to give Cheever any room as the American attempted to go through the gap between the other Alfa and the Williams. In a trice, Eddie's car had bounced off its stablemate and careered into the Williams, punting an astonished Mansell into the guard rail with quite an impact.

Mansell was left to trundle round in the team's unloved FW09B spare for the remainder of the afternoon, but the Williams mechanics totally repaired his FW10 in time for final qualifying on Saturday, using up almost their entire stock of nose cone and front suspension components in the process. Nigel wound up a somewhat disappointed ninth on 1m 23.594s, but minor problems with lack of traction due to a broken exhaust diffuser undertray could be quickly shrugged aside when compared with Friday's problems. At least the

new car had been repaired!

Ferrari new-boy Stefan Johansson found his debut for the Maranello team a little difficult, but he was relieved to find his established colleague Michele Alboreto confirming his concern over the bumpy ride imparted by their 156/85s. Michele assured him that this was a new development as the chassis had handled perfectly in Brazil. Johansson came to Estoril fresh from some testing at Fiorano and was a little bewildered when he found that the Ferraris had problems getting their qualifying rubber up to temperature.

Despite complaining about shortage of traction, Alboreto qualified a respectable fifth on 1m 22.577s. Johansson was obliged to take the spare for a period on both Friday and Saturday, owing to gearbox problems and rotor arm failure respectively on his race car. He found some problems fitting the cockpit of the *muletta* as it was fitted out for Michele's comfort but eventually coaxed his 'unbelievably nervous' machine round to an eleventh quickest 1m 23.652s.

Copying Lotus's aerodynamic front strakes and side aerofoils looked like a desperate attempt by the Renault Elf team to hit on a formula which would magically transform the difficult-to-drive RE60s to some semblance of competitiveness. Although Warwick emerged in a relatively respectable sixth place on 1m 23.084s, he confessed that his fastest lap was 'chaotic – no finesse at all. I was banging kerbs, crunching gears . . . it

just didn't flow smoothly at all.' Both Derek and team-mate Patrick Tambay were worried about lack of grip, and while Patrick was quite perky after trying the latest, more torquey EF15 engine in his race car on Saturday morning, this was then put on one side and he could only manage a disappointing 12th quickest 1m 24.11s in the EF4B-engined spare.

In the Pirelli camp there was endless speculation as to why Ligier's overweight JS25 seemed so effective on the unpredictable Italian rubber, many observers reckoning that the car's surplus kilos provided the ideal way to work up to correct temperatures! The irrepressible Andrea de Cesaris opposite-locked his way round to an eighth quickest 1m 23.02s, although this was more than two seconds away from the Goodyear pole time. Running with Candy identification for the first time, the indications were that the French cars from Vichy were being massaged into some semblance of competitive shape, even though the happy-go-lucky Jacques Laffite found himself down in a lowly 18th slot on 1m 24.943s, his Friday best. Clutch failure spoiled his chances of improvement and he had to wait for a turn in Andrea's race car on Saturday as the spare chassis didn't have a qualifying-spec engine installed.

Nelson Piquet lined up a somewhat crestfallen 10th on 1m 23.618s, explaining that when he got a clear lap he wasn't running sufficient boost pressure – and when he ran sufficient boost, he got

A jubilant Ayrton Senna, his seat harness already undone, splashes back towards the pits and a celebration of his first Grand Prix victory.

enna

Turbo

ecial RE

OLYMPUS
CAMERAS

April
René Arnoux leaves Ferrari; replaced by Stefan Johansson.

tangled up in traffic. On Friday he suffered an engine problem, the BMW four-cylinder seeming reluctant to run cleanly at the top end when the boost was turned up, but that was successfully rectified for Saturday. The team was non-committal about the performance of Pirelli's qualifying rubber, but it's worth mentioning that Piquet was fastest through the start/finish line speed trap at 194.291 mph – some 40 mph more than the Cosworth-engined Tyrrells! François Hesnault suffered with a serious misfire and a whole lot of niggling little problems, creeping into the race in a lowly 19th place.

In between trading insults through third parties, the Alfa Romeo drivers proved a well-matched pair, Patrese and Cheever qualifying 13th and 14th despite their very public tangle. Eddie reckoned that work on the front suspension of the John Gentry-designed chassis had proved its worth during recent tests at Balocco, but his chance of a really quick run on Saturday was spoiled when the 185T broke its engine and he was obliged to qualify the updated 184TB spare.

Thierry Boutsen and Gerhard Berger were disappointed not to be better placed, for both drivers reckoned that the revised wide track rear suspension fitted to their Arrows A8s was a worthwhile improvement. Thierry's intention of qualifying in the top six ended when a freshly installed engine broke on his first lap during

Saturday qualifying and the spare car did not handle anywhere near as well. Berger suffered an engine failure on Friday and wound up 17th, one place behind his team-mate.

Race tyres were proving quicker than qualifiers as far as RAM's Pirellis were concerned but Manfred Winkelhock made some worthwhile progress on Saturday to line up 15th on 1m 24.721s; so, with Alliot 20th on 1m 26.187s, John Macdonald was certainly living up to his assurance to his sponsors that his cars would qualify in the top 20 on most occasions.

Just out of the top 20 were the nimble Tyrrell 012s of Stefan Bellof and Martin Brundle, both drivers agreeing that the cars were a touch too nervous right on the limit for their taste, although they looked moderately encouraging on full tanks.

Jonathan Palmer's debut outing in the very attractive Zakspeed earned him 23rd place on 1m 28.166s and it might have been even quicker had not the car ground to a halt with master switch failure on its first Saturday qualifying lap. Jonathan had found his mount a little lively over the bumps on Friday, so it had been softened up slightly, correct gear ratios chosen and a fresh engine installed. Against Palmer's advice, the team's mechanics worked on the car away from the pits in an attempt to get it going again – earning a 3000 dollar fine from the stewards, just as their driver had feared!

Rounding off the grid were Pierluigi Martini's Cosworth DFV-engined Minardi and the unlucky Piercarlo Ghinzani who had to rely on his Friday best after his Saturday times were disallowed following a rear wing height infringement during that final hour.

FERRARI SENSATION AS JOHANSSON REPLACES ARNOUX

It had been known for some while that the Commendatore was disappointed with René Arnoux's form over the latter half of the 1984 season, but when the plucky little Frenchman came whistling through from 19th to fourth at Rio following a pit stop, most people felt that he was back in the competitive groove once again. Sadly, this Indian summer had come too late to prevent the axe falling and Arnoux found himself invited to Maranello for a 'conference' with Mr Ferrari on the Friday following the Brazilian Grand Prix.

It seems that the exchange got heated and bitter and Arnoux stormed off in a huff, not making himself available for testing at Fiorano the following day. More debate and discussion followed and, by the following Tuesday, official sources announced that Arnoux had asked to be released from his contracts following problems with his leg muscles that had required surgery during the off-season.

This patently transparent euphemism fooled nobody but it seems that it was the prescribed form of words necessary for both parties to disentangle themselves from Arnoux's contract with honour: Ferrari had kept his reputation for fair play intact, René still retained custody of the lion's share of his reputed million-dollar driving

fee for the '85 season.

Through the good offices and sheer generosity of Toleman MD Alex Hawkridge, Stefan Johansson was released from any further commitment to the troubled Witney team and immediately flew to Maranello where a deal was struck for him to take over Arnoux's place in the team. Unofficial sources indicate that, in a 'straw poll' taken amongst leading lights in the Ferrari racing department over the winter, the slightly built Swede was at the top of everybody's list to fill any possible vacant seat in the team. Now the moment had come.

Stefan's meeting with the Old Man was brief but to the point. Ferrari simply asked him: 'Are you a fighter?' Johansson replied that he'd had to fight hard for everything he had. Thus Maranello recruited its first ever Swedish Formula 1 driver. A few days later, Stefan made a hesitant debut in the Estoril rain; just over a fortnight later he was to become Italy's darling at Imola, his position in the team apparently secure.

Arnoux, for his part, treated the whole affair remarkably philosophically. Privately, he may have shared the relief expressed by some of his close friends that Ferrari might have done him a favour in the long run. His driving had certainly been erratic and unpredictable for much of 1984 – hardly a formula for personal safety in the volatile world of Ferrari Formula 1 politics.

Bernard Asset/Agence Vandystadt.

Prost parks it. Alain Prost climbs from his damaged car after the McLaren had aquaplaned out of third place while following de Angelis *(right)*.
'Pinch me, Michele; I'm dreaming.' From reserve bench to best seat in the house, Stefan Johansson was as stunned as the rest of the pit lane when Ferrari sacked René Arnoux and nominated the Swede for the rest of the season *(below)*.
A brilliant drive by Nigel Mansell more than made up for his gaff in Rio two weeks previously. Starting from the pit lane, Mansell conquered a viciously narrow power band on the Honda V6 to keep the Williams in the running for fifth place on a day when Keke Rosberg spun his FW10 into retirement *(opposite top)*.
The atrocious conditions were guaranteed to bring out the best in Stefan Bellof, the Tyrrell-Cosworth driver apparently scarcely bothered about the lack of either horsepower or downforce. Bellof, his Tyrrell showing signs of a brush with Winkelhock's RAM *(following)*, almost took fifth place from Nigel Mansell on the line *(opposite bottom)*.

RACE

On Sunday morning Estoril briefly basked under blue skies but by the time the cars rolled out for the half-hour warm-up it was clouding over and, as predicted, rain began falling shortly before the start. Formula 1 admission price levels were clearly beyond the reach of most of the locals, so the grandstands and trackside enclosures were very sparsely populated – the crowd total was later estimated at a meagre 11,000.

In race trim the McLaren-TAGs looked strong as usual, with Prost quickest in the warm-up from de Angelis, but Senna's 97T suffered transmission failure and needed a fresh engine/gearbox prior to the start. There were some mildly worried faces in the Renault camp, for while Warwick had a quick spin and lightly damaged some bodywork, a rear wishbone pick-up point broke off the gearbox casing on Tambay's sister RE60, so the mechanics had to take the gearbox off the spare car and fit it to Patrick's race machine during the interval. On full tanks Alboreto and Johansson were third and fourth while Palmer's Zakspeed raised some eyebrows with a ninth quickest lap, designer Paul Brown hurriedly pointing out that this was with race boost and a reasonable fuel load.

Shortly before the cars departed on their warming-up lap the rain intensified and Mansell, stabbing hard at the throttle of his Williams-Honda in an attempt to clear a misfire, lurched into a spin which damaged the FW10's nose section against a barrier. He came into the pit lane for repairs, as did Martini after a quick pirouette in the Minardi.

Meanwhile, down on the grid the Alfa mechanics took it upon themselves at this late stage to take out a screw connection in the turbos of Cheever's Alfa which lead to the cockpit turbo temperature read-outs. The intention was to replace them with purpose-made plugs blanking off the connection, the curious reasoning being that there is no time for the driver to monitor turbo temperature in the race, but one of these plugs cross-threaded and wouldn't go in properly. Thus, at the last minute Eddie found himself sitting on the grid with an unwanted hole in one of his turbochargers! There was nothing else for him to do but leap from the cockpit, sprint down the pits, climb aboard the spare 184TB and line up with Mansell and Martini, waiting to join in the race from the pit lane once it had started.

With the rain steadily intensifying, Senna led the parade lap round to the starting lights, Derek Ongaro pressed the button and the battle was on. With well-judged sensitivity, Ayrton edged into the lead on the run down to the first corner, but behind him Keke Rosberg let his rough-running Honda engine go off the boil and stalled in his tracks. Amazingly, everybody weaved round the stationary Williams without a major accident, but Palmer's weekend continued in its luckless vein: the Zakspeed's right-front wheel just glanced the Williams's left-rear. At the end of the second lap the German car came in to retire, with a damaged rim and also deranged suspension.

At the end of the opening lap Senna was already several lengths clear of de Angelis, Prost, Alboreto, Warwick, Lauda, de Cesaris, Tambay, Piquet, Johansson, Patrese, Boutsen, Winkelhock, Bellof, Berger, Alliot, Laffite, Ghinzani, Hesnault, Cheever (from the pit lane), Baldi, Brundle, Mansell (from the pit lane), Martini (from the pit lane), the recovering Rosberg who had taken time off for a quick spin, and the crippled Palmer.

De Angelis was doing everything in his power to keep pace with his team-mate, but Senna's super-confident progress was inexorable and, after half a dozen laps, the Brazilian began to pull away steadily, handling his Lotus on the increasingly treacherous track surface with all the assurance of a veteran. Prost gradually hauled up onto Elio's tail, bringing with him a drenched Alboreto whose Ferrari was sitting a few lengths behind the McLaren.

Warwick's Renault was quickly gobbled up by Lauda's McLaren, although the World Champion was unable to keep pace with the leading bunch, worried about the response of his carbon-fibre brakes in the cool conditions and hampered by a TAG turbo reluctant to pull much over 10,000 rpm. De Cesaris and Tambay were tramping along next in line, Patrick about to displace the Ligier, while Piquet's early spurt was over and the Brabham team leader dropped back through the field like a stone, unable to get anything like competitive grip from his Pirelli wets.

It wasn't long before Nelson was being crowded by the circumspect Johansson and the erratic Patrese and, at the start of lap four, the two Italian cars slipped through – only for Patrese to ram Stefan from behind, spinning both cars to the outside of the first corner. Johansson mercifully kept the engine running and continued way down the field but Patrese's Alfa had stalled and that was the end of his race.

Early retirements included the miserable Hesnault, who was spared any more humiliation at the tail of the field when his BT54 misfired its way out of the contest, both Alliot and Martini spun off, while Gerhard Berger's Arrows chimed on song with such abruptness on lap 13 that the Austrian found himself catapulted against a barrier!

Senna seemed to be revelling in the conditions, the black-and-gold ball of spray pulling further and further away from its pursuers, but these diabolical conditions proved less attractive to some of the older hands in the Formula 1 business. On lap 16 Jacques Laffite pulled into the pits and drove straight into his garage. Climbing out, the normally jaunty Frenchman made it quite clear that, as far as he was concerned, the whole thing was a precarious waste of time. Recounting just how difficult to drive the JS25 had proved on those Pirelli wets, he finished his sermon by suggesting that his team-mate be signalled to stop – if the team wanted de Cesaris's car to have any wheels still attached by the end of the afternoon. After some consideration, as the weather deteriorated by the lap, Andrea was flagged in on lap 30 . . .

De Angelis was still doing an absolutely magnificent job fending off Prost's McLaren and the whole second place battle seemed to be coming down to a question of which driver would crack first under the strain. Despite taking some

unconventional lines under braking for some corners, Elio continued to fend off the McLaren, until, in the height of the downpour, with even Senna signalling to officials that the race should be stopped, Alain suddenly hit a particularly deep puddle on the start/finish straight . . .

The McLaren spun like a top before it even left the tarmac, spearing off towards the guard rail opposite the pits at apparently undiminished speed. Just when it seemed that the car would hit the barrier head-on, it suddenly flicked round and took its rear wing tail flap off in a glancing blow before stopping, more or less undamaged, on the grassy run-off. Prost, happy to be intact, hopped out very promptly!

With Niki's sister MP4/2B succumbing to piston failure, the McLaren mould was broken at last, no matter who won through in the end. Picking his way through the tail-enders, Senna's concentration didn't flag for the slightest moment, despite his involuntary trip down the grass on one particularly fraught lap. In fact, it was de Angelis who lost concentration for a couple of seconds. Relieved that Prost was no longer on his tail, he left the door wide open for Alboreto to poke the Ferrari through into second place on lap 43 and, a

couple of corners later, the Lotus slid wide onto the dirt, puncturing a front tyre which was to slow Elio further in the closing stages of the race.

Gaining in confidence with every lap he negotiated, Patrick Tambay took only 13 laps to get the better of his team-mate and stormed through to take an eventual third place, aided by de Angelis slowing up quite dramatically towards the end. Rosberg's progress through the field, though briefly thwarted by a quick stop to change a tyre deflated in the impact with Palmer, saw the Finn eventually displace Warwick for sixth place. Then the Finn's Honda engine chimed in full power – 'I spent most of the time with 7000 bhp, or nothing!', quoth Keke afterwards – and the FW10 slammed backwards into the barrier at the right-hander before the pits. As the steering wheel whipped out of his hand, Rosberg sustained a broken bone in his right thumb, but thankfully no lasting harm.

Rosberg's departure promoted Warwick back into sixth place but Derek then spun and clanged the barriers, stopping for fresh rubber and a check-over before continuing to an eventual seventh, two laps behind the winning Lotus. In fifth place, behind de Angelis, Nigel Mansell had

driven with just the right blend of fire and determination to take two World Championship points, while Stefan Bellof's Tyrrell, its nose cone rumpled in an earlier head-to-head with Winkelhock's spinning RAM, came home sixth a few lengths behind. Martin Brundle had sadly succumbed to gear selector trouble on lap 29.

Cheever's race through the field in the spare Alfa came to a disappointing end with engine failure. Johansson finished classified eighth, five laps adrift having glanced Winkelhock's stationary machine (which had spun again!) and stopped for a seized left-front brake to be freed, as well as having fresh tyres fitted. Manfred was still trailing round at the finish, almost at walking pace on his uncompetitive tyres, but the frustrated Piquet, after half a dozen pit stops for tyres (and a change of overalls!) called it a day on lap 29.

Michele Alboreto became the only other competitor not to have been lapped by Senna, but Ayrton made the performance almost perfect with fastest race lap. It looked as though Formula 1 had been raised to a new standard when it came to wet weather driving.

The only unanswered question was – could he duplicate that form in the dry? A. H.

TECHNICAL FILE

Cars were prepared in Rio prior to shipment directly to Estoril. As a result, very little technical change in many cases.

McLAREN
Fitted Gleason differential (first seen in Monaco, 1984).

TYRRELL
Nothing new. Maurice Phillippe worked on 014 in England.

WILLIAMS
Different IHI turbocharger; inlet duct in side pod now a permanent feature. Tried 'Lotus' front suspension aerodynamics in wind tunnel, but not seen in Portugal. Lower rear wing in two sections with a small flap.

BRABHAM
New chassis (number 4) flown out to replace (2) damaged in Brazil.

RAM
Longer underwing profile and a four-piece rear wing. Alternated between small and large Holset turbos on Hart engines.

LOTUS
Ran same aerodynamic devices seen in Brazil. Fitted larger side plates to rear wing on Saturday. Lotus/Brembo calipers used for carbon brakes (which differed from other Brembo calipers).

RENAULT
Jean-Pierre Jaussaud tested different aerodynamics and revised electronics (to improve fuel consumption) at small airfield near Renault factory. Fitted front aerodynamic 'Lotus' fins but with different profiles. Tambay tested new front suspension upright, Warwick tried revised rear suspension with different top wishbone. Front suspension mod discarded but both cars had revised rear for Saturday. Reduced size of radiator outlet.

ARROWS
New chassis (number 4) flown to Portugal. Boutsen's car and T-car fitted with exhausts sweeping through rear suspension (similar to Brabham). Boutsen tried revised rear track on Friday; fitted to Berger's car for Saturday. Boutsen also tried brief unsuccessful run without wastegate on Friday.

SPIRIT
No change.

ALFA ROMEO
Produced revised exit for radiators; new front suspension geometry and different rear wing. Briefly tried new pick-up point for rear shock absorbers on Saturday; retained for the race. Cheever tried reprofiled rear undertray (similar to Williams) on Saturday.

OSELLA
Fitted wider front track.

LIGIER
Water tank moved from side pod to position above driver's feet.

FERRARI
Tested winglets mounted at rear of side pods (similar to, but larger than, Lotus versions) at Fiorano. Abandoned because any improvement cancelled by disturbed airflow to turbo inlet duct mounted at the same point. Trials with a smaller duct on Saturday morning proved unsuccessful. Johansson ran with cast-iron disc brakes on Friday; carbon-fibre used on Saturday. Continued to use electronically controlled system which kept turbo running at high speed even when throttle pedal not depressed, thus improving engine response.

MINARDI
Continued to run heavy aluminium modifications to accept Cosworth DFV.

ZAKSPEED
First race for conventional, well-made chassis. Brought five Zakspeed engines to Estoril.

GP

Gran Premio di San Marino

The San Marino Grand Prix produced some of the best racing seen for a long time but the high standard of driving was to be devalued by the rule book.

The last few laps were a joke; the two hours following the Grand Prix became a farce as the world's press waited to discover who had won this race. In the end, Elio de Angelis was declared the winner but, in truth, the final result had no bearing whatsoever on what had gone on before. Apart from a few laps in the early stages, the JPS Lotus driver had never been in the reckoning.

His team-mate, on the other hand, had dominated the proceedings before the Renault V6 consumed the last drop of Elf, four laps from the finish. A pity, but never mind because now we had Stefan Johansson in the lead. This was another excellent performance, the Ferrari driver having worked his way through the field from 15th place on the grid. Johansson's first taste of running at the front of a Grand Prix was to last but half a lap, the Ferrari running out of fuel.

Cruising into the lead came Alain Prost, the Marlboro McLaren driver having battled wheel to wheel with the unflappable Senna before dropping back as a concession to racing with 220 litres of Shell on a track notorious for its heavy demands on fuel consumption. Now Prost was leading. To finish first, first you must finish and it seemed Prost had read the situation correctly as he took the flag, his car spluttering to a halt on the slowing down lap. Hardly the way to go racing – but he had won.

Or had he? The post-race weigh-in showed the McLaren to be under the minimum weight limit. The team had made a miscalculation; Prost was out.

Thus de Angelis, without brakes but with petrol, was first. Second place went to Thierry Boutsen as the Belgian's Barclay Arrows straddled the finishing line, its tank dry. Patrick Tambay, never higher than eighth until three laps from the end, was third and the Renault-Elf would have been second had he arrived at the line three seconds earlier. Niki Lauda, in serious gearbox trouble, took fourth place, the McLaren a lap ahead of Nigel Mansell's Canon Williams Honda. Sixth place was awarded eventually to Johansson. Senna, seventh on paper, did not even gain the satisfaction of a championship point. But at least he had shown that he could run just as confidently in the dry as he had in the wet in Portugal two weeks before. Come the day of reckoning at the end of the season, these were nine points which Lotus could ill-afford to throw away.

ENTRY AND PRACTICE

Before the start of practice, Ayrton Senna was unfamiliar with the Imola circuit and what little he knew of the place did not impress him. By the end of the preliminaries, he proved to be the master of the Autodromo Dino Ferrari – and he liked it even less.

Senna's experience had been limited to a few laps in the wet the previous year when the Toleman team carried out the unseemly public washing of their dispute with Pirelli. Ayrton did not qualify on that occasion. In 1985, he was fastest in both timed sessions.

'I have to admit I don't really like this circuit', he confessed. 'It's all chicanes; you're hard on the brakes, turn in, accelerate out. Not very interesting; a sort of power circuit really. What we need is more fast corners that you can really *drive* through.'

Whatever the combination of corners, the combination of Ayrton Senna and the Lotus 97T proved equal to their demands. Interestingly, his quick qualifying times at Imola were set using race tyres rather than qualifiers.

The aforementioned chicanes helped bottle up the traffic during practice and, as a result, overtaking was difficult; a clear lap hard to find. Most of the Goodyear runners reasoned that it was better to run soft race tyres which would be good for several laps rather than attempting one

banzai hope-no-one-gets-in-my-way run on qualifiers. On top of that, the qualifiers were not reaching working temperature that easily and there was the added complication of the rear tyres, churned by the turbo power, 'coming in' before the front tyres had warmed up properly.

Lotus, for the first time, had the use of the latest EF15 engine, one of the long-stroke units being made available for Elio de Angelis. The Italian ran it on Friday morning and was suitably impressed by the improved response and torque, the plan being to keep the engine for the race and use the T-car with the EF4 unit for qualifying.

That idea was cancelled when Elio lost a turbo on the T-car and was forced to qualify a race chassis which was not set up for the task. Elio was 12th at the end of Friday's practice and in a bid to move up the grid he opted to use two sets of qualifiers on Saturday. He claimed third place with his first set before waiting to try the final set of qualifiers. A light fall of rain half-way through practice spoiled any chance of improvement.

Keke Rosberg opted to run qualifiers on both days. The surprise was that he was able to drive at all bearing in mind the nasty gash on his left hand, received when he spun off in Portugal. Indeed, he was more concerned about an engine misfire on Friday but the Finn was nevertheless in third place at the end of the day. Keke's mechanics changed the ancillary equipment overnight, but with little success, and he stepped into the T-car

Ayrton Senna remained cool under relentless pressure from Alain Prost and the Brazilian did not relinquish the lead until his Lotus ran out of fuel a few laps from the end. Prost crossed the line first but was later disqualified when the McLaren was found to be below the minimum weight limit.

on Saturday morning. That kept blowing off a turbo pipe so the team set to and changed the Honda V6 on his race car in time for the final session. Success at last; it ran perfectly.

On his first set of qualifiers, Rosberg caught his team-mate but misjudged the fact that Mansell was about to start his quick lap too, the pair then circulating in tandem. On his second set, Rosberg caught Patrese's Alfa Romeo three corners from home but since the Alfa was also on a quick lap, he had no option but to fall in behind – and record second fastest time, missing pole by less than a tenth of a second.

Mansell's practice was not without its dramas. On Friday, he misjudged his braking for the final chicane and shot down the escape road – which also happened to be the entrance to the pits. He motored through and began another attempt – only to run out of fuel. On Saturday, his best lap was ruined by Hesnault wandering across the middle of the track, totally oblivious to the Englishman's approach. The Williams pit, listening on the radio link, were aware of a problem when the silence was shattered by a torrent of abuse delivered in a broad Birmingham accent.

The Italian newspapers had been peering through the fence at Fiorano during the run up to Imola and their reports indicated that Ferrari had been testing a quadruple turbo arrangement. Of this there was no sign when practice began at Imola and, judging by Michele Alboreto's perform-

ance on Friday, they had no need of it, the Italian setting second fastest time.

That was as good as calling the faithful to worship and on Saturday the enclosures vibrated in anticipation of a Ferrari on pole. It was not to be. A broken turbo collector chamber put paid to his first run and rain killed any chance in the T-car. Michele was 15th fastest in the session but his time from Friday was good enough for fourth overall.

Stefan Johansson was worse off. The weekend had started in the best possible manner, the Swede setting a time of 1m 29.639s in the unofficial session. Qualifying, however, would present a series of niggling problems and he would not approach that time again. On Friday afternoon, the rear undertray came loose during a run on qualifiers. He went out on race tyres but Piquet spun in front of him and, a little later, Boutsen did the same. The tyres by then were past their best. On Saturday, Johansson ran qualifiers – only to find a spinning Winkelhock. On his second set (of qualifiers) he hit traffic and the engine began to misfire. He was 15th – in Italy. He hoped the press and the fans would understand . . .

The Barclay Arrows team had caused a stir during pre-season testing when Thierry Boutsen set the pace. There was the faint suspicion that the Belgian's performance may have been aided by a full-house BMW engine but, when it really mattered, the team was on the pace during

qualifying. Adjustments to the suspension produced better traction and, at the end of the first day's practice, Gerhard Berger was fifth, Boutsen sixth. A split fuel pipe on Saturday meant that Berger would rely on that time for his grid position while Boutsen improved further in spite of throttle lag which obliged him to slip the clutch through slow corners.

Sixth place for the winner of the previous year's race was not what Alain Prost would have wished for but it was just about what he expected, bearing in mind the inability of the McLaren-TAG to run with qualifying boost. Apart from being slow through the speed trap, Prost missed a gear and had a soft brake pedal to contend with on Friday but larger turbos for Saturday's session helped him find another half-second. Niki Lauda had more urgent problems to attend to throughout practice, his car stopping with a deflating tyre on Friday morning after a rear caliper had scored through a rim. The following morning, his TAG V6 began to make nasty noises and an engine change meant he did not get out in the final session until 20 minutes from the end; by this time the track was damp. None the less, he found another second and moved into eighth place ahead of Nelson Piquet.

Piquet had been breaking the timing beam on the pit straight at 164 mph (compared with Lauda's 157 mph best), yet the Olivetti Brabham was a tenth of a second slower overall and half a

A close battle between Mansell, Boutsen and Cheever matched the drama at the front *(right)*. Nelson Piquet, one of the fastest drivers on the track after his pit stop for fresh Pirellis, would have finished in the top three had he not run out of fuel *(top, far right)*. Elio de Angelis; no brakes – but adequate fuel for nine points *(far right)*. Andrea de Cesaris crashed his Ligier soon after a pit stop for tyres *(below right)*.

April:
Snow forces cancellation of Nürburgring Formula 3000 race; Monza 1000 km stopped when tree falls across track.

May:
Closure of Mount Fuji Speedway announced.
March Engineering receive Duke of Edinburgh's Prize for Design.
Attilio Bettega killed on Tour de Corse.

second away from Boutsen's BMW-powered Arrows. Nelson complained of very little grip from his Pirellis, a fact demonstrated graphically when he spun on Friday. And if Piquet could not tame the BT54/Pirelli combination, what chance was there for François Hesnault? The poor Frenchman looked out of his depth and his humour was not improved when he managed to crash the spare Brabham during his first lap on Saturday morning. The fact that the car had an experimental TV camera on board did not do much for Mr Ecclestone's humour either . . .

Patrick Tambay proved to be the faster of the works Renault-Elf drivers despite a visit to the sand run-off area at *Tosa* on Friday and running out of fuel on Saturday. It was Derek Warwick's turn to have the EF15 engine, this being set to one side for the race, forcing the Englishman to use the spare car during qualifying on Saturday. Problems with the braking were eventually traced to an incorrectly adjusted brake balance bar, thus enabling Warwick to find a full second in the final session.

The Benetton Alfa Romeo drivers were encouraged by the arrival, at long last, of Bosch Motronic systems on their race cars. However, their enthusiasm was blunted on Friday morning when both cars suffered problems as they tried to get to grips with the engine management systems. There was a spare car for each driver but a distributor failure on Saturday afternoon meant Cheever and Patrese had to share a spare car for qualifying! They had their race cars for Saturday, Eddie qualifying 12th while Patrese spun his way down to 18th on the damp track.

Neither Ligier driver was happy with Pirelli qualifying tyres which would last no more than half a lap. Jacques Laffite used race tyres on Saturday while Andrea de Cesaris had his best lap blocked by Alliot's RAM. As if to underline Laffite's problems, Jonathan Palmer was just a fraction slower in the Zakspeed – and this after hardly any laps on Friday. Most of the morning had been spent changing an engine and the Englishman was then stranded out on the circuit when his throttle cable broke half-way through his first lap in the afternoon. On Saturday, the German team ran conservative boost so, all in all, 17th place was an excellent effort.

And if the West-Zakspeed's performance had been noteworthy, then 19th place for the Simod Minardi with its Motori Moderni engine was nothing short of remarkable. Apart from breaking

a fuel pump belt on Saturday, Carlo Chiti's engine never missed a beat throughout practice and the heavy car, with its inexperienced driver, caused some embarrassment by beating Hesnault's Brabham and the entire Skoal Bandit team.

Alliot was the quicker of the RAM drivers even though he had to rely on Friday's time (set with the T-car) after losing a turbo in the final session. Winkelhock had a fresh engine for Saturday but a loss of boost pressure meant 23rd place for the German driver. The Kelemata Osella team presented their new car at Imola but fuel injection pump problems meant Piercarlo Ghinzani had to rely on the FA1F in both timed sessions. Spirit had repaired the car damaged at Estoril but Mauro Baldi's times were so far off the pace that, had there been more than 26 cars practising, he most surely would not have qualified. As it was, he was roundly beaten by the Tyrrell-Cosworths on this, a power circuit.

Stefan Bellof's only problem had been a tyre which been punctured when he made contact with Boutsen's Arrows on Friday afternoon. Martin Brundle, on the other hand, was fortunate to emerge unscathed from a head-on shunt at *Tosa* on Saturday morning. Brundle reported that the brake pedal went to the floor initially. He managed to find enough pressure to lock the front brakes but there was no time to spin the car before it ploughed across the sand run-off area and into a tyre barrier. Brundle's only complaint was a sore back caused by a full tank of fuel surging forward

and thumping the rear of the driver's seat.

The tub was undamaged but when the car was returned to the pits, a rear brake pad was found to be missing. Tyrrell and his mechanics set out to walk from the corner before the pits (where the carbon-fibre brakes had been perfect) to *Tosa* in a bid to find the pad and solve the mystery. Their efforts were repaid when an eagle-eyed spectator, who had spotted the pad flying off at *Tosa*, came forward with his souvenir. Tyrrell rewarded the boy with tickets for the race . . .

RACE

At first light, a heavy rain shower seemed to signal a repeat of Portugal two weeks previously. By the time the warm-up took place, the rain had stopped but the track was damp and teams learned very little about set-ups for what, by now, looked like being a dry race. Complicating the already difficult calculations over fuel consumption and tyre wear, the rain had washed the track clean and the cool, overcast conditions were perfect for a fast race. The resulting demands on fuel consumption indicated a low-boost race with victory going to the frugal rather than the swift.

For Palmer and Zakspeed, it seemed they might not have a race at all, the four-cylinder turbo misfiring throughout the warm-up and continuing during the run onto the grid. Frantic work failed to solve the problem and Palmer wisely decided not to take the start with a car which would prove a hazard to those behind. Therefore,

the Zakspeed's race was even shorter than in Portugal; the trouble was diagnosed eventually as a problem with the engine timing.

Ayrton Senna's timing was perfect at the start, the black-and-gold Lotus making a clean getaway with its sister car slotting into second place. Mindful of the tricky characteristics of the Honda engine and his stalled start in Portugal, Rosberg made what was, for him, a conservative start and the Williams driver was quite happy to find himself in fifth place at the end of the lap.

Alboreto had quickly moved around Rosberg to slot into third place while Prost had shot through from the third row to take fourth spot ahead of the two Williams drivers. Lauda was seventh, ahead of Cheever and Boutsen, the Belgian due to spend most of the race regretting his slow start as he became embroiled in a scrap with the Alfa and Mansell's Williams.

The Lotus drivers made an impressive sight as they demonstrated excellent balance and traction but it was clear that de Angelis, in his efforts to keep up with Senna, was using the kerbs rather more than the Brazilian. A few seconds behind them, Alboreto was busy keeping Prost at bay, the Ferrari driver actually forcing Prost onto the grass as they accelerated out of *Tosa* on one occasion. Parked on the grass already was the Spirit of Baldi, out with turbo trouble. Berger had retired his Arrows with an electrical problem; Patrese's race had ended with a blown turbo on lap four while Bellof was circulating slowly, shortly to

quit with a broken valve on the Cosworth DFY.

The first four cars had broken away from the rest of the field and, at the 10-lap mark, Alboreto and Prost had caught de Angelis as the Lotus driver began to feel the effects of fading brakes. By lap 12, Elio was fourth while behind him the field had been diminished further, Hesnault stopping with engine trouble and de Cesaris crashing his Ligier immediately after calling for a fresh set of Pirellis.

Piquet had also made a stop for tyres on lap 11, the Brabham driver having worked his way impressively from 10th to sixth place. In fact, Piquet had at one stage overhauled Lauda but the reigning World Champion soon reasserted himself and, on lap 12, Niki was in fifth place and gaining rapidly on de Angelis. By lap 17, the McLaren was fourth, six seconds behind his team-mate.

Prost continued to pile the pressure on Alboreto's Ferrari while, at the front, Senna controlled the race beautifully. None the less, the Ferrari was always within striking distance and this kept the expectant crowd on their toes.

On lap 23, a crisis of major proportions swept the hillsides; the Ferrari was slowing. A lap later and Alboreto was in the pits, the mechanics working feverishly on an electrical problem. Alboreto rejoined at the back of the field, a fresh set of Goodyears helping him set fastest lap but, not long after, the problem returned and Michele parked the red car for good. So much for a Ferrari victory.

A lonely race for Patrick Tambay brightened considerably during the closing laps, the Renault jumping from eighth to third as others fell by the wayside *(right)*.
Thierry Boutsen pushes his Arrows to safety after rolling to the line with a dead engine. The Belgian was eventually classified second *(far right)*.

Not quite. The crowd quickly turned their attention to number 28. Johansson had attacked from the start, working his way from 15th to join a battle for eighth place between Mansell, Cheever and Boutsen. These three had circulated nose-to-tail for some laps but Johansson soon found his way through, Boutsen taking the opportunity to pass Cheever at the same time.

Alboreto's pit stop moved Johansson into fifth place behind de Angelis and it was obvious to the crowd that the Swede was reducing the deficit by a second a lap. Further ahead, Lauda was pulling away from de Angelis, having passed the Lotus on lap 17, but the Austrian's progress was suddenly interrupted by a spin. The computer on the TAG engine had been playing tricks, causing the engine to cut in and out and it was just such a moment at the chicane leading onto the pit straight which produced the unexpected gyration. From then on, the problem grew worse and, on top of that, Lauda lost fifth gear and eventually had to hold fourth in place.

But at least he was still running; an important factor in a race which would eventually be decided by counting those still fortunate enough to have petrol in their tanks at the end. Out for the day were Martini (turbo wastegate), Laffite, (a spectacular turbo blaze at the rear of the Ligier), Rosberg (a combination of erratic brakes and a broken throttle assembly) and the RAM drivers (both with engine trouble).

These retirements went largely unnoticed, for at the front we were seeing a battle of renewed intensity as Prost attacked Senna. Frequently the McLaren would tuck under the rear wing of the Lotus before darting out and running alongside under braking for *Tosa*. On one occasion, Prost was alongside as they swept through *Villeneuve* but Senna refused to be intimidated as he held his line for *Tosa*.

Any doubts that Ayrton Senna could handle pressure were dispelled instantly. He drove with such coolness, it was as though he had been leading Grands Prix all his life. The fact remained, however, that the furious pace was doing little for the fuel consumption of either car yet Prost was refusing to let go. Senna had to settle the problem one way or the other and an opportunity presented itself as the leaders caught Tambay's slow Renault.

Senna passed the Frenchman on the exit of *Tosa* and then slowed the pace fractionally; enough to prevent Prost from lapping the Renault before *Piratella*. Then Ayrton put the hammer down. For the next few laps, he increased his pace by over a second, setting his fastest lap of the race. By the time Prost had got past Tambay, he realised it would be fruitless to give chase. Senna, for his part, cut his revs and relied heavily on his brakes and gearbox – and continued to pull away from the McLaren. Since he had no cockpit-mounted computer, Senna could only hope that there would be enough fuel to do the job.

Lauda fell behind de Angelis once more and the McLaren was soon caught and passed by Johansson. The Ferrari driver had dutifully followed team instructions by turning down his boost after 30 laps but that did not prevent him from trying as

hard as he was able. By lap 41, he was hard on the heels of the Lotus although de Angelis held the upper edge when it came to acceleration. Johansson, his Ferrari working exceptionally well under braking, waited for his chance.

The battle between Mansell, Boutsen and Cheever had been resolved when Nigel missed a gear on the exit of *Acque Minerali* and it was all Boutsen needed to nose alongside. From then on, Mansell wisely concentrated on his Mobil Economy Run and let Boutsen get on with chasing Piquet's sixth place. The Arrows caught and passed the Brabham but Nelson was back in front again as de Angelis and Johansson approached.

The four cars arrived at *Tosa*, Johansson running round the outside of de Angelis, momentarily boxing in the Lotus. Then Boutsen, following his line, moved in front of the Ferrari at the exit of the corner and de Angelis tried to return the compliment by trapping Johansson behind the Arrows. Johansson would have none of it, the Swede moving left and forcing the Lotus to give way. It was a classic piece of opportunism, much appreciated by the crowd.

A Ferrari was now third – and at Prost's conservative rate of going there was every chance that Johansson would be second. By lap 54, the Ferrari had taken the place from Prost and Stefan went on to set his fastest lap of the race. The gap to Senna was 10 seconds and dwindling rapidly. Then, on lap 57, the Lotus slowed; by the time

Senna had reached the stadium before the pits, Johansson had swept into the lead.

The delirium in the enclosures had barely gained a hold when a terse announcement from the public address system broke the news that Johansson was also in trouble. The Ferrari, its tanks dry, rolled to a halt . . . and Prost cruised into the lead.

Prost's last lap was some 14 seconds slower than his best effort earlier in the afternoon but it was good enough to see him take the chequered flag before finishing his fuel immediately afterwards. De Angelis, now without brakes, was surprised to find himself in second place while Boutsen, out on his own thanks to Piquet having emptied his tank, was heading for third place when the BMW drank the last of its fuel as the Belgian accelerated out of the final corner. Boutsen freewheeled towards the line, the front of the Arrows j-u-s-t triggering the timing beam. Thierry jumped out and pushed his car to safety, although the fact that his rear wheels had not crossed the line before he stopped raised an interesting question: when is a competitor deemed to have completed a lap? Is it when his timing sensor (mounted in the nose) breaks the Longines beam, or is it when all four wheels have crossed the line?

Tambay, never higher than eighth, suddenly found himself in fourth place, the Frenchman taking it easy on the last lap since he was under the impression that Boutsen was half a minute

ahead. In the event, he failed to catch the trickling Arrows by three seconds! Derek Warwick, having had a miserable race punctuated by a spin and then a stop to attend to a loose electrical wire, brought the other Renault home at the back of the field, on the same lap as Brundle, the Tyrrell driver having lost time changing a punctured rear tyre. Still running, but not classified, Piercarlo Ghinzani had made a long stop to cure gearbox trouble on the Osella.

As Prost, de Angelis and Lauda (thinking he had finished third) set off on their victory lap, the abandoned cars were gathered up and returned for scrutineering. The winning McLaren was found to be two kilogrammes below the minimum weight. Knowing their car was underweight, the McLaren management had been keen to weigh the cars before the start of the race but could find no one in charge of the scales when they presented their car. Taking a chance, they estimated how much ballast to add – and their calculations probably would have been correct had Prost pulled up immediately after crossing the line and not drained the tank of fuel.

In any event, the car was under the minimum limit and a second attempt at checking the scales had the same effect. Prost was out. De Angelis was first. And Grand Prix racing, so absorbing for 56 of the 60 laps, looked anything but Grand at the end of the day.

M.H.

TECHNICAL FILE

FERRARI
Tubular support inside nose for front wing (different to previous arrangement to overcome difficulty experienced while changing Johansson's nose wing during Portuguese Grand Prix). Quadruple turbo arrangement and electronic control on wastegate tested at Fiorano but not seen at Imola.

McLAREN
Nothing new.

LOTUS
De Angelis tried a second rear wing (at gearbox level, similar to Williams) during practice. New rear duct for brakes. Tried different aerodynamic set-up (minus front vertical wings). For the race, both cars had front vertical wings but no winglets at rear of side pods.

BRABHAM
New rear wing; an extra 10 cm in chord length. Tried larger side plates for rear wing but reduced size for race. Rear bodywork 15 cm longer.

RENAULT
All three cars present had new rear suspension, first seen in Portugal. Tambay used larger front wing. Stiffer mounting points for rear shock absorbers. Warwick tried different exhaust arrangement (one pipe) on Friday but reverted to triple arrangement. New ducting for turbo (similar to Lotus) meant vent in side pod and scrapping of vertical system; as a result, engine cover narrower, giving improved aerodynamics. Front uprights lighter and stiffer.

WILLIAMS
Third FW10 chassis available for Rosberg. Work done on springing and mechanical reliability. New, smaller turbos.

ALFA ROMEO
Third 185T for Cheever. Two additional exits in side pods to improve cooling. Bosch fully electronic injection on chassis 2 and 3. (Injection system differed from standard layout; injectors staggered in inlet manifold as opposed to being equally spaced.) All cars had rear suspension modification first seen in Portugal.

ARROWS
Boutsen tried new four-section rear wing with tall leading edge, quite unlike anything seen before.

LIGIER
Tried winglets in front of rear wheels (similar to Lotus) and vertical plate on undertray (similar to Williams).

Carlo Chiti's Motori Moderni engine ran faultlessly in the Minardi throughout practice.

OSELLA
New car (FA1G). 568 kg; 10 kg lighter than FA1F. Different aerodynamics. Side radiator and vertical intercooler similar to Toleman. Revised ducting for turbo and different exhaust system. Wider front track. Alfa Romeo engine same as Alfa team used in Brazil.

MINARDI
Revised side plates to rear wing. Motori Moderni engine used throughout practice and for the race after 700 km of trouble-free testing. Used Lucas/Ferrari ignition.

RAM
New car for Winkelhock. Tried rear wing with long side plates.

ZAKSPEED
Different side pod exit for radiator to improve cooling.

SPIRIT
New car, but to same specification as before.

TYRRELL
Nothing new.

GP

Grand Prix de Monaco

It was perhaps the most unobtrusively efficient race of Alain Prost's career; and coming only a fortnight after his disqualification at Imola, his second successive Monaco Grand Prix triumph was by just as slender a margin as it had been twelve months earlier. In 1984, Alain's McLaren had fended off Ayrton Senna's Toleman by a few seconds in a rain-soaked, prematurely stopped chase through the streets of the Principality. This year Prost went the full distance in the dry to win by a couple of kilogrammes from Michele Alboreto's Ferrari 156/85.

That was the margin by which the Marlboro McLaren cleared the 540 kg minimum weight limit during post-race scrutineering. Not a reflection, it should be said, of a desire to cut things fine on the part of McLaren International, merely the product of sky-high fuel round oil consumption caused by a sticking turbo wastegate on one bank of the TAG V6 engine.

This technical malfunction made the car enormously difficult to drive through Monaco's twists and turns, but Alain Prost did his job superbly, refusing to be ruffled by temporary set-backs on the way. After pole man Ayrton Senna's JPS Lotus 97T blew its Renault V6 coming up to complete lap 13, Prost and Alboreto swapped the lead, Michele's initial stint at the head of the field thwarted by a slide into the

Nelson Piquet and Riccardo Patrese were lucky to emerge unscathed from a horrific accident when the Brabham and Alfa Romeo tangled as they fought for ninth place.
Photo: Franco Villani

Ste. Devote escape road on oil dropped as the result of a spectacular Piquet/Patrese tangle. Then, after fighting back to pass Prost again, a deflated rear Goodyear sent the Ferrari into the pits and lost the Italian all chance of coming back at the leading McLaren. At the end of the day Michele's hard-fought second place was a worthy reward for his sterling efforts, but the quiet air of impending success which seemed to hang over McLaren number two all afternoon was, overall, the most impressive aspect of a race which almost didn't happen at all, thanks to the machinations of the politicians who control our sport's destiny.

Elio de Angelis, unable and unwilling to be drawn into a flat-out sprint against his faster team-mate, settled for a mature display of immaculate self-discipline which saw the surviving Lotus driver rewarded with third place at the flag and a sustained advantage at the head of the Drivers' Championship points table. Emphasising the old adage that if you keep out of trouble at Monaco, you'll probably finish in the points, the top six was completed by the Pirelli-shod Ligier JS25s of Andrea de Cesaris and Jacques Laffite, fourth and sixth, sandwiching Derek Warwick's fifth place Renault Elf RE60. By all accounts it was a good race: Prost's performance may have been one of his best.

ENTRY AND PRACTICE

After last year's saturated extravaganza, the whole question of the Monaco Grand Prix's continued existence turned into a political football of gigantic proportions. The big argument centred round the AC Monaco's apparent reluctance to assign its television coverage rights to FISA, as it was required to do within the terms of the Concorde Agreement (the official charter governing Formula 1 racing worldwide), despite the fact that it had been breached more frequently than Hadrian's Wall. It seemed utterly inconceivable that Grand Prix racing's most glamorous public relations exercise could be seriously jeopar-

dised, but the details of the dispute were further clouded, and the problem aggravated, by a continuing personality clash between ACM top dog Michel Boeri and the fiery FISA President Jean-Marie Balestre. In the early months of 1985 it seemed as though there was no solution to the tedious, much-vexed affair and there came a time when Formula 1 aficionados were seriously writing off this classic event in their own minds.

Thankfully, the whole business was resolved a couple of months before the race, but an unfortunate by-product of battle of political polemics was that much-needed circuit alterations, in the interests largely of spectator safety, had to be shelved. Monaco may well be motor racing's most glittering public showcase, but it's also the place at which everybody is obliged to close their eyes for a weekend and ignore all established parameters of circuit safety. As World Champion Niki Lauda remarked thoughtfully: 'Here I am rushing round exactly the same circuit in an 800 bhp McLaren

that I drove in a 400 bhp BRM only eleven years ago . . . in honesty, it doesn't make sense. But what can you do? Not much, is the answer to that!'

Eddie Cheever expressed his thoughts in a slightly different way: 'Take the chicane for example. I'm going so quickly that I hardly see it. Can you believe that? Out of the tunnel running flat-out, a dab on the brakes, a twitch on the wheel and I'm through it, into the braking area for *Tabac*. You wouldn't need much to go wrong . . .' In qualifying, for certain, the cars did look dauntingly fast, even to the casual observer. But FISA circuit safety inspector Derek Ongaro emphasised that the Monaco organisers had been seriously thinking in terms of improvements, notably in the area of the chicane where a new complex of (much slower) corners was planned for 1986 on land reclaimed from the harbour.

When official qualifying got underway on Thursday afternoon, all eyes were firmly focused on Ayrton Senna's Lotus 97T. Star of the soaking '84 show at the wheel of his Toleman, Senna's exploits in the first three races of the new season had marked him down as *the* man. Despite the fact that he confessed that Monaco scared him 'more than any other track I've raced on', the mild-mannered, calm Brazilian rocketed round in an amazing 1m 21.630s to set fastest lap at an average speed of just over 90 mph!

Playing down his own personal contribution to the equation, Ayrton simply shrugged: he'd had a few lucky breaks in traffic, was his explanation. Not quite true. He had read the circuit just right, watching for the gap in the traffic, noting who was in the pit lane and when; it all added up to another chapter in the making of a quite outstanding racing talent. And out on the circuit, well, it was sheer joy to watch: the meticulous smoothness of

Prince Rainier and Princess Caroline distanced themselves from the political turmoil which threatened their Grand Prix.

Prost spiced with a dash of extrovert flair, a touch of opposite lock at *Tabac*, but no sudden movements of the wheel to disrupt the 97T's graceful progress. History in the making . . .

During final qualifying on Saturday afternoon Senna held onto his pole position, improving his time to 1m 20.450s, but his efforts were clouded by accusations that he'd had run an unnecessary number of laps in a deliberate attempt to baulk his rivals. A cursory glance through his individual laps tended to support this theory because he did in fact run a total of 16 laps on two marked sets of tyres: however, a closer examination revealed he did one run on race tyres, a run on qualifiers and then a third run on a 'mixed bag' during which he actually set second fastest time of the session as well. Only right near the end was he persuaded to go out and defend pole position, so crucial at Monaco, and Ayrton made it quite clear that he didn't want to be asked to do that again . . . ever!

The two men he upset the most were Michele Alboreto and Niki Lauda. The Italian got so angry with what he saw as Senna's deliberate baulking that he forced the Lotus into the escape road on the tight right-hander immediately before the pits. That was Latin temperament at its most extreme! Lauda had to weave round the Lotus coming out of *Tabac*, a manoeuvre which looked far less spectacular from the sidelines than from the McLaren's cockpit. 'Ask him what the bloody hell he thought he was doing', growled an unusually irritated Niki. Senna went to apologise. Niki told him to get lost. Ayrton was chastened, confused. Later, at Ricard testing, Lauda came up to him and said he was sorry he'd gone over the top about the incident. How many others would have apologised?

Elio de Angelis, cast again in a supporting role, was handling his personal PR with dignity and grace. Clearly no match for Senna in terms of out-and-out qualifying pace, the Italian wound up a disappointed ninth on 1m 21.465s, feeling that his engine was slightly down on power. He had also switched back to steel brake discs on Saturday after feeling less than totally confident about the carbon discs he had used on Thursday.

Second place on the front row was snatched by Nigel Mansell's Williams FW10, the Englishman revelling in the challenge of Monaco on Saturday after a troubled first session on Thursday. After lightly glancing a barrier and breaking a driveshaft on Thursday morning, Mansell had a nightmare qualifying session with major throttle response dramas – the Honda engine wouldn't shut off cleanly when he came off the pedal!

'The car was impossibly difficult to drive', he shrugged, 'I'm happy to be fifth but I can't say I'm happy heading straight for the barrier going into Casino Square when the throttle won't come back. I've never been scared in a racing car before, but I was today . . .' Happily the engine response problem was rectified in time for Saturday and Mansell emerged grinning from ear to ear after taking his place on the front row. 'It's transformed – as good today as it was bad on Thursday . . .'

Team-mate Keke Rosberg confessed that Monaco was a circuit which tested a driver's age but his Thursday efforts were also hampered by two turbo failures, one on his race car, one on the spare. Saturday saw him get badly held up by de Cesaris's Ligier 'and then I found Johansson's Ferrari in the wall, so that was it'. Rosberg qualified seventh on 1m 20.855s.

Michele Alboreto challenged strongly for pole position, eventually qualifying third after his contretemps with Senna during the final session. He managed a 1m 20.563s and admitted that his machine had quite a lively ride, particularly through the section by the swimming pool on the harbour front where a car is required to deal with frequent sudden changes of direction.

Stefan Johansson had a nasty moment while trying carbon-fibre brakes on Thursday. 'As I slowed for the chicane, the car suddenly jerked to the left. I just managed to haul it away from the guard rail only for it to clatter down the escape road against the rail on the opposite side!' Emerging tenth from the first session, Stefan's efforts on Saturday were ruined when Teo Fabi's Toleman moved over on him, bouncing the Ferrari into the barrier opposite the pits. 'I just don't think he saw me coming', mused a crestfallen Johansson, now down on 15th slot on 1m 22.635s.

A couple of days testing at Balocco had suffused both Eddie and Cheever and Riccardo Patrese with enormous optimism about their Alfa Romeos' potential for Monaco. 'We're now beginning to understand our Bosch electronic injection', explained a beaming Cheever, 'and what we should and shouldn't do with it.' Aerodynamics are of little overall significance as compared with the ability to 'manhandle' a time out of any given car – and Patrese did just that on Thursday, emerging second only to Senna in the first qualifying session despite complaining that his

fifth gear was a bit too short to get the best out of his high-boost qualifying engine.

Cheever had a problem with his engine's reluctance to pull cleanly over 11,000 rpm on Thursday and he got ticked off by the stewards for passing a couple of cars under the yellow flag after Hesnault spun his Brabham in front of him on Saturday morning. In the final hour he stormed into fourth place with a 1m 20.729s, emerging from the cockpit with a broad grin on his face. 'We're looking good; on full tanks this morning we were pulling 600 rpm more than we were without much fuel aboard on Thursday . . .'

Prost was an unobtrusive fifth on 1m 20.885s, complaining first of excessive understeer on Thursday, then of oversteer on Saturday after an excessive chassis adjustment to compensate. The TAG turbo's reluctance to accept massive doses of qualifying boost also helped keep Niki out of the front-running picture, the World Champion qualifying 14th on 1m 21.997s after running wide at one corner and missing a gear during his best Thursday run, and then having his much-publicised contretemps with Senna on Saturday!

Thierry Boutsen upheld BMW honour admirably after an untroubled couple of days with the Arrows A8, the Belgian taking sixth place on the grid, while his precarious-looking team-mate Gerhard Berger kept away from the barriers (against the predictions of many observers!) to line up a heartening 11th, impressive for a man making his first visit to the Principality in a Formula 1 machine . . .

Behind Rosberg in eighth place was a commendably tidy Andrea de Cesaris in his latest lightweight Ligier JS25, the Italian making up for crashing the heavier spare car quite hard at *Massanet* during the Saturday morning untimed

session. Not only did this make him the quickest Pirelli runner, it also meant that there were three Renault-powered cars (two Lotuses and a Ligier) ahead of the Régie's best-placed works runner, the 10th-placed RE60 of Derek Warwick.

Life wasn't going smoothly in the Renault Elf camp, Warwick's catalogue of troubles ranging from being held up badly by both Brundle and Laffite, excessive understeer and an engine response problem so serious he was having to slip the clutch to get round the two tightest hairpins on the track. Tyrrell driver Martin was apologetic but responded. 'Well, he paid me back by chopping me quite dramatically . . . anyway, I was flat-out trying to get a place on the grid as well!'

Tambay's RE60 wound up a lowly 17th on 1m 22.912s, the Frenchman sliding into the barrier by the swimming pool as he strove to improve his time on Saturday afternoon. Both drivers expressed themselves concerned over the way in which the cars' handling tended towards increasing understeer as the fuel load lightened, a worrying portent for the race on a tight circuit such as this.

Patrese got badly baulked in traffic and could only qualify his Alfa in 12th, one place ahead of Nelson Piquet, the twice World Champion being neither fastest Pirelli, nor fastest BMW runner on this humiliating occasion. A quick trip over to Paul Ricard on Friday to test some brand new Pirelli qualifiers didn't produce any miracles for final qualifying and the BMW engine's tendency to misfire when running high boost frustrated him still further. As for François Hesnault, the Frenchman failed to qualify, never looking remotely at home in the BT54's cockpit. His most spectacular moment of the weekend was a spin in the tunnel!

Behind Johansson in 16th place came Laffite's Ligier, then Brundle's Tyrrell 18th behind Tambay, while the final row was made up by Palmer's understeering Zakspeed and Teo Fabi in the debutant Toleman-Hart TG185, at last making its race debut on Pirelli rubber after months of political machinations behind the scenes.

A combination of minor accidents, engine and gearbox troubles prevented either RAM 03 from making the 20-car grid, while Bellof and Ghinzani could perhaps be regarded as surprising absentees. Right at the bottom of the list was Pierluigi Martini whose Minardi crashed at *Ste. Devote* on Saturday morning and did not take part in final qualifying.

Guy Ligier and Gerard Larrousse had reason to smile when de Cesaris finished fourth and Jacques Laffite brought his Ligier home in sixth place.

A frustrated Stefan Johansson explains to engineer Tomaini how his best practice lap was destroyed by a shunt with Fabi's Toleman.

RACE

By race morning the sunny conditions prevailing throughout the previous three days had vanished, to be replaced by dank and overcast conditions, although the heavy rain thankfully held off until half an hour after the end of the Grand Prix. Prost's McLaren, as usual, was quickest in the half-hour warm-up, but there were problems with several of the Renault-engined runners. Tambay opted to use the EF4B-engined RE60 spare after finding his race car's EF15 engine response very disappointing. Both Lotuses began the day fitted with EF15 units but Elio complained that his felt very sluggish, so an EF4B was hurriedly installed in the Italian's car only to suffer mechanical fuel pump failure when it was being warmed up in the lunch break. As a result, de Angelis was strapped into Ayrton's spare 97T/1 for the race, also equipped with an EF4B.

Pole man Senna went to the line a little worried about his tyres. One of the electric blankets used to pre-heat the Lotus race covers had overheated and blistered his front tyres slightly so they were replaced and he went into the race prepared to cope with a degree of understeer from the unheated replacements in the opening stages. That didn't prevent the Brazilian from storming straight into the lead on the sprint to *Ste. Devote*, Mansell slotting in behind him and giving Senna space to breath until the end of the opening tour when Alboreto went charging through into second place. Already three cars were in trouble. Unable to get cleanly off the starting grid, Berger's Arrows got bogged down, Johansson pulled out of line to avoid him and the Ferrari was hit up the rear by Tambay's Renault. Berger staggered as far as *Ste. Devote* run-off area where he retired with ignition trouble, as did Patrick's RE60 with a brake master cylinder damaged in the impact with the Ferrari. Johansson stopped at the end of lap one, changed all four tyres, but retired on lap two after the problem was found to be more serious: the impact had broken a damper rod on one of the Italian car's rear shock absorbers.

The opening sprint was simply a two-horse race with Alboreto initially closing in on Senna, then easing back slightly to run a few lengths off the Lotus's gearbox, content to let the Brazilian set the pace. Unbeknown to the spectators, Ayrton's engine probably started the race doomed to failure: during the warm-up he had inadvertently over-revved after changing from fifth to second and, although the V6 felt healthy enough to start with, it abruptly expired as he came through *Tabac* on lap 13. Senna trailed gently into the pits where a detailed examination of the engine revealed water and oil mixed in one of the cylinders. Ayrton climbed from the car to be consoled by his colleagues . . .

Alboreto now took over at the head of the field, shadowed discreetly by Prost who had quickly moved into third place as Mansell fell away down the field. Cheever's Alfa 185T briefly held fourth place, 'but then it began to misfire and all the warning lights began flashing in the cockpit, so I knew I wasn't going much further', shrugged

Alain Prost made up for the misfortunes of the previous race by scoring a narrow victory over Michele Alboreto.

Paul Henri Cahier

Eddie. First de Angelis then Rosberg nipped by the American's car, Cheever trailing into the pits at the end of lap 12 to retire with alternator problems.

With Boutsen calling in early for fresh rubber, by lap 15 the race order had settled down with Alboreto, Prost, de Angelis, Rosberg, Mansell and de Cesaris occupying the first six places. Then came Warwick and the fast-rising Niki Lauda who had just shaken himself free after being bottled up behind Riccardo Patrese's Alfa for several laps.

'I got alongside him in the tunnel when he missed a gear and he just tried to chop me into the guard rail, so I can't say I was surprised over what eventually happened', said Lauda later, alluding to the impending major accident which happened shortly afterwards between Patrese and Piquet. 'Eventually I got past him up the hill from *Ste. Devote*, but he still tried to bang wheels with me even when I was alongside . . .'

As Niki sprinted away in eighth place, Patrese was now holding up Piquet and Laffite to the extent that Fabi quickly caught this trio and turned it into a quartet. Coming up to complete lap 16, Nelson tried to slip by Patrese on the right as the two cars approached the start/finish line but as he nosed level with the Alfa's rear wheels, the Italian drove him into the right-hand guard rail.

The initial impact broke the Brabham's left front suspension, throwing up a shower of sparks from its magnesium skid plates as the monocoque bottomed out on the track. Patrese's car then cannoned from guard rail to guard rail, enveloping the circuit in a wall of flame for a second as the contents of its ruptured oil tank ignited. Laffite spun wildly on the debris almost before the two other wrecked cars were catapulted to rest in the *Ste. Devote* run-off area, miraculously in the ideal place to prevent both men being very badly hurt.

Laffite continued but Fabi stopped at the pits next time round to retire with turbo failure. Following this, there were to be a couple more incidents as a direct result of the Piquet/Patrese shunt. Alboreto lost his lead briefly when he slid off at *Ste. Devote*, stopping his Ferrari nose-in to the barrier but, thankfully, not stalling his engine. By contrast, Niki Lauda came sailing in, made exactly the same mistake – 'and by the time I'd opened my eyes and discovered that I hadn't hit the barrier, the engine had stalled and I had to abandon a perfectly healthy car. I couldn't believe what a stupid thing I'd done', explained Niki in a self-mocking tone.

Prost went back into the lead for six laps until Michele slammed the Ferrari back in front, locking his rear brakes in a risky-looking dive down inside the McLaren into *Ste. Devote*. Once ahead, it seemed that Alain would not be able to respond and, troubled by that sticking wastegate, there was nothing he could do. But on lap 32 he was handed a bonus when Alboreto slowed with a deflating left-rear tyre. Prost went back into the lead while the Ferrari limped to the pits for fresh rubber: from then on, assuming he didn't make a mistake and the car lasted, Alain Prost had it in the bag.

Alboreto resumed in fourth place and spent

May:
Toleman and Benetton join forces; Spirit agree to withdraw from Formula 1, giving Toleman their allocation of Pirelli tyres.

Pancho Carter (March-Buick 85C) takes Indy pole at an average of 212.583 mph.

Gordon Johncock retires.

Pierre-Henri Raphanel (Martini-Alfa Romeo MK45) wins Monaco Formula 3 race.

several laps scrubbing in his new tyres. He displaced de Cesaris in a spectacular move at *Mirabeau*, then got his head down and chipped away at de Angelis's second place advantage. Meanwhile, Prost had sufficient in hand to ease back, adapt himself completely to the quirky, sudden-response characteristics of the engine, and stroke his way home to victory.

It was on lap 64, with only 14 laps left, that Alboreto got through ahead of de Angelis into second place. There wasn't sufficient time, even aided by a few spots of light rain that began to fall 10 laps from the end. At the chequered flag only Prost, Alboreto and de Angelis – three very worthy runners indeed – had managed to complete the full race distance.

De Cesaris's fourth place was just reward for the Italian's well-judged blend of forceful driving and self-control, while Warwick was happy to take his first points of the season in the Renault, although that irritating ever-increasing understeer crept in, as expected, as the fuel load lightened in the second half of the race. Both Williams drivers were suffering from brake trouble within 20 laps of the start but it looked as though Mansell would hang onto sixth place to the finish. Alas, despite trying like mad and actually glancing the guard rail in the tunnel in the closing stages, Laffite nipped through to take sixth place only six laps from the end. Rosberg, with similar brake trouble, stopped for fresh rubber and eventually wound up eighth.

Boutsen was ninth after a second stop for tyres, Brundle tenth after a delay fixing a leaking rear brake pipe and Palmer, who'd made the TV screens by spinning his Zakspeed in front of the leaders at *Ste. Devote* and recovering by dint of a fancy full throttle-induced spin in the other direction, brought the Zakspeed home 11th.

AH

TOLEMAN: BACK ON THE ROAD AGAIN!

After months of behind-the-scenes negotiation and what might best be described as time-consuming horse trading, Toleman Group Motorsport made its return to the Formula 1 stage for the first time since Ayrton Senna finished third in the 1984 Portuguese Grand Prix. Since Toleman had bought out the ailing Spirit team's Pirelli tyre contract as the only means of getting back on the Grand Prix bandwagon there was sufficient rubber available for just one entry, and with sponsorship coming from the Benetton clothing concern, 1982 Toleman team member Teo Fabi was nominated driver of the debutant Rory Byrne-designed TG185.

The team arrived in Monaco after a shakedown session at Paul Ricard on the way down but although the car performed reasonably enough considering how much testing time Toleman had lost, the main interest centred on speculation that the Benetton/Toleman partnership amounted to a trailer for a longer-term link with Alfa Romeo. This was cautiously denied at the time, but Eddie Cheever's enthusiasm to move his home to the Oxford area of England suggested that plans for 1986 may in fact have been heading in that direction!

A misjudgement by Niki Lauda saw the McLaren driver slide off on the oil of the Patrese/Piquet accident. Although his car was unmarked Lauda could not restart his stalled engine.

The financial mechanics of the deal necessarily involved Benetton acquiring a financial stake in Toleman Group Motorsport but as the diminutive Fabi struggled to make last place on the grid after qualifying sessions plagued by engine misfires and handling problems, it became clear that there was rather more to this new partnership than met the eye at first glance. What's more, it looked increasingly unlikely that the overall equation would include a drive for John Watson, one of Toleman's originally nominated drivers in addition to Stefan Johansson.

On the day, Fabi raced competently and lapped quicker than the Ligiers on similar rubber in the early stages. However, he retired when the turbo's exhaust turbine seized after its back plate had moved forward by a minuscule amount. Fabi was thus effectively left with a 1500 cc unturbocharged engine, so it was time to call a halt to his participation in the race.

AH.

TECHNICAL FILE

FERRARI
Modified rear suspension with lower mounting point for top wishbone. Smaller turbos used for power at low revs. Larger front brake ducts. No bypass between intercooler and wastegate, as seen before.

LOTUS
Four chassis on hand (like Ferrari). Retained vertical front aerofoils but no winglets at rear of side pods. Used additional low-mounted rear wing (similar to Williams). When running carbon brakes, used Brembo at front and Brembo/Lotus calipers at rear. De Angelis favoured steel brakes for Monte Carlo, as fitted to his spare car. Forced to race Senna's spare car – fitted with carbon brakes.

McLAREN
Ran smaller front wing. Tested at Zolder and discovered cause of problem with electronics which had bothered Lauda at Rio and Imola. Revised turbos and other modifications to engines.

RENAULT
Four cars, including a new chassis with new front uprights. Smaller radiators – part of a 'B' package to be seen later. Lighter bodywork (including underwings) reduced weight from 589 to 570 kg.

BRABHAM
Three cars at Monte Carlo with a fourth at Ricard for a test session on Friday when Piquet tried three different Pirelli qualifiers. BMW produced a revised airbox which protruded through the rear bodywork thanks to longer trumpets. Tried during practice and testing. 1984-style airbox flown from England for Saturday; returned to Thursday configuration for race.

WILLIAMS
Mansell flew to Japan after Imola to test modified Honda engine in FW09 chassis. No major changes for Monaco. Ran two flaps under rear wing and lower wing.

RAM
Nothing new.

ARROWS
Revised rear suspension geometry. New rear wing for both race cars. Also, tested additional low-mounted rear wing.

ALFA ROMEO
Ran larger three-piece rear wing. Fitted vertical plates beneath underbody (similar to Williams) but curved around rear wheels. Fully electronic Bosch ignition on race cars to complement major development by Alfa Romeo on engines.

LIGIER
New chassis for de Cesaris brought JS25 to weight limit. Lighter radiators, bodywork, underbody and rear suspension. Tried winglets at rear of side pod and secondary low-mounted rear wing.

MINARDI
Revised fixing point for rear anti-roll bar otherwise chassis unchanged as development continued with Motori Moderni engine.

OSELLA
Shorter exhaust layout.

TYRRELL
Bigger rear wing and side plates.

TOLEMAN
First appearance at a Grand Prix. Three-piece rear wing. Front wings sculpted at sides to allow air to side pods. Front brake ducts angled to the side, taking air by suction from area in front of tyres.

ZAKSPEED
Tested vertical front aerofoils beside front wheels.

GP

At 7.45 p.m. on Saturday 1 June 1985, the FISA Stewards at the Belgian Grand Prix made history. They postponed a major Formula 1 event, something which neither politics nor boycotts had managed to achieve in the past. The most startling aspect of this unfortunate affair was that the problem had been caused by nothing more than the most fundamental and crass error of judgement by the Belgian organisers; they had resurfaced the entire track a matter of weeks before the event.

Their reasoning had been sound, since the new surface contained excellent drainage qualities designed to rid Spa-Francorchamps of serious aquaplaning problems, but their methods showed a deplorable lack of foresight. By the end of the first day's practice, the track was crumbling.

Remedial work on Friday evening did not prove satisfactory, the drivers stopping practice after just 25 minutes when the track proved potentially lethal. For the rest of Saturday, there was very little activity and, when it became clear the organisers had no ready solution, the Stewards of the Meeting, in accord with a deputation of drivers led by Niki Lauda, made the inevitable decision to call off the race.

As the Formula 1 teams returned to base, the organisers ran a Formula 3000 race. Within three or four laps, the track, completely relaid in parts, was barely able to sustain the less powerful single-seaters and several drivers spun off. The race should never have been run. In fact, a decision should have been made to call off the Belgian Grand Prix long before the teams assembled and Formula 1 was seen to make a collective fool of itself once more.

ENTRY AND PRACTICE

After the restrictions of Monte Carlo, everyone looked forward to the uncluttered expanses of Spa-Francorchamps. Now considered to be one of the best circuits in the world, the Ardennes track represented everything a driver could wish for. The initial response to the rich black asphalt lining the entire 4.3 miles of track was favourable but, when it became clear that work had been completed just 10 days before, doubts began to creep in. Past experiences with Formula 1 cars ripping at uncured surfaces had not been good;

Dallas the previous year sprang readily to mind.

Derek Ongaro, FISA Safety Inspector, was more concerned than most. The fresh surface was news to him. As far as FISA were concerned, they had been asked by the Belgian authorities in October 1984 if it would be permissible to resurface Spa-Francorchamps. FISA had replied in the affirmative – provided the work was completed at least 60 days before the Grand Prix.

Then the cumbersome decision-making machinery employed by the *Intercommunale du Circuit de Spa-Francorchamps* took over and winter had arrived by the time full approval had

been given. Harsh weather delayed proceedings further and work was not started until the beginning of May.

The first hint of trouble came when FISA learned that a scheduled test session had been cancelled because of 'modifications' to the circuit. It could be argued that this should have triggered off warning bells within FISA. But it did not. Someone, somewhere, should have taken the time to enquire exactly what form these 'modifications' were taking. Arriving at the circuit the night before practice was due to commence and then expressing horror at the work of the well-

Up in smoke. Jonathan Palmer's spectacular turbo failure on the Zakspeed at Spa summed up a disastrous weekend in general.

intentioned organisers was just as short-sighted as the methods employed by the Belgians themselves.

In the meantime, practice got under way as planned and the dramatic reduction in lap times underlined drivers' comments concerning the impressive grip offered by the rubberised asphalt.

At the end of timed practice, Michele Alboreto had lapped his Ferrari in 1m 56.046s, a speed of 133.970 mph and some eight seconds under Prost's pole time in 1983. The prospects of a superb battle in qualifying were clearly defined when the Lotus-Renaults of Elio de Angelis and Ayrton Senna were within half a second of Alboreto and just one-tenth of a second ahead of Patrick Tambay's Renault.

De Angelis had various minor problems during qualifying (electrical and a loss of boost pressure) but the 97T had enough power to reach a speed of 199 mph at the top of the hill before braking for *Les Combes*. Senna had explored the track on foot on Wednesday as he jogged and walked round its entire length and he felt he was still discovering the correct lines when practice finished for the day.

Patrick Tambay's enthusiasm for Spa was mirrored in an unaccustomed place in the top four, the Frenchman having a new and slightly stiffer chassis at his disposal. Johansson took fifth place despite missing a gear on one set of qualifying tyres while Rosberg, running a revised Honda engine in the morning session, found his qualifying tyres were finished before the end of the lap.

Seventh place for Nelson Piquet came from a more competitive performance than of late, although the fact that the Brabham-BMW was just two-tenths faster than the next Pirelli runner, Andrea de Cesaris, gave an indication that the problem was down to more than simply tyres.

Surprisingly, Gerhard Berger was the fastest Arrows driver on Thierry Boutsen's home circuit, the Austrian taking ninth place ahead of Niki Lauda and Nigel Mansell. Derek Warwick, troubled by brake vibrations and then a loss of boost (due to a hose clip working loose), could do no better than 13th while Toleman were encouraged by the neat performance of Teo Fabi, over a second slower than the Renault.

Of the rest, the Alfa Romeos, quick at Monaco, did not have the top-end power for Spa. Cheever and Patrese just squeezed in ahead of Marc Surer, who had replaced François Hesnault at Brabham after the Frenchman and Bernie Ecclestone had mutually parted company following Hesnault's massive accident during testing at Paul Ricard the week before.

Although three seconds slower than the Brabham, Jonathan Palmer did an impressive job in the Zakspeed despite an engine pick-up problem and a turbo fire. The Cosworth-powered Tyrrells of Bellof and Brundle were not languishing at the back of the grid as everyone (Ken Tyrrell included) had expected but the one surprise was to find Alain Prost at the bottom of the list. The Frenchman had suffered no less than three engine failures (two in the unofficial session) and the McLaren driver failed to record a single timed lap. Neither, for that matter, did Philippe Alliot as the RAM driver had crashed in the unofficial session and was forced to make way for Manfred Winkelhock after the German had experienced engine trouble with his car.

THE FIRST HINT OF TROUBLE

In the light of what was to follow during the next 24 hours, the two most significant occurrences during timed practice on Friday were a puncture for Nigel Mansell and a cracked visor on Nelson Piquet's helmet. Both were indicative of problems out on the circuit as the surface began to succumb to the fat rear tyres as they searched for grip. The situation was not helped by clear skies and temperatures in the Seventies and it was obvious that work would be required at three corners on the downhill loop linking the public road sections.

By Saturday morning, the officials had worked on the three trouble-spots – and a lot more besides.

The new surface turned out to be very slippery and, within 25 minutes, the drivers were back in the pits, their lap times over 20 seconds off the pace, their comments indicating the dangerous nature of the track. There was no exaggeration when they said it was impossible to drive – at any speed. Proof of their complaints could be found by simply grinding your heel into the asphalt and lifting the surface with one hand.

At first, work was to take place, followed by an inspection at 2.00 p.m. with the final hour of qualifying half an hour later. That came and went and the deadline was pushed back to 5.00 p.m. Apart from some cosmetic brushwork, nothing was done out on the track. But at least the drivers were giving the organisers time.

To the amazement of all and sundry, the Renault Alpine GT cars were allowed out onto the track at 4.40 p.m. After that brief session, a group of Grand Prix drivers climbed aboard a mini-bus and set off on a tour of inspection.

When they returned, it seemed there was no way the race could be held. Discussions with FISA and the organisers began.

In the meantime, the organisers took it upon themselves to make a public announcement (in French and English) to the effect that there would be no further practice but that the race-day schedule would go ahead as planned. It was 5.50 p.m. The world's press, with a decision at last, ran to the phones while the spectators filed home, disappointed but at least secure in the knowledge that there would be a race.

That announcement amounted to deceit. The organisers *knew* that discussions were continuing, and, at the time the statement was made Lauda and FISA's John Corsmit were attempting to reach Jean-Marie Balestre by telephone. The FISA President said he relied on the judgement of Corsmit and he gave backing to the drivers' views.

The drivers were keen to have a decision that night. They knew from past experience (Dallas 1984) that if they waited until race morning the pressures would be too great. They would have to race, come what may. But this was not Dallas. Instead of lapping at 80 mph, they would be lapping at 135 mph.

Finally, the Belgian Steward who, not unnaturally, had been keen to delay the decision-making until the organisers had carried out another night's work, agreed with his colleagues. At 7.45 p.m., the following statement was issued:

'Having inspected the track following the Renault practice, we have decided that in its present condition, the track is unsuitable for Formula 1 cars. Therefore, the Formula 1 practice schedules for this afternoon and the entire Formula 1 programme for June 2nd 1985 is hereby postponed in accordance with Article 141 of the International Sporting Code, for safety reasons. We deeply regret the necessity of this action.
Signed
FISA Stewards of the Meeting:
John Corsmit,
Roger Peart,
Jean-Luc Hendrickx van den Bosch.'

May:

Danny Sullivan (March-Cosworth 85C) wins Indy 500.

Brands Hatch confirm Grand Prix of Europe for 22 September.

Circuit data
Circuit de Spa-Francorchamps
Circuit length: 4·3179 miles/6·949 km
Scheduled race distance: 43 laps, 185·669 miles/298·807 km

Race cancelled and rescheduled for 15 September (see report on pages 170-5).

Spa on Sunday morning, had a Monday feel about it. The pits and paddock were deserted while, down the hill, the Formula 3000 teams, having been held in abeyance all weekend, waited patiently to see if they would be called upon to race. With the contractors continuing to lay fresh tarmac, it seemed not.

However, they practised and raced according to schedule. The decision to allow the Formula 3000 cars – essentially detuned versions of the machines Martin Brundle and Stefan Bellof had been excluded from racing – made little sense. We were told that a different group of Stewards handled Formula 3000 but, in the light of the spinning cars in the race, the decision appeared to be no more than a political sop to television and those unfortunate spectators who had returned to the track thanks to the totally inaccurate information given out the previous day.

And the final irony? All three days were blessed with brilliant sunshine – as unheard of at Spa as the decision to actually postpone a Grand Prix.

M.H.

TECHNICAL FILE

McLAREN
Lauda tested engine with minor modifications. Two of three engines which failed during practice had Monaco GP and Ricard test mileage; problems found to be connected with electronics programming.

WILLIAMS
Running modified Honda engines; longer stroke and different pistons and valves. Double duct to rear brakes.

RENAULT
New, lighter and stiffer chassis for Tambay. New gearbox, five-speed instead of six, fitted to race cars. Smaller radiators, as seen in Monaco. Three EF15 engines available.

BRABHAM
New chassis for Piquet to replace car destroyed at Monaco. Revised top bodywork on all three cars; running winglets at rear of side pods. Tested Garrett turbo after Monaco but continued with KKK in Belgium.

LOTUS
EF15 engines for both drivers. Very small modifications. Tried running with and without rear winglets and lower, secondary rear wing. Senna tried rear brake caliper fitted to bottom of disc (similar to Minardi and Arrows).

LIGIER
Two EF15 engines available. Tested rear winglets at Ricard but not seen at Spa.

ARROWS
Wider front track and different rear wing. Garrett turbo believed tested at Ricard.

ALFA ROMEO
New airboxes, similar to Ferrari. Larger exits to exhaust pipes. Revised rear wing – less chord.

MINARDI
Tried high rear deflector, shaped around rear tyres to send cleaner air to rear wing.

RAM
Fitted small duct in side pod to send air to rear shock absorbers.

OSELLA
Different rear wing; otherwise no change since Monaco.

ZAKSPEED
Ran front vertical deflectors on single car present at Spa.

TYRRELL
No change. New car due to be unveiled.

FERRARI
New chassis for Johansson; tested computer with fuel consumption analysis during practice. Figures could not be read from cockpit. Considered to be one of the best systems but delicate to adjust and not yet accurate enough. Revised front suspension geometry and new casting on gearbox to accommodate suspension pick-up points and new rear wing support. Used electronic control on wastage, tested before Imola.   GP

Grand Prix Labatt du Canada

When Harvey Postlethwaite left Spa following the abortive Belgian Grand Prix weekend he was in a confident mood. Having finalised the detail specification of Ferrari's 156/85 just prior to that unhappy weekend in the forests of the Haut Fagne, Maranello's English designer knew that this would have to be good enough to carry the cars through the helter-skelter of a brief, two-race North American tour followed by the hard slog of a frantic European season stretching right through the summer. No major modifications could really be fed into the design system before Monza, at the earliest, and possibly not before Brands Hatch. It was thus with some pleasure that he had watched as Michele Alboreto set fastest time in the one, abortive, official qualifying session to be held on the crumbling Spa surface. It might not have been truly representative, but Harvey was keeping his fingers crossed . . .

Two weeks later, everybody at Maranello was smiling broadly. For not only had Michele Alboreto produced a splendid victory in the Canadian Grand Prix at Montreal, but his new team-mate Stefan Johansson passed the chequered flag in his wheel tracks – the first Ferrari 1-2 since René Arnoux and Patrick Tambay managed such a feat at Zandvoort back in '83. It had been an all-Lotus front row at the Circuit Gilles Villeneuve, but with Ayrton Senna encountering an early turbo problem which delayed him in the pits for five laps and pole man Elio de Angelis gradually fading after an initial spurt, the only real opposition to the Ferraris came from Alain Prost's McLaren MP4/2B. But while Michele and Stefan clearly had few worries when it came to fuel efficiency, to the extent that they both imperiously completed the slowing-down lap in victorious formation and still had fuel left in their tanks, Prost faced one of the most frustrating afternoons of his career. For much of the race his eyes remained riveted to the digital consumption readouts in the cockpit of his McLaren, to the point where it was only in the closing stages that he could allow himself off the leash for a crack at Johansson's second place. On the last lap, he was planning to turn up the boost and surprise Johansson going through the last couple of corners, but Andrea de Cesaris's brake-troubled Ligier lurched into his path. The McLaren ace lost at least a second, maybe more, so that was the end of any slim chance to break up the symmetry of a long-overdue Maranello grand slam.

ENTRY AND PRACTICE

Although the setting of the Circuit Gilles Ville-neuve is most attractive, amidst the former Olympic facilities on the Ile Notre Dame a mere subway ride from downtown Montreal, the track configuration is something of an acrobatic chal-lenge for the drivers and few rate it highly in terms of pure enjoyment. World Champion Niki Lauda, struggling to come to grips with the difficult medium-speed S-bends, admitted: 'I hate the place . . . I just can't get into any sort of rhythm at all here'. And, to a greater or lesser extent, most of his colleagues echoed these sentiments. The daunting, high-speed S-bend beyond the pits may well separate the men from the boys, but it has virtually nothing in the way of run-off areas and prompted more than a passing degree of concern from many competitors. By the end of the weekend one of them counted himself lucky to have survived unscathed a simply enormous accident on this section of the circuit.

The first day's qualifying took place in cool, overcast conditions with an occasional rain squall to keep everybody on their toes. Most people quickly found that the conditions were strangely unsuited to the use of very soft qualifying rubber: the rears were wearing out before the fronts had warmed up to operating temperature, so event-ually soft race compounds seemed to be the most effective order of the day, offering the added attraction of allowing upwards of half a dozen consecutive laps rather than the normal single 'banzai' stab at a good qualifying time.

Alboreto turned a 1m 25.127s to be quickest on the first day, beaming expansively that his car 'handled like a Rolls-Royce' when compared to the 126C4 he drove last season. Michele used race tyres to set his time, but expressed confidence that qualifiers would be faster the following afternoon when much warmer weather conditions were expected. When it came to it, his prospects of setting a quicker time on Saturday were spoiled after an oil-line became disconnected on his first run and the rear of the car suddenly became wreathed in flame. Michele hurriedly pulled off and went back to the pits, but after a brief sortie at the wheel of the spare 156/85, he was resigned to the fact that he was not going to improve his time in that machine and called it a day.

Without Alboreto to keep up the pressure, Team Lotus enjoyed something of a field day with the on-form Elio de Angelis out-fumbling Senna to grab pole position by slightly less than three-tenths of a second. Ayrton, who had earlier somewhat modestly remarked 'the car may be capable of taking the esses beyond the pits flat – but I'm not!', offered no excuses for the fact that his team-mate had pipped him during that final session. Elio had run two sets of qualifiers on Friday, but switched to soft race rubber for his pole position run the following day. The Lotuses looked very stable under braking and quick out of the slow corners: on the face of it, it was difficult to

see how they could fail.

Johansson started the weekend on a troubled note, spinning gently into one of the many unyielding walls and breaking a steering arm during Friday's untimed session. He limped slowly back to the pits for repairs, then suffered clutch trouble and transferred to the spare which proved extremely nervous over the bumps. By his own admission, Stefan could not get into a proper rhythm with the very nervous chassis and Saturday morning didn't look much better for the genial Swede when a wastegate failure on his race car forced him into the *muletta* yet again. However, backing off some wing 'and living with it' made the car much more manageable during that final hour: using two sets of soft race tyres, he completed a total of 18 laps, the tenth of which earned him a 1m 25.170s for fourth place on the grid. After all his qualifying disappointments at Estoril, Imola and Monaco, Johansson had at last got everything together . . .

A whole series of minor problems beset the McLaren-TAGs in both qualifying sessions, Alain Prost being held up by a slower car on his best Friday run and then spinning at the hairpin before the pits. He was hard on the heels of team-mate Lauda at the time and dived far too deep inside de Cesaris's Ligier as he tried to stay with the Austrian: Prost's MP4/2B swapped ends and finished up nose-to-nose with the bemused Andrea, more used to creating these unusual situations himself! Prost blamed a soft brake pedal

Stefan Johansson may have enjoyed success in North America but his expression sums up the decline which was about to set in for Ferrari.

113

Michele Alboreto keeps Elio de Angelis at bay after taking the lead from the Lotus driver on lap 16. The Ferrari driver went on to take an untroubled victory (except for a late challenge from his team-mate!) while de Angelis slipped to an eventual fifth place.

for at least part of the problem, but already had a 1m 25.557s in the bag. That was good enough for fifth fastest, which is where he stayed after a second try on qualifying rubber failed to produce a quicker time thanks to an engine failure which left him stranded out on the circuit.

Niki Lauda had a simply dismal time at Montreal, complaining that he still could not get into the frantic swing of qualifying. 'I just can't break the habits of a lifetime and screw the car up for a single quick lap. I've always disciplined myself to drive neatly and that's all there is to it.' Lauda also punctuated one of his Saturday runs by coming in to complain 'there's a beaver on the track at the hairpin!' He could see that Ron Dennis had little sympathy with what sounded a pretty fatuous explanation, but a picture in the following morning's newspaper vindicated Lauda's apparently fragile tale: there they were, Rat and Beaver, together on the track at the hairpin!

Niki's eventual 1m 28.126s, set on Friday, none the less seemed pretty tame and the feeling in the team was that he could not go on for ever excusing his inability to qualify well on the basis that he was unable to master a one-lap qualifying technique. To those doubters, Niki merely replied 'wait for the faster circuits...' The World Champion lined up in 17th position.

In the Renault camp there was cause for a small degree of jubilation on Friday when the hitherto perpetually understeering RE60 actually showed the first signs of oversteer in Derek Warwick's hands. Derek was fifth fastest on Friday after his first run, but a slipping clutch spoiled his chances of improvement on his second run. Warwick consolidated sixth place overall with a 1m 25.622s on Saturday, his time virtually the same on soft race tyres as on out-and-out qualifiers. 'If you were allowed 84 sets, it might be possible to work out an ideal balance', he reflected, 'but, in reality, it doesn't feel too bad at all today. I'm quite optimistic about a place on the rostrum'. By contrast, team-mate Tambay complained of abiding understeer for much of qualifying, spoiled his Friday efforts with a half spin over the kerb at the hairpin before the pits and could not get the car balanced out to his taste the following day. He wound up tenth on 1m 26.340s.

Thierry Boutsen qualified seventh on 1m 25.846s, using the spare Arrows A8 after spinning into the guard rail with his race car on the second corner of his first lap of the Friday morning untimed session. The race car was repaired quite quickly, but Thierry concentrated his efforts on the spare thereafter as the team didn't want to risk using a chassis which might not be quite up to scratch after suffering that impact. Gerhard Berger returned a respectable 1m 26.995s for 12th place on the grid, his Friday efforts being hampered by a troublesome clutch during the first qualifying session.

Williams drivers Keke Rosberg and Nigel Mansell were finding the sudden surge of power from the Honda engines keeping them more than occupied out of the slower hairpins: 'for the first 25 yards nothing happens, then it's fluttering against the rev limiter and you can't change gear quick enough', grinned Rosberg. A head gasket

failure on Friday morning saw Keke consigned to the team's spare car on Friday afternoon, setting fourth fastest time, but Mansell's progress was hampered by braking problems and then a misfire intervened as he went for a fast time on qualifiers. On Saturday, Rosberg squeezed in a 1m 26.097s for eighth place on the grid, despite selecting second instead of fourth on one of his runs when the FW10 jumped out of gear. Meanwhile, Mansell had another bout of irritating setbacks. He managed a 1m 27.728s on hard race tyres, despite gear selection troubles, then one of the turbos ingested its protective gauze shield and he stopped his smoking car in front of the pit wall, unable to improve any further.

The Alfa Romeo 185Ts opened the weekend with a bout of major turbocharger problems, Cheever suffering two big failures on both his race and the spare car, while Riccardo Patrese had a single failure during the Friday timed session. All

'If he can do it...' John Macdonald's hopes of emulating Ron Dennis (left) and the McLaren International operation were thwarted yet again by a mixture of mechanical problems and accidents for Alliot and Winkelhock.
One of the best dices of the race was between de Angelis and Johansson. The Lotus started from pole position and lost top end power while the Ferrari, starting from the second row, had a misfire but nevertheless finished a fine second.

three were major productions on a grand scale, with the rear bodywork of the cars catching fire and marshals having to douse them with extinguishant. Several other runners had moments on the oil swathes laid by the Italian cars, but Pierluigi Martini had more cause than most to remember these incidents as he crashed his Minardi quite heavily thanks to the debris dropped by Patrese's machine.

Saturday saw Cheever suffering electrical problems and he lined up a disappointed 11th on 1m 26.354s, two places ahead of his team-mate, and convinced that the handling was good enough to earn a top six placing on the grid – had everything else been equal to the task.

Nelson Piquet spent most of his time on Pirelli race tyres, qualifying ninth on 1m 26.301s after a rear suspension problem had caused the BT54's right-rear wheel to collapse mid-way round a quick lap on Saturday afternoon. Miraculously, Nelson's out-of-control machine tobogganed to a halt alongside the circuit without making contact with anything firm, and the crestfallen Brazilian sat out the rest of the session in company with the spectating Alain Prost. Marc Surer had picked up some sort of influenza and did not feel particularly well all weekend, dragging his BT54 reluctantly round to a 20th fastest 1m 29.473s.

In the RAM camp Philippe Alliot gave the team's morale something of a boost by emerging tenth fastest in Friday's untimed session, but a couple of suspected valve failures on Saturday morning meant that he was obliged to qualify the spare car and could not improve on his Friday best, 21st overall. Winkelhock squeezed in a brave 1m 27.403s for 14th fastest, quicker than either of the Ligiers, de Cesaris and Laffite qualifying 15th and 19th respectively and complaining constantly about lack of Pirelli grip.

Teo Fabi's two Toleman TG185s suffered three turbo failures between them during practice and the reluctance to accept much boost was allied to a frustrating degree of understeer, keeping the little Italian down in 18th place. Outside the money-earning top 20, in addition to Alliot, were Piercarlo Ghinzani's Osella FA1G, the out-gunned Tyrrell-DFYs of Stefan Bellof and Martin Brundle and the novice Martini's Minardi. The Tyrrells ran almost faultlessly, but Martin suffered a puncture on Friday afternoon and later abandoned his car out on the circuit with electrical trouble. After running all the way back to the pits he found he only had three marked tyres left, so that was the end of his efforts! Bellof ran like a train, apart from a broken driveshaft on Saturday, his amazing, split-second clutchless gear-changes earning him admiration from just about everybody.

RACE

The race morning warm-up saw the Renault EF15 V6 in Senna's Lotus start leaking water, so the mechanics hurriedly changed it before the start, while Lauda wiped his critics in the eye by setting fastest time with his McLaren in its race set-up. In the Toleman camp just about every ancillary had been changed on Teo's TG185 race car, but it still wouldn't sustain the requisite turbo boost pressure. De Angelis's car was fitted with new turbos as he was worried about lack of crisp response from the engine, the Williams team was in an optimistic frame of mind and the Ferrari drivers cautiously confident.

A fuel pump leak eventually obliged Fabi to start in his spare car from the pit lane, but apart from that everybody got away cleanly with de Angelis out-accelerating his team-mate as they went away from the grid, completing lap one comfortably in command with Senna, Alboreto, Johansson, Warwick, Prost and Rosberg leading the pursuit at the end of the opening lap. Far from moving in to challenge his team-mate, Senna sat back and conserved both himself and his car, mindful that this was a long race which would take a heavy toll on fuel consumption. The time to run hard was later in the proceedings, using all the fuel that could be saved by taking things

Prost had what he described as an average race as he stroked into third place after taking care of his fuel consumption. A plan to attack the Ferraris on the last lap was thwarted by a back-marker.

gently in the opening phase.

Warwick was cursing his Renault, finding that a perfectly good-handling car now seemed to have been transformed into an ill-handling beast, and he spun in the middle of the pack coming up the return leg of the circuit on lap three, recovering to continue in a miserable 12th place. It was only long after the race had finished that Derek's problem was traced to a seized rear anti-roll bar – by which time his RE60 had ended its race with two broken wheels, wedged firmly against the guard rail into which it had spun after 26 laps.

At the end of lap six Senna's Lotus came hurtling into the pits where the agitated Brazilian explained that he was losing turbo boost pressure: a quick examination revealed a clip retaining a pipe between the compressor and the turbo on one bank had come adrift, and although the problem could be rectified it lost Ayrton five laps on the leaders. It says a great deal for his tenacity that he then went straight back into the race and kept up the pressure all the way to the chequered flag. Although there was no way he could improve on 16th place, he shattered the lap record, leaving it at 1m 27.445s.

On the same lap, de Cesaris spun his Ligier at one of the S-bends on the return leg of the circuit, pirouetting drunkenly in a misguidedly spectacular attempt to get the car facing the correct way – in the course of which he managed to wipe Winkelhock's RAM into the barrier in a manoeuvre which looked like something out of the Keystone Cops! Andrea pitted for a fresh nose section before continuing on his way unabashed, leaving a furious Manfred to abandon his rumpled car by the side of the circuit!

At the end of lap eight Rosberg hurtled into the pits for attention to his cockpit boost control switch, resuming well down the field after a quick stop, while Niki Lauda began his steady progress through the field, out-braking Warwick's Renault at the end of lap 11 at the hairpin before the pits. By lap 12, as Senna returned to the fray, Alboreto was moving in to challenge de Angelis for the lead. Elio parried a couple of attempts on lap 15 by sticking to the inside line and forcing Michele to go the long way round, then as they went into lap 16, the Ferrari team leader ran round the outside of the Lotus going into the S-bends beyond the pits – a most assertive move! – and that was the end of that.

By lap 22 Alboreto had taken full advantage of slower traffic to break de Angelis's challenge and Ferrari number 27 (an evocative number here at the Circuit Gilles Villeneuve) looked well in command of the proceedings. On lap 29 Alliot's RAM crashed badly when exiting the kink beyond the pits, scattering debris all over the circuit. The white flag appeared for a few laps as a tow truck was sent out to recover the wreck but, thankfully, nobody picked up any punctures and the race continued without further major incident.

Tambay's early spurt in the Renault pushed the fuel-conscious Prost down to fifth place, but the Frenchman eventually got the Renault back again towards the finish when Patrick lost third gear and the McLaren slipped ahead again on lap 50. De Angelis's early pace had taken its toll on his

front tyres, and by the time Alboreto got by his Lotus was suffering from an increasing degree of unwanted understeer, a problem later aggravated by an engine response problem, particularly in third and fourth gears. Even so, it took a long time for Johansson's third-place Ferrari (misfiring audibly) to make up the ground, but when Stefan finally got through at the start of lap 52, he stayed there for the rest of the race.

But for that slight misfire, Johansson might have made a serious bid for the lead. Unaware of any official team orders in such situations, Stefan piled on as much pressure as he could and moved right onto Michele's tail with eight laps left to run. Then the Italian simply turned up the boost pressure and sprinted away from him down a couple of straights. 'He got the message', smiled Alboreto on the winner's rostrum.

Either way, Johansson was only 1.9s down at the chequered flag after a performance which must have convinced Enzo Ferrari of the strength of his current driver pairing. Prost's plans for a last-corner assault on the second Ferrari were thwarted by de Cesaris, the Ligier driver limping round almost brakeless thanks to a split caliper, so the best-placed McLaren had to settle for third. Niki Lauda had been knocking at the door of the top six when his MP4/2B began to overheat and he pulled in for good at the end of lap 38.

One of the outstanding stars of the race was unquestionably Keke Rosberg. Having lost that initial ground with one pit visit, he then spun at

June:
New York GP cancelled. Brands Hatch confirmed as substitute race.

Alfa Romeo bench test four-cylinder turbo.

Emanuele Pirro tests Brabham at Silverstone.

Tyrrell unveil 014-turbo Renault at Silverstone.

Klaus Ludwig/Paulo Barilla/'John Winter' (Joest Porsche 956B) win Le Mans 24-Hrs.

the hairpin before the pits as he attempted an ambitious dive inside Warwick's Renault. That necessitated another stop for fresh rubber but, thus equipped, the Finn was an absolute revelation, storming through to take an eventual fourth place at the chequered flag – and on the same lap as the winner. That left the thoroughly disheartened de Angelis to fade to a disappointed fifth place at the flag, just ahead of the hard-driving Mansell who, for many laps, had been involved in a wheel-to-wheel tussle with Cheever's Alfa until the Italian car had been delayed with the latest in a sequence of seemingly endless electrical problems.

Outside the top six, Tambay's gearbox problems caused him to slump to eighth place, but when Laffite was docked a minute for jumping the start, Patrick moved back ahead of the Ligier driver in the final classification. Boost control problems kept Boutsen back in ninth place ahead of Patrese, Bellof and Brundle, while de Cesaris's braking problems dropped him to 14th behind Berger. Still feeling below par, Surer had only a partly-opening throttle on his Brabham BT54, but he ground round to finish a cheerless 15th, three laps down on Alboreto. His team mate had been spared any such embarrassment: Piquet's gearbox packed up almost as the starting signal was given and the man who had won the previous year's Canadian Grand Prix in champion style staggered through the first couple of corners before his race came to an end. How times change . . .   A. H.

TECHNICAL FILE

FERRARI
Used Valeo water radiator on Friday but returned to IPRA for remainder of weekend. Tested fuel consumption computer (revised since Spa; now with cockpit readout) but discarded for the race since it was felt this could upset electronics on rest of car. No bypass between heat exchanger and turbo but ran electronic control on wastegate. Raced with very flat rear wing, suggesting good aerodynamics at rear of car.

ALFA ROMEO
Tested inlet duct for turbos (similar to Ferrari) at Balocco; not seen in Montreal. Also wind tunnel tested side pods with side exit and tried front vertical wings (similar to Lotus). Continued using exhausts with large exits. Used same fuel computer as McLaren. Known to have bench tested four-cylinder engine. During practice, tried running wastegate with rigid valve setting. As a result, turbo revved to 180,000 instead of 140,000 and caused failures. (Intention was to run for a single lap with wastegate in this state but drivers completed too many fast laps.)

WILLIAMS
Ran AP brake calipers and double cooling ducts at rear. On Friday, Rosberg used revised Honda engine seen at Spa (known as 'D' version) while Mansell ran latest 'E' spec. 'E' had better fuel consumption with more power at low revs, the power band running from 8500 rpm (previously 9500) to 11,500 rpm. Rosberg had 'E' spec engine on Saturday. Used fuel computer manufactured by Honda which indicated number of litres left in tank.

LOTUS
EF15 engines for both drivers. Still running without on-board computer but Renault working on it. Did not run rear trim tabs but continued with secondary rear wing.

TOLEMAN
Tested at Mallory Park after Spa. New electronic ignition on one car at Montreal. Ballast moved to new location towards rear of chassis.

ARROWS
Stiffened rear mounting points on chassis.

RAM
Secondary, low-mounted rear wing. Longer side plates (first seen at Monte Carlo) on all three cars.

MINARDI
Did not continue with flaps around rear wheels; needed wind tunnel work to find the correct position.

Another fresh Renault engine for Lotus. Elio de Angelis had engine problems, while Ayrton Senna lost five laps as a broken clip was attended to but drove a spirited race into 16th place.

TYRRELL
Nothing new.

LIGIER
Laffite's car fitted with new bodywork, retaining same design but using fewer sections and fixing points; also incorporated the lighter components seen on de Cesaris's car at Monte Carlo. Ligier, in common with other Renault users, ran EF4B engines without wastegates during practice.

OSELLA
Tried lower, secondary rear wing. Brought four engines to North America. Waiting for new electronic ignition similar to system used by Alfa Romeo in Brazil.

McLAREN
Tried revised rear suspension but Lauda preferred old set-up. Used large turbos in practice and smaller versions for race.

BRABHAM
No change; continued with rear flaps seen at Spa.   G.P.

United States Grand Prix Detroit

'The thing about this place', said Keke Rosberg, nodding towards the concrete walls, 'is that the margin for error is non-existent. Apart from that, there isn't much more to say.'

Rosberg, however, had a lot to say when his team called him in 13 laps from the end of the race. The Canon Williams Honda had a lead of 25 seconds over Stefan Johansson's Ferrari but he was bothered by rising temperatures caused by a plastic bag lodged across the right-hand air intake. His tyres, however, were perfect. Rosberg had been the only driver to choose the soft Goodyears and, in retrospect, this had been the correct decision.

Rosberg's surprise can be imagined therefore when he dashed in to the pit lane to have the obstruction removed – and found the mechanics throwing themselves onto his car and changing tyres. The radio airwaves between Rosberg and his crew were blue but it was a shrewd move, although Keke failed to see the wisdom of it at the time as he rejoined just two seconds ahead of Johansson.

The additional grip from the Goodyears helped Rosberg set his fastest lap of the race, while a brake problem for Johansson finally settled the issue and brought Stefan six points for the second race in succession.

Third place for Michele Alboreto helped the Ferrari driver maintain his lead of the championship, the Italian having been severely embarrassed earlier in the race by an electrifying drive from Martin Brundle. The Tyrrell driver was eventually eliminated while lapping a back-marker and it was left to Stefan Bellof to give the Ford-Cosworth its last competitive run and take fourth place.

Elio de Angelis scored points once again for JPS Lotus while Nelson Piquet, winner of the race the year before, scored the Brabham team's first point of the year by finishing sixth, a lap behind the leader.

Many of the fancied runners had spent the afternoon proving Rosberg's theory about the margin of error although, to be fair, the track at Turn Three, the corner which caught Senna, Mansell, Tambay and Prost, had broken up badly. Elsewhere, cars were parked with their transmissions thrashed by the uneven streets of Detroit.

Rosberg's Williams had survived and this victory was attributed to a professional driver and an equally professional team. The only surprise was that the Detroit Grand Prix represented their first victory in almost a year; the last win having come at Dallas. That race had been run under similar conditions: a race with a non-existent margin of error.

ENTRY AND PRACTICE

In a moment of enthusiasm, a reporter on one of the Detroit morning newspapers, searching desperately for superlatives to describe the bland street circuit, compared Detroit with Monte Carlo.

True, both races are run on public thoroughfares but there the comparison ends. Monte Carlo may have its faults but at least the circuit rises and falls; snakes through a variety of corners. Detroit is mainly flat with the majority of corners being ninety degrees, as dictated by the grid pattern of streets in American cities. You either liked it or loathed it. At least it added variety to the calendar as a whole and the organisers were always willing, if occasionally lacking. And one last point; Monte Carlo may have gone in for rather tasteless renovation work in recent years but they had nothing to compare with the appalling glass and concrete jungle known as the Renaissance Centre, the hub of 'Detroit Grand Prix IV'.

The drivers who disliked the circuit were even less enchanted by the place when it was discovered that the organisers had only carried out resurfacing work at one or two of the very worst bumps. Elsewhere, the ravages of a late and harsh winter were obvious as the cars bounced along the straights. It was clear that the transmissions would take a pounding as the drivers applied the turbo power.

Ayrton Senna's lack of enthusiasm for Detroit was deepened, perhaps, by the fact that he had crashed twice during his first visit in 1984. None the less, the Brazilian put all that behind him as he went out on Friday afternoon and set a time which was over a second faster than anyone else. The forecasters said it would rain on Saturday and Ayrton took them at their word, buttoning up the overnight pole by using race rubber rather than qualifiers. In fact, he did use qualifiers but made self-confessed errors on that lap, vindicating the decision to use a set of soft race tyres which allowed time to find a clear lap.

The decision to rely on the weather forecasters was also correct, only seven cars taking to the streaming track on Saturday afternoon. Friday's times, therefore, determined the grid.

At one stage on Friday, Senna had sat quietly in the pits, watching the Longines monitor to see if anyone would approach his time. Nigel Mansell, revelling in the special demands of a street circuit, came closest as he made the most of continued development with the Honda. Like Senna, he had set his time on Cs, a run on qualifiers almost ending in disaster as he took to an escape road. The Williams ran into a tyre barrier and, remarkably, damage was confined to a bent end plate on the nose wing. Switching back to the race tyres, Mansell set his best time on his very last lap.

This was Senna's fourth pole position of the season and the fifth for Lotus. On this occasion, however, Elio de Angelis was back in eighth place, the Italian forced to use the T-car, which had been fitted with the EF15 engine in readiness for the race. An EF4B had, as usual, been allocated for practice and it was that car which Elio crashed during the unofficial session on Friday morning.

Running a set of qualifiers near the end of the session, de Angelis blasted through a left-hander, the concrete walls obscuring Patrick Tambay as the Frenchman made his way slowly on a set of cold tyres. There were no warning flags for either driver and de Angelis, committed to his line, crashed into the Renault, causing severe damage to both cars. The front-left corner was torn off the Lotus and the mechanics toiled in the early hours of Saturday morning as they rebuilt the car. The rain meant their urgency was in vain.

The Ferrari team, on a high following their clean sweep in Montreal the previous weekend,

The 9.5 seconds which won the race. The Williams mechanics spring into action while Patrick Head reaches down to move rubbish from the right-hand side pod. Rosberg rejoined just two seconds ahead of Johansson but held off the Ferrari to score his first win since Dallas in 1984.

David Hutson

Keke Rosberg gave his sponsors full coverage in Detroit.
Michele Alboreto took four more points in spite of
severe problems with the brakes on his Ferrari.

looked to be in trouble as the red cars showed a dislike of the many bumps but Michele Alboreto nevertheless managed to set third fastest time. Stefan Johansson was down in ninth place, the Swede complaining of a lack of traction and understeer caused by a soft front roll bar. Johansson was confident that he would improve when more rubber was laid on the track surface on Saturday but the rain cancelled that plan.

One driver very happy to see the wet conditions on Saturday was Alain Prost. The Detroit circuit is the Frenchman's bogey track and his impressions of the place were not helped when he crashed and jarred his right wrist. This was within 15 minutes of the start of practice, a loss of fluid having caused the rear brakes to fail, leaving Prost resting against a tyre barrier.

Willi Dungl strapped the wrist and Alain took to the T-car although his progress in that was hampered by problems with fourth and fifth gears. His race car was repaired in time for a run at the end of official practice so Prost gritted his teeth and his brave effort was rewarded by fourth place. Using race tyres, Prost found the business of completing four or five laps on the trot quite painful but he took a brief rest before making his last, successful attempt in the race car. Rain on Saturday meant his place was secure and gave the Frenchman time to rest his injury.

With 63 laps ahead of him on Sunday, Prost needed all the help he could get. So, too, did Lauda, the World Champion disappointed that he was unable to improve on 12th place, his lowly position being accounted for by fifth gear continually jumping out during the official session on Friday afternoon.

Sixth place for Derek Warwick was something of a surprise since the Renault looked far from stable on the bumps. Warwick's practice on Friday morning was curtailed by a broken output shaft from the gearbox but that was easily fixed, unlike the car of his team-mate. Patrick had to use the spare (fitted with the less suitable EF15) for the afternoon session and he was hoping to improve on 15th place on Saturday.

Happy with seventh place, Eddie Cheever's position reflected the continuing development with the Alfa Romeo – during practice at least. The Italian cars continued to be unreliable when it came to running a race distance but Cheever was out there in the rain on Saturday, two seconds faster than anyone else in the morning session. Riccardo Patrese took 14th place on the grid, the Italian having the misfortune to run into Berger's Arrows on Friday morning. Berger was having his own accident when he collected Patrese but, even so, Patrese was no match for his team-mate on a circuit where Cheever had a good track record.

Nelson Piquet's record at Detroit was equally impressive, the Brabham driver having scored a brilliant win here the previous year. In 1985, however, he was five seconds off his practice time from the year before! True, the circuit was bumpier and a little tighter at one point (to make way for a column supporting a 'people mover' which was under construction) but the deficit was down to a woeful lack of grip from the Pirellis. Marc Surer was next up, the Swiss taking 11th place and distinguishing himself by spinning four times as he explored the limits of the Pirelli wets on Saturday afternoon.

An engine change on Teo Fabi's car meant the Italian had to use the spare on Friday afternoon but at least he was comfortably ahead of the Pirelli-shod Ligiers of Jacques Laffite and Andrea de Cesaris in 16th and 17th places, both drivers running EF15 engines on Friday. They reckoned the more favourable torque characteristics of the new engine were better than sheer horsepower but their decision to run a mixture of qualifying and race tyres (at the same time!) proved to be something of a novelty.

Behind the blue French cars sat the blue British Tyrrells, Martin Brundle out-qualifying Stefan Bellof. In truth, the Tyrrell lads had hoped to be further up the grid since Detroit represented the last chance for the ubiquitous Ford-Cosworth to score points. Apart from a touch too much understeer, Brundle had no worries and it was clear that the young Brit was keen to do well after the disqualification in 1984.

It was surprising to find the Arrows team at the back of the grid among the RAMs and Piercarlo Ghinzani's Osella. Thierry Boutsen could do no better than 21st slot in the T-car after his regular car had stopped with electrical problems but Berger was lucky to be able to drive at all after a series of accidents. Apart from his spin and subsequent brush with Patrese, the Austrian hit the wall in a big way during the afternoon session. He walked back to the pits but, in view of the neck injuries incurred in a road accident the previous winter, he wisely took the precaution of having a check-up in hospital. He was fit enough to do some serious work in the wet on Saturday and actually set the fastest time in the afternoon – to move from 25th to 24th place at the expense of Pierluigi Martini, who did not manage a single timed lap all weekend due to a misfire on the Minardi.

RACE

You can't beat the American people when it comes to enthusiasm and, as had become the habit, Detroit went 'partying' to celebrate their Grand Prix. Fortunately, the weather smiled on their efforts, clear blue skies and temperatures in the high Seventies tempered with a fresh breeze blowing off the Detroit River.

The teams had no time to notice the colourful jamboree surrounding them as they tackled the morning warm-up. With Saturday's practice having been rained off, there was much work to be squeezed into the 30-minute session.

For a start, there had been no time to try running full tank tests and the most pressing question of all was that of brakes. Would the

Once again, Ayrton Senna led a Grand Prix but the wrong choice of tyres would necessitate two pit stops. The Lotus driver eventually crashed on the crumbling track surface. Rosberg and Mansell follow during the opening laps.

carbon discs be equal to the task on a circuit which did not possess straights long enough to allow the discs and pads to cool properly?

Williams, for example, sent Mansell out on carbon brakes but the high wear rate convinced them of the need for steel. Senna, on the other hand, was keen to switch back to carbon fibre although opinions generally seemed to favour the heavier discs. Some teams, such as McLaren, had no provision to switch from carbon even though Prost, his wrist still troubling him, would have preferred the conservative choice.

Tyres, too, were something of a gamble but, in the end, the majority chose either As or a combination of A and B. The Tyrrells, of course, could afford to run Cs all round. Rosberg, significantly, was the only turbo runner to choose the softer B compound all round. That was to be the shrewdest decision of the weekend . . .

The field rolled onto the grid at the appointed hour, Mansell getting the drop on Senna as they rushed into the first left-hander. By the end of the following straight, however, Ayrton was in the lead with Prost third and a remarkable start by Rosberg having pushed the Williams ahead of Alboreto and Warwick. Keke wasn't finished either. During the course of the first lap, he took Prost and his team-mate, the order at the end of the tour being: Senna, Rosberg, Mansell, Prost, Alboreto, Warwick, de Angelis, Johansson, Piquet, Lauda and Fabi. Then came the Tyrrells of Brundle and Bellof as the blue cars started the first lap the way they meant to go on – absolutely flat-out.

Cheever, running steel brakes and in a confident mood before the start, peeled into the pits with a puncture at the end of the lap, while Ghinzani's race was run, the Osella parked against a wall with broken suspension.

Senna began to ease away from Rosberg, the Williams showering sparks as the skid pads grounded on the bumps. After a few laps it became

clear that the gap, if anything, was diminishing and, sure enough, at the end of lap seven, they were nose to tail. Senna's choice of As all round was proving to be the incorrect tactic.

At the end of lap eight, Ayrton powered into the pit lane, the Lotus getting very sideways as he did so. A quick stop had him on his way again in 14th place and he soon began to work his way past the midfield runners – but not as quickly as we might have expected. Indeed, his lap times were around two seconds off Rosberg's pace and that was directly attributable to the fact that he had been given another set of As! Lotus did not possess a radio link between driver and pit; Williams did – and it would be small details like that which would help win this race.

June:
Ford confirm three-year deal with Beatrice Formula 1 team for Ford-Cosworth turbo engine.

A high rate of attrition was expected and the list of retirements grew by two when Winkelhock stopped with a blown turbo and Fabi crept into the pits with a broken clutch. Lauda, not at home on this track, was happy to call it a day when the brakes (carbon) faded on lap 11 while, at the same time, Martini's slow performance at the back of the field was mercifully ended by turbo trouble.

By this stage, Rosberg held a comfortable lead of 11 seconds over his team-mate who, in turn, was eight seconds ahead of de Angelis, the Lotus having moved ahead of Prost and then Alboreto as the McLaren and Ferrari drivers began to experience brake problems. In the early laps, Warwick had held a confident sixth place but, after 10 laps, it became clear that brake problems (carbon) were causing the Renault to slide down the lap chart, his progress being arrested finally

by a broken driveshaft. Warwick, with just two championship points on the board, was not amused.

Neither, for that matter, was his team-mate. The additional work necessitated by his lowly grid position had been compounded when Surer made a slow getaway and Tambay finished the first lap in 20th place. Duly fired up, Patrick began to work his way through to 13th position but, on lap 16, the carbon brakes faded and he spun on the rapidly disintegrating surface at Turn Three. The left-rear corner of the Renault hit the wall and that was that although Tambay seemed hell-bent on destruction as he crabbed his way (against the flow of traffic on the exit of a blind corner!) to the safety of an escape road.

Rosberg continued to pull away from Mansell but, lapping just as quickly as the Finn, Elio de Angelis reeled in and passed Mansell on lap 20. The Englishman was beginning to feel the effects of brake and tyre trouble and he duly made a stop for tyres four laps later. The brakes, however, could not be improved and Mansell was caught out by the advanced state of decay at Turn Three. Unfortunately for Nigel, the Williams drove headlong into a section of concrete wall laid bare of protection earlier in the race when the rear of Senna's Lotus had clipped a pile of tyres and flicked them out of position. Mansell was momentarily concussed and the fierce impact jarred his right thumb.

The run-off area at this corner now resembled a dead car-park, Prost having crashed when his brakes faded on lap 20. At least his McLaren was safely tucked away but the zealous marshals made a meal of removing Mansell's damaged car. For four laps they struggled and no progress was made until Ayrton Senna's manager, spectating at that corner, hurdled the barrier and knocked the Williams out of gear. A crane, positioned and handled as expertly as those at Monte Carlo, would have solved the inefficient marshals'

Ferrari were on the pace again, Johansson and Alboreto finishing second and third .
Alain Prost's dislike of Detroit was not helped by a brush with the wall (caused by brake trouble) during
practice. Willi Dungl attends to the McLaren driver's sprained wrist.

problems within seconds.

Mansell was understandably disappointed but Prost was on his way to the airport, happy to be finished with this circuit for another year. Apart from that, he had been completely humbled by Martin Brundle as the Tyrrell driver made full use of his nimble car.

Attacking continuously, the Tyrrells sounded like busy wasps as they dashed and darted, Bellof the more untidy of the two. At one stage, Stefan removed his nose cone against the rear of Brundle's car but eventually Martin pulled away as he hounded the likes of Lauda and Piquet and passed Prost with insolent ease. He then set about taking fifth place from Alboreto, the Ferrari driver's progress being hindered by fading brakes so much that he had been unable to prevent his team-mate from moving ahead on lap 15.

Once in front of Alboreto, Brundle was able to move into fourth place after Mansell's demise, and he then set after Johansson. In view of his performance the year before when he finished second, it seemed there would be no stopping the Tyrrell on the only circuit which suited the normally aspirated Ford-Cosworth. However, he dropped back to fifth again when Alboreto, having allowed his brakes to cool, put on a spurt and caught Brundle by surprise. In fact, Michele had dropped so far behind that Brundle was sure the Ferrari had made a pit stop and was at least one lap behind. It wasn't and that development would play a crucial part a few laps later.

In the meantime, the Ferrari and the Tyrrell each moved up one place when de Angelis, lying in second place 27 seconds behind Rosberg, came into the pits on lap 29. The Lotus had been trying to lap Berger as the Arrows did battle with Surer at the back of the field and the result of a passing move was a broken nose wing for de Angelis. The team fitted the wings taken from the spare car (set up for Senna) and a furious de Angelis continued in ninth place, aiming now for a finish and points.

Looking for a place on the rostrum at least, Brundle continued to chase Alboreto and, on lap 31, they came upon the RAM of Philippe Alliot. The Frenchman had been plagued with engine problems during the morning warm-up and the RAM team responded by changing both his and Winkelhock's engine in time for the race. A

misfire for Alliot meant he was 15 seconds off the pace as the Ferrari and Tyrrell approached, the RAM duly moving to the right and letting Alboreto through. Assuming one glance in his mirror would be enough, Alliot moved back on line for the next corner – and hit Brundle as the Tyrrell attempted to come through. Both retired instantly. It was the end of a superb drive for Brundle and a miserable weekend for the RAM team. The bulk of the blame lay with Alliot but perhaps Brundle should have made allowances. On the other hand, if he had made allowances, he would not have been lying fourth at the time . . .

That left Bellof, now fourth behind Rosberg, Johansson and Alboreto, to carry the Tyrrell hopes although it was clear he would be no match for Senna as the Lotus, having stopped yet again and finally received the correct tyres, came slicing through the field. Setting fastest lap of the day, Senna drove beautifully even though his brakes (carbon) now required regular pumping on the approach to corners. He dealt with Bellof on lap 45 and quickly caught Alboreto. There were 13 laps remaining; at this rate of going, he might take second from Johansson.

Hysterics from the commentator – 'Rosberg is in the pits!' Suddenly, it seemed possible that Senna might win!

Of more immediate importance was the reason for Rosberg's unexpected stop. For several laps, Keke had noticed the temperatures running high and, suspecting some of the rubbish swirling around the circuit might have gathered in a cooling duct, he radioed his pits. They confirmed that a yellow plastic bag was lodged in the right side pod. The temperatures continued to climb and now the Honda was losing power. His advantage over Johansson was 25 seconds; Patrick Head made the decision to bring Rosberg in.

Then, slight confusion. Rosberg was very happy with his tyres but Head misunderstood his driver and thought they needed changing. Rosberg

Bernard Asset

arrived in his pit – and flew into a rage when the mechanics started removing the near-perfect tyres. No one, it seemed to Keke, was clearing away the rubbish!

In fact, Head had reached down and removed the obstruction and there was certainly no confusion over the tyre change, the Williams lads sending Keke on his way in 9.5 seconds. Laying rubber all the way down the pit lane, a furious Rosberg rejoined just two seconds ahead of Johansson.

Minutes later, Turn Three claimed another victim, Ayrton Senna crashing into the wall while looking for a way past Alboreto. The Brazilian was honest enough to admit that, in the excitement, he had forgotten to pump his brakes and, dehen the pedal went to the floor, he knew he was in for a nasty bump. Lifting his legs clear of the pedals, his only injury was a jarred hand. Once again, a fine performance – but no points for Senna.

Sensing there were nine points to be had, Johansson pushed Rosberg hard but, even though his front tyres had yet to warm sufficiently, Keke was determined not to lose this race. He opened the gap and, almost unbelievably, the turbo temperatures began to rise again – and down

TECHNICAL FILE

There were few innovations at Detroit, the teams having moved directly from Canada to the United States.

WILLIAMS
Tried running lower rear wing in two pieces but reverted to one. Both race cars had latest E-spec engines. T-car, always fitted with steel disc brakes, had older spec engine. Rain on Saturday cancelled opportunity for Mansell to run with steel discs and large side plates to front wing. Rosberg tried steel discs on Sunday morning, Mansell switching from carbon for the race.

McLAREN
Ran smaller turbos during practice. Lauda and Prost had different rear suspension set-ups and different stiffness in rear shock absorbers. Both cars ran larger brake cooling ducts, in common with the rest of the teams.

LOTUS
Fitted rear trim tabs once more. T-car fitted with steel discs. Both drivers tried steel discs during Sunday morning warm-up, while the T-car had been changed to carbon. Senna opted for carbon.

FERRARI
Engineer Caruso arrived in Detroit on Friday with new alternators following the discovery that the alternators used in Canada were about to fail.

TYRRELL
Brought one large rear wing as seen on 014 turbo model.

LIGIER
De Cesaris ran carbon brakes on Friday but both drivers chose steel for the race.

ALFA ROMEO
Used same rear wing as seen at Monaco. Continued experimentation with revised air-box.

GP

The world of Formula 1 pivoted around Detroit's Renaissance Centre for three days in June. Steady improvements by the organisers have made the street race an accepted part of the calendar.
Nigel Mansell's promising start from the front of the grid came to nothing when the Williams developed brake trouble. Mansell was concussed briefly when he hit the wall.
The Last Hurrah. The Tyrrell-Cosworths put on a stunning display as Martin Brundle and Stefan Bellof made the most of their nimble cars in the tight confines of the street circuit. Brundle was eliminated while lapping a back-marker but Bellof finished fourth despite a broken clutch.

Paul Henri Cahier

Mike Levasheff

came the gap to Johansson. Two things resolved the battle. The fresh piece of paper resting in the duct blew away and Johansson's right-front disc brake more or less exploded with just three laps remaining. Winding his brakes to the rear, Stefan nursed his car to the line, Alboreto doing the same with his Ferrari. Unfortunately for Bellof, a slipping clutch meant he was unable to do anything about the hobbled Ferraris and he came home fourth ahead of de Angelis. A lap behind, Nelson Piquet scored his first point of the season after stopping to have rubbish removed from his side pod as early as lap 12. Surer, coping with brake problems, finished eighth behind Boutsen, the Arrows driver struggling without one nose wing for most of the race.

To finish this race had been a tribute to both the driver and his machinery. Rosberg had driven brilliantly in difficult conditions, the Finn remaining alert to the end of the race and right through to the excellent press conference. As Rosberg sat down, he deftly removed the bottles of Pepsi which had been placed on the table. When you are on a large retainer from Marlboro, whose subsidiaries include 'Seven Up', a rival of Pepsi, there's no room for error at Detroit . . .   M.H.

Grand Prix de France

'You know, I think we'll go well where it's hot and fast. We haven't been in as bad shape as everybody thinks . . . I reckon we might well have won Brazil and we were in a position to win Imola in terms of competitiveness until we ran out of fuel. Just wait . . .' Was Nelson Piquet expressing his true thoughts, or was it simply a subtle piece of gamesmanship to wind up his rivals prior to the French Grand Prix at Paul Ricard? Certainly, with all that pre-season testing in hot weather at Kyalami under their belts, Brabham and Pirelli *should* have been in a position to shine under the French sun at Paul Ricard. Still, you never could be really sure until the race started . . .

At the end of the day, it was Goodyear, not Pirelli, that slunk away licking its wounds! After qualifying a respectable fifth on the grid, Piquet completed the opening lap of the French Grand Prix in third place behind Keke Rosberg's Williams and Ayrton Senna's Lotus 97T. On lap seven he was up to second place, and on lap 10 he was through into the lead: from that point onwards everybody else was firmly cast in a supporting role.

As Nelson staged another Brabham demonstration run, all too familiar in the days when Bernie's cars ran on Michelins, Rosberg's performance was simply heroic. Up to just beyond half distance he fought manfully to keep the McLaren-TAGs of Niki Lauda and Alain Prost behind him. Niki retired on lap 30 with transmission failure and, after Prost had nipped through into second place 10 laps later, Keke stopped for fresh tyres. He then made up lost ground with brilliant aplomb to deprive a troubled Prost of second place on the very last lap, crowning a splendid weekend's endeavour. With Stefan Johansson hurtling round the *Signes* right-hander at the end of the daunting *Mistral* straight, overtaking de Angelis to gain fourth place on the last lap, this was truly a race for heroic gestures.

Sixth place fell to Patrick Tambay's revamped Renault RE60B but the Régie's front runner, Ayrton Senna, had a bad time with his Renault-powered Lotus 97T which had started from the front row alongside Rosberg's pole-position Williams. Gear selection trouble sent Senna into the pits early on and he was charging back through the field when his engine failed spectacularly at *Signes* and he crashed on his own oil slick.

After months of being eclipsed by his younger compatriot, Formula 1's most experienced Brazilian had re-established himself at the pinnacle of Grand Prix achievement.

ENTRY AND PRACTICE

The Championship trail certainly provides contrasts! Two weeks after the precarious acrobatics of Detroit's bumpy street circuit, complete with painful excursions into unyielding concrete barriers and a high level of mechanical mayhem, the Formula 1 fraternity brushed the cement dust out of its hair and settled down to savour the challenge of Paul Ricard. With a photoflood of Mediterranean sunshine keeping the weather uniformly sweltering throughout the three-day meeting, the French Grand Prix turned into a gruelling battle where breathtaking straightline speed and brute engine power were every bit as important as good handling chassis and a capable driving technique.

Speculation had been going on for weeks as to just what sort of figures would be recorded on Ricard's daunting, mile-long *Mistral* straight. When Keke Rosberg opened proceedings with a 207 mph terminal velocity turning into the right-hander at *Signes* during Friday's untimed session, it was clear that second generation turbos really had brought a new dimension in terms of performance to the super-fast southern French track. Later during the weekend, Marc Surer's Brabham BT54, running with plenty of boost pressure through its BMW engine's new Garrett turbocharger, raised the informal record to 213 mph. From the touchlines, amidst the sun-soaked, dusty scrubland, it looked as blindingly quick as it

appears on paper . . .

Central to the issue of qualifying at every Grand Prix so far had been Lotus team-leader Ayrton Senna, and Paul Ricard proved to be no exception to this black-and-gold pattern. Using a Renault EF4B qualifying engine as usual, the Brazilian dominated his first ever official practice session at Paul Ricard with a 1m 32.835s on Friday afternoon, beating the hitherto fastest-ever Formula 1 lap at the French track – René Arnoux's 1m 34.406s which had earned the Frenchman pole position for the 1982 Grand Prix at the wheel of a ground-effect Renault RE30C.

With typical modesty, Senna reckoned that neither of his Friday runs were particularly good, and that he would hold onto pole position without much problem. 'I missed a gear on my first run and, to judge by the lack of wear on those qualifiers when I got back to the pits, all I can say is that I couldn't have been pushing them hard enough! I tried to push harder on my second run, but there was a cross-wind at *Signes* which kept my attention pretty dramatically.' Only two weeks after badly bruising his right hand in an uncharacteristically silly accident at Detroit, Ayrton was now shrugging aside the obvious discomfort: 'It only hurts when I think about it', he joked confidently.

Alas for Lotus, Senna's pole-position challenge came to a sudden end the following afternoon when, straining every sinew to regain fastest time

from Keke Rosberg's impressive Williams FW10, his 97T's V6 blew up spectacularly on a fast right-hand swerve just before the pits. 'All I could do was to kick out the clutch and coast into the pit lane', mused Senna reflectively: 'a pity, because I reckon that lap would have been even better than my Friday best.'

Rosberg, buoyed up with confidence in the latest long-stroke Honda engine after his victory at Detroit, was in fine form on the long straights and fast curves of Paul Ricard. On Friday he set second fastest time, 'which was pretty pleasing, considering that I used up my tyres by the end of my best lap'. Interestingly, that experience tempted him to throw thoughts of tyre conservation to the wind, the Finn simply 'going for it' in a big way on Saturday afternoon to slice six-tenths of a second off his previous best and grasp pole position with a 1m 32.462s.

The Williams team's delight over Keke's performance was unhappily tempered by concern over Nigel Mansell's accident during Saturday morning's untimed session. The Englishman was another survivor of the Detroit wall-banging antics, and had a painfully swollen right wrist to prove it when he arrived at the French circuit. However, there was even more misfortune in store for this stoic campaigner. Between pain-killing sprays on Friday he had managed a seventh fastest 1m 34.191s lap, but then plunged off the circuit at *Signes* the following morning when a

July:
FISA issue written reprimand to Patrese and Piquet over incident during Monaco Grand Prix.

David Purley killed in plane crash.

European Grand Prix at Brands Hatch moved from 22 September to 29 September — then, 6 October.

Back on the rostrum. Nelson Piquet scored his first win in over a year as he took Brabham and Pirelli to a commanding victory. It was the first Grand Prix win for Pirelli since 1957.

left-rear Goodyear flew apart as his Williams approached this very quick corner.

Running with a full fuel load on 'B' compound rubber, Mansell was still doing all of 200 mph when he lost control. The flailing rubber strands destroyed the FW10's left-rear corner, shedding its suspension which, in turn, ripped off the rear wing. As it plunged headlong towards the guard rail, the FW10's left-front wheel caught a plastic catch-fence pole, the base of which was set firmly in concrete. Rather than the pole snapping under impact, it uprooted its foundations and this effort was sufficient to break the left-front suspension, allowing the wheel to flip backwards to catch Nigel's helmet a severe glancing blow.

Nigel was lifted unconscious from the wrecked car and taken to the circuit medical centre for an initial examination before being transferred to a Marseilles hospital for further attention. He was quite clearly suffering from very bad concussion, but there was no serious, lasting damage and he was flown home to the Isle of Man the following day. There was obviously no chance of his taking part in the French Grand Prix, so now all his efforts were focussed on making a complete recovery in time for Silverstone.

Goodyear was obviously concerned about this failure, but there was no question of withdrawing the batch of rubber concerned as the tyre which had broken up on Mansell's car was of a construction which had been in regular use since

the start of the season with no problems whatsoever. There was an obvious possibility that the incident could have been caused by the tyre developing a slow puncture, but there were no untoward signs which pointed to the need for precipitate action on the part of the tyre company.

Pre-Ricard testing at Fiorano saw Ferrari produce a new front suspension geometry for its 156/85s, two of which were built up around revised monocoques featuring removable access panels to the inboard front spring/damper units. A couple of engine failures, put down to a faulty batch of pistons, hampered the team's progress on Friday and both drivers reported on an irritating degree of understeer with this new set-up.

Michele Alboreto reverted to his spare car on Saturday, equipped with the 'old spec' suspension geometry, and immediately went over a second and a half quicker than he had managed on Friday, qualifying third overall with a 1m 33.267s. Stefan Johansson, recovering from a bout of chicken pox and still feeling slightly under the weather, was also hoping to have a crack in a second spare fitted with the older suspension arrangement, but his mechanics could not change a broken engine in this car in time for him to use it during final qualifying. He thus ran his first set of Saturday qualifiers in his new car, wasn't very happy with it, so opted to wait for a crack in Michele's spare once the Italian had finished with it. Unfortunately, on his final run he missed

John Townsend

The Mistral straight allowed the turbocharged cars
to reach speeds in excess of 200 mph. Nigel Mansell
was lucky to escape with nothing more than
concussion when a tyre failed during unofficial
practice.

fourth gear twice and wound up a disappointed 15th on 1m 36.140s.

Revised front suspension geometry with new front uprights was also to be seen on the McLaren MP4/2Bs. This system had been tried out with promising results in Alain Prost's hands during testing at Silverstone the previous week. Both he and Niki Lauda were delighted with the way their cars were handling round Paul Ricard. Although Niki confirmed yet again that the TAG turbo does not like massive doses of qualifying boost ('I turned it up sharply at one point during Saturday qualifying and immediately lost about 200 rpm!'), the two cars qualified fourth and sixth. Alain managed a 1m 33.355s to line up alongside Michele's Ferrari, while the World Champion, baulked at the fast kink beyond the pits on his very fastest run, started alongside Nelson Piquet's Brabham BT54 on the outside of row three on 1m 33.860s.

It should not perhaps have come as any great surprise that Pirelli managed to produce a respectable qualifying performance in the heat of Paul Ricard: Nelson Piquet had completed the lion's share of the Italian firm's tyre testing last winter in the similarly warm conditions of Kyalami, so if a Pirelli qualifier wasn't going to work in hot conditions it probably wasn't going to work anywhere! The BMW four-cylinder engines had been given an even sharper performance edge by the use of new Garrett turbochargers, and although the BT54 chassis looked something of a handful through the fast swerves beyond the pits, Nelson managed a 1m 33.812s lap for an encouraging fifth place on the grid. On Friday, the Brazilian's BT54 twice suffered a small fire when a fuel line came adrift and a fuel pick-up problem the following afternoon made it necessary for him to do his qualifying runs with about 12 gallons on board. It was a heartening showing from Ecclestone's number one – a performance not quite matched by Marc Surer who could think of no specific problems, but failed to improve on a 14th fastest 1m 35.572s.

Elio de Angelis was in a somewhat grumpy mood after qualifying his Lotus 97T seventh on 1m 34.022s, running throughout qualifying with an EF15 Renault V6 rather than an EF4B qualifying unit as employed by his Brazilian team-mate.

Elio lined up alongside Gerhard Berger's Arrows A8, the determined Austrian being promoted to the fourth row after the withdrawal of Mansell's entry, this new-boy surviving a suspension breakage on the *Mistral* straight without so much as batting an eyelid! Berger set his 1m 34.674s on Friday, out-qualifying colleague Thierry Boutsen – who's no slouch – in a confident display of spectacularly controlled extrovert driving. Boutsen suffered engine problems on Friday, improving to 1m 35.488s for 11th place on the grid the following afternoon, despite being quite badly baulked in the process.

With Renault Director General, Georges Besse, expected in the pits for Saturday qualifying, France's national Formula 1 team was pinning its hopes on the revamped RE60B for a morale-boosting race on home soil. Visually very similar to any other '85-spec Renault, the RE60B was built up round the same carbon-fibre composite monocoque but featured major changes in every other design area. Only one such machine was ready for Patrick Tambay's use at Ricard and was equipped with a special qualifying version of the EF15 V6 since the chassis would only accept one of the latest Renault engines. Patrick managed a 1m 34.680s on Friday but reported a worrying degree of fluctuating boost pressure at the top end. He reverted to the EF4B-engined RE60 spare for final qualifying but was unable to improve his time and lined up a somewhat disappointed ninth. Immediately behind him was team-mate Derek Warwick, whose RE60 also had boost pressure problems on Saturday and lost 400 rpm as a result.

Andrea de Cesaris's Ligier JS25 qualified 12th on 1m 35.571s, the Italian suffering boost control problems on Friday and missing a gear on his best Saturday run. Jacques Laffite performed quite

respectably in front of his home crowd and was helped to 14th place on the grid by a brand new lightweight chassis. Immediately behind Johansson's Ferrari were the Alfas of Riccardo Patrese and Eddie Cheever, the Italian grumbling about electrical problems on Friday and, not unreasonably, a little perturbed when the steering column began to move from side to side in his hands the following afternoon. One of the steering column retaining brackets had broken, so Riccardo retired to the cool of the pits content with his 16th fastest time.

Eddie Cheever ran through his now-familiar programme of turbo failures (one before his car had even reached the exit of the pit lane!) and actually dropped a couple of wheels onto the dirt on the very fast *Signes* right-hander, emerging a somewhat disgruntled 17th just ahead of Teo

Fabi's Toleman. Revised intercooling and a smaller rear wing helped the TG185's performance on this very fast circuit, but detonation problems with the Hart 415T engine were still causing concern. The same problems were evident in the RAM camp, where John Macdonald was wearing a very concerned look and expressing some doubts about his ability to complete the season's racing programme.

Manfred Winkelhock lined up his RAM 03 immediately behind Fabi, while Martin Brundle was wrestling with the unsorted Tyrrell-Renault 014 on the new car's maiden outing. 'The learning curve with these turbos is much steeper than I'd ever anticipated', smiled Martin thoughtfully, after qualifying a lowly 20th on 1m 40.015s. The Englishman grappled with an irritating amount of understeer and had to swap to the totally

TECHNICAL FILE

McLAREN
Engine problems in Belgium and Detroit discovered to have been caused by fuel manufactured in France. At Paul Ricard, McLaren used fuel supplied by Shell Germany. Revised front suspension geometry helped cure understeer problem. Both drivers used larger turbos during qualifying.

TYRRELL
Two new 014 Renault turbo chassis. Straightforward and well engineered, the chassis followed the 012 theme with similar suspension. Incorporated rear inlet ducts for turbos similar to Ferrari.

WILLIAMS
Honda engines incorporated pistons with ceramic heads. Revised turbos and intercoolers. Longer underbody profiles that had been tried during testing at Silverstone not seen at Paul Ricard.

BRABHAM
Garrett turbos used by Brabham at a race meeting for the first time. Spent time on Friday checking turbo performance details with on-board instrumentation. Larger air inlet to improve throttle response. Tried new engine cover, revised air intakes and a heavier nose cone during testing at Silverstone; not seen at Ricard. Fitted winglets to rear of side pods.

RAM
Alliot's car fitted with a different fuel pump and a spray system for intercooler. Larger water tank incorporated as a result.

LOTUS
Both race cars fitted with rear inlet ducts for turbos (similar to Ferrari). Ran without rear winglets and lower rear wing. Front brakes fitted with Brembo caliper; rear calipers made by Brembo but designed by Lotus.

RENAULT
New RE60B for Tambay. Weigh-in during practice on Friday showed car to be exactly on 540 kg limit. Chassis same as RE60 but electrics moved from top of fuel tank to inside cockpit, allowing 15 cm lower engine cover. Smaller radiators permitted shorter side pods. New uprights and wishbones although

geometry remained much as before. Caliper placed in front of rear disc. Slimmer nose cone. Produced EF15 qualifying engine since RE60B would not accept EF4B. Used new rims made by Dymag.

ARROWS
Boutsen's car featured a 5 cm longer wheelbase thanks to a spacer between the engine and gearbox. Engine mounting points strengthened further.

TOLEMAN
Ran a new intercooler in left-hand side pod to cool air for engine.

ALFA ROMEO
New turbo inlet ducts, incorporating a scoop cut into top of side pod and a fin to direct passage of air. Bodywork in front of rear tyre modified to allow hot air to escape more efficiently. Shorter profile to underbody. Exhausts shorter with larger diameter pipes.

LIGIER
New lightweight chassis, with lighter bodywork, for Laffite. Underbody at rear of de Cesaris's car reduced in length for race.

ZAKSPEED
A second car available with a stiffer chassis and minor revisions to tub shape, side pods and underbody. The chassis was heavier but, overall, the car was lighter.

FERRARI
Two new chassis featuring modifications to front suspension. Front shock absorbers had revised lower mounting points and an opening cut in top bodywork to facilitate their removal. Different mounting point for lower front wishbone. Modifications tested on Friday, along with a smaller inlet duct for turbo. Opted to use 'standard' T-car (079) for remainder of weekend. Another unmodified car (081 – used for Silverstone test) brought into action. All cars had new rear wing fixing points on mounting tube.

MINARDI
Brought chassis repaired after shunt in Canada. A problem with pressure at the turbo wastegate meant adjustments had to be made by hand and not mechanically as before. GP

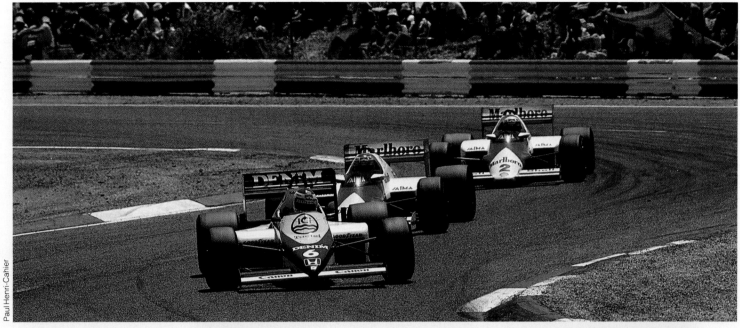

Paul Henri-Cahier

Wing Commander. Keke Rosberg engaged in a superb battle with the McLarens of Niki Lauda and Alain Prost, the Williams driver, running less rear wing than his rivals, proving difficult to pass on the straights.

The End is Nigh. Drastic revision of the Renault RE60 failed to change the French team's fortunes at home.

Gordon Murray (opposite) helped mastermind a commanding victory for Nelson Piquet, Brabham and Pirelli.

Agence de Presse Rougier

untested spare 014 after a turbo failure and fire on Friday afternoon, a problem which repeated itself the following day. Team-mate Stefan Bellof resigned himself to a tail-end weekend with the sole Cosworth car in the race and lined up at the back – a full 12 seconds slower than Rosberg's pole-position Williams!

Fading turbo boost pressure also hampered Formula 1 returnee Jonathan Palmer. The Doc was now equipped with a spare Zakspeed 841 for the first time, which featured a six-speed gearbox and digital instrumentation. He qualified respectably just behind Brundle and ahead of Philippe Alliot's RAM, while Piercarlo Ghinzani's minimally financed works Osella and Pierluigi Martini's Minardi completed the grid ahead of the turbo-less Bellof!

RACE

Notwithstanding the sweltering weather, the attraction of the French Grand Prix was sufficient to lure the spectators away from the tempting nearby beaches in their droves, an enormous crowd clogging up the inadequate turnstiles outside the circuit from an early hour. The warm-up followed a familiar pattern with Prost and Lauda at the head of the pack, but Piquet was third from de Angelis and the two Ligiers. Clearly, things were looking up for Pirelli . . .

At the end of the first warm-up lap, Nelson Piquet drove straight into the pits to confer with Gordon Murray: his BT54's gearchange did not feel quite right, so the decision was made to transfer him to the spare car which was all ready and waiting for just such a contingency. It was a promising omen: Piquet's last victory, at Detroit a year earlier, had been scored at the wheel of his spare BT53 after his race car had been 'wiped out' in the multiple startline accident.

With Rosberg and Senna crouching ominously together on the front row, the Williams and Lotus rivals led the 25 cars out of the slow right-hander and up to the starting light gantry. They paused, the light blinked red, then green, and they were away – Senna just getting the jump on his rival as they passed the end of the pits, but Keke easing into the fast kink at the head of the pack. Down near the back of the grid, Fabi, Brundle and Palmer all had difficulty getting off the line, but eventually scampered away amidst the course cars which pursued the field on its first frantic lap.

Down the *Mistral* straight Rosberg pulled out about ten lengths on Senna, the Williams-Honda blaring through to complete the opening lap well ahead of the Lotus, with Piquet third, then Alboreto, de Angelis, Lauda, Prost, de Cesaris, Berger, Warwick, Tambay and the rest. Second time round, on a clean track surface, Piquet set his own personal fastest race lap and most other front runners also recorded their individual quickest laps in that opening sprint on new tyres before any debris went down.

Paying the penalty, perhaps, of trying to run excessive boost pressure to produce a good showing in front of the home crowd, the Ligier JS25s both expired a few miles into the race. Laffite was out on lap three with turbo failure, while de Cesaris stopped in front of the pits with a broken driveshaft two laps later. By the end of lap four Rosberg had pulled out a couple of seconds' lead over his rivals, but he was to need every bit of this advantage as Piquet was sizing up Senna for second place, the Brabham eventually nipping through in a dramatic run down the inside of the *Signes* braking area on lap seven. This was a particularly ambitious thing to do bearing in mind that Alboreto's Ferrari had expired in a dramatic cloud of oil smoke at this point two laps earlier, generously lubricating the surface of the 190 mph corner and spelling *finis* to the prospect of any more really quick laps for the time being.

On lap nine Piquet came through on Rosberg's tail, having closed the gap to the Williams with no difficulty at all, while Senna's run was punctuated by a quick pit visit to sort out a sticking third gear, this delay losing him virtually a full lap on the leading Williams. Undaunted, Ayrton rejoined at the tail of the field and began lapping with all the

purpose of a race leader . . .

Rosberg pulled every trick in the book to stay ahead of the Pirelli-shod Brabham, fighting like a tiger through the twisty infield section, but it was to no avail. The Williams-Honda was a match for the Brabham-BMW in terms of straightline speed, but Piquet had significantly better grip through the infield. When it came to displacing Rosberg, the Brabham team leader simply drove inside him just before the apex of a tricky right-hander shortly before the pits. Sliding wide over the kerb, Keke tried to come back immediately at his rival but Piquet had equal power with superior grip. That was the end of the battle.

'From that point onwards I could dictate the pace of the race', confessed Nelson afterwards: 'it was really no problem'. And that's the way it looked from the sidelines as Rosberg now occupied himself by fending off the advances from Lauda and Prost when the McLaren duo drew up onto the Williams's tail in tight red-and-white formation. Niki was slightly quicker through the infield, but there was nothing in it in terms of straightline speed. On a couple of occasions, the World Champion poked his McLaren's nose alongside Keke's right-rear wheel as they went into *Signes*, but it was going to take a more aggressive move than this to worry the unflustered Finn.

With 20 laps completed de Angelis was fifth behind the two McLarens, while Derek Warwick's early stint in sixth place had come to an end when he stopped for fresh tyres. The Englishman had started the race on softer 'B' compound Goodyears as his RE60 had proved 'so awful on the harder race rubber when I tried it in practice'. Derek was well aware that he would have to stop for fresh tyres, but spent the balance of the race wondering why he had bothered when the replacement set lost grip so quickly that the delay seemed hardly worth his while!

Warwick's delay briefly allowed Tambay's RE60B up into sixth place, but the Frenchman was suffering from bronchitis and oversteer in fairly equal doses, so it wasn't long before Surer's Brabham nipped past. Boutsen was now eighth ahead of Johansson's wildly understeering Ferrari, followed by Berger, the recovering Warwick and then Brundle with Fabi quite close behind. The ill-handling Alfas were now a long way back, their drivers working out their frustrations on each other in a time-wasting, wheel-banging battle which raged for the first part of the race.

On lap 16 Martini nearly took Lauda out of the race when he chopped across in front of the McLaren at the fast kink beyond the pits, Niki veering up the kerb as he sought to avoid the wayward Italian car. The young Italian pulled the same stunt on Tambay's Renault a few laps later before eliminating both his Minardi and Berger's Arrows in a tangle on the 21st lap. Neither man was hurt, but Gerhard walked away seething with indignation.

By the end of lap 30 Piquet had built up a 16-second advantage over Rosberg. On the same lap, Lauda's McLaren suffered transmission failure as he went back on the power turning out of the right-hander before the pits and he coasted to an immediate stop opposite the timing line. That left Prost with a clear run at Rosberg and since Alain had opted for a harder left-front tyre compound than Keke, it wasn't long before the Frenchman was scrambling all over the Williams. On lap 40, Prost eventually sprinted through on the inside going into the *Verrerie* kink beyond the pits in a manoeuvre which even impressed Rosberg. Keke immediately took the decision that fresh rubber was required and dived straight into the pit lane to change – a fine piece of judgement which would pay off in the dying seconds of the race!

Meanwhile, Senna's afternoon had come to a spectacular end on lap 27 as he climbed back through the mid-field runners. The engine of his Lotus blew up spectacularly going into *Signes* and he spun violently on his own oil! The 97T hurtled through the catch-fencing and into the tyre barrier on the outside of the corner as Ayrton kept his head down 'and took my hands off the wheel

remembering what happened to me at Detroit . . .' He stepped out unscathed and the monocoque stood up extremely well to the impact.

With a clear track ahead of him to Piquet's Brabham, Prost began making inroads into the Brazilian's advantage once he had passed Rosberg, though this progress was to last for only five or six laps. Alain suddenly found that his engine had developed a tendency to die at low revs, so he was having to keep his right foot on the throttle whilst braking and gear changing, this frantic ballet reducing his progress towards the leading Brabham.

Rosberg, now back in ferocious action on fresh rubber, began rattling off a whole series of fastest race laps in the sprint to the finish. Prost, far from challenging Piquet, now had to sit there and watch his second place advantage being gobbled up relentlessly by the Williams. As Piquet cruised home to a convincing and worthy victory, Alain was unable to prevent Rosberg from slamming by on the very last lap to take second place. 'It couldn't have been easy for him', remarked Keke generously afterwards, 'but he was never tempted to make it difficult for me'.

De Angelis, who later complained that turning up the boost pressure made precious little difference to his flat-as-a-pancake engine, must have known how Prost felt. On the very last lap Elio saw Johansson's Ferrari coming up behind on the *Mistral* straight and he 'wound the boost off the dial' to stay ahead. It didn't work. Stefan lunged his way round the outside at *Signes* in an audacious manoeuvre which was rewarded with fourth place. De Angelis, distraught and irritated, just couldn't believe what was happening to him . . .

Sixth place fell to Tambay's unimpressive Renault RE60B, while Warwick was seventh and Marc Surer a lapped eighth. The other BT54 had been up to fifth at one point, but Marc had opted for too soft a choice of rubber and found his BMW over-revving madly when running in the slipstream of another car. This eventually led to a valve-spring breakage, so he was lucky to stagger home at all.

Boutsen was classified ninth ahead of Cheever and Patrese, both Alfas having stopped for fresh tyres during the race. Winkelhock was three laps behind in 12th spot, grappling with gear selection trouble and boost pressure which almost faded to nothing at one point, while Bellof was 13th and Fabi classified 14th despite running out of fuel four laps from the finish. Alliot's RAM had been an early retirement with loss of fuel pressure, while Brundle's Tyrrell succumbed to gear selection trouble following his climb through the field to hold 10th place briefly behind Warwick's Renault.

A.H.

Paul Henri-Cahier

Marlboro British Grand Prix

This was the half-way mark in the season and a mere 78 minutes of racing were all that was needed to encapsulate what had been going on during the previous 15 weeks.

Alain Prost won by over a lap and the nine points put the consistent Frenchman into a strong second place in the Championship. He was now five points behind Michele Alboreto, the Ferrari driver never in serious contention at Silverstone but yet poised to pick up a rather fortunate six points for second place.

In fact, the race should have belonged to Ayrton Senna, the Lotus driver making a brilliant start and fending off challenges from Keke Rosberg's pole sitting Williams and Prost's McLaren. A broken wire on his Renault engine was to rob Senna yet again and, while this may have followed the familiar pattern of events, Elio de Angelis was destined to break his consistent run of points scoring with a mysterious electrical problem which would make the Lotus team's miserable day complete.

Rosberg's record-breaking pole position lap of 160.90 mph indicated that the race would be one of fuel consumption figures and tactical driving but carefully laid plans were to be upset by a last-minute piece of ineptitude by the RAC as their man with the chequered flag elected to stop the race one lap too soon.

This action ensured that Jacques Laffite took third place since the Ligier driver was destined to roll to a halt two corners later while Derek Warwick was also blessed by circumstance as he coasted across the line, his Renault out of fuel but safely into fifth place. Had the race run the full distance, Nelson Piquet, classified fourth, would have demoted Laffite. As it was, the three points moved Piquet into sixth place in the Championship but the failure of the other leading contenders to score allowed Alboreto and Prost to pull away slightly at the head of a table which, until now, had been notable for its unpredictability.

British bungling. Alain Prost receives the chequered flag one lap too soon, but the nine points moved the McLaren driver into serious contention for the Championship.

ENTRY AND PRACTICE

Friday's practice was nothing short of a shambles and it set the scene for what would be a muddled weekend terminated by organisational bungling. The warm weather which usually attends Silverstone deserted the Grand Prix, grey cloud swirling across the flat expanses of Northamptonshire as the teams waited for practice to start at 10 a.m. on Friday morning. The low cloud prevented the medical helicopter from arriving and the untimed practice was postponed. In any case, sheeting rain would have made venturing out an unpleasant business and the track remained silent until lunchtime.

It was announced that the 90-minute session had been cancelled and, in its place, there would be an untimed half hour at 1.45 p.m. with the hour of qualifying taking place at four. This did not appeal to some teams who, understandably, did not wish to have their mechanics working all hours of the night.

A revised schedule was then issued. There would be 20 minutes of untimed practice, followed by a 10-minute break, with the qualifying session at 2.15. This appeased the original objectors and raised criticism from other quarters. But it would be the same for every team and the conditions would obviously suit the most professional, quick-witted members of the pit lane.

The drivers were barely comfortable in their cars when the untimed session was over. Very little had been learned and, even so, there was no time to implement changes for the qualifying session. A driver's ability to go out and make the most of what was available to him would be all-important; ideal conditions for Keke Rosberg.

As the track began to dry, Keke recorded 1m 17.055s, followed by de Angelis, Surer and Johansson. The times, as such, were not truly representative and everyone hoped better weather on Saturday would allow the leaders to approach the magic 160 mph mark hinted at during testing.

In fact, the weather the following day fluctuated from rain to bouts of sunshine but the all-important final hour started dry. Then, after 20 minutes, there came a light shower with the track drying rapidly as the session drew to an end; conditions which would provide a spectacular finish to an unsettled two days.

All eyes were on Rosberg as he set off on the dry track with his first set of qualifiers. The rain was beginning to fall as he reached Woodcote, the lap of 1m 5.967s ending with a kerb-thumping moment which must have hindered rather than helped. In fact, we were to learn later that the left-front tyre on the Williams was deflating slowly but, whatever his problem, Rosberg had reached the 160 mph barrier. The rain which followed seemed to have sealed his pole position.

However, the fresh winds soon dispersed the clouds and the racing line began to dry. With nine minutes remaining, Piquet took to the track. He had no choice since his practice on Friday had been disrupted by an engine failure and he needed to improve on 11th place. With the track still damp at the 150 mph Stowe corner, Nelson cut a superb

lap of 1m 6.249s. Not long after, Senna produced a 1m 6.794s. Rosberg reached for his helmet. There were five minutes left.

In one of those brilliant virtuoso displays which had become the Finnish driver's hallmark, he lapped the still-damp 2.932-mile track in 65.591 seconds.

The crowd rose to applaud such brilliance. It had been worth waiting to see and, with rumours gathering force that the Silverstone track would soon be altered in the interests of safety, there was the feeling that those present had witnessed Rosberg carve himself a slice of history. This was the fastest lap ever recorded by a formula 1 car at any circuit during a race meeting.

No sooner had Rosberg set his time than the session was over. It was time to assess the rest of the grid.

July:
Ferrari threaten switch to CART racing due to FISA's suggested unscheduled changes to F1 technical rules (pop-off valves, reduction in turbocharger size, the introduction of 1200 cc engines in 1987 instead of 1988) to cut costs and speeds.

WEC teams say they will not participate in two races which clash with Grands Prix on rescheduled F1 calendar unless dates are changed. Brands Hatch WEC round is subsequently changed but Fuji organisers remain firm.

Roberto Moreno tests Toleman at the Nürburgring.

Michigan 500 CART race postponed because of tyre failures during practice.

Williams re-sign Mansell for 1986

Piquet retained second place, his time having been achieved in spite of the need to run round the outside of Patrese – at Stowe! With the memories of Ricard still lingering, the Piquet/Brabham-BMW/Pirelli combination was something of a wild card, provided the conditions were warm.

Alain Prost's form was more predictable, particularly as the McLaren was to be found on the second row. The surprise was that the Frenchman had set this time on Friday (after using a set of race tyres before finally recording his time on qualifiers). On Saturday, he found the spare car (fitted with the larger turbos for qualifying) to be down on power, so he sat out the rest of the session knowing that it would be a waste of time attempting to improve with the race car.

However, Prost's anticipated confidence for Sunday was eroded by worries about the handling of his car in race trim, a concern which was shared by team-mate Niki Lauda. The Austrian was down in tenth place with a time from Friday, as he had been unable to run the larger KKK turbos. There was no hope of improving in the final session: not only was his engine a thousand revs down, but also he was baulked by Patrese.

Ayrton Senna had similar problems with traffic on Saturday but his two days of practice had been littered with a series of mechanical problems which conspired to keep the favourite for the race in fourth place. Ayrton's time had been set on Friday, the frustration of trying to operate in half the time usually available having been compounded by engine problems with his qualifying car, a switch to the race car with the less favourable EF15 engine, locking brakes and a slide on oil while setting his time with, incidentally, Cs on the left and qualifying tyres on the right of his 97T! Saturday was more straightforward. The handling was good but the Renault engine cut out and his left-rear qualifier had lost its grip before the end of his lap.

As for Elio de Angelis, he was in eighth place (again, with Friday's time). There had been no time to fit the larger Garrett turbos for the first qualifying session and, when they were added for final practice, Elio guessed wrongly on his gear ratios, particularly third which was too long to give him maximum power while exiting the chicane.

Fifth place for Nigel Mansell was a tribute to the Englishman's tenacity and resilience. Not only was his lap of 1m 6.675s on Saturday an excellent time in the circumstances (the third fastest on the day) but it also represented a great psychological victory as Mansell recovered from his accident during practice for the French Grand Prix. Although he had been pronounced fit, shrugging off the effects of a 200 mph accident is not the work of a moment. Mansell needed time behind the wheel, which is why he chose to run two sets of race tyres on Friday although, even then, his progress was halted by an exploding clutch. There were no such problems on Saturday and his lap merited unstinted praise from Rosberg.

Mansell's performance pushed Alboreto into sixth place and underlined the problems being experienced by Ferrari as they appeared to lose their competitive edge. Apart from switching from

Basking in an Indian Summer. Jacques Laffite gave his usual enthusiastic performance on race day to take third place for Ligier (far left).
Photo: John Colley
Memorable moment – Keke Rosberg setting a stunning 160 mph pole-position lap (left).
Photo: John Townsend
Prost, happy to finish first; Alboreto, lucky to finish second.
Rostrum photo: Nigel Snowdon
Johansson, hardly got started.
Main picture: John Colley

the understeer (which had plagued them in France) to sudden bouts of oversteer, the Ferraris were also losing out in the horsepower stakes, a problem which was aggravated when larger rear wings were fitted on Saturday to cure the oversteer. Alboreto did not improve but the extra two-tenths found by Johansson were only good enough for 11th place.

A wholesale improvement for Andrea de Cesaris early in the final session saw the Ligier driver jump from 21st to seventh, Andrea expressing himself pleased with the Pirelli qualifiers although he had reservations about their race rubber. Jacques Laffite, with no major problems to report on Saturday, was down in 16th place.

Taking a backward step on Saturday, Teo Fabi slipped from sixth to ninth place, which was a pity since the Toleman looked impressive through the corners. Any hopes of improving had been ruled out when the team missed the dry start to the final session thanks to a late finish to a gear ratio change. Renault, by comparison, were suffering from severe handling problems with the RE60B, a fact confirmed by Derek Warwick since he now had a new chassis at his disposal. His experience with the new car had been limited to a few laps of Donington and any hopes of running through basic setting-up procedures on Friday were dashed by the rain. Warwick complained that he was unable to take either Maggotts or Abbey flat-out while Tambay had a turbo fail on Friday. Patrick improved on Saturday but the French cars were due to start from 12th and 13th places; hardly an encouraging prospect in view of the continuing rumours over the team's future.

Euroracing were in a similar state of unease over their future and things were not helped by the usual spate of turbo failures, necessitating Cheever and Patrese to share cars from time to time. Eddie's rash of engine problems meant he had to sit out the dry part of Saturday while a turbo was changed and his very last lap of qualifying was just good enough for 22nd place. Riccardo was slightly better off in 14th place, half a second quicker than Marc Surer who suffered rear wheel bearing failures on both days of practice.

The Arrows team were surprisingly far back, Gerhard Berger and Thierry Boutsen split by the RAM-Hart of Manfred Winkelhock. The Belgian had suffered a major engine failure on Friday but, generally, the Barclay cars had handling bothers while Winkelhock's two days of practice had been riddled with problems ranging from an electrical fault to engine misfires and, finally, an engine failure and a small fire. Team-mate Alliot had to contend with a broken fuel pump drive belt and a misfire. The Frenchman took 21st place.

Martin Brundle and the Tyrrell team continued to feel their way with the 014 turbo although Martin briefly lost his sense of direction on Friday when he spun at the exit of Woodcote! The curtailed practice meant a loss of valuable development time although Brundle felt he would have been higher than 20th had his front qualifying tyres not gone off by the time he reached the last corner on what was his best lap. Stefan Bellof, meanwhile, persevered with the

160 mph Man. Keke Rosberg waits in the pits between record-shattering performances during practice. Mechanical problems dropped the Williams-Honda from contention in the race.

DFY, the 012 being almost 30 mph slower than Rosberg's Honda through the speed trap on the start/finish line.

Pierluigi Martini, 23rd fastest in the Minardi, added to his already dubious reputation by parking his blown-up car at the apex of Copse on Saturday morning and then thoughtfully walking off with the steering wheel. Doubtless he had become accustomed to such precautions while racing in Italy! In the meantime, his action meant marshals were unable to remove the stricken car and practice had to be stopped . . .

That left Piercarlo Ghinzani, struggling with the dreadfully under-financed Osella, and Jonathan Palmer whose practice was filled with a number of irritating problems such as a loose timing gear, fuel mixture problems, gear selection difficulties and a loss of turbo boost during qualifying.

In the meantime, the media eulogised Rosberg's performance and it took a rather sombre Frank Williams to put everything in perspective. 'Yes, it's good', he agreed. 'But tomorrow is far more important.'

RACE

A quick glance along the pit lane during the race morning warm-up gave an accurate indication of what was in store later in the day. There was ordered calm in the McLaren pit as overnight changes to the cars appeared to have been successful; Prost and Lauda setting the pace. Meanwhile, there was all manner of drama down at Lotus. De Angelis had returned with his right-rear wheel at a drunken angle, this as a result of Pierluigi Martini making an abysmal attempt to tuck in behind the Lotus as de Angelis went by. Elio was transferred to the spare car but was soon back to have a loose fixing on the instrument panel attended to. Meanwhile, mecha-

nics dived into the cockpit of Ayrton Senna's car in an attempt to ease a stiff gear linkage.

Lotus mechanics had straightened out Elio's car in time for the start but Rosberg was to make a last-minute swap to his spare car when a freshly installed Honda engine misfired. Similarly, Teo Fabi switched to his T-car when a gearbox oil cooler split during the final warm-up lap.

The morning session had shown four Pirelli-shod cars in the first eight and, as far as Goodyear were concerned, all their runners chose the C compound, with the exception of Mansell who opted to use the harder B.

Brundle was stranded on the grid as the field began the final parade lap but the Renault technician managed to coax the V6 into life in time for Martin to take off in pursuit of the rest. He caught them on Hanger Straight but the Tyrrell driver wisely resisted the temptation to slide easily into his rightful position. As Watson had found to his cost in South Africa in 1983, that could lead to disqualification. Brundle started from the back.

At the front, Senna made a beautiful start from the outside of the second row, the Lotus driver powering past Piquet and confidently taking his line into Copse to ease Rosberg into second place. Realising he had to fight back immediately, otherwise the black-and-gold car would be out of sight, Keke attacked into Becketts and made serious moves to out-brake into Stowe. Senna was unmoved. He held his line – and the lead.

Tambay, meanwhile, had lost his line at the first corner. Running round the outside after a storming start, Patrick lost control, the Renault slewing sideways before shooting into the middle of the pack. Johansson saw the accident coming but was powerless to prevent the impact as the Renault smashed into the left-hand side pod of the Ferrari. Tambay limped onto the grass while his right-front wheel bounced across the track, causing Alliot to take drastic avoiding action, bringing him into collision with the hapless Ghinzani. First corner – and four cars out.

Johansson, in fact, had carried on since he could see little damage from the cockpit and all his wheels appeared to be attached to the car. Unwittingly, he was depositing oil around the circuit and the V6 seized solid just as he reached the pit lane.

Senna had a clear view of the oil and he moved off line where necessary. He was rather alarmed, however, to note that the slippery surface did little to deter Rosberg from darting and weaving in his mirrors as they pulled away from Mansell and Prost. The McLaren driver was thinking seriously about attacking the Williams when he suddenly found Johansson's oil on the braking area for Becketts and he did well to scramble round the third-gear corner. In the meantime, de Cesaris had moved into a remarkable fourth place while Prost had recovered in time to hold off Piquet.

De Angelis was seventh, having overtaken Alboreto on lap 2; Warwick was ninth ahead of Fabi (soon to retire with a broken pinion), Surer, Cheever (an incredible start, the Alfa making up nine places in the first lap!), Berger, Patrese, Lauda (already making up for a dreadful start),

Philippe Alliot gets his RAM broadside and collects
Ghinzani's Kelemata Osella after avoiding
Tamhay's front wheel (left).
Williams attack. Rosberg attempts to wrest the lead
from Senna while Mansell and Prost dispute third
place during the opening lap. All bar Prost were due
to retire (below left).
Derek Warwick's first outing with the Renault
RE60B ended in silence, the Englishman coasting
into fifth place. Bernie Ecclestone (extreme right)
appears to object to the impromptu parking below
the Brabham pit (bottom).

Laffite, Boutsen, Palmer (soaring ahead with
plenty of boost knowing that his engine was
unlikely to last), Brundle (having made a swift
start from the back but dropping two places when
he understeered on the oil at Stowe), Winkelhock,
Bellof and Martini.

After four laps, Senna and Rosberg had pulled
out five seconds on Mansell as the Williams, whose
B compounds were struggling for grip on the
greasy surface, fell back towards the Ligier and
the McLaren. Soon they were ahead of Mansell,
Prost then neatly out-braking de Cesaris for third
place at the end of lap nine. With a clear track
ahead of him, Prost set about establishing new
records by the lap as he closed on the leaders.

Just as it looked as though it would be a
three-way fight for the lead, Rosberg took the
decision to ease off. 'At the speed Senna was
running', said Keke, 'I couldn't stay with him – not
without destroying my tyres. I had to let him go.
There was nothing else for it.' By lap 14, Prost was
on Rosberg's tail and into second place two laps
later. Ahead lay Senna, motoring on serenely with
a cushion of several seconds. Would the Lotus
last?

The first chink in the JPS armour had come on
lap 13. And, against all odds, it was Elio de Angelis
who crept slowly into the pit lane, his engine dead.
Assuming his race was run, Elio climbed from the
car and walked towards the motor-home to
contemplate his first failure to finish in the points
since the 1984 European Grand Prix. The Renault
technicians removed the monitoring equipment in
the hope of finding an explanation. There was
none. They then tried firing up the engine. It burst
into life with no trouble at all. After a delay of 34
minutes, de Angelis returned to the track, his car
running better than ever . . .

Meanwhile, we had lost Mansell, the Englishman retiring from fifth place with a repeat of the
clutch trouble which had bothered Williams
during practice. A pity, in view of Mansell's brave
recovery and the fact that his hard B tyres were
now coming into their own. And that was not all.
Four laps later, Rosberg disappeared from the lap
charts, his FW10 pulling off when a cracked
exhaust pipe (manufactured by Williams) caused
a loss of boost.

The exit of the Williams team gave the
leader-board a new look. After 22 laps, Senna led
Prost by five seconds; Lauda had slipped unobtrusively into third place; de Cesaris was next, with
Piquet fifth and Alboreto not far behind in sixth
place. Eight laps later and the entire field bar
these had been lapped by the leaders as Senna and
Prost set a furious pace.

Each time Prost closed, Senna would ease away,
fuelling speculation that he was turning up the
boost to do so. Subsequent examination of the
on-board monitoring equipment would show Peter
Warr and his colleagues that Senna was leaving
Prost behind on sheer driving skill alone.

On lap 28, Alboreto caught and passed Piquet,
the only piece of racing the Ferrari driver would
take part in all afternoon, and this purely because
Nelson's fuel monitoring device had broken and he
had no idea how much fuel remained in the BT54's
tank. As the Monte Carlo neighbours had their

TECHNICAL FILE

McLAREN
Briefly tried vertical aerofoils behind front wheels on Friday (used fixing plates rather than tubes seen on Lotus). Total of 13 TAG engines present at Silverstone.

TYRRELL
Used front wings with a Delta section. One chassis fitted with AP carbon-fibre discs.

WILLIAMS
New chassis for Mansell to replace car destroyed in France. Now the only team running without 'snorkel' air intake for turbos (although Williams had tried them in Brazil). Honda engines had single inlet from plenum chamber instead of two.

Not again! A broken wire on the Renault engine robbed Ayrton Senna of a place on the rostrum after the Lotus driver had dominated most of the race. The stunned Brazilian abandons his car in front of the Tyrrell and Toleman pits.

private battle, they soon became embroiled in the story of the race as the leaders closed in, locked in a superb duel of tactics and racecraft.

The pressure was firmly on Senna: one wrong move while lapping a slower car and Prost would box him in, overtake and force Senna to use boost and fuel to get back on even terms. Ayrton, despite his relative inexperience, made no mistakes. Approaching Woodcote, he took Piquet who then denied Prost room at the following corner. By Stowe, Senna had passed Alboreto while Prost languished behind Piquet. Clearly, the pressure was on the McLaren now. He took Piquet at Woodcote and swooped past Alboreto at Copse but, by now, Senna was seizing his advantage. Prost had no option but to turn up his boost and give chase, setting his fastest lap as he did so.

On lap 48, Senna recorded his fastest lap of the race to pull out a gap of two seconds over Prost. Then, two laps later, the complexion of the race began to change; Senna's engine sounded flat as he passed the pits. The problem cleared itself almost immediately only to return as he left Copse on lap 58. Prost was on his tail in an instant, darting into the lead as they swept through Becketts. Senna's race was run.

Or was it? Once again, the engine cleared and Ayrton hauled back into contention. Completing the lap nose-to-tail, the leaders swept past the long-since abandoned Ligier of de Cesaris, an exploding clutch having ended the Italian's fine run. As Prost and Senna carried on their breathtaking duel, there were two more retirements: Boutsen crashed without injury when his throttle jammed at Becketts, and Lauda's electronics played up causing the third-place man to slow just as he was about to be lapped.

Indeed, Niki inadvertently caused Prost to lift slightly as they powered through Becketts and that was all Senna needed to take a shot at passing the McLaren on the approach to Stowe. The crowd were on their feet.

Senna led the next lap but then, leaving Copse, the engine faltered once more and Prost was through. This time, there would be no remission, a stunned Senna crawling round to coast to a poignant halt under the noses of the shocked Lotus team.

What had gone wrong this time? A wire running from the heat sensor on the right-hand exhaust had broken and, as a result, the electronic fuel injection had caused the right-hand bank of the V6 to run rich. The Lotus, quite simply, had run out of fuel.

Prost was now a lap clear of the next man who was . . . let's see, Senna out, Lauda retired, de Cesaris retired, Rosberg out, Mansell retired . . . it had to be Alboreto. It could have been anyone since the Ferrari driver's race bore no resemblance to what had been going on at the front of the field. With Prost some four miles ahead of the Italian it was hardly surprising that the man with the chequered flag became confused.

Ignoring the multi-million pound computerised back-up in nearby race control, the official assumed his lap chart was correct – and waved the chequered flag one lap too soon. Adopting a more professional approach, Prost noted that the official's counterpart on the left-hand side of the track had not waved his flag and this supported the McLaren pit board informing Prost that there was one lap to go. He wisely completed another tour before pulling up at the end of the pits.

Alboreto duly collected his 'bonus' six points while Jacques Laffite found himself in third place as he passed the chequered flag. Jacques blessed the official's incompetence as the Ligier rolled to a halt out of fuel and the Brabham team were quick to instigate a protest since Piquet and Surer were fourth and sixth on the road and each would have moved up one place had the race run its prescribed distance.

The verdict at the end of the day was 'human error' – in which case, sorry chaps, but the results stand. It left Prost to speculate on the 'human error' which caused his car to be a couple of kilogrammes below the limit at Imola. The officials took nine points from him for that indiscretion. But, at least there were no mistakes today and the well-earned points put him back in serious contention for the Championship.

M.H.

BRABHAM

All three cars fitted with Garrett turbos. Piquet's car fitted with driver-activated electronic system in nose to monitor engine. Spare car new to replace chassis destroyed by fire during testing at the Nürburgring.

RAM

New chassis with stiffer construction for Winkelhock. Tried carbon-fibre brakes.

LOTUS

All three cars fitted with turbo air inlet ducts at rear of side pods. Used secondary rear wings but only de Angelis opted to use rear winglets. Both race cars fitted with vertical front wings.

RENAULT

Both drivers now had RE60B chassis with EF15 qualifying engines available. Tried 'snorkel' turbo air inlets.

ARROWS

All three cars fitted with lower, secondary rear wing. Continued with KKK turbos. Additional heat protection around gearbox.

TOLEMAN

Continued testing with electronic injection. Not used for race.

ALFA ROMEO

Reverted to '84-spec cars. Cheever ran chassis used in winter testing and in Brazil featuring 1984 chassis and front suspension but with 1985 rear suspension and side pods. This was the result of back-to-back testing at Balocco. Prepared to try carbon-fibre brakes on Patrese's car but plans abandoned because of rain during practice.

OSELLA

Shorter underbody profile. Used gas Koni shock absorbers.

LIGIER

All three cars fitted with lighter bodywork (T-car still had heavier chassis). Fitted vertical front aerofoils for race.

FERRARI

New chassis seen at Ricard not brought to Silverstone. Radiator position moved to allow more air to flow to intercooler. Tried different type of intercooler and different rear wings.

MINARDI

New chassis. Fitted 'snorkel' air inlet ducts on side pods.

ZAKSPEED

T-car fitted with a new electronic ignition made by Zakspeed in Detroit and used in IMSA racing; it proved unsuccessful during practice. Six-speed gearbox fitted. New exhaust and rear wing.

Nigel Snowdon

Grosser Preis von Deutschland

Michele Alboreto was in an emotional mood as he walked into the Marlboro motor-home after the German Grand Prix. Coming face to face with team-mate Stefan Johansson he grabbed him by the arm. 'I'm so sorry', said Michele, 'I just couldn't believe what was happening. I thought "Oh no, not Stefan . . . anybody but Stefan . . ." But there was no way I could avoid you.' The Swede just shrugged his shoulders. 'Don't worry about it. At least you won the race for us.'

That was how Alboreto and Johansson debated the unfortunate first-corner incident which deprived the Swede of any chance of victory in a race at where he had started from second place on the front row. As he dived into the first right-hander, holding third place behind Ayrton Senna's Lotus 97T and Keke Rosberg's Williams FW10, Johansson was savaged from behind by his team-mate. The left-hand nose fin of Alboreto's Ferrari sliced the right-rear Goodyear on Johansson's sister car, sending Stefan into the pit lane at the end of the opening lap. When he resumed, running just ahead of the leaders but almost a lap behind them, Johansson pulled away in commanding fashion. It was one of the great 'might have been' episodes of the 1985 season.

So Michele Alboreto won the German Grand Prix – after Senna's Lotus suffered driveshaft troubles; after Rosberg's Williams had brake trouble; after de Angelis's Lotus blew up; after Prost's down-on-power McLaren spun due to fading brakes. Smoking gently on right-handers, Alboreto's Ferrari survived.

And survival was what this 67-lap thrash round the new Nürburgring was all about . . .

Michele Alboreto survived a first-corner brush with his team-mate, as well as constant attacks during the race, to score a somewhat fortunate nine points once Rosberg and Senna had retired (left).
In view of the political conflict at the beginning of the season, Teo Fabi and the Toleman team took great pleasure from keeping pole position for Pirelli when it rained during the final practice session.

ENTRY AND PRACTICE

Nine months earlier, the focal point of everybody's attention had been on the Prost-versus-Lauda fight for the '84 title. Now, in the height of a German summer, the Grand Prix fraternity was back in the Eifel mountains for the German Grand Prix, not the Grand Prix of Europe, as the new circuit's Formula 1 debut had been titled the previous autumn. A stone's throw away from the old *Nordschleife* in geographical terms, the new Nürburgring might well be on another planet as far as concept and detail design is concerned. The ultimate in sanitised, anaesthetised autodromes, the track may indeed endure into the 1990s unchanged from the point of view of safety and security. But, for all that, it is unlikely to become a place the dyed-in-the-wool enthusiast will warm to. It remains bland and featureless, notwithstanding its atmosphere of Teutonic order and efficiency.

However, no amount of technical planning could protect the track from the vagaries of the Eifel weather. Those ready to go – and to go quickly – on Friday found themselves richly rewarded. Others, grappling with technical problems and difficult handling, faced a cold wall of steady rain for much of Saturday's two sessions. And the man who set the paddock on its ear on Friday afternoon was the diminutive Teo Fabi. The introspective little Italian with the morose expression found his Pirelli-shod Toleman TG185 just the ticket for the fast sweeps of this artificial track, squeezing every ounce of performance from his Hart-propelled bolide to grab what was to remain pole position for the German Grand Prix.

It was an impressive performance, without doubt. Nelson Piquet's Michelin-shod Brabham BT53 had buttoned-up pole for the '84 GP of Europe with a 1m 18.871s best but Fabi improved on that by more than a second to take the first Formula 1 pole of his career. For Toleman, mentally bruised and battered after being used as a political football during the off-season, it was a sweet, sweet moment. They were on pole – on Pirellis. And that was a feat that Brabham, Pirelli's big-budget, prestige frontline operation, had yet to manage.

Fabi's performance was the result of no sudden, magic ingredient. The Toleman-Hart partnership had simply caught up much of the ground lost during the great tyre supply crisis earlier in the year. Fabi's form in the following few races was to prove this no fluke.

Not that the team was without its problems, of course. With pole in the bag, Fabi lost control of the spare TG185 in the rain the following afternoon as he accelerated through the right-hander onto the pit straight. As the Italian changed up, the car snapped away from him as it hit a puddle, plunging off into the guard rail on the right. Unfortunately the TG185 nose box slipped under the bottom of the guard rail (where the gap was too large) and the leading edge of the monocoque took the brunt of the impact, writing the car out of the team's equation for the rest of the weekend. That left Fabi with his race car plus a second spare which, en route to a test at Monza,

was diverted to the Nürburgring to take over its new role.

There was a touch of irony over the fact that Stefan Johansson's Ferrari joined Fabi on the front row: the genial Swede had been released from his Toleman contract in order to go to Maranello at a time when it seemed unlikely the TG185 would ever see the light of competitive day. Johansson admitted he was pretty pleased with his car's balance at the Nürburgring: 'a touch of understeer, perhaps, but nothing really to worry about. I reckon we're going to be in pretty good shape.' His 1m 18.616s was still more than a second slower than Fabi!

By contrast, Michele Alboreto just didn't seem to be able to balance out his Ferrari to his liking. He couldn't put his finger on anything in particular, and he was only half a second slower than his team-mate. But that was sufficient to ensure that he lined up eighth on the outside of the fourth row.

Nestling on the inside of row two, never to be ignored, Alain Prost was moderately happy with his 1m 18.725s best. 'In Friday's untimed session I was very concerned because the brake pedal seemed to be going down to the floor after five or six laps', mused the Frenchman, 'but we managed

August:
Mario Andretti, injured in CART Michigan 500 race, replaced by Alan Jones in Beatrice Lola.
Rumours of Ferrari Indycar project gather strength.
Piercarlo Ghinzani tests Toleman and is confirmed as driver of the second car.
Disagreement between Renault and Ligier over the supply of engines for 1986.

to cure the problem for the afternoon. It'll be OK . . .'

By contrast, World Champion Niki Lauda dismissed his own qualifying efforts with ruthless candour. 'I'm a complete idiot', insisted the Rat. 'I messed up one set of qualifiers all on my own and then I got held up by Bellof on the other set. Ran E qualifiers both runs . . . the car is good. All my fault . . .' His reward for mismanaging his two runs was an unimpressive 12th quickest 1m 19.652s.

The Williams-Honda squad had not tested previously at the Nürburgring with its FW10s, so setting up the latest cars proved something of a lottery from which Keke Rosberg was quite happy to emerge with fourth place overall. 'I spent most of Friday's untimed session trying to set up the car for the circuit and chose one set of qualifiers, one set of race rubber.' Then the programme was thrown into chaos by the rain on Saturday, making it impossible to evaluate overnight changes made to his car's set-up.

Nigel Mansell found himself experiencing dire brake trouble from the word go on Friday morning, 'to the extent where I could hardly stop for the marshal at the end of the pit lane'. The mechanics bled the braking system twice during that untimed session before a faulty master cylinder was diagnosed to be the problem. It was changed with commendable speed, but Mansell's FW10 was only ready to go again 15 minutes before the end of the timed session. Under the circumstances his tenth fastest 1m 19.475s was a very respectable effort. The following day, having worked out a competitive wet-weather set-up, Mansell was fastest of all when the rain was at its heaviest.

The bland fact that Ayrton Senna recorded fifth quickest time on 1m 18.792s masked a truly outstanding performance from the Brazilian. He managed this time in an initial two-lap run before returning to the pit lane, ready to respond to any dramatic challenge later in the session.

When his Lotus 97T's Renault engine was fired up preparatory to its second run, the French V6 would just not run cleanly. Although Ayrton eventually staggered out of the pit lane, frantically blipping the throttle in an attempt to keep the engine running at all, it was a vain effort and he trickled straight back into the pit lane at the end of that single lap. Later detailed examination of the fuel system showed that a non-return valve in the mechanical fuel pump had become blocked with shreds from a rubber washer: the problem was thus cleared up for Saturday's sessions, by which time it was all too late.

Elio de Angelis was similarly annoyed after recording a seventh quickest 1m 19.120s. His car felt fine on its first, fastest run, but then refused to pull properly on its second run just when Elio was confident he could make it into the 1m 18s bracket. Behind the scenes he was bursting with indignation about the way in which the Renault technicians had readjusted his engine's electronic management system between runs. Second time out it wouldn't pull the skin off a rice pudding!

Anxious to produce a good performance on home ground, Nelson Piquet flew the BMW

M/Power flag to sixth place on the grid with a 1m 18.802s, but the Brazilian emerged from the cockpit in a pensive mood. 'We did a 1m 19.5s on race boost quite easily during testing', said Nelson thoughtfully, 'but this time it was just undrivable. Paul [Rosche] has altered the engine's response characteristics and there's no flexibility at all.' The engine adjustments were duly changed again for Saturday practice, but there was no chance to improve. A pity, reflected Piquet, because they were banking on a high boost run in the mid 1m 16s bracket!

Marc Surer qualified 11th in the second BT54 while Riccardo Patrese gave Alfa Romeo a brief surge of optimism during qualifying, taking a leaf out of Eddie Cheever's book by trying an interim 184TB like the American had used at Silverstone. Eddie had reckoned the 'TB' was better than the later 185T in the fast corners, 'but the front end of mine's too loose here by far', reflected the Italian. None the less Patrese managed a ninth quickest 1m 19.338s, while Cheever languished down in 18th slot the best part of two seconds slower after a couple of turbo failures, one in the 'TB' and one in the spare 185T.

The Ligier JS25s occupied their customary mid-grid positions with Laffite just out-qualifying de Cesaris for 13th place on the grid and then delighting the spectators by setting quickest time of all in Saturday's soaking untimed warm-up session. The JS25 performance meant that the works Renault outfit was made to look stupid yet again, although it has to be said that the French team hardly helped its own cause by fielding three cars on this occasion, a third original-spec RE60 'camera car' being pressed into service in the hands of former Brabham teamster François Hesnault.

This third Renault entry required the agreement of all rival teams if it was to start, boosting the field to 27 cars, but everybody accepted its presence with good grace. Patrick Tambay was the fastest RE60B qualifier, turning an unimpressive 16th quickest 1m 19.917s despite being hampered by an oil leak on Friday. Derek Warwick, worried about the prospect of rain on the first afternoon, managed only one run in 1m 21.237s for 20th spot before a rear wishbone pick-up point casting on the gearbox casing broke and pitched him into a fourth-gear spin on one of the fastest downhill sections of the circuit. It took Derek's breath away, but the car was beefed up and repaired in time for Saturday. Hesnault was right down in 23rd place, taking things easy with the camera car.

In the Tyrrell camp it was Stefan Bellof's turn to try the Renault-engined 014 which Brundle had used initially at Paul Ricard and Silverstone. Despite a turbocharger oil leak and boost control problems, Brundle qualified 19th on 1m 21.219s, trying both the team's 014s in the course of qualifying. 'At Silverstone we were four and a half seconds away from pole and here we're only three seconds away – that means progress!', beamed the optimistic German.

The RAM 03s of Philippe Alliot and Manfred Winkelhock qualified 21st and 22nd despite suffering their customary cross-section of mechanical maladies, ranging from soft brake pedals to misfires. Brian Hart's multiple checking computer had been installed on the team's spare car in order to get to the bottom of why the team has suffered so many engine problems so far this season.

Jonathan Palmer's Zakspeed qualified just behind Hesnault's Renault, the English doctor anxious for a reasonable showing at his team's home circuit. Unfortunately, a leaking plenum chamber prevented him from improving on 1m 24.217s on Friday and Saturday saw the team suffer a couple of engine failures caused by excessively lean fuel mixture. The only runners to qualify behind him were Huub Rothengatter,

Martin Brundle, tear-off visors in place, prepares to give the Tyrrell-Cosworth its last race.
Photo: Paul-Henri Cahier

145

making a return to Formula 1 almost a year out of the cockpit, as Ghinzani's paying successor in the Osella line-up, Martin Brundle's non-turbo Tyrrell 012 and Pierluigi Martini's tardy Minardi. He had an engine failure on one car and a crash with the other on Friday morning, leaving him with nothing left for dry qualifying and he had to do his grid time in the wet on Saturday!

RACE

Although a total of 67,000 spectators were claimed on race day, it must have been just a little disappointing for the AVD when they reflected on the great days of the old Nürburgring when campers came in their droves and made a weekend party of the whole affair. The half-hour warm-up session saw Rosberg's Williams FW10 pip Prost's McLaren at the top of the timing sheets, with Teo Fabi down in seventh place, sharing his rival Pirelli runners' concern that the weather might not be sufficiently warm to get the best out of their race rubber.

Fabi proudly led the field round the parade lap, but proved unable to match Toleman's first pole position with the marque's first stint in the lead of a Grand Prix. It seemed like an age before the green light came on, by which time Fabi was creeping slightly and had to dip the clutch to check his car's progress. At that moment the green light came on and Johansson initially sprinted into the lead, Fabi bogging down and finding himself engulfed by cars on both sides.

Stefan found his Ferrari hesitating slightly on the first couple of up-changes, so he too was passed by Senna and Rosberg by the time the field arrived at the first tight right-hander. Then Alboreto suddenly came from nowhere, front tyres locked up, and tried to squeeze inside Johansson at the same point. The two cars made contact, the left-front nose fin on the Italian's 156 just slicing the right-rear Goodyear on Stefan's machine, deflating the tyre and sending him straight into the pits at the end of the opening lap. Mid-way round the opening lap Rosberg blasted past Senna in a great surge of Honda power and Keke came through in the lead first time round with Ayrton still right on his tail.

Running third was the lucky Alboreto from de Angelis, Prost, Piquet, Mansell, Fabi, Patrese, Laffite, Boutsen, Lauda, Cheever, Tambay, Berger, Surer, Warwick, Bellof and the rest of the pack. Johansson trailed into the pits for fresh rubber, while de Cesaris was already out, unintentionally nudged by team-mate Laffite at the first corner. Andrea slid to a halt with a broken steering arm, so that was the end of that!

As the pack settled down into a steady order at the front of the field, Johansson resumed immediately in front of Rosberg and Senna, quickly pulling away as a reminder of what might have been. Hesnault's camera car was down at the tail of the field dicing gently with the Zakspeed, but Palmer was out after nine laps with a broken alternator belt and the cameras stopped rolling a lap later when Hesnault's clutch, slipping from the start, finally slipped out of business altogether and stranded him out on the circuit. The RAMs also expired early on, Alliot with fading oil pressure and Manfred with an engine failure.

By the end of the 10th lap, Rosberg and Senna had pulled away comfortably from a tight threesome – Alboreto, de Angelis and Prost – while Mansell was hanging on in sixth place. Next up was Piquet, but the Brabham team leader had his hands full fending off the nimble Toleman which was crowding him through the corners even though Nelson's BMW M/Power enabled him to squirt away on the straights. This necessitated the liberal use of the cockpit boost control and Piquet eventually paid the penalty with turbo failure on lap 24. In fact, it wasn't a good day for Bernie's boys as Surer had over-revved his BT54 going away from the line. From the outset his car had no real power at all and he had dropped to 15th when the engine turned rough on lap 16 so he prudently called it a day.

By lap 15, Senna was coming back steadily at Rosberg's leading Williams, the Brazilian unsuc-

cessfully attempting to outfumble Keke as the pair of them lapped Martini's Minardi. Rosberg kept him covered, but Senna finally slipped by going into the lower hairpin next time round. By this stage Rosberg was losing grip; nevertheless, he hung on gamely and refused to let the Lotus get away.

Although Ayrton was in a confident mood, he privately doubted whether he could keep ahead of a healthy Williams-Honda for the full race distance, but the question became academic on lap 27 when a driveshaft constant velocity joint overheated and failed. As Peter Warr remarked ruefully, 'we fitted revised rear uprights for this race in an effort to get more air to the rear brakes – but in doing that, we caused the c/v joint to overheat and that was the source of the failure'.

With 30 laps completed Rosberg now had a

Elio de Angelis's expression sums up his second retirement in succession. The engine failure on his Lotus-Renault, which was handling perfectly and was poised to finish in the top three, was another blow to Elio's increasingly slim Championship chances.

Early leaders Ayrton Senna and Keke Rosberg were sidelined by mechanical problems after dominating the first half of the race.

A highlight of the closing stages was a battle for third place between Nigel Mansell and Jacques Laffite. Mansell gained the upper hand, only to have his Honda engine suddenly lose boost, leaving the Ligier driver to step onto the rostrum for the second race in succession.

Lock out. Bernie Ecclestone scales the gates to gain admission to the inner sanctum. Judging by the size of the meagre crowd in the public enclosures, there was no need to lock the paddock gates.

four-second lead over the tight Alboreto/de Angelis/Prost trio, the Frenchman struggling to hang on at the back of the bunch with a down-on-power engine, the cause of which was later traced to a fractured pipe between a turbo and its intercooler. Mansell was fifth and World Champion Niki Lauda had just moved into sixth spot before pitting with a loose rear wheel caused by a heat deflector on a rear brake moving slightly. The irritated Austrian tore back into the fray in 12th place on his fresh set of tyres.

Despite the fact that his Lotus 97T was handling superbly, de Angelis knew that his race was doomed from lap 32 onwards. 'The oil pressure warning light began flickering in the corners, so I knew I wasn't going to make it.' On lap 41 the Renault V6 expired in an expensive cloud of smoke. 'A shame', concluded Elio, 'because Michele was actually holding me up'.

That disappointment prevented the Lotus from joining the three-way dispute for the lead which now developed as Alboreto and Prost hauled up onto Keke's tail. On lap 45 the Williams team leader got into a huge slide coming off the final S-bend (Veedol) coming up towards the uphill right-hander before the pits. This offered Alboreto the chance he was waiting for: although it looked like an outside chance, Michele launched an ambitious run up the inside of the Williams. Rosberg wasn't expecting him to try it on and the two cars bumped wheels as Alboreto bounced off the inside kerb as he elbowed his way past. Rosberg ran wide and immediately dropped to third as Prost also took the opportunity to nip through.

Now Michele had it in the bag, for although Prost was an ever-present threat, the McLaren driver was now suffering with a soft brake pedal to add to that gutless engine. With 10 laps to go those deteriorating brakes pitched him into an inelegant pirouette at the very same point which saw Lauda spin at last year's GP of Europe. That lost him the best part of 10 seconds, allowing Alboreto a comfortable cushion with which to canter home to an easy victory, Ferrari's team leader not in the least hampered by a mysterious oil leak which only manifested itself on right-hand corners.

Rosberg pitted for fresh rubber on lap 57, resuming fifth behind Mansell and Laffite who were enjoying a right royal tussle from which the Ligier driver emerged on top. Just when he thought he had the upper hand, Nigel's Honda V6 lost turbo boost pressure and he dropped back to finish sixth behind Thierry Boutsen's efficient Arrows and the fast-driving Lauda who performed admirably after his earlier delay.

Five laps from the finish Keke's great drive finally came to an end when a leaking left-rear brake seal finally took its toll and, with no retardation, he pulled into the pits for good. Johansson drove with tremendous verve, pulling back the best part of a lap on the leaders and looked certain to finish in the points when fading brakes pitched him into a spin 10 laps from the flag. 'The pedal just went to the bulkhead', said Stefan. 'I just didn't have a chance. Round she went . . .'

None of the Renaults went the distance. Tambay, suffering badly with neck cramps again, spun off on lap 20 and was unable to restart while the electrics went haywire on Warwick's RE60B and it eventually would hardly run properly at all. Patrese's Alfa expired with gearbox trouble, Cheever's after one of its almost-inevitable turbo failures. Fabi's Toleman suffered a sudden transmission breakage and Rothengatter's Osella broke its gearbox.

Outside the top six Gerhard Berger's Arrows finished seventh ahead of Bellof's Tyrrell, the German having stopped on his own initiative for fresh rubber and gained over two seconds a lap as a result.

Alboreto emerged from the German GP with a five-point advantage over Alain Prost in the Championship struggle. By any objective standards, he had been lucky. Lucky, that is, to have Ferrari's legendary reliability on his side.

A.H.

TECHNICAL FILE

McLAREN
KKK turbos in different positions so now symetrical. Prost tested larger front brake ducts on Friday. Revised brake calipers fitted with thin metal plates to help circulation of air across discs. (It was this plate which caused the incorrect mounting and gradual loosening of Lauda's rear wheel in the race.) Both cars raced with vertical front aerofoils.

TYRRELL
014 fitted with new front uprights and double rear wing.

WILLIAMS
Race cars fitted with single chamber airbox (to avoid variation in pressure found with twin chambers). By race day, T-car also had this arrangement. T-car equipped with metal brakes. New air ducts for rear brakes. Additional plates, added to sides of monocoque, made chassis dimensions legal.

BRABHAM
Addition of secondary lower rear wing meant mirrors had to be mounted on stalks on top of side pods. Alterations to airbox led to lower and slimmer engine cover. Piquet again used electronic monitoring system to check engine and turbo during practice.

RAM
Winkelhock tried AP carbon brakes. T-car equipped with sophisticated electronic system (made by Luptronics) to check engine for a six-minute run in an effort to solve detonation problems. Underbody profile shortened on Alliot's car. Both cars fitted with double rear wings.

LOTUS
Renault had now supplied fuel consumption monitoring devices. De Angelis's car equipped with on-board radio and a narrower front wing. (both cars had these wings for race). Senna's car fitted with revised rear upright to improve brake cooling.

RENAULT
Tambay tried smaller rear wing on Friday. All three cars to 'B' specification. An additional car for Hesnault (RE60) fitted with on-board television camera.

ARROWS
Ran vertical aerofoils which were in two stages and half the size of the more common 'Lotus' type used elsewhere. Race cars had shorter underbodies; Berger's car incorporated small revision to rear suspension geometry.

TOLEMAN
Hart engine fitted with new electronic ignition system. Development Hart engine run by Fabi on Saturday.

ALFA ROMEO
Following lead set by Cheever at Silverstone, both race cars were 1984 184Ts. Bench tests had been carried out with four-cylinder engine.

LIGIER
Used air ducts for turbos ('snorkel' type fitted to top of side pods). Both cars used carbon brakes on Saturday.

FERRARI
Position of intercooler changed. Additional oil radiator placed in horizontal position at rear of engine cover. All three cars incorporated revised radiator positions (less angle – as seen at Silverstone). Tested different rear wings and modification to brake calipers.

ZAKSPEED
Electronic fuel injection, as seen during testing, not used. GP

Grosser Preis von Österreich

Practice was dominated by news of Niki Lauda's decision to retire at the end of the season. The race was dominated for the most part by the man himself but we were to be denied a fairytale ending when Niki's Marlboro McLaren rolled to a halt with a broken turbo.

Lauda's retirement from his last home Grand Prix also denied us the opportunity of a rare wheel-to-wheel confrontation between the Austrian and his team-mate. Alain Prost had lost the lead when he stopped for tyres at half-distance but he was gaining a second a lap on Lauda as the race ran towards its conclusion and with the diminishing gap came the hope of a lively finish to what had been an otherwise dull race.

Mind you, things had got off to a dramatic start. Four cars tangled on the grid and officials took the dubious decision to stop the race. This allowed Michele Alboreto, among others, to switch to his T-car and the Ferrari driver's luck continued into the race as he picked up a distant and rather fortunate third place. Second, but glad of a finish with a difficult car and engine, Ayrton Senna brought his JPS Lotus-Renault into the points for the first time since his win in Portugal, Elio de Angelis giving Lotus two more points by taking fifth (in his T-car) behind the Ferrari of Stefan Johansson.

Both Ferrari and Lotus had been hopelessly off the pace and it seemed that the Canon Williams Honda team (second and fourth fastest in practice) would give McLaren a run for their money. Engine failures for Keke Rosberg and Nigel Mansell meant that McLaren utterly dominated this 10th round of the championship. After all the early promise of a varied season, it was beginning to look like 1984 all over again.

ENTRY AND PRACTICE

As ever at this time of year, paddock chat centred on the forthcoming season rather than the here-and-now details of practice. Naturally, the news of Niki Lauda's impending retirement added spice to the speculation since his departure would leave another gap in the driver market. Of more immediate importance was the question of team orders within McLaren. Would Niki be willing to assist Alain in his bid for the Championship? Lauda gave little indication that he would and he underlined his determination to retire on a high note by taking third place on the grid – his highest starting position in over a year! And, but for a fine effort by Nigel Mansell on Saturday afternoon, Lauda would have been on the front row alongside Prost . . .

Both McLaren drivers set their times during a dry qualifying session on Friday and Lauda was one of the few to venture out in the final session, Niki managing just one flying lap before the arrival of rain which washed out the remainder of the session.

Bearing in mind the difficulties of persuading the TAG turbo to accept qualifying boost, it was a surprise to see a McLaren on pole for the first time this season. The reason for this lay in the fact that the magnificent Österreichring, with its predominance of fast corners, favoured a car with good balance and sure-footed handling. Aerodynamics outweighed sheer horsepower here, as witnessed by the high speed of Piquet's Brabham-BMW, some 30 kph faster than the McLaren, yet nearly a second slower overall.

Prost had spent the first unofficial session (when he was fastest, incidentally) carrying out back-to-back tests with the modified rear suspension fitted to the race car. He found little advantage but neither did it seem to hinder his progress and Prost decided to stick with it for the remainder of practice. Twelve minutes into the

final qualifying session, Prost knew his pole position was secure as the rain began to fall – which was just as well, perhaps, since fuel accidently spilt onto the back of his overalls in the morning was causing discomfort. As for Lauda, his only major problem had been a shaft failure on one of his turbos on Friday morning. It was, he was told, a rare failure on the KKK. Lauda would experience one more before the weekend was out . . .

As Lauda discounted the theory that he was incapable of throwing himself into the specialised requirements of qualifying, so Nigel Mansell dispelled the belief that he could only shine on street circuits. Revelling in the demands of the

Österreichring, the Williams driver cut just one timed lap on Saturday afternoon as the rain began to fall and this was good enough for the front of the grid alongside Prost. Mansell had spent Friday running race tyres since his morning session had been interrupted by routine work but, even then, he managed a respectable fourth fastest time. His run on qualifiers on Saturday was the first occasion he had used them all weekend.

Doubts about qualifying tyres lasting for a whole lap led Keke Rosberg to use Cs for his first run on Friday and he set a time of 1m 26.333s. Switching to qualifiers, he attempted to improve but a typically dramatic drive was heightened further by the rear wing suddenly tilting as a support wilted under pressure. Assuming his tyres were giving up the ghost, Rosberg pressed on undaunted! And that lap was worth 1m 26.860s . . .

Piquet had an even more dramatic practice. Electing to run just one set of qualifying tyres, Nelson's lap ended in a spin at the *Boschkurve* where he found oil dropped by yet another Ferrari engine failure. Miraculously, the Brabham merely tapped the barrier at a corner where the run-off area is non-existent and Piquet trundled back to the pits to take over the T-car which now had the race tyres (used earlier in the session) in place. Gathering himself up for a very brave lap, Piquet rushed round to take fifth place. That would remain his starting position despite the fact that he shaved a tenth off before the rain fell on Saturday. Marc Surer was ninth fastest on Friday but an engine change was not completed in time for the dry period in the final session and the Swiss slipped to 11th place.

If handling and aerodynamics were to play an important part in Austria then one look at Teo Fabi's Toleman-Hart through the *Boschkurve* told you that here was a combination which would thrive, despite the fact that the Hart engine lacked power – in qualifying trim at least. Teo was

Niki Lauda's hopes for a final home win were dashed by a turbo failure as he passed the pits at the end of the 39th lap.

Nelson Piquet survived a spin at the *Boschkurve* during practice, but retired from third place with a broken exhaust on his Brabham.
Photo: Paul-Henri Cahier

sixth fastest after minor problems on Friday while, for the first time this season, the Benetton-sponsored team had entered a second car, driven by Piercarlo Ghinzani. Revelling in a car which was infinitely superior to the Osella with which he had struggled for so long, the Italian set 15th fastest time on Friday but slipped to 19th when he failed to get out promptly in the final session.

The folly of missing a test session at the Österreichring was apparent when the Lotus drivers finished Friday's practice desperately unhappy about the handling of their cars – an unusual complaint for the team which had dominated such a large part of the season up to this point. Ayrton Senna went so far as to say he would crash if he tried any harder, such was the unpredictable nature of his 97T on the bumps. Elio de Angelis was the better placed of the two, the Italian taking seventh place with Friday's time despite not feeling in the best of health. For Senna, Friday had been a struggle as he tried both the race and spare cars but could do no better than 10th. On Saturday morning he had improved his car enough to set third fastest time and he was raring to go once the pit lane opened for the final session. One lap later and he was back in the pits, more angry than ever since one bank of the V6 was down on boost. Improvements by others meant that he slipped to 14th place. Then the rain came . . .

Patrick Tambay did manage to improve his time on Saturday although it made no difference to his grid position. None the less, eighth place wasn't bad for a team which had been in the doldrums; Patrick was much happier than he had been the previous day.

A misfire on Derek Warwick's car on Friday led him to step into Tambay's RE60B (the spare car having an EF15 'race' engine in it) once the Frenchman had set his time and declared himself

very satisfied with the car. Not realising Tambay had wound on plenty of front wing to combat understeer, Warwick promptly spun the car into the barrier under braking for the *Hella-Licht* chicane. Tambay was livid and stormed out of the circuit before practice had ended. After a short time he had calmed down and phoned the circuit to apologise to Warwick. The car was repaired. All was well; except that an improvement by Warwick on Saturday was still only good enough for 13th place.

In terms of the Championship battle between Alain Prost and Michele Alboreto, the most significant aspect of practice was the poor performance of the Ferraris. Apart from not handling well over the bumps, Alboreto was plagued with a run of engine failures. On Friday morning, he lost a V6 in his race car and a switch to the T-car for qualifying resulted in the same problem. By now, his race car was ready to run again but, incredibly, the fresh engine blew as he entered the *Bosch-kurve*. Finally, Michele took Johansson's car and struggled into 19th place. He made the most of the brief period when the track was dry on Saturday by setting just one flying lap – good enough for a jump to ninth place – but two seconds off Prost's time. Stefan Johansson also improved, although 12th place was little to get enthusiastic about as the Swede struggled with the nervous handling and heavy steering.

It was as much a surprise to see the Ferraris so far down the grid as it was to see Riccardo Patrese up in 10th place, particularly in view of the Alfa Romeo drivers' comments about their cars. Both complained about appalling handling and a lack of power and Patrese's time, set on one flying lap on Saturday, was a good effort under the circumstances. Eddie Cheever, meanwhile, resorted to clipping the barrier on the exit of the *Rindtkurve* as he fought the understeer but failed to improve on 20th place. He then went out and enjoyed himself by throwing the Alfa around in the rain.

Jacques Laffite, never one to become unduly upset about practice, accepted his 15th place with a shrug after the rain had put paid to his hopes of improving. Andrea de Cesaris, on the other hand, was far from happy and a check on his car on Friday had found the suspension settings to be incorrect. Even so, Andrea found the car to be undriveable on Saturday and he intended to take over Laffite's car once Jacques had finished with it. That plan was cancelled when it rained and the initial problem with Andrea's car was thought to be faulty shock absorbers.

The lacklustre handling of the Barclay Arrows meant that Thierry Boutsen and Gerhard Berger were 16th and 17th, the Austrian being particularly disappointed since this was his home Grand Prix and the first anniversary of his Grand Prix debut. Meanwhile, down at the far end of the pit lane, the Skoal Bandit RAM team were still reeling at the shock of Manfred Winkelhock's fatal accident at Mosport. Kenny Acheson, fresh from a Formula 2 victory in Japan, had been drafted in as a replacement and the Ulsterman set about playing himself in. He almost didn't make it. An engine failure at the end of Friday's unofficial

session meant the fresh unit was not installed in time for qualifying (the spare car had gearbox trouble). On Saturday, therefore, Acheson had to go out immediately and record a time on soft race tyres. He took 23rd place while Philippe Alliot, now enjoying a Hart engine with the ignition programme used by Toleman, took 21st place.

Between the green-and-white cars sat the Tyrrell-Renault of Stefan Bellof, the German struggling with handling problems while Martin Brundle thrashed the Cosworth-powered 012 for all it was worth. It was a hopeless task although Brundle almost qualified since Martini, who had crashed his Minardi on Friday, just squeezed in a quick lap before the rain fell on Saturday. That left Huub Rothengatter in the Osella and Jonathan Palmer in the Zakspeed, the Englishman struggling with appalling throttle response problems.

The end of a brilliant team? News of Nelson Piquet's move to Williams signalled the end of his successful partnership with Gordon Murray. Piquet's Brabham held third place behind the McLarens before retiring with a broken exhaust. Faced with a massive increase in the price of grandstand seats, these spectators built their own vantage point, complete with a suspended bar in the top-deck lounge.

August:

Manfred Winkelhock dies of injuries received in World Endurance Championship race at Mosport.

Jaguar XJR-6 Group C car makes debut at Mosport.

Kenny Acheson replaces Manfred Winkelhock at RAM.

Niki Lauda announces decision to retire at the end of 1985.

Keke Rosberg signs for Marlboro McLaren.

---

continued on page 154

Michael Keppel

MANFRED WINKELHOCK

Manfred Winkelhock died from injuries received when he crashed his Porsche 962C during a round of the World Endurance Championship at Mosport in Canada on 11 August.

Those were the facts which robbed Grand Prix racing of a colourful and complex-free driver and the irony is that he lost his life, not while passing time in a lesser formula, but while making up time by driving flat-out in a category of racing which he thoroughly enjoyed.

Manfred Winkelhock did not spend his waking hours scheming a way to win the World Championship. In fact, he did not have a burning desire to be a racing driver in the first place, his introduction to the sport being due to the persuasion of friends who realised Manfred's antics on the public roads ought to be channelled into a competitive force on the race tracks.

BMW snapped up the home-grown talent to foster a relationship which took Winkelhock through saloon cars and into Formula 2 with the works March team in 1979 and 1980.

As a winner of German championships with BMW and Ford, Manfred found himself in line for the ATS Formula 1 drive (after an abortive attempt to qualify an Arrows at Imola in 1980). Amid scenes of despair and frustration, compounded by the erratic behaviour of a team owner whose pit lane performances often overshadowed those of his cars on the track, Winkelhock remained largely unaffected and he never failed to give his best when the shouting stopped and the real work had to be done.

The record book shows he scored two points in Brazil in 1982 but the record book takes no account of drives such as Zolder in 1984 when he ran a strong fourth until the inevitable mechanical failure intervened.

Not the most naturally gifted of drivers, Winkelhock nevertheless knew how to *race* – an attribute which, aligned with a complete absence of Superstar temperament, fitted perfectly the requirements of John Macdonald's RAM team for 1985.

Again, the machinery let Winkelhock down but he never stopped trying; never complained and never failed to give a smile or a playful slap on the back as he made his jaunty way along the pit lane.

Written appreciations are never adequate and the most touching tribute came from John Macdonald when interviewed in Austria a few days after the accident. 'Manfred', he said, 'was what I would call a normal, proper person'. In a world where Proper People are thin on the ground, Manfred Winkelhock's loss was sorely felt in the paddock at the Österreichring.

M.H.

Nigel Mansell, on the front row at the Österreichring, was lying a handy third when his Honda engine failed.

Paul Henri-Cahier

RACE

The rain, which had started during the final untimed practice, gathered strength in the afternoon and, by early evening, thunder rumbled across the Styrian foothills. It would continue through the night and into race morning, turning the car parks and camp sites into an appalling mess, rivers of muddy water flowing through tents and swirling around car door sills. The average motor racing enthusiast puts up with a lot, what with astronomic admission charges and equally high fences around the paddock, but this was testing their endurance to the limit. Thankfully, by the time the cars took to the track for the warm-up at 10.30, the sun was shining and the track was drying. The rest of the Österreichring steamed gently in the rising temperatures.

Prost was fastest but the apparent ease of his customary race morning performance masked a major drama right at the end of the session. Approaching the *Hella-Licht* on his last lap, the throttle jammed open, sending the McLaren across the kerb and straight up a bank. Damage was confined to the right-front suspension and the nose but it was an unsettling incident just before a race at the 145 mph circuit.

Three hours later, as Prost completed his exploratory laps before forming on the grid, it was noticed that the right-rear universal joint had more play than normal. Prost wanted to change to the T-car but he was persuaded that everything was in order.

Once on the grid proper, Prost made a good start but Lauda made a better one, darting to the right and making the most of a dreadful getaway by Mansell. The Honda V6 eventually picked up revs but, behind the Williams, there was chaos.

Fabi, on the inside of row three, had stalled; de Angelis, on the outside of row four, was crawling off the line and the narrow gap caused a predictable bottleneck. Tambay squeezed through but, along the way, Alboreto's Ferrari damaged its front suspension and, as a queue of cars formed behind Fabi, Berger lost his front wheels. The damaged cars were parked on the right-hand side of the track but they were proving difficult to remove and the officials took a decision to stop the race. Lauda, three car lengths ahead of Prost, raised his hand and slowed. Tambay, fourth behind Rosberg at the end of the first lap, shook his fist with understandable fury. In his opinion, there was enough room to continue the race in safety, a view shared by most observers. But, stopped it was and now the arguments started.

Initially, it was thought the race would be shortened to 48 laps with no refuelling. Then, it was announced that there would be a completely fresh start, with refuelling. And, since it was a 'new race', spare cars could be used – a blessing for Alboreto. Marco Piccinini, of course, had been well to the fore in the discussion over what should happen. This let Fabi and Berger back in the race as well, and de Angelis was able to swap to his T-car. Prost also took the opportunity to switch to his T-car since he felt that the dubious universal joint might not survive another start. Further-

more, he changed his mind over tyre choice, reverting to Cs all round (in line with everyone else on Goodyears) rather than keeping the harder B on the left side.

At the second start, Mansell's engine again hesitated and the Williams was engulfed although, this time, Prost made a better start while Rosberg, squeezing between his team-mate and the pit wall, eased Lauda back to third spot. At the end of the lap, Piquet was fourth, de Angelis fifth with Mansell sixth ahead of Tambay who, this time, had not made such a lightning getaway. For Piercarlo Ghinzani, however, there would be no start since his Hart engine had over-revved on that first lap. Of course, the officials now said that lap had never happened. The race had never started. Try telling that to a disappointed Ghinzani as he walked back . . .

Bearing in mind Rosberg's charge past Senna on the opening lap at the Nürburgring, Prost watched his mirrors carefully. The Williams remained in close proximity but did not pass. By lap four, it was gone, failing oil pressure sending Keke into the pits.

Now Lauda closed on his team-mate and, by the end of lap five, they had pulled out 11 seconds on Piquet. This was 1984 all over again. While the McLarens set about having their own race, a major battle was developing for third as Piquet held off de Angelis and Mansell while Fabi soon joined them after passing Tambay on lap six. Patrick was to drop from contention three laps later when he came into the pits with a punctured left-rear tyre, the Renault rejoining in 21st place to start a drive which would earn fifth fastest lap

of the race.

Senna took eight laps to deal with Alboreto and Tambay's mishap moved the Lotus into seventh place. Johansson, having worked his way past Surer and Warwick, was closing on his team-mate while the Ligiers of de Cesaris and Laffite began to reel in the Renault. At the end of lap 14, Laffite came past on his own, the Frenchman making a spinning gesture to his pit to indicate the fate of de Cesaris. It was not that simple. Not even with two hands could Jacques have indicated the magnitude of Andrea's latest escapade.

Powering through the *Texaco Schikane*, the Italian had put a rear wheel on the grass – and kept his foot on the throttle. The Ligier slid sideways, the rear catching the sloping bank to begin a series of rolls and flips before crashing upside down and then rolling back onto the two wheels which remained attached to the chassis. After a few moments, Andrea, his helmet splattered in mud, undid his belts and climbed out. It was a miraculous escape, even by the standards of Andrea de Cesaris.

On lap 18 Mansell was finally able to get past de Angelis, the Italian not finding the handling of the T-car to his liking. The Williams pulled away immediately and set after Piquet's third place but he need not have worried for the Brabham was soon to retire with a broken exhaust. The battle behind the leaders was well and truly dissolved now for Fabi had suddenly dropped away, his engine sounding flat as a prelude to a series of pit stops to sort out the electrics. All this allowed Alboreto to creep into sixth place, closely followed by Johansson. At the front, however, there were also signs of a change.

As he completed lap 25, Prost tapped his helmet; a signal to his pit that he was coming in for tyres. The spare car was not set up to the fine degrees favoured by the Professor and he found his tyre wear to be more than he would have liked. Reasoning that it would be better to come in, take on fresh tyres and be in good shape at the end of the race, Prost headed for the pit lane as Lauda swept into the lead.

The McLaren mechanics made the change in 11.5 seconds and, by the time Prost rejoined, Lauda was 30 seconds ahead. There were 26 laps to go; exactly half distance.

Already out of contention were Palmer (a broken alternator belt) after a spirited dice with the slow-starting Patrese; Alliot (engine) after a first-lap pit stop to have someone's brake duct removed from his front suspension; Cheever and Patrese (turbo) – and then, on lap 26, Mansell as his Honda seized with an oil pressure problem.

The order on Lap 27 appeared as: Lauda, Prost, Senna, de Angelis, Alboreto, Johansson, Surer, Warwick, Laffite, Boutsen, Berger, Tambay, Bellof, Acheson (about to stop when the engine cut out without warning), Rothengatter, Martini and, a long way back, Fabi.

Warwick's lively tussle with Laffite ended shortly afterwards when the Renault retired with a blown engine. The rapidly diminishing field shrunk even further when Berger stopped with a blown turbo on lap 34.

The Arrows team ran in tandem for much of the race. Gerhard Berger retired from his home Grand Prix while Thierry Boutsen (18) struggled home when a loss of boost pressure dropped the Belgian to 8th place.

Prost was pulverising the lap record as he reduced the gap on Lauda to 17 seconds and a quick calculation was enough to show that battle would be joined before the end. There were no team orders and both drivers clearly wanted to win. Besides, there was no threat from behind since Senna was half a lap away and too concerned about a vibration from his car to even contemplate improving. Ayrton had moved ahead of his team-mate shortly before Elio stopped for tyres and now de Angelis was some distance behind the Ferraris, who appeared to be having their own private battle for fourth place. Time and again, Johansson would take a run down the inside of the T-car but Alboreto's rather ruthless tactics made it clear what his feelings were. Rather than risk two bent Ferraris and no points, a bemused Johansson backed off.

Lauda and Prost, on the other hand, were doing anything but; Lauda setting his fastest lap only to have it bettered by Prost on lap 39. The gap was 15 seconds. Then on lap 40 it was all over.

Lauda suddenly switched off as he passed the pits, the McLaren coasting to a halt at the foot of the hill. The cause? A broken shaft on the KKK turbo . . .

Flicking off his belts, Lauda was out of the car and away before many of the spectators had realised what had happened. On learning of Niki's retirement, most of the crowd went home too.

Apart from the lack of excitement at the front, there was little to watch elsewhere as the retirements grew. Laffite stopping when the right-front wheel came off just after he had made a stop for tyres. Tambay's spirited drive ended when his engine failed, the oil spinning the Renault to a conclusive halt. Earlier, Tambay had been running ahead of Piquet and Mansell, an indication that he could have finished second had he not had his problems.

As it was, that place belonged to Ayrton Senna – just. The vibrations were so bad that Senna was taking one hand off the steering wheel when he could and he completed every lap thinking the engine was about to expire. The Ferraris were still third and fourth with de Angelis fifth but the remainder of the field looked a tired collection of cars as they struggled to reach the finish. Some didn't even manage that, Bellof running out of fuel, but Surer's impressive drive, although spoiled by a broken exhaust in the closing stages, at least brought him a point for sixth place. Bellof was classified seventh ahead of Boutsen, a chronic loss of boost pressure committing the Arrows to a walking pace as he completed his final lap ahead of the equally tardy Rothengatter, the Osella sounding as though it had breathed its last several laps before the finish.

Two laps from the finish, the McLaren team had shown Prost that he had 37 seconds on Senna and 43 on Alboreto. Not only did that sum up a domination which put him in joint first place with the Ferrari driver at the head of the Championship, it also summed up the way the tide of the Championship was turning in Prost's favour – with or without the help of his team-mate.

M.H.

Technical File

McLAREN
Revised rear suspension on Prost's car; alteration to fixing point for forward arm of lower wishbone. Airflow ducts across brake discs seen in Germany removed.

TYRRELL
Two 014 turbos (for Bellof) with detail modifications. Bellof's race car fitted with AP carbon-fibre discs drilled with numerous radial holes.

WILLIAMS
Both race cars equipped with stiffer top rocker arms (as tested by Mansell at Monza) and larger front brake ducts.

BRABHAM
Removed driver-adjustable flap controlling air flow to intercooler; declared a moveable aerodynamic device by FISA. Revised rear wing and winglets.

RAM
Acheson's car fitted with carbon-fibre discs and revised rear suspension geometry.

LOTUS
T-car ran revised front and rear suspension; new uprights with lower wishbone and upper links at the rear and new uprights at the front with a variety of fixing points for lower wishbone.

RENAULT
Brought along a new twin-section rear wing but did not use it. Used different suspension geometry on T-car to help anti-dive and anti-squat.

ARROWS
New chassis for T-car stiffer but slightly heavier. Berger tried revised rear suspension geometry. Wastegate position on T-car turned through 180 degrees to exit inside bodywork.

TOLEMAN
Became apparent that secret of excellent handling came from clever design on bottom of chassis. Tub made with a 3-cm step built into front section. Leading edges of V-shaped step acted like skirts to deflect air and create partial vacuum under chassis. Front wing side plates fitted with additional deflectors to add to effect.

ALFA ROMEO
Both drivers had 184T chassis with revised fixing points for upper rear wishbones.

OSELLA
Revised front suspension geometry and double rear wing.

LIGIER
Nothing new.

FERRARI
Chassis revisions tried during testing at Monza not seen in Austria. Continued experiments with engines; suffered four failures in three days.

MINARDI
Ran additional rear wing, mounted very low.

ZAKSPEED
Revisions to suspension geometry.

G.P.

Alain Prost took the spare McLaren to victory once
Lauda had retired.

'I drove just as hard as I needed to keep the other guy behind me. I had to work bloody hard over the last three or four laps, I can tell you that for sure!' World Champion Niki Lauda's eyes twinkled with a mischievous air of self-satisfaction as he discussed his victory in the Dutch Grand Prix at Zandvoort. 'What's more', he continued enthusiastically, 'there were *no* team orders. Alain is good enough to win his own races – he doesn't need any help from me. Sure, I'll help him to win his World Championship. But later in the year. Not yet . . .'

Roughly translated, all the bets were now off. Niki Lauda, having spent much of the season in the wilderness, had tasted success yet again and liked its flavour. More relaxed than ever and secure in the knowledge that he was quitting at the end of the season, he had now made up his mind to go for as many wins as possible on the remaining high-speed circuits which suited his delicate, precise style. He'd issued a stern warning at the Österreichring and now he had backed it up with a fine victory, the first time Lauda had beaten Prost in an all-McLaren fight.

True, Niki didn't actually *pass* the Frenchman, but he timed his race tactics to absolute perfection. On an abrasive track surface where just about everybody was expected to make at least one stop for fresh rubber, Lauda calculated that it was best to stop early (lap 20 out of 70) and he was absolutely right. Prost stopped on lap 33, the McLaren mechanics didn't quite service him with their customary split-second slickness, and by the time Alain accelerated back into the fray, Niki was comfortably through into the lead. The mathematics of the closing laps might not have appeared very promising for the Austrian as Prost devoured his lead with controlled ferocity, but there was still the problem of passing McLaren Number One when he hauled up onto its tail. The last couple of laps were like some novice Formula 3 battle as the two team-mates ducked and dived, dropped wheels on dirt and locked brakes. And Niki kept ahead . . .

More significant still, on the evening after the 1985 Dutch Grand Prix, the McLaren drivers had between them amassed a total of 45 victories. The remainder of the field – all 24 of them – could only muster a collective total of 35 victories. *That* made you think!

Charles Knight

Grote Prijs van Nederland

ENTRY AND PRACTICE

Zandvoort is everybody's favourite time of the Grand Prix year! Not only is the John Hugenholtz-designed circuit, which wends its way through the seaside sand dunes near Haarlem, one of the most challenging on the international calendar, but the pit lane is always full of gossip about 'who drives what' for the coming season. The format of the track has barely changed since it was first laid out in the immediate post-war years, although the inclusion of a couple of well designed chicanes on the fast back section have not only served to slow the cars down slightly, but also provide excellent overtaking opportunities. And the flat-out blast down the start/finish straight into the braking area for the spectacular 180-degree *Tarzan* corner remains one of the truly outstanding sections of Grand Prix circuit anywhere in the world.

Nelson Piquet was well in the news with his rumoured (soon to be confirmed) transfer from Brabham to Williams after a seven-year stay with Bernie Ecclestone's team. Piquet had been one of the quickest in recent Zandvoort testing and clearly wasn't in the mood to rest on his laurels now he had a new project to look forward to in 1986. As it turned out, only Friday effectively counted for grid positions, the blustery dry weather giving way to heavy rain on Saturday with the result that those not organised for first qualifying paid a penalty in disappointment.

Piquet got off to a bad start during Friday's untimed session, leaving his braking too late on cold rubber at *Tarzan* and sliding inelegantly into the tyre barrier on the outside of the corner. This BT54, his race car, suffered only minor damage and Nelson nipped straight back to the pits to take over his spare. In the afternoon he traded times with Prost and Keke Rosberg, eventually proving that the Brabham-BMW partnership still had the legs on everybody, at least in qualifying trim, and wrapped up pole with a fine 1m 11.074s. He was half a second clear of his closest rival.

Rosberg, last of the late brakers in classic style, was an absolute joy to watch as he hurled his Williams-Honda FW10 deep into the *Tarzan* braking area, qualifying Goodyears chirping in protest. 'My top gear was too short', he reflected after setting a second-fastest 1m 11.647s, 'but the fact is that Nelson is quicker – period!' Over in the McLaren camp, Alain Prost was slightly hampered by the TAG turbo's reluctance to accept massive helpings of boost pressure for qualifying purposes, but he wound up a contented, unobtrusive third on 1m 11.801s.

The other McLaren, Niki Lauda's, finished in 10th place after what seemed on the face of it a typically cautious qualifying performance on the part of the current title holder. In fact, Niki had been in trouble. 'I got blocked by Fabi on one run', reported the Rat, 'but, to be honest, the engine felt a little on the flat side. When we took a close look at it after the session, we found that it had lost compression on one of its cylinders . . .'

Ayrton Senna qualified his Lotus 97T fourth on 1m 11.837s, but put his name into the paddock headlines for a different reason during Friday's

Paul Henri-Cahier

Out on their own. It was 1984 all over again, only this time the McLarens actually engaged in superb wheel-to-wheel combat. Prost closes in on Lauda to dispute the lead *(left)*.
Teo Fabi put the Toleman on the inside of the third row and held third at the end of the first lap before assuming a comfortable fifth place ahead of Mansell, Warwick and de Angelis. The Benetton car retired eventually when a wheel worked loose *(above)*.

untimed session. Negotiating the twisty section behind the paddock, a turbo fire set light to the Lotus's rear bodywork and, in what Senna saw as a totally understandable move to save his car, he pulled off to the right into an access road on the apex of the *Hugenholtzbocht* hairpin behind the pits and drove back into the paddock.

All hell suddenly appeared to cave in around his ears! He was summoned to the race stewards where it was pointed out that the Formula 1 regulations state that 'only the track may be used by drivers during practice and the race'. Furthermore, they added, 'during the practice sessions and the race the only access to the pits is permitted through the deceleration zone. The penalty for a breach of this rule shall be exclusion from the race'. Notwithstanding any explanation from the driver, the stewards imposed a severe reprimand and a 5000 dollar fine on the rather bewildered Brazilian!

'I wonder who would have paid if I'd just left it burning by the side of the track?' mused Senna as he prepared himself for first qualifying. In the afternoon he managed his grid time by dint of an on-the-limit run, 'although I have to admit it wasn't quite perfect . . . I touched a kerb where I shouldn't at one point. It was also my first crack on qualifying rubber. Because of the time we lost this morning after the fire, I wasn't able to try them earlier.'

Team-mate Elio de Angelis had both his runs spoiled by slower traffic and the rain intervened to preclude improvement the following day. 'First it was a RAM, then the Zakspeed . . . right in the middle of the circuit. But the chassis feels pretty good and I'm reasonably optimistic.' His best time was 1m 13.078s.

On the inside of the third row sat Teo Fabi's Toleman TG185, the fine-handling car from

August:
Renault announce plans to disband their Formula 1 team at the end of 1985.
Ligier fire Andrea de Cesaris; Philippe Streiff to act as replacement.
South African Grand Prix date changed from 16 November to 19 October.
Bobby Rahal rumoured to drive for Ferrari at Indianapolis in 1986.

Witney producing a 1m 12.310s best during a trouble-free run. Ghinzani wasn't anywhere near as quick, but at least had the satisfaction of qualifying in front of the two ill-handling Ferrari 156s which were providing an appalling ride over the bumps and ripples of the dune-lined circuit.

Patrick Tambay squeezed a very respectable 1m 12.486s out of his Renault RE60B to qualify sixth, raising the hopes of the French team in the wake of its sad notice of intent to retire at the end of the year. But Derek Warwick's consistently miserable season continued in a disappointing vein: during the untimed Friday morning session he found his RE60B savaged by Riccardo Patrese's Alfa 184TB in a silly coming together at the hairpin behind the paddock.

'I followed him round Tarzan after he came out of the pits in front of me', explained an irritated Warwick, 'and I was absolutely sure he'd seen me coming up inside him as we went into the hairpin. I mean, he was running on a wide line, so I went inside him and, as I drew level, he simply drove into me!'

The Alfa's left-rear wheel made contact with the Renault's right-front and, on this occasion, French engineering came off worst! While there wasn't

even a scratch on the Italian car, the impact tore off Warwick's right-front wheel as well as ripping out the suspension mounting points to leave a gaping hole in the monocoque. 'I went out and found Patrese afterwards', fumed Derek, 'and all he said was "I'm sorry, I didn't see you . . ." I told him he always says that when he's made another bloody silly mistake . . .' Sadly, it was Warwick who suffered the most from this drama, being obliged to take over the Renault spare fitted with an EF15 spec race engine. It wasn't a match for his team-mate's EF4B, so the Englishman's best was a 1m 13.289s, 12th quickest.

Nigel Mansell admitted that he hadn't made the best use of his two sets of Goodyear qualifiers on Friday, and although his 1m 12.614s fastest stood him in as seventh quickest, he maintained a revised chassis set-up was needed to get the optimum performance from the FW10. The wet weather put an end to that idea on Saturday, so he had to be content with his initial position.

Thierry Boutsen joined Mansell on the fourth row, the Belgian capitalising on his Arrows' impressive straightline speed to put himself well in contention. The quiet Arrows driver was extremely satisfied to have pipped Marc Surer's Brabham BT54 in the line-up, the Swiss qualifying ninth immediately ahead of Lauda's McLaren on 1m 12.856s.

'It just couldn't seem to get the boost pressure up to its working level properly', explained Surer, 'and by the time I'd got that sorted out I'd blown my chances because I'd used up my two sets of qualifying rubber . . . it's very frustrating indeed!'

Jacques Laffite amused himself on Saturday afternoon by setting fastest time in the rain, emphasising the quality of Pirelli's wet weather rubber, but the best he could manage in the dry was a 13th quickest 1m 13.435s. That put him just ahead of Zandvoort first-timer Gerhard Berger in the other Arrows, but Andrea de Cesaris was badly off-form, languishing down in 18th place on 1m 13.797s. The Italian was feeling just a touch jaded after his spectacular end-over-end accident in the previous weekend's Austrian Grand Prix, not to say somewhat indignant that Guy Ligier had decided to dispense with his services immediately following the Zandvoort race. Some observers couldn't see the sense in this. With the Italian Candy domestic appliance concern as one of the Ligier co-sponsors, what sense did it make kicking out his only Italian driver a week before Monza?

After a steady performance at the Österreichring, the Ferrari 156/85s were completely out of the picture at Zandvoort and neither Michele Alboreto nor Stefan Johansson could produce a lasting solution to their difficulties. The Italian cars were bouncing about precariously over the bumps, suffering from appalling wheel-spin and unpredictable handling. Expressions were glum and preoccupied in the Ferrari garage when Alboreto and Johansson could only qualify 16th and 17th — more than 2.5 seconds away from Piquet's pole time. Johansson briefly tried a new, low-mounted rear wing beneath the car's undertray in an attempt to improve its traction, but this

Eddie Cheever spent more time out of his car than in, the Alfa Romeo retiring with a blown turbo after one lap.

wasn't the answer and the team continued to flounder from problem to problem throughout the weekend.

Still, at least the Ferraris *just* managed to stay ahead of the Alfa Romeos! In 19th and 20th position on the grid were the two Benetton-liveried 184TBs of Riccardo Patrese and Eddie Cheever, on 1m 14.240s and 1m 14.912s respectively. Referring to his tangle with Warwick, Patrese said simply: 'I apologised to him and agreed it was my fault. I'm sorry. What more does he want me to say?' The Italian V8s were running erratically as usual, both drivers complaining about poor grip and unpredictable handling, while Eddie had the added complication of an engine which refused to run cleanly over 8000 rpm with the result that the American was forced into the unloved spare 185T for a time on Friday.

Although there was no spare Tyrrell 014 on hand, Ken Tyrrell decided to give his two drivers a crack with Renault power at the same time, both cars fitted with EF4 Renault V6s. Stefan Bellof's was only to race specification, precluding him from running as much boost pressure as team-mate Martin Brundle. The Englishman qualified 0.3s faster and the two blue cars from Ripley shared the 21st row of the grid. Brundle was troubled by second gear jumping out on the over-run, an irritating gremlin which cost him a few tenths here and there.

Completing the Zandvoort line-up was Jonathan Palmer in the Zakspeed, the Doc expressing himself guardedly optimistic about the performance of the latest specification German engine which now revved to 11,000 rpm, an increment of 800 rpm over the older units. He lined up right behind the Tyrrells, while Pierluigi Martini's Minardi M185 was next from Philippe Alliot's RAM 03 and local star Huub Rothengatter in the lone Osella-Alfa.

The RAM team had a fraught time, Kenny Acheson being the lone non-qualifier and not allowed in when McLaren International's Ron Dennis declined to agree to the prospect of a 27th runner – just as he had done to Brundle at the Österreichring. The RAM problems began when Alliot's car went straight on at *Tarzan* after only four laps in Friday's untimed session. Repaired, the car then lost sixth gear in the afternoon and, since Acheson's engine had expired, Kenny had to wait until Philippe's car was repaired. He did a 1m 20.429s on his first lap with qualifiers. Then the engine broke . . .

RACE

Race morning brought with it the customary Zandvoort procedure which meant that no racing cars could go out on the circuit until the local church service was over. Lauda and Prost confidently headed the times for the half-hour session in race trim, but the Renault camp was plunged into a state of chaos when Tambay's RE60B careered off the circuit at *Tarzan* as a result of severe damage to the left-front suspension under hard braking. Eventually, it was to transpire that the RE60B's components had undergone what might best be described as

RENAULT ended months of speculation and eight years of attempting to win the World Championship when, on the day after the Dutch Grand Prix, they revealed their decision to disband the team at the end of 1985.

The announcement came as no surprise in the light of a poor season for the team and heavy losses incurred by the parent company.

Renault made their Grand Prix debut at Silverstone in July 1977 and the French team were the first to explore the turbocharging alternative offered by the regulations. After a hesitant start, when the yellow cars with their persistent trails of oil and smoke were the butt of pit lane jokes, Renault finally came good when Jean-Pierre Jabouille scored a historic victory in 1979 – appropriately enough in the French Grand Prix.

Renault went from strength to strength and it soon became apparent that turbocharged engines were capable of producing prodigious power at the expense of the 3-litre normally-aspirated engines. At this point, Renault should have capitalised on their advantage.

They claimed 31 pole positions and won 15 Grands Prix to come within an ace of taking the Championship with Alain Prost in 1983. By 1984, it was too late. The competition had made rapid development and the cumbersome decision-making process at Renault could not hope to keep pace with the rapid reactions required by Formula 1.

At the end of 1984, Gérard Larrousse, the erstwhile Director of Renault Sport, and Michel Tétu, the team's underrated designer, left to join Ligier. Bernard Hanon, the Régie's President and a supporter of their involvement in motor sport, was replaced by Georges Besse, a known hard-liner charged with the task of turning around the company's sagging fortunes.

Charged with boosting morale within Renault Sport, Gérard Toth arrived from sporting obscurity to assume command but the self-opinionated former Assistant Director of Automobile Research and Development singularly failed in his task; the results in this book speak for themselves.

Although despised by the more traditionally minded stalwarts in the pit lane, Renault added considerable colour and charm to the pit lane as they set about altering the face of Grand Prix racing in the Eighties. Their presence will be missed by a sport which needs the participation of major manufacturers; their failure to win the Championship merely underlining the fact that Grand Prix racing is competitive enough to stand its ground without being bowled over by a constructor backed by a huge budget.

Niki Lauda showed he had lost none of his forcefulness or guile by taking an excellent victory, the 25th of his career.

cursory static rig testing and the whole affair left some very worried faces indeed in the pit lane. There was no question of repairing this car as it was a second spare which had been flown in to supplement team strength after Warwick's collision with Patrese on Friday. Patrick's mechanics busied themselves changing turbos on his race car and the two remaining RE60Bs had additional strengthening 'lozenges' welded to their lower-front wishbones prior to the start.

Tambay's problems were *still* not over. After a couple of warm-up laps, he pulled into the pits for a misfire to be cured and then found that he was too late to be allowed out of the pit lane to join the grid. Wondering whether anything else might be in store for him, he lined up at the end of the pit lane and prepared to chase after his rivals once the grid was unleashed.

When the starting light flashed green, Nelson Piquet did what he has done on several previous occasions: stalled the pole-position Brabham-BMW. On the other side of the grid Thierry Boutsen all but stalled his Arrows, forcing some phenomenal avoiding manoeuvres as the pack scattered in all directions! Astonishingly, no two cars made contact and Rosberg led the scramble through *Tarzan*, round the twists at the back of the pits and out over the hill into the country.

Teo Fabi had given his Toleman's Hart engine a healthy bootful of revs at the start, amazing himself with an absolutely stunning getaway from the third row and the little Italian came through at the end of the opening lap in third place behind Keke and Senna's Lotus 97T. Fourth was Prost from Lauda, Mansell, Warwick, Surer, de Angelis, Laffite, Johansson, Alboreto, Berger, Bellof,

Brundle, Ghinzani, de Cesaris, Palmer, Alliot, Tambay, Boutsen and Piquet. Second time round both Alfas expired, with turbo failure as usual, while Martini made a mess of braking for one of the chicanes and piled the Minardi firmly into the barrier, removing a couple of wheels, but was able to hop out unhurt.

Prost nipped past Fabi on the second lap and quickly moved in onto Senna's tail, Lauda was moving up towards the Toleman and Mansell still held Warwick back in seventh place. Tambay was absolutely flying through the back-markers, out-braking car after car into *Tarzan* with a tremendous zest which set people thinking that perhaps all wasn't as it might have been. Was the Renault running with a light fuel load, not wanting to risk another suspension breakage on full tanks? Patrick eventually fought his way to a magnificent fourth place, immediately behind his team-mate, when the RE60B succumbed to 'transmission failure' out on the circuit. An examination of his individual lap times revealed that Tambay had recorded a 1m 17.335s as early as lap 15. Only the McLarens and Mansell's Williams bettered that time, and then only much later in the race after pit stops for fresh tyres and running with a light fuel load. A light fuel load? Most people left Zandvoort feeling that they knew the answer to that Renault performance.

By lap 12 the first four were still in close touch in the order Rosberg, Senna, Prost, Lauda, while Fabi led the rest in a comfortable fifth place. The TG185 seemed to be running like a precision watch on this occasion, so it was with a sense of great disappointment that Fabi trailed in to retire on lap 19. It appears that the rear wheels worked

loose, Teo got himself into a dramatic 'fishtail' under braking for the first chicane and the Toleman launched itself over the kerbing, damaging the underside of its nose section and ripping away its brake cooling ducts.

On lap 21 Rosberg's dominant Williams expired with a smoky Honda engine failure, allowing Prost through into the lead with Lauda ducking into the pits for a well-timed tyre change. That put Senna back into second place from Warwick, the soon-to-retire Tambay, Michele Alboreto's stealthy Ferrari and Marc Surer who was driving with unobtrusive smoothness and now knocking on the door of the points-scoring positions. Johansson's Ferrari had departed with engine failure, while similar fates had befallen Ghinzani, Palmer and Laffite.

De Angelis stopped for tyres as early as lap 19, while Mansell's Williams was in at the end of lap 24, followed by Senna on lap 26. Gearbox trouble claimed Warwick's Renault on lap 28, just as Derek poked its nose into a brief second place, but by lap 30 it was the lucky Alboreto who headed Prost's pursuit with Niki now back to third and Surer getting to grips with Senna's Lotus, the Renault engine of which was showing signs of overheating and losing power.

On lap 32 Alboreto made his stop for tyres, dropping down to eighth, so Lauda suddenly found himself second. It was all set up nicely for the Rat. His McLaren was running well, his tyres felt good and he had only his team-mate in front of him – who had yet to make his stop for fresh tyres. He'd got it made!

At the end of lap 33 Prost was in, but the stop took around 18 seconds and he resumed in third

Keith Sutton

place behind Lauda and Senna. It took him until lap 48 before he could find a path inside Senna under braking for *Tarzan*, from which moment all the stopwatches in Zandvoort were turned to the riveting task of plotting the gap between the two McLarens.

On lap 51 Niki was 7.1s ahead, but over the next few tours Alain closed the gap relentlessly: 6.6s, 5.8s, 4.1s, 3.4s, 3.2s . . . finally 2.6s on lap 61 and the two cars took up nose-to-tail formation. Would Niki concede – or would Prost force a way past? The remaining 10 laps were absolutely spellbinding as the crowd was treated to a touch of rare vintage Lauda, the World Champion controlling the pace of the two McLarens just as he pleased, holding Prost back when it looked as though they might lap slower cars at awkward moments, easing away slightly when he himself got through and the Frenchman was momentarily delayed.

Finally, off came the gloves for the last three laps as Prost realised he was going to have to fight for it. Lauda, knowing, perhaps, that Prost was not going to do anything too dramatic to jeopardise his own Championship aspirations, simply concentrated on driving smoothly and regularly, legitimately baulking his rival by taking slightly unhelpful lines under braking for the chicanes.

Suddenly, it was all over. Through the last, fast right-hander they came, Lauda still ahead, and Niki swept past the chequered flag to take his 25th Grand Prix triumph, equalling Jim Clark's record in the process. It was epic stuff!

Grappling with a down-on-power motor, the water temperature 'off the clock' and the oil pressure warning light flashing ominously in the corners, Senna just hung on to third place, although the Brazilian was less than impressed with Alboreto's tactics after the Ferrari team leader nudged his Lotus quite hard under braking on the last lap. That Michele should have survived to finish fourth is a quite remarkable testimony to Maranello reliability, particularly when the Ferrari team's practice form is considered.

De Angelis came through to take an undramatic fifth while Mansell might have been higher than sixth had it not been for a second tyre stop. 'At my first stop we changed to Bs and they were too hard, so I had to come in again for a set of Cs. After that it was fine, although the clutch pedal didn't seem to want to work for a few laps and I had a big vibration problem . . .'

Marc Surer seemed destined to finish fifth or sixth before a broken exhaust intervened, and his Brabham-BMW lost turbo boost pressure. He slipped back to 10th at the end behind Martin Brundle's Tyrrell 014, the recovering Nelson Piquet and Gerhard Berger in the sole surviving Arrows. Thierry Boutsen's A8 succumbed to broken rear suspension, Bellof's Tyrrell had engine failure and de Cesaris's Ligier career came to an unremarkable end when his JS25's Renault V6 also expired.

It had been a fascinating race of changing fortunes, where good luck and timing mattered almost as much as good driving. Sadly for his rivals, Niki Lauda managed to display all three . . .   A.H.

Lukas Gorys

TECHNICAL FILE

McLAREN
Both race cars fitted with revised rear suspension seen in Austria. Prost's car equipped with larger, slimmer front brake ducts tested in wind tunnel.

TYRRELL
Both drivers had 014 turbos; no T-car. Tried double twin-section rear wings.

WILLIAMS
Spare car now fitted with new top rocker arms seen in Austria.

BRABHAM
No change since Austria except for double rear wing tried in testing at Zandvoort.

RAM
Nothing new for Zandvoort.

LOTUS
Revised suspension, seen on T-car in Austria, not fitted in Holland.

RENAULT
Chassis 7 badly damaged in practice on Friday. Chassis 5 brought to Holland for use as T-car.

ARROWS
Shuffled chassis around, giving Boutsen new car (number 5). All three cars had revised wastegate position seen in Austria.

TOLEMAN
Nothing new.

ALFA ROMEO
Nothing new.

OSELLA
No change since Austria.

LIGIER
Built new car to replace chassis crashed in Austria. De Cesaris took chassis number 3, fitted with new-spec bodywork.

FERRARI
Tried low-mounted additional rear wing on Friday to improve extraction of air from underbody and increase downforce. Tried revised air boxes on race cars.

MINARDI
Low-mounted rear wing seen in Austria abandoned.

ZAKSPEED
Nothing new.   G.P.

Gran Premio d'Italia

Ben Horne, a member of the Marlboro McLaren pit crew, took his life in his hands on race day at Monza. Holding a pit board reading 'Prost – Laud – Albo – John', he taunted the *Tifosi*, simmering behind the wire mesh fencing on the opposite side of the track. A few minutes later, Bellentani of Ferrari held aloft his board showing the predicted order to be 'Michele – Stefan'. The mob, passified for the time being, applauded loudly. It would be as near as they would get to seeing a home victory.

Ferrari, despite a week of testing at Monza and heavy revisions to their cars, were severely trounced. Michele Alboreto retired from a distant fifth position with engine failure, Stefan Johansson then salvaging the place even though his car had run out of fuel on the last lap.

To make matters worse, Alain Prost scored his fifth win of the season to move 12 points clear of Alboreto although, in truth, he did not expect this victory. The race belonged to Keke Rosberg, the Canon Williams Honda pulling away at the start, losing the lead while making a stop for tyres, surging ahead of Prost again – only to retire eight laps from the finish.

Ayrton Senna's brilliant pole-position lap came to nothing. The JPS Lotus driver, hampered by fuel consumption and engine problems, was literally powerless to prevent Nelson Piquet from storming into an excellent second place after an early stop for Pirellis. Giving Brabham a healthy result in front of their Italian sponsor, Marc Surer took fourth place when de Angelis, also in engine trouble, slipped to sixth.

The fastest man on the track was classified 11th, Nigel Mansell retiring four laps from the end after what had been a determined drive through the field. The Williams-Honda had been forced out of second place in the opening stages to pit for a replacement electronic control box. With precious little to gain, Mansell had driven flat-out and recorded fastest lap.

With everything to gain, Alain Prost had cruised into another nine points. Even Alboreto had to admit the Ferrari was no match for the McLaren. Ben Horne had been right after all.

ENTRY AND PRACTICE

As the final practice session on Saturday afternoon drew to a close, it seemed the Williams team had tied up the front row of the grid. Nelson Piquet, the man who had been fastest on Friday, was struggling with a turbo boost problem and Keke Rosberg's time of 1m 25.230s looked like being the benchmark for 1985. Then, to their surprise, Ayrton Senna shaved another tenth off that time to take his fifth pole position of the season.

It was a surprise for two reasons. Senna had never driven at Monza before and, during the course of that brilliant lap, he had understeered off at the first *Lesmo*! The grass-cutting moment had cost him, he reckoned, about three-tenths of a second but, even so, it was a brilliant performance by the man who, on Friday, had arrived at a chicane flat in fifth – simply because he had forgotten it was there! Clearly, by Saturday afternoon, he had got to know the Monza autodrome quite well . . .

On the first day of practice, both Lotus drivers had been within a fraction of each other. On Saturday, however, Ayrton improved by around two seconds while Elio de Angelis found just one second after hitting a kerb while running his second set of qualifiers.

Keke Rosberg regretted that he had used all of his qualifiers by the time Senna snatched pole. The Williams driver felt he could have found more time, particularly in view of a slipping clutch and a brake pedal which went to the floor at *Parabolica*. Keke reduced speed by jamming the gearbox from sixth to third, the engine bouncing off the rev limiter but he still made it to the line two-tenths faster than his team-mate.

Nigel Mansell's practice had also been fraught even though things started well enough when the Englishman set fastest time on Friday morning. During the same session on Saturday, a left-rear tyre exploded, the repeat of his terrifying Ricard incident sending the Williams off the track. This time, Mansell emerged unscathed but it meant driving the spare car for the first time in the final qualifying session. Both Williams drivers had looked strong and competitive throughout practice so second and third places were an appropriate reward.

According to the speed traps, the Honda engines were bettered only by the BMWs mounted in the Brabham BT54s and it was no surprise to see Nelson Piquet take the provisional pole with a last-minute, high boost run after his mechanics had completed an engine change on Friday. Piquet was obviously the man the Williams team feared most and, while Nelson did improve slightly, his engine appeared to be down on boost. A change of turbo made little difference and a last do-or-die attempt in the closing minutes of practice was thwarted when Boutsen's Arrows dumped its oil on the circuit. Marc Surer, troubled with understeer and a misfire on high boost, claimed ninth place, three-tenths faster than Johansson's Ferrari.

The story of the weekend, of course, was the battle between Ferrari and McLaren, Alboreto and Prost. The Championship contenders were side-by-side, sixth and seventh, on Friday but Prost quickly dispelled any hopes the Italians may have held when he improved to fifth place while Alboreto dropped from sixth to seventh on Saturday. What's more, Prost reckoned he could

have had a shot at pole had he not chosen to run one set of soft race tyres (C) and one set of qualifiers (E). 'It was a mistake', he said afterwards. 'I didn't think the qualifiers would last a full lap. But they did. I should have used two sets.'

Niki Lauda made a similar choice on Saturday and had similar regrets even though he was more concerned about a problem with the electronics which caused the V6 to cut out intermittently. He was unable to improve on Friday's time and dropped from 12th to 16th place.

The presence of Gianni Agnelli, President of Fiat, represented another turn of the screw for Ferrari, desperate to perform well on their home circuit and recoup some of the ground lost to McLaren in recent races. Indeed, while Stefan Johansson had taken part in the test session at Brands Hatch, Michele Alboreto had been pounding round Monza and the result of his efforts was evident in the substantial changes to the cars (see Technical File, p. 167).

Michele had recorded a 1m 28s lap during testing and he felt there was more to come. Indeed there was – but not enough. A lack of grip compounded a shortfall in horsepower and, to add to his troubles, Alboreto had engine failures at the end of the unofficial sessions each day.

Johansson had a similar problem; only his was during qualifying on Friday. And, since there was only one spare car available, this had been set aside for Alboreto. Once Michele had finished his runs, Johansson was allowed to use the T-car and with just four minutes to go the Swede got the crowd on their feet by tearing out of the pit lane, his final set of qualifiers leaving rubber smoke hanging in the air. He completed one warm-up lap and, as he prepared for his final flyer, a nameless

Graham Smith

Rearguard action. Kenny Acheson was called in to replace the late Manfred Winkelhock at RAM. A severe shortage of engines thwarted the Ulsterman's hopes of establishing a Formula 1 reputation.

official hung out the chequered flag! Needless to say, the crowd were on their feet once more, but in a less charitable frame of mind this time. Stefan did find an improvement on Saturday but it was only good enough for 10th place.

An excellent effort in a less than excellent car saw Patrick Tambay split the Ferraris; this in the spare Renault after his regular car had been damaged during a terrifying shunt on Friday. Going for a time on qualifiers, Tambay came across a Ligier at the 150′ mph second *Lesmo*. Thinking it might be Streiff, Tambay assumed the novice might not have seen him and he took avoiding action. In fact, it was Laffite: he had seen Patrick and he did move over. Tambay took to the grass, the rough ride severely damaging the bottom of the chassis. A few places further back, Warwick was 12th, the Englishman preferring the feel of his car on full tanks to its skittish behaviour during qualifying.

Thanks to the power of their BMW engines, the Arrows drivers were nudging the 200 mph mark during qualifying although both drivers slipped down the order slightly in the final session, a misfire keeping Gerhard Berger in 11th spot while Thierry Boutsen's engine failure meant he had to make do with Friday's time.

Major changes to the Alfa Romeos did not seem to bring about any improvement in track performance or reliability as Riccardo Patrese walked in from his car, abandoned on Friday morning due to a turbo failure. A last-minute effort by the Italian moved him into 13th place while Eddie Cheever's best efforts on Saturday could only elevate the American into 17th spot.

This was what we had come to expect from the Benetton cars but the Italian sponsor's other representative, Toleman, had of late done rather better than take 15th (Teo Fabi) and 21st (Piercarlo Ghinzani). Doubtless the chassis were performing well but the Hart engines could not hope to match the BMWs and Hondas in qualifying trim, added to which Ghinzani had a faulty distributor which caused his engine to misfire through the final session.

Saddened by the loss of Stefan Bellof, Tyrrell entered just one car and quietly got on with the business of sorting the 014-Renault. A new car was on hand but this refused to fire up on Friday and, as a result, Martin Brundle was unable to test and compare the changes made to the new chassis. He did manage to run this car on Saturday and, in the course of one lap, he improved by five seconds to take 18th place.

Andrea de Cesaris was present to see Philippe Streiff take his place in the Ligier team, the young Frenchman beating his more experienced teammate by a tenth of a second, neither of them managing to improve on Saturday. Streiff had got off to a bad start by damaging his car during the unofficial session on Friday and the necessary repairs to the suspension and gearbox meant he had to use the spare car later in the day. Laffite took over the T-car when a turbo failed on his race car in the final session.

Behind the Ligiers and the Toleman of Ghinzani came Huub Rothengatter (forced to use the spare after gearbox troubles had sidelined his regular

Kelemata car) and Pierluigi Martini's Minardi. And behind them came the RAM team and the new Beatrice-Lola, Hart users all.

The RAMs of Philippe Alliott and Kenny Acheson suffered detonation problems on Friday and, with the engines being in short supply, both drivers had to suffer the ignominy of running race boost and tyres as well as half a tank of fuel in the final qualifying session.

Splitting the Skoal Bandit cars at the back of the grid was hardly an auspicious return for Alan Jones. The Beatrice team had not expected an easy ride, but neither had they anticipated practice sessions as fraught as this. There was much muttering about engines not lasting as long as the qualifying tyres although, according to the much-maligned Brian Hart, the FORCE-run team suffered overheating with one engine, a transmission failure with another, while the third 415T succeeded in blowing its oil out. This gave Jones no opportunity to dial out understeer and, to add to their problems, an overheating CV joint curtailed progress even further. Jones had to rely on his time from Friday, as problems on Saturday reduced his qualifying to the final 20 minutes and a time some nine seconds slower than the previous day. To get on terms with the pole-position man, Jones actually needed to go *nine* seconds faster. Welcome back . . .

August/September:
Stefan Bellof killed during Spa 1000 Km.
Jonathan Palmer injured during practice for Spa 1000 Km.
Rothmans Porsche clinch the World Endurance Championship of Teams at Spa.
Jacques Laffite re-signs with Ligier.

RACE

Hope springs eternal in the hearts of the Italian fans and they streamed into the Autodrome in their usual numbers at the start of a typically hot and hazy Monza day. The warm-up times provided little sustenance, however, since the McLarens of Prost and Lauda were wedged firmly in their usual place at the top of the list. Alboreto was sixth, a full two seconds off the pace. There was a wide variation in tyre choice for the day, Piquet opting for soft tyres and a planned stop, others gambling on harder tyres and a straight-through run.

After hours of careful work by his mechanics and much discussion over tyre choice, Ayrton Senna almost threw it all away at the first corner. He had made a good start but Rosberg surged forward as they approached the chicane, the Lotus on the inside, the Williams very slightly ahead on the outside. By the time Senna realised that Keke *really* meant business, it was too late and the Lotus was forced to take to the kerb as the Williams came across his bows. Showering sand onto the track, Senna then bounced over the kerb on the outside of the corner and somehow maintained second place. Even more surprising was the fact that no one else became involved as the rest, some of whom were almost at a walking pace, filed through.

Taking advantage of Senna's lost momentum and the Honda's exceptional power, Mansell rushed into second place. By the end of the lap, the Williams team had begun to pull away from Prost and Senna (side-by-side), de Angelis, Alboreto, Piquet, Tambay and Johansson. Parked by the side of the start line was the Toleman of Ghinzani, the Italian having stalled on the grid and then panicked himself into submission by throwing

John Townsend

every switch he could find and fouling up any chance of restarting the Hart. Acheson, also in trouble at the start, did at least get going but the cause of his trouble, a broken clutch, would send the Ulsterman into retirement and a state of disillusionment over his team's efforts. Martini had retired with engine failure half-way round the first lap and the next car to visit the pits belonged to Alan Jones.

Realising his race might be a short one, Jones tried to make the most of it, the red car darting and weaving as he picked up a few places on the first lap. He also picked up rubbish in the cooling ducts and a quick stop at the end of lap two saw the paper removed. The Beatrice ran for another four laps before the overheating returned and the final act was a distributor failure which caused Jones to park his car just before the pits. After such a dismal start, the only way was up.

While Jones was having his problems at the back of the field, there was trouble at the front, Mansell's engine suddenly sounding as though it was running on three cylinders as he passed the pits at the end of lap three. He completed a lap at slow speed, the mechanics changing the electronics before sending the Englishman on his way. The car was perfect again but he was exactly two laps behind as he rejoined in the slipstream of his team-mate.

Prost was seven seconds behind Rosberg and comfortably ahead of de Angelis, the Italian having moved ahead of his team-mate as Senna struggled with hard tyres and a down-on-power engine. Alboreto was fifth but that was not to last long, the crowd watching helplessly as the Italian was demoted by Piquet's Brabham on lap eight. As if to underline the problems afflicting the Ferrari drivers, Johansson had lost eighth place on the same lap as Lauda came by, the Austrian enjoying

STEFAN BELLOF: SO MUCH TO GIVE
Stefan Bellof began his Formula 1 career the way he meant to go on. Refusing to be depressed by niggling problems during practice for the 1984 Brazilian Grand Prix, Bellof floored the throttle of his Tyrrell-Cosworth on the green light and moved from 22nd on the grid to 13th in the space of two laps.

It was our first indication that a driver of startling reflexes and co-ordination was about to brighten the Formula 1 scene; and that was not confined to his energy at the wheel.

Bellof's booming laugh in the paddocks and restaurants became as familiar as his opposite lock on the track. He was fun-loving yet took his racing very seriously indeed – a rare combination in the hyped-up Eighties – and he thoroughly enjoyed the ambience of the race track.

Shunning the late arrival techniques of his more blasé seniors, Bellof often made an early start and breakfasted at the circuit with the mechanics, a habit which he had adopted since Dijon in 1984 when he became stuck in the notorious traffic. Abandoning the queue, he simply drove his Porsche across ploughed fields, grinning all the way.

The mechanics loved that story. On one occasion, he made a note of their shoe sizes, offering to provide samples of his sponsor's training shoes. To everyone's surprise, he fulfilled his promise and such a thoughtful act endeared him to the team as much as his ability to put their car through its paces.

Bellof had to bide his time with the Tyrrell-Cosworth until the middle of 1985, but not before turning in an exhilarating drive in

the wet at Monaco in 1984 and finishing an excellent fourth at Detroit in '85 despite a broken clutch.

His future was about to blossom with the arrival of the turbo 014; the speed and flair shown in Endurance Racing was about to be put to good effect.

The Rothmans Porsche team had signed Bellof for 1983 and 1984 after an excellent year with the Maurer in Formula 2. Once again, Bellof went into the attack immediately, taking pole position and winning at Silverstone with Derek Bell, the driver with whom he would share great success in Group C.

Stefan Bellof won the Driver's category in 1984 and, along the way, took a fine victory at Spa. Twelve months later, he returned to Belgium to dispute the lead with Jacky Ickx. Keen to get by, Bellof attempted a rash move at *Eau Rouge*.

It would have been hailed as pure Bellof had it come off. But it did not and the 27-year old German died of injuries received when his Brun Porsche cannoned into the barrier.

A week later, the Grand Prix teams, barely over the shock of Winkelhock's fatal accident, assembled at Monza. Given Bellof's exuberant style, there was a reluctant acceptance of what had happened. Down in the Tyrrell pit, the loss of a friend was felt more keenly, the premature departure of a driver of such ability causing frustration and sadness in equal amounts.

One mechanic, seasoned but not immune to the larcenous nature of motor racing, summed it up: 'The accident, everything about it; it's bloody annoying', he said. 'Stefan had so much to give.'

M. H.

More oil and more speed required for the Beatrice-Lola. Alan Jones spent more time in the pits than on the track during the team's debut. Teddy Mayer (left) looks on. Neil Oatley, designer of the THL 1, confers with Brian Hart.

one of his famous charges from the rear of the grid. A lap later and he had dispensed with Tambay's Renault; now it seemed Alboreto's sixth place would not last long either.

It was a bad day for Italy in general, what with Ghinzani and Martini out on the first lap and Patrese making frequent pit stops to attend to brake trouble on the Alfa Romeo. Eventually he would retire with a broken exhaust to join his team-mate, who had stopped running after just four laps with a broken engine. Then there was Fabi, into the pits at the end of lap 11 to have a rear tyre replaced after Berger had sliced the Pirelli with his nose wing, the Arrows now running with a lop-sided look about it. Fabi was back at the end of the next lap, asking to have the rear of the car checked more thoroughly. Nothing was found to be amiss and he was sent on his way, last and behind Mansell.

As the Williams pair continued to run in tandem on the road, Prost was happy to run in second place since he knew he could run all day at that pace while Rosberg was sure to stop. Indeed, the first driver to make a tyre change was Piquet, the Brabham stopping as early as lap 12 and dropping from fifth to 11th place in the process. That pit stop should have elevated Alboreto back to fifth – except that the Ferrari had just been passed by Lauda and the Austrian was quickly catching Senna's Lotus, Niki taking fourth on lap 15. One lap later and he had devoured the Lotus of de Angelis. That left his team-mate, not too far ahead – but running on harder tyres than Lauda.

Further retirements included Warwick (broken crown wheel and pinion), Berger (gearbox trouble), Alliot (no boost on his RAM-Hart) and Rothengatter, after a steady run in the Osella was ended by engine failure.

Lauda's great charge appeared to have ended on lap.26 when he made for the pits but the problem was confined to sagging nose wings on the McLaren. He received new tyres while a replacement nose cone was fitted and the delay dropped Niki to 10th. As Lauda rejoined, Alboreto arrived at the Ferrari pit for fresh tyres, Rosberg doing likewise at the end of his 28th lap.

That, of course, left Prost in the lead and, for a while, it seemed the cushion of 17 seconds to Rosberg might provide the setting for an interesting race. No chance. From just past half-distance, it took the determined Rosberg just 10 laps to haul himself onto the McLaren's tail, Keke continually smashing the lap record as he did so. By lap 40, he was leading again.

Senna was third now, despite his struggle with the hard Goodyears and poor response from his engine, while de Angelis was dropping back in fourth place as he heeded the fuel monitoring device which warned of high consumption – wrongly, as it turned out. Johansson held a temporary fifth place, temporary because he was about to be passed by the rapid Piquet and the Swede had yet to make a stop for tyres. Surer, had been in reasonable shape all afternoon and was not far behind his team-mate, keeping a safe distance ahead of the unhappy Alboreto. Resolutely making up ground once more, Lauda was closing on the Ferrari when the TAG engine emitted a trail of smoke and the man who had done so much for Ferrari in the past ended his last race in Italy to a round of sympathetic applause from the stands.

There was little sympathy for Mansell as he charged along by himself, almost unnoticed, in 14th, then 13th place. Along the way he set the fastest lap, racing no one but never losing heart.

Rosberg's performance at the front merely underlined what might have been: Mansell might have been second. Then, at the end of lap 45, it became clear he might have *won*.

Rosberg was in the pits, a broken head gasket causing the Honda engine to lose its water and any chance of victory.

Assuming an equally easy win, Prost found himself over a minute ahead of Piquet, the Brabham having displaced Senna a few laps earlier. Surer was now fourth and closing on the Lotus but all of that became a matter of secondary importance at the end of lap 45; Ferrari number 27 was crawling into the pits with a broken engine. Alboreto's dismal weekend was over just as he looked like salvaging a few points.

All this drama moved Johansson into fifth place as he passed de Angelis and it was the Italian's Lotus which would form an impromptu taxi as Stefan, desperately hitching a ride, returned to the pits after his car had run out of fuel on the last lap. Elio, fearing the same fate was about to befall him, was not amused to find there was in excess of 20 litres in his tank at the end of the race.

Tambay took a dispirited seventh place in the Renault after running behind Brundle's Tyrrell during the second half of the race. Brundle would have kept the place had he not suffered a severe vibration once he had collected debris on his hard compound left-rear tyre.

The hard Goodyears on Prost's McLaren had not caused the slightest bother under the circumstances but then, of course, he had not been under pressure and neither had he challenged for the lead. The nine points more or less fell into his lap and there was no sweeter place to savour them than the victory rostrum at the *Autodromo Nazionale di Monza*.   M.H.

Nothing to smile about. Subdued Ferrari supporters wait by the paddock gates.

Every move by Ferrari was watched and recorded. At the end of the weekend, however, there was nothing to say.

TECHNICAL FILE

McLAREN
Chassis 5, damaged during French GP, repaired and used by Prost. Brake discs equipped with close-fitting plates to give aerodynamic effect (as seen in Germany). John Barnard not present at Monza.

TYRRELL
New chassis 014 (3) for Brundle. Revised rear suspension; uprights modified to give different angle to pullrods and top wishbones. Shorter side pods.

WILLIAMS
Major development continuing with engines at Didcot and in Japan. Strengthened exhaust systems.

BRABHAM
Fitted carbon-fibre skirts under nose, following the same principle as Toleman. Surer used them for the first day's practice; Piquet's car so equipped for the race.

RAM
Ran latest specification Hart engine with larger Holset turbo.

LOTUS
Cut off side plates to rear underbody to counteract porpoising effect. Senna tried T-car with rear suspension revisions (seen in Austria) during unofficial practice sessions.

RENAULT
Front upper wishbones stiffened following failure at Zandvoort. Tried new rear wing.

ARROWS
Tried revised rear wings. All three cars fitted with revised wastegate position.

TOLEMAN
Apart from a more efficient spray to intercooler, no major chassis changes.

ALFA ROMEO
Major changes for Monza included fitting of 1985 rear suspension to '84 chassis and the adoption of lower side pods and revised radiator positions. Larger pipes from intercooler to engine. Bosch electronic box moved from top of fuel tank to side pod, allowing longer and lower engine cover. New front brake ducts to give aerodynamic effect. Ran vertical aerofoils behind front wheels. Modified steering rack position.

OSELLA
Revised rear suspension (different angle to top wishbone) to improve anti-squat.

LIGIER
Streiff's car fitted with front vertical aerofoils.

FERRARI
Brought three cars instead of the traditional four chassis for Monza. All three heavily revised. Suspension had different fixing points, front and rear, for pullrods. Also, different fixing points for front shock absorbers with appropriate holes in chassis top (as seen at Ricard) to allow access. Side rads almost parallel to tub; larger intercooler with second exit resulted in different side pod shape. Revised position for wastegate allowed narrower and shorter rear bodywork to improve airflow. Engine cover lower and without duct for gearbox oil cooler. Revised air intake for engine. Underbody profile shortened to reduce porpoising experienced at Zandvoort. Tried secondary rear wing, mounted very low.

MINARDI
Ran double rear wing. Fitted manometer to monitor engine temperatures.

BEATRICE
First race appearance for this car with its traditional rather than radical design. Taller and narrower side pods allowed a 5 cm platform to extend at lower edge to maximum width permitted, giving extra downforce. Bodywork cut and flattened at top of cockpit section to give additional stiffness. NACA duct on top of side pod cooled Holset turbo.

G.P.

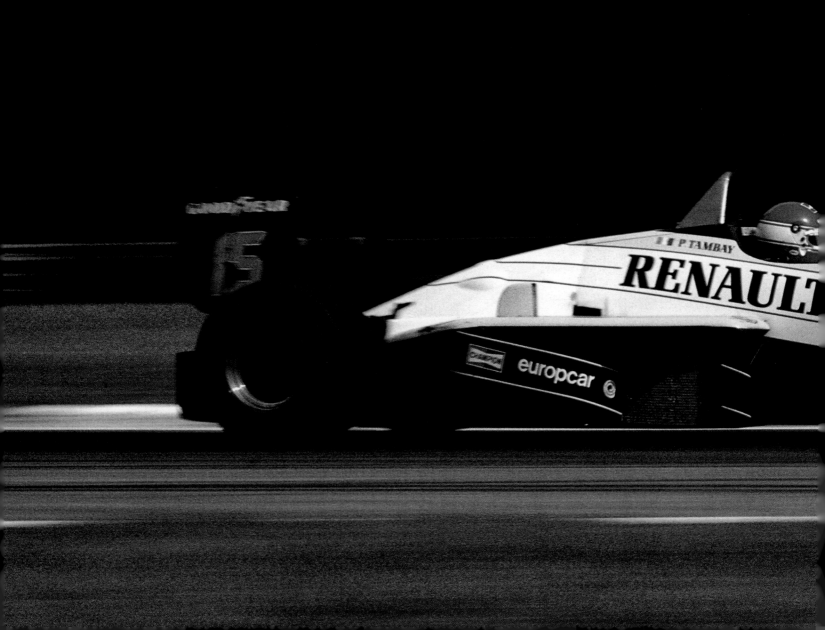

Grand Prix
of Belgium

Paul-Henri Cahier

Alain Prost finished third; Michele Alboreto retired after three laps to give the Marlboro McLaren driver a lead of 16 points in the Championship. With three races remaining, the identity of the car destined to carry Number 1 in 1986 was becoming increasingly obvious.

That feeling of anticlimax at Spa-Francorchamps was encouraged when Ayrton Senna completely overshadowed the fight for the title by producing a display of undeniable brilliance to take his second win of the season. Like the victory in Portugal, this was achieved in tricky conditions as the track changed from wet to dry with the added complication of a treacherous shower half-way through.

Senna lost the lead only once, when he stopped for tyres, and up to that time he had been under pressure from both the Canon Williams of Mansell and Prost's McLaren. Then, the JPS Lotus team played their master stroke by fitting pre-heated and scrubbed slicks to give Senna an advantage which would render him untouchable for the rest of the afternoon.

Mansell, nursing a broken rib, survived an attack from his team-mate, a spin and two off-course excursions to finish second and score his best result to date. Third place for Prost was no more than average – but good enough to consolidate his Championship lead.

You would have thought, therefore, that it had been an easy cruise into the points. Not so. The Frenchman, fastest in all four practice sessions, was convinced he had a car capable of winning. He had to spend the race talking himself into a circumspect drive which had the Championship rather than a wheel-to-wheel fight for the lead as its ultimate aim. Bearing in the mind his previous experiences when on the brink of success, Prost was not about to risk anything now.

A rare moment. Ayrton Senna gets out of shape under braking for *La Source* during the opening stages. Apart from a pit stop to change to slicks, the Lotus led all the way. Prost, lying second, dropped to third in the race to make sure of scoring points.

Patrick Tambay (*previous page*) and Derek Warwick raced hard in the tricky conditions at Spa, the Englishman scoring his first points in five races for Renault-Elf.

ENTRY AND PRACTICE

Grand Prix racing returned to Spa in September to have another crack at the Belgian Grand Prix following the fiasco earlier (see pages 110-111). In the intervening three months, the track surface had been repaired and there had been major changes in Formula 1 as the teams worked their way through eight races.

In June, Michele Alboreto had been fastest during the one day of practice while Alain Prost, plagued with engine failures, had languished at the back of the grid. At the time, Alboreto shared joint second place in the Championship with Prost, two points behind de Angelis.

In September, de Angelis was third, Prost led Alboreto by 12 points and, this time, the McLaren was quickest in all four practice sessions. Ferrari, as had become the norm, were in trouble.

It was Prost's first pole position of the season, hardly a surprise in view of McLaren's attendant problems in raising the TAG turbo boost to the high pressure required for qualifying. Indeed, Prost was some 20 kph down when it came to measuring speed at the top of the hill, a shortcoming which merely underlined the excellent quality of the MP4/2B chassis elsewhere – even if Prost did express himself less than satisfied with the car's overall performance.

Prost would be the McLaren team's sole representative following an incident involving Niki Lauda on Friday morning. The Austrian was cruising back to the pits when the throttle stuck open, the subsequent impact with the barrier whipping the steering wheel and, with it, Lauda's right wrist. An X-ray revealed that nothing was broken but Lauda clearly had no wish to continue, the Austrian returning almost immediately to Vienna.

If Prost had been in trouble with blown engines in June, then it appeared to be Ayrton Senna's turn in September, certainly during Friday's practice. In the morning he had problems with the gearbox and then an engine change was required for the timed session. He used the spare car, fitted with race tyres as a stop-gap measure while he waited for a run on qualifiers with the more favourable race car. Proceedings were delayed when a flash fire in the garage burnt out an oil line on the race car. This was repaired in time for a run at the end of the session, until half-way round his lap a turbo blew. Senna was a very unhappy 18th.

Twenty-four hours later, he was second fastest, just one-tenth slower than Prost in the course of 4.3 miles! According to Ayrton, the car was not balanced properly, a fact which accounted for his rear qualifiers losing their edge three corners before the end of the lap.

The same reason gave Elio de Angelis difficulty in making his qualifiers last although gradual development work – such as adding more front wing to reduce the understeer – helped him move from 11th to ninth place in the final session.

Nelson Piquet may have been a couple of tenths slower than Senna but, judging by his progress in the twitchy Brabham-BMW, he had to work much harder than the Lotus driver. The speed trap (an indicated 200.862 mph on the approach to *Les Combes* at the top of the hill!) showed that German horsepower was responsible for working the BT54 into third place on the grid . . . on the understanding, of course, that it took a driver of Piquet's skill to keep the car under control. Marc Surer, for example, put everything into an impressive lap on Saturday but the Swiss driver's satisfaction with 12th place evaporated when he discovered that Piquet was two seconds faster. It put Nelson's ability into true perspective, at least, as far as Marc Surer was concerned.

The Ferrari drivers proved to be more of a match although Michele Alboreto's superior grid position did not give a true indication of practice form. Stefan Johansson had been second fastest overall on Friday and a misfire on Saturday meant a drop to fifth place on the grid. Alboreto, meanwhile, had been busy with back-to-back comparisons between his race car and the T-car (in the older configuration with which he had set fastest time in June) before deciding that the revised 156 seen at Monza was the better of the two. On Friday, he had been sixth fastest with a car which looked ill at ease through *Eau Rouge* but, in the final session, he improved to take fourth despite the fact that he was blocked by slower cars while running his second set of qualifiers, a problem which had also troubled Johansson.

The relatively smooth nature of the Spa circuit suited the Barclay Arrows team since it did not highlight the handling problems which had been experienced elsewhere. Gerhard Berger was fifth fastest on Friday with Thierry Boutsen 12th but, in the final session, the order was reversed as the local lad found over two seconds to improve to sixth while a major mechanical failure led to Berger slipping to eighth. Powering through *Eau Rouge* on his first set of qualifiers, the plenum chamber on the BMW suddenly exploded with enough force to smash the engine cover and fling bits of BMW over the track.

Keke Rosberg hurled his Williams across the

September:

FISA confirms South African Grand Prix will go ahead in spite of political unrest.

Renault withdraw their entry for Kyalami.

FOCA agrees five-year deal to run a Grand Prix at Budapest.

Watson called in to replace injured Lauda at Spa; Ferrari will not agree to last-minute substitution.

Alan Jones banned from driving for a year in the UK due to a drink-driving charge in London.

Wally Dallenbach Jnr (Mercury Capri) wins SCCA Bendix TransAm Championship.

Bertrand Fabi (Reynard 84SF) wins EFDA Formula Ford 2000 Euroseries.

Al Holbert (Porsche 962) wins IMSA Camel GT Championship.

track in his usual manner but on this occasion it failed to produce the results, Keke taking a disappointing 10th place even though the power and handling of the FW10 had no obvious shortcoming. In fact, for the fourth time this season, Rosberg was beaten by Nigel Mansell, a feat which was even more significant in view of problems experienced by the Englishman during practice.

In keeping with a decision made by Rosberg on Friday, Mansell opted to use a set of Cs and one set of qualifiers. It was while he was using his race tyres that Mansell had the terrifying experience of a broken steering wheel – in the middle of one of the downhill sweepers. He wrestled the car to a safe speed and, in the course of his struggle, he aggravated a chest injury incurred at Monza. He returned to the pits where the wheel with the broken spoke was replaced and the race tyres were replaced with 'E' qualifiers. Mansell set fourth fastest time and that would be his best of the weekend as Saturday's efforts on two sets of Es were thwarted by a combination of clutch trouble and slower cars. Mansell slipped to seventh.

Teo Fabi took 11th place with a Toleman which lacked the straightline speed to match its deft handling. Apart from a wastegate problem on Friday, the Italian had no major dramas, Piercarlo Ghinzani's practice being equally straightforward (apart from an engine failure on Saturday morning) although his performance was only good enough for 16th place.

Had Patrick Tambay been able to repeat the 1m 56.486s set in June, then he would have been fifth fastest. Of course, the track was offering nothing like the grip which came with the fresh surface three months previously but Patrick was nevertheless disappointed to be in 13th place with the Renault-Elf on a circuit which he thoroughly enjoyed.

Tambay did not improve on his Friday time thanks to gear selection bothers on his first run and an inattentive Philippe Streiff later in the session. Derek Warwick did find another second on Saturday but even that was slower than Tambay's time as the Englishman continued to fight the 'understeer in, oversteer out' habit of his RE60B.

If the Renault drivers were feeling despondent with their lot, they were positively joyful compared with Eddie Cheever as he attempted to put together one good lap with the troublesome Alfa Romeo. There was a broken turbo on Friday and a blown engine on Saturday morning, the subsequent mechanical work meaning that Cheever lost half an hour of the final session. And, when he did finally take to the track, the clutch was slipping. He took 19th place, a second slower than Riccardo Patrese.

The Benetton cars sandwiched the equally unhappy Ligier Gitanes drivers as Jacques Laffite took 17th place with a car whose understeering characteristics did not inspire confidence in the fast corners – particularly when the JS25 suddenly switched to oversteer. Streiff took 18th place but at least he felt he would have been better off had he not been baulked by Tambay as the

Paul-Henri Cahier

Renault driver engaged in an unnecessary tit-for-tat exchange after their earlier incident.

The Skoal Bandit RAM team confined themselves to one car for Spa, Kenny Acheson deciding that the desperate shortage of engines was doing nothing for his Formula 1 aspirations. By switching to a new blend of fuel, however, RAM appeared to have eliminated a few of their problems as Philippe Alliot took an exceptional 13th place on Friday, the Frenchman enjoying the excellent handling of the Gustav Brunner-designed car. On Saturday, a loss of boost saw no improvement and he dropped to a more accustomed 20th.

Since this was the scene of Bellof's fatal accident just a few weeks before, no one needed reminding of the reason why the Tyrrell team were continuing with just one car for Martin Brundle. It was not a happy time for the Englishman since he had been present on that fateful day and now, to make things worse, the Tyrrell was handling poorly, Brundle having a high-speed brush with the barrier on Friday.

Spa had also claimed the services, albeit temporarily, of Jonathan Palmer and, in his place, the German team chose their countryman and recently crowned Formula 3000 Champion, Christian Danner. He had to be satisfied with Friday's practice time since the final session saw both the West sponsored cars stop with misfires and broken turbos although it is doubtful whether Danner could have made up the four seconds between himself and Brundle. But at least he was ahead of those perennial back-markers, Huub Rothengatter in the Osella and Pierluigi Martini, the latter looking painfully slow and out of his depth with the Minardi on a circuit which highlighted a driver's lack of skill and commitment.

RACE

Alain Prost must have grimaced when he pulled back his curtains on Sunday morning. He wanted a straightforward race where he could get on with scoring a handful of points to strengthen his position at the top of the table. The last thing he needed was the element of chance, forcing him to make decisions without the benefit of his usual forethought, testing and analysis. In other words, it was a typical Spa day: rain, with the chance of sunshine later . . . then, maybe, more rain. And to think that the sun was splitting the trees on the aborted race day back in June.

The organisers must have had similar thoughts. As it was, they faced a low-key weekend. The handful of spectators present during practice indicated that people were unwilling to come back to Francorchamps after paying out to see a Formula 3000 race in June and then a Group C race a few weeks before the rescheduled Grand Prix.

The problems facing the organisers were the last thing on Michele Alboreto's mind; he had difficulties of his own during the warm-up. A persistent misfire gave the Italian no chance to find out about Spa in the streaming conditions and he looked resigned rather than angry.

For Nigel Mansell and Williams, things looked good as the Englishman set the fastest time, followed by de Angelis, Senna, Rosberg and Johansson.

The rain had eased a little by the time they formed on the grid but there was no question of fitting slicks. And, for Alboreto, there was no question of using his race car. He had completed his exploratory lap in the T-car and found, to his extreme consternation, a fuel leak! This was fixed in time for the start; as was a fuel pump problem on Alliot's race car, saving the Frenchman from having to make the anticipated switch to his spare chassis.

Christian Danner, meanwhile, made the unprecedented move of slipping into the pit lane at the end of the formation lap and switching to his spare car after the Zakspeed's gearbox had begun to give trouble. He took the start from the pit lane while, on the other side of the barrier, the rest of the field made a clean getaway, Senna powering into an immediate lead while Prost fell to third place behind Piquet.

The leaders rounded *La Source* and there was instant mayhem as Piquet applied the power and promptly spun to the left before rolling back into the middle of the track. Prost managed to miss the Brabham, as did the Ferraris, Alboreto and Johansson somehow moving far enough to the right in the short time they had available to react. The rest fanned out on either side, those on the left taking to the dirt.

All of which gave Senna, the only man untroubled by Piquet's gyration, breathing space as he slithered up the hill to *Les Combes*. Prost soon gave chase, however, with Mansell emerging from the spray to challenge the McLaren for second place. Alboreto was fourth but at the end of the second lap, he was in eighth place and struggling. The McLaren team were quick to relay the news to Prost.

Sensing that there was no real urgency today, Prost was not too bothered when Mansell neatly out-braked the McLaren into *Les Combes* on lap four. By the end of that lap his hunch had been proved right, for Alboreto was out, his Ferrari parked by the barrier with a broken clutch and deranged gearbox.

The line was now quite dry in places and, since this had been declared a Wet Race, the onus was on the drivers to make the decision when to stop for slicks. It was not easy. The top end of the circuit may have been manageable on slicks but there

Alain Prost sweeps through the magnificent Ardennes circuit to take pole position. His car was perfect but rain on race day prevented him from using it to good effect, as the McLaren driver preferred to race with Championship points in mind.
Thierry Boutsen, sixth on the grid, lost a well-earned place in the points when his Arrows-BMW retired, much to the disappointment of the home crowd.

International Press Agency

was still a lot of water to be found under the trees and around the start/finish area. None the less, Rosberg made the decision to come in at the end of lap three, the first driver to do so.

His lap times subsequently proved this was the right move and it took the rest of the field a considerable time to get the message. Piquet and Streiff came in at the end of the next lap, but the leading three, Senna, Mansell and Prost, continued to circulate in close company.

Johansson stopped at the end of lap six but his race was destined to be brief when his V6 seized at the top of the hill and sent the Ferrari off the circuit. The end of a miserable weekend for Ferrari went almost unnoticed since the leaders had chosen the same lap to make their stops.

The Williams crew won the tyre-change race, sending Mansell out of the pit lane just ahead of Senna. But it was Lotus who won the tactical battle. While Mansell struggled for grip on the run down to *Eau Rouge*, Senna calmly pulled out of his slipstream and drove past – in the wet. The Lotus team had given Ayrton a set of heated and scrubbed Goodyears; Mansell had a shiny, unscrubbed set and the difference provided the Brazilian with a three-second lead at the end of the lap.

While the leading trio had been in the pits, de Angelis and Boutsen had assumed command, the Arrows driver making his stop at the end of the next lap. De Angelis, however, pressed on, a strange decision since his team-mate was over 10 seconds per lap quicker on slicks. Elio did make his stop at the end of lap 10 but this was to prove an academic exercise for the pit crew since the Renault engine was to expire with turbo failure not long after.

The rest of the field had changed tyres by now and, for some, it would mean the end of the race as they showed a surprising lack of common sense in the tricky conditions. Both Ghinzani and Alliot spun into the barrier as they accelerated too hard, too soon after leaving the pits, the latter incurring the justifiable wrath of John Macdonald since the Frenchman had been running strongly in the mid-field up to this point.

As if to emphasise the delicate approach required, Mansell spun under braking for *La Source* at the end of lap 10 but he kept the engine running and, although he was no longer in close company with Senna, he did not lose second place. Prost, who had also been given unscrubbed slicks, had relinquished his third place to Rosberg as the Finn continued at his usual electrifying pace.

Prost was not in danger since Boutsen was almost half a minute behind in fifth place though managing to pull away gradually from Tambay's Renault. De Angelis's demise let Warwick take seventh, the Renault coming under attack from Cheever as the Alfa driver set the fastest lap and made the most of the only conditions which would suit his difficult car.

During the course of the next few laps, the honour of setting the fastest lap changed hands as the track continued to dry and Prost closed on Rosberg. Senna, however, was not hanging around either and he went even faster as he pulled

out an 11-second lead over Mansell. The race seemed to be settling down.

But not for long. Lap 19 was marked by a short, sharp shower in the pits area; heavy enough to send plumes of spray from the slicks and to cause the team managers to order preparations for further pit stops to change back to wets. But no one came in. It was a case of typical Spa weather, the very thing which had given this magnificent circuit in its old form such a chilling reputation. Drivers went from sunshine to showers and never knew what to expect next.

No one fell off, however, and the order remained the same although Rosberg continued to close on Mansell. The gap was reduced considerably on lap 25 when Surer went off the track at *Les Combes* and returned in front of Mansell, causing the Williams to take drastic avoiding action.

Now the Williams pair ran nose to tail, Keke ducking and diving; Mansell remaining resolute; the pit crew watching with interest since team orders would not be applied. For six laps, Rosberg

kept this up then, at the start of lap 31, he dropped away suddenly. For some time, the left-front brake duct had been breaking up and the effect was to give uneven braking as the right disc received proper cooling while the left ran much hotter than normal. Rosberg decided enough was enough and a pit stop was inevitable when the duct finally snapped off.

Mansell, meanwhile, arrived at *Les Combes*, still racing the now imaginary Rosberg. He looked in his mirrors. Nothing. He looked again – and missed his braking point. The Williams bounced across the kerb as Mansell straightlined the corner before regaining the track. Fortunately there was no damage done. Rosberg eventually made his stop; the mechanics tore off the right duct and gave Keke a fresh set of tyres while they were at it.

Rosberg rejoined 17 seconds down on Prost who, in turn, was half a minute behind Mansell, the Williams being much the same distance behind the Lotus of Senna. The first four positions would

Nelson Piquet caused mayhem at the first corner. Everyone managed to avoid the Brabham driver and he recovered to finish fifth.
'What Williams?' Marc Surer inadvertently sends Nigel Mansell onto the grass at *Les Combes*. The Williams driver drove an excellent race to finish second.

not change during the course of the final 11 laps and it seemed that Senna was simply cruising home.

In fact, he was going as hard as he could since the Renault engine had developed the unnerving habit of cutting out every so often. With Mansell only 28 seconds behind, he wanted to keep as comfortable a cushion as possible. For Nigel, he was in pain from a cracked rib, caused by his kerb bashing incident when a tyre failed at Monza and aggravated by his incident during practice at Spa. The only man who was cruising easily was Prost – which was the last thing he wanted to do. Once the track dried, he found his car to be perfect and yet he had to resist the urge to charge to the front. Championship points were the final arbiter in this instance.

The only change to the leaderboard occurred when Thierry Boutsen's excellent run in fifth place began to crumble as he lost two gears and the differential began to pack up. First he was passed by Warwick (suffering from too short a fifth gear) and then by Piquet, the Brabham really motoring now that Nelson had got rid of the ineffectual intermediate Pirelli wets. Indeed, with five laps remaining, he took fifth place from Warwick.

The hapless Boutsen stopped two laps from the end to sympathetic applause from the handful of spectators, allowing his team-mate Berger (who had stopped even later than de Angelis to change tyres) to take seventh ahead of Surer (struggling with an engine which would not pick up cleanly, making the Brabham difficult to drive in the slippery conditions). None the less, the Swiss set second fastest lap and held off Streiff, now the only Ligier representative following Laffite's untimely crash into the barrier after holding a steady eighth place for the second half of the race. At the back came Brundle, the Tyrrell driver losing all the ground he had made up in the wet as the handling of the 014 became extremely difficult in the dry, Martin spinning twice and making an extra pit stop to see if anything could be done.

Among the retirements were Cheever whose dramatic drive ended with a gearbox failure, a similar problem for Tambay being caused by a broken oil line. Fabi had lost an unimpressive mid-field position with a deranged throttle assembly and Patrese, never in serious contention, retired with ignition trouble. Still running were the struggling Rothengatter and Martini's Minardi, both of whom managed to keep out of the leaders' way on the five or six occasions they were lapped.

Senna admitted this victory was not as sweet as Portugal but it meant enough to have the Brazilian brush aside the marshals as they tried to wave him into *parc fermé* rather than let him complete a lap of honour. With the lap measuring in excess of four miles, he clearly had no worries about the Lotus running out of fuel since the wet conditions had reduced the pace considerably.

Prost, though, was taking no chances. He duly parked his car as directed and collected the four points which made the Championship almost a formality.
M.H.

TECHNICAL FILE

McLaren
New titanium anti-roll bars. Revised profiles to lower edge of front wing side plates.

Tyrrell
New one-piece carbon-fibre air ducts for turbos. Both cars have shorter side pods but only one chassis fitted with revised rear suspension.

Williams
No changes to cars due to one-week interval between Monza and Spa.

Brabham
Piquet's car fitted with small skirts under nose section. Brabham brought back adjustable flap to regulate airflow to radiators and intercoolers in spite of device being declared illegal as moveable aerodynamic device. This was a form of protest by Brabham against the brake ducts used by Ferrari, McLaren, Williams, RAM, Alfa Romeo, Tyrrell and Minardi. The ducts in question acted as an aerodynamic aid and were cooling ducts in name only.

RAM
Used same fuel as Toleman began using at French Grand Prix in a bid to cure detonation problems.

Lotus
Suspension modifications seen at Monza not used at Spa. All three cars fitted with rear trim tabs on side pods and vertical front wings.

Renault
No changes to cars at Spa.

Arrows
In common with majority of teams, cars transported directly to Spa but chassis Number 1 brought from England to replace chassis 2 damaged on Monza kerbs.

Toleman
Nothing new.

Alfa Romeo
Cheever's car fitted with vertical front wings; abandoned after Friday's practice. Patrese tried lower secondary rear wing fitted to gearbox on Friday.

Osella
No change to cars for Belgium.

Ligier
Both cars fitted with vertical front wings.

Ferrari
Brought two modified chassis (as per Monza) and one chassis as seen at Spa in June. Revised cars ran additional wing profile at rear and vertical front wings. Alboreto's race car fitted with skirts under nose section (Friday only). Revised cars had duct running from turbo inlet to rear shock absorbers made by Marzocchi. Black box, fixed to nose section above driver's legs, monitored engine performance (revs, fuel consumption etc.) during race.

Minardi
Nothing new.

Zakspeed
Four-piece rear wing.

Beatrice
Not present at rescheduled Spa since team not entered for original race.
G.P.

'I said in my preview there was as much chance of John Watson making a comeback as there was of Derek Warwick scoring points in that Renault or Nigel Mansell winning a race! I'll probably be proved wrong as usual. . .' The indefatigable Murray Walker chats with Nigel Mansell, who finished second, and Derek Warwick who collected his first points in five races.

Shell Oils Grand Prix of Europe

This was the perfect day; Alain Prost finally won the World Championship and Nigel Mansell finally won a Grand Prix.

Leading up to their successes, we had a fascinating race, full of tension, incident, pleasure, anger, competition and, to add further interest, praise for drivers unaccustomed to sharing the limelight. At the end, though, we had a new World Champion, a cruise into fourth place being sufficient to make Prost the first Frenchman to win the title. And we had a new winner, an almost faultless drive leading Mansell to victory – the first Englishman to win a Grand Prix since 1977.

A few moments after the start, however, it did not look as though it would work out that way as both Mansell and Prost spent some time motoring off the circuit. The Canon Williams Honda had been disputing the first corner with the JPS Lotus of Ayrton Senna while a slow start by Mansell's team-mate, Keke Rosberg, had caused Prost to take to the grass. The irony was, that as Prost dropped to 14th place, Rosberg suddenly found grip and rocketed off to play a decisive part in shaping the outcome of the race.

Mansell's excursion across the kerbs let Rosberg into second place and a battle with Senna ended, temporarily, when Keke spun and accidently removed Nelson Piquet's Olivetti Brabham. Pitting to replace a punctured tyre, Rosberg rejoined in front of the leaders, Senna and Mansell and, venting his fury, Rosberg slowed Senna to let Mansell into a lead he was never to lose.

Senna went on to finish second and Rosberg charged through the field to take third place. Prost's frustration at the start was compounded when he saw Michele Alboreto ahead of him. However, the Ferrari was running true to form and could offer no resistance as Prost moved ahead, Ferrari's dismal decline being exacerbated a few laps later by a massive turbo fire for Alboreto.

The Championship issue was not yet clear cut as Marc Surer and Jacques Laffite worked their way into the top three – superb drives which were denying Prost valuable points. Unfortunately, both the Brabham and the Ligier were destined to retire to allow Prost to take the title, an achievement which was as overdue as Nigel Mansell's maiden Grand Prix victory.

ENTRY AND PRACTICE

The challenge presented by the Brands Hatch circuit is such that *any* lap good enough for pole position over the years has been, by definition, something of a spectacle. Ayrton Senna's lap in the final practice session for the Shell Oils Grand Prix of Europe was no exception; the Brazilian was simply outstanding as he shattered the seemingly unbeatable standard set by Keke Rosberg's ground-effect Williams FW08C in 1982.

It had been clear from the outset that Senna felt comfortable with his Lotus 97T. This was due in part to a busy day of testing by Derek Warwick, the Englishman having been released from his Renault contract when neither Senna (in Brazil) nor Elio de Angelis (unwell) was available. According to Senna, the car felt *safe*; a necessary prerequisite for a fast lap on a circuit which allows no room for error.

Senna set the ball rolling on his first set of qualifiers when he recorded a 1m 09.66s – and that was while avoiding Capelli's Tyrrell, a manoeuvre which Ayrton reckoned cost him 1000 revs and a loss of boost. The second run proved the point when he lapped Brands in 1m 08.020s. But there was more to come. The Lotus was understeering slightly and he had not been as precise as he would have liked. On Saturday? 'Low sevens, no problem.' For Senna's rivals, who

Alain Prost finally won the World Championship and Nigel Mansell finally won his first Grand Prix.

thought the low eights would be adequate for pole, this was disconcerting news . . .

'The car is fantastic, the best I've had all year.' And with that assurance, Ayrton climbed into the 97T on Saturday and cut a 1m 07.786s. That, it seemed, would be that.

Nelson Piquet, with BMW qualifying horsepower reckoned to be in excess of 1200 bhp, was not about to give up without a fight. In one of those typical Piquet laps – the Brazilian's head cocked to the side, the BMW pumping out a haze of black smoke – the Brabham BT54 covered the 2.614 miles in 1m 07.482s. Senna, watching the Longines monitor, knew what he had to do on his last set of qualifiers.

With 10 minutes of the session remaining, Senna went out and raised his own exceptional standards with a lap of 1m 07.169s, a shade over 140 mph. Piquet knew the Brabham had no answer; his lap had been on the limit. He did try again, in fact, by buffing his Pirellis once they had been used. Nelson managed five quick laps in total but he had to be satisfied with a place on the outside of the front row; a starting position which was more favourable thanks to the sloping grid.

Third, a Williams-Honda. But not, as you might expect, Keke Rosberg. Following a disappointing day on Friday, when a misfire forced him to use the spare car (not fitted with the modified rear suspension), Nigel Mansell made amends on

Good Guy? Bad Guy? Keke Rosberg warms his tyres after his early pit-stop while Nigel Mansell prepares to dive inside Ayrton Senna as the Lotus driver tries to decide what Rosberg will do next.

Saturday. The FW10 had not been handling to his satisfaction in the morning but the mechanics changed everything and Mansell knew immediately that their hard work had not been in vain when he cut 1m 08.786s. Fitting his final set, he hustled the Williams round in 1m 08.059s, beating his team-mate in the process.

Keke Rosberg found the suspension modifications to be a definite improvement and he was reasonably pleased with fourth fastest, offering no excuses for a time one-tenth slower than Mansell. Keke was less than pleased, however, when Ivan Capelli wandered in front of the Williams as they approached Paddock Bend during unofficial practice on Friday. Keke promptly gave the poor Tyrrell driver a 'brake test', a stupid move which merely served to cause damage to the front of Capelli's car, even if it did relieve Rosberg of some of his understandable frustration.

Brands Hatch was no place for a novice, struggling to become familiar with the circuit *and* a turbocharged Formula 1 car and it was hardly surprising to find the young Italian in 26th place on Friday evening. However, it *was* surprising to find Philippe Streiff in sixth place. He may have won a Formula 2 race at Brands Hatch at the end of the previous season but that had been in the wet and this was merely his second drive in the Ligier Formula 1 car. Was sixth fastest a fluke? Indeed not, because the Frenchman improved to take a remarkable fifth place overall on Saturday. The Ligier Gitanes team had been testing at Brands Hatch and the adjustments seemed to be working although Streiff survived a frightening moment when the bell-housing appeared to break and the gearbox seized solid, on the approach to Hawthorns! He spun twice – and lived to tell the tale…

Had Streiff not produced such an excellent performance, Jacques Laffite would have received praise for 10th fastest time. Taking into account his relative lack of interest in qualifying, that performance said much about the suitability of the JS25/Pirelli combination at Brands Hatch. Indeed, Pirelli were hopeful of a good result and further proof was provided by Marc Surer taking seventh place in the Brabham. In fact, he should have been higher, having slipped from fourth place on Friday (when he was within a half-second of Piquet) to seventh thanks to problems with traffic in the final session.

In some respects, Surer's performance went unnoticed since the attention this weekend was focused firmly on Champion Elect Alain Prost and his rival, Michele Alboreto. The pressure on Prost was enormous, besieged as he was by interviewers asking how it felt to be close to the Championship yet again, bearing in mind his disappointments during previous seasons. That was the last thing Prost needed since he was clearly struggling with his McLaren. During testing, the team had bolted on a set of qualifying tyres at the end of the day and Prost had recorded a nine-three with no apparent effort. Now, when it really mattered, he could not approach that time in a car which was set up almost identically. It was a mystery but at least the team, accustomed to lacking the necessary pace during qualifying, were reasonably confident for the race. And then there was the comforting thought that Ferrari were in deeper trouble still . . .

By taking a miserable 15th place, Michele Alboreto was more or less conceding the Championship before the race had started. Struggling with a lack of traction, his problems were compounded by engine failures during both unofficial sessions and a broken turbo when he used the spare car on Friday afternoon. Although two places ahead of his team-mate, Stefan Johansson was just as unhappy, the Swede agreeing with Michele about the inability of the Ferrari to put the power down without provoking sudden oversteer.

The Renault-Elf drivers were also unaminous about the inability of the RE60B to cope with Brands Hatch – or anywhere else for that matter – but Derek Warwick really carried the car on his back as he threw it round Brands to record a creditable eighth fastest. Patrick Tambay admitted his mind was on other things (it was revealed at Brands Hatch that the Frenchman would be joining Beatrice in 1986) and he finished practice in 17th place. One positive point about the Renault operation was the successful use of an on-board Thomson camera beaming live television pictures which were of a superb quality. Indeed, we were able to follow Tambay's efforts for the full 1m 10.934s as he struggled to defeat a car which appeared to have a mind of its own.

The tricky nature of Brands Hatch caught out Elio de Angelis on the first day of practice when the Italian crashed at Westfield. Damage to the Lotus was confined to the nose box and front suspension and the team somehow managed to have the 97T repaired in time for the afternoon session. However, the impact had cricked his neck and the subsequent delay while receiving medical attention meant Elio had completed very few laps. He therefore ran a set of race tyres and one set of qualifiers on Friday and then improved on his time in the final session to take ninth fastest time. In all, though, it was an unhappy practice for Elio since he was almost three seconds away from his frustratingly quick team-mate.

There was also a considerable gap between the Benetton Alfa Romeo drivers, Riccardo Patrese taking 11th place on a circuit he enjoys whereas a turbo failure near the end of a quick lap kept Eddie Cheever in 18th place. Thierry Boutsen had been keeping company with Patrese on Friday but the Barclay Arrows driver made only a fractional improvement in the final session and slipped to 12th place. Team-mate Gerhard Berger went from 16th to 19th place after spending time switching chassis since he felt more at ease in the spare car. None the less, that was not the answer and the Austrian was unable to improve on Saturday.

Piercarlo Ghinzani managed to split the Ferraris as well as recording the fastest time for the Benetton Toleman team. The practice dramas of the weekend were confined to his team-mate, Teo Fabi crashing heavily on the exit of Druids on Friday afternoon and then going off at Paddock in the final qualifying session. Fabi's first shunt had been an almost carbon copy of Martin Brundle's accident during testing but, this weekend, there were no such problems as the Tyrrell driver made the most of a chassis which had been improved considerably during that test session. In fact, he was a little disappointed with 16th place.

The same could be said for Alan Jones in 22nd

Unaccustomed as we are . . . Marc Surer and Jacques Laffite ran second and third, making the most of their Pirellis before two excellent drives were halted by mechanical problems.
Marc Surer and Christian Danner return on foot from opposite ends of the field, Surer having held second place while Danner's Zakspeed had run at the tail of the field.

John Colley

Riccardo Patrese's Alfa Romeo was to take ninth place.

Alan Jones ... frustrations.

place, the Beatrice driver struggling with gear selection bothers on Friday and a general lack of balance. He split both qualifying sessions by using a set of Cs and and set of Es, the Australian admitting he was finding difficulty in getting into the swing of using the qualifiers, a similar problem also afflicting John Watson, his partner on the 11th row.

Problems with making his Pirellis reach a decent working temperature notwithstanding, Philippe Alliot's 23rd place was a major disappointment for RAM boss John Macdonald since this would be the team's last race and they wanted to salvage something from a miserable season which had been rounded off by a decision by Skoal Bandit not to renew their contract in 1986. The back row belonged to Christian Danner (deputising once more for the injured Jonathan Palmer in the Zakspeed) and Pierluigi Martini's Minardi. Huub Rothengatter was the one and only non-qualifier, the Osella driver having suffered the embarrassment of executing a spin on Brabham Straight in view of the entire pit lane.

RACE

When the date for Brands Hatch was finally settled after much prevarication by FISA, it seemed that the favourable weather which had attended every Grand Prix at the Kent circuit would be hard-pushed to repeat itself so late in the year. But, true to form, the day dawned windy – but dry. Rain was the last thing Alain Prost wanted. Come to that, it was the last thing Nelson Piquet and Pirelli needed, particularly as the Brabham had been quickest in the morning warm-up, his time of 1m 12.333s being more than a second clear of Senna, Prost, Rosberg and Surer. Mansell was over two seconds off the pace and expressing worries about the handling of his car. The mechanics immediately set about undoing adjustments which had been made to cope with a full fuel load.

All was well in time for the race, Mansell completing at least four warm-up laps before pulling onto the grid to have his three Cs and a B left-rear covered by pre-heated blankets. It was a clever move by the Williams team which paid off as Mansell made the best start of all to run round the outside of Senna on the approach to Paddock. The Lotus driver took his line, running out to the kerb at the exit to force Mansell onto the dirt. By the time Nigel had recovered, Rosberg was diving

up the inside on the approach to Druids and, before he knew it, Mansell had understeered off line and was running around the kerb on the outside of the corner, losing third place to Piquet in the process.

From the foregoing, you might assume that Rosberg had made an equally scorching start from the second row. Alain Prost would tell you otherwise. The Williams had, in fact, been so slow that Prost pulled left and put two wheels on the grass rather than become stuck behind the Finn. And, irony of ironies, no sooner had he done that than Rosberg's rear Goodyears suddenly gripped and Keke rocketed forward while Prost was left struggling on the grass.

By the time Alain had regained the track, half of the grid had rushed by, including Michele Alboreto. At the end of the first lap, Prost was 14th and he faced the unenviable prospect of working his way through the field.

As far as Rosberg was concerned, he merely wanted to move ahead of Senna since Piquet was beginning to apply pressure in third place. The Williams was quicker than the Lotus through the fast corners but Senna's advantage lay in the ability to brake late and deep; that, and the fact that he was leading! Try as he might, Rosberg could not find a way through, Senna taking the inside line for Druids and Hawthorns. Rosberg would complain later that Senna's weaving tactics on the back straight were of a Formula 3 standard but, whatever the rights and wrongs of Senna's techniques, he left Rosberg with no option but to try a risky move under braking for Surtees on lap seven.

The Williams dived inside but Senna took his line and the two cars touched, Rosberg spinning into the path of the hapless Piquet. At first, it looked as though Nelson would avoid the Williams but, unfortunately, the left-front wheel of the Brabham clipped Rosberg's left-rear. The impact bent the Brabham's suspension and punctured Rosberg's tyre. As Piquet remained stationary, Rosberg set off to complete his lap.

When the Williams reached the pits the tyre was in tatters, and a 20-second stop saw Rosberg emerge from the pit lane just in front of the leaders, Senna and Mansell.

Despite his cold tyres, Rosberg managed to take the inside line to Druids and give Senna a taste of his own medicine. However, going through Bottom Bend, the Williams appeared to hesitate long enough to cause Senna to back off. Ayrton floored the throttle again and moved to Rosberg's right but in the instant it had taken him to do that, Mansell was on Senna's left and into the lead.

Later, there would be talk of Mansell overtaking under the yellow since the warning flags were in operation as marshals removed Piquet's Brabham. However, a video subsequently showed that Mansell had more or less passed Senna by the time they had reached the first yellow flag (stationary), never mind the waved yellow at the scene of the incident.

While Rosberg stuck to his line, Mansell made his escape and, by the end of lap nine, he had pulled a couple of lengths over Rosberg. Senna, meanwhile, began to drop back as Keke's tyres found extra grip.

Concerning the rest of the field, de Angelis was third but the Lotus was being caught by Surer's Brabham as the Pirelli tyres began to reach working temperature. Johansson had lost a place to the Brabham, while Prost was making up for his slow start by moving into sixth place after passing Alboreto's Ferrari.

The red cars had made the most of the chaos at the start but Michele was finding his own level as he slipped down through the field. With Prost now in front, there was little hope of taking the Championship and a disconsolate Alboreto pulled into the pits for tyres on lap 11. One lap later he was back, under rather more dramatic circumstances.

Half-way round the circuit, a turbo had failed and, as Alboreto made his way slowly towards the pits, the ensuing fire really took a hold. Judging by the driver's fairly relaxed pace, he did not

181

John Watson: burning off the rust

John Watson returned to Grand Prix racing at Brands Hatch knowing that, no matter how competent his performance, he was likely to come off second best. Watson had been asked to deputise for Niki Lauda, still unfit after injuring his wrist at Spa. At first, it seemed a golden opportunity for Watson, out of Formula 1 racing since the end of 1983 when McLaren dismissed the Ulsterman in favour of Prost. The irony of a return, thanks to the team which brought his career to a halt in the first place, paled into insignificance once Watson took the wheel of the MP4/2B for two test sessions. Watson was 2.4 seconds off the pace set by Prost at Donington and suddenly the idea of a comeback did not seem so clever.

As Watson deliberated over the wisdom of achieving a mediocre result in a car which, ultimately, would show the driver in a bad light, McLaren attempted to persuade Renault to release Derek Warwick from his contract. The French team, not surprisingly, refused, by which time Watson had completed another test session and improved his time.

Watson's expectations assumed a more realistic level and he agreed he had set himself a tough standard by comparing himself to the man who was about to win the World Championship. Prost, not averse to scoring a psychological point over the man who had once been his team leader, had put the McLaren on its ear at Donington; Watson, his experience limited to Endurance Racing and the odd IROC race, could not possibly hope to match such a performance from a man familiar with the car and driving at the peak of his form.

Watson spent practice at Brands Hatch playing himself in and his lack of recent experience showed when he found difficulty in turning on the performance necessary to make the most of a set of qualifying tyres. He qualified in 21st place.

In the race, his confidence returned by the lap but, judging by his lengthy efforts at passing Tambay's Renault, he was still feeling his way. Two years earlier and the overtaking manoeuvre would have been the work of a moment.

By the end of the race, Watson was closing on sixth place and the championship point would have brought a reasonable conclusion. It was not to be and Watson would admit quietly that his Formula 1 future after his return was no brighter than it had been at the outset.

realise the full extent of the blaze and there were worrying moments as he pulled into the pit lane where the fire was finally extinguished – as were Michele's Championship hopes.

However, it was not that straightforward for Prost. Of course the news of Alboreto's retirement was encouraging but, for the moment, he was cursing the wrong choice of tyres (B on the left, C on the right). Ideally, Prost would have preferred to have stopped but the pre-race plan had been for the Frenchman to receive exactly the same tyres if he came in before half-distance. And that was the last thing Prost wanted. He would have to wait until lap 38 before he could receive a more suitable mix without going through a lengthy explanation to his team.

In the meantime, Prost was struggling and, by lap 19, he was out of the points again as none other than Jacques Laffite steamed by, the Ligier, like Surer's Brabham, running well on Pirellis.

Out for the day were: Martini, demonstrating his usual flair for spinning, although this time the Minardi driver had managed to stay out of trouble for at least three laps; Warwick, his unhappy time with the ill-handling Renault ending with a chronic misfire on lap four; Jones, a holed radiator in the Beatrice after a superb start had taken him round the outside of several drivers on the first lap, only for his progress to be halted briefly by a loose wheel; Ghinzani, whose low-key performance was terminated by oil pressure prob-

Philippe Streiff shook the establishment by qualifying in the top six in his Ligier.
The frustrations and hardships endured by Nigel and Rosanne Mansell over the years were swept away by an emotional victory at Brands Hatch.

lems, while engine trouble accounted for Fabi's Toleman not long after.

By half-distance, the order at the front had changed considerably as Surer caught and passed Senna to take second place. And, with all due respect to the Swiss driver, if he could manage that, where would Nelson Piquet have been had he not been involved in someone else's accident?

Adding further to Senna's discomfort, Laffite took third place but there seemed little chance of him catching Surer who, in turn, had been unable to do anything about reducing the 15-second gap to Mansell.

As the Williams driver picked his way through the traffic, it became clear he was looking after his tyres and had no immediate plans to make a stop. Prost, on the other hand, was in at exactly half-distance to collect three Cs and a B left-rear for the McLaren and returned to the race with the loss of just one place, to Martin Brundle. After two more laps, Prost reclaimed seventh as the blue Tyrrell crept towards the pits. Brundle had been running easily on Cs all round as he hauled in Johansson's slithering Ferrari but a broken water pipe had ended an excellent drive. Not long after Brundle had reached the pits, Capelli reversed his 014 into the catch-fencing after missing a gear and locking his brakes.

As the race reached the 50th lap, there were questions about the durability of the Pirellis. Senna had closed on Laffite and, sure enough, the Ligier came into the pits for what would be a lengthy stop. Jacques returned in eighth place, the Frenchman setting fastest lap before a fine day's work was ended by a smoking engine. Equally disappointing had been the retirement a few laps earlier of Johansson. The Ferrari driver

had given his usual energetic performance to overcome the inadequacies of his car and had worked his way into a worthwhile fourth place, but an alternator failure would give the management another difficult phone call to the Old Man back in Maranello.

The Ferrari's retirement more or less assured Alain Prost of the Championship since he had now moved ahead of de Angelis to take what had become fourth place and, with it, the three points necessary to take the title.

The only doubt remaining was whether the meteoric progress of Rosberg – who had quickly unlapped himself and set off at a blistering pace – would pull the Williams into the top four and deny Prost the points. It was clear that Prost was running for a finish when he got down to the tricky business of lapping a mid-field battle between Streiff, Boutsen and Patrese. As Prost carefully picked his way through, Rosberg caught the lot of them and the gaggle of cars barely broke Keke's stride as he rushed through, taking fourth place from Prost in the process. Alain was not bothered, however. He had passed the blazing Brabham of Marc Surer a few moments before and that meant he was fourth once more.

This was perhaps the saddest retirement of the lot. The Swiss had given the best drive of his career but lost a certain second place with a turbo failure. It remained to be seen, however, whether Surer's tyres would have allowed him to maintain the seven-second gap to Senna.

With all this drama surrounding the closing laps, it was easy to forget Mansell as he maintained an 18-second gap over Senna. The concentration required was enormous but he did not make a single mistake. Indeed, the Williams

team decided against showing Mansell the number of laps remaining but this scarcely mattered since Mansell could tell victory was close at hand from the reaction of the 75,000 strong crowd. It was a moment to savour and the emotion welling up inside Mansell was something which perhaps could only have been appreciated by John Watson who had once been in a similar situation.

Brands Hatch 1985 was a far cry from Silverstone 1981 as Watson struggled along at the back of the field, the Ulsterman taking a woefully long time to pass Tambay's cumbersome Renault. Once on his way, however, Watson began to settle into a rhythm and he was closing rapidly on Boutsen's Arrows at the end. Claiming one point would have been a suitable reward for both Watson and McLaren but it was not to be.

Instead, everyone's attention was riveted to McLaren number 2 as Prost crossed the line in fourth place to become World Champion... at last.

Third, every lap driven as though it had been a qualifying lap, a tired Keke Rosberg, while Ayrton Senna was pleased to have finished second with a car which, he admitted later, was no match for the Williams Honda. Rosberg and Senna remained tactfully restrained afterwards, Senna merely hinting that there had been no need for Keke to block the Lotus in order to let Mansell through. 'Nigel would have won today, even without Rosberg's help. He deserved it', said Ayrton. That seemed to sum up a victory which had been so close yet so far in the past – just like Alain Prost's elusive Championship. Everything came right at Brands Hatch on 6 October: a perfect day.

M.H.

TECHNICAL FILE

McLAREN
Ran modified front brake ducts to conform with revised dimensions agreed at Spa. Used rear brake ducts for the first time. On Saturday, returned to large front brake duct and removed rear to complete back-to-back test with set-up used during test session at Brands Hatch. Returned to new configuration for the race.

TYRRELL
New chassis for Brundle. Both cars had shorter side pods but ran without revised rear suspension seen in Italy and Belgium. Ran aerodynamic brake ducts.

WILLIAMS
New rear suspension for race cars. Double wishbone replaced rocker arm and required new gearbox casting to carry suspension mounting points (in place of a frame used previously). New uprights; rear brakes had caliper mounted at the rear. Smaller plenum chamber allowed new engine cover, 10 cm lower, improving airflow to rear wing. Fitted smaller front brake ducts.

BRABHAM
New chassis for Piquet to replace number 8 which appeared to have an inherent balance problem. Lower position for airbox. Fitted rear trim tabs as usual. Piquet's car fitted with deflectors under nose section.

RAM
No change; the last race of the season for the British team.

LOTUS
De Angelis tried four-piece biplane rear wing with short chord seen during 1984. Did not use rear trim-tabs but fitted vertical front aerofoils. T-car had revised suspension tested in Austria, Holland and Italy.

RENAULT
Tambay's race car fitted with Thomson television camera.

ARROWS
Ran secondary low-mounted rear wing.

TOLEMAN
Not in favour of new dimensions for brake ducts and continued with their large versions. Eventually signed agreement.

ALFA ROMEO
Nothing new.

OSELLA
Repaired chassis damaged at Spa.

LIGIER
Chassis number 1, damaged by de Cesaris in Austria, repaired and used as T-car since this was lighter than previous spare car (number 3).

FERRARI
New chassis for Johansson. All three cars had three rear wings (with different profiles to those seen in Belgium) and shortened underbody. Fitted larger rear anti-roll bar. Did not run brake ducts. Major work carried out on engine oil systems. Mention made of special fuel used for qualifying. Alboreto tested revised KKK turbos that subsequently failed on Saturday.

MINARDI
Fitted revised front suspension after successful test at Misano.

ZAKSPEED
Fitted double rear wing. Modifications to turbo and engine for improved reliability.

BEATRICE
Modified front and rear suspension; improved the installation of engine accessories. New position for gearbox radiator with small duct provided at rear of engine cover. G.P.

Under pressure. Nigel Mansell leads the McLarens
of Alain Prost and Niki Lauda out of Clubhouse.
Stefan Johansson, having stopped for tyres,
latches on to the leading trio.
Photo: Diana Burnett

Southern Sun Hotels Grand Prix of South Africa

'In many ways, it was more difficult than Brands Hatch. I took the lead early in that event and all I had to do was to keep concentrating and making sure that I kept out of trouble for the rest of the race. This time I was under pressure all the way. I must admit, I can't help smiling about it all: I mean, it was even more rewarding from a satisfaction point of view than the Grand Prix of Europe. I think I've nailed this thing about not being a winner once and for all...'

Nigel Mansell lolled against a partition as he chatted aboard the British Airways 747 which was winging him through the night northwards from Johannesburg a few hours after stepping off the Kyalami rostrum. The airline staff were fêting him as something of a hero and he was indulging himself 'up at the pointed end' to celebrate his second GP success.

By any standards, it had been a truly impressive victory for the Englishman. His pole-position qualifying lap will be talked about for many a month; his start was terrific and his performance flawless under pressure from World Champion Alain Prost. When team-mate Keke Rosberg pirouetted off on oil dropped by an expiring Toleman at Crowthorne, Nigel avoided the same fate by the skin of his Goodyears, but he never really put a wheel badly out of place from flag to flag.

He finally beat his frustrated, frantic team-mate Keke Rosberg by just over seven seconds at the flag, the Finn making up for two tyre stops to Nigel's one by pummelling the lap record into submission on the penultimate tour. But, just as at Brands Hatch, the day belonged to Nigel Mansell – deservedly so!

ENTRY AND PRACTICE

The essence of achieving a competitive lap time round Kyalami involves a major compromise: the ability to run as quickly as possible down that daunting main 'straight' from Leeukop through the flat-out right-hand kink before the pits, over the crest of the hill and down into the challenging Crowthorne corner, while at the same time retaining sufficient downforce for the fast swerves and tricky corners which make up the balance of the circuit. Whatever the individual feelings about the political creed practised by South Africa, it has to be said that a visit to Kyalami is regarded by most of the Grand Prix fraternity as a high spot on the international calendar. And the circuit itself, situated some 5700 feet above sea level in the rolling veldt a short distance from Johannesburg, is arguably the best on which Formula 1 cars regularly race.

Bearing in mind the form displayed by the Williams-Honda squad at Brands Hatch and the fact that the Brabham team seemed to have spent most of the previous winter tyre testing at the South African track, it was no surprise that the frantic battle for pole position was waged between GP of Europe winner Nigel Mansell, Keke Rosberg and two-times Kyalami pole-sitter Nelson Piquet. Two years ago Rosberg took the very first Williams-Honda FW09 to a cautiously optimistic fifth place in a race dominated by Brabham-BMWs. Now these two arch-rival teams faced each other as they were level pegging, and the ferocity of their battle was awesome.

As usual, the race was scheduled to take place on the Saturday, so Thursday and Friday were enlivened with the regular qualifying sessions. Keke Rosberg set the pace with fastest time on the first day, despite starting the weekend with an acute pain in his neck, something which he initially wondered might have been caused by his opposite-lock excesses as he pounded up through the field at Brands Hatch. More probably it had been brought about by sitting in a draught in the cockpit of his Lear Jet during a flight from Italy to Ibiza the week following the Brands Hatch race.

'I felt so bad during the week prior to coming out here that I attended a Frankfurt clinic for some injections to alleviate the pain.' Happily, once he got into the swing of things in the cockpit of his FW10B, this discomfort quickly slipped to the back of his mind. In Thursday's session Rosberg rocketed round in 1m 3.073s to set a target for his rivals to aim at, while Nigel Mansell all but matched him with a 1m 3.188s. The Englishman set this first session time at his third attempt, using a mixed set of Goodyear qualifiers. He reckoned he could have been even quicker if he'd had a third set available; 'maybe by as much as half a second...'

None the less, Mansell continued his determined battle into Friday's timed session and, as the advantage fluctuated between himself, his team-mate and Piquet's Brabham, he finally settled the argument beyond question with a stupendous 1m 2.366s on his second run. By any standards, it was a classic lap.

Straightline speed was no problem to the Williams-Honda, Mansell slamming through the trap just before Crowthorne at 206.996 mph. Nigel's car control was taxed the whole length of that 'switchback' section round the back of the circuit between Barbecue and the tricky, climbing uphill right-hander at Leeukop.

Mansell described it as a 'perfect nine-tenths of a lap. I grabbed sixth for a second after the Jukskei kink then slammed it back into fifth and went through Sunset without braking – and that really frightened me when I thought about it afterwards, I can tell you. The engine was fluttering against the rev limiter in fifth on the short straight down to Clubhouse, then it was through the Esses and up to Leeukop. As I turned in I felt the car begin to understeer, but rather than back off, I decided to drive through it...with the result that I came out of the corner, running wide along the kerbing. I thought I'd just glanced the wall, but in fact I missed it...'

Keke Rosberg, not Mansell's greatest fan when they joined up as team-mates at the start of the '85 season paid the ultimate tribute: 'I didn't know they made balls that big...McLaren must be beginning to wonder whether they've signed the wrong Williams driver for the next season!' Rosberg lined up third behind Piquet, his Williams running through the speed trap at 208.864 mph, the Finn unable to improve on his 1m 2.504s best from Thursday. But Nelson pulled every trick in the book in a vain attempt to win his third successive Kyalami pole in a Brabham-BMW.

By dint of running on a combination of buffed down Pirelli qualifiers, Nelson managed to make four serious runs in both timed sessions. On Thursday he was very badly baulked at Jukskei by Berger's Arrows and Streiff's Tyrrell, but finished the day third and hauled himself onto the front row with a 1m 2.409s on Friday. Right at the end of the session, with the track virtually empty, Nelson went out for a final banzai effort at grabbing pole. But despite the fact that the BT54 proved capable of 210.965 mph on the straight, electrical problems intervened on that last run and the BMW engine detonated, so second place was his final reward.

For once, Ayrton Senna was out of this battle for pole position, though only by a whisker. He extracted the absolute maximum from his Lotus 97T's chassis to compensate for giving away the best part of 10 mph to Piquet's Brabham on the run down into Crowthorne. On Thursday the Brazilian had been troubled by fluctuating turbo boost pressure on his Renault V6 engine and was unable to break 1m 4.5s at a time when Rosberg was almost nudging the upper 1m 2s bracket. The problem was rectified the following day allowing Ayrton to take full advantage of a 'superbly handling chassis' and record a splendid fourth quickest 1m 2.825s, running like Piquet on a virtually empty circuit at the end of the session.

Marc Surer followed up his excellent Brands Hatch race performance with a fine fifth qualifying time at Kyalami, taking the second Brabham BT54 round in 1m 4.088s. In the process, he survived a nasty moment at the Jukskei kink when Ghinzani's Toleman lurched into his path, the Italian hardly impressing any of his rivals with

Just Williams. Keke Rosberg and Nigel Mansell dominated the South African Grand Prix – Rosberg with a brilliant comeback drive, Mansell with his second win in succession.

his use of rear-view mirrors.

Elio de Angelis had not been totally satisfied with the balance of his 97T on Thursday, but improvements were made for Friday's qualifying session and he improved to a sixth fastest 1m 4.129s. It was a satisfactory performance by the Italian, but it, when hard facts are examined, he was fortunate not to be bumped off the third row by Teo Fabi's Toleman TG185.

The Tolemans both looked rock steady, as usual, through the fast Kyalami swerves, and Ghinzani raised a few eyebrows by holding top spot in the timing lists for much of Friday's untimed session. Fabi wound up fastest at the end of that session, but the team encountered a whole series of minor problems which prevented Fabi realising the car's true potential.

For a start, there was an annoying disparity between the straightline performance of the Hart 415T engines: on Friday afternoon, Teo was obliged to run the spare car following an engine problem in the morning, and it would only pull 196.051 mph on the straight whereas Ghinzani was topping 200 mph in the same session. Fabi none the less managed a seventh fastest 1m 4.215s before briefly trying his team-mate's machine right at the end of the session. He confirmed that the engine felt much stronger than that in the spare, but the tiny Italian could barely reach the pedals in a cockpit tailored for Ghinzani, let alone press them effectively.

In the McLaren International camp Niki Lauda was back in the fold, recovered from his Spa practice shunt and entertaining the pit lane with the tale of how he survived a taxi shunt in Zurich a week or so before the Kyalami race. It seems that the Rat's taxi was T-boned by a fast-moving Jaguar, but the Austrian emerged unscathed, hopped out and settled his fare with the shaken driver, leaving him to sort out the mess! As if one personal drama wasn't enough, Alain Prost found himself stranded in Geneva on the Tuesday evening prior to the race when he missed his Swissair flight after failing to read the small print of his airline schedule in sufficient detail: 'an hour earlier from 1 October'! The net result of that little delay was that the new World Champion had to charter an executive jet to whisk him to Heathrow in time to catch the Wednesday evening South African Airways 747 flight, arriving at Johannesburg's Jan Smuts airport a little more than an hour prior to the start of the first untimed session. A helicopter hop later he was in the paddock and dressed in his togs: a little jaded, perhaps, but right on the button when he climbed

October:
FISA agrees to keep 1500 cc engine formula until 1990.

Jean-Marie Balestre elected President of the FIA, to replace the retiring Prince Paul von Metternich, and re-elected President of FISA.

Mauricio Gugelmin (Ralt RT30-VW) wins British Formula 3 Championship.

into the cockpit.

The McLaren team was experimenting with revised turbochargers and turbo compressors at Kyalami, but suffered throughout the weekend with a variety of altitude related problems such as overspeeding. Prost was hampered by fluctuating boost pressure on Thursday using the new turbos and switched back to the original spec 'large' turbos for his Friday qualifying run. Lauda, who got the MP4/2B spare car allocated to him only after a strenuous debate with team boss Ron Dennis, used the 'small' turbos to good effect, outqualifying Prost for only the second time in their two-season partnership, the Rat turning a 1m 4.283s for eighth fastest slot, the new Champion lining up right behind on 1m 4.376s.

The two Arrows A8 drivers produced well-matched performances, as did the Alfa 184TB pilots. Thierry Boutsen had a trouble-free couple of days, lapping in 1m 4.518s to pip Gerhard Berger, the Austrian suffering no fewer than three engine failures on Thursday. The Alfas managed to get through both days of practice without a single turbo failure, thereby establishing something of a record in Euroracing circles, but Cheever's 184TB only ran properly after the ignition pack from Patrese's machine was fitted after Riccardo's two runs in the final session. 'Once that was done, it suddenly ran smoothly and picked up more than 8 mph on the straight', beamed Eddie. Patrese qualified 12th, Cheever 14th, split by yet another Benetton-backed car, the other Toleman TG185 of Piercarlo Ghinzani.

In the Ferrari camp, the mood was one of panic and dismay. To say that the 156/85s were hopeless round Kyalami would be to flatter them. It was difficult to believe that Michele Alboreto had been a winner this season, let alone a challenger for the Championship, as the 156s yawed their unpredictable path round the circuit. Both men complained unceasingly about the classic 'no grip' syndrome: wandering understeer going into the corners, terminal oversteer and dramatic wheel-spin on the way out. In addition, Johansson's engine was hampered by a peculiar 'surging' as the revs built up towards their maximum during Thursday's qualifying session, a gremlin which also afflicted Alboreto's on Friday. Add to that the miserable slowness of the Ferraris in a straight line – approaching Crowthorne at barely 195 mph – and the final result was that Michele and Stefan lined up in 15th and 16th position respectively.

With the Ligier team joining Renault in its boycott of the proceedings, thereby reducing the field to 21 cars, Philippe Streiff was recruited to partner Martin Brundle for the weekend, Martin comfortably outqualifying his team-mate to the tune of 0.6s. After an encouraging performance in the GP of Europe at Brands Hatch, Brundle was looking forward to a good showing at Kyalami, but was sadly disappointed. He found himself having to run such soft springs in order to achieve a reasonable degree of grip that the car yawed and rolled all over the place in a disconcerting fashion.

Streiff had a few problems working into the swing of things, qualifying behind Alan Jones's Beatrice Lola THL185 but taking his place on the grid when the Australian pulled out on race morning suffering from a particularly nasty bout of flu which had been affecting him for most of the previous week. Right at the back, sharing the tenth row, were usual tail-enders Pierluigi Martini and Huub Rothengatter.

RACE

Race morning saw a huge crowd pour into Kyalami, the organisers' estimate of around 85,000 people putting the numbers far in excess of those recorded for recent SAGPs. Piquet's Brabham set the cat amongst the pigeons with a 1m 6.856s in the half-hour warm-up session, a second and a half faster than Senna's Lotus, but it subsequently transpired that the Brazilian was running relatively soft Pirelli rubber rather than the hard compound the team was destined to use for the race.

If Mansell had any nerves about starting from

Alain Prost crept across the line with a seized engine *(left)*.
Uncomfortable three-some as the Alfa Romeos of Eddie Cheever and Riccardo Patrese sandwich the Toleman of Piercarlo Ghinzani. Both Alfas were destined to spin off and retire *(right)*.
Ken Tyrrell hired Philippe Streiff, but the Frenchman spun out of the race *(below)*.
In trouble again. Pierluigi Martini spun his Minardi on Ghinzani's oil but otherwise had an uneventful race *(bottom)*.

pole, there was no trace of them in public and his Williams simply catapulted into the lead once the green light blinked on its gantry. A wheel-locking Piquet just scrambled into Crowthorne in second place from Surer, while Senna grabbed third midway round the opening lap with a breathtaking inside dive at Sunset, almost rubbing wheels with the startled Swiss driver in the process. Meanwhile, down at the tail of the field, Ghinzani's Toleman pitched Cheever's Alfa into team-mate Patrese, the two Italian V8s pirouetting down the dusty outfield into immediate retirement. With both 184TBs out of the race, their indignant drivers conducted an animated post-mortem on the bank above their abandoned machines.

At the end of the opening lap Mansell was comfortably in the lead from Piquet, de Angelis, Senna, Rosberg, Lauda, Surer, Prost, Alboreto, Fabi, Berger, Brundle, Johansson, Boutsen, Streiff and the trailing Martini. Rosberg was not idling along; he quickly climbed through to second place, despatching Senna, de Angelis and Surer on consecutive laps before taking over second place from whence he steadily began to whittle away at Mansell's lead.

From the beginning of lap nine, Rosberg had hauled right up onto Mansell's tail by using more turbo boost pressure early in the race. Nigel obligingly waved him by as they crested the rise by the pits, confident that he would be able to come back at his team-mate later. Unfortunately, by the time Keke led Nigel down into Crowthorne one lap later, Ghinzani's Toleman had dumped most of the contents of its sump all through that corner on the racing line and, since the marshals were just a touch tardy with the oil warning flags, Keke was left to spin like a top onto the sandy outfield. Mansell ducked through again into the lead after a close moment of his own under hard braking, leaving Keke to gather up his sand-streaked FW10B and chase off in sixth place.

From that moment onwards, Mansell never relinquished the lead as, one by one, his potential challengers dropped by the wayside. Surer's BT54 had been in trouble almost from the start, expiring at the end of lap four with a valve breakage, and Piquet fell victim to the same fate two laps later. The oil pump drive failed on Fabi's Toleman, and Senna's Lotus expired with an expensive-looking engine failure on lap nine. This followed an ambitious outside dive round de Angelis going into Crowthorne, which had fired up the Italian with so much indignation that he went looking for Ayrton with a purpose, once his own 97T had succumbed to a similar mechanical fate later in the race.

At the start of lap 10 Prost dived up the inside of Elio going into Crowthorne, the McLaren taking the dry inside line whilst forcing de Angelis to brake hard on the oil-slicked racing line. The Italian got into such a twitch that Niki also pulled past him just beyond the apex of the corner.

This left the order Mansell, Prost, Lauda, de Angelis, Rosberg and Brundle, with Johansson's seventh place Ferrari gradually hauling up onto the Tyrrell's tail. Alboreto's challenge evaporated thanks to a broken engine, rounding off an

ignominious weekend for Maranello, but neither car had ever proved a threat. The main issue was now between Mansell and the two McLarens, as Prost and Lauda eased steadily closer to their intended quarry with every lap that passed.

By lap 25 the leading trio was running nose-to-tail, Mansell bumping his Williams' left-front wheel up the kerb exiting Leeukop with increasing frequency as Prost stepped up the pressure. 'I was anxious that he should keep Niki behind him', grinned Nigel reflectively after it was all over, 'because I could see that he was potentially quicker than both of us.'

At the end of lap 26 both Rosberg and Johansson took turns to stop for fresh rubber, as scheduled for every Goodyear runner in the sweltering conditions, and Stefan insolently tagged onto the leading bunch as it lapped him, his fresh tyres enabling him to keep pace with the McLarens and Williams on their increasingly worn covers.

Niki came in at the end of lap 32, a frustrating 15.8s tyre stop losing him more time than intended, but when Prost took over 18s for his similar tyre stop, Niki emerged with a net advantage on the track in second place. Experienced Kyalami observers reckoned the Rat was shaping up to take one of his famous 'tactical' victories, but just as he seemed poised to take the lead when Mansell stopped on lap 36, his boost pressure faded and he pulled in to retire with a blown turbo, leaving Prost to carry the McLaren torch on his own.

Mansell's Williams had been changed from four B compound Goodyears to three Cs and a B for the sprint to the finish and, with 40 laps completed, he had only to worry about Prost. Rosberg was third, but pressed his second set of tyres so blisteringly hard (literally!) that he was obliged to stop and change again before the finish. Thus, when Prost's McLaren began stuttering intermittently from just beyond half-distance, its electrical warning light hinting at a possible computer malfunction, all Nigel had to do was to concentrate on finishing.

To be fair, Mansell handled himself excellently, threading a skilful path through slower traffic, making the lapped cars work for him in building up a slight cushion over the McLaren. And all the time he was watching his engine temperature gauge, the needle of which was gradually creeping further across the face of the dial: for the last 20 laps or so Nigel was keeping his fingers firmly crossed, anxious about the 120-degree reading and the slight loss of sharp throttle response through the corners.

By lap 60 it was pretty clear that Prost was not going to challenge him and, as the McLaren gradually slipped further behind with its stammering engine, Rosberg came swathing into contention after his second tyre stop. On lap 70 Keke slammed round the outside of Sunset to take second place from the ailing McLaren. The Detroit winner finished with a flourish as he rode the kerbs in mind-boggling style for the last few laps, finally establishing a new circuit record on the penultimate tour, but unable to get within even striking distance of his team-mate as Nigel strode home to a brilliant second victory.

Prost's McLaren took so long over its final lap that it was disallowed as being too slow, but Alain still collected third place ahead of Johansson, the Swede running just as gently as he dared, keeping an eye on his fuel read-out, to beat Gerhard Berger's Arrows A8 by a few lengths past the flag. Sixth and seventh, both having made two pit stops for tyres, were Thierry Boutsen in the other Arrows and Martin Brundle's sole surviving Tyrrell. Streiff spun off at Clubhouse, Martini's Minardi suffered engine failure at Crowthorne and Rothengatter expired with electrical trouble. So who needs 26 cars?

A.H.

TECHNICAL FILE

McLAREN
New chassis for Prost, the first to be built entirely at McLaren International factory. Fitted small ducts for front brakes; large ducts at rear.

TYRRELL
Used EF15 engine (Brundle) for the first time. No modifications since Brands Hatch. Continuing to use short side pods.

WILLIAMS
Smaller front brake ducts. All three cars equipped with revised rear suspension and other modifications seen at Brands Hatch. Revised position for gas cylinder serving rear shock absorbers.

LOTUS
Only de Angelis's car fitted with winglets at rear of side pods.

ARROWS
Did not bring chassis 5; Berger preferred to use number 2.

TOLEMAN
Finally removed large aerodynamic front brake ducts. Rory Byrne absent due to work on 1986 car.

ALFA ROMEO
Fitted larger radiator. Ran smaller front wings.

FERRARI
Tried smaller rear anti-roll bar. Fitted new side plates to front wings to cover space left by removal of large brake ducts. Alboreto's car fitted with old style undertray with long rear profile and single rear wing. Johansson's car and T-car ran short undertray and additional rear wing with long side plate to upper rear wing.

Other teams (with the exception of Renault, Ligier and RAM who were absent from Kyalami) remained unchanged.

G.P.

The Mitsubishi Australian Grand Prix

'Goodbye innocent Adelaide, hello international city!' bellowed the headlines of one Australian daily newspaper the morning after Keke Rosberg had romped to a brilliant victory in the inaugural Australian Grand Prix.

The final round of the World Championship took place in a country new to the title trail, yet steeped in racing history and tradition. Most enthusiasts have believed that Australia's place on the F1 international calendar has been long overdue, but well worth waiting for. Held round a superbly conceived circuit in Adelaide's suburbs, the race organisation matched that of the best run established events in the Championship, and seriously embarrassed many of the others.

The 2.347-mile Victoria Park Circuit, running through parkland, city streets and through part of the horse racing track was the backdrop to one of the very best races of the season with Rosberg's Williams FW10B battling for much of the distance with pole winner Ayrton Senna's Lotus 97T, the pair of them surviving pit stops for tyres, off-track excursions and even a minor collision with each other. Rosberg held the upper hand for much of the tussle, Senna demonstrating a quite remarkable degree of uncharacteristically erratic behaviour as he grappled with fading carbon-fibre brakes and worn tyres. The Brazilian eventually retired with a major engine failure after three spectacular trips off the track.

Retiring triple World Champion Niki Lauda briefly poked his McLaren MP4/2B into the lead to celebrate his Championship swansong but the possibility of a sensational last-time-out victory evaporated when snatching rear brakes sent him headlong into the retaining wall, so the day was left to Rosberg without question. The great street circuit improvisor added victory at Adelaide to his previous successes in similar surroundings at Monaco, Dallas and Detroit over the past few seasons. He built up a full lap's advantage over Jacques Laffite's Ligier JS25 before allowing himself the luxury of a third tyre stop in the race's closing stages, cantering home to win easily from his former team-mate and rounding off his Williams career on the highest possible note.

82 laps of a difficult street circuit; ideal Rosberg territory.

ENTRY AND PRACTICE

Never has a race been anticipated with so many misgivings – yet, on the day, been accepted with so many unqualified accolades of international approval. A trip to the other side of the world was not generally deemed to be high on the list of the average F1 mechanic's priorities at the end of a gruelling season which had kicked off in Brazil seven months earlier. The South Australian government had really pushed the boat out as far as promotion and packaging of its first Grand Prix was concerned, but mention of 'a new road circuit' mid-season was sufficient to produce furrowed brows from competitors who recalled the Dallas fiasco in the summer of '84. The wisdom of holding Grand Prix races on totally new circuits without any sort of warm-up race, seemed, on the face of it, to be gambling heavily against the odds.

Thankfully, the pessimists were proved to be completely wrong in their predictions. This was a major project designed to put South Australia on the map. Premier John Bannon had rustled up a good deal of financial support for the project and the event even attracted the patronage of the country's Prime Minister, Bob Hawke. In terms of media exposure, Adelaide was being put firmly on the country's map at a time when it was ranged against plenty of rival international *glitterati*.

The whole circuit, together with its excellent facilities, was completed in good time prior to the event, surprising those who recalled the first year at Long Beach, Detroit and the only year at Dallas. 'The impression is not one of a street circuit because, with working conditions like this, they are better than we have just about anywhere', explained Keke Rosberg candidly. 'As a facility, it has got to be the best street circuit we have ever seen. This is a natural environment for a Formula 1 race.' Later in the weekend Rosberg would be challenged about his praise of Adelaide: wasn't he just being polite in front of the locals, he was asked? 'Take it from me', he replied, 'the F1 fraternity is one of the rudest in the world. If we thought it was bad, don't worry – we would have said so. But we think it's the best . . .'

With the temperature consistently nudging 90°F throughout the four days of the meeting, with appropriately blue and cloudless skies to accompany it, the Australian spring weather was well received by the European racing fraternity seeking shelter from the onset of autumn in the Northern Hemisphere. The track surface was extremely slippery from the outset and it did not take long for many competitors to discover that one pair of race tyres on the rear would last as long as three sets of qualifiers on the front. This total of eight covers was not only an ingenious method of using up the allotted maximum number of covers per session, but also a means of balancing tyre wear on a track where, compounds being equal, the rear qualifiers tended to go off long before the fronts had even worked up to temperature.

An untimed familiarisation session on Thursday afternoon saw Senna set the pace in the mid-1m 24s bracket, but it was Keke Rosberg who emerged with provisional pole position at the end of the first hour of official qualifying the following afternoon. Lap speeds were proving something of a lottery on Friday, because the track felt slow with minimal grip at the start of Friday's untimed morning session, speeded up towards the end of the 90 minutes, only for a stint by historic rɔɔrs during the lunch break to leave the track with less grip again by the start of first qualifying. Thus those who left their runs latest tended to go quickest.

For much of first qualifying, Nigel Mansell held sway at the top of the timing lists, running a set of E compound qualifiers to turn a 1m 22.564s best, holding onto his advantage almost until the end of the session when his team-mate and Senna bettered this time in the closing moments.

Saturday afternoon's session followed in similar vein with Senna throwing down a firm challenge by posting 1m 21.053s, followed immediately by Mansell pulling a 1m 20.537s out of the bag. Ayrton was clearly not in a mood to let matters rest there and the Brazilian responded with a breathtaking 1m 19.843s, a full 0.7s quicker than the Brands and Kyalami winner who lined up beside him. 'It was very difficult indeed to be tidy today', he reflected: 'it was just like driving on ball bearings or ice. I don't really recall much because my best lap was over so quickly!'

Mansell had one of his Saturday runs messed up after Thierry Boutsen's Arrows A8 skittered past his Williams going into the chicane immediately beyond the pits, bouncing across the sandy apex and almost collecting the FW10B as it lurched back onto the circuit again. Mansell survived involvement in this incident by the skin of his teeth, but Boutsen duplicated the manoeuvre next time round, reflecting the fact that the A8's rear brakes were playing up badly. As a result, Mansell's best Saturday run, and second place on the grid, were produced from a set of C compound soft race tyres, while both Senna and Rosberg produced their personal bests on E compound qualifiers.

Keke was an uncomplaining third on the grid, recording a 1m 21.887s. 'OK, so perhaps I was blown off. Perhaps I should have followed Nigel in my choice of tyre. It seemed to work OK for Senna, but it didn't quite work for me. But we should be in pretty good shape once the race starts . . .'

Alain Prost availed himself of one pair of rear race tyres and three sets of front qualifiers, the new World Champion having to put up with a cut rear tyre throughout the session after spinning on his first run. Prost looked unusually ragged, and the McLaren quite a handful, so for Alain to qualify fourth on 1m 21.889s was, in the circumstances, an absolutely outstanding performance.

Niki Lauda found that his tyres were taking five or six laps to warm up on Friday, thwarting his efforts to improve on a 13th quickest 1m 24.691s

---

November:

BMW announce plans to supply engines to the Benetton (née Toleman) team.

Niki Lauda reaffirms plans to retire after holding discussions with Brabham over $6m deal for 1986.

---

on the first day. On Saturday he stayed in the spare throughout qualifying after encountering serious electrical problems during the morning's untimed session. He improved to 1m 23.941s, yet dropped three places in the overall line-up and emerged in a pretty glum frame of mind.

Over in the Ferrari camp the team was experimenting with revised rear aerofoils as well as redesigned turbos which were first tried on Stefan Johansson's machine on Friday. Stefan switched to his spare car after the first untimed session, simply 'because it felt better', and both Ferraris were fitted with the revised turbos to provide improved top end response, in time for Saturday qualifying. They helped Michele Alboreto, much happier than of late, towards a fine fifth fastest 1m 22.337s, but Stefan had a miserable time complaining that his adhesion problems seemed more serious than most. 'I had to turn down the boost pressure in an effort to get some traction, but the rear wheels were still spinning in fifth gear', mused a reflective Stefan: 'really disappointing'.

Reducing boost pressure in an attempt to get more grip was a method employed by Nelson Piquet on Friday when the Brazilian returned fourth quickest time on 1m 23.018s. He did this time on a buffed-down mixture of used tyres, but suffered with an erratic misfire on Saturday caused by a sticking butterfly in the induction system. By the time the team had pinpointed the precise problem, Nelson had used up all his tyres, so a switch to the spare car was to little avail. Although he actually improved his time to 1m 22.718s, he none the less dropped back to ninth place in the final line-up.

Marc Surer continued to impress in the other Brabham entry, the genial Swiss lining up sixth on 1m 22.561s, despite coming in on five separate occasions during the final session to check an apparent grounding problem which turned out to be the collapsed nose wings which were touching the ground at high speed.

Fellow BMW users, Arrows, seemed to be on the receiving end of a non-stop catalogue of minor tribulations; Alan Rees's plaintive speculation on Friday, 'it can't get any worse', proved sadly optimistic. On Friday morning Boutsen's A8 stopped out on the circuit with a metering unit malfunction and, by the time the car was retrieved and the problem diagnosed, there was no time left to fix it for first qualifying. Meanwhile, Gerhard Berger's car had broken its gearbox, so the two men had to share Berger's repaired machine at the end of the session.

Then on Saturday morning, Berger's car blew a head-gasket and Boutsen's developed a misfire, so both BMW engines had to be changed for final qualifying. Gerhard did a spectacularly erratic job, including a spin, to line up an eventual seventh on 1m 22.592s, while Boutsen, suffering the aforementioned braking problems, turned a 1m 23.196s for 11th place on the grid.

Lack of power (seriously!) on the slippery track surface enabled the Alfa 184TBs of Cheever and Patrese to exploit their chassis' good handling to the accompaniment of a minimum of wheelspin on Friday, but with the track providing more grip the

Mansell takes the lead at the start but a challenge
from Senna three corners later would end the
Williams driver's hopes of scoring three wins in a
row.

following afternoon, they faded to 13th and 14th behind Derek Warwick's ill-handling Renault RE60B and Johansson's Ferrari. The Renault team, incidentally, exuded the atmosphere of a wake on its last F1 outing. Patrick Tambay opted for the spare chassis early in the proceedings (as he felt it handled significantly better than his assigned race car) and proved this by lining up eighth on 1m 22.683s, 0.8s – four grid places ahead of the disconsolate Englishman.

In the Tyrrell camp there was a dire shortage of gearboxes by Saturday morning after Martin had crashed getting off-line as Piquet came out of the pits in front of him during first qualifying. 'I locked up a wheel and round I went', shrugged Brundle. Ivan Capelli had earlier crashed one car on Thursday afternoon, so after Martin's shunt, it meant that the team was down to only two serviceable gearboxes for the remainder of the weekend. Just to be on the safe side, Capelli was not allowed to practice on Saturday, Martin turning an eventual 1m 24.241s 'which was over half a second slower than I thought we might be able to manage', said a disgruntled Martin. 'It was the same old story – no traction.'

Neither Ligier JS25 driver seemed able to get it together round Adelaide, Philippe Streiff's second qualifying session spoiled when electrical problems stranded him on the circuit and he had to take the EF15 race-engined spare. He lined up 18th, Jacques Laffite 20th, the two French cars split by Alan Jones's Beatrice Lola THL-1. Clearly A.J. was hoping for better things on home soil and the Lola's understeer had been reduced by the fitting of a bigger lip on the front aerofoils. He eventually worked his way down to a 1m 24.369s, 'getting more out of the car than it's got to give', mused a pensive Carl Haas.

Jones suffered a series of Hart engine problems, as did the Toleman TG185s of Teo Fabi and Piercarlo Ghinzani. However, the Tolemans' abiding problem was lack of Pirelli grip and they qualified right down at the tail end of the grid, in amongst Capelli, Pierluigi Martini's Minardi and the lone Osella-Alfa of Huub Rothengatter.

RACE

By the time Senna led the field round its parade lap to the final grid in the Sunday afternoon heat, every seat in the house had been sold and Adelaide even produced the unlikely sight of ticket touts hanging round the gates offering cash for any spare entrance tickets! It was hardly likely, though, that anybody with a ticket was going to pass up a chance of attending what was undoubtedly Adelaide's sporting occasion of the year . . .

Finally, that year of planning and organisation reached its glorious conclusion for Australian fans as FISA's Derek Ongaro flicked the button to turn the starting lights to green and Nigel Mansell sprinted away from the front row to lead the jostling pack into that first chicane. Alan Jones stalled his Beatrice Lola and it had to be push-started after the pack had departed, but everybody else managed to get through that first corner without untoward contact and Mansell led up the hill with Senna's Lotus crawling all over his

Williams's gearbox.

Mid-way round the opening lap, the Brazilian chose to dive down the inside of Mansell on a ridiculously tight line as the two cars went into a 90-degree left-hander, Senna elbowing the Williams out over the kerbing in a most unruly fashion. Senna was to claim that Mansell had attempted to stay with him round the outside where there was insufficient room, while a furious Nigel dismissed his rival as 'an idiot' for such an outlandish piece of driving so early in the race. Even if Senna was technically in the right, it was a foolish manoeuvre to execute on full tanks in the first few crowded moments of a Grand Prix – and it was not to be the first such stunt Senna would produce during this ferocious afternoon's racing!

Mansell cruised round to the pits, eventually retiring after one additional lap with three teeth stripped off the Williams's crownwheel. Suppressing a burning desire to take the matter up with the Lotus team management, Nigel bit the bullet and left the circuit for his hotel long before the finish.

Rosberg completed the first lap ahead of Senna, these two already opening a gap from the on-form Alboreto, then Prost, Berger, Surer, Tambay, de Angelis, Piquet, Cheever, Boutsen and the rest. This would be the pattern for the opening stages of the race, as Keke controlled the pace, confident about the performance of his cast-iron brake discs in the extremely hot conditions compared with the carbon-fibre discs sported by Senna and a few others.

It did not take long for the abrasive surface to exact its toll as many of the leading runners' tyres displayed signs of rolling and graining within a few laps. Hardly had Cheever's Alfa expired on lap six with engine failure and Brundle's Tyrrell stuttered slowly round with little more than 2000 rpm after its electronics went haywire, than the pit lane became crowded with the first spate of visitors for fresh rubber.

Berger, whose Arrows moved up confidently from fifth to fourth on lap seven, dropped to sixth on lap nine as his tyres lost grip and he came in to change them next time round. Prost had stopped a lap before, while at the end of lap 12 Tambay and both Ferraris felt they could wait no longer for new rubber. Boutsen was in on lap 13, then Warwick on lap 14. At the same time, a worried Piquet vacated his smoking Brabham for good out on the circuit. An electrical short circuit had set the battery alight and, since the BT54's battery is situated beneath the driver's legs, he was distinctly anxious to move to a place of safety!

All this early activity resulted in Lauda and Jones moving up to sixth and seventh respectively, although an electrical misfire was due to blight the Beatrice Lola's challenge just when Jones was beginning to look a likely points scorer. But at the head of the field it was Rosberg who continued to set the pace, watching his mirror carefully to track Senna's progress, speeding up slightly on the straights when necessary while allowing the Lotus to get as close as Ayrton liked on the twisty bits where there was no hope of getting through.

De Angelis found himself black-flagged from

A steady drive from Ivan Capelli brought the Tyrrell
novice three points for fourth place (below).
Gerhard Berger; an excellent practice followed by
an eventful race (below right).
Jacques Laffite finished second, despite the best
efforts of his team-mate! (bottom)

Kev Koala meets The Rat. Niki Lauda entered permanent retirement while leading the Australian Grand Prix.

fifth place as a belated response, 17 laps into the race, for transgressing the rules by 'catching up' to his original grid position after being delayed on the parade lap. Although this was a quite justified penalty, consistently applied these days, it begged the question why a driver must risk himself for 17 laps before being disqualified. Either he broke the rules or he didn't. A debate amongst the stewards seemed an unnecessary waste of time.

On lap 18 Surer briefly passed Prost, but the McLaren regained what had become third place on lap 25 before retiring a couple of laps later with a spectacular engine failure. This put Surer back in third place with Lauda fourth, then Alboreto ahead of Philippe Streiff's Ligier.

By lap 26 Rosberg had opened out a 9.8s advantage over Senna, the Brazilian now nursing his tyres, but Ayrton chiselled his way back onto the Williams's tail, despite a couple of wild old moments riding the bevelled kerbs around the circuit, one of which was sufficiently spectacular to toss the Lotus into the air like a leaf. But they make Lotus chassis very strong and Senna's lightning reactions were always well up to the task of fielding the catches dropped by his own increasingly erratic driving. Finally, on lap 42, Senna excelled himself.

As Rosberg suddenly slowed to pull into the pits for fresh tyres, Ayrton's Lotus touched the rear of the Williams, wiping off the right-front aerofoil against the Williams's left-rear wing side plate. Next time round, instead of slowing to come into the pits himself, Ayrton found himself locked into a violently understeering slide which took him across the kerbing onto the grass on the outside of the circuit, from where he autocrossed back onto the track the other side of the hairpin. On the following lap, he came in for fresh tyres, a new nose section and a general 'clean out' of the radiator and intercooler ducting.

Meanwhile, Surer's race had ended when his engine cut out and failed to restart as he was limping back to the pits with a deflated left-front tyre sustained in a fleeting brush with Ghinzani's hiccupping Toleman. Further down the field, Boutsen's progress was terminated when an oil line came adrift, spraying lubricant over his rear tyres, causing him to spin violently. Both Renaults expired with crownwheel and pinion

breakages, Ghinzani's clutch packed up, and Jones conceded defeat with his misfiring Lola.

By lap 46 the order was Rosberg, Lauda and Senna, but Ayrton took back second place from the outgoing World Champion on lap 50 and inherited the lead when Keke stopped for his third set of tyres three laps later. A sticking left-front wheel-securing nut cost the Williams the best part of half a minute, and as the grip on Senna's Goodyears faded once more and his brakes lost their edge, Lauda surged through into the lead on lap 56. It looked as though we were in for a fairy-tale ending to his illustrious career.

Sadly, Niki's moment of glory was brief. 'I had been having trouble with my brakes for 10 laps or so', recounted Lauda after the race, 'and was having to pump the pedal really hard in order to get much response. As I was braking for the tight right-hander at the end of the longest straight, the rears locked up and that was the end of it all!' The Lauda McLaren speared off gently into the concrete wall on the left-hand side of the circuit, rumpling its left-front suspension in the process.

This left us effectively where we started, with Senna and Rosberg battling ferociously at the head of the field. Keke was almost seven seconds down, but he was already making definite inroads into the Brazilian's advantage when the Lotus's engine suddenly spewed most of a piston into its inlet tract. There was a puff of blue smoke and Senna slowed dramatically as Rosberg had him in his sights. He trailed into the pits for a detailed assessment of the damage: after one more slow lap Ayrton retired for good, so the race was handed to Rosberg on a plate.

Not that he didn't deserve the subsequent victory, of course. Keke had driven like a king to notch up his second victory of the season, and the lack of fuss with which he made yet another 'precautionary' stop for a fourth set of tyres in the closing stages, mirrored the level of his ruthless confidence. On this day, in these circumstances, he had been unbeatable.

Laffite and Streiff rough-and-tumbled their way to second and third for Ligier, Philippe 'misunderstanding' the team's pit signals as an excuse for challenging Jacques closely over the last two laps – too closely, as it turned out, for he rammed Jacques at the end of the back straight and was lucky to hobble home with his JS25's left front wheel hanging off. Fourth was Capelli's Tyrrell, this Dustin Hoffman lookalike keeping his nose clean, while Stefan Johansson's Ferrari pipped Berger's Arrows to complete the top half-dozen. Ferrari's last chance of clinching the Constructors' Championship ended when Alboreto lost third place shortly before the finish, a bolt falling out of the 156's gearchange lever in the cockpit.

So McLaren won the Constructors' crown for the second year in succession, adding this to Alain Prost's own 1985 achievement. Rosberg had triumphed for the fifth time in his World Championship GP career. But the real winners in this last race of the '85 season had proved to be the Adelaide organisers and Australia itself.

Good on yer' cobber!

A.H.

TECHNICAL FILE

McLAREN
Used front brake ducts seen at Brands Hatch with large ducts for rear brakes. Ran vertical front aerofoils.

TYRRELL
Brought new chassis to Australia to act as spare car. All three cars had the short side pod configuration.

WILLIAMS
Mansell's car had radiator venting enlarged in side pod; Rosberg's car fitted with a deflector rather than cutting larger duct. Tried carbon-fibre and cast-iron discs; settled for cast-iron. Additional cooling ducts for brakes, in common with other teams.

BRABHAM
Tried revised turbo wastegate to give less brutal response. Found to be an improvement and used on both race cars.

LOTUS
Additional brake ducts, front and rear. Senna ran carbon discs in race; de Angelis, cast-iron.

RENAULT
Last race for the French team; no technical changes. Tambay's car ran with on-board television camera.

ARROWS
Ran triple rear wing arrangement.

TOLEMAN
Did not run additional intercooler seen in South Africa. Fitted rubber skirts under front wing side plates.

ALFA ROMEO
Continued with larger radiator seen in South Africa. Ran larger front brake ducts and additional duct at rear.

BEATRICE
Last race with Hart engines; Ford turbo bench-tested and ready to run in test hack.

MINARDI
Used engine with revised electronics seen in South Africa.

FERRARI
Alboreto's car ran longer underbody profile and rear wing similar to type used at the beginning of the season. Johansson's car and T-car fitted with shorter underbody profile and triple rear wing arrangement. On Saturday, Johansson switched to single rear wing. Alboreto's car ran larger turbochargers. Both cars fitted with extra cooling duct for clutch. Johansson ran cast-iron brakes in race; Alboreto used carbon.

G.P.

If there was such a thing as the Chassis Economist Award for 1985, McLaren International would win handsomely. Continuing their efficient long-term programme with the carbon-fibre MP4/2 chassis, McLaren merely modified tubs built for 1984 and, thanks to the mature skills of Prost and Lauda, these cars lasted through the season. Indeed, McLaren built only two brand new chassis for 1985, a remarkable record when their Championship winning achievements are considered.

Lotus enjoyed a straightforward season with four cars but, elsewhere, the chassis building departments barely paused for breath. Brabham and Ferrari each built no less than nine new cars while Renault worked their way through eight.

Thanks to the introduction of the 195-litre fuel capacity limit in 1986, the cars listed below are now obsolete. We are indebted to Giorgio Piola, Denis Jenkinson and the various team managers and mechanics who helped in the preparation of the following information.

Alfa Romeo

Had two 1985 cars and a modified 184T at start of season.

184T
1 Spare car at Rio, Estoril, Imola and Monaco.

185T
1 New for Cheever at Rio. For Cheever at Estoril. Spare car at Imola. For Cheever at Monaco. Spare car at Spa, Montreal, Detroit and Paul Ricard.

2 New for Patrese at Rio. For Patrese at Estoril, Imola, Monaco, Spa, Montreal, Detroit, Paul Ricard and Silverstone.

3 New for Cheever at Imola. Spare car at Monaco. For Cheever at Spa, Montreal, Detroit and Paul Ricard. Spare car at Nürburgring. Reverted to 1984 184T chassis mid-season.

184T
1 Spare car at Monza, Spa, Brands Hatch, Kyalami and Adelaide.

2 For Patrese at Nürburgring, Österreichring, Zandvoort, Monza, Spa, Brands Hatch, Kyalami and Adelaide.

3 For Cheever at Silverstone, Nürburgring, Österreichring, Zandvoort, Monza, Spa, Brands Hatch, Kyalami and Adelaide.

Arrows

Began the season with three new A8 models

A8
1 New for Boutsen at Rio. Spare car at Estoril, Imola, Monaco and Spa. Spare car at Spa (15 Sep), Kyalami and Adelaide.

2 New for Berger at Rio. For Boutsen at Spa. Spare car at Montreal, Detroit, Paul Ricard, Silverstone, Nürburgring, Monza (raced by Berger) and Brands Hatch. For Berger at Kyalami and Adelaide.

3 New at Rio (spare car – raced by Berger). For Berger at Estoril, Imola, Monaco, Spa, Montreal, Detroit, Paul Ricard, Silverstone, Nürburgring and Zandvoort.

4 New for Boutsen at Estoril. For Boutsen at Imola, Monaco, Montreal, Detroit, Paul Ricard, Silverstone, Nürburgring, Österreichring, Zandvoort, Monza, Spa, Brands Hatch, Kyalami and Adelaide.

5 New at Österreichring (spare car – raced by Berger). Spare car at Zandvoort. For Berger at Monza, Spa and Brands Hatch.

Beatrice-Lola

New to Formula 1. Cars designed and built by FORCE. First race at Monza.

THL-1
001 Spare car at Monza (raced by Jones), Brands Hatch (raced by Jones), Kyalami and Adelaide.

002 For Jones at Monza, Brands Hatch, Kyalami and Adelaide.

Brabham

As usual, had three brand new cars ready for start of season.

BT54
1 New for Hesnault at Rio. For Hesnault at Estoril, Imola and Monaco. Damaged by Hesnault during testing at Paul Ricard.

2 New at Rio (spare car – raced by Piquet and damaged. Became wind tunnel car.)

3 New for Piquet at Rio. Spare car at Estoril and Imola. Became test car but brought back into service for Surer at Spa. For Surer at Montreal, Detroit, Paul Ricard, Silverstone and Nürburgring.

4 New for Piquet at Estoril. For Piquet at Imola and Monaco (damaged in race).

5 New at Monaco (spare car). Spare car at Spa, Montreal, Detroit and Paul Ricard (raced by Piquet). Destroyed by fire in testing accident at Nürburgring.

6 New for Piquet at Spa. For Piquet at Montreal, Detroit, Paul Ricard, Silverstone, Nürburgring, Österreichring, Zandvoort, Monza and Spa. For Surer at Brands Hatch, Kyalami and Adelaide.

7 New at Silverstone (spare car). Spare car at Nürburgring, Österreichring, Zandvoort, Monza, Spa, Brands Hatch, Kyalami and Adelaide.

8 New for Surer at Österreichring. For Surer at Zandvoort, Monza and Spa. This chassis thought to have inherent handling deficiency; used as show car.

9 New for Piquet at Brands Hatch. For Piquet at Kyalami and Adelaide.

Ferrari

Introduced 156/85 in New Year. Continued chassis numbering sequence from 1984 C4 series.

156/85
78 Winter test car. Spare car at Rio, Estoril, Imola, Monaco (Johansson), Silverstone and Nürburgring. For Alboreto at Österreichring. Spare car at Zandvoort and Spa.

79 New for Alboreto at Rio. For Alboreto at Estoril. For Johansson at Imola and Monaco. For Alboreto at Paul Ricard. For Johansson at Silverstone, Nürburgring, Österreichring and Zandvoort.

80 New for Arnoux at Rio. For Johansson at Estoril. Spare car at Monaco (Alboreto), Spa, Montreal and Detroit. For Alboreto at Nürburgring. Spare car at Österreichring (raced by Alboreto). For Alboreto at Zandvoort.

81 New for Alboreto at Imola. For Alboreto at Monaco, Spa, Montreal and Detroit. For Johansson at Paul Ricard. For Alboreto at Silverstone.

82 New for Johansson at Spa. For Johansson at Montreal and Detroit.

83 New for Alboreto at Paul Ricard (became spare car). For Johansson at Monza and Spa. Spare car at Brands Hatch. For Alboreto at Kyalami and Adelaide.

84 New for Johansson at Ricard (practice only). Spare car at Monza, Kyalami and Adelaide.

85 New for Alboreto at Monza. For Alboreto at Spa and Brands Hatch.

86 New for Johansson at Brands Hatch. For Johansson at Kyalami and Adelaide.

Ligier

Three completely new cars for Rio.

JS25
01 New for de Cesaris at Rio. For de Cesaris at Estoril. For Laffite at Spa, Montreal and Detroit. Spare car at Silverstone, Nürburgring and Österreichring (raced by de Cesaris). Spare car at Brands Hatch and Adelaide.

02 New for Laffite at Rio. For Laffite at Estoril and Imola. Spare car at Monaco.

03 New at Rio (spare car). Spare car at Estoril and Imola. For Laffite at Monaco. Spare car at Spa, Montreal, Detroit and Paul Ricard. For de Cesaris at Zandvoort. For Streiff at Monza and Spa.

04 New for de Cesaris at Imola. For de Cesaris at Monaco, Spa, Montreal, Detroit, Paul Ricard, Silverstone, Nürburgring and Österreichring. Spare car at Zandvoort, Monza and Spa. For Streiff at Brands Hatch and Adelaide.

05 New for Laffite at Paul Ricard. For Laffite at Silverstone, Nürburgring, Österreichring, Zandvoort, Monza, Spa, Brands Hatch and Adelaide.

Lotus

Three new 97Ts ready for Brazil.

97T
1 New for winter testing. Spare car at Rio, Estoril, Imola (raced by de Angelis) and Monaco (raced by de Angelis). Became test car.

2 New for Senna at Rio. For Senna at Estoril, Imola, Monaco, Spa, Montreal and Detroit. Spare car at Paul Ricard, Silverstone, Nürburgring, Österreichring (raced by de Angelis), Zandvoort, Monza, Spa, Brands Hatch, Kyalami and Adelaide.

3 New for de Angelis at Rio. For de Angelis at Estoril, Imola, Monaco, Spa, Montreal, Detroit, Paul Ricard, Silverstone, Nürburgring, Österreichring, Zandvoort, Monza, Spa, Brands Hatch, Kyalami and Adelaide.

4 New at Monaco (spare car for de Angelis during practice). Spare car at Spa, Montreal and Detroit. For Senna at Paul Ricard, Silverstone, Nürburgring, Österreichring, Zandvoort, Monza, Spa, Brands Hatch, Kyalami and Adelaide.

McLaren

Development of MP4/2 using existing chassis from 1984.

MP4/2B
2 For Prost at Silverstone, Nürburgring, Österreichring, Zandvoort and Brands Hatch.

3 Spare car at Rio, Estoril, Imola, Monaco, Spa, Montreal, Detroit, Paul Ricard, Silverstone, Nürburgring, Österreichring (raced by Prost), Zandvoort (raced by Prost), Monza, Spa, Brands Hatch, Kyalami and Adelaide.

4 For Lauda at Rio, Estoril, Monaco, Spa, Montreal, Detroit, Paul Ricard, Silverstone, Nürburgring, Zandvoort, Monza and Spa. For Watson at Brands Hatch. For Lauda at Kyalami and Adelaide.

5 New for Prost at Rio. For Prost at Estoril, Imola, Monaco, Spa, Montreal, Detroit, Paul Ricard, Monza and Spa.

6 The first carbon-fibre chassis to be built entirely at Woking. New for Prost at Kyalami. For Prost at Adelaide.

Minardi

Joined Formula 1 with new car which had been unveiled with Alfa Romeo engine. Adapted to suit Cosworth V8 for first race and then altered to take Motori Moderni engine at Imola.

M/85
1 For Martini at Rio and Estoril. Spare car at Imola and Monaco. For Martini at Montreal, Detroit and Paul Ricard. Spare car at Monza, Spa, Brands Hatch, Kyalami and Adelaide.

2 Spare car at Spa, Montreal, Detroit, Paul Ricard, Silverstone, Nürburgring, Österreichring and Zandvoort.

3 New for Martini at Imola. For Martini at Monaco and Spa.

4 New for Martini at Silverstone. For Martini at Nürburgring, Österreichring, Zandvoort, Monza, Spa, Brands Hatch, Kyalami and Adelaide.

Osella

Modified 1984 FA1F while waiting for 1985 FA1G.

FA1F
01 Spare car at Rio and Estoril.

02 For Ghinzani at Rio and Estoril. Spare car at Imola (raced by Ghinzani), Monaco, Spa, Montreal, Detroit, Paul Ricard, Silverstone, Nürburgring, Österreichring, Zandvoort, Monza, Spa (raced by Rothengatter), Brands Hatch, Kyalami and Adelaide.

FA1G
01 New for Ghinzani at Imola. For Ghinzani at Monaco, Spa, Montreal, Detroit, Paul Ricard and Silverstone. For Rothengatter at Nürburgring, Österreichring, Zandvoort, Monza, Spa, Brands Hatch, Kyalami and Adelaide.

'Sorry!...SORRY!...I'll give you sorry, mate!'
Derek Warwick, his damaged Renault parked on the grass, prepares to interview the third party.

RAM

Built two new 1985 03 models for start of season.

03

1 New for Alliot at Rio. For Alliot at Estoril, Imola, Monaco, Spa and Montreal (damaged during race).

2 New for Winkelhock at Rio. For Winkelhock at Estoril. Spare car at Imola, Monaco, Spa and Montreal. For Alliot at Detroit, Paul Ricard, Silverstone and Nürburgring. Spare car at Österreichring and Zandvoort. For Acheson at Monza and Spa. Spare car at Brands Hatch.

3 New for Winkelhock at Imola. For Winkelhock at Monaco, Spa, Montreal, Detroit and Paul Ricard. Spare car at Silverstone and Nürburgring. For Acheson at Österreichring and Zandvoort. Spare car at Monza (raced by Acheson) and Spa.

4 New for Winkelhock at Silverstone. For Winkelhock at Nürburgring. For Alliot at Österreichring, Zandvoort, Monza, Spa and Brands Hatch.

Renault

1985 RE60 models ready for start of season.

RE60

1 Test car.

2 New at Rio (spare car – raced by Tambay). Spare car at Estoril, Imola and Monaco (for Warwick).

3 New for Warwick at Rio. For Warwick at Estoril, Imola, Monaco, Spa, Montreal, Detroit and Paul Ricard. Uprated to RE60B-specification. For Warwick at Monza, Spa, Brands Hatch and Adelaide.

4 New for Tambay at Rio. For Tambay at Estoril, Imola and Monaco. Spare car at Spa, Montreal, Detroit and Silverstone. For Hesnault at Nürburgring.

5 New at Monaco (spare car – raced by Tambay). For Tambay at Spa, Montreal and Detroit. Spare car at Paul Ricard. Uprated to RE60B-specification. Spare car at Nürburgring, Zandvoort, Monza, Brands Hatch and Adelaide.

RE60B

6 New for Tambay at Paul Ricard. For Tambay at Silverstone, Nürburgring, Österreichring, Zandvoort and Monza (damaged during practice).

7 New for Warwick at Silverstone. For Warwick at Nürburgring, Österreichring and Zandvoort (written off during practice).

8 New at Österreichring (spare car). Spare car at Zandvoort (raced by Warwick), Monza (raced by Tambay). For Tambay at Spa, Brands Hatch and Adelaide.

Spirit

Modified 1984 chassis for start of season.

101D

2 For Baldi at Rio and Estoril (damaged in race).

3 New for Baldi at Imola.

Toleman

Had four 1985 chassis ready by the time they had their first race of the season at Monaco.

TG185

1 Test car then spare car at Spa (15 Sep), Kyalami and Adelaide.

2 Spare car at Monaco, Spa, Montreal, Detroit and Silverstone (raced by Fabi).

3 For Fabi at Monaco, Spa, Montreal, Detroit, Paul Ricard, Silverstone and Nürburgring. Spare car at Österreichring (raced by Fabi), Zandvoort, Monza (raced by Fabi) and Brands Hatch. For Fabi at Kyalami and Adelaide.

4 Spare car at Paul Ricard and Nürburgring (crashed during practice). For Ghinzani at Österreichring, Zandvoort, Monza, Spa, Brands Hatch, Kyalami and Adelaide.

5 New for Fabi at Österreichring. For Fabi at Zandvoort, Monza, Spa and Brands Hatch.

Tyrrell

Sold 012 (1) and (4) to Baron Racing for F3000. Chassis (2) and (3) written off in 1984. Retained (5) for 1985 and

built two new chassis before starting work on 014 turbo car.

012

5 Spare car at Rio, Estoril, Imola, Monaco, Spa, Montreal and Detroit. For Bellof at Paul Ricard and Silverstone. For Brundle at Nürburgring and Österreichring.

6 New for Brundle at Rio. For Brundle at Estoril, Imola, Monaco, Spa, Montreal and Detroit.

7 New for Johansson at Rio. For Bellof at Estoril, Imola, Monaco, Spa, Montreal and Detroit. Spare car at Paul Ricard, Silverstone and Nürburgring.

014

1 New for Brundle at Paul Ricard. For Brundle at Silverstone. For Bellof at Nürburgring and Österreichring. For Brundle at Zandvoort. Spare car at Monza and Spa (crashed by Brundle).

2 New at Paul Ricard (spare car). Spare car at Silverstone, Nürburgring and Österreichring. For Bellof at Zandvoort. For Capelli at Brands Hatch. For Streiff at Kyalami. For Capelli at Adelaide.

3 New for Brundle at Monza. For Brundle at Spa, Brands Hatch, Kyalami and Adelaide.

4 New at Adelaide (spare car).

Williams

Prepared two 1985 FW10 cars for start of season, using 1984 FW09 as back-up.

FW09

8 Spare car at Rio and Estoril.

FW10

1 New for Rosberg at Rio. For Rosberg at Estoril. Spare car at Imola and Monaco. For Rosberg at Spa. Spare car at Montreal and Detroit.

2 New for Mansell at Rio. For Mansell at Estoril, Imola, Spa, Montreal and Detroit.

3 New for Rosberg at Imola. For Rosberg at Monaco. Spare car at Paul Ricard, Silverstone (raced by Rosberg), Nürburgring, Zandvoort, Monza, Spa, Brands Hatch, Kyalami and Adelaide.

4 New at Spa (spare car). For Rosberg at Montreal, Detroit, Paul Ricard, Silverstone and Nürburgring.

5 New for Mansell at Paul Ricard (crashed during practice).

6 New for Mansell at Silverstone. For Mansell at Nürburgring, Österreichring, Zandvoort, Monza, Spa, Brands Hatch, Kyalami and Adelaide.

7 New for Rosberg at Österreichring. For Rosberg at Zandvoort, Monza, Spa, Brands Hatch, Kyalami and Adelaide.

Zakspeed

New to Formula 1. First race at Estoril with car unveiled in 1984.

ZAK841

1 For Palmer at Estoril, Imola, Monaco, Spa. Spare car at Paul Ricard, Silverstone, Nürburgring, Österreichring, Zandvoort, Spa (raced by Danner) and Brands Hatch.

2 New for Palmer at Paul Ricard. For Palmer at Silverstone, Nürburgring, Österreichring and Zandvoort. For Danner at Spa and Brands Hatch.

During 1985, 36 drivers from 13 countries participated in the season's 16 Formula 1 races (there were no non-championship events). They were seen in 17 different makes of car powered by 10 makes of engine. Eleven drivers took part in all 16 races. Alain Prost scored points 12 times, Elio de Angelis 11 and Michele Alboreto nine. Ayrton Senna won seven pole positions but scored points on just six occasions. Prost took two pole positions and set four fastest laps. Keke Rosberg claimed two pole positions and three fastest laps.

1985 Formula 1 Drivers' Statistics

Driver	Nat.	Date of birth	Car	Rio de Janeiro	Estoril	Imola	Monte Carlo	Montreal	Detroit	Paul Ricard	Silverstone	Nürburgring	Österreichring	Zandvoort	Monza	Spa-Francorchamps	Brands Hatch	Kyalami	Adelaide	World Championship points	No. of Grands Prix started	1st	2nd	3rd	No. of Grand Prix pole positions
Kenny Acheson	GB	27/11/57	RAM-Hart	–	–	–	–	–	–	–	–	–	R	NQ	R	–	–	–	–	0	3	–	–	–	–
Michele Alboreto	I	23/12/56	Ferrari	2	2	R	2	1	3	R	2	1	3	4	13*	R	R	R	R	53	73	5	6	4	2
Philippe Alliot	F	24/7/54	RAM-Hart	8	R	R	NQ	R	R	R	R	R	R	R	R	R	R	–	–	0	26	–	–	–	–
Elio de Angelis	I	26/3/58	Lotus-Renault	3	4	1	3	5	5	5	NC	R	5	5	6	R	5	R	D	33	104	2	2	5	3
René Arnoux	F	4/7/48	Ferrari	4	–	–	–	–	–	–	–	–	–	–	–	–	–	–	–	3	96	7	9	6	18
Mauro Baldi	I	31/1/54	Spirit-Hart	NC	R	R	–	–	–	–	–	–	–	–	–	–	–	–	–	0	36	–	–	–	–
Stefan Belloff†	D	20/11/57	Tyrrell-Cosworth Tyrrell-Renault	W	6	R	NQ	11	4	13	11		8	7*	R					4	20	–	–	–	–
Gerhard Berger	A	27/8/59	Arrows-BMW	R	R	R	R	13	11	R	8	7	R	9	R	7	10	5	6	3	20	–	–	–	–
Thierry Boutsen	B	13/7/57	Arrows-BMW	11	R	2	9	9	7	9	R	4	8	R	9	10	6	6	R	11	41	–	1	–	–
Martin Brundle	GB	1/6/59	Tyrrell-Cosworth Tyrrell-Renault	9	R	9	10	12	R	R	7	10	NQ	7	8	13	R	7	NC	0	22	–	–	–	–
Ivan Capelli	I	24/5/63	Tyrrell-Renault	–	–	–	–	–	–	–	–	–	–	–	–	R	–	–	4	3	2	–	–	–	–
Andrea de Cesaris	I	31/5/59	Ligier-Renault	R	R	R	4	14	10	R	R	R	R	R	–	–	–	–	–	3	73	–	2	1	1
Eddie Cheever	USA	10/1/58	Alfa Romeo	R	R	R	R	17	R	10	R	R	R	R	R	R	11	R	R	0	85	–	2	5	–
Christian Danner	D	4/4/58	Zakspeed	–	–	–	–	–	–	–	–	–	–	–	–	R	R	–	–	0	2	–	–	–	–
Teo Fabi	I	9/3/55	Toleman-Hart	–	–	–	R	R	R	14*	R	R	R	R	12	R	R	R	R	0	32	–	–	1	1
Piercarlo Ghinzani	I	16/1/52	Osella-Alfa Romeo Toleman-Hart	12	9	R	NQ	R	R	15	R		DNS	R	R	R	R	R	R	0	36	–	–	–	–
François Hesnault	F	30/12/56	Brabham-BMW Renault	R	R	R	NQ	–	–	–	–	–	R	–	–	–	–	–	–	0	19	–	–	–	–
Stefan Johansson	S	8/9/56	Tyrrell-Cosworth Ferrari	7		8	6*	R	2	2	4	R	9	4	R	5	R	4	5	26	28	–	2	–	–
Alan Jones	AUS	2/11/46	Beatrice-Hart	–	–	–	–	–	–	–	–	–	–	–	R	–	R	DNS	R	0	100	12	7	5	6
Jacques Laffite	F	21/11/43	Ligier-Renault	6	R	R	6	8	12	R	3	3	R	R	R	11*	–	–	2	16	167	6	9	15	7
Niki Lauda	A	22/2/49	McLaren-TAG	R	R	4	R	R	R	R	R	5	R	1	R	W	–	R	R	14	171	25	20	9	24
Nigel Mansell	GB	8/8/54	Williams-Honda	R	5	5	7	6	R	DNS	R	6	R	6	11*	2	1	1	R	31	74	2	1	5	2
Pierluigi Martini	I	23/4/61	Minardi-Cosworth Minardi-Motori Moderni	R	R	R	NQ	R	R	R	R	11*	R	R	R	12	R	R	8	0	15	–	–	–	–
Jonathan Palmer	GB	7/11/56	Zakspeed	–	R	DNS	11	–	–	R	R	R	R	R	–	–	–	–	–	0	23	–	–	–	–
Riccardo Patrese	I	17/4/54	Alfa Romeo	R	R	R	R	10	R	11	9	R	R	R	R	9	R	R	R	0	128	2	2	4	2
Nelson Piquet	BR	17/8/52	Brabham-BMW	R	R	8	R	R	6	1	4	R	R	8	2	5	R	R	R	21	110	13	9	7	18
Alain Prost	F	24/2/55	McLaren-TAG	1	R	(1)	1	3	R	3	1	2	1	2	1	3	4	3	R	73	89	21	9	7	15
Keke Rosberg	SF	6/12/48	Williams-Honda	R	R	R	8	4	1	2	R	12*	R	R	R	4	3	2	1	40	98	5	7	4	4
Huub Rothengatter	NL	8/10/54	Osella-Alfa Romeo	–	–	–	–	–	–	–	–	R	9	NC	R	R	NQ	R	7	0	14	–	–	–	–
Ayrton Senna	BR	21/3/60	Lotus-Renault	R	1	7*	R	16	R	R	10*	R	2	3	R	1	2	R	3	38	30	2	3	4	7
Philippe Streiff	F	26/6/55	Ligier-Renault Tyrrell-Renault	–	–	–	–	–	–	–	–	–	–	–	10	9	8	R	3	4	6	–	–	1	–
Marc Surer	CH	18/9/51	Brabham-BMW	–	–	–	15	8	8	6	R	6	10*	4	8	R	R	R	R	5	77	–	–	–	–
Patrick Tambay	F	25/6/49	Renault	5	3	3	R	7	R	6	R	R	10*	R	7	R	12	–	R	11	100	2	4	5	5
Derek Warwick	GB	27/8/54	Renault	10	7	10	5	R	R	R	7	5	R	R	R	6	R	–	R	5	58	–	2	2	–
John Watson	GB	4/5/46	McLaren-TAG	–	–	–	–	–	–	–	–	–	–	–	–	–	7	–	–	0	152	5	6	9	2
Manfred Winkelhock†	D	6/10/52	RAM-Hart	13	NC	R	NQ	R	R	12	R	R	–	–	–	–	–	–	–	0	47	–	–	–	–

† Deceased
* Retired but classified as a finisher
DNS = Qualified, did not start
NC = Running at finish, not classified
NQ = Did not qualify
R = Retired
D = Disqualified
W = Entry withdrawn

Grand Prix Super Grid

by John Taylor

By adding together the length of all 16 circuits used in this year's Grand Prix World Championship, we arrive at a circuit with a length of 47·45 miles/76·36 km. If we then add together the best official practice times of each of the 13 drivers who achieved a qualifying time in each event, we arrive at a hypothetical grid for the season.

Keke Rosberg (Williams FW10/FW10B)
22m 18·792s, 127·592 mph/205·339 km/h

Ayrton Senna (Lotus 97T)
22m 12·275s, 128·217 mph/206·345 km/h

Nigel Mansell (Williams FW10/FW10B)
22m 24·339s, 127·066 mph/204·492 km/h

Alain Prost (McLaren MP4)
22m 21·615s, 127·324 mph/204·908 km/h

Michele Alboreto (Ferrari 156/85)
22m 28·902s, 126·636 mph/203·800 km/h

Nelson Piquet (Brabham BT54)
22m 25·537s, 126·953 mph/204·311 km/h

Thierry Boutsen (Arrows A8)
22m 46·940s, 124·965 mph/201·111 km/h

Elio de Angelis (Lotus 97T)
22m 30·089s, 126·525 mph/203·622 km/h

Riccardo Patrese (Alfa Romeo 184TB/185T)
22m 54·781s, 124·252 mph/199·964 km/h

Stefan Johansson (Tyrrell 012/Ferrari 156/85)
22m 51·714s, 124·530 mph/200·411 km/h

Gerhard Berger (Arrows A8)
23m 11·758s, 122·737 mph/197·526 km/h

Eddie Cheever (Alfa Romeo 184TB/185T)
22m 58·876s, 123·883 mph/199·370 km/h

Martin Brundle (Tyrrell 012/014)
23m 42·943s, 120·047 mph/193·196 km/h

Points per start average (career)

Position	Name	Nationality	Starts	Points	1st	2nd	3rd	4th	5th	6th	Pole	F. lap	Points average
1	Alain Prost	F	89	286·5	21	9	7	4	2	4	15	15	3·219
2	Niki Lauda	A	171	420·5	25	20	9	7	7	5	24	24	2·459
3	Nelson Piquet	BR	110	236	13	9	7	8	5	3	18	13	2·145
4	Alan Jones	AUS	100	202	12	7	5	7	5	1	6	13	2·020
5	René Arnoux	F	96	164	7	9	7	3	5	3	18	12	1·708
6	Ayrton Senna	BR	30	51	2	3	4	–	–	2	7	4	1·700
7	Michele Alboreto	I	73	119·5	5	6	3	4	2	3	2	5	1·637
8	Ivan Capelli	I	2	3	–	–	–	1	–	–	–	–	1·500
9	Keke Rosberg	SF	98	137·5	5	7	4	7	7	1	4	3	1·403
10	Jaques Laffite	F	167	214	6	9	15	7	8	8	7	6	1·281
11	Elio de Angelis	I	103	122	2	2	5	11	17	6	3	–	1·184
12	John Watson	GB	152	169	5	6	9	9	7	11	2	5	1·112
13	Stefan Johansson	S	28	29	–	2	–	4	2	1	–	–	1·036
14	Patrick Tambay	F	100	101	2	4	5	6	7	7	5	2	1·010
15	Nigel Mansell	GB	74	69	2	1	5	4	2	8	2	2	0·932
16	Philippe Streiff	F	6	4	–	–	1	–	–	–	–	–	0·667
17	Derek Warwick	GB	58	37	–	2	2	3	3	2	–	1	0·638
18	Eddie Cheever	USA	85	50	–	2	5	3	3	3	–	–	0·588
19	Riccardo Patrese	I	126	73	2	4	4	2	2	5	2	4	0·579
20	Thierry Boutsen	B	41	16	–	1	–	1	2	3	–	–	0·390
21	Andrea de Cesaris	I	73	27	–	2	1	2	1	3	1	1	0·370
22	Teo Fabi	I	32	9	–	–	1	1	1	1	1	–	0·281
23	Marc Surer	CH	76	17	–	–	–	2	2	7	–	1	0·224
24=	Gerhard Berger	A	20	4	–	–	–	–	1	2	–	–	0·200
24=	Stefan Bellof	D	20	4	–	–	–	1	–	1	–	–	0·200
26	Mauro Baldi	I	36	5	–	–	–	–	1	3	–	–	0·139
27	Piercarlo Ghinzani	I	36	2	–	–	–	–	–	1	–	–	0·056
28	Manfred Winkelhock	D	47	2	–	–	–	–	–	1	–	–	0·043

Laps led (drivers)

Driver	Races led	Laps led (no./per cent)	Miles (to nearest mile)	Km (to nearest km)
Ayrton Senna	9	270 (26·16)	823	1325
Keke Rosberg	8	232 (22·48)	638	1026
Alain Prost	7	178 (17·25)	523	841
Nigel Mansell	2	141 (13·66)	364	586
Michele Alboreto	4	99 (9·59)	265	427
Niki Lauda	3	52 (5·04)	150	242
Nelson Piquet	1	43 (4·17)	155	250
Elio de Angelis	2	16 (1·55)	45	73
Stefan Johansson	1	1 (0·10)	3	5

Laps led (manufacturers)

Manufacturer	Races led	Laps led (no./per cent)	Miles (to nearest mile)	Km (to nearest km)
Williams	9	373 (36·14)	1002	1612
Lotus	10	286 (27·71)	869	1398
McLaren	8	230 (22·29)	673	1083
Ferrari	5	100 (9·69)	269	432
Brabham	1	43 (4·17)	155	250

Total laps/miles/km in season = 1032 laps/2970 miles/4780 km

Points per start average (season)

Position	Name	Nationality	Starts	Points	1st	2nd	3rd	4th	5th	6th	Pole	F. lap	Points average
1	Alain Prost	F	16	76	5	2	4	1	–	–	2	5	4·750
2	Michele Alboreto	I	16	53	2	4	2	1	–	–	2	2	3·313
3	René Arnoux	F	1	3	–	–	1	–	–	–	–	–	3·000
4	Keke Rosberg	SF	16	40	2	2	1	2	–	–	2	3	2·500
5	Ayrton Senna	BR	16	38	2	2	2	–	–	–	7	3	2·375
6	Nigel Mansell	GB	15	31	2	1	–	–	2	3	1	1	2·067
7	Elio de Angelis	I	16	33	1	–	2	1	6	1	1	–	2·063
8	Stefan Johansson	S	16	26	–	2	–	3	2	1	–	–	1·625
9	Ivan Capelli	I	2	3	–	–	–	1	–	–	–	–	1·500
10	Nelson Piquet	BR	16	21	1	1	–	1	1	1	1	1	1·313
11	Jacques Laffite	F	15	16	–	1	2	–	–	2	–	1	1·067
12	Niki Lauda	A	14	14	1	–	–	1	–	–	1	1	1·000
13	Philippe Streiff	F	5	4	–	–	1	–	–	–	–	–	0·800
14	Patrick Tambay	F	15	11	–	–	2	–	1	1	–	–	0·733
15	Thierry Boutsen	B	16	11	–	1	–	1	–	2	–	–	0·688
16	Stefan Bellof	D	9	4	–	–	–	1	–	1	–	–	0·444
17	Marc Surer	CH	12	5	–	–	–	1	–	2	–	–	0·417
18	Derek Warwick	GB	15	5	–	–	–	–	2	1	–	–	0·313
19	Andrea de Cesaris	I	11	3	–	–	–	–	1	–	–	–	0·273
20	Gerhard Berger	A	16	3	–	–	–	–	1	1	–	–	0·188

Meadowlands: 'a miserably unattractive race amid cement walls and chainlink fencing'.
Photo: Gary Gold

Unser and Son

by Gordon Kirby

As *Autocourse* went to press, CART's PPG Industries-sponsored Indycar World Series remained a wide-open proposition. With two of 15 races to run, Bobby Rahal was in the midst of a late-season Championship assault, closing fast on points leader Al Unser Jnr and second-placed Al Unser Snr. Defending Champion Mario Andretti was hanging on in fourth place while Emerson Fittipaldi and Danny Sullivan also figured as possibilities for the 1985 Indycar title.

Whatever the outcome, the 1985 Indycar season will go down as one of the most competitive in the 76-year history of American national championship automobile racing. Eight different drivers won races during the first 13 rounds of the year and every race had a character entirely its own. With 95 per cent of the field aboard similar March 85C- or Lola T900-Cosworth DFXs, the championship developed into a fascinating battle of drivers, which was comparatively uncomplicated by variables in chassis, engines and tyres.

This translated into a summer full of superb wheel-to-wheel motor racing on both oval tracks and road courses. Sixteen drivers led races legitimately, under the green flag. The Championship itself developed into an intriguing, ever-changing battle between three 'veterans' (Mario Andretti, Al Unser Snr and Emerson Fittipaldi) and three 'newcomers' (Bobby Rahal, Danny Sullivan and Al Unser Jnr).

By the middle of the season the Unsers were adding another dimension to the Championship as the father and son act (46 and 23 years of age), began to control the leading positions in the tight points race. In four of those first 13 races 'Big Al' and 'Little Al' shared the victory podium alongside one other driver.

At the time of writing Unser Snr (in his third year with Penske Racing, aboard a March 85C) had not won a race although he had come desperately close on two occasions and had otherwise strung together a typically consistent collection of strong finishes among the first three. It was Unser Jnr's first year with Doug Shierson's

Domino's Pizza/Lola team) and his driving reflected a style similar to his father's. By his own admission, he was lucky to win two races, which thereby gave him a small advantage over his father, and he was able to maintain this precarious lead.

Meanwhile, as the season neared its end, Bobby Rahal was emerging as the fastest man in Indycar racing. He was on pole for four races in succession and won three of them convincingly, leading most laps in each race. With momentum on his side, Rahal and the TrueSports/Budweiser/March team looked like a favourite to overhaul both Unsers although the blend of speed, consistency and race-smart thinking evident in the latter would clearly take some beating.

Defending Champion Mario Andretti began the '85 season where his '84 season ended. He won at Long Beach, was a fighting second at Indianapolis and won again at Milwaukee and Portland in June. Luck then seemed to desert Andretti and after a series of DNFs he crashed near the end of the Michigan 500, breaking a collarbone and cracking a hip socket.

After missing one race, Andretti returned to finish a dogged seventh in the Pocono 500. That was to be a high point, however. In a series of four races he fell by the wayside just as he looked ready to record a good, points-earning finish. When his Lola caught fire three laps from the end of round 13 at Laguna Seca in October, Mario's luck seemed to have all but run out. With two races to go he was in fourth place, 20 points behind Championship leader Unser Jnr with a maximum of 44 points available (20 for a win plus one point apiece for pole position and the man who leads most laps in each race).

Also holding theoretical chances to win the Championship were Emerson Fittipaldi and Danny Sullivan. Fittipaldi made a good start to his first full season in Indycars, driving for CART co-founder Pat Patrick's team. He was second at Long Beach, ran well at Indianapolis before dropping out near the end, and scored a rather

Al Unser Jnr, fighting with Dad for the title *(below)*. The start at Long Beach, led by Mario Andretti *(left)* and Bobby Rahal *(bottom)*.

lucky mid-summer victory in the Michigan 500. A persistent finisher through the middle stages of the season, Fittipaldi faded in the last part of the year as he struggled both with reliability and from starting regularly from the mid-field.

Sullivan switched from Shierson to Penske Racing for his second year in Indycars and after a busy winter of testing he was sharp and ready for the start of the season. He led at Long Beach before running out of fuel and finishing third. He won spectacularly at Indianapolis after a giant spin during his first attempt to pass Mario Andretti for the lead.

The rest of Sullivan's season, however, was an anticlimax. In eight of the races that followed he was on the front row but, despite leading five of those races, he all too rarely finished. He was second at Mid-Ohio in September but otherwise there was always some kind of mechanical or handling problem which dropped him down the field or into retirement. When he was blackflagged for leaking oil while running second with only four laps to go at Laguna Seca in October, his chances for the Championship all but vanished.

In addition to the six drivers in the championship battle, a good many more enjoyed days in the sun. Rick Mears for example, started only five races as he recovered from foot injuries incurred in September 1984. Continuing with Penske Racing, he won the Pocono 500, was on the pole for the Michigan 500 and set the fastest lap in the Indianapolis 500.

Also scoring single victories last year were Jacques Villeneuve and Johnny Rutherford. In his second year of Indycar racing, Villeneuve secured his first win in the category at Road America in mid-summer. He also challenged for the lead at Long Beach, Cleveland and Sanair but a couple of crashes during practice at Indy convinced the French-Canadian and his team to stay away from the season's four, major super-speedway races.

Veteran Rutherford was something of a contrast to Villeneuve, adopting a conservative make-the-flag approach to road races and running powerfully, particularly on the big ovals. He was competitive in the three 500-mile races only to hit several problems in each race. Rutherford was a rather lucky winner of the bizarre, crash-strewn race at Sanair in Quebec, recording his first win in five years. 1986 would see his second year with Alex Morales' small but effective team.

Unser Snr aside, the most successful driver who failed to win a race was Geoff Brabham. After four years in Indycars, Brabham finally landed a number one seat for 1985, replacing Al Unser Jnr in Rick Galles' two-car team. Brabham ran near the front in many races, leading at Cleveland and featuring in battles for the lead in a couple of other races. Reliability, however, was rarely on his side.

Brabham shared a couple of team-mates during the year. Pancho Carter drove Galles' second car in all the oval races and often ran hard among the leaders. At Indianapolis, using a USAC-specification 'big boost' Buick V6 engine, Carter qualified on pole, although in the race he and second-starting Scott Brayton were early victims of burned Buick pistons.

Reverting to Cosworth power for the rest of the year, Carter continued to show excellent oval track form. He was remarkably quick at Milwaukee, was in with the leaders in both races at the Michigan super-speedway and was briefly a disputed winner (ultimately confirmed as second to Rutherford) at Sanair.

Roberto Moreno stepped into Carter's car for most road races and proved very quick. He stole the lead from Sullivan at Road America and ran with the leaders in every race he started. For 1986, the ambitious Galles planned to run three cars for Brabham, Carter and Moreno!

Also running two cars with race-leading, if not winning, potential was the Kraco Car Stereos team owned by Maurie Kraines. In business as an Indycar team owner for four years, Kraines ran Michael Andretti and Geoff Brabham in '84, replacing Brabham with Kevin Cogan for '85.

As in his rookie year, young Andretti continued

to run at the front but the team still lacked depth and reliability. Michael seized the lead at the start of the Pocono 500 and later led in similar style at September's 200-mile sprint race on the Michigan super-speedway. Cogan fought to recover from painful heel injuries sustained in August '84, and came on strong as the summer wore on. At the end of the year he was running quickly on a regular basis and sometimes leading, but like his younger team-mate, Cogan never enjoyed the right combination of luck and reliability.

The same was true of the other teams and drivers who occasionally insinuated themselves among the leaders. Least lucky of all, perhaps, was Roberto Guerrero. The young Colombian (a father in September) continued for a second year of Indycar racing with Dan Cotter's team but, despite his evident speed, frequently he was very fragile. If the engine didn't blow up (which happened far too often), then Roberto himself would throw away his opportunity. 1986 will surely be better.

Also enjoying the worst combination of poor reliability and bad luck was young Mexican Josele Garza. In his fifth year of Indycars (he's only 24!), young Garza was often a contender on all types of tracks. He led the Michigan 500 for example, but his Machinists' Union-owned car was rarely around at the finish. In a better team, Garza might quickly develop into a race winner.

The Machinists' Union (full mouthful is International Association of Machinists and Aerospace Workers) ran a second car in most races. Various drivers – Pete Halsmer, Chip Ganassi and Rupert Keegan – took the wheel without much luck.

Seat-swopping became a common practice among some teams with Patrick Racing being the most consistent practitioner of this artless theory. Joining Emerson Fittipaldi from time to time in the CART co-founder's frustratingly unsuccessful team were Bruno Giacomelli, Don Whittington and sprint car ace Sammy Swindell.

Patrick's 'guest driver' seat opened up after long-time team leader Gordon Johncock decided to retire on the eve of qualifying at Indianapolis. As Patrick searched for a replacement, Johncock walked the pit lane at Indianapolis, announcing his retirement to the spectators and taking congratulations all round.

A smaller team able to achieve some success last year was the Milwaukee-based outfit owned by veal producer Aat Groenevelt. Super Vee champion Arie Luyendyk moved into Indycars with Groenevelt's team and had a pretty good year. He was seventh at Indianapolis and won the race's 'rookie of the year' award. After a mixture of good and bad races, Luyendyk was becoming a regular mid-field/front runner and, at the time of writing,

Rick Mears, uninhibited by injury: Al Unser Snr, uninhibited by age *(top)*.
Eric Broadley, keeping the Lola name to the fore.

he was the apparent winner of CART's season-long 'rookie of the year' prize.

A couple of drivers who showed they still deserve a chance were Raul Boesel and Jim Crawford. Boesel joined the team run by veteran driver Dick Simon, starting about half the races. Next year Boesel will spend a full season with Simon, who intended to retire. Crawford started the season with old friend Bob Fernley and the pair later merged with Jacques Villeneuve's Canadian team. In the few races he started, Crawford showed a lot of speed but had no results.

Occasional starters from among the ranks of Indycar veterans were A. J. Foyt and Danny Ongais. Foyt was nowhere; Ongais, on the other hand, was on the pace in a number of races although he scored no real results. Trying to find work for 1986 after starting only the Indy 500 in 1985 was Derek Daly. After breaking a leg in a terrible accident at the Michigan super-speedway in September of '84, the Irishman made his comeback in a team put together only days before the start of practice at Indianapolis. Following various dramas, Daly made the field and the finish of the race only to see the team fall apart and leave him a spectator for the rest of the year.

All the aforementioned drivers and many more

(in fact, totalling 52 names) drove on one or more occasions a variant of either the March 85C or Lola T900. These two British manufacturers produced 45 and 25 respectively of their 1985 Indycar chassis, and the Cosworth DFX turbo V8s mated to these chassis meant that the American national championship continued to be dominated by British equipment.

This state of affairs has applied for nearly a decade and, with the 'March spec-car revolution' sweeping the Indycar tracks in the past three years, the British grip has tightened still further. However, most fans of the sport in America have become steadily less happy with the situation. Now that many of the drivers come from some kind of European racing background, CART's 'Indycar Car World Series' is viewed with great suspicion from the grass roots of the sport.

Meanwhile, the man who stands, more than anyone, for the Stars and Stripes in Indycar racing today is Dan Gurney. The good-humoured, often irascible Gurney wears the same twinkle in his eyes that he wore in Formula One 20 years ago and still approaches life with a boyish innocence and enthusiasm. Last year Gurney's All-American Racers operation built three new Eagles, fielding the cars in most races for Tom Sneva and Ed Pimm.

Occasionally the team's spare car – a Lola T900 – was pressed into service but otherwise Gurney persisted with the latest Eagle design. Completed just in time for the start of the season, the new Eagles were light-years behind March and Lola in development and track testing but by the middle of the year the team was making progress, despite a series of accidents. Sneva finished second at Milwaukee but otherwise had a miserable year, disagreeing with the team's approach and continuing to have a hard time in road races. In the second half of the year Sneva was overshadowed by his younger team-mate Ed Pimm who rose to the job of sorting out the Eagle and began consistently to outpace Sneva.

CHANGING TIMES

Not only have the Indycar projects from March and Lola been flourishing, but the fierce competition of the past few years has been encouraged by restrictions on tyre sizes and compounds, on turbo boost pressure and to single turbos. These combine to act as a performance barrier for all Indycars.

This most recent (fleeting?) Golden Age of Indycar racing has been financed by a series of new races with substantially increased purses, together with PPG Industries' annual commitment of some $2 million per year in additional prize money and the first complete television package to cover the entire Indycar championship.

Increased competition has of course brought about increased costs and the escalation has reached the point where a new round of growth is required both in purses and media-marketing. However, none of these appears to be on the horizon. In fact, poor television ratings, thin coverage in the daily newspapers and an increasingly unstable schedule seem to be severely restricting the potential growth of CART's package.

In retrospect, it may be that 1985 was a high point for Indycar racing. A handful of teams seemed ready to fold and many mid-field teams were grumbling noisily about their inabilities to attract sponsorship.

There was also a lot of political wrangling. Many of the smaller teams complained they were being ignored in terms of planning and policy decisions by the larger teams, represented by the six elected CART Board members: Roger Penske, Pat Patrick, Jim Trueman, Carl Haas, Doug Shierson and Rick Galles. Between them, they fielded 10 cars in most races last year. (Also on the Board, incidentally, are mechanics' representative Steve Horne, from TrueSports, and drivers' rep Al Unser Snr.) A matter of hot debate throughout the summer was CART's 1986-89 rules package which was announced in July but remained disputed and

Danny Sullivan, who won spectacularly at Indianapolis (below).
Jacques Villeneuve challenged for the lead at Long Beach and won at Road America (opposite).

Lisa Newsome

Paul Webb

unratified in mid-October.

There were other arguments over new races and venues, date changes and the shift in the balance between oval and road courses. The 1986 Indycar schedule was expected finally to push the weight in favour of road courses.

Many of these 'road courses' are in fact 'city event' races run either on streets or through parking lots. In the case of Cleveland, a very bumpy airport course forms the course. For the second year in a row, the Meadowlands Sports Complex in metropolitan New Jersey ran a miserably unattractive race amid cement walls and chainlink fencing in the parking lots of the complex.

Some of the other new races may have been run in less hostile environments but none the less failed to interest many long-time fans of Indycar racing. The shrinking number of oval track races was increasingly lamented; indeed, in 1985 only six ovals staged Indycar races, two of these being at Roger Penske's awesomely fast Michigan International Speedway.

Another matter of some concern in 1985 was CART's standard of officiation. Persistent problems continued with lap scoring and pace car placement at oval track races. A good many disputed black flag 'stop and go' penalties were also meted-out in the year. A more sinister development seemed to be the constant revision of rules to eliminate small innovations or neat tricks designed to outwit the rule book.

All this quibbling came before the public eye at Sanair, a tiny, 0.833-mile trioval in southern Quebec. Following a crash-strewn race on the frenetic little track ('why are we racing here?', many people asked) it appeared that the 300-km race would end under a yellow flag. However, against all forms of oval racing logic and convention, the race was restarted with barely one-tenth of a lap remaining as the field came off the last turn on the last lap!

In response, Pancho Carter passed apparent race-winner Johnny Rutherford and after a very confused evening (poorly managed by CART in the formal post-race interview) the race became a

matter of protest and then appeal by Rutherford's team. In the end the victory was given to Rutherford with Carter placed second. CART's illogical and heavy-handed methods of handling this affair did not go down very well with the public or the media.

Another hot end-of-season debate concerned a mooted supporting series utilising F3000-based March chassis, and unturbocharged Buick V6 engines. Rejected by the CART Board but supported by Board member Pat Patrick and by appointed Board Chairman John Frasco (the sharp-eyed lawyer who negotiates CART's contracts), the formula was being pushed to take effect in 1986 with the cars being leased (!) to prospective teams in the interests of cost-control.

This last item has become a matter of increasing concern and is likely to be of paramount importance over the next few years. Coming in 1986 is a new Roger Penske-inspired Chevrolet V8 four-cam racing engine designed in Northampton by Ilmor (Mario Ilien and Paul Morgan) Engineering. The Penske and Patrick teams plan to race the engine in '86 with the power plant made available to all teams on a commercial basis in 1987.

Meanwhile, Jim Trueman has been romancing Enzo Ferrari (and vice versa?) as the *Commendatore* considers the benefits of Indycar racing in 1986. Heavily rumoured as an Indycar contestant for 1987 is McLaren International, in company with their sponsor, Marlboro. Porsche, Honda and others are also known to be taking a hard look at building Indycar engines.

After the entry in 1979 of Championship Auto Racing Teams, the Indycar waters are becoming awfully hot!

Super-Bill versus the Dreaded Darrell

The other major championship in the United States is of course NASCAR's Winston Cup Grand National series. The pinnacle of American 'stock car' racing, the Grand National Championship continued to thrive in its 37th year.

'Stock car' racing is the most broad-based and widespread type of automobile racing in America; last year, NASCAR's top series regularly

attracted full, 40-car fields to all 28 Championship races. The series also captured a large share of the market – in the grandstands, on television and radio and in the newspapers.

In fact, NASCAR continues to outwit CART at attracting both media and public attention. Good marketing, a decade and a half of sponsorship from Winston cigarettes and a historically stable schedule and series has made the Winston Cup Grand National Championship the most widely recognised motor sport in America. For the majority of race fans and motor racing writers/columnists/commentators across the USA, it is NASCAR's major series *not* CART's which is considered to be the National Championship.

Last year, Winston announced an increased prize money package, equalling PPG Industries' expenditure of $2 million per year on the CART championship. Meanwhile, the package of contingency money associated with NASCAR completely outstrips that offered by CART. In total, NASCAR offers a much better business proposition for its 3700 lb 600 bhp tube-frame 'stock cars', than any other form of automobile racing anywhere in the world.

One drawback to NASCAR is that most of the races take place in the south-eastern United States, far away from major population centres. This has led to accusations of regionalism and in an effort to expand beyond this limited base, NASCAR is looking to move into new venues, including road courses. In 1986, Grand National cars will race at Watkins Glen in mid-summer and the following year a handful of road and 'city event' races for slightly smaller cars are scheduled to be included within the Winston Cup championship.

The 1985 Winston Cup was dominated for most of the year by one man: Bill Elliott. Based in Georgia, Elliott and his family have raced Fords in NASCAR for nine years but it has only been in the past three years that the team has enjoyed the sponsorship required to mount a full-blown effort. Elliott finally established himself as a regular front-runner and race winner in 1983 and '84, and in 1985 he and his brothers took Grand National

205

racing by storm.

Driving one of the latest generation of Ford Thunderbirds, Elliott started the season with a dominant victory in the Daytona 500. He went on to dominate most races run on super-speedways and by mid-season looked unbeatable in the Championship stakes. In fact he had won 10 races by mid-October and also scooped a million-dollar bonus from Winston for winning three of the four major races of the year.

On the half-mile and one-mile 'short tracks' which compromise almost half the 28-race NASCAR schedule, however, Elliott was nothing like as fast. He did not win a single short-track race and because of this Elliott came under pressure for the title from Darrell Waltrip.

Driving as he has since 1981 for Junior Johnson's all-powerful Chevrolet-equipped team, Waltrip is a master of the smaller tracks and in the latter half of the year he was able to catch and overhaul Elliott in the points tables. Winston Cup Champion in 1981 and '82, Waltrip looked capable of defeating Elliott for the '85 title.

1984 Champion Terry Labonte had a miserable year, winning only once and never really featuring in the Championship reckoning. Nor did '83 Champion Bobby Allison who split with DiGard Racing in mid-summer, finishing the year in his own, privately run car.

Another veteran to have had a bad year was seven-times NASCAR Champion Richard Petty. For only the third season in his long career, the 48-year old Petty failed to win a race and by late summer news broke that Petty was planning to revive his family team which had been closed down at the beginning of 1985. A little unlucky he may have been, but clearly he harboured no thoughts of retirement . . .

Despite Elliott's domination of NASCAR's victory circles, a total of eight drivers won races last year. Among the race winners were Harry Gant (third in the points), Waltrip's team-mate Neil Bonnett, Cale Yarborough (Ford-mounted like Elliott, and the only driver to beat Elliott in a super-speedway race), Dale Earnhardt, Labonte and newcomer Greg Sacks. Incidentally, 25 drivers won at least $100,000 with Elliott carting home more than $2 million!

Getting Better all the Time

Completely dominating the American road racing theatre at present is John Bishop's IMSA organisation. After leaving the SCCA some 15 years ago, Bishop and his operation have gone from strength to strength while the SCCA has continued to flounder and recede.

In recent years, IMSA's flagship series for GTP (Grand Touring Prototypes) has begun to boom as result of good marketing and an expansion of manufacturer interest. In the past two years, most IMSA races have been dominated by Porsche 962s although there is increasing competition from a variety of other cars.

Last year, Ford's neat, tidy Probe showed it was capable of running with the Porsches although it suffered from being underpowered and unreliable. Other challengers included Bob Tullius's superb fleet of Group 44 Jaguars as well as a handful of turbo Buick V6-powered Marches.

Nevertheless, the Championship was carried by Porschemeister Al Holbert. After a year of Indycar racing, Holbert returned full-time to IMSA. As Porsche's racing agent in the USA, he ran a 962 with Derek Bell co-driving. His team also constructed their own version of a 962 and in a handful of races Holbert ran two cars, with Al Unser Jnr joining the team as a third driver. Holbert won half of the 17 races and wrapped up his fourth IMSA title.

Further full-blooded GTP cars entered the IMSA wars as the season wore on. Although many were fielded and driven by amateurs, the starting fields usually made an impressive sight as Bishop showed his organisation could exist very happily without any involvement or meddling by FISA.

The once-powerful SCCA, on the other hand, struggled for survival in the professional racing theatre. Focusing most of its failing energy on the TransAm series, the SCCA's reputation continued to fade with a series of questionable rulings allied to the club's celebrated inability to cope with real-world marketing and promotion.

For the second successive year the TransAm was dominated by Mercury Capris fielded by a pair of Ford-backed teams. Champion was 22-year old Wally Dallenbach Jnr who defeated the rapid Willy T. Ribbs and '84 Champion Tom Gloy. Other contenders included Buick-mounted Elliott Forbes-Robinson and Nissan-mounted Paul Newman. Although he didn't run all the races, 60-year old Newman showed he could fight it out with the youngsters!

Near the end of the year, word leaked out that Ford planned a drastic cut-back in its TransAm involvement for 1986. Poor administration by the SCCA pushed Ford to concentrate on IMSA and it will therefore be interesting to see how the SCCA survives as a major professional racing series in 1986.

The SCCA's celebrated ineptitude has had a dire effect on the 'farm system' of American racing. The club has ignored and abused Formula Atlantic for many years while Super Vee survives primarily because the category is run as a support event at most CART races.

As in the mid-Seventies, Formula Atlantic has been taken over by an organisation comprising the leading teams. A thriving West Coast-based series has consequently developed, complemented last year by a new East Coast series. Champion of the category in 1985 was Jeff Wood who battled for the title with Dan Marvin.

The Super Vee series, sponsored by the Robert Bosch Corporation, was fiercely contested on both ovals and road courses. Seven different drivers won races during the year with 21-year old Ken Johnson emerging as champion over Davy Jones. Jeff Andretti, Mike Groff and Cary Bren also showed their ability to progress in the sport while Europeans Didier Theys and Hans-Peter Pandur surprised many with their speed.

The Group 44 Jaguar: to the fore once more.

US TOP TEN

1 Bobby Rahal
Champion or not, Bobby Rahal emerged as the most complete Indycar driver of 1985, particularly in the second half of the season. A race leader and winner on both ovals and road courses, he was a front-runner in all but one race last year and established himself in September and October, on every weekend, as *the* man to beat.

Last year was Rahal's fourth in Indycars. He and team owner Jim Trueman got together in 1981 in order to move from CanAm to Indycar racing, and the partnership thrived. Trueman owns a thriving motel chain as well as the Mid-Ohio Sports Car Course. He races IMSA GTP cars and is a CART Board member – one of the strongest and most influential directors of the organisation in fact.

The team is aggressive and well-organised, having been managed since the start by Steve Horne and enjoying the services of March's chief Indycar engineer Adrian Newey in 1984-85. In company with them, Rahal has put his stylishly precise driving to the very best use. As he enters his fifth year of Indycar racing, Rahal, 33, is a supremely fast, thinking driver at the top of his profession.

2 Al Unser Snr
Approaching his 21st season of Indycar racing, 46-year old Al Unser Snr was consigned to the role of a third-string, back-up driver. Replaced for 1985 by Danny Sullivan, the 1970 and '83 Indycar Champion – a remarkably honest, uncomplicated man – was scheduled to drive a third Penske Racing entry in the three 500-mile races and serve as a replacement driver in early-season road races for Rick Mears. It turned out, however, that Mears' injured feet prevented the Penske team leader from running *any* road races last year.

As a result Unser was kept busy in most races, missing only Milwaukee, and by the middle of the season his clean, workmanlike technique had brought him enough points to rate as a Championship contender. He was extremely competitive in every oval race he started and used his patient, car-conserving style to collect a series of good finishes in road races.

As the season wore on, Unser really got the bit between his teeth and was the dominant man in three oval track races. By soundly defeating his son Al Jnr, Mario Andretti, Danny Sullivan and Bobby Rahal in a magnificent race-winning performance at Phoenix in October he assured himself of finishing at least second in the '85 Championship . . .

3 Al Unser Jnr
23-year old Al Unser Jnr was challenging his father for the Indycar title when *Autocourse* closed for press. In his third season of Indycar racing, the second-generation driver utilised a style

similar to his father's – canny, somewhat conservative, usually quicker in the race than in qualifying. His father aside, Unser Jnr was the most consistent finisher among the first three places and by the middle of the season he had solidly established himself near the top of the points tables.

Even a broken ankle in August failed to get in Junior's way, an accident in the rain on slicks while leading caused the injury, but Unser was back in action at the next race, sporting a brace on his right ankle. Despite this handicap, he fought for the lead in that race and finished an excellent second!

Faster on road circuits than his dad, Junior could not quite match his father's combination of finesse and speed on ovals. Nevertheless his immense, family-bred talent is just now coming into full bloom.

4 Mario Andretti
It hardly seems correct to rate Mario Andretti so far down the list. He started the season in great form, winning three of the first four races and looking for a while like an easy repeat Champion. Then Andretti suddenly lost momentum amid a sea of ill-fortune.

He crashed with Bobby Rahal while running second at the Meadowlands, had his car catch fire while leading at Cleveland and then crashed heavily near the end of the Michigan 500, breaking a collarbone and cracking a hip socket. After missing one race (the first he's missed through injury in his career!), Andretti returned, taped and sore yet able to finish a dogged seventh in the Pocono 500.

Thereafter, however, he ran out of luck completely and failed to finish four races in a row despite running among the top five places. After an excellent 1984 season, '85 was an anti-climax but Andretti's familiar driving force remained fiercely undiminished.

5 Danny Sullivan
Most of Danny Sullivan's 1985 season comprised a similar anti-climax. Joining Penske Racing for his second season of Indycar racing, he battled Andretti in the Long Beach season-opener and then defeated the man, scoring a sensational win in the Indy 500. Sullivan and his agents made full use of the victory to establish him as a 'media personality'. In the meantime, however, his racing efforts floundered.

Sullivan was on the front row nine times and led six races but a series of un-Penske-like mechanical problems kept him from scoring many results. Not as competitive in most oval races as he was at Indianapolis, Sullivan is not yet as mature an Indycar driver as some of his peers. If he can remain unaffected by his busy schedule of self-promotion, Sullivan should put it all together in 1986.

6 Rick Mears
After smashing both feet in an accident at Sanair, Quebec, in September 1984, Rick Mears was able to run only on oval tracks last year. Insufficiently strong to withstand the rigours of road racing, Mears' feet were useable on ovals where much less pedalwork is required. From the five races he started Mears collected a win, a second and a third as well as four, front row starts. As quick and competitive as ever on ovals, he plans to run the full schedule in '86.

7 Geoff Brabham
Recognition finally and deservedly came to Geoff Brabham last year. The California-domiciled Australian didn't win a race but he often was among the leaders and was a contender on both ovals and road circuits. At Cleveland and Laguna Seca he featured in the fight for the lead although mechanical failures kept him from finishing all but four races.

8 Michael Andretti
Despite poor reliability and inconsistent performance from his car, 22-year old Michael Andretti showed race-winning potential last year. He led two super-speedway races at Pocono and Michigan and finished a good second in tricky weather conditions at Road America. Sharp and worldly-wise in the manner of his father, the eldest of Mario's two sons has a big future ahead of him.

9 Emerson Fittipaldi
In his first full season of Indycar racing, the unretired Brazilian had a good year. Following a strong start, Fittipaldi's competitiveness tended to trail off and after challenging for the Championship in mid-season, he and Patrick Racing floundered in the second half of the year. Surprisingly, Fittipaldi was more competitive in most oval races than road races. A persistent finisher, he scored a rather lucky yet canny victory in the Michigan 500.

10 Kevin Cogan
A serious heel injury and number two seat gave Kevin Cogan a difficult first half to the '85 season. However, he often showed well in the second half of the year and from time to time was very competitive on both ovals and road courses. Recuper-ation from his August '84 accident at Pocono may have helped breed a combination of patience and tough-mindedness which Cogan previously lacked.

Gérard Vandystadt

Traumatic Times

by Quentin Spurring

The Martini-Lancia LC2s led every race they
contested and achieved 10 finishes from 14 starts.

Robert Newsome

Hans-Joachim Stuck and Derek Bell claimed the
Drivers' title while Rothmans Porsche won the first
FIA World Endurance Championship of Teams.

TRAUMATIC TIMES

The bald statistics are: Rothmans-Porsche, the factory establishment, won the first FIA World Endurance Championship of Teams; and two of its drivers, Hans-Joachim Stuck and Derek Bell, claimed a shared Drivers' title, with their team-mates, Jacky Ickx and Jochen Mass, runners-up. The team monopolised the front row on four occasions, secured three one-two finishes, and won five of the first nine races.

The same old story, you might say.

Yet there is much more to the story than meets the eye, quite apart from the struggle the works Porsches had in order to achieve these results. FIA sports car racing was in fact more competitive than it has been for a decade, and it also had a traumatic year.

The season, sadly, will be remembered as one that claimed the lives of two of Germany's finest motor racing stars. Manfred Winkelhock and Stefan Bellof both died in privately entered Porsches – the latter, the reigning World Champion in this class of racing, universally acknowledged as its fastest driver.

These tragedies, occurring in successive races mid-season, were the most distressing of a series of setbacks suffered by Group C racing in 1985. The Championship was also assaulted by the elements: bitter cold, excessive heat (causing serious fires), gale-force winds, fog, torrential rain, flooding and even an earthquake; all were experienced by the sports car racing teams in a year most will be happy to put behind them.

The Championship consisted of 10 races, with the old Makes title – which Porsche dominated numerically once again – replaced by one for Teams. Mugello, Silverstone, Le Mans, Hockenheim, Mosport Park, Spa Francorchamps and Fuji were the races counting towards both championships; Monza, Brands Hatch and a new race at Shah Alam, Malaysia (which took place after this was written), gained points towards the Drivers'

series only. The WEC series temporarily lost its Australian fixture when the Sandown Park promoters could not find the finance, and it remained crucially without a race in the USA.

Infuriated by a clash between Le Mans and the Canadian Grand Prix, which deprived several teams of their best drivers, the team managers subsequently flexed their muscles by threatening to boycott two races when they coincided with rescheduled Formula 1 events. Gaining strong support, they succeeded in having Brands Hatch moved (although the race then clashed with a German national event!), but not Fuji.

As well as Rothmans Porsche, races were won by Lancia, Nissan-March and the private Kremer and Joest Porsche teams, while the score in the tyre war was six wins for Dunlop, and one each for Michelin, Bridgestone and Goodyear.

There were, essentially, eight cars competing regularly in the series that were genuinely capable of winning races, and on the track there was very little to choose between them. These were the two Rothmans Porsche 962Cs; the two factory Martini Lancia LC2s; the Brun Motorsport Porsche 962C and the similar car of the Kremer team; New Man Joest Racing's Porsche 956B (a 1984 chassis); and Richard Lloyd Racing's Canon Porsche 956 GTI (a specially built, honeycomb chassis version of the 1984 model). Each led on many occasions during the season, and only three of them failed to carry off a victory.

Peter Falk's Rothmans Porsche team, after two seasons with the same type 956 chassis, finally built new cars. Nevertheless, it retained its productive links with its cigarette sponsor (which went to great lengths to promote the championship), Dunlop tyres and Shell fuel and oil. The 962C had to comply with a new rule, stipulating that pedals should be located behind the line of the front wheel centres. The factory version differed from the car supplied to the customer teams, in that the works cars were fitted with 17 in.

diameter front wheels and 19 in. rears, whereas the private entries were on 16 in. wheels all round.

As well as being taller, the special rear tyres produced by Dunlop were also narrower, enabling the works team, with a major rework of the suspension geometry, to build in air tunnels that were both wider and deeper. The idea was to create substantially more downforce so as to offset the turn-in difficulties inherent in the longer-wheelbase 962C design. At first, the Rothmans cars were visibly twitchy in the medium and fast corners, but the team was able to dial out this problem as the season wore on.

The normal race engine – the famous 2.6-litre flat-six, with twin KKK turbochargers – was retained, producing about 630 bhp on race boost pressures. The team was unable to bring its 3-litre version into play because of the reduced Group C1 fuel allowance that also came into force for the 1985 season. The old allowance was reduced by 15 per cent to only 510 litres for the 1000-kilometre races that predominated, sending Porsche's neighbour in Stuttgart, Bosch, into renewed work on the Motronic electronic engine management systems.

Race-managed by Norbert Singer, Walter Naeher and Klaus Bischoff, the works 962Cs started the season with both handling and fuel consumption problems, but the writing was surely on the wall when the team achieved an unexpected victory at the Mugello series opener. Although not always having the fastest nor the most fuel-efficient cars, the ever-impressive works team had brought its 1985 tally to five victories when the WEC entourage made its way to Malaysia for the end-of-season party at Shah Alam.

The series started disastrously for Bell and Stuck (codenamed BEST in the language of the team's race management computer) when Peter Falk made a very rare mistake on a bitterly cold, windy day at Mugello. They had been running in

Paul-Henri Cahier

Under the bonnet. The Martini-Lancias were the
most fuel-efficient of the front-running cars during
the first half of the season.

third place, suffering for much of the race with serious fuel consumption problems, until Stuck parked it near the end, the tank virtually dry. The driver was waiting for the winner to take the flag so that he could lurch across the line. However, the team had forgotten about a rule (designed to remove the hazard of seriously stricken cars) stating that each car's final lap must be completed within 400 per cent of the pole position time. This Stuck failed to do, and the BEST entry was excluded.

The sister car of Mass and Ickx (the 1982-83 Champion), meantime, came through to win, having been raced over most of the distance under a very tight fuel economy rein. The MIX crew relied almost entirely on the fragility of some of the fastest cars and on rivals slowing during the final stages to conserve fuel, and it paid off.

Things went from bad to worse for BEST at Monza, where Stuck was lucky to escape a practice fire (caused by a suspected fuel leak) which burned out his 962C before help arrived from the fire marshals. The drivers had to race an untried hybrid, a spare type 956 chassis onto which had been grafted the rear end of the 962C. This car was not a force in qualifying, but it served BEST well in the race, finishing second, challenging hard. The regular, higher-drag MIX 962C was less fuel-efficient and was fortunate to finish fourth, the drivers again hogtied by the need for economy.

With the works team apparently in unaccustomed disarray, it came as a surprise when MIX and BEST pulled off a one-two at Silverstone. Again, the MIX car was held on a tight rein until three-quarters distance, and picked up the win when faster cars were delayed or retired. BEST was convinced it would have won had it not been for a loosened windscreen, which cost a minute in the pits.

Although they were best of the field under high-boost qualifying conditions, both cars were outpaced by the Joest and Canon privateers in the Le Mans fuel economy run, while MIX suffered a succession of gearbox problems and could finish only 10th. But BEST, briefly delayed by a seized wheel-bearing, survived to finish a strong third.

With three solid, points-scoring finishes in the bag, Bell and Stuck now made their mid-series bid for the title, winning handsomely at both Hockenheim and Mosport. In the well-supported German event, it seemed that Bosch had at least managed to achieve a substantial improvement in the economy-versus-power game, and the Rothmans cars were on a par with their rivals. Mass – defeating Stuck for once – was on pole but BEST led the final third of the race and ran out an easy winner when other cars fell by the wayside. The win was remarkable in that it showed the determination of the works team, which had suffered a cruel blow during the first refuelling halt by MIX.

In the extremely hot conditions, the pressure had built up in the near-empty fuel tank, and unfortunately the refuelling mechanic opened his valve a moment before his colleague with the overflow bottle had released the venting valve on the far side of the car. The result was a blowback of fuel up the refuelling hose, which caused the (full) tank on top of the fuel-rig to overflow. Something set it alight, and there was instantly a terrifying fireball.

Before the blaze was extinguished, team manager Norbert Singer, engineer Helmut Schmidt and four mechanics had been burned, Singer seriously. He spent many weeks in hospital but was well enough to attend the Fuji 1000 at season's end.

Amazingly, the MIX Porsche itself was hardly damaged, but later went out with a turbo failure, one of the team's two retirements for mechanical reasons, from 20 starts.

Bell and Stuck now led the Championship as none of their closest rivals finished at Hocken-

heim. Mass and Ickx none the less gave them a fight at Mosport, the Canadian race which was so poorly supported, especially relative to Hockenheim. There were no team orders at Rothmans Porsche, and a spectacular battle endured for the entire distance. It was resolved when Mass made a rare error and missed his line by a few inches in the final corner, getting onto the marbles and socking the trackside wall a glancing blow that broke a rear wheel and burst the tyre. A works one-two was still the result, however.

Returning to Europe for the classic race at Spa, Rothmans Porsche knew that it had virtually now clinched the Teams' title, and that at last the cars were a match in terms of performance for all their rivals. Ickx was dicing for the lead of his 'home' race when poor Stefan Bellof drove into him, the German losing his life in the accident that inevitably followed. The MIX 962C was also very badly damaged, but thankfully Ickx was unhurt, although deeply distressed. The BEST car finished second to the Lancia which was leading when the race was stopped out of respect.

With the German privateers absent from Brands Hatch, the team had only to beat the Lancias, and BEST – both drivers particularly on-form this day – defeated MIX by a dozen seconds after another race-long fight.

Pressed by Nissan far harder than expected, Rothmans Porsche responded with another Stuck-Mass front row at Fuji but, like all the other European teams, declined to take part in the shortened race because of the dangerous flooding on the track. MIX still had a slim mathematical chance of beating BEST to the Championship, but this decision put the title beyond their reach with only one round remaining.

The works team fielded a third car on two occasions. At Le Mans, Al Holbert, Vern Schuppan and John Watson shared a standard 962C and ran second for many hours, but fell foul of an engine failure. At Brands Hatch, Holbert/

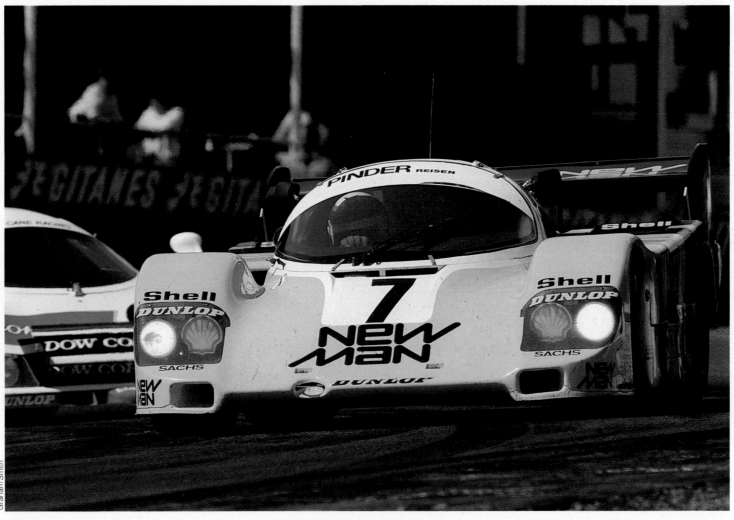

Graham Smith

A second straight win at Le Mans for the New Man
Joest Racing Porsche.

Schuppan appeared with a car fitted with the experimental PDK transmission, a twin-clutch device with electronic controls. This was designed to allow the drivers to make shifts without lifting from the throttle, thus eliminating the problem of turbo lag. Apart from a brief switch circuit fault, the PDK unit (modified since its disastrous debut at Imola the year before) worked well, and the car finished fifth.

This was the works team's fourth and last full season of Group C racing, and certainly its most difficult. It overcame unaccustomed adversity to secure both the prime championships, and this may legitimately be perceived as a measure of the experience and skill of its drivers and engineers, under a diligent and committed director.

Although they trailed their team-mates at first, Stuck and Bell became worthy champions, claiming the first FIA track racing title to be shared. Stuck's pace was evident from the start as he replaced Stefan Bellof, and the formerly under-rated German drove three of the team's four poles, only once failing to qualify among the three fastest cars. Stuck also displayed firm self-discipline in the races themselves, and soon created a formidable partnership with the vastly experienced Bell, who proved that he can still turn it on when the situations demand.

Cesare Fiorio's Martini Lancia team, which had to achieve much during the 1985 series if it was to remain in Group C, conducted a Europe-only programme with modified versions of its existing cars. Under its new chief engineer, Claudio Lombardi, the Abate (near Turin) based team produced a lot of winter development, basing the modifications on the original monocoque so as not to be compelled to extend the wheelbase.

Wider bodywork on redesigned suspension front and rear increased both underbody and top surface downforce considerably, and the car was now on 16 in. diameter wheels all round. Many of the changes were made to make the cars compatible with the radial tyres from Lancia's new supplier, Michelin, whose withdrawal from Formula 1 meant that Group C was its only international track racing programme.

The 3-litre V8 engine, designed and built by Ferrari but maintained in Abate, featured greatly improved electronic gadgetry from Weber-Marelli, and could race with about 640 bhp forced by its two turbochargers. Indeed, the Lancias were the most fuel-efficient of the front-running cars during the first half of the season.

Riccardo Patrese was normally paired with Alessandro Nannini, while Bob Wollek partnered Mauro Baldi. The team employed an Italian-born Australian, Lucio Cesario, as test driver, and gave him a race at Le Mans, where Henri Pescarolo was also drafted in to replace Patrese who was racing in Canada. Andrea de Cesaris, recently fired from Formula 1, joined the team in its final race, at Brands Hatch.

This time, Lancias presented a very solid-looking package, and it seemed that several wins had to come when Patrese began the series with three stunning, record-breaking poles. At Hockenheim, Patrese proved his pace once more in the unofficial testing, but it was Fiorio who left the pole to Porsche, spending both qualifying sessions earnestly doing fuel consumption tests. However, Patrese was again impressively fastest at Spa and Brands Hatch. The type 308C engine clearly takes much more boost pressure than the Porsche unit, for Patrese's achievement was five poles from his six races.

Unfortunately for Lancia, though, sports car racing is not all about brute horsepower. With one or other of its cars, Lancia Martini led every race it contested, sometimes making all opposition seem pedestrian. But reliability, although much improved relative to 1984, remained the Italian team's weak point. This time, retirements were rare (the team achieved 10 finishes from its 14 starts) but it was normal for the cars to be delayed during the races.

The Patrese/Nannini car, usually Lancia's 'hare' in the early-race battles of nerves, was halted at Mugello by an engine failure but looked the best bet for winning Monza when the race was stopped prematurely. At Silverstone, where it was again heavily involved in the front-running action, it was hampered by a wheel-bearing failure and again finished third. At Le Mans, where Wollek was drafted in with Nannini, a stone damaged a turbo and cost half an hour, sixth place the result. Nannini, striving to catch the leader in the dying minutes, ran it out of fuel at Hockenheim. An engine electronics failure and a collision with its sister car (Patrese versus de Cesaris in the silliest incident of the year) were the respective delays at Spa and Brands Hatch, finishing fourth on both occasions.

For Wollek/Baldi, the story was similar, but the season was highlighted by a very fine win under the sad circumstances at Spa. This was a tense race Lancia would almost certainly have won, even if it had not been stopped 23 laps ahead of schedule, so it was a fair exchange for Monza, where the team felt it had been robbed of a sure victory.

Otherwise, however, no race was incident-free: Mugello, a handling imbalance, fourth; Monza, Baldi forced off the road in a clash with Marc Surer's Kremer Porsche, retirement; Silverstone, an overheated gearbox just as the car was about to take the lead, 12th; Le Mans (where Pescarolo joined Baldi), excessive fuel consumption relative to the ultra-low drag Porsches, seventh; Hockenheim, again conserving fuel, fourth; and Brands Hatch, short brake life and overheating tyres, third.

The understandable frustration of the drivers, afflicted by such a wide variety of mechanical problems, was aggravated by Lancia losing its initial fuel economy advantage by mid-season, but alleviated by noticeably improved pitwork by

The Jaguar XJR-6 – an impressive package which
made everyone sit up when Martin Brundle led at
Mosport.

Graham Smith

Fiorio's team. It was a shame that the Spa victory
could not be acclaimed as decisive, and just as
disappointing that the team was unable to prove
itself at Brands Hatch three weeks later, when the
attractive LC2 cars were outpaced by the works
Porsches.

The best of the private Porsche teams were
those that scored no wins, namely Brun Motorsport and Richard Lloyd Racing. Swiss Walter
Brun's new type 962C, crewed by Stefan Bellof
and Thierry Boutsen, was arguably the best
driven Group C car of all, and these talented
young men also led more laps and more miles than
any other crew until the dreadful tragedy at Spa.

Managed by Peter Reinisch, and sponsored in
the first four events by the Torno construction
company, the Dunlop-shod Brun Porsche was a
front runner from the start, handling better than
predicted on its 'customer-standard' rear end. In
the Italian races, it fell foul of high fuel consumption after reckless opening shifts, and at Silverstone it was curiously delayed when it twice lost a
front wheel. With its regular drivers busy in
Canada, it was raced in other hands at Le Mans,
and destroyed in a high-speed accident on the
straight caused, it was believed, by a seized
transmission; Joel Gouhier was lucky to escape
unhurt.

Bellof and Boutsen, still more than capable of
leading, switched to the team's older type 956B for
Hockenheim and Spa, running in the colours of
Schiesser underwear. The car looked as strong as
ever in Germany but was reportedly sabotaged,
someone putting water in the reserve fuel tank,
and Bellof ran out of fuel. The Kremer brothers'
programme was ended by the appalling accident
at Spa, when Bellof's error of judgement at *Eau
Rouge* at half-distance cost him his life as the car
careered off Jacky Ickx's and into the barrier.

The British-owned Canon team did not enter
the series until Monza, but its very rigid,
honeycomb-chassis 956 immediately emerged as

the fastest Porsche, taking the fight to the works
Lancias in Italy, and beyond them into a sure lead
at Silverstone. On both occasions, Jonathan
Palmer's efforts with this visibly 'chuckable' car
were thwarted by lost road wheels, a very
contentious failure that angered several customers.

Jan Lammers inexplicably then left the team, so
as to take up the offer of a second-rate Indycar
drive in the USA. He was replaced at Le Mans by
James Weaver who did a good job, sharing a
memorable performance as the British pair
finished second, delayed by a Motronics fault but
beating all the factory cars nevertheless.

Team manager Keith Greene, however, did not
feel that Weaver was the man he needed for the
shorter races, which were becoming increasingly
competitive. He recruited David Hobbs, the very
experienced veteran, but at Hockenheim progress
was oddly hampered by unsuitable Goodyear
tyres, and the team's third-fifth placing of the year
resulted.

In the right conditions, the Goodyears did a fine
job for the Canon team, but it appears that it was a
front tyre failure that caused the accident that
ended Palmer's season during practice at Spa. He
broke two bones in his right leg in the incident,
and damage to the car was extensive.

The team had a new chassis built, and presented
a virtually new car at Fuji, where recruits Kenny
Acheson and Johnny Dumfries had an abortive
trip.

The team run out of Köln by Erwin and Manfred
Kremer was another to use Goodyears, this time
on a new 962C sponsored by Barclay cigarettes
and driven by Marc Surer and Manfred Winkelhock – another fast pairing, which quickly
established itself as a candidate for the title.
Second place at Mugello was immediately followed
by a fortunate victory at Monza, where the race
was halted at four-fifths distance when a large
tree, felled by gale-force winds, blocked the track.

At that moment, the Kremer Porsche was two
laps out from a pit stop which would have cost it
the lead.

With a strong third place at Silverstone, the
Swiss-German crew remained on target but lost
out in the clash between the Canadian GP and Le
Mans, where their car was raced in Kenwood hi-fi
livery by Mike Thackwell, Jean-Pierre Jarier and
Franz Konrad, finishing ninth. But the Silverstone points were to be their last, anyway.

Racing well at Hockenheim, Winkelhock smel-
led fuel leaking into the cockpit and headed for the
pits, where the second big fire of this race erupted.
This time, no one was hurt, but the car was quite
badly damaged.

It was repaired for Mosport, but the trip to
Canada ended in tragedy. Delayed by Surer's
early collision with a back-marker, Winkelhock
was charging hard when, at one-third distance, he
lost control in a fourth-gear, downhill left-hander,
and hit a concrete retaining wall. Apparently no
bones were broken, but the driver died later from
head injuries, presumably caused by the sheer
force of the impact. No cause for this accident has
been identified.

In all three of these serious Porsche accidents –
those of Winkelhock, Bellof and Palmer – the cars
were folded inwards by collision with the barrier,
trapping the drivers by their legs. This phen-
omenon not only placed a question mark over the
future participation of Grand Prix drivers in
Group C: it also shook the confidence of many in
the basic Porsche design. Most observers agreed
that any vehicle would have been similarly
affected, because all three accidents took place at
about 140 mph. Even so, Porsche engineers
instigated a study of the strength of the car,
including crash-testing.

The star performer among Porsche's privateers
in the results tables was New Man Joest Racing,
which carried off the prestige prize of the year:
victory at Le Mans. Not only that, but it was a

Keith Sutton

Five class wins in eight races by the Spice-Tiga
secured the Group C2 Driver World Championship
for Gordon Spice and Ray Bellm.

second straight win in the 24 Hours by Reinhold Joest's team from Abtsteinach, Germany. Its Porsche 956-117 became only the second car in the history of the great race to win in successive years, a feat previously achieved by JW Automotive's famous Ford GT40-1075, in 1968-69.

By any standard, it was a remarkable performance. Klaus Ludwig (his third Le Mans win) and Paolo Barilla, joined by 'Johnny Winter' for a single shift, drove immaculately, and their car never once let them down. It was the fastest car in the race, and also the most fuel-efficient.

In allocating fuel for the 1985 Le Mans, FISA got the sums wrong, allowing the C1 teams only 4.3-times the amount permitted in the 1000-kilometre events. While every other team struggled to come through the marathon under these conditions, the yellow 956B left them far behind and completed over 5000 kilometres. And it had more than 140 litres to spare at the finish!

The Joest team and its efficient manager, Domingos Piedade, held on to their secrets, but the performance was certainly aided by a special, slippery underbody and possibly also by a purpose-written electronic chip in the car's Motronics box. But essentially it resulted from highly disciplined and skilful race management and driving.

Most of Joest's New Man fashion budget was spent at Le Mans and, although the Dunlop-equipped team attended five other races, it concentrated otherwise on winning the German national title for Jochen Mass. Good World series finishes were, however, achieved with third placings at Hockenheim and Spa.

The Joest, Kremer and Brun teams all ran second-string Porsches in the World Championship, but only the Brun entry showed real class. The multi-sponsored 956, driven by Oscar Larrauri and Massimo Sigala and managed by the clever Tomas Vogelgesang, often came through the good positions later in the races, although a fine second place at Hockenheim was the only real

reward in a season punctuated by accidents.

The Obermaier team reappeared with its Goodyear-shod Porsche, but the Fitzpatrick team ran a much-reduced programme, its highlight being a fourth place at Le Mans for Yokohama, its tyre supplier.

Porsche 956 engines propelled Yves Courage's stylish new Cougar and Costos Los's Cosmik March 84G, the latter attempting a full season with F3000 star Christian Danner among the drivers. The Courage-constructed, Michelin-tyred Cougar, however, was very much a flat-bottom 'Le Mans special' while the Gordon Horn-managed, Yokohama-shod March was overweight.

It was a March, though, that scored the only WEC victory of the season that wasn't claimed by a Porsche or Lancia. Significantly for the future of the series, it was one of the Japanese entered 85G models powered by the latest, production-based Nissan VG-30 engine, and officially backed by the factory.

Hoshino Racing's entry shook the works Porsche team when it outqualified both its cars at record-breaking speed in the first session at Fuji. Stuck and Mass had to pull out all the stops to demote the car to the second row the next day. But race day (which followed a major earthquake in the region) dawned with torrential rain, flooding the circuit.

The presence of no fewer than 25 Group C1 entries rendered the conditions very dangerous and, represented and united by the new OSCAR organisation, all the European teams withdrew. This left the experienced and talented Hoshino to score a superb victory on his exceptional Bridgestone storm tyres, in a race shortened to two hours by the water and fog.

The Nissan VG-30 is a 3-litre, twin-turbo V6, developed by Nismo (the company's sporting arm) in association with the US company, Electramotive. Obviously powerful and apparently fuel-efficient, hopefully it will bring Nissan into

Europe next year for more World Championship events, including Le Mans.

In terms of manufacturer participation, however, the most significant event of 1985 was the arrival of the Jaguar XJR-6 cars, built and run on behalf of the factory by Tom Walkinshaw Racing of Kidlington, near Oxford. The cars, designed by Tony Southgate and managed by Roger Silman, entered the series at Mosport in August, and made everyone sit up when Martin Brundle did the early leading.

The XJR-6 package is impressive: an all-embracing monocoque central structure of composite materials, advanced suspension, the latest Dunlop tyres, and a 6-litre race version of the atmospheric V12 engine, driving through a new, March-developed transmission. The team's short 1985 programme showed that the cars were slightly overweight and a little underpowered by their two-valve engines, but solutions to both problems are in the pipeline. It is to be hoped that the TWR Jaguar project will stay on target and produce real results in 1986.

The Jaguar drivers were Brundle, Mike Thackwell, Hans Heyer and Jean-Louis Schlesser, and the team secured a third placing at Mosport and fifth at Spa, the engine on its last legs on both occasions. Brundle was later banned by his Formula 1 employer, Ken Tyrrell, from taking part in sports car racing, reacting to the spate of accidents. When Thackwell raced in a clashing F3000 fixture, Alan Jones and Jan Lammers were drafted in at Brands Hatch, but both cars were retired with engine problems.

With massive air tunnels, the Jaguars created clearly superior downforce and grip. For the TWR team, it was a pity that these beautiful cars never got to race in the rain.

The entry of Jaguar into Group C was on altogether a higher plane than that of Aston Martin three years earlier. However, Steve O'Rourke's Emka, designed by Len Terry, proved that it had been substantially improved, and led Le Mans memorably if briefly in the hands of Tiff Needell. Backed by Dow Corning silicones and prepared and managed by Michael Cane, the Emka had closer assistance from the Tickford engine company than did the Gatoil Cheetah G-604, Chuck Graemiger's composite chassis car which attempted a full programme under the management of Mike Brunt. Initially unreliable, the Cheetah eventually came good but its 550 bhp compared unfavourably to the 620 horsepower of the Jaguars, so the Aston Martin V8 cars were always fighting a losing battle.

The factory-supported, 2.1-litre Toyota turbo-powered Dome cars from Japan raced at Le Mans and Fuji but achieved little, also overweight and underpowered. The appealing little WM cars from France did Le Mans as always, with their twin-turbo, 2.8-litre Peugeot V6 engines. The American built Group 44 Racing Jaguar XJR-5 GTP cars also attended Le Mans (struggling more than most on fuel consumption), while the Swiss constructor, Peter Sauber debuted his new car there, powered by the very promising 5-litre Mercedes V8. Unluckily, however, the Sauber C-12 was lost in a qualifying accident when John Nielsen flew into the air at over 200 mph, emerging shocked but unhurt.

Otherwise, no significant chassis-engine combinations appeared in the World series in 1985 which, in terms of new cars, would have been another season of little progress had it not been for Jaguar. With the works Porsche team planning a reduced programme in 1986, the way is open for Jaguar and Lancia to take on the Porsche privateers, and thus to boost public enthusiasm for sports car racing towards the level of 15 years ago.

It is of vital importance that FISA, the circuits and the teams substantially improve promotion for the renamed Sportscar World Championship. The format of the 1986 series – which will include up to four 'supersprint' races – will lend itself to a measured publicity campaign, and particularly to television coverage. Provided real efforts are made to stimulate public and media interest, the opportunity is there for sports car racing to accept once again a larger share of the available sponsorship and other commercial resources.

It may be up to OSCAR (the association which currently represents the teams in administrative matters) to accept the promotional and political challenge, and to place itself at the centre of efforts to put sports car racing back on the map.

GROUP C2: THE COSWORTH LIVES

The normal-induction Ford-Cosworth DFL sports car racing engine, while no match for the turbos in the Group C1 class, had a new lease of life during 1985 in Group C2, the alternative FIA category. The C2 rules are essentially the same as those governing C1, except for the 700-kilogramme minimum weight (150 kilos lighter) and 330 litres fuel allowance (180 litres less).

Under these conditions, the 3.3-litre version of the DFL, with about 480 bhp available, is ideal equipment. In its first two seasons, the FIA Group C2 Cup points table had been topped by the turbocharged Alba cars but, as the Cosworth began to appear in good C2 chassis, the Italian team reacted by abruptly losing its previously much-envied reliability, leaving the field clear for the atmospheric V8-powered entries.

The class car in C2 was Spice Engineering's Tiga GC85, a Howden Ganley design built and prepared by Gordon Spice's emerging team at Silverstone. The Spice Tiga was ingeniously managed by Jeff Hazell and sponsored by several companies, notably Jaeger and Holts. Running on Avon tyres in a class dominated by this supplier, the car won four victories in the Teams series events: Mugello, Le Mans, Mosport and Spa. Hazell also threw in the Drivers' event at Monza for good measure.

With these five wins from eight races, the team secured an easy Drivers' World Championship (the first in the category) for Gordon Spice and Raymond Bellm, whose win at Le Mans was shared with Mark Galvin. So effective was the ground-effect Tiga that the Spice team was able on five occasions to achieve finishes in the top ten overall.

The Spice Tiga failed to finish only at Brands Hatch (a suspension failure) where the class fell to Ecurie Ecosse, the only team to offer any kind of a realistic challenge to the champions. Hugh McCaig's project (which is a genuine revival of the famous Le Mans team of the Fifties) was not as well financed, and the car did only six races.

Also powered by a 3.3 DFL and equipped with Avons, the neat Ecosse was engineered by Ray Mallock and managed by Richard Williams.

Sponsored by Bovis construction, it was driven by Mallock (who finished third in the Championship), Mike Wilds and David Leslie. It was beaten by the Spice Tiga into second place at Monza, but gained its revenge by reversing the result at both Silverstone and Hockenheim. It also led handsomely at Le Mans, but was sidelined by a sheared oil pump drive.

The 1983-84 series winning Alba team raced its latest, composite chassis AR-6 with its powerful, 1.8-litre, four-cylinder Carma turbo engine. But the Martino Finotto-financed team had a wretched series, a second at Mugello and a third at Hockenheim the only rewards for Finotto and the evergreen Carlo Facetti.

The Japanese AutoBeaurex team picked up its second straight C2 win at Fuji, in the absence of the European cars, with its quick, 3.5-litre BMW powered Lotec – Yokohama's only success of the 1985 World series.

Consistency paid off for the Ark Racing team, backed by Arthur Hough Pressings, and its unusual Ceekar, underpowered by a 2-litre Cosworth BDG. The team made it 1-2-3 for Britain in the Teams' table, a triumph for the low-budget project and regular drivers Max Payne and Chris Ashmore.

Also Cosworth DFL powered, Fritz Gebhardt's neat C2 car from Germany placed the 'works' team fourth in the table, with a couple of second places and a fourth. But unreliability spoiled the competitive drives by the talented Frank Jelinski and John Graham in the entry sponsored by Labatt's beer. The team's 1984 Gebhardt-Cosworth, now owned by Ian Harrower's ADA Engineering, scored a fine second at Le Mans with John Sheldon – badly burned in the Nimrod the year before – among its drivers.

The other regular runners, attempting a full C2 series, were Roy Baker's intriguing Tigas (propelled by the 1.7-litre Ford turbo four-cylinder from the RS200 rally car project) and Jens Winther's straight-six URD-BMW. The factory Mazda team's rotary engined C2 cars had three outings but needed more power to repeat their previous successes in the category.

215

As an international formula for touring cars, Group A has continued to make progress in many ways.

The European Touring Car Championship is more widely publicised now than ever before and has developed into a marketing exercise, with strong backing for contracted teams not only from oil, tyre, and cigarette companies but also from the car manufacturers themselves.

Only the marking system prevents the struggle for outright victory from being reflected fully in the end-of-season results. As in recent years, the Alfa Romeo teams dominated the 1.6 to 2.5 litre class on sheer numbers. Just occasionally, the GTV6 was outpaced, with Winni Vogt's BMW 323i taking two of the mid-season rounds and other marques (notably the Mercedes-Benz 190E) giving warning of future danger. However, Alfa Romeo once again assured itself of the Manufacturers' title which is based upon class performance alone. Neither VW or Toyota could hope to succeed because, in the sub-1.6 litre category, they were so closely matched. The same applied among the over-2.5 class, because the BMWs, the Rovers, and the Volvos gained no extra points for their outright victories.

The Drivers' Championship system is better, even if Lella Lombardi and Rinaldo Drovandi may not have shared that view. Despite their consistent performances, victory in the 'Alfa' class rarely earned them any of the extra points available to those who finish in the top six of the general classification, as happens in Formula 1.

The fact remains that manufacturers *can* get plenty of publicity from the Drivers' Championship – especially if their drivers are first past the chequered flag most often. There is nothing quite like being first 'on the road'.

The racing was marvellous for most of the time, frequently providing close finishes. It was a shame that a shadow persisted throughout the season, concerning Volvo and the eligibility of its 240 Turbo in 'evolution' form. The eligibility question was one of interpretation: once 500 examples of an 'evolution' model have been seen to be built, do they have to be seen to be sold too? The answer would appear to be obvious, wouldn't it? In fact, this particular area was so grey that, as the end of the season approached, the matter was far from resolved. If it should be decided that the 'evolution' Volvo never should have been homologated in the first place, then the blame cannot be placed solely at the manufacturer's door. On the other hand, much has changed since the first great era of Volvo participation in competitions; throughout 1985's summer months when official comment upon the corporation's attitude was being sought, the Gothenburg giant proved impenetrable.

By contrast, the Austin Rover Group's E.T.C. communications were admirable. After all, the TWR-prepared Rover Vitesse had not lived up to earlier promise when, in 1984, the big V8-powered saloon had failed to score a single E.T.C. victory. With Tom Walkinshaw committed to becoming champion for Jaguar, it had not been possible for him to have the cake and eat it. So 1984 had been Jaguar's year. 1985 saw the TWR Jaguars being

Tom Walkinshaw.

tested and then cocooned for transit to Australia, in readiness for the spectacular 1000 Km of Bathurst, which was switching to Group A. This enabled TWR's touring car specialists, by this time thoroughly versed in E.T.C., to concentrate on bringing Rover the long-distance race wins which the marque had been seeking for so long.

On the whole, the 1985 season proved to be a needle match between the Rovers and the Volvos and by mid-September, with 11 races gone, they had won five races each.

Zolder, in late September provided the Volvo with another win, however, after Tom Walkinshaw's Rover had been tapped into a first-corner spin when leading – to be written off by (according to Tom) no fewer than three BMWs. After that, the Eggenberger Volvo team stayed in Europe to concentrate on ETC, rather than take up the entry it had for Bathurst. Tom Walkinshaw, however, took some of his 1985 ETC Rover team members to Australia while the Vitesses were refurbished for the Spanish round.

At Bathurst, Group A took a more-than-ever international turn, and benefited from what is probably the world's best 'actuality' TV coverage. In a classic battle of attrition, John Goss and Armin Hahne took a fine victory, having lain second for most of the 1000 km to Walkinshaw/Percy in a similar TWR/Works Jaguar XJ-S, until the latter had to change a leaking oil cooler.

After Bathurst, the TWR team reverted to Rovers for the final stages of ETC '85.

Reigning champion Tom Walkinshaw and his co-driver, Win Percy, were the winners at Monza, Vallelunga, Donington, Silverstone and Nogaro, strongly backed in their Texaco-Bastos Vitesse by such very fast team men as Jeff Allam, Armin Hahrne, Jean-Louis Schlesser, Steve Soper and other well-established names. Outstanding handling characteristics were aided more than a little by Dunlop's latest tyre technology and, as often as not, these advantages compensated for the amazing power of the 'evolution' Volvo turbos whose victories came at Anderstorp, Brno, Zeltweg, Salzburg and the Neue Nürburgring.

The regular Volvo attack came from two Pirelli-shod cars, beautifully prepared and presented by Switzerland's Rudi Eggenberger (who had taken a brave decision to switch from BMW), and from Ulf Granberg's Magnum team car. The latter came into its own at Brno by taking pole position and winning the race. With steady support from former champions Pierre Dieudonné and Sigi Müller Jnr, the Eggenberger team leader Gianfranco Brancatelli and Thomas Lindström had built up a strong championship lead between them, aggregating four wins and good placings in all but the opening round at Monza.

Typical of the season was the Brancatelli versus Walkinshaw duel of the opening laps. Sometimes it would last for a whole race cheered on by the pit crews and co-drivers, Win Percy and Thomas Lindström; sometimes, though, the Rovers would have to be over-driven to stay with the Volvos and reliability would suffer. At these moments, Tom Walkinshaw's patience would be stretched to the limit, for havering in high places ensured that, as month followed month, postponements continued to keep the Volvo issue in the air. One place where it *did* seem certain the result would go the Scot's way was the Salzburgring. There, the Number One Rover had been second 'on the road' behind the lead Volvo, which had been allowed to start pending an appeal concerning the mountings of its front suspension – an issue quite separate from the wider one of possibly incorrect homologation.

Grand Prix racing without Ferrari and sports car racing without Porsche are hard to imagine; the situation is similar with BMW and touring car events. For years the Bavarian marque has been a leading force in this branch of the sport and, although the BMW 635CSi is at the limit of this particular development, it is still not far off the pace. It has noteworthy reliability, too, and the Italian-run CiBiEmme team provided the most reminders of this in 1985 with regular high placings, usually in the top six. The works/Schnitzer team's cars were even quicker but were not always entered. They were 'saved up' for Belgium where they took an impressive 1-2 in the single most prestigious touring car race in the northern hemisphere – the 24 Hours of Francorchamps. That victory alone made sure that BMW means to keep its hard-won reputation.

October witnessed a flurry of activity as Group A in Europe clashed with Group A in Australia, forcing weary pit crews and drivers to flit between continents. It was all a sign of the lively state of touring car racing, epitomised earlier by the tooth-and-nail fight between the Rovers and the Volvos in the 80th-anniversary TT at Silverstone. In over three hours of racing, less than a quarter of a minute separated the first three finishers! The winners? – undoubtedly, Eddie Hinckley and the TWR pit crew. In 1984, the TWR Jaguars had lost the TT in the pits; this time TWR Rovers came 1st and 2nd *thanks* to the pitwork.

The TT and other late-season events showed that 1986 will be producing more competition and even more exciting races. In a series which should have easily interpreted rules, it is to be hoped that 1985's lesson was the last of its kind.

Progress Under a Shadow

by Andrew Whyte

No.1 on the track.

 **AUSTIN ROVER**

BY APPOINTMENT
TO HM THE QUEEN
MANUFACTURERS OF ROVER CARS
AND AUSTIN CARS
AUSTIN ROVER GROUP LIMITED
COVENTRY

NOW WE

In December 1984, the FIA European Formula 2 Championship Trophy was presented for the last time. A day later, detailed technical regulations were announced for the first European Formula 3000 Championship which was to begin just 3½ months later. The sporting regulations were published in June 1985 when the inaugural series was half-way through.

Formula 3000 had a difficult and premature birth but it pulled through, thanks to sometimes over-the-top financial commitment and dedication from those involved. By the second half of the season, the quality of the racing was simply superb and the quality and quantity of the cars constantly increasing. The potential of the Formula as a public spectacle – motor *racing* – is tremendous; where it suffers, like most areas of the sport if one is honest, is from unprofessional promotion.

The best driver did not win the Championship, but the best driver in the best chassis/tyre combination did, and most significant and pleasing of all was that it represented a true privateer effort. In Formula 2, Christian Danner had developed into a fast, consistent and reliable driver without ever quite showing a winner's aggression. But after his breakthrough maiden win at Pau, that changed. It is often said that winning is an attitude of mind and, armed with confidence in the second half of the year, the 27-year old German looked – and was – a winner thereafter.

The March 85B chassis was a superb and elegant car, especially given the unrealistic design time. Bob Sparshott Automotive showed themselves to be a team of thoroughbred, instinctive racers and, using Danner's testing skills, they were the first team to reach a proper understanding of how to get the best out of their off-the-shelf car and over-the-counter Bridgestone tyres. They placed their faith in Danner, who had a sponsorship budget which would not have given him half a British Formula 3 season, and he rewarded them and his own self-belief with a total of four wins and the Championship title. For Danner, Sparshott, March and Bridgestone, as well as the Formula, it was the right result.

The interest that the idea of Formula 3000 generated was considerable but the delay in the regulations, and the paucity of relevant information about the Formula, stifled it in the crucial weeks before the opening race. The manufacturers had a near impossible race against time and the fact that there were no real cars running until three weeks before Silverstone gave it a very uncertain air.

In the midst of all this was a wrangle about the Formula's tyre regulation. Bridgestone had announced that they would sponsor and exclusively supply the works Ralt team in the Formula with their radial tyres. This was against the spirit of the regulations and, with the only alternative supplier being the internationally unknown quantity of Avon's cross-ply tyres, the potential entrants agitated like mad. A compromise was reached whereby any tyre supplier must provide a minimum of 30 per cent of the entries with equal

An Encouraging Start

by Ian Phillips

and similar equipment. The system worked remarkably well and ultimately the field was split about 50/50. The feared disparity between the theoretically ill-matched radial and cross-ply constructions never became apparent. Twelve people led the 11 races during the year, six of them on Bridgestones and six on Avons although the Japanese company's stronger depth in teams gave them the lion's share of the honours – nine victories to two.

On the chassis front, Ralt to a greater degree, and March to a slightly lesser one, relied on updated versions of their existing Formula 2 designs. AGS built a most attractive all-new car while Lola returned to the European fray with a design based on their successful Indycar chassis. Individual teams opted to convert Formula 1 chassis which had been successful with Cosworth power in F1, to suit the Formula. Going into the season nobody really had a clue which was the right way to go.

Ralt and the March Oynx team had both covered in excess of 3000 testing miles with a prototype chassis from November onwards, using, respectively, Bridgestone and Avon tyres. Ron Tauranac's finalised car, exclusively for his works team, used replica F2 aluminium honeycomb monocoque (and later in the year the actual F2 winning chassis) and front suspension. The DFV engine was mated to the bigger gearbox via a Williams oil tank/bell-housing. The rear suspension, pullrod operated, had the spring damper units mounted horizontally on the gearbox top. The unknown quantity was the flat-bottomed car's aerodynamics, which were fettled throughout the year.

March already had a completed flat-bottom wind tunnel programme on the shelf and Ralph Bellamy and Tim Holloway adapted this to suit a modified version of the F2 842 monocoque. The concept of the aluminium honeycomb bathtub and carbon-fibre top section was retained and refined, the most obvious changes being that it had slab sides and was two inches longer. The packaging of the DFV was typical of Bellamy's tidy design and the whole car was small, under the 540 kg weight limit, and very neat. The first 85B did not appear until 21 days before the first race and at the time only three had been ordered. The company's commitment to the Formula, however, was justified immediately and nine cars were at the first race and 15 at the last.

Lola had seven orders for their car, which was announced at the end of January, but only two appeared at the first race and four in total over the season. The car turned out to be big and heavy against its contemporaries and was not a success. Rather to everyone's surprise, the F1-based cars were similarly unsuccessful although the smallest of them, the Tyrrell 012, began to look promising before the team gave up the struggle against the development cost.

The AGS was the only totally new and very striking design. It was a completely carbon-fibre composite chassis with some interesting suspension systems. Initially, it was very fragile and aerodynamically inferior but, by the end of the

season, it was a potential race winner.

There were 17 cars at the opening race which, considering the time scale, was very encouraging, being due in the main to the March production miracle. For the second race 21 cars practised, including five F1 based cars, but it was not until the final round at Donington that the number of cars reached that level again (with only one F1 car this time). As always, money was very tight and unfortunately those teams which had made the wrong choice of chassis were in no position to change and they gradually faded away, the performance gap being too great for any ambitious driver to want to pursue that line of development.

When Mike Thackwell led home John Nielsen in a Ralt 1-2 at the first race it was too easy for the Formula's detractors to write it off as a reborn Formula 2. Rain obscured the real pattern of play although it helped to make it a good and spectacular event which, above all, was what was needed. Looking deeper into it, the signs were encouraging. For instance, Michel Ferté had never seen or driven a Formula 3000 car until three days beforehand yet he was on pole position and led the race in the Marlboro Oreca March on Avon tyres.

As expected, Thackwell soon became the dominant driver in the series, which he was doing with a slight reluctance, but the heavy Ralt was by no means the force it had been the previous year. The development programme with Bridgestone was naturally affected by the Japanese company's late, compulsory, commitment to 30 per cent of the field and their 'unfair advantage' was nullified. At Thruxton, three Avon-tyred Marches, driven by Ferté, Tomas Kaiser and ultimate winner, Emanuele Pirro in the Marlboro Onyx car, led the race. Pole-man Thackwell stopped for a new nose on the third lap but showed his brilliance by carving his way back to be in a position to challenge for the lead on the last lap.

So far so good. The third round was to be the first of four rounds run as a supporting event to a European Grand Prix, this time at Estoril. The idea of running at GP events was to present the Formula to a ready-made crowd and media gathering. This first attempt was an unmitigated disaster which set back the growth of the Formula harshly. With teams still trying to understand their cars, they were given almost no practice time on a circuit which was unfamiliar to almost everyone. Everything was horribly compromised and a wholly unprepared act put on a second-rate show which was the fault of incompetent organisation. As an illustration of how miserable it all was, the F3000 passes did not allow anyone access to the one and only toilet block in the paddock!

Thackwell was again on pole and led by four seconds on the first lap only to have the controversial Monk rev limiter fail completely on lap two. There had been problems with this untried and untested device in the first two races but only in practice. Now it had significantly affected the outcome of a race and naturally everyone became very nervous of it. After Thackwell's unfortunate demise, team-mate John Nielsen was able to score a very comfortable win.

After Thackwell had taken his third successive pole at the Nürburgring a week later, the race was snowed off. The New Zealander was on pole again at Vallelunga, but in the race, the Ralts were no match for the Marches of Pirro and Ferté (the latter being denied second place by a Monk box failure). The Avon-shod Marches confirmed their early season potential with a dominant display, but Danner also achieved his best result here (third) with his first race on Bridgestones. He made the switch because he could not get used to driving on cross-ply tyres and not because, at that stage, he or anyone else could see a performance advantage. His was the most professionally run of the Marches on Bridgestones and, after one decent test session at Donington, he was able to use softer rubber than the Ralts.

Pirro was on pole at Pau and dominated the race while the likes of Thackwell, the Ferté brothers, Alain and Michel, and Nielsen dropped out very early on. A mechanical problem in qualifying put Danner way down the grid but he was easily the quickest man on the track. Pirro was slowed by an overheating engine towards the end and Danner took his first win comfortably. It had been five years since his single-seater debut in Formula 2 and this was his first win. He liked the taste of victory champagne and from now on was win-hungry on the track as well as off it.

In terms of organisation, the second F1 support event was a success. The limited practice time was still disliked, but as drivers and crews came to terms with their machinery the restrictions did not affect the racing. Michel and Alain Ferté in their Avon Marches shared the front row, on a track that had begun to crumble seriously. The race was postponed on Saturday and was eventually held on a very questionable surface to replace Sunday's GP. Eleven cars spun off in the conditions and it was the cool Thackwell who won by an impressive 50 seconds from Alain Ferté and Danner, who was the only man not to have any incident in the race. The race merely confirmed Thackwell's skill and the view that it should never have taken place.

At Dijon a month later it was a Bridgestone/ March benefit. The Ralts filled the front row (Nielsen first) but they were forced to run very hard tyres in the race. They were pushed down to fourth and fifth at one stage as Danner stormed away to win but, with others hitting problems, Thackwell came in second to share the points lead with Danner.

Thackwell was again on pole at Enna and he won the race by dint of some very intelligent driving. Ralt were again forced to run a very hard tyre and, as Lamberto Leoni (Avon/March) and Danner fought for the lead, Thackwell got pushed to the back of a six-car bunch. But he hung in there and when Danner's fuel bag collapsed causing a severe misfire, Thackwell beat Pirro in a sprint to the line, with Danner an unrepresentative and distant third.

At the Österreichring, Danner took his first pole just ahead of Pirro with Thackwell fourth. All three main Championship contenders had a bad result in a great race which saw undoubted Rookie

Christian Danner and the Sparshott March: a true privateer effort which won the inaugural Formula 3000 Championship.

of the Year Ivan Capelli (March/Bridgestone) pip Nielsen to the flag by half a second. Thackwell was handicapped when a wheel started to fall off on the first lap while he was lying second to Danner. Danner himself spun off when second behind Streiff, while Pirro had deranged his suspension with a spin on the wet warming-up lap and could only struggle round to fourth place.

Ron Tauranac took a leaf out the Williams F1 book and decided to run his cars very low to the ground at Zandvoort the following week. Nielsen had done the only test on this set-up and was on the front row next to pole-man Danner, the team now in a position to match Danner on race rubber choice. Thackwell was only fifth on the grid and entirely unconvinced by the new arrangement. Rain before the start of the race provided the let-out to his confusion and he went for a conventional full wet set-up.

In the very wet early conditions that prevailed, Pirro blew the initial advantage offered by his Avons and this had a knock-on effect through a race which became really dry too long after his early stop for slicks. Fifth place, however, still kept him in the Championship picture. After a slick pit stop, Thackwell had a healthy lead which, had he been able to retain it, would have virtually assured him of the title. But Danner's standard dry settings (with no rear anti-roll bar) gave him all the wet traction he needed. After his late change of tyre he was virtually in qualifying trim and he dramatically kept his title hopes alive with a storming late run to overtake Thackwell two laps from the end.

And so to the final round of the series with seven

points separating Thackwell, Danner and Pirro in the title chase. The Ralt team worked hard and refined their low-ride height settings to a point where they could run softer race tyres than the Marches. Thackwell was confidently on pole by half a second with Danner fourth and Pirro a hundredth of a second behind in fifth place. The Onyx team had gambled on what had to be a win-or-nothing race by combining the respective development lines of Ralt and the BS team. This Avon runner was suddenly back in contention, right on cue.

Sadly, the title battle fizzled out when Thackwell and Pirro touched in a classic first-corner pincer movement which eliminated them both virtually on the spot. All Danner had to do was to finish third or higher but initially he found himself stuck in the now traditional seven- or eight-car leading F3000 train. He kept a cool head while others lost theirs in the excitement, and the German took his fourth win and the title in style.

The BS team gave Danner a mechanical edge in the series when it counted most and he deserved his title for his part in the development of it and then for making best use of it. Now that he has a winning mentality to go with his speed and consistency, he is a worthy champion.

It was never going to be easy for Mike Thackwell to follow his F2 Championship season but he was *the* consistently quick man throughout the season. While the Ralt chassis was still extremely effective, its development potential after three seasons was limited and on occasions, when it was not entirely compatible with the sponsor's product, Thackwell's flair more than

made up for it. Certainly he is no less talented for being pipped at the post this year.

Emanuele Pirro's season peaked a little early when, after two wins, he came within minutes of being a Brabham F1 driver. A bad race for the team and Avon at Dijon knocked the stuffing out of their Championship challenge for a while and they lost their technical direction just as others found theirs. They got it back for the last race and the advantage previously credited to the opposition's Bridgestone rubber evaporated. Pirro is quick and young and perhaps would have been better partnered by a driver able to stimulate him and contribute to the development programme.

John Nielsen is one of the game's true professionals who does a great job uncomplainingly in any circumstances. Being in Thackwell's shadow is no easy task but he emerged from the season with great credit.

Of the rest of the 33 drivers who took part in the series, Ivan Capelli was the most impressive. Although the reigning European F3 champion won only once, he looked a potential winner two or three times. His Genoa Racing team could not afford their own truck, let alone any testing, but at 22-years old he shows great potential. Philippe Streiff tried as hard as ever but the AGS let him down too often. Michel Ferté looked very good early on but then made too many mistakes; also, he was overshadowed by his elder brother Alain, who had a variety of drives in the year and each time showed how under-rated he is. Gabriele Tarquini was the other newcomer to show good potential and he should be able to capitalise on this year's experience (his first in racing!) in 1986.

John Nielsen emerged from the season with great credit in the ageing but effective Ralt chassis.

Formula 3000 is essentially for flat-bottomed F2-size cars producing an additional 125 bhp. The regulations call for a 3-litre racing engine restricted to 9000 rpm. For everyone this meant the now F1-redundant Cosworth DFV fitted with an electronic rev limiter/cut-out device devised by Glen Monk.

The engine was the heart and success of the Formula. As well as being readily available, it had the great advantage of being some 60 per cent cheaper to run than a BMW F2 engine . . . and was 100 per cent more reliable. The Monk box, after early teething troubles, worked well and the 1986 Mk 2 version should be trouble-free.

The tyre regulation was effective but the strongest lobby for 1986 will push for a single supplier to the series, to make it even more competitive and, for some, probably cheaper too.

The biggest gripe of the year centred on the Grand Prix supporting events but these became

steadily more acceptable as the year went on and, at venues where the Formula can be properly accommodated, should be continued perhaps three times in a season. The races brought with them guaranteed television, increased media coverage and better spectator attendance than anywhere but at a properly promoted meeting (Pau was the best of the year with a two-day crowd of 60,000 people which showed what a professional approach can do).

If FISA or FOCA do not grab this excellent opportunity to exploit such a cost-effective racing formula then the future of the sport looks bleak. In race conditions, F3000 cars are on the pace with the slowest F1 cars and a season of racing with 3000 miles of testing costs £250,000. Who needs to spend a million dollars for each second per lap gained just to say they are competing in Grand Prix racing? In every respect Formula 3000 makes sense.

For 1985 Formula 3 underwent an important change, with ground effect banned and flat-bottomed chassis *de riguer*. In terms of competition it had little effect; the restricted induction two-litre single-seaters still provided close enough racing and a useful index of driver talent.

However, one significant effect of the change was to encourage several Ford 2000 teams into the formula, with Pegasus Motorsport, Richard Dutton Racing, Madgwick Motorsport and Swallow Racing all making the step up for the new season. That injected some fresh blood into the formula and broke up the 'monopoly' the best teams – West Surrey Racing, David Price Racing, Eddie Jordan Racing, Intersport Racing and Murray Taylor Racing – had previously enjoyed. It also meant Ralt's stranglehold on the formula was challenged seriously for the first time since 1981 as far as the Marlboro British Championship was concerned. Three of the new teams had experience of Adrian Reynard's creations and were naturals to run his much vaunted Formula 3 offering, the controversial carbon-fibre 853.

With Reynards and Ralts fighting it out, grids swelled massively, the bad old days of 11-car grids from 1983 merely unpleasant memories. Formula 3, 1985 style, regularly saw grids of 25 to 40 cars.

On the driving front no single pilot stood out above his rivals as Johnny Dumfries had done in 1984, or Ayrton Senna and Martin Brundle had the year before that. Instead we had a situation akin to 1980, where any one of about half a dozen drivers could produce winning style. From 1984 came Russell Spence, Ross Cheever and Dave Scott, all yardsticks by which newcomers such as Andy Wallace, Mauricio Gugelmin, Gerrit van Kouwen and Tim Davies were judged.

Wallace, a 24-year old from Oxford, rocked everyone with a dominant performance in a Swallow Racing Reynard to win the series opener at Silverstone in March, and had no trouble thereafter convincing onlookers of his potential. Never a consistent winner in FF2000 he took to Formula 3 like the proverbial duck to water and his fluid style seemed better suited to the cars at first than that of team-mate Davies. The Welshman could match him for speed and racked up a highly impressive record in qualifying, but somehow victory eluded him and he then had to suffer the indignity of being dropped by Swallow just before the British GP support race. Tim Stakes had virtually set up his team around Davies, so the blow was all the harder to take.

As Davies went on to try Tom Alpern's Richard Dutton-run Reynard Alfa Romeo, before switching to Madgwick's Volkswagen-engined example for the final race, Wallace consolidated his position. He won again at Donington in April and took his third win at Thruxton in May, but that was to be the Reynard's last success. With Davies absent, setting up the 853 suffered initially and as Reynard began to let up mid-season and dreamed prematurely of an F3000 contender for 1986, the Leicester-based team ran into real trouble. When Gugelmin finally won at Silverstone in June, Wallace struggled for sixth and writing was

A Year of Change

by David Tremayne

beginning to appear on the wall.

The 22-year old Brazilian's season began with a disappointing string of minor placings despite the relationship he struck with West Surrey Racing guru Dick Bennetts. The facts were simple. The Reynard, despite shortcomings that would become apparent later, worked straight out of the box.

The Ralt RT30, brainchild of Ron Tauranac and developed from the highly successful RT3 which had dominated the series since 1980, did not.

Gradually, however, Bennetts and Intersport's Glenn Waters kept chipping away on development. In April at Thruxton, Gugelmin looked to have it made until a combination of late-race rain

continued on page 226

1st Marlboro British Formula 3 Championship — Mauricio Gugelmin. Ralt/Volkswagen

2nd Marlboro British Formula 3 Championship — Andy Wallace. Reynard/Volkswagen

For once we didn't mind finishing 3rd in the championship. We didn't even mind coming 2nd. But we were delighted to finish 1st. Powered by a modified Golf engine we have won 35 consecutive races.

Date	Circuit	Driver	Car
4 March 1984	Silverstone	Johnny Dumfries (GB)	Ralt/Volkswagen
11 March 1984	Thruxton	Johnny Dumfries (GB)	Ralt/Volkswagen
1 April 1984	Silverstone	Johnny Dumfries (GB)	Ralt/Volkswagen
15 April 1984	Zolder	Russell Spence (GB)	Ralt/Volkswagen
23 April 1984	Thruxton	Johnny Dumfries (GB)	Ralt/Volkswagen
7 May 1984	Thruxton	Johnny Dumfries (GB)	Ralt/Volkswagen
20 May 1984	Donington	Johnny Dumfries (GB)	Ralt/Volkswagen
28 May 1984	Silverstone	Mario Hytten (GB)	Ralt/Volkswagen
1 July 1984	Snetterton	Johnny Dumfries (GB)	Ralt/Volkswagen
8 July 1984	Donington	Russell Spence (GB)	Ralt/Volkswagen
18 August 1984	Oulton Park	Russell Spence (GB)	Ralt/Volkswagen
6 May 1985	Thruxton	Gary Rvans (GB)	Ralt/Volkswagen

Volkswagen Motorsport

3rd Marlboro British Formula 3 Championship — Russell Spence. Reynard/Volkswagen

Date	Circuit	Driver	Car	
27 August 1984	Silverstone	Johnny Dumfries (GB)	Ralt/Volkswagen	VW
1 September 1984	Spa-Francorchamps	Ross Cheever (USA)	Ralt/Volkswagen	VW
16 September 1984	Zandvoort	Ross Cheever (USA)	Ralt/Volkswagen	VW
23 September 1984	Brands Hatch	Ross Cheever (USA)	Ralt/Volkswagen	VW
30 September 1984	Thruxton	Johnny Dumfries (GB)	Ralt/Volkswagen	VW
11 October 1984	Silverstone	Johnny Dumfries (GB)	Ralt/Volkswagen	VW
3 March 1985	Silverstone	Andy Wallace (GB)	Reynard/Volkswagen	VW
10 March 1985	Thruxton	Russell Spence (GB)	Reynard/Volkswagen	VW
24 March 1985	Silverstone	Russell Spence (GB)	Reynard/Volkswagen	VW
8 April 1985	Thruxton	Russell Spence (GB)	Reynard/Volkswagen	VW
14 April 1985	Donington	Andy Wallace (GB)	Reynard/Volkswagen	VW
21 April 1985	Zolder	Russell Spence (GB)	Reynard/Volkswagen	VW
27 May 1985	Thruxton	Andy Wallace (GB)	Reynard/Volkswagen	VW
9 June 1985	Silverstone	Mauricio Gugelmin (BR)	Ralt/Volkswagen	VW
23 June 1985	Brands Hatch	Ross Cheever (USA)	Ralt/Volkswagen	VW
21 July 1985	Silverstone	Gerrit Van Kouwen (NL)	Ralt/Volkswagen	VW
28 July 1985	Donington	Dave Scott (GB)	Ralt/Volkswagen	VW
11 August 1985	Snetterton	Gerrit Van Kouwen (NL)	Ralt/Volkswagen	VW
17 August 1985	Oulton Park	Gerrit Van Kouwen (NL)	Ralt/Volkswagen	VW
26 August 1985	Silverstone	Dave Scott (GB)	Ralt/Volkswagen	VW
1 September 1985	Spa-Francorchamps	Ross Cheever (USA)	Ralt/Volkswagen	VW
14 September 1985	Zandvoort	Mauricio Gugelmin (BR)	Ralt/Volkswagen	VW
13 October 1985	Silverstone	Mauricio Gugelmin (BR)	Ralt/Volkswagen	VW

Mauricio Gugelmin

and Russell Spence's hard driving in the treacherous conditions snatched success away. Later, again at Thruxton, a pole start was negated by gear selection problems on the line. Gugelmin, they began to say, just wasn't a winner. It took him until that day at Silverstone to prove the pundits wrong, but even after the breakthrough a string of wins failed to follow.

By that stage, Spence's challenge was beginning to show very slight signs of cracking. Blisteringly fast on occasions in 1984, the Yorkshireman made one major mistake early on; at the behest of sponsor Warmastyle, he split with Glenn Waters. Had he stayed with him he would more than likely have dominated the series, in Reynard or Ralt. As it was, he joined forces with Peter Macintosh and PMC Motorsport.

After finishing second to Wallace first time out, he took his Reynard to a string of successes that included two wins at Thruxton, one at Silverstone and one at Zolder, with numerous minor placings. A gritty, determined driver, Spence always looked the one who might pull something out of the bag against the odds, as he did by rattling Gugelmin at Thruxton. However, at the same venue in late May his fearlessness to mix it with anyone led to his eventual downfall when he tangled with Davies while dicing for second place. His subsequent retirement cost him a minimum four points, a possible nine and, as it transpired, his shot at the title.

By mid-season the cracks in his relationship with Macintosh were all too apparent and the two parties split acrimoniously, PMC to sink into voluntary liquidation, Spence to set up Team Warmastyle. Besides the internal problems, however, he had to cope with Reynard's flagging development. After further frustrations it seemed sensible to switch to a Ralt, with all that that entailed in terms of the team catching up on

sorting and development experience. As hindsight has shown, that was just when Reynard belatedly decided to concentrate on its Formula 3 programme once more with the result that the 853 began to regain its form.

Going into the penultimate race at Zandvoort, Gugelmin, now the series leader, the deposed Spence and Wallace looked set for a tooth and nail fight to the wire, the former still at his consistent best despite picking up only one point for fastest lap after disasters at the previous round at Spa, the latter pair getting back into their rhythm. But when Spence was punted into retirement on the first lap his challenge was ended, Gugelmin and Wallace going to Silverstone as the only runners with a chance after finishing first and second respectively.

On 13 October Gugelmin revealed just how strongly he had developed. Consistency was always his key, not only in terms of race results but also of lap times, and from pole he lead every lap to rack up his third win of the year and clinch the title in deserving style. Wallace put in a brave performance, but ultimately had to settle for runner-up slot in both race and Championship. It was the fourth title in six seasons for Dick Bennetts of West Surrey Racing, and literally saved the day for Ralt, for whom it was the sole Championship in an otherwise barren year.

The man who upset everyone's applecart mid-season was van Kouwen, the tall Dutchman who had dominated the Formula Ford Festival at Brands Hatch the previous autumn. In his Pegasus Motorsport Ralt he blew everyone away to win the prestigious British GP supporting race, then repeated the feat at Snetterton and Oulton Park to explode the other distinguishing feature of the 1985 season: the backbiting and controversy that raged behind the scenes.

The stage had been set for this at Thruxton in March when three of the top five regular teams known as the Famous Five – MTR, WSR and EJR – protested the Reynards on the most footling of grounds. They argued that the nosebox was made from aluminium and the chassis constructed of carbon fibre, thereby contravening regulations which say both must be of the same material. The regulations do not, however, state a ratio, so thereafter the Reynards appeared with postage stamp sized carbon-fibre pads – beneath the nosebox where they were not easily detected by rivals.

That ridiculous little scenario was an indication of the apprehension with which the Establishment, with its close working relationship with Ralt, regarded the upstart FF2000 newcomers and the innovative Reynard, both of which represented a threat to business.

When van Kouwen began winning regularly the atmosphere turned uglier, with the pit lane accusations that Pegasus was cheating. Brian de Zille's team did nothing to help the situation by continually winding up its rivals, but in truth who could blame it? When it won it was cheating; when it was beaten it was only because it didn't dare use its trick device, the logic went. But what *was* the device? Vivid imaginations from those who should

have known better spoke of special bolts attaching the manifold to the engine. These fabulous bolts were equipped with a memory programmed to expand them at just the right time to permit more than the regulation amount of air into the engine . . . Others contended the fire extinguishers were full of nitrous oxide, but did not elect to explain why there wasn't any piping to feed it into the combustion chambers.

It sounded silly then, although it had virtually everyone going at the time, and it sounds sillier now. After a protest at Spa led to an inspection which cleared Pegasus's second-placed car and Andy Wallace's third-place Reynard (the disease was spreading), the air was finally cleared. Suffice it to say van Kouwen is as good as he often looked and that he must start favourite for the 1986 series.

When the Dutchman wasn't dishing out the beatings, Ross Cheever could be found at the sharp end, the talented American taking wins at Brands Hatch and Spa, where he ousted van Kouwen fair and square. Sadly, though, he still let psychological pressure get to him on occasions and his practice performance at Zandvoort where he spun many times in a few laps was just plain crazy, especially after his splendid showing at Spa. Ross has all the speed, what he needs is a mature brain to accompany it.

Dave Scott, once a shooting star in Formula 3, was another double winner once he'd sorted his 1985 programme. He did a couple of early races in Dutton's RT3 before buying a Ralt RT30, and was quick and consistent at most venues. He won at

Ross Cheever

'These fabulous bolts were equipped with a memory programmed to expand them at just the right time'

Donington in July and Silverstone in August and his points tally suggested he might have been a real threat had he done the full season. The final winner was Briton Gary Evans, who shook everyone at Thruxton in May by giving the RT30 its first British win. Driving for MTR he was inconsistent; at times he could mix it with the best, at others he was merely an also-ran.

Of the rest Davies was the most deserving of a win on his early showings but somehow things never gelled for him. If he can calm himself and get rid of a tendency to collide with anyone who has just overtaken him he could still make the F3 grade. Norwegian Harald Huysman proved disappointing for EJR, gaining a reputation for hitting other cars and triggering accidents, and little else, while Cathy Muller beat all of the top guys on one occasion or other but never managed to bring her DPR Reynard into the top three. Andrew Gilbert-Scott, who ran under the Systime/Racing for Britain scheme, was another to disappoint, his best showing until then being fourth at Oulton Park which was disallowed because of a wing infringement. He did however hit the national headlines with an airborne roll at Donington caused by Huysman, and then rather redeemed himself with a fine third at Silverstone's finale.

On the technical front it was business as usual for Johnny Judd's highly successful Volkswagen engine which also won in Italy and Japan, but the Reynard Saab venture run jointly by Madgwick's Robert Synge and Scan-Sport's Bob Moore was a bold effort. Maurizio Sandro Sala put one car on

Gerrit Van Kouwen

Cathy Muller

pole at Zolder and both he and team-mate Anthony Reid scored a few points, but as development lagged the promise disappeared and neither driver, nor Julian Bailey who joined the team late in the season, had the means of demonstrating their true ability. However, Rome took more than a few days to build so hopefully Saab will stay in racing. Faint heart fair maiden never won, and all that . . .

Further afield the demise of the European Formula 3 Championship focused more attention on national series. In France, Pierre-Henri Raphanel underlined his talent by winning the domestic championship and Monaco's support race in a Martini Alfa Romeo, while Yannick Dalmas in a similar car, Dominique Delestre (EJR Ralt), Michel Trollé (Ralt) and Paul Belmondo (DPR Reynard) all had moments of glory. In Germany Volker Weidler was equally dominant in a Martini Alfa, with Dane Kris Nissen showing plenty of flair. Franco Forini clinched the Italian title in his intriguing carbon-fibre Dallara VW after a season of battles with Fabrizio Barbazza's Alfa-powered version, Alex Caffi's Martini Alfa and Dallara Alfa, and Marco Apicella's Reynard Alfa. In Sweden, Formula 3 also proved strong, Thomas Danielsson winning for Reynard Saab, albeit against negligible opposition.

Once again, though, it was the Marlboro British Championship that drew the real attention. While Spence was fiery and Wallace smooth both had to contend with that hurtful and consequently unsettling mid-season slump, while Gugelmin simply continued on his consistent way, showing real speed just when it mattered. Formula 3 had a crest of a wave year in 1985 despite the acrimony, but the signs are clear it won't have quite the stepping stone status in the future that it has enjoyed in the past. After its successful inaugural season F3000 looks set to become officially established as the category through which Formula 3 drivers must pass *en route* to Formula 1.

Class B: Successful beyond expectations
One of the contributory factors in the Marlboro British series' full grids was the strength of the Class B or Pre-1984 category, which succeeded beyond the wildest expectations in its second season.

At the end of a hard-fought year Manchester-based Jamaican Carlton Tingling emerged a battered but deserving champion in his Ralt RT3 VW (he missed the last races after sustaining injuries in a shunt in the only testing session he could afford to attend). He struggled all year on a financial shoestring, like the majority of his rivals, and racked up three wins. His tally was topped only by find-of-the-year Giles Butterfield, who graduated from karting, survived a nasty shunt which broke an ankle, and took five wins to mark himself as a man to watch.

Other impecunious Brits to win a race apiece were Mike Wright (Jupiter Racing RT3), Mark Goddard (Solar/Savoir Fare RT3) and Steve Kempton (Worldwide Dryers RT3). The popular Richard Dutton équipe provided race-winning RT3s, Paul Stott and Sean Walker taking victory on one-off outings and FF2000 man Ross Hockenhull winning twice. Regular RDR runner Ray Stover from Denver thoroughly enjoyed his full season, picking up the laurels at Zolder. Finally, Dick Parsons came out of retirement, the former F3/F5000 racer quickly finding his feet again to give Rob Arnott's Solar Racing RT3 VW a brace of wins.

While 18 drivers scored points in Class A, 22 did so in Class B at one stage or other and the standard of driving was, if anything, even more entertaining. And 1986 looks even better if current interest is sustained.

'Formula 3 had a crest of a wave year in 1985 despite the acrimony'

A Brazilian and two Englishmen. A 22-year old from Curitiba, a 24-year old from Oxford and a 25-year old from Bradford. Mauricio Gugelmin, Andy Wallace and Russell Spence. Between them they accounted for 10 of the 18 races in the 1985 Marlboro British Formula 3 Championship. All three have very different personalities and driving styles, but they had one thing in common: the superb two-litre Volkswagen engine developed by John Judd at his Rugby-based Engine Developments concern.

All three had spells as Championship leader. Quiet-spoken Wallace showed his hand first, creating something of a sensation by winning the opening race at Silverstone in March (his first ever race in the formula!) and giving Swallow Racing and Adrian Reynard's highly innovative carbon-

Andy Wallace

fibre Reynard 853 victory first time out. When Wallace was forced to miss the second race at Thruxton, Spence, also driving a Reynard, made the most of the opportunity and won convincingly. He then won again at Silverstone, Thruxton and Zolder, while Wallace kept on the boil with further wins at Donington and Thruxton. Until Oulton Park in August, Spence held sway at the top of the points table.

Gugelmin's challenge took longer to develop. He looked a likely victor at Thruxton as early as April before spinning down to third in a late-race rain shower. On that occasion Spence's impressive ability to drive quickly on slick tyres in damp conditions reaped dividends as he applied strong pressure. Initially the Ralt RT30 was no match for the Reynard, but by Silverstone in June West Surrey Racing had got it right and Gugelmin was dominant. Nevertheless, as an indication of just how tough Formula 3 was in 1985 the Brazilian had to wait until the final pair of races, at Zandvoort in September and Silverstone in October, before he again took the chequered flag ahead of his rivals. On the latter occasion, as he clinched the Championship, the Volkswagen engine competed its second clean sweep in the

series and took its 35th consecutive win.

Wallace for Reynard, Gugelmin for Ralt. That was how the eventual Championship battle shaped up prior to Silverstone's finale. Wallace was back in the hunt after the Reynard had lost its edge during the middle of the year; Gugelmin's incredible consistency, as much a product of West Surrey Racing's ability as his own smooth style, was edging him ever closer to his final triumph.

But what about Spence?

By the end of the year he would be the only driver in the formula with race experience of both the Reynard 853 and the Ralt RT30. His season began with the former, run for him by PMC Motorsport in conjunction with his sponsor, Warmastyle Racing. Up to the June race at Silverstone, where Gugelmin finally won for the first time, his Reynard was a competitive proposition. However, whereas Wallace enjoyed a good relationship with Swallow Racing's boss Tim Stakes and team manager Colin Essex, and Gugelmin had forged a superb partnership with Dick Bennetts of West Surrey Racing – the man who had masterminded the Formula 3 Championship successes of present-day Grand Prix drivers Stefan Johansson (1980), Jonathan Palmer (1981) and Ayrton Senna (1983) – Spence's relations with Peter Macintosh of PMC became steadily more strained. Eventually, the two parted company in July amid some acrimony. Still backed by the enthusiastic and understanding Bill Blandford of Warmastyle, Team Warmastyle was set up by Spence to continue running a Reynard.

The red-haired Yorkshireman is in some ways a stereotype: outgoing, big-hearted, quick-tempered . . . and forthright. When the Reynard continued to struggle mid-season as its early cutting edge became blunter, harsh views were exchanged and a further upheaval was inevitable. After an appalling race at Snetterton in August, Spence bought a Ralt. Sadly, however, it was not to prove the palliative everyone hoped, for one simple reason. Spence first raced it at Oulton Park in the week following Snetterton, then again at weekly intervals at Silverstone and Spa. At the latter venue he brought it home an encouraging fourth but the sheer pace of the racing schedule frustrated the team's chances of making up ground on its Ralt rivals who had run the car all season and therefore had greater experience to draw on for development. At Zandvoort another

Mauricio Gugelmin

driver collided with Spence and his Championship aspirations died in the sand dunes on the first racing lap. At Silverstone he was much closer to Gugelmin's pace, but it was too late. For the second successive year he had to be content with third overall in the Championship.

While his year had its highs and lows, however, his one real constant was the support of Volkswagen. That and an unquenchable determination to succeed. It is that determination which has characterised his career to date. From his first foray into racing with a hillclimb Mini in 1980, through his seasons in Formula Ford 2000 – where he took the Donington, Golden Lion and European Championships – Spence has always gone racing to win. Last year in Formula 3 there were occasional lapses after late-night partying, and the boisterous off-track activity tended to obscure an otherwise impressive series of on-track performances. In 1985 the potential was more obvious and the Spence attitude far more professional. The raw speed, car control and even a degree of latent charisma is all there and with each season Spence's rough edges become smoother

For 1986 there is already talk of Mauricio Gugelmin following in the footsteps of fellow countrymen Emerson and Wilson Fittipaldi, Carlos Pace, Nelson Piquet and the good friend with whom he and his wife Stella share a house, Ayrton Senna. It is no secret the latter would dearly love to have him as his team-mate in the Lotus team. Failing that, a season of Formula 3000 with West Surrey Racing seems likely, in which case it is probable there will be further battles between the Brazilian, Andy Wallace and Russell Spence, for both Englishmen have their sights set firmly on the Grand Prix scene and see the category as the next logical stepping stone. If all three succeed their careers will owe much to the British Formula 3 Championship of 1985.

To say nothing of the encouragement and support they received from Volkswagen Audi Group.

Russell Spence

Mauricio Gugelmin

Russell Spence

FORMULA ONE GRANDS PRIX STATISTICS 1985

Entries and practice times

No.	Driver	Nat	Car	Tyre	Engine	Entrant	Practice 1	Practice 2
1	Niki Lauda	A	Marlboro McLAREN MP4/2B	G	TAG P01 (TTE P01)	Marlboro McLaren International	1m 30·716s	**1m 29·984s**
2	Alain Prost	F	Marlboro McLAREN MP4/2B	G	TAG P01 (TTE P01)	Marlboro McLaren International	1m 30·253s	**1m 29·117s**
3	Martin Brundle	GB	TYRRELL 012	G	Ford-Cosworth DFY	Tyrrell Racing Organisation	1m 36·225s	**1m 36·152s**
4	Stefan Johansson	S	TYRRELL 012	G	Ford-Cosworth DFY	Tyrrell Racing Organisation	1m 37·799s	**1m 37·293s**
5	Nigel Mansell	GB	WILLIAMS FW10	G	Honda RA163–E	Canon Williams Team	1m 31·211s	**1m 28·848s**
6	Keke Rosberg	SF	WILLIAMS FW10	G	Honda RA163–E	Canon Williams Team	1m 32·135s	**1m 27·864s**
7	Nelson Piquet	BR	Olivetti BRABHAM BT54	P	BMW M12/13	Motor Racing Developments Ltd	1m 31·364s	**1m 29·855s**
8	François Hesnault	F	Olivetti BRABHAM BT54	P	BMW M12/13	Motor Racing Developments Ltd	1m 34·742s	**1m 32·904s**
9	Manfred Winkelhock	D	RAM 03	P	Hart 415T	Skoal Bandit Formula 1 Team	1m 36·239s	**1m 32·560s**
10	Philippe Alliot	F	RAM 03	P	Hart 415T	Skoal Bandit Formula 1 Team	**1m 35·726s**	1m 37·409s
11	Elio de Angelis	I	John Player Special LOTUS 97T	G	Renault EF4	John Player Special Team Lotus	**1m 28·081s**	—
12	Ayrton Senna	BR	John Player Special LOTUS 97T	G	Renault EF4	John Player Special Team Lotus	1m 28·705s	**1m 28·389s**
15	Patrick Tambay	F	Elf RENAULT RE60	G	Renault EF4	Equipe Renault Elf	**1m 30·254s**	1m 30·516s
16	Derek Warwick	GB	Elf RENAULT RE60	G	Renault EF4/EF15	Equipe Renault Elf	1m 31·533s	**1m 30·100s**
17	Gerhard Berger	A	ARROWS A8	G	BMW M12/13	Barclay Arrows BMW	1m 34·919s	**1m 34·773s**
18	Thierry Boutsen	B	ARROWS A8	G	BMW M12/13	Barclay Arrows BMW	1m 32·207s	**1m 30·953s**
19	Stefan Johansson	S	TOLEMAN TG185	—	Hart 415T	Toleman Group Motorsport		Entry withdrawn
20	John Watson	GB	TOLEMAN TG185	—	Hart 415T	Toleman Group Motorsport		Entry withdrawn
21	Mauro Baldi	I	SPIRIT 101D	P	Hart 415T	Spirit Enterprises	**1m 41·330s**	—
22	Riccardo Patrese	I	Benetton ALFA ROMEO 185T	G	Alfa Romeo 890T	Benetton Team Alfa Romeo	1m 32·107s	**1m 31·790s**
23	Eddie Cheever	USA	Benetton ALFA ROMEO 185T	G	Alfa Romeo 890T	Benetton Team Alfa Romeo	1m 33·094s	**1m 33·091s**
24	Piercarlo Ghinzani	I	Kelemata OSELLA FA1G	P	Alfa Romeo 890T	Osella Squadra Corse	1m 38·272s	**1m 36·743s**
25	Andrea de Cesaris	I	LIGIER JS25	P	Renault EF4	Equipe Ligier	1m 37·803s	**1m 31·411s**
26	Jacques Laffite	F	LIGIER JS25	P	Renault EF4	Equipe Ligier	1m 37·803s	**1m 32·021s**
27	Michele Alboreto	I	Fiat FERRARI 156/85	G	Ferrari 126C	Scuderia Ferrari SpA	1m 28·899s	**1m 27·768s**
28	René Arnoux	F	Fiat FERRARI 156/85	G	Ferrari 126C	Scuderia Ferrari SpA	1m 30·813s	**1m 29·612s**
29	Pierluigi Martini	I	Simod MINARDI M/85	P	Ford-Cosworth DFV	Minardi Team SpA	**1m 44·046s**	—

Friday morning and Saturday morning practice sessions not officially recorded.

G – Goodyear, P – Pirelli.

Fri p.m. Hot, dry Sat p.m. Hot, dry

Starting grid

27 ALBORETO (1m 27·768s)
Ferrari

6 ROSBERG (1m 27·864s)
Williams

11 DE ANGELIS (1m 28·081s)
Lotus

12 SENNA (1m 28·389s)
Lotus

5 MANSELL (1m 28·848s)
Williams

2 PROST (1m 29·117s)
McLaren

28 ARNOUX (1m 29·612s)
Ferrari

7 PIQUET (1m 29·855s)
Brabham

1 LAUDA (1m 29·984s)
McLaren

16 WARWICK (1m 30·100s)
Renault

15 TAMBAY (1m 30·254s)
Renault

18 BOUTSEN (1m 30·953s)
Arrows

25 DE CESARIS (1m 31·411s)
Ligier

22 PATRESE (1m 31·790s)
Alfa Romeo

26 LAFFITE (1m 32·021s)
Ligier

9 WINKELHOCK (1m 32·560s)
RAM

8 HESNAULT (1m 32·904s)
Brabham

23 CHEEVER (1m 33·091s)
Alfa Romeo

17 BERGER (1m 34·773s)
Arrows

10 ALLIOT (1m 35·726s)
RAM

3 BRUNDLE (1m 36·152s)
Tyrrell

24 GHINZANI (1m 36·743s)
Osella

4 JOHANSSON (1m 37·293s)
Tyrrell

21 BALDI (1m 41·330s)
Spirit

29 MARTINI (1m 44·046s)
Minardi

Results and retirements

Place	Driver	Car	Laps	Time and Speed (mph/km/h)/Retirement	
1	Alain Prost	McLaren-TAG t/c V6	61	1h 41m 26·115s	112·795/181·527
2	Michele Alboreto	Ferrari t/c V6	61	1h 41m 29·374s	112·716/181·4
3	Elio de Angelis	Lotus-Renault t/c V6	60		
4	René Arnoux	Ferrari t/c V6	59		
5	Patrick Tambay	Renault t/c V6	59		
6	Jacques Laffite	Ligier-Renault t/c V6	59		
7	Stefan Johansson	Tyrrell-Cosworth V8	58		
8	Martin Brundle	Tyrrell-Cosworth V8	58		
9	Philippe Alliot	RAM-Hart t/c 4	58		
10	Derek Warwick	Renault t/c V6	57		
11	Thierry Boutsen	Arrows-BMW t/c 4	57		
12	Piercarlo Ghinzani	Osella-Alfa Romeo t/c V8	57		
13	Manfred Winkelhock	RAM-Hart t/c 4	57		
	Gerhard Berger	Arrows-BMW t/c 4	51	Broken suspension	
	Ayrton Senna	Lotus-Renault t/c V6	48	Electrical	
	Eddie Cheever	Alfa Romeo t/c V8	42	Engine	
	Pierluigi Martini	Minardi-Cosworth V8	41	Engine	
	Niki Lauda	McLaren-TAG t/c V6	27	Fuel metering	
	Andrea de Cesaris	Ligier-Renault t/c V6	26	Accident	
	Riccardo Patrese	Alfa Romeo t/c V8	20	Puncture	
	Keke Rosberg	Williams-Honda t/c V6	10	Turbo	
	François Hesnault	Brabham-BMW t/c 4	9	Accident	
	Nigel Mansell	Williams-Honda t/c V6	8	Broken exhaust/accident damage	
	Mauro Baldi	Spirit-Hart t/c 4	7	Turbo/misfire	
	Nelson Piquet	Brabham-BMW t/c 4	2	Transmission	

Fastest lap: Prost, on lap 34, 1m 36·702s, 116·378 mph/187·292 km/h.
Lap record: Alain Prost (F1 McLaren MP4/2-TAG t/c V6), 1m 36·499s, 116·622 mph/187·686 km/h (1984).

Past winners

Year	Driver	Nat	Car	Circuit	Distance miles/km	Speed mph/km/h
1972*	Carlos Reutemann	RA	3·0 Brabham BT34-Ford	Interlagos	183·01/294·53	112·89/181·68
1973	Emerson Fittipaldi	BR	3·0 JPS/Lotus 72-Ford	Interlagos	197·85/318·42	114·23/183·83
1974	Emerson Fittipaldi	BR	3·0 McLaren M23-Ford	Interlagos	158·28/254·73	112·23/180·62
1975	Carlos Pace	BR	3·0 Brabham BT44B-Ford	Interlagos	197·85/318·42	113·40/182·50
1976	Niki Lauda	A	3·0 Ferrari 312T/76	Interlagos	197·85/318·42	112·76/181·47
1977	Carlos Reutemann	RA	3·0 Ferrari 312T-2/77	Interlagos	197·85/318·42	112·92/181·73
1978	Carlos Reutemann	RA	3·0 Ferrari 312T-2/78	Rio de Janeiro	196·95/316·95	107·43/172·89
1979	Jacques Laffite	F	3·0 Ligier JS11-Ford	Interlagos	197·85/318·42	117·23/188·67
1980	René Arnoux	F	1·5 Renault RS t/c	Interlagos	195·70/314·95	117·40/188·93
1981	Carlos Reutemann	RA	3·0 Williams FWO7C-Ford	Rio de Janeiro	193·82/311·92	96·59/155·45
1982	Alain Prost	F	1·5 Renault RE t/c	Rio de Janeiro	196·95/316·95	112·97/181·80
1983	Nelson Piquet	BR	1·5 Brabahm BT52-BMW t/c	Rio de Janeiro	196·95/316·95	108·93/175·30
1984	Alain Prost	F	1·5 McLaren MP4/2-TAG t/c	Rio de Janeiro	190·69/306·89	111·54/179·51
1985	Alain Prost	F	1·5 McLaren MP4/2B-TAG t/c	Rio de Janeiro	190·69/306·89	112·79/181·53

*Non-championship

Circuit data

Autodromo Internacional do Rio de Janeiro, Baixada de Jacarepaguá
Circuit length: 3·126 miles/5·031 km
Race distance: 61 laps, 190·692 miles/306·889 km
Race weather: Hot, dry.

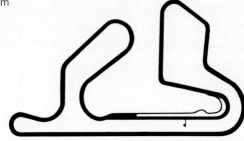

Lap chart

1st LAP ORDER	Laps 1–61
6 K. Rosberg	6 6 6 6 6 6 6 6 6 27 27 27 27 27 27 27 27 2 2 2 2 2 2 2 2 2 2 2 2 2 2 2 2 2 2 2 2 2 2 2 2 2 2 2 2 2 2 2 2 2 2 2 2 2 2 2 2 2 2 2 2
27 M. Alboreto	27 27 27 27 27 27 27 27 27 2 2 2 2 2 2 2 27 27 27 27 27 27 27 27 27 27 27 12 27 27 27 27 27 27 27 27 27 27 27 27 27 27 27 27 27 27 27 27 27 27 27 27 27 27 27 27 27 27 27 27 27
2 A. Prost	2 2 2 2 2 2 2 12 12 12 12 1 1 1 1 1 1 1 1 12 12 12 12 12 27 12 12 12 12 12 12 12 12 12 12 12 12 12 12 12 11 11 11 11 11 11 11 11 11 11 11 11 11 11 11 11 11
12 A. Senna	12 12 12 12 12 12 12 12 12 1 1 1 12 12 12 12 12 12 12 1 11 20 20 11 11 11 11 11 11 11 11 11 11 11 11 11 11 11 11 11 11 11 11 11 11 15 15 20 20 20 20 20 20 20 20
11 E. de Angelis	11 11 11 11 11 11 11 11 11 1 11 11 11 11 11 11 11 11 11 11 11 11 28 25 10 10 23 23 23 23 23 23 23 15 15 15 15 15 15 15 15 28 28 15 15 15 15 15 15 15 15 15
28 R. Arnoux	28 28 28 28 28 28 28 1 1 6 28 28 28 28 28 28 28 28 28 28 28 28 25 11 11 23 23 23 10 15 15 15 15 15 15 15 23 23 26 26 28 28 28 28 28 26 26 26 26 26 26 26 26 26
7 N. Piquet	7 7 1 1 1 1 1 28 28 25 25 25 25 25 25 25 25 25 25 25 25 15 15 15 15 15 15 10 10 26 26 26 26 26 28 28 26 26 26 26 10 10 4 4 4 4 4 4 4 4
1 N. Lauda	1 1 22 25 25 25 25 25 22 22 22 22 22 22 22 26 15 15 15 10 10 10 17 18 18 26 26 10 10 28 28 23 10 10 10 10 10 3 3 3 3 3 3 3 3 3
22 R. Patrese	22 22 22 22 22 22 22 22 22 15 15 15 26 26 26 26 15 18 18 18 23 23 18 26 26 18 18 18 18 18 10 10 10 18 3 3 3 3 18 4 10 10 10 10 10 10 10
25 A. de Cesaris	25 25 15 15 15 15 15 15 15 26 26 26 15 15 15 15 18 10 10 10 17 17 28 17 4 4 3 3 28 28 28 18 18 18 3 18 18 18 18 4 18 18 18 18 18 18 16
15 P. Tambay	15 15 23 23 23 23 23 26 23 23 23 23 23 23 17 17 17 17 23 4 18 4 4 3 4 28 3 3 3 3 3 3 23 4 4 4 4 17 17 17 9 9 9 9 9 18
26 J. Laffite	26 23 26 26 26 26 26 26 23 18 18 18 18 18 18 18 10 9 9 23 4 9 26 9 9 9 9 28 9 9 9 9 4 4 4 4 9 17 17 17 9 9 24 24 24 16 16 7
23 E. Cheever	23 26 16 16 16 16 8 8 8 18 16 17 17 17 17 17 17 9 4 23 9 9 18 4 3 28 28 28 9 4 4 4 4 9 9 9 9 17 9 9 9 24 24 16 16 16 24 24
3 M. Brundle	3 3 3 3 8 8 16 16 16 16 17 16 16 16 10 10 10 4 23 4 4 26 26 9 28 24 24 24 24 24 17 17 17 17 17 17 17 24 24 24 24 16 16 16
9 M. Winkelhock	9 16 17 8 3 3 3 3 3 3 3 3 10 16 9 9 23 24 26 26 3 3 24 28 17 17 17 17 24 24 24 24 24 24 16 16 16 16 16 16
16 D. Warwick	16 17 8 17 17 17 18 18 17 9 9 9 10 9 4 4 4 26 18 3 3 3 24 24 16 16 16 16 16 16 16 16 16 16 16 16 16
17 G. Berger	17 9 9 9 9 18 18 18 17 9 4 10 10 9 4 24 24 24 24 26 24 24 16 16 29 29 29 29 29 29 29 29 29 29 29 29 29 29 29 29
8 F. Hesnault	8 8 4 4 4 9 9 9 9 4 10 4 4 4 3 24 3 3 3 29 29 29 29 29 1 1 1
4 S. Johansson	4 4 24 18 18 4 4 4 4 10 24 24 24 24 24 3 29 29 29 29 16 16 16 16 16 29 29 29
24 P. Ghinzani	24 24 10 24 24 10 10 10 10 24 29 29 29 29 29 16 16 16 16
10 P. Alliot	10 10 18 10 10 24 24 24 24 29
29 P. Martini	29 18 29 29 29 29 29 29 29
18 T. Boutsen	18 27 21 5 5 5 5 5
21 M. Baldi	21 21 5 21 21 21
5 N. Mansell	5 5

Fastest laps

Driver	Time	Lap
Alain Prost	1m 36·702s	34
Michele Alboreto	1m 36·925s	37
Niki Lauda	1m 38·098s	15
René Arnoux	1m 38·349s	39
Ayrton Senna	1m 38·440s	32
Keke Rosberg	1m 38·678s	2
Elio de Angelis	1m 39·080s	31
Derek Warwick	1m 39·715s	32
Nigel Mansell	1m 39·996s	2
Andrea de Cesaris	1m 40·008s	7
Patrick Tambay	1m 40·459s	59
Nelson Piquet	1m 40·558s	2
Jacques Laffite	1m 40·572s	24
François Hesnault	1m 41·151s	5
Thierry Boutsen	1m 41·809s	30
Riccardo Patrese	1m 41·812s	2
Eddie Cheever	1m 41·855s	24
Stefan Johansson	1m 41·926s	36
Piercarlo Ghinzani	1m 42·234s	43
Gerhard Berger	1m 42·588s	39
Martin Brundle	1m 42·606s	17
Philippe Alliot	1m 43·115s	23
Manfred Winkelhock	1m 44·236s	8
Pierluigi Martini	1m 45·662s	27
Mauro Baldi	1m 47·046s	2

Points

WORLD CHAMPIONSHIP OF DRIVERS

1	Alain Prost	9 pts
2	Michele Alboreto	6
3	Elio de Angelis	4
4	René Arnoux	3
5	Patrick Tambay	2
6	Jacques Laffite	1

CONSTRUCTORS' CUP

1=	McLaren	9 pts
1=	Ferrari	9
3	Lotus	4
4	Renault	2
5	Ligier	1

Entries and practice times

No.	Driver	Nat	Car	Tyre	Engine	Entrant	Practice 1	Practice 2
1	Niki Lauda	A	Marlboro McLAREN MP4/2B	G	TAG P01 (TTE P01)	Marlboro McLaren International	1m 23·670s	**1m 23·288s**
2	Alain Prost	F	Marlboro McLAREN MP4/2B	G	TAG P01 (TTE P01)	Marlboro McLaren International	1m 23·887s	**1m 21·420s**
3	Martin Brundle	GB	TYRRELL 012	G	Ford-Cosworth DFY	Tyrrell Racing Organisation	1m 28·694s	**1m 27·602s**
4	Stefan Bellof	D	TYRRELL 012	G	Ford-Cosworth DFY	Tyrrell Racing Organisation	**1m 27·284s**	1m 27·474s
5	Nigel Mansell	GB	WILLIAMS FW10	G	Honda RA163–E	Canon Williams Honda Team	1m 26·459s	**1m 23·594s**
6	Keke Rosberg	SF	WILLIAMS FW10	G	Honda RA163–E	Canon Williams Honda Team	—	**1m 21·904s**
7	Nelson Piquet	BR	Olivetti BRABHAM BT54	P	BMW M12/13	Motor Racing Developments Ltd	1m 25·580s	**1m 23·618s**
8	François Hesnault	F	Olivetti BRABHAM BT54	P	BMW M12/13	Motor Racing Developments Ltd	—	**1m 25·717s**
9	Manfred Winkelhock	D	RAM 03	P	Hart 415T	Skoal Bandit Formula 1 Team	1m 34·876s	**1m 24·721s**
10	Philippe Alliot	F	RAM 03	P	Hart 415T	Skoal Bandit Formula 1 Team	1m 27·430s	**1m 26·187s**
11	Elio de Angelis	I	John Player Special LOTUS 97T	G	Renault EF4	John Player Special Team Lotus	1m 22·306s	**1m 22·159s**
12	Ayrton Senna	BR	John Player Special LOTUS 97T	G	Renault EF4	John Player Special Team Lotus	1m 21·708s	**1m 21·007s**
15	Patrick Tambay	F	Elf RENAULT RE60	G	Renault EF4	Equipe Renault Elf	1m 25·718s	**1m 24·111s**
16	Derek Warwick	GB	Elf RENAULT RE60	G	Renault EF4/EF15	Equipe Renault Elf	1m 24·538s	**1m 23·084s**
17	Gerhard Berger	A	ARROWS A8	G	BMW M12/13	Barclay Arrows BMW	1m 26·154s	**1m 24·842s**
18	Thierry Boutsen	B	ARROWS A8	G	BMW M12/13	Barclay Arrows BMW	**1m 24·747s**	1m 26·695s
19	Stefan Johansson	S	TOLEMAN TG185	—	Hart 415T	Toleman Group Motorsport		Entry withdrawn
20	John Watson	GB	TOLEMAN TG185	—	Hart 415T	Toleman Group Motorsport		Entry withdrawn
21	Mauro Baldi	I	SPIRIT 101D	P	Hart 415T	Spirit Enterprises Ltd	1m 30·231s	**1m 28·473s**
22	Riccardo Patrese	I	Benetton ALFA ROMEO 185T	G	Alfa Romeo 890T	Benetton Team Alfa Romeo	1m 24·519s	**1m 24·230s**
23	Eddie Cheever	USA	Benetton ALFA ROMEO 185T	G	Alfa Romeo 890T	Benetton Team Alfa Romeo	1m 24·880s	**1m 24·563s**
24	Piercarlo Ghinzani	I	Kelemata OSELLA FA1F	P	Alfa Romeo 890T	Osella Squadra Corse	**1m 30·855s**	
25	Andrea de Cesaris	I	LIGIER JS25	P	Renault EF4	Equipe Ligier	1m 24·723s	**1m 23·302s**
26	Jacques Laffite	F	LIGIER JS25	P	Renault EF4	Equipe Ligier	**1m 24·943s**	1m 26·181s
27	Michele Alboreto	I	Fiat FERRARI 156/85	G	Ferrari 126C	Scuderia Ferrari SpA	1m 23·831s	**1m 22·577s**
28	Stefan Johansson	S	Fiat FERRARI 156/85	G	Ferrari 126C	Scuderia Ferrari SpA	1m 25·136s	**1m 23·652s**
29	Pierluigi Martini	I	Simod MINARDI M/85	P	Ford-Cosworth DFV	Minardi Team	1m 31·205s	**1m 28·596s**
30	Jonathan Palmer	GB	West ZAKSPEED ZAK 841	G	Zakspeed	West Zakspeed Racing	**1m 28·166s**	—

Friday morning and Saturday morning practice sessions not officially recorded.

G – Goodyear, P – Pirelli.

Fri p.m.	Sat p.m.
Cool, dry, occasional drizzle	Warm, dry

Starting grid

	12 SENNA (1m 21·007s) Lotus
2 PROST (1m 21·420s) McLaren	
	6 ROSBERG (1m 21·904s) Williams
11 DE ANGELIS (1m 22·159s) Lotus	
	27 ALBORETO (1m 22·577s) Ferrari
16 WARWICK (1m 23·084s) Renault	
	1 LAUDA (1m 23·288s) McLaren
25 DE CESARIS (1m 23·302s) Ligier	
	*5 MANSELL (1m 23·594s) Williams
7 PIQUET (1m 23·618s) Brabham	
	28 JOHANSSON (1m 23·652s) Ferrari
15 TAMBAY (1m 24·111s) Renault	
	22 PATRESE (1m 24·230s) Alfa Romeo
*23 CHEEVER (1m 24·563s) Alfa Romeo	
	9 WINKELHOCK (1m 24·721s) RAM
18 BOUTSEN (1m 24·747s) Arrows	
	17 BERGER (1m 24·842s) Arrows
26 LAFFITE (1m 24·943s) Ligier	
	8 HESNAULT (1m 25·717s) Brabham
10 ALLIOT (1m 26·187s) RAM	
	4 BELLOF (1m 27·284s) Tyrrell
3 BRUNDLE (1m 27·602s) Tyrrell	
	30 PALMER (1m 28·166s) Zakspeed
21 BALDI (1m 28·473s) Spirit	
	*29 MARTINI (1m 28·596s) Minardi
24 GHINZANI (1m 30·855s) Osella	

* Started from the pit lane.

Results and retirements

Place	Driver	Car	Laps	Time and Speed (mph/km/h)/Retirement	
1	Ayrton Senna	Lotus-Renault t/c V6	67	2h 00m 28·006s	90·198/145·160
2	Michele Alboreto	Ferrari t/c V6	67	2h 01m 30·984s	89·415/143·9
3	Patrick Tambay	Renault t/c V6	66		
4	Elio de Angelis	Lotus-Renault t/c V6	66		
5	Nigel Mansell	Williams-Honda t/c V6	65		
6	Stefan Bellof	Tyrrell-Cosworth V8	65		
7	Derek Warwick	Renault t/c V6	65		
8	Stefan Johansson	Ferrari t/c V6	62		
9	Piercarlo Ghinzani	Osella-Alfa Romeo t/c V8	61		
	Manfred Winkelhock	RAM-Hart t/c 4	50	Running, not classified	
	Niki Lauda	McLaren-TAG t/c V6	49	Engine	
	Eddie Cheever	Alfa Romeo t/c V8	36	Engine/misfire	
	Alain Prost	McLaren-TAG t/c V6	30	Spun off	
	Andrea de Cesaris	Ligier-Renault t/c V6	29	Tyres/handling	
	Thierry Boutsen	Arrows-BMW t/c 4	28	Water in the engine/electrics	
	Nelson Piquet	Brabham-BMW t/c 4	28	Tyres/handling	
	Martin Brundle	Tyrrell-Cosworth V8	20	Gear linkage	
	Mauro Baldi	Spirit-Hart t/c 4	19	Spun off	
	Keke Rosberg	Williams-Honda t/c V6	16	Spun off	
	Jacques Laffite	Ligier-Renault t/c V6	15	Tyres/handling	
	Gerhard Berger	Arrows-BMW t/c 4	12	Spun off	
	Pierluigi Martini	Minardi-Cosworth V8	12	Spun off	
	Riccardo Patrese	Alfa Romeo t/c V8	4	Spun off	
	Philippe Alliot	RAM-Hart t/c 4	3	Spun off	
	François Hesnault	Brabham-BMW t/c 4	3	Electrics	
	Jonathan Palmer	Zakspeed t/c 4	2	Suspension damage	

Fastest lap: Senna, on lap 15, 1m 44·121s, 93·455 mph/150·401 km/h.
Lap record: Niki Lauda (F1 McLaren MP4/2-TAG t/c), 1m 22·996s, 117·242 mph/188·683 km/h (1984).

Past winners

Year	Driver	Nat	Car	Circuit	Distance miles/km	Speed mph/km/h
1958	Stirling Moss	GB	2·5 Vanwall	Oporto	233·01/375·00	105·03/169·03
1959	Stirling Moss	GB	2·5 Cooper T51-Climax	Monsanto	209·00/336·35	95·32/153·40
1960	Jack Brabham	AUS	2·5 Cooper T53-Climax	Oporto	256·31/412·50	109·27/175·85
1984	Alain Prost	F	1·5 McLaren MP4/2-TAG t/c	Estoril	189·21/304·50	112·18/180·54
1985	Ayrton Senna	BR	1·5 Lotus 97T-Renault t/c	Estoril	181·09/291·45	90·19/145·16

Circuit data

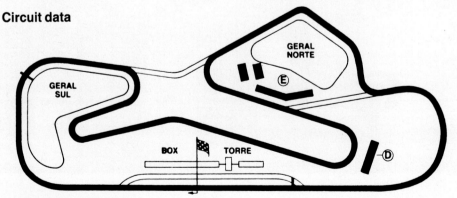

Autodromo do Estoril

Circuit length: 2·703 miles/4·350 km
Race distance: 67 laps, 181·098 miles/291·450 km
(Scheduled to run 69 laps but reduced in accordance with two-hour rule.)
Race weather: Cold, very wet

Lap chart

1st LAP ORDER	Laps 1 → 67
12 A. Senna	12 12 12 12 12 12 12 12 12 12 12 12 12 12 12 12 12 12 12 12 12 12 12 12 12 12 12 12 12 12 12 12 12 12 12 12 12 12 12 12 12 12 12 12 12 12 12 12 12 12 12 12 12 12 12 12 12 12 12 12 12 12 12 12 12 12 12
11 E. de Angelis	11 11 11 11 11 11 11 11 11 11 11 11 11 11 11 11 11 11 11 11 11 11 11 11 11 11 11 11 11 11 11 11 11 11 11 11 11 11 11 11 11 11 11 11 11 11 27 27 27 27 27 27 27 27 27 27 27 27 27 27 27 27 27 27 27 27 27
2 A. Prost	2 2 2 2 2 2 2 2 2 2 2 2 2 2 2 2 2 2 2 2 2 2 2 2 2 2 27 27 27 27 27 27 27 27 27 27 27 27 11 11 11 11 11 11 11 11 11 11 11 11 11 11 11 11 11 11 11 11 11 11 15 15 16 15 15 15 15
27 M. Alboreto	27 27 27 27 27 27 27 27 27 27 27 27 27 27 27 27 27 27 27 27 27 27 27 15 15 15 15 15 15 15 15 15 15 15 15 15 15 15 15 15 15 15 15 15 15 15 15 15 15 15 15 15 15 15 15 15 11 11 11 11 11 11 11 11 11 11 11
16 D. Warwick	16 16 1 1 1 1 1 1 1 1 1 1 1 1 15 15 15 15 15 15 15 15 15 15 15 15 15 15 1 1 1 1 1 1 1 1 1 1 1 1 5 5 5 5 5 5 5 5 5 5 5 5 5 5 5 5 5 5 5 5 5 5 5 5 5 5 5
1 N. Lauda	1 1 16 16 16 16 16 16 16 16 16 16 15 15 1 1 1 16 16 1 1 1 1 1 1 1 1 1 5 5 5 5 5 5 5 5 5 5 5 5 5 1 4 4 4 4 4 4 4 4 4 4 4 4 4 4 4 4 4 4 4 4 4 4 4 4 4
25 A. de Cesaris	25 25 25 15 15 15 15 15 15 15 16 16 16 16 16 1 1 16 5 5 5 5 5 5 5 5 23 23 4 4 4 4 4 4 4 4 4 4 1 1 1 16 16 16 16 16 16 16 16 16 16 16 16 16 16 16 16 16
15 P. Tambay	15 15 15 15 25 25 25 23 23 23 23 23 23 5 5 5 5 5 23 23 23 23 23 23 23 23 4 23 23 16 16 16 16 16 16 16 16 16 16 16 16 16 1 28 28 28 28 28 28 28 28 28 28 28 28 28
7 N. Piquet	7 7 28 7 7 18 18 18 25 5 5 5 5 5 23 23 23 23 23 4 4 4 4 4 4 16 16 16 16 23 28 28 28 28 28 28 28 28 28 28 28 28 24 24 24 24 24 24 24 24 24 24
28 S. Johansson	28 28 7 28 18 17 23 23 18 17 17 17 18 28 28 28 3 3 3 4 18 18 16 16 16 16 16 24 28 28 28 28 24 24 24 24 24 24 24 24 24 24 24 9
22 R. Patrese	22 22 22 29 17 23 17 17 17 18 28 18 28 18 18 18 18 4 4 18 16 16 18 18 18 24 24 28 24 24 24 24 9 9 9 9 9 9 9 9 9 9 9 9
18 T. Boutsen	18 18 18 18 23 7 7 5 5 28 18 28 3 3 3 4 4 18 18 24 24 24 24 24 24 28 28 9 9 9 9 9
9 M. Winkelhock	9 9 9 9 5 5 5 28 28 25 3 3 3 4 4 4 28 7 24 24 7 28 28 28 28 28 18 25 9
4 S. Bellof	4 4 4 4 26 26 26 7 3 3 4 7 7 7 6 25 24 7 7 25 25 25 25 25 25 25 25 9
17 G. Berger	17 17 17 17 24 24 28 3 7 4 7 7 25 25 6 25 7 28 25 25 28 7 7 7 7 9 9
10 P. Alliot	10 10 10 23 3 3 3 26 4 7 25 25 26 26 25 7 24 25 28 28 9 9 9 9 9 9 7 7
24 P. Ghinzani	24 24 23 24 21 28 4 4 26 26 26 26 6 6 26 24 9 9 9 9
26 J. Laffite	26 23 24 26 28 21 24 24 24 24 6 24 24 24 9 21 21 21
8 F. Hesnault	8 26 26 3 4 4 21 21 21 21 6 24 9 9 9 21
23 E. Cheever	23 8 8 5 29 29 29 29 6 6 9 9 21 21 21
21 M. Baldi	21 21 21 21 9 9 6 6 29 9 21 21
3 M. Brundle	3 3 3 29 6 6 9 9 9 29 29 29
5 N. Mansell	5 5 5 6
29 P. Martini	29 29 29
6 K. Rosberg	6 6 6
30 J. Palmer	30 30

Fastest laps

Driver	Time	Lap
Ayrton Senna	1m 44·121s	15
Michele Alboreto	1m 44·864s	5
Alain Prost	1m 44·901s	8
Elio de Angelis	1m 45·212s	13
Keke Rosberg	1m 45·717s	14
Derek Warwick	1m 45·985s	63
Patrick Tambay	1m 46·290s	52
Stefan Johansson	1m 46·297s	11
Niki Lauda	1m 46·633s	4
Nigel Mansell	1m 46·697s	62
Stefan Bellof	1m 47·861s	11
Eddie Cheever	1m 47·908s	14
Martin Brundle	1m 48·395s	14
Gerhard Berger	1m 48·561s	11
Thierry Boutsen	1m 49·518s	13
Andrea de Cesaris	1m 49·658s	3
Manfred Winkelhock	1m 50·480s	3
Jacques Laffite	1m 50·491s	5
Philippe Alliot	1m 50·643s	3
Nelson Piquet	1m 51·619s	5
Riccardo Patrese	1m 51·658s	3
Piercarlo Ghinzani	1m 51·747s	3
François Hesnault	1m 53·975s	3
Mauro Baldi	1m 54·588s	3
Pierluigi Martini	1m 56·040s	3
Jonathan Palmer	2m 55·894s	1

Points

WORLD CHAMPIONSHIP OF DRIVERS

	Driver	Points
1	Michele Alboreto	12 pts
2=	Alain Prost	9
2=	Ayrton Senna	9
4	Elio de Angelis	7
5	Patrick Tambay	6
6	René Arnoux	3
7	Nigel Mansell	2
8=	Jacques Laffite	1
8=	Stefan Bellof	1

CONSTRUCTORS' CUP

		Points
1	Lotus	16 pts
2	Ferrari	15
3	McLaren	9
4	Renault	6
5	Williams	2
6=	Ligier	1
6=	Tyrrell	1

Gran Premio di San Marino, 5 May/statistics

Entries and practice times

No.	Driver	Nat.	Car	Tyre	Engine	Entrant	Practice 1	Practice 2
1	Niki Lauda	A	Marlboro McLAREN MP4/2B	G	TAG P01 (TTE P01)	Marlboro McLaren International	1m 29·413s	**1m 28·399s**
2	Alain Prost	F	Marlboro McLAREN MP4/2B	G	TAG P01 (TTE P01)	Marlboro McLaren International	1m 28·604s	**1m 28·099s**
3	Martin Brundle	GB	TYRRELL 012	G	Ford-Cosworth DFY	Tyrrell Racing Organisation	**1m 36·397s**	1m 36·661s
4	Stefan Bellof	D	TYRRELL 012	G	Ford-Cosworth DFY	Tyrrell Racing Organisation	1m 35·774s	**1m 35·653s**
5	Nigel Mansell	GB	WILLIAMS FW10	G	Honda RA163–E	Canon Williams Honda Team	1m 29·756s	**1m 28·202s**
6	Keke Rosberg	SF	WILLIAMS FW10	G	Honda RA163–E	Canon Williams Honda Team	1m 28·347s	**1m 27·354s**
7	Nelson Piquet	BR	Olivetti BRABHAM BT54	P	BMW M12/13	Motor Racing Developments Ltd	1m 29·427s	**1m 28·489s**
8	François Hesnault	F	Olivetti BRABHAM BT54	P	BMW M12/13	Motor Racing Developments Ltd	**1m 33·142s**	1m 33·160s
9	Manfred Winkelhock	D	RAM 03	P	Hart 415T	Skoal Bandit Formula 1 Team	1m 34·936s	**1m 34·579s**
10	Philippe Alliot	F	RAM 03	P	Hart 415T	Skoal Bandit Formula 1 Team	**1m 34·201s**	2m 05·041s
11	Elio de Angelis	I	John Player Special LOTUS 97T	G	Renault EF4/EF15	John Player Special Team Lotus	1m 30·325s	**1m 27·852s**
12	Ayrton Senna	BR	John Player Special LOTUS 97T	G	Renault EF4	John Player Special Team Lotus	1m 27·589s	**1m 27·327s**
15	Patrick Tambay	F	Elf RENAULT RE60	G	Renault EF4/EF15	Equipe Renault Elf	**1m 29·102s**	1m 29·654s
16	Derek Warwick	GB	Elf RENAULT RE60	G	Renault EF4	Equipe Renault Elf	1m 30·440s	**1m 29·466s**
17	Gerhard Berger	A	ARROWS A8	G	BMW M12/13	Barclay Arrows BMW	**1m 28·697s**	1m 29·102s
18	Thierry Boutsen	B	ARROWS A8	G	BMW M12/13	Barclay Arrows BMW	1m 28·829s	**1m 27·918s**
19	Stefan Johansson	S	TOLEMAN TG185	–	Hart 415T	Toleman Group Motorsport	Entry withdrawn	
20	John Watson	GB	TOLEMAN TG185	–	Hart 415T	Toleman Group Motorsport	Entry withdrawn	
21	Mauro Baldi	I	SPIRIT 101D	P	Hart 415T	Spirit Enterprises Ltd	**1m 36·922s**	1m 38·235s
22	Riccardo Patrese	I	Benetton ALFA ROMEO 185T	G	Alfa Romeo 890T	Benetton Team Alfa Romeo	1m 31·388s	**1m 31·108s**
23	Eddie Cheever	USA	Benetton ALFA ROMEO 185T	G	Alfa Romeo 890T	Benetton Team Alfa Romeo	1m 30·605s	**1m 29·259s**
24	Piercarlo Ghinzani	I	Kelemata OSELLA FA1G	P	Alfa Romeo 890T	Osella Squadra Corse	1m 34·974s	**1m 34·209s**
25	Andrea de Cesaris	I	LIGIER JS25	G	Renault EF4	Equipe Ligier	1m 30·339s	**1m 29·406s**
26	Jacques Laffite	F	LIGIER JS25	P	Renault EF4	Equipe Ligier	1m 31·625s	**1m 30·982s**
27	Michele Alboreto	I	Fiat FERRARI 156/85	G	Ferrari 126C	Scuderia Ferrari SpA	**1m 27·871s**	1m 30·637s
28	Stefan Johansson	S	Fiat FERRARI 156/85	G	Ferrari 126C	Scuderia Ferrari SpA	1m 30·240s	**1m 29·806s**
29	Pierluigi Martini	I	Simod MINARDI M/85	P	Motori Moderni	Minardi Team	**1m 32·770s**	1m 48·391s
30	Jonathan Palmer	GB	West ZAKSPEED ZAK 841	G	Zakspeed	West Zakspeed Racing	2m 30·990s	**1m 31·028s**

Friday morning and Saturday morning practice sessions not officially recorded.

Fri p.m. Warm, dry
Sat p.m. Cool, dry

G – Goodyear, P – Pirelli.

Starting grid

12 SENNA (1m 27·327s) Lotus
6 ROSBERG (1m 27·354s) Williams

11 DE ANGELIS (1m 27·852s) Lotus
27 ALBORETO (1m 27·871s) Ferrari

18 BOUTSEN (1m 27·918s) Arrows
2 PROST (1m 28·099s) McLaren

5 MANSELL (1m 28·202s) Williams
1 LAUDA (1m 28·399s) McLaren

7 PIQUET (1m 28·489s) Brabham
17 BERGER (1m 28·697s) Arrows

15 TAMBAY (1m 29·102s) Renault
23 CHEEVER (1m 29·259s) Alfa Romeo

25 DE CESARIS (1m 29·406s) Ligier
16 WARWICK (1m 29·466s) Renault

28 JOHANSSON (1m 29·806s) Ferrari
26 LAFFITE (1m 30·982s) Ligier

*30 PALMER (1m 31·028s) Zakspeed
22 PATRESE (1m 31·108s) Alfa Romeo

29 MARTINI (1m 32·770s) Minardi
8 HESNAULT (1m 33·142s) Brabham

10 ALLIOT (1m 34·201s) RAM
24 GHINZANI (1m 34·209s) Osella

9 WINKELHOCK (1m 34·579s) RAM
4 BELLOF (1m 35·653s) Tyrrell

3 BRUNDLE (1m 36·397s) Tyrrell
21 BALDI (1m 36·922s) Spirit

Did not start:
*30 Palmer (Zakspeed), engine misfire on warm-up lap.

Results and retirements

Place	Driver	Car	Laps	Time and Speed (mph/km/h)/Retirement	
1	Elio de Angelis	Lotus-Renault t/c V6	60	1h 34m 35·955s	119·177/191·798
2	Thierry Boutsen	Arrows-BMW t/c 4	59		
3	Patrick Tambay	Renault t/c V6	59		
4	Niki Lauda	McLaren-TAG t/c V6	59		
5	Nigel Mansell	Williams-Honda t/c V6	58		
6	Stefan Johansson	Ferrari t/c V6	57	Out of fuel	
7	Ayrton Senna	Lotus-Renault t/c V6	57	Out of fuel	
8	Nelson Piquet	Brabham-BMW t/c 4	57		
9	Martin Brundle	Tyrrell-Cosworth V8	56		
10	Derek Warwick	Renault t/c V6	56		
	Eddie Cheever	Alfa Romeo t/c V8	50	Out of fuel	
	Piercarlo Ghinzani	Osella-Alfa Romeo t/c V8	46	Running, not classified	
	Michele Alboreto	Ferrari t/c V6	29	Electrics	
	Manfred Winkelhock	RAM-Hart t/c 4	27	Engine	
	Philippe Alliot	RAM-Hart t/c 4	24	Engine	
	Keke Rosberg	Williams-Honda t/c V6	23	Throttle linkage/brakes	
	Jacques Laffite	Ligier-Renault t/c V6	22	Turbo	
	Pierluigi Martini	Minardi-Moderni t/c V6	14	Turbo	
	Andrea de Cesaris	Ligier-Renault t/c V6	11	Spun off	
	Mauro Baldi	Spirit-Hart t/c 4	9	Electrics	
	François Hesnault	Brabham-BMW t/c 4	5	Engine	
	Stefan Bellof	Tyrrell-Cosworth V8	5	Engine	
	Gerhard Berger	Arrows-BMW t/c 4	4	Electrics/engine	
	Riccardo Patrese	Alfa Romeo t/c V8	4	Engine	

Fastest lap: Alboreto, on lap 29, 1m 30·961s, 123·945 mph/199·47 km/h (record).
Previous lap record: Nelson Piquet (F1 Brabham BT53-BMW t/c 4), 1m 33·275s, 120·869 mph/194·521 km/h (1984).
Note: Alain Prost (McLaren-TAG t/c V6), 1h 33m 57·118s; disqualified after finishing first (car found to be below minimum weight limit at post-race scrutineering).

Past winners

Year	Driver	Nat.	Car	Circuit	Distance miles/km	Speed mph/km/h
1981	Nelson Piquet	BR	3·0 Brabham BT49C-Ford	Imola	187·90/302·40	101·20/162·87
1982	Didier Pironi	F	1·5 Ferrari 126C2 t/c V6	Imola	187·90/302·40	116·63/187·70
1983	Patrick Tambay	F	1·5 Ferrari 126C2/B t/c V6	Imola	187·90/302·40	115·25/185·48
1984	Alain Prost	F	1·5 McLaren MP4/2-TAG t/c	Imola	187·90/302·40	116·35/187·25
1985	Elio de Angelis	I	1·5 Lotus 97T-Renault t/c V6	Imola	187·90/302·40	119·17/191·79

234

Lap chart

1st LAP ORDER	1 2 3 4 5 6 7 8 9 10 11 12 13 14 15 16 17 18 19 20 21 22 23 24 25 26 27 28 29 30 31 32 33 34 35 36 37 38 39 40 41 42 43 44 45 46 47 48 49 50 51 52 53 54 55 56 57 58 59 60
12 A. Senna	12 12 12 12 12 12 12 12 12 12 12 12 12 12 12 12 12 12 12 12 12 12 12 12 12 12 12 12 12 12 12 12 12 12 12 12 12 12 12 12 12 12 12 12 12 12 12 12 12 12 12 12 12 12 12 12 28 2 2 2
11 E. de Angelis	11 11 11 11 11 11 11 11 11 11 27 27 27 27 27 27 27 27 27 27 ? ? ? ? ? ? ? ? ? ? ? ? ? ? ? 2 2 2 2 2 2 2 2 2 2 2 2 2 2 2 2 2 2 2 28 28 28 2 11 11 11
27 M. Alboreto	27 27 27 27 27 27 27 27 27 11 2 2 2 2 2 2 2 2 2 2 27 1 1 1 1 1 1 1 1 1 1 1 1 1 1 11 11 11 11 11 11 11 11 11 11 11 11 11 11 11 11 11 28 28 28 28 2 2 2 12 18 18
2 A. Prost	2 2 2 2 2 2 2 2 2 2 11 11 11 11 11 1 1 1 1 1 1 1 11 11 11 11 11 11 11 11 11 11 11 1 1 28 28 28 28 28 28 28 28 28 28 28 11 11 11 11 11 11 11 11 11 11 11 11 15 15
6 K. Rosberg	6 6 6 6 6 1 1 1 1 1 1 1 1 1 1 11 11 11 11 11 11 11 28 28 28 28 28 28 28 28 28 28 28 28 1 1 1 1 1 1 1 1 1 1 1 1 1 7 7 7 7 7 7 7 1 1
5 N. Mansell	5 5 5 5 1 6 / / / / / 6 6 6 6 6 28 28 28 28 27 7 7 7 7 7 7 7 7 7 7 7 7 7 7 7 7 7 10 10 10 10 10 7 7 7 1 18 18 18 18 18 5 6
1 N. Lauda	1 1 7 1 7 7 0 0 0 0 0 5 20 20 20 20 20 0 0 0 0 0 0 7 5 5 5 5 5 5 5 5 5 5 5 5 19 18 18 18 7 7 7 7 7 18 18 18 18 1 1 1 1 1
23 E. Cheever	23 7 1 7 5 5 5 5 5 5 5 23 28 5 5 5 5 5 5 5 5 5 5 5 18 18 18 18 18 18 18 18 18 18 18 18 18 23 5 5 5 5 5 5 5 5 5 5 5 5 5 15 15 15 15 15
18 T. Boutsen	18 18 18 23 23 23 23 23 23 23 28 18 18 18 18 18 18 18 18 18 7 18 23 23 23 23 23 23 23 23 23 23 23 23 5 23 23 23 23 23 23 23 23 23 23 15 15 15 15 15 5 5 5 5 5
7 N. Piquet	7 23 23 18 18 18 18 18 18 28 18 23 23 23 23 23 23 23 7 18 23 15 15 15 15 15 15 15 15 15 15 15 15 15 15 15 15 15 15 15 15 15 15 15 15 15 15 23 23 3 3 3 3 3 3
25 A. de Cesaris	25 25 25 25 25 25 25 28 28 18 15 15 15 15 15 15 7 7 7 23 16 16 16 16 16 16 16 16 16 16 16 16 16 16 16 3 3 3 3 3 3 3 3 3 16 16 16 16 16 16
17 G. Berger	17 22 22 28 28 28 28 28 25 25 15 26 26 26 26 26 7 15 15 15 16 9 9 9 3 3 3 3 3 3 3 3 3 3 3 3 3 16 16 16 16 16 16 16 16
22 R. Patrese	22 17 17 17 15 15 15 15 15 26 7 7 7 7 7 26 26 26 26 16 9 3 3 27 27 24 24 24 24 24 24 24 24 24 24 24 24 24 24
28 S. Johansson	28 28 28 22 26 26 26 26 26 25 16 16 16 16 16 16 16 16 16 9 3 27 27 27 24 24
15 P. Tambay	15 15 15 15 16 16 16 16 16 16 9 9 9 9 9 9 9 9 9 9 9 3 10 24 24 24
16 D. Warwick	16 16 16 26 10 10 10 10 10 9 9 24 3 3 3 3 3 3 3 3 10 24
26 J. Laffite	26 26 26 16 24 24 9 9 9 24 24 3 29 29 10 10 10 10 10 10 10 24
4 S. Bellof	4 4 4 10 9 9 24 24 24 3 3 29 10 24 24 24 24 24 24 24
3 M. Brundle	3 3 10 24 3 3 3 3 3 29 10 24 24
10 P. Alliot	10 10 3 3 8 29 29 29 29 10 10
24 P. Ghinzani	24 24 24 9 29 21 21 21 21
9 M. Winkelhock	9 9 9 8 21
29 P. Martini	29 29 8 29 4
8 F. Hesnault	8 8 29 21
21 M. Baldi	21 21 21

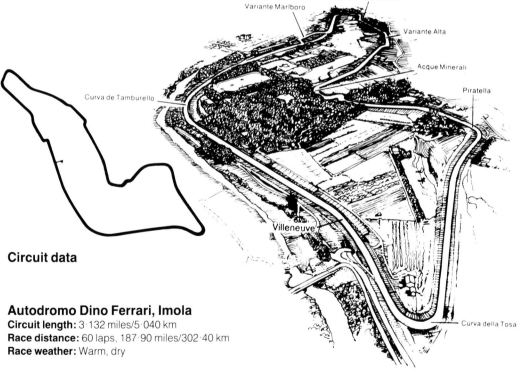

Circuit data

Autodromo Dino Ferrari, Imola

Circuit length: 3.132 miles/5.040 km
Race distance: 60 laps, 187.90 miles/302.40 km
Race weather: Warm, dry

Fastest laps

Driver	Time	Lap
Michele Alboreto	1m 30.961s	29
Stefan Johansson	1m 31.017s	56
Elio de Angelis	1m 31.411s	55
Nelson Piquet	1m 31.424s	50
Ayrton Senna	1m 31.549s	37
Alain Prost	1m 31.925s	26
Niki Lauda	1m 32.198s	25
Thierry Boutsen	1m 33.448s	47
Patrick Tambay	1m 33.514s	55
Derek Warwick	1m 33.702s	45
Nigel Mansell	1m 33.891s	33
Keke Rosberg	1m 34.084s	20
Eddie Cheever	1m 34.128s	34
Philippe Alliot	1m 35.013s	20
Jacques Laffite	1m 35.245s	20
Andrea de Cesaris	1m 35.856s	8
Gerhard Berger	1m 36.239s	3
Riccardo Patrese	1m 36.422s	3
Manfred Winkelhock	1m 36.708s	8
Piercarlo Ghinzani	1m 36.858s	26
Martin Brundle	1m 37.887s	51
Pierluigi Martini	1m 38.203s	14
Stefan Bellof	1m 38.437s	3
François Hesnault	1m 38.906s	3
Mauro Baldi	1m 39.686s	4

Points

WORLD CHAMPIONSHIP OF DRIVERS

1	Elio de Angelis	16 pts
2	Michele Alboreto	12
3	Patrick Tambay	10
4=	Alain Prost	9
4=	Ayrton Senna	9
6	Thierry Boutsen	6
7	Nigel Mansell	4
8=	René Arnoux	3
8=	Niki Lauda	3
10=	Jacques Laffite	1
10=	Stefan Bellof	1
10=	Stefan Johansson	1

CONSTRUCTORS' CUP

1	Lotus	25 pts
2	Ferrari	16
3	McLaren	12
4	Renault	10
5	Arrows	6
6	Williams	4

Entries and practice times

No.	Driver	Nat.	Car	Tyre	Engine	Entrant	Practice 1	Practice 2
1	Niki Lauda	A	Marlboro McLAREN MP4/2B	G	TAG P01 (TTE P01)	Marlboro McLaren International	1m 22·897s	**1m 21·907s**
2	Alain Prost	F	Marlboro McLAREN MP4/2B	G	TAG P01 (TTE P01)	Marlboro McLaren International	1m 22·270s	**1m 20·885s**
3	Martin Brundle	GB	TYRRELL 012	G	Ford-Cosworth DFY	Tyrrell Racing Organisation	1m 26·499s	**1m 23·827s**
4	Stefan Bellof	D	TYRRELL 012	G	Ford-Cosworth DFY	Tyrrell Racing Organisation	1m 26·214s	**1m 24·236s**
5	Nigel Mansell	GB	WILLIAMS FW10	G	Honda RA163–E	Canon Williams Honda Team	1m 22·650s	**1m 20·536s**
6	Keke Rosberg	SF	WILLIAMS FW10	G	Honda RA163–E	Canon Williams Honda Team	1m 23·099s	**1m 21·320s**
7	Nelson Piquet	BR	Olivetti BRABHAM BT54	P	BMW M12/13	Motor Racing Developments Ltd	1m 23·548s	**1m 21·817s**
8	François Hesnault	F	Olivetti BRABHAM BT54	P	BMW M12/13	Motor Racing Developments Ltd	1m 27·505s	**1m 25·068s**
9	Manfred Winkelhock	D	RAM 03	P	Hart 415T	Skoal Bandit Formula 1 Team	1m 26·182s	**1m 24·764s**
10	Philippe Alliot	F	RAM 03	P	Hart 415T	Skoal Bandit Formula 1 Team	1m 28·026s	**1m 24·763s**
11	Elio de Angelis	I	John Player Special LOTUS 97T	G	Renault EF4	John Player Special Team Lotus	1m 23·319s	**1m 21·465s**
12	Ayrton Senna	BR	John Player Special LOTUS 97T	G	Renault EF4/EF15	John Player Special Team Lotus	1m 21·630s	**1m 20·450s**
15	Patrick Tambay	F	Elf RENAULT RE60	G	Renault EF4/EF15	Equipe Renault Elf	1m 24·473s	**1m 22·912s**
16	Derek Warwick	GB	Elf RENAULT RE60	G	Renault EF4	Equipe Renault Elf	1m 23·524s	**1m 21·531s**
17	Gerhard Berger	A	ARROWS A8	G	BMW M12/13	Barclay Arrows BMW	1m 24·293s	**1m 21·665s**
18	Thierry Boutsen	B	ARROWS A8	G	BMW M12/13	Barclay Arrows BMW	1m 24·510s	**1m 21·302s**
19	Teo Fabi	I	TOLEMAN TG185	P	Hart 415T	Toleman Group Motorsport	1m 26·243s	**1m 23·965s**
21	Mauro Baldi	I	SPIRIT 101D	P	Hart 415T	Spirit Enterprises Ltd	Entry withdrawn	
22	Riccardo Patrese	I	Benetton ALFA ROMEO 185T	G	Alfa Romeo 890T	Benetton Team Alfa Romeo	1m 22·145s	**1m 21·813s**
23	Eddie Cheever	USA	Benetton ALFA ROMEO 185T	G	Alfa Romeo 890T	Benetton Team Alfa Romeo	1m 22·755s	**1m 20·729s**
24	Piercarlo Ghinzani	I	Kelemata OSELLA FA1G	P	Alfa Romeo 890T	Osella Squadra Corse	1m 26·230s	**1m 24·071s**
25	Andrea de Cesaris	I	LIGIER JS25	P	Renault EF4/EF15	Equipe Ligier	1m 22·992s	**1m 21·347s**
26	Jacques Laffite	F	LIGIER JS25	P	Renault EF4	Equipe Ligier	1m 26·681s	**1m 22·880s**
27	Michele Alboreto	I	Fiat FERRARI 156/85	G	Ferrari 126C	Scuderia Ferrari SpA	1m 22·630s	**1m 20·563s**
28	Stefan Johansson	S	Fiat FERRARI 156/85	G	Ferrari 126C	Scuderia Ferrari SpA	1m 23·163s	**1m 22·635s**
29	Pierluigi Martini	I	Simod MINARDI M/85	P	Motori Moderni	Minardi Team	6m 41·037s	—
30	Jonathan Palmer	GB	West ZAKSPEED ZAK 841	G	Zakspeed	West Zakspeed Racing	1m 41·564s	**1m 23·840s**

Thursday morning and Saturday morning practice sessions not officially recorded.

G – Goodyear, P – Pirelli.

Thu p.m.	Sat p.m.
Hot, dry	Hot, dry

Starting grid

		12 SENNA (1m 20·450s) Lotus
5 MANSELL (1m 20·536s) Williams		
		27 ALBORETO (1m 20·563s) Ferrari
23 CHEEVER (1m 20·729s) Alfa Romeo		
		2 PROST (1m 20·885s) McLaren
18 BOUTSEN (1m 21·302s) Arrows		
		6 ROSBERG (1m 21·320s) Williams
25 DE CESARIS (1m 21·347s) Ligier		
		11 DE ANGELIS (1m 21·465s) Lotus
16 WARWICK (1m 21·531s) Renault		
		17 BERGER (1m 21·665s) Arrows
22 PATRESE (1m 21·813s) Alfa Romeo		
		7 PIQUET (1m 21·817s) Brabham
1 LAUDA (1m 21·907s) McLaren		
		28 JOHANSSON (1m 22·635s) Ferrari
26 LAFFITE (1m 22·880s) Ligier		
		15 TAMBAY (1m 22·912s) Renault
3 BRUNDLE (1m 23·827s) Tyrrell		
		30 PALMER (1m 23·840s) Zakspeed
19 FABI (1m 23·965s) Toleman		

Did not start:
24 Ghinzani (Osella), 1m 24·071s, did not qualify
4 Bellof (Tyrrell), 1m 24·236s, did not qualify
10 Alliot (RAM), 1m 24·763s, did not qualify
9 Winkelhock (RAM), 1m 24·764s, did not qualify
8 Hesnault (Brabham), 1m 25·068s, did not qualify
29 Martini (Minardi), no time recorded – knee injury during practice.

Results and retirements

Place	Driver	Car	Laps	Time and Speed (mph/km/h)/Retirement	
1	Alain Prost	McLaren-TAG t/c V6	78	1h 51m 58·034s	86·018/138·434
2	Michele Alboreto	Ferrari t/c V6	78	1h 52m 05·575s	85·935/138·3
3	Elio de Angelis	Lotus-Renault t/c V6	78	1h 53m 25·205s	84·941/136·7
4	Andrea de Cesaris	Ligier-Renault t/c V6	77		
5	Derek Warwick	Renault t/c V6	77		
6	Jacques Laffite	Ligier-Renault t/c V6	77		
7	Nigel Mansell	Williams-Honda t/c V6	77		
8	Keke Rosberg	Williams-Honda t/c V6	76		
9	Thierry Boutsen	Arrows-BMW t/c 4	76		
10	Martin Brundle	Tyrrell-Cosworth V8	74		
11	Jonathan Palmer	Zakspeed t/c 4	74		
	Niki Lauda	McLaren-TAG t/c V6	17	Spun off, could not restart	
	Riccardo Patrese	Alfa Romeo t/c V8	16	Accident with Piquet	
	Nelson Piquet	Brabham-BMW t/c 4	16	Accident with Patrese	
	Teo Fabi	Toleman-Hart t/c 4	16	Turbo	
	Ayrton Senna	Lotus-Renault t/c V6	13	Engine	
	Eddie Cheever	Alfa Romeo t/c V8	10	Alternator	
	Stefan Johansson	Ferrari t/c V6	1	Accident damage	
	Patrick Tambay	Renault t/c V6	0	Accident damage	
	Gerhard Berger	Arrows-BMW t/c 4	0	Accident damage	

Fastest lap: Alboreto, on lap 60, 1m 22·637s, 89·654 mph/144·284 km/h (record).
Previous lap record: Riccardo Patrese (F1 Arrows A3-Cosworth DFV), 1m 26·058s, 86·089 mph/138·548 km/h (1980).
*See page 123, Autocourse 1980/81.

Past winners

Year	Driver	Nat.	Car	Circuit	Distance miles/km	Speed mph/km/h
1950	Juan Manuel Fangio	RA	1·5 Alfa Romeo 158 s/c	Monte Carlo	197·60/318·01	61·33/98·70
1952*	Vittorio Marzotto	I	2·7 Ferrari 225MM	Monte Carlo	195·42/314·50	58·20/93·66
1955	Maurice Trintignant	F	2·5 Ferrari 625	Monte Carlo	195·42/314·50	65·81/105·91
1956	Stirling Moss	GB	2·5 Maserati 250F	Monte Carlo	195·42/314·50	64·94/104·51
1957	Juan Manuel Fangio	RA	2·5 Maserati 250F	Monte Carlo	205·19/330·22	64·72/104·16
1958	Maurice Trintignant	F	2·0 Cooper T45-Climax	Monte Carlo	195·42/314·50	67·99/109·41
1959	Jack Brabham	AUS	2·5 Cooper T51-Climax	Monte Carlo	195·42/314·50	66·71/107·36
1960	Stirling Moss	GB	2·5 Lotus 18-Climax	Monte Carlo	195·42/314·50	67·48/108·60
1961	Stirling Moss	GB	1·5 Lotus 18-Climax	Monte Carlo	195·42/314·50	70·70/113·79
1962	Bruce McLaren	NZ	1·5 Cooper T60-Climax	Monte Carlo	195·42/314·50	70·46/113·40
1963	Graham Hill	GB	1·5 BRM P57	Monte Carlo	195·42/314·50	72·43/116·56
1964	Graham Hill	GB	1·5 BRM P261	Monte Carlo	195·42/314·50	72·64/116·91
1965	Graham Hill	GB	1·5 BRM P261	Monte Carlo	195·42/314·50	74·34/119·64
1966	Jackie Stewart	GB	1·9 BRM P261	Monte Carlo	195·42/314·50	76·51/123·14
1967	Denny Hulme	NZ	3·0 Brabham BT20-Repco	Monte Carlo	195·42/314·50	75·90/122·14
1968	Graham Hill	GB	3·0 Lotus 49B-Ford	Monte Carlo	156·34/251·60	77·82/125·24
1969	Graham Hill	GB	3·0 Lotus 49B-Ford	Monte Carlo	156·34/251·60	80·18/129·04
1970	Jochen Rindt	A	3·0 Lotus 49C-Ford	Monte Carlo	156·34/251·60	81·85/131·70
1971	Jackie Stewart	GB	3·0 Tyrrell 003-Ford	Monte Carlo	156·34/251·60	83·49/134·36
1972	Jean-Pierre Beltoise	F	3·0 BRM P160B	Monte Carlo	156·34/251·60	63·85/102·75
1973	Jackie Stewart	GB	3·0 Tyrrell 006-Ford	Monte Carlo	158·87/255·68	80·96/130·29
1974	Ronnie Peterson	S	3·0 JPS/Lotus 72-Ford	Monte Carlo	158·87/255·68	80·74/129·94
1975	Niki Lauda	A	3·0 Ferrari 312T/75	Monte Carlo	152·76/245·84	75·53/121·55
1976	Niki Lauda	A	3·0 Ferrari 312T-2/76	Monte Carlo	160·52/258·34	80·36/129·32
1977	Jody Scheckter	ZA	3·0 Wolf WR1-Ford	Monte Carlo	156·41/251·71	79·61/128·12
1978	Patrick Depailler	F	3·0 Tyrrell 008-Ford	Monte Carlo	154·35/248·40	80·36/129·33
1979	Jody Scheckter	ZA	3·0 Ferrari 312T-4	Monte Carlo	156·41/251·71	81·34/130·90
1980	Carlos Reutemann	RA	3·0 Williams FW07B-Ford	Monte Carlo	156·41/251·71	81·20/130·68
1981	Gilles Villeneuve	CDN	1·5 Ferrari 126CK	Monte Carlo	156·41/251·71	82·04/132·03
1982	Riccardo Patrese	I	3·0 Brabham BT49D-Ford	Monte Carlo	156·41/251·71	82·21/132·30
1983	Keke Rosberg	SF	3·0 Williams FW08C-Ford	Monte Carlo	156·41/251·71	80·52/129·59
1984	Alain Prost	F	1·5 McLaren MP4/2-TAG t/c	Monte Carlo	63·80/102·67	62·62/100·77
1985	Alain Prost	F	1·5 McLaren MP4/2B-TAG t/c	Monte Carlo	160·52/258·34	86·02/138·30

*Non-championship (sports cars)

Lap chart

1st LAP ORDER	1	2	3	4	5	6	7	8	9	10	11	12	13	14	15	16	17	18	19	20	21	22	23	24	25	26	27	28	29	30	31	32	33	34	35	36	37	38	39	40	41	42	43	44	45	46	47	48	49	50	51	52	53	54	55	56	57	58	59	60	61	62	63	64	65	66	67	68	69	70	71	72	73	74	75	76	77	78
12 A. Senna	12	12	12	12	12	12	12	12	12	12	12	12	12	12	27	27	27	2	2	2	2	2	27	27	27	27	27	2	2	2	2	2	2	2	2	2	2	2	2	2	2	2	2	2	2	2	2	2	2	2	2	2	2	2	2	2	2	2	2	2	2	2	2	2	2	2	2	2	2	2	2	2	2	2	2	2	2	2
5 N. Mansell	5	27	27	27	27	27	27	27	27	27	27	2	2	2	2	2	2	27	27	27	27	2	2	2	2	2	2	11	11	11	11	11	11	11	11	11	11	11	11	11	11	11	11	11	11	11	11	11	11	11	11	11	11	11	11	11	11	11	11	11	11	11	11	11	11	27	27	27	27	27	27	27	27	27	27	27	27	27
27 M. Alboreto	27	5	2	2	2	2	2	2	2	2	2	11	11	11	11	11	11	11	11	11	11	11	11	11	11	11	11	27	25	25	25	25	25	27	27	27	27	27	27	27	27	27	27	27	27	27	27	27	27	27	27	27	27	27	27	27	27	11	11	11	11	11	11	11	11	11	11	11	11	11	11	11	11	11	11	11	11	11
2 A. Prost	2	2	23	23	23	23	11	11	11	11	11	11	11	12	6	6	6	6	6	6	6	6	6	6	6	6	25	25	27	27	27	27	27	25	25	25	25	25	25	25	25	25	25	25	25	25	25	25	25	25	25	25	25	25	25	25	25	25	25	25	25	25	25	25	25	25	25	25	25	25	25	25	25	25	25	25	25	25
23 E. Cheever	23	23	5	5	11	11	23	6	6	6	6	6	6	5	5	25	25	25	25	25	25	25	25	25	25	25	16	16	16	16	16	16	16	16	16	16	16	16	16	16	16	16	16	16	16	16	16	16	16	16	16	16	16	16	16	16	16	16	16	16	16	16	16	16	16	16	16	16	16	16	16	16	16	16	16	16	16	16
11 E. de Angelis	11	11	11	11	6	6	6	5	5	5	5	5	5	25	25	16	16	16	16	16	16	16	16	16	16	16	6	6	6	6	6	6	6	6	6	6	6	6	6	6	6	6	6	6	6	6	6	6	5	5	5	5	5	5	5	5	5	5	5	5	5	5	5	5	5	5	5	5	5	5	5	5	5	5	5	5	26	26
18 T. Boutsen	18	18	18	6	5	5	5	18	18	18	18	25	16	16	16	5	6	5	5	5	5	5	5	5	5	5	5	5	5	5	5	5	5	5	5	5	5	5	5	5	5	5	5	5	5	5	5	6	6	6	26	26	26	26	26	26	26	26	26	26	26	26	26	26	26	26	26	26	26	26	26	26	26	26	26	26	5	5
6 K. Rosberg	6	6	6	18	18	18	18	25	25	25	25	16	16	1	1	1	1	1	3	3	3	3	3	3	3	26	26	26	26	26	26	26	26	26	26	26	26	26	26	26	26	26	26	26	26	26	26	26	26	26	26	6	6	6	6	6	6	6	6	6	6	6	6	6	6	6	6	6	6	6	6	6	6	6	6	6	6	6
25 A. de Cesaris	25	25	25	25	25	25	25	16	16	16	16	16	1	1	22	22	3	30	26	26	26	26	26	26	26	30	30	30	30	30	30	30	30	30	30	30	30	30	30	30	30	30	30	30	30	30	30	30	30	30	30	18	18	18	18	18	18	18	18	18	18	18	18	18	18	18	18	18	18	18	18	18	18	18	18	18	18	18
16 D. Warwick	16	16	16	16	16	16	16	22	22	22	1	1	22	7	7	19	26	30	30	30	30	30	30	30	18	18	18	18	18	18	18	18	18	18	18	18	18	18	18	18	18	18	18	18	18	18	18	30	30	30	30	30	30	30	30	30	30	30	30	30	30	30	30	30	30	30	30	30	30	30	30	30	30	30	30	30		
22 R. Patrese	22	22	22	22	22	22	22	1	1	1	22	22	7	7	26	26	30	18	18	18	18	18	18	18	3	3	3	3	3	3	3	3	3	3	3	3	3	3	3	3	3	3	3	3	3	3	3	3	3	3	3	3	3	3	3	3	3	3	3	3	3	3	3	3	3	3	3	3	3	3	3	3	3	3	3	3	3	3
1 N. Lauda	1	1	1	1	1	1	1	7	7	7	7	7	26	26	19	19	26																																																											
7 N. Piquet	7	7	7	7	7	7	7	26	26	26	26	26	19	19	3	3	18																																																									
26 J. Laffite	26	26	26	26	26	26	26	19	19	19	19	19	3	3	30	30																																																									
3 M. Brundle	3	3	3	3	19	19	19	3	3	3	3	30	30	18	18																																																									
19 T. Fabi	19	19	19	19	3	3	3	30	30	30	30	30	18	18																																																									
30 J. Palmer	30	30	30	30	30	30	30	23	23	23	23	23																																																										
28 S. Johansson	28	28																																																																								

Fastest laps

Driver	Time	Lap
Michele Alboreto	1m 22·637s	60
Alain Prost	1m 23·898s	66
Elio de Angelis	1m 24·434s	47
Andrea de Cesaris	1m 24·554s	58
Keke Rosberg	1m 24·617s	62
Nigel Mansell	1m 24·673s	59
Jacques Laffite	1m 24·788s	51
Ayrton Senna	1m 24·803s	7
Derek Warwick	1m 25·305s	42
Thierry Boutsen	1m 25·631s	43
Niki Lauda	1m 25·842s	16
Martin Brundle	1m 26·131s	57
Eddie Cheever	1m 26·548s	10
Jonathan Palmer	1m 26·653s	57
Teo Fabi	1m 26·717s	9
Nelson Piquet	1m 27·124s	5
Riccardo Patrese	1m 27·723s	6
Stefan Johansson	2m 31·095s	1

Points

WORLD CHAMPIONSHIP OF DRIVERS

1	Elio de Angelis	20 pts
2=	Michele Alboreto	18
2=	Alain Prost	18
4	Patrick Tambay	10
5	Ayrton Senna	9
6	Thierry Boutsen	6
7	Nigel Mansell	4
8=	René Arnoux	3
8=	Niki Lauda	3
8=	Andrea de Cesaris	3
11=	Derek Warwick	2
11=	Jacques Laffite	2
13=	Stefan Bellof	1
13=	Stefan Johansson	1

CONSTRUCTORS' CUP

1	Lotus	29 pts
2	Ferrari	22
3	McLaren	21
4	Renault	12
5	Arrows	6
6	Ligier	5
7	Williams	4
8	Tyrrell	1

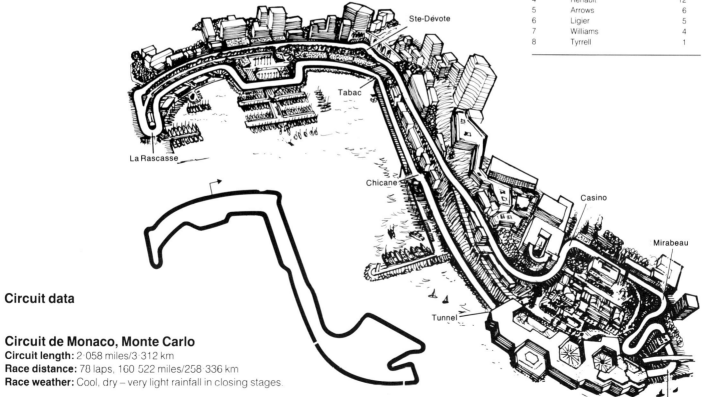

Circuit data

Circuit de Monaco, Monte Carlo

Circuit length: 2·058 miles/3·312 km
Race distance: 78 laps, 160·522 miles/258·336 km
Race weather: Cool, dry – very light rainfall in closing stages.

Entries and practice times

No.	Driver	Nat.	Car	Tyre	Engine	Entrant	Practice 1	Practice 2
1	Niki Lauda	A	Marlboro McLAREN MP4/2B	G	TAG P01 (TTE P01)	Marlboro McLaren International	**1m 28·126s**	1m 28·130s
2	Alain Prost	F	Marlboro McLAREN MP4/2B	G	TAG P01 (TTE P01)	Marlboro McLaren International	1m 25·997s	**1m 25·557s**
3	Martin Brundle	GB	TYRRELL 012	G	Ford-Cosworth DFY	Tyrrell Racing Organisation	1m 32·760s	**1m 31·923s**
4	Stefan Bellof	D	TYRRELL 012	G	Ford-Cosworth DFY	Tyrrell Racing Organisation	1m 32·586s	**1m 31·733s**
5	Nigel Mansell	GB	WILLIAMS FW10	G	Honda RA163–E	Canon Williams Honda Team	1m 28·367s	**1m 27·728s**
6	Keke Rosberg	SF	WILLIAMS FW10	G	Honda RA163–E	Canon Williams Honda Team	1m 26·255s	**1m 26·097s**
7	Nelson Piquet	BR	Olivetti BRABHAM BT54	P	BMW M12/13	Motor Racing Developments Ltd	1m 27·004s	**1m 26·301s**
8	Marc Surer	CH	Olivetti BRABHAM BT54	P	BMW M12/13	Motor Racing Developments Ltd	1m 30·206s	**1m 29·473s**
9	Manfred Winkelhock	D	RAM 03	P	Hart 415T	Skoal Bandit Formula 1 Team	1m 31·147s	**1m 27·266s**
10	Philippe Alliot	F	RAM 03	P	Hart 415T	Skoal Bandit Formula 1 Team	**1m 29·501s**	1m 36·960s
11	Elio de Angelis	I	John Player Special LOTUS 97T	G	Renault EF4/EF15	John Player Special Team Lotus	1m 26·895s	**1m 24·567s**
12	Ayrton Senna	BR	John Player Special LOTUS 97T	G	Renault EF4/EF15	John Player Special Team Lotus	1m 25·399s	**1m 24·816s**
15	Patrick Tambay	F	Elf RENAULT RE60	G	Renault EF4/EF15	Equipe Renault Elf	1m 26·959s	**1m 26·340s**
16	Derek Warwick	GB	Elf RENAULT RE60	G	Renault EF4/EF15	Equipe Renault Elf	1m 26·801s	**1m 25·622s**
17	Gerhard Berger	A	ARROWS A8	G	BMW M12/13	Barclay Arrows BMW	1m 30·826s	**1m 26·743s**
18	Thierry Boutsen	B	ARROWS A8	G	BMW M12/13	Barclay Arrows BMW	1m 28·241s	**1m 25·846s**
19	Teo Fabi	I	TOLEMAN TG185	P	Hart 415T	Toleman Group Motorsport	1m 29·910s	**1m 28·625s**
22	Riccardo Patrese	I	Benetton ALFA ROMEO 185T	G	Alfa Romeo 890T	Benetton Team Alfa Romeo	1m 27·638s	**1m 26·995s**
23	Eddie Cheever	USA	Benetton ALFA ROMEO 185T	G	Alfa Romeo 890T	Benetton Team Alfa Romeo	1m 27·638s	**1m 26·354s**
24	Piercarlo Ghinzani	I	Kelemata OSELLA FA1G	P	Alfa Romeo 890T	Osella Squadra Corse	1m 32·299s	**1m 31·576s**
25	Andrea de Cesaris	I	Gitanes LIGIER JS25	P	Renault EF4/EF15	Equipe Ligier Gitanes	1m 28·746s	**1m 27·403s**
26	Jacques Laffite	F	Gitanes LIGIER JS25	P	Renault EF4	Equipe Ligier Gitanes	1m 29·730s	**1m 28·750s**
27	Michele Alboreto	I	Fiat FERRARI 156/85	G	Ferrari 126C	Scuderia Ferrari SpA	**1m 25·127s**	1m 25·832s
28	Stefan Johansson	S	Fiat FERRARI 156/85	G	Ferrari 126C	Scuderia Ferrari SpA	1m 27·870s	**1m 25·170s**
29	Pierluigi Martini	I	Simod MINARDI M/85	P	Motori Moderni	Minardi Team	**1m 34·985s**	1m 47·148s

Friday morning and Saturday morning practice sessions not officially recorded.

G – Goodyear, P – Pirelli.

Fri p.m. — Warm, dry
Sat p.m. — Hot, dry

Starting grid

11 DE ANGELIS (1m 24·567s) Lotus

12 SENNA (1m 24·816s) Lotus

27 ALBORETO (1m 25·127s) Ferrari

28 JOHANSSON (1m 25·170s) Ferrari

2 PROST (1m 25·557s) McLaren

16 WARWICK (1m 25·622s) Renault

18 BOUTSEN (1m 25·846s) Arrows

6 ROSBERG (1m 26·097s) Williams

7 PIQUET (1m 26·301s) Brabham

15 TAMBAY (1m 26·340s) Renault

23 CHEEVER (1m 26·354s) Alfa Romeo

17 BERGER (1m 26·743s) Arrows

22 PATRESE (1m 26·995s) Alfa Romeo

9 WINKELHOCK (1m 27·266s) RAM

25 DE CESARIS (1m 27·403s) Ligier

5 MANSELL (1m 27·728s) Williams

1 LAUDA (1m 28·126s) McLaren

*19 FABI (1m 28·625s) Toleman

26 LAFFITE (1m 28·750s) Ligier

8 SURER (1m 29·473s) Brabham

10 ALLIOT (1m 29·501s) RAM

24 GHINZANI (1m 31·576s) Osella

4 BELLOF (1m 31·733s) Tyrrell

3 BRUNDLE (1m 31·923s) Tyrrell

29 MARTINI (1m 34·985s) Minardi

* Started from pit lane.

Results and retirements

Place	Driver	Car	Laps	Time and Speed (mph/km/h)/Retirement	
1	Michele Alboreto	Ferrari t/c V6	70	1h 46m 01·813s	108·544/174·68
2	Stefan Johansson	Ferrari t/c V6	70	1h 46m 03·770s	108·491/174·6
3	Alain Prost	McLaren-TAG t/c V6	70	1h 46m 06·154s	108·491/174·6
4	Keke Rosberg	Williams-Honda t/c V6	70	1h 46m 29·634s	108·056/173·9
5	Elio de Angelis	Lotus-Renault t/c V6	70	1h 46m 45·162s	107·807/173·5
6	Nigel Mansell	Williams-Honda t/c V6	70	1h 47m 19·691s	107·248/172·6
7	Patrick Tambay	Renault t/c V6	69		
8	Jacques Laffite	Ligier-Renault t/c V6	69		
9	Thierry Boutsen	Arrows-BMW t/c 4	68		
10	Riccardo Patrese	Alfa Romeo t/c V8	68		
11	Stefan Bellof	Tyrrell-Cosworth V8	68		
12	Martin Brundle	Tyrrell-Cosworth V8	68		
13	Gerhard Berger	Arrows-BMW t/c 4	67		
14	Andrea de Cesaris	Ligier-Renault t/c V6	67		
15	Marc Surer	Brabham-BMW t/c 4	67		
16	Ayrton Senna	Lotus-Renault t/c V6	65		
17	Eddie Cheever	Alfa Romeo t/c V8	64		
	Pierluigi Martini	Minardi-MM t/c V6	57	Accident	
	Niki Lauda	McLaren-TAG t/c V6	37	Engine	
	Piercarlo Ghinzani	Osella-Alfa Romeo t/c V8	35	Engine	
	Philippe Alliot	RAM-Hart t/c 4	28	Accident	
	Derek Warwick	Renault t/c V6	25	Accident	
	Manfred Winklehock	RAM-Hart t/c 4	5	Accident	
	Teo Fabi	Toleman-Hart t/c 4	3	Turbo	
	Nelson Piquet	Brabham-BMW t/c 4	0	Transmission	

Fastest lap: Senna, on lap 45, 1m 27·445s, 112·812 mph/181·554 km/h (record).
Previous lap record: Didier Pironi (F1 Ferrari 126C2 t/c V6), 1m 28·323s, 111·691 mph/179·749 km/h (1982).

Past winners

Year	Driver	Nat	Car	Circuit	Distance miles/km	Speed mph/km/h
1961*	Pete Ryan	CDN	2·5 Lotus 19-Climax	Mosport Park	245·90/395·74	88·38/142·23
1962*	Masten Gregory	USA	2·5 Lotus 19-Climax	Mosport Park	245·90/395·74	88·52/142·46
1963*	Pedro Rodriguez	MEX	3·0 Ferrari 250P	Mosport Park	245·90/395·74	91·55/147·34
1964*	Pedro Rodriguez	MEX	4·0 Ferrari 330P	Mosport Park	245·90/395·74	94·36/151·86
1965*	Jim Hall	USA	5·4 Chaparral 2B-Chevrolet	Mosport Park	245·90/395·74	93·78/150·92
1966*	Mark Donohue	USA	6·0 Lola T70 Mk 2-Chevrolet	Mosport Park	209·02/336·38	101·87/163·94
1967	Jack Brabham	AUS	3·0 Brabham BT24-Repco	Mosport Park	221·31/356·16	82·99/133·56
1968	Denny Hulme	NZ	3·0 McLaren M7A-Ford	St Jovite	238·50/383·83	97·22/156·47
1969	Jacky Ickx	B	3·0 Brabham BT26A-Ford	Mosport Park	221·31/356·16	111·19/179·93
1970	Jacky Ickx	B	3·0 Ferrari 312B/70	St Jovite	238·50/383·83	101·27/162·98
1971	Jackie Stewart	GB	3·0 Tyrrell 003-Ford	Mosport Park	157·38/253·27	81·96/131·90
1972	Jackie Stewart	GB	3·0 Tyrrell 005-Ford	Mosport Park	196·72/316·59	114·28/183·92
1973	Peter Revson	USA	3·0 McLaren M23-Ford	Mosport Park	196·72/316·59	99·13/159·53
1974	Emerson Fittipaldi	BR	3·0 McLaren M23-Ford	Mosport Park	196·72/316·59	117·52/189·13
1976	James Hunt	GB	3·0 McLaren M23-Ford	Mosport Park	196·72/316·59	117·84/189·65
1977	Jody Scheckter	ZA	3·0 Wolf WR1-Ford	Mosport Park	196·72/316·59	118·03/189·95
1978	Gilles Villeneuve	CDN	3·0 Ferrari 312T-3/78	Ile Notre-Dame	195·72/314·98	99·67/160·40
1979	Alan Jones	AUS	3·0 Williams FW07-Ford	Ile Notre-Dame	197·28/317·52	105·35/169·54
1980	Alan Jones	AUS	3·0 Williams FW07B-Ford	Ile Notre-Dame	191·82/308·70	110·00/177·03
1981	Jacques Laffite	F	3·0 Ligier JS17-Matra	Ile Notre-Dame	172·62/277·83	85·31/137·29
1982	Nelson Piquet	BR	1·5 Brabham BT50-BMW t/c	Ile Notre-Dame	191·82/308·70	107·93/173·70
1983	René Arnoux	F	1·5 Ferrari 126C2/B t/c	Ile Notre-Dame	191·82/308·70	106·04/170·66
1984	Nelson Piquet	BR	1·5 Brabham BT53-BMW t/c	Ile Notre-Dame	191·82/308·70	108·17/174·08
1985	Michele Alboreto	I	1·5 Ferrari 156/85 t/c	Ile Notre-Dame	191·82/308·70	108·54/174·68

* *Non-championship (sports cars)*

Lap chart

1st LAP ORDER		1	2	3	4	5	6	7	8	9	10	11	12	13	14	15	16	17	18	19	20	21	22	23	24	25	26	27	28	29	30	31	32	33	34	35	36	37	38	39	40	41	42	43	44	45	46	47	48	49	50	51	52	53	54	55	56	57	58	59	60	61	62	63	64	65	66	67	68	69	70
11	E. de Angelis	11	11	11	11	11	11	11	11	11	11	11	11	11	11	11	11	11	27	27	27	27	27	27	27	27	27	27	27	27	27	27	27	27	27	27	27	27	27	27	27	27	27	27	27	27	27	27	27	27	27	27	27	27	27	27	27	27	27	27	27	27	27	27	27	27	27	27	27	27	27
12	A. Senna	12	12	12	12	12	27	27	27	27	27	27	27	27	11	11	11	11	11	11	11	11	11	11	11	11	11	11	11	11	11	11	11	11	11	11	11	11	11	11	11	11	11	11	11	11	11	11	11	11	11	20	20	20	20	20	20	20	20	20	20	20	20	20	20	20	20	20	20	20	20
27	M. Alboreto	27	27	27	27	27	12	28	28	28	28	28	28	28	28	28	28	28	28	28	28	28	28	28	28	28	28	28	28	28	28	28	28	28	28	28	28	28	28	28	28	28	28	28	28	28	28	28	28	28	28	11	11	11	11	11	11	11	11	11	11	2	2	2	2	2	2	2	2	2	2
16	D. Warwick	16	16	28	28	28	28	15	15	15	15	15	15	15	15	15	15	15	15	15	15	15	15	15	15	15	15	15	15	15	15	15	15	15	15	15	15	15	15	15	15	15	15	15	15	15	15	15	15	15	15	2	2	2	2	2	2	2	2	2	11	11	11	11	11	11	6	6	6	6	6
28	S. Johansson	28	28	15	15	15	15	2	2	2	2	2	2	2	2	2	2	2	2	2	2	2	2	2	2	2	2	2	2	2	2	2	2	2	2	2	2	2	2	2	2	2	2	2	2	2	2	2	2	2	15	15	15	15	6	6	6	6	6	6	6	6	6	6	6	6	11	11	11
2	A. Prost	2	15	2	2	2	6	23	23	23	23	23	23	23	23	23	23	23	23	23	5	5	5	5	5	5	5	5	5	5	5	5	5	5	5	5	5	5	5	5	5	5	5	5	5	5	5	6	6	15	15	15	5	5	5	5	5	5	5	5	5	5	5	5	5	5	5
15	P. Tambay	15	2	6	6	6	6	23	18	5	5	5	5	5	5	5	5	5	5	5	5	5	23	23	23	23	23	23	23	23	23	23	23	23	23	23	23	6	6	6	6	6	6	6	6	6	6	5	5	5	5	15	15	15	15	15	15	15	15	15	15	15	15	15	15	15	26	26
6	K. Rosberg	6	6	18	23	23	18	5	18	18	18	18	18	18	18	18	18	1	1	1	1	1	1	1	1	1	1	1	1	1	1	6	6	6	23	23	23	23	23	23	23	23	23	23	26	26	26	26	26	26	26	26	26	26	26	26	26	26	15	15
23	E. Cheever	23	23	23	18	18	5	6	22	22	22	22	22	22	22	1	1	18	18	18	18	18	18	18	18	18	18	18	18	18	6	6	18	18	18	18	26	26	26	26	26	26	26	26	26	25	25	25	18	18	18	18	18	18	18	18
18	T. Boutsen	18	18	5	5	5	5	22	22	16	16	1	1	1	1	1	22	22	22	22	22	22	22	22	22	22	22	22	22	22	18	18	22	22	22	22	22	18	18	18	18	18	25	25	25	18	18	18	18	18	25	25	22	22	22	22	22
22	R. Patrese	22	22	22	22	22	16	16	1	1	16	16	16	16	16	16	16	16	16	16	16	16	16	26	26	26	6	6	6	6	22	26	26	26	26	22	22	22	22	22	22	22	22	25	25	18	18	18	22	22	22	22	22	25	25	4	4	4
5	N. Mansell	5	5	16	16	16	16	1	1	17	17	17	17	6	6	6	6	6	6	6	6	26	26	26	6	6	26	26	26	26	26	25	25	25	25	25	25	25	25	25	25	25	22	22	22	22	22	23	4	4	4	4	4	4	4	3	3	3
9	M. Winkelhock	9	9	9	9	1	1	17	26	26	26	6	17	17	26	26	26	17	17	17	17	17	17	17	17	17	17	17	25	17	17	17	17	17	17	17	17	17	17	17	17	17	17	4	4	17	3	3	3	3	25	17	17
1	N. Lauda	1	1	1	25	17	4	26	4	4	6	26	26	26	17	17	17	17	6	6	8	8	8	8	25	25	25	25	17	8	8	8	8	8	8	8	8	8	8	8	8	8	4	4	17	3	3	17	17	17	17	17	25
25	A. de Cesaris	25	25	25	25	9	4	26	4	8	6	4	4	8	8	8	8	8	8	8	8	8	4	4	25	25	8	8	8	8	8	8	4	4	4	4	4	4	4	4	4	4	8	8	8	3	3	8	8	8	8	8	8
17	G. Berger	17	17	7	17	17	26	8	8	6	8	8	8	4	4	4	4	4	4	4	4	4	4	3	25	25	4	4	4	4	4	3	3	3	3	3	3	3	3	3	3	3	3	3	3	3	8	8	12	12	12	12	12	12
4	S. Bellof	4	4	4	4	4	8	3	3	3	3	3	3	3	3	3	3	3	3	3	3	3	3	25	3	3	3	3	3	3	3	12	12	12	12	12	12	12	12	12	12	12	12	12	12	12	12	12	23	23	23	23	23
26	J. Laffite	26	26	26	26	3	10	10	10	10	10	10	10	10	25	25	25	25	25	24	24	24	24	24	24	12	12	29	29	29	29	29	29	29	29	29	29	29	29	29	29	29	29	29	29	29	29	29
8	F. Hesnault	8	8	8	8	25	24	24	24	24	24	24	24	24	24	24	24	24	24	10	10	10	12	12	12	12	29	29	29
3	M. Brundle	3	3	3	3	24	29	29	29	29	25	25	25	25	10	29	29	29	10	10	10	12	12	29	29	29	29
24	P. Ghinzani	24	24	24	24	10	25	25	25	25	29	29	29	29	29	10	10	10	10	29	12	12	29	29
29	P. Martini	29	29	29	10	10	29	12	12	12	12	12	12	12	12	12	12	12	12	12	29	29
10	P. Alliot	10	10	10	29	29
19	T. Fabi	19	19	19	19	19

Fastest laps

Driver	Time	Lap
Ayrton Senna	1m 27·445s	45
Keke Rosberg	1m 27·611s	51
Eddie Cheever	1m 28·481s	64
Michele Alboreto	1m 28·637s	28
Stefan Johansson	1m 28·651s	44
Alain Prost	1m 28·755s	64
Patrick Tambay	1m 28·863s	46
Elio de Angelis	1m 29·156s	38
Nigel Mansell	1m 29·331s	50
Andrea de Cesaris	1m 30·070s	45
Jacques Laffite	1m 30·324s	54
Niki Lauda	1m 30·433s	29
Derek Warwick	1m 31·367s	22
Thierry Boutsen	1m 31·688s	6
Gerhard Berger	1m 31·735s	15
Riccardo Patrese	1m 31·978s	24
Marc Surer	1m 32·286s	40
Philippe Alliot	1m 32·325s	25
Martin Brundle	1m 32·485s	55
Stefan Bellof	1m 33·085s	56
Manfred Winkelhock	1m 33·690s	4
Piercarlo Ghinzani	1m 35·136s	5
Teo Fabi	1m 35·539s	2
Pierluigi Martini	1m 36·757s	7

Points

WORLD CHAMPIONSHIP OF DRIVERS

1	Michele Alboreto	27 pts
2=	Alain Prost	22
2=	Elio de Angelis	22
4	Patrick Tambay	10
5	Ayrton Senna	9
6	Stefan Johansson	7
7	Thierry Boutsen	6
8	Nigel Mansell	5
9=	René Arnoux	3
9=	Andrea de Cesaris	3
9=	Keke Rosberg	3
9=	Niki Lauda	3
13=	Derek Warwick	2
13=	Jacques Laffite	2
15	Stefan Bellof	1

CONSTRUCTORS' CUP

1	Ferrari	37 pts
2	Lotus	31
3	McLaren	25
4	Renault	12
5	Williams	8
6	Arrows	6
7	Ligier	5
8	Tyrrell	1

Circuit data

Circuit Gilles Villeneuve, Ile Notre Dame, Montreal, Quebec
Circuit length: 2·74 miles/4·41 km
Race distance: 70 laps, 191·82 miles/308·70 km
Race weather: Cool, dry

United States Grand Prix (Detroit), 23 June/statistics

Entries and practice times

No.	Driver	Nat.	Car	Tyre	Engine	Entrant	Practice 1	Practice 2
1	Niki Lauda	A	Marlboro McLAREN MP4/2B	G	TAG P01 (TTE P01)	Marlboro McLaren International	1m 46·266s	—
2	Alain Prost	F	Marlboro McLAREN MP4/2B	G	TAG P01 (TTE P01)	Marlboro McLaren International	1m 44·088s	—
3	Martin Brundle	GB	TYRRELL 012	G	Ford-Cosworth DFY	Tyrrell Racing Organisation	1m 47·563s	—
4	Stefan Bellof	D	TYRRELL 012	G	Ford-Cosworth DFY	Tyrrell Racing Organisation	1m 47·911s	—
5	Nigel Mansell	GB	WILLIAMS FW10	G	Honda RA163–E	Canon Williams Honda Team	1m 43·249s	—
6	Keke Rosberg	SF	WILLIAMS FW10	G	Honda RA163–E	Canon Williams Honda Team	1m 44·156s	—
7	Nelson Piquet	BR	Olivetti BRABHAM BT54	P	BMW M12/13	Motor Racing Developments Ltd	1m 45·194s	—
8	Marc Surer	CH	Olivetti BRABHAM BT54	P	BMW M12/13	Motor Racing Developments Ltd	1m 45·979s	—
9	Manfred Winkelhock	D	RAM 03	P	Hart 415T	Skoal Bandit Formula 1 Team	1m 47·926s	—
10	Philippe Alliot	F	RAM 03	P	Hart 415T	Skoal Bandit Formula 1 Team	1m 50·455s	2m 24·814s
11	Elio de Angelis	I	John Player Special LOTUS 97T	G	Renault EF4/EF15	John Player Special Team Lotus	1m 44·769s	—
12	Ayrton Senna	BR	John Player Special LOTUS 97T	G	Renault EF4/EF15	John Player Special Team Lotus	1m 42·051s	—
15	Patrick Tambay	F	Elf RENAULT RE60	G	Renault EF4/EF15	Equipe Renault Elf	1m 47·028s	—
16	Derek Warwick	GB	Elf RENAULT RE60	G	Renault EF4/EF15	Equipe Renault Elf	1m 44·163s	—
17	Gerhard Berger	A	ARROWS A8	G	BMW M12/13	Barclay Arrows BMW	—	2m 05·307s
18	Thierry Boutsen	B	ARROWS A8	G	BMW M12/13	Barclay Arrows BMW	1m 48·023s	—
19	Teo Fabi	I	TOLEMAN TG185	P	Hart 415T	Toleman Group Motorsport	1m 46·546s	—
22	Riccardo Patrese	I	Benetton ALFA ROMEO 185T	G	Alfa Romeo 890T	Benetton Team Alfa Romeo	1m 46·592s	—
23	Eddie Cheever	USA	Benetton ALFA ROMEO 185T	G	Alfa Romeo 890T	Benetton Team Alfa Romeo	1m 44·231s	2m 05·540s
24	Piercarlo Ghinzani	I	Kelemata OSELLA FA1G	P	Alfa Romeo 890T	Osella Squadra Corse	1m 48·546s	2m 11·904s
25	Andrea de Cesaris	I	Gitanes LIGIER JS25	P	Renault EF4/EF15	Equipe Ligier Gitanes	1m 47·393s	2m 12·268s
26	Jacques Laffite	F	Gitanes LIGIER JS25	P	Renault EF4/EF15	Equipe Ligier Gitanes	1m 47·267s	—
27	Michele Alboreto	I	Fiat FERRARI 156/85	G	Ferrari 126C	Scuderia Ferrari SpA	1m 43·748s	—
28	Stefan Johansson	S	Fiat FERRARI 156/85	G	Ferrari 126C	Scuderia Ferrari SpA	1m 44·921s	—
29	Pierluigi Martini	I	Simod MINARDI M/85	P	Motori Moderni	Minardi Team	3m 04·446s	—

Friday morning and Saturday morning practice sessions not officially recorded.

G – Goodyear, P – Pirelli.

Fri p.m.	Sat p.m.
Warm, dry	Cool, wet

Starting grid

12 SENNA (1m 42·051s)
Lotus

    5 MANSELL (1m 43·249s)
    Williams

27 ALBORETO (1m 43·748s)
Ferrari

    2 PROST (1m 44·088s)
    McLaren

6 ROSBERG (1m 44·156s)
Williams

    16 WARWICK (1m 44·163s)
    Renault

23 CHEEVER (1m 44·231s)
Alfa Romeo

    11 DE ANGELIS (1m 44·769s)
    Lotus

28 JOHANSSON (1m 44·921s)
Ferrari

    7 PIQUET (1m 45·194s)
    Brabham

8 SURER (1m 45·979s)
Brabham

    1 LAUDA (1m 46·266s)
    McLaren

19 FABI (1m 46·546s)
Toleman

    22 PATRESE (1m 46·592s)
    Alfa Romeo

15 TAMBAY (1m 47·028s)
Renault

    26 LAFFITE (1m 47·267s)
    Ligier

25 DE CESARIS (1m 47·393s)
Ligier

    3 BRUNDLE (1m 47·563s)
    Tyrrell

4 BELLOF (1m 47·911s)
Tyrrell

    9 WINKELHOCK (1m 47·926s)
    RAM

18 BOUTSEN (1m 48·023s)
Arrows

    24 GHINZANI (1m 48·546s)
    Osella

10 ALLIOT (1m 50·455s)
RAM

    17 BERGER (2m 05·307s)
    Arrows

29 MARTINI (3m 04·446s)
Minardi

Results and retirements

Place	Driver	Car	Laps	Time and Speed (mph/km/h)/Retirement	
1	Keke Rosberg	Williams-Honda t/c V6	63	1h 55m 39·851s	81·702/131·486
2	Stefan Johansson	Ferrari t/c V6	63	1h 56m 37·400s	81·0/130·3
3	Michele Alboreto	Ferrari t/c V6	63	1h 56m 43·021s	81·0/130·356
4	Stefan Bellof	Tyrrell-Cosworth V8	63	1h 56m 46·076s	80·9/130·196
5	Elio de Angelis	Lotus-Renault t/c V6	63	1h 57m 06·817s	80·7/129·9
6	Nelson Piquet	Brabham-BMW t/c 4	62		
7	Thierry Boutsen	Arrows-BMW t/c 4	62		
8	Marc Surer	Brabham-BMW t/c 4	62		
9	Eddie Cheever	Alfa Romeo t/c V8	61		
10	Andrea de Cesaris	Ligier-Renault t/c V6	61		
11	Gerhard Berger	Arrows-BMW t/c 4	60		
12	Jacques Laffite	Ligier-Renault t/c V6	58		
	Ayrton Senna	Lotus-Renault t/c V6	51	Accident	
	Martin Brundle	Tyrrell-Cosworth V8	30	Accident with Alliot	
	Philippe Alliot	RAM-Hart t/c 4	27	Accident with Brundle	
	Nigel Mansell	Williams-Honda t/c V6	26	Accident	
	Alain Prost	McLaren-TAG t/c V6	19	Brakes/accident	
	Riccardo Patrese	Alfa Romeo t/c V8	19	Electrics	
	Derek Warwick	Renault t/c V6	18	Transmission	
	Patrick Tambay	Renault t/c V6	15	Accident	
	Pierluigi Martini	Minardi-MM t/c V6	11	Engine	
	Niki Lauda	McLaren-TAG t/c V6	10	Brakes	
	Teo Fabi	Toleman-Hart t/c 4	4	Clutch	
	Manfred Winkelhock	RAM-Hart t/c 4	3	Turbo	
	Piercarlo Ghinzani	Osella-Alfa Romeo t/c V8	0	Accident	

Fastest lap: Senna, on lap 51, 1m 45·612s, 85·2175 mph/137·144 km/h (record).
Previous lap record: Derek Warwick (F1 Renault RE50 t/c), 1m 46·221s, 84·729 mph/136·358 km/h (1984).

Past winners

Year	Driver	Nat.	Car	Circuit	Distance miles/km	Speed mph/km/h
1982	John Watson	GB	3·0 McLaren MP4B-Ford	Detroit	154·57/248·75	78·20/128·85
1983	Michele Alboreto	I	3·0 Tyrrell 011-Ford	Detroit	150·00/241·40	81·16/130·61
1984	Nelson Piquet	BR	1·5 Brabham BT53-BMW t/c	Detroit	157·50/253·47	81·68/131·45
1985	Keke Rosberg	SF	1·5 Williams FW10-Honda t/c	Detroit	157·50/253·47	81·70/131·48

Lap chart

1st LAP ORDER		1 2 3 4 5 6 7 8 9 10 11 12 13 14 15 16 17 18 19 20 21 22 23 24 25 26 27 28 29 30 31 32 33 34 35 36 37 38 39 40 41 42 43 44 45 46 47 48 49 50 51 52 53 54 55 56 57 58 59 60 61 62 63
12	A.Senna	12 12 12 12 12 12 12 6 6 6 6 6 6 6 6 6 6 6 6 6 6 6 6 6 6 6 6 6 6 6 6 6 6 6 6 6 6 6 6 6 6 6 6 6 6 6 6 6 6 6 6 6 6 6 6 6 6 6 6 6 6 6 6
6	K.Rosberg	6 6 6 6 6 6 6 12 6 6 6 6 6 6 6 6 6 5 11 11 11 11 11 11 11 11 11 28 28 28 28 28 28 28 28 28 28 28 28 28 28 28 28 28 28 28 28 28 28 28 28 28 28 28 28 28 28 28 28 28 28 28 28
5	N.Mansell	5 5 5 5 5 5 5 5 27 27 11 11 11 11 11 11 11 11 11 5 5 28 28 28 28 28 28 11 27 27 27 27 27 27 27 27 27 27 27 27 27 27 27 27 27 27 27 27 27 27 27 27 27 27 27 27 27 27 27 27 27 27 27
2	A.Prost	2 2 2 27 27 27 27 11 11 27 27 27 20 20 20 20 20 20 20 5 5 3 3 3 3 3 27 3 4 4 4 4 4 4 4 4 4 4 4 4 4 4 4 12 12 12 12 12 12 4 4 4 4 4 4 4 4 4 4 4 4 4 4
27	M.Alboreto	27 27 27 11 11 11 11 11 2 2 2 2 20 20 20 27 27 27 27 3 3 3 27 27 27 27 3 1 12 12 12 12 12 12 12 12 12 12 12 12 12 12 12 4 4 4 4 4 4 11 11 11 11 11 11 11 11 11 11 11 11 11 11
16	D.Warwick	16 16 11 2 2 2 2 2 28 28 28 28 2 2 2 2 3 3 27 27 27 27 5 4 4 4 4 12 26 11 11 11 11 11 11 11 11 11 11 11 11 11 11 11 11 11 7 7 7 7 7 7 7 7 7 7 7 7
11	E.de Angelis	11 11 16 16 16 16 16 28 16 16 16 16 3 3 3 2 2 2 4 4 4 4 12 12 12 12 12 26 26 26 26 7 7 7 7 7 7 7 7 7 7 7 7 7 8 8 8 8 8 8 8 8 8 8 8 8 8 8
28	S.Johansson	28 28 28 28 28 28 16 7 7 7 3 3 12 12 12 12 12 12 12 12 26 26 26 26 26 18 11 18 18 7 7 26 26 26 26 26 26 26 26 18 18 8 8 25 25 25 25 25 25 25 23 23 23
7	N.Piquet	7 7 7 7 7 7 7 1 1 1 4 4 16 4 4 4 4 18 26 26 26 26 5 5 18 18 18 11 7 7 7 18 18 18 18 18 18 18 18 18 18 26 8 26 26 23 23 23 23 23 23 25 25 25
1	N.Lauda	1 1 1 1 1 1 1 1 3 3 3 12 12 4 16 16 16 16 26 18 18 18 18 18 18 7 7 7 8 8 8 8 8 8 8 8 8 8 8 8 8 8 8 8 26 25 25 25 26 17 18 18 18 18 18 18 18 18
19	T.Fabi	19 19 19 19 3 3 3 3 4 4 4 7 26 18 18 18 18 26 7 7 7 7 7 7 8 8 8 17 17 25 25 25 25 25 25 25 25 25 25 25 25 25 17 23 17 18 17 17 17 17 17 17 17 17 17
3	M.Brundle	3 3 3 3 4 4 4 26 26 26 26 18 26 26 26 26 8 8 8 8 8 8 8 17 17 17 25 25 17 23 23 23 23 23 23 23 23 23 23 23 23 23 17 18 26 26 26 26 26 26
4	S.Bellof	4 4 4 26 26 26 26 12 12 12 18 15 15 15 8 8 8 7 17 17 17 17 17 17 25 25 25 25 23 23 23 17 17 17 17 17 17 17 17 17 17 17 17 18 18
22	R.Patrese	22 26 26 26 18 18 18 18 18 18 15 8 8 8 7 7 7 17 23 23 23 23 23 23 23 23 23
26	J.Laffite	26 18 18 18 22 22 22 15 15 15 15 8 7 7 7 17 17 17 23 25 25 25 25 25 25 25 10
18	T.Boutsen	18 25 25 25 15 65 22 22 8 8 17 17 17 17 25 25 25 25 10 10 10 10 10 10 10
9	M.Winkelhock	9 9 22 22 15 8 8 8 8 17 23 23 23 23 23 23 23 10 22
25	A.de Cesaris	25 22 9 15 8 17 17 17 23 23 25 25 25 25 10 10 10 22
10	P.Alliot	10 15 15 8 17 23 23 23 22 25 10 10 10 22 22 22
15	P.Tambay	15 17 8 17 19 10 10 10 25 25 10 22 22 22 22
17	G.Berger	17 8 17 10 23 29 29 25 10 10 22
8	F.Hesnault	8 10 10 23 10 25 25 29 29 29 29
29	P.Martini	29 29 29 29 29
23	E.Cheever	23 23 23

Fastest laps

Driver	Time	Lap
Ayrton Senna	1m 45·612s	51
Keke Rosberg	1m 47·311s	58
Michele Alboreto	1m 47·518s	43
Elio de Angelis	1m 47·572s	43
Stefan Johansson	1m 47·797s	56
Eddie Cheever	1m 47·916s	33
Nelson Piquet	1m 48·045s	40
Nigel Mansell	1m 48·241s	6
Thierry Boutsen	1m 48·554s	6
Stefan Bellof	1m 48·681s	12
Jacques Laffite	1m 48·702s	6
Alain Prost	1m 49·001s	8
Martin Brundle	1m 49·073s	15
Derek Warwick	1m 49·485s	4
Niki Lauda	1m 49·489s	6
Andrea de Cesaris	1m 49·603s	57
Patrick Tambay	1m 49·931s	6
Marc Surer	1m 49·998s	5
Gerhard Berger	1m 50·576s	21
Riccardo Patrese	1m 50·729s	6
Teo Fabi	1m 51·211s	3
Philippe Alliot	1m 53·752s	6
Pierluigi Martini	1m 55·446s	7
Manfred Winkelhock	1m 55·649s	2

Points

WORLD CHAMPIONSHIP OF DRIVERS

1	Michele Alboreto	31 pts
2	Elio de Angelis	24
3	Alain Prost	22
4	Stefan Johansson	13
5	Keke Rosberg	12
6	Patrick Tambay	10
7	Ayrton Senna	9
8	Thierry Boutsen	6
9	Nigel Mansell	5
10	Stefan Bellof	4
11 =	René Arnoux	3
11 =	Niki Lauda	3
11 =	Andrea de Cesaris	3
14 =	Derek Warwick	2
14 =	Jacques Laffite	2
16	Nelson Piquet	1

CONSTRUCTORS' CUP

1	Ferrari	47 pts
2	Lotus	33
3	McLaren	25
4	Williams	17
5	Renault	12
6	Arrows	6
7	Ligier	5
8	Tyrrell	4
9	Brabham	1

Circuit data

Detroit Grand Prix Circuit, Detroit, Michigan

Circuit length: 2·50 miles/4·0233 km
Race distance: 63 laps, 157·500 miles/253·471 km
Race weather: Hot, dry

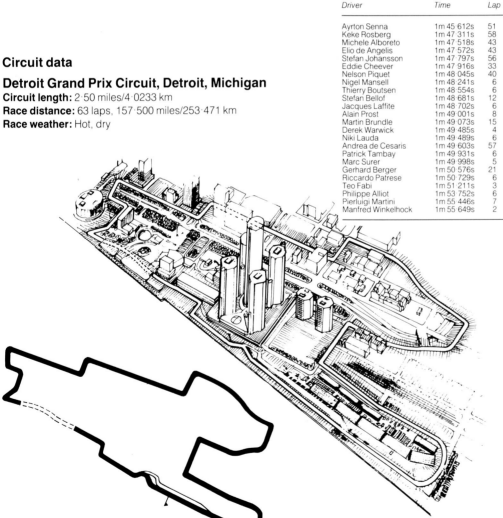

Entries and practice times

No.	Driver	Nat.	Car	Tyre	Engine	Entrant	Practice 1	Practice 2
1	Niki Lauda	A	Marlboro McLAREN MP4/2B	G	TAG P01 (TTE P01)	Marlboro McLaren International	**1m 33·860s**	1m 34·166s
2	Alain Prost	F	Marlboro McLAREN MP4/2B	G	TAG P01 (TTE P01)	Marlboro McLaren International	1m 33·547s	**1m 33·335s**
3	Martin Brundle	GB	TYRRELL 014	G	Renault EF4	Tyrrell Racing Organisation	1m 40·486s	**1m 40·015s**
4	Stefan Bellof	D	TYRRELL 012	G	Ford-Cosworth DFY	Tyrrell Racing Organisation	**1m 44·404s**	1m 45·478s
5	Nigel Mansell	GB	WILLIAMS FW10	G	Honda RA163–E	Canon Williams Honda Team	**1m 34·191s**	—
6	Keke Rosberg	SF	WILLIAMS FW10	G	Honda RA163–E	Canon Williams Honda Team	1m 33·484s	**1m 32·462s**
7	Nelson Piquet	BR	Olivetti BRABHAM BT54	P	BMW M12/13	Motor Racing Developments Ltd	1m 33·981s	**1m 33·812s**
8	Marc Surer	CH	Olivetti BRABHAM BT54	P	BMW M12/13	Motor Racing Developments Ltd	**1m 35·572s**	1m 35·640s
9	Manfred Winkelhock	D	RAM 03	P	Hart 415T	Skoal Bandit Formula 1 Team	**1m 37·654s**	1m 45·628s
10	Philippe Alliot	F	RAM 03	P	Hart 415T	Skoal Bandit Formula 1 Team	**1m 41·647s**	1m 44·221s
11	Elio de Angelis	I	John Player Special LOTUS 97T	G	Renault EF4/EF15	John Player Special Team Lotus	**1m 34·022s**	1m 34·227s
12	Ayrton Senna	BR	John Player Special LOTUS 97T	G	Renault EF4/EF15	John Player Special Team Lotus	**1m 32·835s**	1m 33·677s
15	Patrick Tambay	F	Elf RENAULT RE60B	G	Renault EF15	Equipe Renault Elf	**1m 34·680s**	1m 36·339s
16	Derek Warwick	GB	Elf RENAULT RE60	G	Renault EF4/EF15	Equipe Renault Elf	**1m 34·976s**	1m 35·190s
17	Gerhard Berger	A	ARROWS A8	G	BMW M12/13	Barclay Arrows BMW	**1m 34·674s**	1m 37·455s
18	Thierry Boutsen	B	ARROWS A8	G	BMW M12/13	Barclay Arrows BMW	1m 36·051s	**1m 35·488s**
19	Teo Fabi	I	TOLEMAN TG185	P	Hart 415T	Toleman Group Motorsport	**1m 37·142s**	1m 37·657s
22	Riccardo Patrese	I	Benetton ALFA ROMEO 185T	G	Alfa Romeo 890T	Benetton Team Alfa Romeo	**1m 36·729s**	1m 38·745s
23	Eddie Cheever	USA	Benetton ALFA ROMEO 185T	G	Alfa Romeo 890T	Benetton Team Alfa Romeo	**1m 36·931s**	1m 38·489s
24	Piercarlo Ghinzani	I	Kelemata OSELLA FA1G	P	Alfa Romeo 890T	Osella Squadra Corse	**1m 42·136s**	1m 42·968s
25	Andrea de Cesaris	I	Gitanes LIGIER JS25	P	Renault EF4/EF15	Equipe Ligier Gitanes	1m 37·335s	**1m 35·571s**
26	Jacques Laffite	F	Gitanes LIGIER JS25	P	Renault EF4/EF15	Equipe Ligier Gitanes	1m 38·173s	**1m 36·133s**
27	Michele Alboreto	I	Fiat FERRARI 156/85	G	Ferrari 126C	Scuderia Ferrari SpA	1m 35·421s	**1m 33·267s**
28	Stefan Johansson	S	Fiat FERRARI 156/85	G	Ferrari 126C	Scuderia Ferrari SpA	1m 37·546s	**1m 36·140s**
29	Pierluigi Martini	I	Simod MINARDI M/85	P	Motori Moderni	Minardi Team	1m 47·523s	**1m 44·350s**
30	Jonathan Palmer	GB	West ZAKSPEED ZAK 841	G	Zakspeed	West Zakspeed Racing	1m 40·498s	**1m 40·289s**

Friday morning and Saturday morning practice sessions not officially recorded.

G – Goodyear, P – Pirelli.

Fri p.m.	*Sat p.m.*
Hot, dry	*Hot, dry*

Starting grid

6 ROSBERG (1m 32·462s)
Williams

    12 SENNA (1m 32·835s)
    Lotus

27 ALBORETO (1m 33·267s)
Ferrari

    2 PROST (1m 33·335s)
    McLaren

7 PIQUET (1m 33·812s)
Brabham

    1 LAUDA (1m 33·860s)
    McLaren

11 DE ANGELIS (1m 34·022s)
Lotus

    17 BERGER (1m 34·674s)
    Arrows

15 TAMBAY (1m 34·680s)
Renault

    16 WARWICK (1m 34·976s)
    Renault

18 BOUTSEN (1m 35·488s)
Arrows

    25 DE CESARIS (1m 35·571s)
    Ligier

8 SURER (1m 35·572s)
Brabham

    26 LAFFITE (1m 36·133s)
    Ligier

28 JOHANSSON (1m 36·140s)
Ferrari

    22 PATRESE (1m 36·729s)
    Alfa Romeo

23 CHEEVER (1m 36·931s)
Alfa Romeo

    19 FABI (1m 37·142s)
    Toleman

9 WINKELHOCK (1m 37·654s)
RAM

    3 BRUNDLE (1m 40·015s)
    Tyrrell

30 PALMER (1m 40·289s)
Zakspeed

    10 ALLIOT (1m 41·647s)
    RAM

24 GHINZANI (1m 42·136s)
Osella

    29 MARTINI (1m 44·350s)
    Minardi

4 BELLOF (1m 44·404s)
Tyrrell

Did not start:
5 Mansell (Williams), 1m 34·191s, accident during practice on Saturday.

Results and retirements

Place	Driver	Car	Laps	Time and Speed (mph/km/h)/Retirement	
1	Nelson Piquet	Brabham-BMW t/c 4	53	1h 31m 46·266s	125·096/201·323
2	Keke Rosberg	Williams-Honda t/c V6	53	1h 31m 52·926s	124·9/201·1
3	Alain Prost	McLaren-TAG t/c V6	53	1h 31m 55·551s	124·9/201·0
4	Stefan Johansson	Ferrari t/c V6	53	1h 32m 39·757s	123·9/199·4
5	Elio de Angelis	Lotus-Renault t/c V6	53	1h 32m 39·956s	123·9/199·4
6	Patrick Tambay	Renault t/c V6	53	1h 33m 01·433s	123·4/198·6
7	Derek Warwick	Renault t/c V6	53	1h 33m 30·478s	122·8/197·6
8	Marc Surer	Brabham-BMW t/c 4	52		
9	Thierry Boutsen	Arrows-BMW t/c 4	52		
10	Eddie Cheever	Alfa Romeo t/c V8	52		
11	Riccardo Patrese	Alfa Romeo t/c V8	52		
12	Manfred Winkelhock	RAM-Hart t/c 4	50		
13	Stefan Bellof	Tyrrell-Cosworth V8	50		
14	Teo Fabi	Toleman-Hart t/c 4	49	Fuel Pressure	
15	Piercarlo Ghinzani	Osella-Alfa Romeo t/c V8	49		
	Martin Brundle	Tyrrell-Renault t/c V6	32	Gearbox	
	Niki Lauda	McLaren-TAG t/c V6	30	Gearbox	
	Ayrton Senna	Lotus-Renault t/c V6	26	Engine failure/accident	
	Gerhard Berger	Arrows-BMW t/c 4	20	Accident with Martini	
	Pierluigi Martini	Minardi-MM t/c V6	19	Accident with Berger	
	Philippe Alliot	RAM-Hart t/c 4	8	Fuel Pressure	
	Jonathan Palmer	Zakspeed t/c 4	6	Engine	
	Michele Alboreto	Ferrari t/c V6	5	Turbo	
	Andrea de Cesaris	Ligier-Renault t/c V6	4	Driveshaft	
	Jacques Laffite	Ligier-Renault t/c V6	2	Turbo	

Fastest lap: Rosberg, on lap 46, 1m 39·914s, 130·077 mph/209·304 km/h (record).
Previous lap record: Riccardo Patrese (F1 Brabham BT50-BMW t/c), 1m 40·075s, 129·868 mph/209·003 km/h (1982).

Past winners

Year	Driver	Nat	Car	Circuit	Distance miles/km	Speed mph/km/h
1950	Juan Manuel Fangio	RA	1·5 Alfa Romeo 158 s/c	Reims-Gueux	310·81/500·20	104·84/168·72
1951	Luigi Fagioli/	I				
	Juan Manuel Fangio	RA	1·5 Alfa Romeo 159 s/c	Reims-Gueux	373·94/601·80	110·97/178·59
1952	Alberto Ascari	I	2·0 Ferrari 500	Rouen-les-Essarts	240·39/386·88	80·13/128·96
1953	Mike Hawthorn	GB	2·0 Ferrari 500	Reims	314·56/506·23	113·64/182·89
1954	Juan Manuel Fangio	RA	2·5 Mercedes-Benz W196	Reims	314·64/506·36	115·97/186·64
1956	Peter Collins	GB	2·5 Lancia-Ferrari D50	Reims	314·64/506·36	122·29/196·80
1957	Juan Manuel Fangio	RA	2·5 Maserati 250F	Rouen-les-Essarts	313·01/503·74	100·02/160·96
1958	Mike Hawthorn	GB	2·4 Ferrari Dino 246	Reims	257·90/415·05	125·45/201·90
1959	Tony Brooks	GB	2·4 Ferrari Dino 246	Reims	257·90/415·05	127·43/205·08
1960	Jack Brabham	AUS	2·5 Cooper T53-Climax	Reims	257·90/415·05	131·80/212·11
1961	Giancarlo Baghetti	I	1·5 Ferrari Dino 156	Reims	268·22/431·66	119·85/192·87
1962	Dan Gurney	USA	1·5 Porsche 804	Rouen-les-Essarts	219·51/353·27	101·84/163·89
1963	Jim Clark	GB	1·5 Lotus 25-Climax	Reims	273·37/439·95	125·31/201·67
1964	Dan Gurney	USA	1·5 Brabham BT7-Climax	Rouen-les-Essarts	231·71/372·90	108·77/175·04
1965	Jim Clark	GB	1·5 Lotus 25-Climax	Clermont-Ferrand	200·21/322·21	89·22/143·58
1966	Jack Brabham	AUS	3·0 Brabham BT19-Repco	Reims	247·58/398·44	136·90/220·32
1967	Jack Brabham	AUS	3·0 Brabham BT24-Repco	Bugatti au Mans	219·82/353·77	98·90/159·16
1968	Jacky Ickx	B	3·0 Ferrari 312/66	Rouen-les-Essarts	243·90/392·52	100·45/161·66
1969	Jackie Stewart	GB	2·0 Matra MS80-Ford	Clermont-Ferrand	190·20/306·10	97·71/157·25
1970	Jochen Rindt	A	3·0 Lotus 72-Ford	Clermont-Ferrand	190·20/306·10	98·42/158·39
1971	Jackie Stewart	GB	3·0 Tyrrell 003-Ford	Paul Ricard	198·56/319·55	111·66/179·70
1972	Jackie Stewart	GB	3·0 Tyrrell 003-Ford	Clermont-Ferrand	190·20/306·10	101·56/163·44
1973	Ronnie Peterson	S	3·0 JPS/Lotus 72-Ford	Paul Ricard	194·95/313·74	115·12/185·26
1974	Ronnie Peterson	S	3·0 JPS/Lotus 72-Ford	Dijon-Prenois	163·49/263·11	119·75/192·72
1975	Niki Lauda	A	3·0 Ferrari 312T/75	Paul Ricard	194·95/313·74	116·60/187·65
1976	James Hunt	GB	3·0 McLaren M23-Ford	Paul Ricard	194·95/313·74	115·84/186·42
1977	Mario Andretti	USA	3·0 JPS/Lotus 78-Ford	Dijon-Prenois	188·90/304·00	113·72/183·01
1978	Mario Andretti	USA	3·0 JPS/Lotus 79-Ford	Paul Ricard	194·95/313·74	118·31/190·40
1979	Jean-Pierre Jabouille	F	1·5 Renault RS t/c	Dijon-Prenois	188·88/304·00	118·88/191·32
1980	Alan Jones	AUS	3·0 Williams FW07B-Ford	Paul Ricard	194·95/313·74	126·15/203·02
1981	Alain Prost	F	1·5 Renault RE t/c	Dijon-Prenois	188·88/304·00	118·30/190·39
1982	René Arnoux	F	1·5 Renault RE t/c	Paul Ricard	194·95/313·74	125·02/201·20
1983	Alain Prost	F	1·5 Renault RE t/c	Paul Ricard	194·95/313·74	124·19/199·87
1984	Niki Lauda	A	1·5 McLaren MP4/2-TAG t/c	Dijon-Prenois	186·53/300·20	125·53/202·02
1985	Nelson Piquet	BR	1·5 Brabham BT54-BMW t/c	Paul Ricard	191·34/307·93	125·09/201·32

Lap chart

1st LAP ORDER — laps 1 to 53

No	Driver	Lap-by-lap progression
6	K. Rosberg	6 6 6 6 6 6 6 6 6 6 7 7 7 7 7 7 7 7 7 7 7 7 7 7 7 7 7 7 7 7 7 7 7 7 7 7 7 7 7 7 7 7 7 7 7 7 7 7 7 7 7 7 7
12	A. Senna	12 12 12 12 12 12 7 7 7 6 6 6 6 6 6 6 6 6 6 6 6 6 6 6 6 6 6 6 6 6 6 6 6 6 6 6 6 6 6 6 2 2 2 2 2 2 2 2 2 2 2 2 6
1	N. Piquet	1 1 1 1 1 1 10 10 10 1 1 1 1 1 1 1 1 1 1 1 1 1 1 1 1 1 1 1 1 1 7 7 7 7 11 11 11 11 11 11 11 11 11 11 11 11 11 11 11 11 11 7
27	M. Alboreto	27 27 27 27 11 11 11 11 11 11 2 2 2 2 2 2 2 2 2 2 2 2 2 2 2 2 2 1 11 11 11 11 11 11 11 11 11 6 6 11 11 11 11 11 11 11 11 11 11 28
11	E. de Angelis	11 11 11 11 1 1 1 1 11 2 11 11 11 11 11 11 11 11 11 11 11 11 11 11 11 11 11 11 0 0 0 0 0 0 0 0 0 0 0 20 20 20 20 20 20 20 20 20 20 11
1	N. Lauda	1 1 1 1 2 2 2 2 1b 1b 1b 1b 1b 1b 1b 1b 8 8 8 8 8 8 8 8 8 8 1b 1b 1b 1b 1b 1b 28 28 28 28 1b 1b 1b 1b 1b 1b 1b 1b 1b 1b 1b 1b 1b
2	A. Prost	2 2 2 16 16 16 16 16 15 15 15 15 16 8 8 8 15 15 15 15 15 15 15 15 15 15 15 15 28 28 28 28 28 15 15 15 15 8 16 16 16 16 8 8 8 16 16 16 16
25	A. de Cesaris	25 25 25 25 17 17 17 17 15 18 18 18 8 8 16 18 18 18 18 18 18 18 18 18 28 28 28 18 18 18 18 18 18 16 16 16 8 8 8 8 16 16 16 8 8
17	G. Berger	17 16 16 16 15 15 15 15 17 17 8 8 8 18 18 18 28 28 28 28 28 28 28 28 18 18 18 18 18 16 16 16 16 16 18 18 19 19 19 19 19 19 19 19 19 18 18 18 18
16	D. Warwick	16 17 17 17 18 18 18 18 8 17 17 28 28 28 28 17 17 17 17 16 16 16 16 16 16 16 16 3 3 19 19 19 19 19 19 19 18 18 18 18 18 18 18 19 23 23 23
15	P. Tambay	15 15 15 15 8 8 8 8 28 28 28 18 17 17 17 16 16 16 16 3 3 3 3 3 3 3 3 3 9 9 9 9 9 9 9 9 22 22 22 22 22 22 22 23 23 23 22 22
18	T. Boutsen	18 18 18 18 28 28 28 28 28 12 3 3 3 3 3 3 3 3 3 19 19 19 19 19 19 19 19 22 22 22 22 22 22 23 23 23 23 23 23 23 23 22 22 9
8	M. Surer	8 8 8 8 27 22 22 22 22 3 22 22 19 19 19 19 19 19 19 9 9 9 9 9 9 9 9 22 22 23 23 23 23 23 23 9 9 9 9 9 9 9 4
26	J. Laffite	26 26 28 28 22 22 23 3 3 22 19 19 9 9 9 9 9 9 9 9 23 23 23 12 22 22 22 22 23 23 24 24 4 4 4 4 4 4 4 4 4 4 4 4 4
28	S. Johansson	28 28 22 22 23 19 19 19 10 10 9 9 22 22 23 23 23 23 22 22 12 22 22 23 23 23 23 24 4 4 24 24 24 24 24 24 24 24 24 24 24 24 24 24
22	R. Patrese	22 22 23 23 19 3 3 23 23 9 23 23 23 23 22 22 22 22 12 12 22 23 4 4 4 24 4 4
23	E. Cheever	23 23 19 19 3 9 9 9 9 23 24 24 4 4 4 4 4 12 12 12 4 4 4 4 4 4 24 24 24 4
9	M. Winkelhock	9 3 3 3 9 30 10 24 24 24 4 4 24 24 24 24 12 4 4 4 24 24 24 24 24
3	M. Brundle	3 9 9 9 30 10 24 4 4 4 29 29 29 29 29 12 24 24 24 24 24 24
10	P. Alliot	10 19 30 30 10 24 4 29 29 29 12 12 12 12 12 29 29 29 29
19	T. Fabi	19 10 10 10 24 4 29 10
30	J. Palmer	30 30 24 24 4 29
24	P. Ghinzani	24 24 4 4 29
4	S. Bellof	4 4 29 29
29	P. Martini	29 29

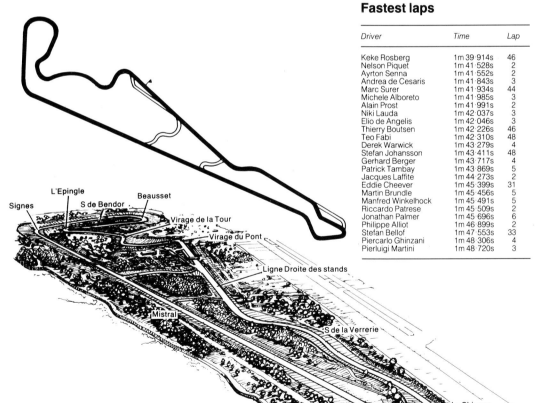

Circuit map labels: L'Epingle · S de Bendor · Beausset · Signes · Virage de la Tour · Virage du Pont · Mistral · Ligne Droite des stands · S de la Verrerie · La Chicane · L'Ecole · Sainte-Baume

Fastest laps

Driver	Time	Lap
Keke Rosberg	1m 39·914s	46
Nelson Piquet	1m 41·528s	2
Ayrton Senna	1m 41·552s	2
Andrea de Cesaris	1m 41·843s	3
Marc Surer	1m 41·934s	44
Michele Alboreto	1m 41·985s	3
Alain Prost	1m 41·991s	2
Niki Lauda	1m 42·037s	3
Elio de Angelis	1m 42·046s	3
Thierry Boutsen	1m 42·226s	46
Teo Fabi	1m 42·310s	48
Derek Warwick	1m 43·279s	4
Stefan Johansson	1m 43·411s	48
Gerhard Berger	1m 43·717s	4
Patrick Tambay	1m 43·869s	5
Jacques Laffite	1m 44·273s	2
Eddie Cheever	1m 45·399s	31
Martin Brundle	1m 45·456s	5
Manfred Winkelhock	1m 45·491s	5
Riccardo Patrese	1m 45·509s	2
Jonathan Palmer	1m 45·696s	6
Philippe Alliot	1m 46·899s	2
Stefan Bellof	1m 47·553s	33
Piercarlo Ghinzani	1m 48·306s	4
Pierluigi Martini	1m 48·720s	3

Points

WORLD CHAMPIONSHIP OF DRIVERS

	Driver	Points
1	Michele Alboreto	31 pts
2=	Elio de Angelis	26
2=	Alain Prost	26
4	Keke Rosberg	18
5	Stefan Johansson	16
6	Patrick Tambay	11
7	Nelson Piquet	10
8	Ayrton Senna	9
9	Thierry Boutsen	6
10	Nigel Mansell	5
11	Stefan Bellof	4
12=	René Arnoux	3
12=	Niki Lauda	3
12=	Andrea de Cesaris	3
15=	Derek Warwick	2
15=	Jacques Laffite	2

CONSTRUCTORS' CUP

1	Ferrari	50 pts
2	Lotus	35
3	McLaren	29
4	Williams	23
5	Renault	13
6	Brabham	10
7	Arrows	6
8	Ligier	5
9	Tyrrell	4

Circuit data

ASA Paul Ricard, near Marseilles
Circuit length: 3·610 miles/5·810 km
Race distance: 53 laps, 191·337 miles/307·928 km
Race weather: Hot, dry.

Entries and practice times

No.	Driver	Nat.	Car	Tyre	Engine	Entrant	Practice 1	Practice 2
1	Niki Lauda	A	Marlboro McLAREN MP4/2B	G	TAG P01 (TTE P01)	Marlboro McLaren International	**1m 07·743s**	1m 09·001s
2	Alain Prost	F	Marlboro McLAREN MP4/2B	G	TAG P01 (TTE P01)	Marlboro McLaren International	**1m 06·308s**	1m 08·532s
3	Martin Brundle	GB	TYRRELL 014	G	Renault EF4	Tyrrell Racing Organisation	1m 10·718s	**1m 09·242s**
4	Stefan Bellof	D	TYRRELL 012	G	Ford-Cosworth DFY	Tyrrell Racing Organisation	1m 17·009s	**1m 16·596s**
5	Nigel Mansell	GB	WILLIAMS FW10	G	Honda RA163–E	Canon Williams Honda Team	1m 09·080s	**1m 06·675s**
6	Keke Rosberg	SF	WILLIAMS FW10	G	Honda RA163–E	Canon Williams Honda Team	1m 06·107s	**1m 05·591s**
7	Nelson Piquet	BR	Olivetti BRABHAM BT54	P	BMW M12/13	Motor Racing Developments Ltd	1m 08·933s	**1m 06·249s**
8	Marc Surer	CH	Olivetti BRABHAM BT54	P	BMW M12/13	Motor Racing Developments Ltd	1m 09·572s	**1m 08·587s**
9	Manfred Winkelhock	D	RAM 03	P	Hart 415T	Skoal Bandit Formula 1 Team	1m 10·299s	**1m 09·114s**
10	Philippe Alliot	F	RAM 03	P	Hart 415T	Skoal Bandit Formula 1 Team	1m 11·162s	**1m 09·609s**
11	Elio de Angelis	I	John Player Special LOTUS 97T	G	Renault EF4/EF15	John Player Special Team Lotus	**1m 07·581s**	1m 07·696s
12	Ayrton Senna	BR	John Player Special LOTUS 97T	G	Renault EF4/EF15	John Player Special Team Lotus	**1m 06·324s**	1m 06·794s
15	Patrick Tambay	F	Elf RENAULT RE60B	G	Renault EF15	Equipe Renault Elf	1m 09·989s	**1m 08·240s**
16	Derek Warwick	GB	Elf RENAULT RE60B	G	Renault EF15	Equipe Renault Elf	**1m 08·238s**	1m 08·604s
17	Gerhard Berger	A	ARROWS A8	G	BMW M12/13	Barclay Arrows BMW	1m 09·870s	**1m 08·672s**
18	Thierry Boutsen	B	ARROWS A8	G	BMW M12/13	Barclay Arrows BMW	1m 09·413s	**1m 09·131s**
19	Teo Fabi	I	TOLEMAN TG185	P	Hart 415T	Toleman Group Motorsport	**1m 07·678s**	1m 07·871s
22	Riccardo Patrese	I	Benetton ALFA ROMEO 185T	G	Alfa Romeo 890T	Benetton Team Alfa Romeo	**1m 08·384s**	1m 10·110s
23	Eddie Cheever	USA	Benetton ALFA ROMEO 185T	G	Alfa Romeo 890T	Benetton Team Alfa Romeo	1m 11·072s	**1m 10·345s**
24	Piercarlo Ghinzani	I	Kelemata OSELLA FA1G	P	Alfa Romeo 890T	Osella Squadra Corse	**1m 16·400s**	—
25	Andrea de Cesaris	I	Gitanes LIGIER JS25	P	Renault EF4/EF15	Equipe Ligier Gitanes	1m 11·082s	**1m 07·448s**
26	Jacques Laffite	F	Gitanes LIGIER JS25	P	Renault EF4/EF15	Equipe Ligier Gitanes	1m 10·756s	**1m 08·656s**
27	Michele Alboreto	I	Fiat FERRARI 156/85	G	Ferrari 126C	Scuderia Ferrari SpA	**1m 06·793s**	1m 07·427s
28	Stefan Johansson	S	Fiat FERRARI 156/85	G	Ferrari 126C	Scuderia Ferrari SpA	1m 08·169s	**1m 07·887s**
29	Pierluigi Martini	I	Simod MINARDI M/85	P	Motori Moderni	Minardi Team	**1m 13·645s**	1m 15·363s
30	Jonathan Palmer	GB	West ZAKSPEED ZAK 841	G	Zakspeed	West Zakspeed Racing	1m 17·856s	**1m 13·713s**

The first session on Friday and Saturday morning practice not officially recorded.

G – Goodyear, P – Pirelli.

Fri p.m. Cool, dry/damp
Sat p.m. Cool, dry

Starting grid

	6 ROSBERG (1m 05·591s) Williams	
7 PIQUET (1m 06·249s) Brabham		
	2 PROST (1m 06·308s) McLaren	
12 SENNA (1m 06·324s) Lotus		
	5 MANSELL (1m 06·675s) Williams	
27 ALBORETO (1m 06·793s) Ferrari		
	25 DE CESARIS (1m 07·448s) Ligier	
11 DE ANGELIS (1m 07·581s) Lotus		
	19 FABI (1m 07·678s) Toleman	
1 LAUDA (1m 07·743s) McLaren		
	28 JOHANSSON (1m 07·887s) Ferrari	
16 WARWICK (1m 08·238s) Renault		
	15 TAMBAY (1m 08·240s) Renault	
22 PATRESE (1m 08·384s) Alfa Romeo		
	8 SURER (1m 08·587s) Brabham	
26 LAFFITE (1m 08·656s) Ligier		
	17 BERGER (1m 08·672s) Arrows	
9 WINKELHOCK (1m 09·114s) RAM		
	18 BOUTSEN (1m 09·131s) Arrows	
*3 BRUNDLE (1m 09·242s) Tyrrell		
	10 ALLIOT (1m 09·609s) RAM	
23 CHEEVER (1m 10·345s) Alfa Romeo		
	29 MARTINI (1m 13·645s) Minardi	
30 PALMER (1m 13·713s) Zakspeed		
	24 GHINZANI (1m 16·400s) Osella	
4 BELLOF (1m 16·596s) Tyrrell		

* Started from back of grid (engine would not start in time for final parade lap).

Results and retirements

Place	Driver	Car	Laps	Time and Speed (mph/km/h)/Retirement	
1	Alain Prost	McLaren-TAG t/c V6	65	1h 18m 10·436s	146·274/235·405
2	Michele Alboreto	Ferrari t/c V6	64		
3	Jacques Laffite	Ligier-Renault t/c V6	64		
4	Nelson Piquet	Brabham-BMW t/c 4	64		
5	Derek Warwick	Renault t/c V6	64		
6	Marc Surer	Brabham-BMW t/c 4	63		
7	Martin Brundle	Tyrrell-Renault t/c V6	63		
8	Gerhard Berger	Arrows-BMW t/c 4	63		
9	Riccardo Patrese	Alfa Romeo t/c V8	62		
10	Ayrton Senna	Lotus-Renault t/c V6	60	Fuel injection electronics	
11	Stefan Bellof	Tyrrell-Cosworth V8	59		
	Niki Lauda	McLaren-TAG t/c V6	57	Electrics	
	Thierry Boutsen	Arrows-BMW t/c 4	57	Spun off	
	Andrea de Cesaris	Ligier-Renault t/c V6	41	Clutch	
	Pierluigi Martini	Minardi-MM t/c V6	38	Transmission	
	Elio de Angelis	Lotus-Renault t/c V6	37	Running, not classified	
	Manfred Winkelhock	RAM-Hart t/c 4	28	Turbo	
	Keke Rosberg	Williams-Honda t/c V6	21	Split exhaust	
	Nigel Mansell	Williams-Honda t/c V6	17	Clutch	
	Eddie Cheever	Alfa Romeo t/c V8	17	Turbo	
	Jonathan Palmer	Zakspeed t/c 4	6	Camshaft drive pinion	
	Teo Fabi	Toleman-Hart t/c 4	4	Crownwheel and pinion	
	Stefan Johansson	Ferrari t/c V6	1	Accident damage	
	Patrick Tambay	Renault t/c V6	0	Spun, then hit by Johansson	
	Philippe Alliot	RAM-Hart t/c 4	0	Accident damage	
	Piercarlo Ghinzani	Osella-Alfa Romeo t/c V8	0	Accident damage	

Fastest lap: Prost, on lap 43, 1m 09·886s, 151·035 mph/243·066 km/h (record).
Previous lap record: Alain Prost (F1 Renault RE40 t/c V6), 1m 14·212s, 142·23 mph/228·896 km/h (1983).

Past winners

Year	Driver	Nat.	Car	Circuit	Distance miles/km	Speed mph/km/h
1952	Alberto Ascari	I	2·0 Ferrari 500	Silverstone	248·80/400·40	90·92/146·32
1953	Alberto Ascari	I	2·0 Ferrari 500	Silverstone	263·43/423·95	92·97/149·62
1954	Froilán González	RA	2·5 Ferrari 625	Silverstone	263·43/423·95	89·69/144·34
1955	Stirling Moss	GB	2·5 Mercedes-Benz W196	Aintree	270·00/434·52	86·47/139·16
1956	Juan Manuel Fangio	RA	2·5 Lancia-Ferrari D50	Silverstone	295·63/475·77	98·65/158·76
1957	Tony Brooks/	GB				
	Stirling Moss	GB	2·5 Vanwall	Aintree	270·00/434·52	86·80/139·69
1958	Peter Collins	GB	2·4 Ferrari Dino 246	Silverstone	219·53/353·30	102·05/164·23
1959	Jack Brabham	AUS	2·5 Cooper T51-Climax	Aintree	225·00/362·10	98·88/159·13
1960	Jack Brabham	AUS	2·5 Cooper T53-Climax	Silverstone	225·00/362·10	108·69/174·92
1961	Wolfgang von Trips	D	1·5 Ferrari Dino 156	Aintree	225·00/362·10	83·91/135·04
1962	Jim Clark	GB	1·5 Lotus 25-Climax	Aintree	225·00/362·10	92·25/148·46
1963	Jim Clark	GB	1·5 Lotus 25-Climax	Silverstone	240·00/386·25	107·75/173·41
1964	Jim Clark	GB	1·5 Lotus 25-Climax	Brands Hatch	212·00/341·18	94·14/151·50
1965	Jim Clark	GB	1·5 Lotus 33-Climax	Silverstone	240·00/386·25	112·02/180·28
1966	Jack Brabham	AUS	3·0 Brabham BT19-Repco	Brands Hatch	212·00/341·18	95·48/153·66
1967	Jim Clark	GB	3·0 Lotus 49-Ford	Silverstone	240·00/386·25	117·64/189·32
1968	Jo Siffert	CH	3·0 Lotus 49B-Ford	Brands Hatch	212·00/341·18	104·83/168·71
1969	Jackie Stewart	GB	3·0 Matra MS80-Ford	Silverstone	245·87/395·69	127·25/204·79
1970	Jochen Rindt	A	3·0 Lotus 72-Ford	Brands Hatch	212·00/341·18	108·69/174·92
1971	Jackie Stewart	GB	3·0 Tyrrell 003-Ford	Silverstone	199·04/320·32	130·48/209·99
1972	Emerson Fittipaldi	BR	3·0 JPS/Lotus 72-Ford	Brands Hatch	201·40/324·12	112·06/180·34
1973	Peter Revson	USA	3·0 McLaren M23-Ford	Silverstone	196·11/315·61	131·75/212·03
1974	Jody Scheckter	ZA	3·0 Tyrrell 007-Ford	Brands Hatch	198·75/319·86	115·74/186·26
1975	Emerson Fittipaldi	BR	3·0 McLaren M23-Ford	Silverstone	164·19/264·24	120·02/193·15
1976	Niki Lauda	A	3·0 Ferrari 312T-2/76	Brands Hatch	198·63/319·67	114·24/183·85
1977	James Hunt	GB	3·0 McLaren M26-Ford	Silverstone	199·38/320·88	130·36/209·79
1978	Carlos Reutemann	RA	3·0 Ferrari 312T-3/78	Brands Hatch	198·63/319·67	116·61/187·66
1979	Clay Regazzoni	CH	3·0 Williams FW07-Ford	Silverstone	199·38/320·88	138·80/223·37
1980	Alan Jones	AUS	3·0 Williams FW07B-Ford	Brands Hatch	198·63/319·67	125·69/202·28
1981	John Watson	GB	3·0 McLaren MP4-Ford	Silverstone	199·38/320·88	137·64/221·51
1982	Niki Lauda	A	3·0 McLaren MP4B-Ford	Brands Hatch	198·63/319·67	124·70/200·68
1983	Alain Prost	F	1·5 Renault RE40 t/c	Silverstone	196·44/316·17	139·22/224·05
1984	Niki Lauda	A	1·5 McLaren MP4/2-TAG t/c	Brands Hatch	185·57/298·64	124·41/200·21
1985	Alain Prost	F	1·5 McLaren MP4/2B-TAG	Silverstone	190·58/306·71	146·27/235·40

Lap chart

1st LAP ORDER	Lap sequence (1–66)
12 A. Senna	12 12 12 12 12 12 12 12 12 12 12 12 12 12 12 12 12 12 12 12 12 12 12 12 12 12 12 12 12 12 12 12 12 12 12 12 12 12 12 12 12 12 12 12 12 12 12 12 12 12 12 12 12 12 12 12 12 12 12 2 12 2 2 2 2 2
6 K. Rosberg	6 6 6 6 6 6 6 6 6 6 6 6 6 6 6 2 2 2 2 2 2 2 2 2 2 2 2 2 2 2 2 2 2 2 2 2 2 2 2 2 2 2 2 2 2 2 2 2 2 2 2 2 2 2 2 2 2 2 2 12 2 12 27 27 27 27
5 N. Mansell	5 5 5 5 25 25 25 25 2 2 2 2 2 2 6 6 6 6 6 6 1 1 1 1 1 1 1 1 1 1 1 1 1 1 1 1 1 1 1 1 1 1 1 1 1 1 1 1 1 1 1 1 1 1 1 1 1 1 27 27 27 26 26 26 26
2 A. Prost	2 25 25 25 5 5 2 2 25 25 25 25 25 25 25 25 25 1 25 25 25 25 25 25 25 25 25 25 25 25 25 25 25 25 25 25 25 27 27 27 27 27 27 27 27 27 27 27 27 27 27 27 27 27 27 27 27 27 27 26 26 26 7 7 7 7
25 P. Ghinzani	25 2 2 2 2 5 5 5 5 5 5 5 5 5 5 1 1 1 25 7 7 7 7 7 27 27 27 27 27 27 27 27 27 27 27 27 1 1 1 1 1 7 7 7 7 7 7 7 7 26 26 7 7 7 16 16 8
7 M. Brundle	7 7 7 7 7 7 7 1 1 1 1 1 1 1 1 1 1 1 20 20 20 20 20 20 1 1 1 20 20 20 20 20 20 20 20 T T 10 10 10 8 8 8 10
27 M. Alboreto	27 11 11 11 11 11 11 7 7 7 7 7 7 7 7 27 27 27 16 16 16 16 16 16 16 26 26 26 26 26 26 26 26 26 19 19 19 16 16 16 16 16 16 16 16 16 16 8 8 11 11 11 11
11 E. de Angelis	11 27 27 27 27 27 27 1 1 1 27 27 27 5 16 16 16 26 26 26 26 26 26 16 16 16 16 16 16 17 17 17 8 8 8 8 8 8 8 8 8 8 17 17 3 3 17
16 D. Warwick	16 16 16 19 1 1 1 27 27 27 16 16 16 16 26 26 26 17 17 17 17 17 17 17 17 17 17 17 17 17 17 17 8 8 8 17 17 17 17 17 17 17 17 17 17 3 3 3 22 22
19 T. Fabi	19 19 19 16 16 16 16 16 16 16 17 17 17 17 17 17 17 18 8 8 8 8 8 8 8 8 8 8 8 8 8 8 8 3 3 3 3 3 3 3 3 3 3 3 3 3 22 22 22
22 R. Patrese	22 8 8 8 23 23 17 17 17 17 17 17 26 26 26 26 8 8 8 18 18 18 18 18 18 18 18 18 18 18 18 18 18 18 18 18 18 18 18 18 18 18 18 18 18 4 4
8 M. Surer	8 23 23 1 17 17 23 23 23 23 23 23 23 23 23 18 18 18 18 3 3 3 3 3 3 3 3 3 3 3 3 3 3 3 3 3 2 22 22 22 22 22 22 22 22 22 22 22 22 22 22 22
23 E. Cheever	23 17 1 23 8 8 8 8 8 8 26 8 8 8 8 3 3 3 22 22 22 22 22 22 22 22 22 22 22 22 22 22 22 22 4 4 4 4 4 4 4 4 4 4 4 4 4 4
17 G. Berger	17 22 17 17 26 26 26 26 26 26 8 18 18 18 18 22 22 9 9 9 9 9 29 29 29 29 29 29 29 29 29 4 4 4
26 J. Laffite	26 1 22 22 22 18 18 18 18 18 18 3 3 3 3 9 9 9 29 29 29 20 20 20 29 4 4 4 4 4 4 4 4 4
30 J. Palmer	30 26 30 26 30 18 22 22 3 3 3 22 22 22 22 29 29 29 4 4 4 4 4 11 11 11 11 11 11 11 11 11 11 11
3 M. Brundle	3 18 26 30 18 30 3 3 22 22 22 22 9 9 9 9 4 4 4 11 11 11 11 11 11 11 11
18 T. Boutsen	18 30 18 18 3 3 9 9 9 9 9 11 29 29 29 29 11 11 11 11
1 N. Lauda	1 3 3 3 9 9 29 29 29 29 29 29 4 4 4 4
9 M. Winkelhock	9 9 9 9 4 4 4 4 4 4 4 4 11 11 11 11 11
4 S. Bellof	4 4 4 4 29 29
29 P. Martini	29 29 29 29
28 S. Johansson	28

RACE STOPPED ONE LAP EARLY

Circuit data

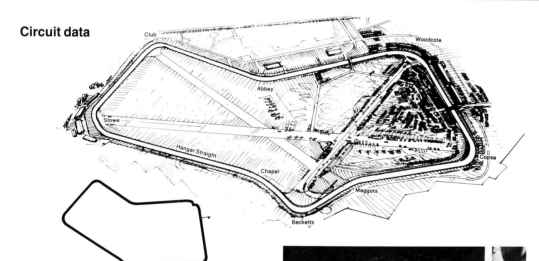

Silverstone Grand Prix Circuit, near Towcester, Northamptonshire

Circuit length: 2·932 miles/4·719 km
Race distance: 65 laps, 190·580 miles/306·708 km (Race scheduled for 66 laps but stopped in error.)
Race weather: Warm, dry

Fastest laps

Driver	Time	Lap
Alain Prost	1m 09·886s	43
Ayrton Senna	1m 10·032s	48
Niki Lauda	1m 10·905s	40
Michele Alboreto	1m 11·290s	56
Jacques Laffite	1m 11·649s	48
Nelson Piquet	1m 11·837s	43
Elio de Angelis	1m 12·068s	18
Andrea de Cesaris	1m 12·089s	36
Marc Surer	1m 12·135s	41
Derek Warwick	1m 12·383s	51
Martin Brundle	1m 12·432s	49
Gerhard Berger	1m 12·765s	38
Keke Rosberg	1m 12·914s	13
Thierry Boutsen	1m 13·021s	48
Riccardo Patrese	1m 13·111s	47
Nigel Mansell	1m 13·532s	16
Manfred Winkelhock	1m 14·486s	26
Eddie Cheever	1m 15·055s	17
Pierluigi Martini	1m 17·486s	24
Jonathan Palmer	1m 17·499s	5
Stefan Bellof	1m 17·854s	52
Teo Fabi	1m 18·250s	4
Stefan Johansson	2m 31·135s	1

Points

WORLD CHAMPIONSHIP OF DRIVERS

1	Michele Alboreto	37 pts
2	Alain Prost	35
3	Elio de Angelis	26
4	Keke Rosberg	18
5	Stefan Johansson	16
6	Nelson Piquet	13
7	Patrick Tambay	11
8	Ayrton Senna	9
9	Thierry Boutsen	6
10	Jacques Laffite	6
11	Nigel Mansell	5
12=	Stefan Bellof	4
12=	Derek Warwick	4
14=	René Arnoux	3
14=	Niki Lauda	3
14=	Andrea de Cesaris	3
17	Marc Surer	1

CONSTRUCTORS' CUP

1	Ferrari	56 pts
2	McLaren	38
3	Lotus	35
4	Williams	23
5	Renault	15
6	Brabham	14
7	Ligier	9
8	Arrows	6
9	Tyrrell	4

Entries and practice times

No.	Driver	Nat.	Car	Tyre	Engine	Entrant	Practice 1	Practice 2
1	Niki Lauda	A	Marlboro McLAREN MP4/2B	G	TAG P01 (TTE P01)	Marlboro McLaren International	1m 19·652s	1m 44·330s
2	Alain Prost	F	Marlboro McLAREN MP4/2B	G	TAG P01 (TTE P01)	Marlboro McLaren International	1m 18·725s	1m 43·088s
3	Stefan Bellof	D	TYRRELL 014	G	Renault EF4	Tyrrell Racing Organisation	1m 21·219s	—
4	Martin Brundle	GB	TYRRELL 012	G	Ford-Cosworth DFY	Tyrrell Racing Organisation	1m 27·621s	1m 47·820s
5	Nigel Mansell	GB	WILLIAMS FW10	G	Honda RA163-E	Canon Williams Honda Team	1m 19·475s	1m 42·050s
6	Keke Rosberg	SF	WILLIAMS FW10	G	Honda RA163-E	Canon Williams Honda Team	1m 18·781s	1m 39·547s
7	Nelson Piquet	BR	Olivetti BRABHAM BT54	P	BMW M12/13	Motor Racing Developments Ltd	1m 18·802s	1m 49·347s
8	Marc Surer	CH	Olivetti BRABHAM BT54	P	BMW M12/13	Motor Racing Developments Ltd	1m 19·558s	1m 38·330s
9	Manfred Winkelhock	D	RAM 03	P	Hart 415T	Skoal Bandit Formula 1 Team	1m 22·607s	1m 51·109s
10	Philippe Alliot	F	RAM 03	P	Hart 415T	Skoal Bandit Formula 1 Team	1m 22·017s	—
11	Elio de Angelis	I	John Player Special LOTUS 97T	G	Renault EF4/EF15	John Player Special Team Lotus	1m 19·120s	1m 29·714s
12	Ayrton Senna	BR	John Player Special LOTUS 97T	G	Renault EF4/EF15	John Player Special Team Lotus	1m 18·792s	1m 36·471s
14	François Hesnault	F	Elf RENAULT RE60	G	Renault EF4	Equipe Renault Elf	1m 23·161s	—
15	Patrick Tambay	F	Elf RENAULT RE60B	G	Renault EF15	Equipe Renault Elf	1m 19·917s	1m 33·373s
16	Derek Warwick	GB	Elf RENAULT RE60B	G	Renault EF15	Equipe Renault Elf	1m 21·237s	1m 46·473s
17	Gerhard Berger	A	ARROWS A8	G	BMW M12/13	Barclay Arrows BMW	1m 20·666s	1m 41·131s
18	Thierry Boutsen	B	ARROWS A8	G	BMW M12/13	Barclay Arrows BMW	1m 19·781s	1m 54·674s
19	Teo Fabi	I	TOLEMAN TG185	P	Hart 415T	Toleman Group Motorsport	1m 17·429s	—
22	Riccardo Patrese	I	Benetton ALFA ROMEO 184T	G	Alfa Romeo 890T	Benetton Team Alfa Romeo	1m 19·338s	—
23	Eddie Cheever	USA	Benetton ALFA ROMEO 184T	G	Alfa Romeo 890T	Benetton Team Alfa Romeo	1m 21·074s	1m 32·376s
24	Huub Rothengatter	NL	Kelemata OSELLA FA1G	P	Alfa Romeo 890T	Osella Squadra Corse	1m 26·478s	—
25	Andrea de Cesaris	I	Gitanes LIGIER JS25	P	Renault EF4/EF15	Equipe Ligier Gitanes	1m 19·738s	1m 39·623s
26	Jacques Laffite	F	Gitanes LIGIER JS25	P	Renault EF4/EF15	Equipe Ligier Gitanes	1m 19·656s	—
27	Michele Alboreto	I	Fiat FERRARI 156/85	G	Ferrari 126C	Scuderia Ferrari SpA	1m 19·194s	1m 41·490s
28	Stefan Johansson	S	Fiat FERRARI 156/85	G	Ferrari 126C	Scuderia Ferrari SpA	1m 18·616s	1m 46·919s
29	Pierluigi Martini	I	Simod MINARDI M/85	P	Motori Moderni	Minardi Team	—	1m 40·506s
30	Jonathan Palmer	GB	West ZAKSPEED ZAK 841	G	Zakspeed	West Zakspeed Racing	1m 24·217s	1m 51·833s

Friday morning and Saturday morning practice sessions not officially recorded.

G – Goodyear, P – Pirelli.

Fri p.m. Cool, dry   *Sat p.m. Cool, wet*

Starting grid

19 FABI (1m 17·429s) Toleman

28 JOHANSSON (1m 18·616s) Ferrari

2 PROST (1m 18·725s) McLaren

6 ROSBERG (1m 18·781s) Williams

12 SENNA (1m 18·792s) Lotus

7 PIQUET (1m 18·802s) Brabham

11 DE ANGELIS (1m 19·120s) Lotus

27 ALBORETO (1m 19·194s) Ferrari

22 PATRESE (1m 19·338s) Alfa Romeo

5 MANSELL (1m 19·475s) Williams

8 SURER (1m 19·558s) Brabham

1 LAUDA (1m 19·652s) McLaren

26 LAFFITE (1m 19·656s) Ligier

25 DE CESARIS (1m 19·738s) Ligier

18 BOUTSEN (1m 19·781s) Arrows

15 TAMBAY (1m 19·917s) Renault

17 BERGER (1m 20·666s) Arrows

23 CHEEVER (1m 21·074s) Alfa Romeo

3 BELLOF (1m 21·219s) Tyrrell

16 WARWICK (1m 21·237s) Renault

10 ALLIOT (1m 22·017s) RAM

9 WINKELHOCK (1m 22·607s) RAM

14 HESNAULT (1m 23·161s) Renault

30 PALMER (1m 24·217s) Zakspeed

24 ROTHENGATTER (1m 26·478s) Osella

4 BRUNDLE (1m 27·621s) Tyrrell

29 MARTINI (1m 40·506s) Minardi

Results and retirements

Place	Driver	Car	Laps	Time and Speed (mph/km/h)/Retirement	
1	Michele Alboreto	Ferrari t/c V6	67	1h 35m 31·337s	118·773/191·147
2	Alain Prost	McLaren-TAG t/c V6	67	1h 35m 42·998s	118·532/190·759
3	Jacques Laffite	Ligier-Renault t/c V6	67	1h 36m 22·491s	117·722/189·456
4	Thierry Boutsen	Arrows-BMW t/c 4	67	1h 36m 26·616s	117·638/189·321
5	Niki Lauda	McLaren-TAG t/c V6	67	1h 36m 45·309s	117·260/188·712
6	Nigel Mansell	Williams-Honda t/c V6	67	1h 36m 48·157s	117·202/188·619
7	Gerhard Berger	Arrows-BMW t/c 4	66		
8	Stefan Bellof	Tyrrell-Renault t/c V6	66		
9	Stefan Johansson	Ferrari t/c V6	66		
10	Martin Brundle	Tyrrell-Cosworth V8	63		
11	Pierluigi Martini	Minardi-MM t/c V6	62	Engine	
12	Keke Rosberg	Williams-Honda t/c V6	61	Brake caliper	
	Eddie Cheever	Alfa Romeo t/c V8	45	Turbo	
	Elio de Angelis	Lotus-Renault t/c V6	40	Engine	
	Huub Rothengatter	Osella-Alfa Romeo t/c V8	32	Gearbox	
	Teo Fabi	Toleman-Hart t/c 4	29	Clutch	
	Ayrton Senna	Lotus-Renault t/c V6	27	c/v joint	
	Derek Warwick	Renault t/c V6	25	Ignition	
	Nelson Piquet	Brabham-BMW t/c 4	23	Turbo	
	Patrick Tambay	Renault t/c V6	19	Spun off	
	Marc Surer	Brabham-BMW t/c 4	12	Engine	
	Manfred Winkelhock	RAM-Hart t/c 4	8	Engine	
	Riccardo Patrese	Alfa Romeo t/c V8	8	Gearbox	
	François Hesnault	Renault t/c V6	8	Clutch	
	Philippe Alliot	RAM-Hart t/c 4	8	Oil pressure	
	Jonathan Palmer	Zakspeed t/c 4	7	Alternator belt	
	Andrea de Cesaris	Ligier-Renault t/c V6	0	Broken steering arm (hit by Laffite)	

Fastest lap: N. Lauda, on lap 53, 1m 22·806s, 122·698 mph/197·464 km/h (record).
Previous lap record: Nelson Piquet (F1 Brabham BT53-BMW t/c 4), 1m 23·146s, 122·196 mph/196·656 km/h (1984).

Past winners

Year	Driver	Nat	Car	Circuit	Distance miles/km	Speed mph/km/h
1950*	Alberto Ascari	I	2·0 Ferrari 166	Nürburgring North	266·78/364·96	77·75/125·13
1951	Alberto Ascari	I	4·5 Ferrari 375	Nürburgring North	283·47/456·20	83·76/134·80
1952	Alberto Ascari	I	2·0 Ferrari 500	Nürburgring North	255·12/410·58	82·20/132·29
1953	Giuseppe Farina	I	2·0 Ferrari 500	Nürburgring North	255·12/410·58	83·91/135·04
1954	Juan Manuel Fangio	RA	2·5 Mercedes-Benz W196	Nürburgring North	311·82/501·82	82·87/133·37
1956	Juan Manuel Fangio	RA	2·5 Lancia-Ferrari D50	Nürburgring North	311·82/501·82	85·45/137·52
1957	Juan Manuel Fangio	RA	2·5 Maserati 250F	Nürburgring North	311·82/501·82	88·82/142·94
1958	Tony Brooks	GB	2·5 Vanwall	Nürburgring North	212·60/342·15	90·31/145·34
1959	Tony Brooks	GB	2·4 Ferrari Dino 256	Avus	309·44/498·00	145·35/230·70
1960*	Jo Bonnier	S	1·5 Porsche 718	Nürburgring South	154·04/247·90	80·23/129·12
1961	Stirling Moss	GB	1·5 Lotus 18/21-Climax	Nürburgring North	212·60/342·15	92·30/148·54
1962	Graham Hill	GB	1·5 BRM P57	Nürburgring North	212·60/342·15	80·35/129·31
1963	John Surtees	GB	1·5 Ferrari 156	Nürburgring North	212·60/342·15	95·83/154·22
1964	John Surtees	GB	1·5 Ferrari 158	Nürburgring North	212·60/342·15	96·58/155·43
1965	Jim Clark	GB	1·5 Lotus 33-Climax	Nürburgring North	212·60/342·15	96·76/160·55
1966	Jack Brabham	AUS	3·0 Brabham BT19-Repco	Nürburgring North	212·60/342·15	86·75/139·61
1967	Denny Hulme	NZ	3·0 Brabham BT24-Repco	Nürburgring North	212·60/342·15	101·41/163·20
1968	Jackie Stewart	GB	3·0 Matra MS10-Ford	Nürburgring North	198·65/319·69	85·71/137·94
1969	Jacky Ickx	B	3·0 Brabham BT26A-Ford	Nürburgring North	198·65/319·69	108·43/174·50
1970	Jochen Rindt	A	3·0 Lotus 72-Ford	Hockenheim	210·92/339·44	124·07/199·67
1971	Jackie Stewart	GB	3·0 Tyrrell 003-Ford	Nürburgring North	170·27/274·02	114·45/184·19
1972	Jacky Ickx	B	3·0 Ferrari 312B-2/72	Nürburgring North	198·65/319·69	116·62/187·68
1973	Jackie Stewart	GB	3·0 Tyrrell 006-Ford	Nürburgring North	198·65/319·69	116·79/187·95
1974	Clay Regazzoni	CH	3·0 Ferrari 312B-3/74	Nürburgring North	198·65/319·69	117·33/188·82
1975	Carlos Reutemann	RA	3·0 Brabham BT44B-bford	Nürburgring North	198·65/319·69	117·73/189·47
1976	James Hunt	GB	3·0 McLaren M23-Ford	Nürburgring North	198·65/319·69	117·18/188·59
1977	Niki Lauda	A	3·0 Ferrari 312T-2/77	Hockenheim	198·27/319·08	129·57/208·53
1978	Mario Andretti	USA	3·0 JPS Lotus 79-Ford	Hockenheim	189·83/305·51	129·41/208·26
1979	Alan Jones	AUS	3·0 Williams FW07-Ford	Hockenheim	189·83/305·51	134·27/216·09
1980	Jacques Laffite	F	3·0 Ligier JS11/15-Ford	Hockenheim	189·83/305·51	137·22/220·83
1981	Nelson Piquet	BR	3·0 Brabham BT49C-Ford	Hockenheim	189·83/305·51	132·53/213·29
1982	Patrick Tambay	F	1·5 Ferrari 126C2 t/c	Hockenheim	190·05/305·86	130·43/209·90
1983	René Arnoux	F	1·5 Ferrari 126C3 t/c	Hockenheim	190·05/305·86	130·81/210·52
1984	Alain Prost	F	1·5 McLaren MP4/2-TAG t/c	Hockenheim	185·83/299·07	131·61/211·80
1985	Michele Alboreto	I	1·5 Ferrari 156/85 t/c	New Nürburgring	189·09/304·31	118·77/191·15

* Non-championship (Formula 2)

Lap chart

The lap chart below records the running order for each of the 67 laps. The "1st LAP ORDER" column lists the starting number and driver; the following columns give the car number at each lap.

1st LAP ORDER	Lap sequence (laps 1–67)
6 K. Rosberg	6 6 6 6 6 6 6 6 6 6 6 6 6 6 6 6 12 12 12 12 12 12 12 12 12 12 12 6 6 6 6 6 6 6 6 6 6 6 6 6 6 6 6 6 6 6 6 6 6 6 6 27 27 27 27 27 27 27 27 27 27 27 27 27 27 27 27
12 A. Senna	12 12 12 12 12 12 12 12 12 12 12 12 6 6 6 6 6 6 6 6 6 6 27 27 27 27 27 27 27 27 27 27 27 27 27 27 27 27 2 2 2 2 2 2 2 2 2 2 2 2 2 2 2 2 2 2 2 2 2 2 2 2 2 2 2
27 M. Alboreto	27 27 27 27 27 27 27 27 27 27 27 27 27 27 27 27 27 27 27 27 11 11 11 11 11 11 11 11 11 11 11 11 11 11 11 11 11 11 2 2 2 2 6 6 6 6 6 6 6 6 6 6 6 6 6 26 5 26 5 5 5 5 26 26 26 26
11 E. de Angelis	11 11 11 11 11 11 11 11 11 11 11 11 11 11 11 11 11 11 11 11 11 11 2 2 2 2 2 2 2 2 2 2 2 2 2 2 2 2 5 5 5 5 5 5 5 5 5 5 5 5 5 5 5 5 5 20 5 20 20 20 20 5 10 10 10
2 A. Prost	2 2 2 2 2 2 2 2 2 2 2 2 2 2 2 2 2 2 2 2 2 2 2 2 2 2 5 5 5 5 5 5 5 5 5 5 5 5 26 26 26 26 26 26 26 26 26 26 26 26 26 26 6 6 6 6 18 18 18 18 5 5 1
7 N. Piquet	7 7 5 5 5 5 5 5 5 5 5 5 5 5 5 5 5 5 5 5 5 5 5 5 5 10 10 1 1 1 10 10 10 10 10 10 10 10 10 10 10 10 10 10 10 10 10 10 10 10 10 10 1 1 1 1 1 1 6
5 N. Mansell	5 5 7 7 7 7 7 7 7 7 7 7 7 7 7 7 7 7 7 7 7 7 7 19 19 1 1 18 18 26 26 26 26 26 18 18 17 17 17 17 17 28 28 28 28 28 28 28 28 28 28 28 28 28 28 28 17 17 17
19 T. Fabi	19 19 19 19 19 19 19 19 19 19 19 19 19 19 19 19 19 19 19 19 1 1 18 18 26 17 17 17 17 17 17 17 17 28 28 28 28 17 17 17 17 17 17 17 17 1 1 17 17 28 28 3
22 R. Patrese	22 22 22 22 22 22 18 18 18 18 18 18 18 18 18 18 18 18 18 18 18 18 26 26 17 17 3 28 28 28 28 28 28 23 23 23 23 1 1 1 1 1 1 1 1 1 1 1 1 17 3 3 3 3 3 28
26 J. Laffite	26 26 18 18 18 18 1 1 1 1 1 1 1 1 1 1 1 1 1 1 1 26 26 26 23 23 17 3 3 28 3 3 3 23 23 23 23 1 1 1 3 3 3 3 3 3 3 3 3 3 3 3 3 3 3 3 29 29 4
18 T. Boutsen	18 18 26 1 1 1 26 26 26 26 26 26 26 26 26 26 26 26 26 26 23 23 17 23 28 28 23 3 3 3 29 29 29 29 29 29 29 29 29 29 29 29 29 29 29 29 29 4 4
1 N. Lauda	1 1 26 26 26 23 15 15 15 23 23 23 23 23 23 23 23 23 17 17 3 3 3 23 23 1 1 1 1 1 1 1 3 29 29 29 4 4 4 4 4 4 4 4 4 4 4 4
23 E. Cheever	23 23 23 23 23 23 15 23 23 17 17 17 17 17 17 17 17 17 3 3 3 28 28 29 29 29 29 29 29 29 29 29 4 4 4
15 P. Tambay	15 15 15 15 15 15 17 17 17 17 3 3 3 3 3 3 3 15 3 3 3 16 28 28 29 29 29 24 24 24 4 4 4 4 4 4
17 G. Berger	17 17 17 17 17 17 3 3 3 8 8 8 15 15 15 15 3 16 16 16 16 28 29 24 24 24 4 4 4
8 M. Surer	8 8 3 3 3 3 22 8 8 8 15 15 15 8 8 16 16 16 16 28 28 28 28 29 29 24 4 4 4
16 D. Warwick	16 3 8 8 8 8 8 16 16 16 16 16 16 16 28 28 28 28 29 29 29 29 24 24 4
3 S. Bellof	3 16 16 16 16 16 16 9 29 29 29 29 28 28 28 29 29 29 29 24 24 24 24 4 4
9 M. Winkelhock	9 9 9 9 9 9 9 14 28 28 28 28 29 29 29 29 24 24 24 4 4 4 4
10 P. Alliot	10 10 14 14 14 14 14 22 24 24 24 24 24 4 4 4 4
30 J. Palmer	30 14 30 30 30 30 29 29 4 4 4 4 4 4
14 F. Hesnault	14 30 29 29 29 29 24 24
29 P. Martini	29 29 24 24 24 24 4 28
24 H. Rothengatter	24 24 4 4 4 28 4
4 M. Brundle	4 4 10 28 28 28 30 10
28 S. Johansson	28 28 28 10 10 10 10

Fastest laps

Driver	Time	Lap
Niki Lauda	1m 22·806s	53
Keke Rosberg	1m 23·481s	59
Thierry Boutsen	1m 23·652s	57
Alain Prost	1m 23·810s	51
Michele Alboreto	1m 24·112s	57
Stefan Johansson	1m 24·185s	16
Ayrton Senna	1m 24·270s	20
Teo Fabi	1m 24·354s	25
Stefan Bellof	1m 24·476s	54
Nigel Mansell	1m 24·486s	5
Elio de Angelis	1m 24·515s	33
Jacques Laffite	1m 24·820s	36
Eddie Cheever	1m 24·937s	39
Nelson Piquet	1m 25·132s	19
Patrick Tambay	1m 25·502s	18
Gerhard Berger	1m 25·555s	5
Riccardo Patrese	1m 25·854s	5
Marc Surer	1m 26·204s	6
Derek Warwick	1m 26·496s	5
Manfred Winkelhock	1m 26·691s	7
Martin Brundle	1m 28·197s	63
Pierluigi Martini	1m 28·341s	38
Philippe Alliot	1m 28·424s	7
François Hesnault	1m 28·671s	6
Huub Rothengatter	1m 29·263s	31
Jonathan Palmer	1m 30·543s	5

Points

WORLD CHAMPIONSHIP OF DRIVERS

1	Michele Alboreto	46 pts
2	Alain Prost	41
3	Elio de Angelis	26
4	Keke Rosberg	18
5	Stefan Johansson	16
6	Nelson Piquet	13
7	Patrick Tambay	11
8	Jacques Laffite	10
9=	Ayrton Senna	9
9=	Thierry Boutsen	9
11	Nigel Mansell	6
12	Niki Lauda	5
13=	Stefan Bellof	4
13=	Derek Warwick	4
15=	René Arnoux	3
15=	Andrea de Cesaris	3
17	Marc Surer	1

CONSTRUCTORS' CUP

1	Ferrari	65 pts
2	McLaren	46
3	Lotus	35
4	Williams	24
5	Renault	15
6	Brabham	14
7	Ligier	13
8	Arrows	9
9	Tyrrell	4

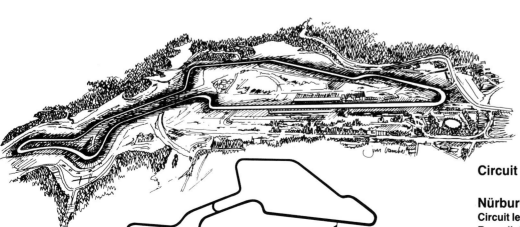

Circuit data

Nürburgring, near Koblenz

Circuit length: 2·822 miles/4·542 km
Race distance: 67 laps, 189·091 miles/304·314 km
Race weather: Cool, dry

Entries and practice times

No.	Driver	Nat.	Car	Tyre	Engine	Entrant	Practice 1	Practice 2
1	Niki Lauda	A	Marlboro McLAREN MP4/2B	G	TAG P01 (TTE P01)	Marlboro McLaren International	**1m 26·250s**	1m 26·727s
2	Alain Prost	F	Marlboro McLAREN MP4/2B	G	TAG P01 (TTE P01)	Marlboro McLaren International	**1m 25·490s**	—
3	Stefan Bellof	D	TYRRELL 014	G	Renault EF4	Tyrrell Racing Organisation	1m 31·022s	**1m 30·514s**
4	Martin Brundle	GB	TYRRELL 012	G	Ford-Cosworth DFY	Tyrrell Racing Organisation	1m 39·247s	**1m 37·317s**
5	Nigel Mansell	GB	WILLIAMS FW10	G	Honda RA163–E	Canon Williams Honda Team	1m 26·453s	**1m 26·052s**
6	Keke Rosberg	SF	WILLIAMS FW10	G	Honda RA163–E	Canon Williams Honda Team	**1m 26·333s**	1m 26·762s
7	Nelson Piquet	BR	Olivetti BRABHAM BT54	P	BMW M12/13	Motor Racing Developments Ltd	1m 26·568s	**1m 26·404s**
8	Marc Surer	CH	Olivetti BRABHAM BT54	P	BMW M12/13	Motor Racing Developments Ltd	**1m 27·954s**	1m 50·796s
9	Philippe Alliot	F	RAM 03	P	Hart 415T	Skoal Bandit Formula 1 Team	1m 32·766s	**1m 29·827s**
10	Kenny Acheson	GB	RAM 03	P	Hart 415T	Skoal Bandit Formula 1 Team	—	**1m 35·072s**
11	Elio de Angelis	I	John Player Special LOTUS 97T	G	Renault EF4/EF15	John Player Special Team Lotus	**1m 26·799s**	—
12	Ayrton Senna	BR	John Player Special LOTUS 97T	G	Renault EF4/EF15	John Player Special Team Lotus	**1m 28·123s**	3m 04·856s
15	Patrick Tambay	F	Elf RENAULT RE60B	G	Renault EF15	Equipe Renault Elf	1m 27·722s	**1m 27·502s**
16	Derek Warwick	GB	Elf RENAULT RE60B	G	Renault EF15	Equipe Renault Elf	1m 30·602s	**1m 28·006s**
17	Gerhard Berger	A	ARROWS A8	G	BMW M12/13	Barclay Arrows BMW	**1m 28·566s**	1m 28·762s
18	Thierry Boutsen	B	ARROWS A8	G	BMW M12/13	Barclay Arrows BMW	1m 28·617s	**1m 28·262s**
19	Teo Fabi	I	TOLEMAN TG185	P	Hart 415T	Toleman Group Motorsport	**1m 26·664s**	—
20	Piercarlo Ghinzani	I	TOLEMAN TG185	P	Hart 415T	Toleman Group Motorsport	**1m 28·894s**	—
22	Riccardo Patrese	I	Benetton ALFA ROMEO 184T	G	Alfa Romeo 890T	Benetton Team Alfa Romeo	1m 29·485s	**1m 27·851s**
23	Eddie Cheever	USA	Benetton ALFA ROMEO 184T	G	Alfa Romeo 890T	Benetton Team Alfa Romeo	**1m 29·031s**	1m 29·608s
24	Huub Rothengatter	NL	Kelemata OSELLA FA1G	P	Alfa Romeo 890T	Osella Squadra Corse	1m 35·329s	1m 58·090s
25	Andrea de Cesaris	I	Gitanes LIGIER JS25	P	Renault EF4/EF15	Equipe Ligier Gitanes	**1m 28·666s**	—
26	Jacques Laffite	F	Gitanes LIGIER JS25	P	Renault EF4/EF15	Equipe Ligier Gitanes	1m 29·181s	**1m 28·249s**
27	Michele Alboreto	I	Fiat FERRARI 156/85	G	Ferrari 126C	Scuderia Ferrari SpA	1m 29·774s	**1m 27·516s**
28	Stefan Johansson	S	Fiat FERRARI 156/85	G	Ferrari 126C	Scuderia Ferrari SpA	1m 28·134s	**1m 27·961s**
29	Pierluigi Martini	I	Simod MINARDI M/85	P	Motori Moderni	Minardi Team	—	**1m 36·765s**
30	Jonathan Palmer	GB	West ZAKSPEED ZAK 841	G	Zakspeed	West Zakspeed Racing	1m 36·060s	**1m 35·787s**

Friday morning and Saturday morning practice sessions not officially recorded.

G – Goodyear, P – Pirelli.

Fri p.m.
Hot, dry

Sat p.m.
Cool, dry,
then wet

Starting grid

2 PROST (1m 25·490s)
McLaren

5 MANSELL (1m 26·052s)
Williams

1 LAUDA (1m 26·250s)
McLaren

6 ROSBERG (1m 26·333s)
Williams

7 PIQUET (1m 26·404s)
Brabham

19 FABI (1m 26·664s)
Toleman

11 DE ANGELIS (1m 26·799s)
Lotus

15 TAMBAY (1m 27·502s)
Renault

27 ALBORETO (1m 27·516s)
Ferrari

22 PATRESE (1m 27·851s)
Alfa Romeo

8 SURER (1m 27·954s)
Brabham

28 JOHANSSON (1m 27·961s)
Ferrari

16 WARWICK (1m 28·006s)
Renault

12 SENNA (1m 28·123s)
Lotus

26 LAFFITE (1m 28·249s)
Ligier

18 BOUTSEN (1m 28·262s)
Arrows

17 BERGER (1m 28·566s)
Arrows

25 DE CESARIS (1m 28·666s)
Ligier

*20 GHINZANI (1m 28·894s)
Toleman

23 CHEEVER (1m 29·031s)
Alfa Romeo

9 ALLIOT (1m 29·827s)
RAM

3 BELLOF (1m 30·514s)
Tyrrell

10 ACHESON (1m 35·072s)
RAM

24 ROTHENGATTER (1m 35·329s)
Osella

30 PALMER (1m 35·787s)
Zakspeed

29 MARTINI (1m 36·765s)
Minardi

Did not start:
3 Brundle (Tyrrell-Cosworth), 1m 37·317s, did not qualify.
*20 Ghinzani (Toleman), engine failure during lap before race was stopped and re-started.

Results and retirements

Place	Driver	Car	Laps	Time and Speed (mph/km/h)/Retirement	
1	Alain Prost	McLaren-TAG t/c V6	52	1h 20m 12·583s	143·618/231·132
2	Ayrton Senna	Lotus-Renault t/c V6	52	1h 20m 42·585s	142·729/229·700
3	Michele Alboreto	Ferrari t/c V6	52	1h 20m 46·939s	142·601/229·494
4	Stefan Johansson	Ferrari t/c V6	52	1h 20m 51·656s	142·462/229·271
5	Elio de Angelis	Lotus-Renault t/c V6	52	1h 21m 34·675s	141·210/227·256
6	Marc Surer	Brabham-BMW t/c 4	51		
7	Stefan Bellof	Tyrrell-Renault t/c V6	49	Out of fuel	
8	Thierry Boutsen	Arrows-BMW t/c 4	49		
9	Huub Rothengatter	Osella-Alfa Romeo t/c V8	48		
10	Patrick Tambay	Renault t/c V6	46	Engine	
	Jacques Laffite	Ligier-Renault t/c V6	43	Accident	
	Pierluigi Martini	Minardi-MM t/c V6	40	Suspension failure	
	Niki Lauda	McLaren-TAG t/c V6	39	Engine	
	Gerhard Berger	Arrows-BMW t/c 4	32	Turbo	
	Teo Fabi	Toleman-Hart t/c 4	31	Electrics	
	Derek Warwick	Renault t/c V6	29	Engine	
	Kenny Acheson	RAM-Hart t/c 4	28	Engine	
	Nelson Piquet	Brabham-BMW t/c 4	26	Exhaust	
	Nigel Mansell	Williams-Honda t/c V6	25	Engine	
	Riccardo Patrese	Alfa Romeo t/c V8	25	Engine	
	Jonathan Palmer	Zakspeed t/c 4	17	Engine	
	Philippe Alliot	RAM-Hart t/c 4	16	Turbo	
	Andrea de Cesaris	Ligier-Renault t/c V6	13	Accident	
	Eddie Cheever	Alfa Romeo t/c V8	6	Turbo	
	Keke Rosberg	Williams-Honda t/c V6	4	Engine	

Fastest lap: Prost, on lap 39, 1m 29·241s, 148·943 mph/239·701 km/h (record).
Previous lap record: René Arnoux (F1 Renault RE20 t/c V6), 1m 32·53s, 143·659 mph/231·197 km/h (1980).

Past winners

Year	Driver	Nat	Car	Circuit	Distance miles/km	Speed mph/km/h
1963*	Jack Brabham	AUS	1·5 Brabham BT7-Climax	Zeltweg	159·07/256·00	96·34/115·04
1964	Lorenzo Bandini	I	1·5 Ferrari 156	Zeltweg	208·78/336·00	99·20/159·65
1965]	Jochen Rindt	A	3·3 Ferrari 250LM	Zeltweg	198·84/320·00	97·13/156·32
1966]	Gerhard Mitter/ Hans Herrmann	D D	2·0 Porsche 906	Zeltweg	312·18/502·40	99·68/160·42
1967	Paul Hawkins	AUS	4·7 Ford GT40	Zeltweg	312·18/502·40	95·29/153·35
1968	Jo Siffert	CH	3·0 Porsche 908/02 Spyder	Zeltweg	312·18/502·40	106·86/171·97
1969]	Jo Siffert/ Kurt Ahrens	CH D	4·5 Porsche 917	Österreichring	624·40/1004·87	115·78/186·33
1970	Jacky Ickx	B	3·0 Ferrari 312B-1/70	Österreichring	220·38/354·67	129·27/208·04
1971	Jo Siffert	CH	3·0 BRM P160	Österreichring	198·34/319·20	131·64/211·85
1972	Emerson Fittipaldi	BR	3·0 JPS/Lotus 72-Ford	Österreichring	198·34/319·20	133·29/214·51
1973	Ronnie Peterson	S	3·0 JPS/Lotus 72-Ford	Österreichring	198·34/319·20	133·99/215·64
1974	Carlos Reutemann	RA	3·0 Brabham BT44-Ford	Österreichring	198·34/319·20	134·09/215·80
1975	Vittorio Brambilla	I	3·0 March 751-Ford	Österreichring	106·12/170·78	110·30/177·51
1976	John Watson	GB	3·0 Penske PC4-Ford	Österreichring	198·29/319·11	132·00/212·41
1977	Alan Jones	AUS	3·0 Shadow DN8-Ford	Österreichring	199·39/320·89	122·98/197·91
1978	Ronnie Peterson	S	3·0 JPS/Lotus 79-Ford	Österreichring	199·39/320·89	118·03/189·95
1979	Alan Jones	AUS	3·0 Williams FW07-Ford	Österreichring	199·39/320·89	136·52/219·71
1980	Jean-Pierre Jabouille	F	1·5 Renault RS t/c	Österreichring	199·39/320·89	138·69/223·20
1981	Jacques Laffite	F	3·0 Ligier JS17-Matra	Österreichring	195·70/314·95	140·23/225·70
1982	Elio de Angelis	I	3·0 Lotus 91-Ford	Österreichring	195·70/314·95	138·07/222·20
1983	Alain Prost	F	1·5 Renault RE40 t/c	Österreichring	195·70/314·95	138·87/223·49
1984	Niki Lauda	A	1·5 McLaren MP4/2 t/c	Österreichring	188·31/303·06	139·11/223·98
1985	Alain Prost	F	1·5 McLaren MP4/2B t/c	Österreichring	191·99/308·98	143·62/231·13

* Non-championship (Formula 1)
† Sports car race

Lap chart

1st LAP ORDER	1	2	3	4	5	6	7	8	9	10	11	12	13	14	15	16	17	18	19	20	21	22	23	24	25	26	27	28	29	30	31	32	33	34	35	36	37	38	39	40	41	42	43	44	45	46	47	48	49	50	51	52
2 A. Prost	2	2	2	2	2	2	2	2	2	2	2	2	2	2	2	2	2	2	2	2	2	2	2	2	2	2	1	1	1	1	1	1	1	1	1	1	1	1	1	1	1	2	2	2	2	2	2	2	2	2	2	2
6 K. Rosberg	6	6	6	1	1	1	1	1	1	1	1	1	1	1	1	1	1	1	1	1	1	1	1	1	1	1	2	2	2	2	2	2	2	2	2	2	2	2	2	2	12	12	12	12	12	12	12	12	12	12	12	12
1 N. Lauda	1	1	1	7	7	7	7	7	7	7	7	7	7	7	7	7	7	7	7	7	7	7	7	6	12	12	12	12	12	12	12	12	12	12	12	12	27	27	27	27	27	27	27	27	27	27	27	27				
1 N. Piquet	7	7	11	11	11	11	11	11	11	11			3	3	3	3	3	11	11	11	11	27	27	27	27	27	27	27	27	27	26	26	26	26	26	26	26	26	26	26	26	26	26	26	26	26	26	26				
11 É. de Angelis	11	11	11	5	5	5	5	5	5	5	5	5	5	5	5	5	5	5	11	11	11	11	11	12	12	12	27	27	27	27	28	28	28	28	28	28	28	28	28	11	11	11	11	11	11	11	11	11	11	11	11	11
5 N. Mansell	5	5	5	15	15	19	19	19	19	19	19	19	19	12	12	12	12	12	12	12	11	11	28	28	28	28	11	11	11	11	11	11	11	11	8	8	8	8	8	8	8	8	8	8	8							
15 P. Tambay	15	15	15	19	19	15	15	15	12	12	12	12	12	19	19	27	27	27	27	27	27	7	8	8	8	8	8	8	8	8	8	8	26	26	15	15	15	15	3	3	3											
19 T. Fabi	19	19	19	27	27	27	27	27	27	27	27	27	27	27	28	28	28	28	28	28	28	8	16	16	26	26	26	26	26	26	26	26	26	26	15	15	26	26	18	18	18	18	18									
27 M. Alboreto	27	27	27	12	12	12	12	12	28	28	28	28	28	28	19	19	19	16	16	16	16	16	26	26	27	17	17	17	17	15	15	15	15	15	18	18	18	18	3	3	3	24	24									
12 A. Senna	12	12	12	16	16	28	28	28	16	16	16	16	16	16	16	16	16	26	26	26	8	8	26	18	18	18	15	15	15	18	18	18	18	18	3	3	3	3	24	24	24											
16 D. Warwick	16	16	16	28	28	16	16	16	25	25	25	25	26	26	26	26	26	8	8	8	26	18	17	17	15	18	18	18	3	3	3	3	3	3	24	24	24	24														
8 M. Surer	8	28	28	25	25	25	25	25	26	26	26	26	8	8	8	8	8	8	19	3	18	17	15	15	15	3	3	3	24	24	24	24	24	24	29																
28 S. Johansson	28	25	25	26	26	26	26	26	15	3	8	8	8	3	3	3	3	3	18	17	17	3	3	3	24	24	24	24	29	29	29	29	29																			
25 A. de Cesaris	25	26	26	23	23	3	3	3	3	8	3	3	18	18	18	18	18	18	17	17	3	3	15	10	10	24	24	29	29	29																						
26 J. Laffite	26	23	23	3	3	18	18	8	8	18	18	18	18	17	17	17	17	17	17	22	22	22	22	10	24	24	24	19	19																							
23 E. Cheever	23	17	3	18	18	8	8	18	18	17	17	17	17	30	22	22	22	22	15	15	15	15	24	29	29	19																										
17 G. Berger	17	3	18	17	17	17	17	17	30	30	30	30	22	30	30	15	15	15	15	10	10	10	10	29	19	19																										
3 S. Bellof	3	18	17	8	8	30	30	30	22	22	22	22	9	9	15	15	10	10	10	10	24	24	24	24	19																											
18 T. Boutsen	18	8	8	30	30	22	22	22	22	9	9	9	9	10	10	10	10	24	24	24	29	29	29	29																												
30 J. Palmer	30	30	30	6	22	24	9	9	9	10	10	10	10	15	15	24	24	29	29	29	29	19	19	19	19																											
24 P. Ghinzani	24	24	24	22	24	29	24	10	10	15	15	15	15	24	24	29	29																																			
29 P. Martini	29	29	22	24	29	9	10	24	24	24	24	24	29	29	9																																					
22 R. Patrese	22	22	29	10	10	22	9	29	29	29	29	29	29																																							
10 K. Acheson	10	10	10	10	9																																															
9 P. Alliot	9	9	9	9																																																

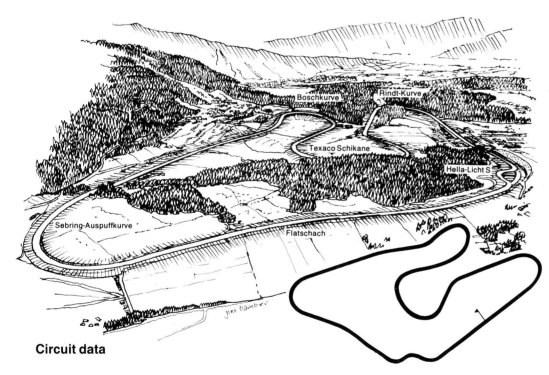

Circuit data

Österreichring, near Knittelfeld
Circuit length: 3·692 miles/5·9424 km
Race distance: 52 laps, 191·993 miles/308·984 km
Race weather: Warm, dry

Fastest laps

Driver	Time	Lap
Alain Prost	1m 29·241s	39
Niki Lauda	1m 30·052s	38
Elio de Angelis	1m 30·949s	40
Teo Fabi	1m 31·089s	26
Stefan Johansson	1m 31·501s	45
Patrick Tambay	1m 31·525s	45
Michele Alboreto	1m 31·536s	40
Ayrton Senna	1m 31·666s	36
Keke Rosberg	1m 31·667s	3
Nelson Piquet	1m 31·816s	22
Nigel Mansell	1m 31·835s	22
Thierry Boutsen	1m 32·758s	34
Marc Surer	1m 32·935s	16
Gerhard Berger	1m 33·663s	33
Derek Warwick	1m 33·677s	22
Jacques Laffite	1m 33·708s	23
Andrea de Cesaris	1m 33·883s	13
Philippe Alliot	1m 34·040s	10
Stefan Bellof	1m 34·219s	29
Riccardo Patrese	1m 34·254s	24
Eddie Cheever	1m 35·522s	3
Jonathan Palmer	1m 35·792s	13
Kenny Acheson	1m 36·491s	17
Huub Rothengatter	1m 38·336s	21
Pierluigi Martini	1m 38·727s	27

Points

CONSTRUCTORS' CUP

1	Ferrari	72 pts
2	McLaren	55
3	Lotus	43
4	Williams	24
5=	Renault	15
5=	Brabham	15
7	Ligier	13
8	Arrows	9
9	Tyrrell	4

WORLD CHAMPIONSHIP OF DRIVERS

1=	Michele Alboreto	50 pts
1=	Alain Prost	50
3	Elio de Angelis	28
4	Stefan Johansson	19
5	Keke Rosberg	18
6	Ayrton Senna	15
7	Nelson Piquet	13
8	Patrick Tambay	11
9	Jacques Laffite	10
10	Thierry Boutsen	9
11	Nigel Mansell	6
12	Niki Lauda	5
13=	Stefan Bellof	4
13=	Derek Warwick	4
15=	René Arnoux	3
15=	Andrea de Cesaris	3
17	Marc Surer	2

Grote Prijs van Nederland, 25 August/statistics

Entries and practice times

No.	Driver	Nat.	Car	Tyre	Engine	Entrant	Practice 1	Practice 2
1	Niki Lauda	A	Marlboro McLAREN MP4/2B	G	TAG P01 (TTE P01)	Marlboro McLaren International	1m 13·059s	—
2	Alain Prost	F	Marlboro McLAREN MP4/2B	G	TAG P01 (TTE P01)	Marlboro McLaren International	1m 11·801s	1m 29·507s
3	Martin Brundle	GB	TYRRELL 014	G	Renault EF4	Tyrrell Racing Organisation	1m 14·920s	1m 32·003s
4	Stefan Bellof	D	TYRRELL 014	G	Renault EF4	Tyrrell Racing Organisation	1m 15·236s	—
5	Nigel Mansell	GB	WILLIAMS FW10	G	Honda RA163–E	Canon Williams Honda Team	1m 12·614s	1m 32·740s
6	Keke Rosberg	SF	WILLIAMS FW10	G	Honda RA163–E	Canon Williams Honda Team	1m 11·647s	—
7	Nelson Piquet	BR	Olivetti BRABHAM BT54	P	BMW M12/13	Motor Racing Developments Ltd	1m 11·074s	—
8	Marc Surer	CH	Olivetti BRABHAM BT54	P	BMW M12/13	Motor Racing Developments Ltd	1m 12·856s	—
9	Philippe Alliot	F	RAM 03	P	Hart 415T	Skoal Bandit Formula 1 Team	1m 18·525s	1m 36·270s
10	Kenny Acheson	GB	RAM 03	P	Hart 415T	Skoal Bandit Formula 1 Team	1m 20·429s	—
11	Elio de Angelis	I	John Player Special LOTUS 97T	G	Renault EF4/EF15	John Player Special Team Lotus	1m 13·078s	1m 30·078s
12	Ayrton Senna	BR	John Player Special LOTUS 97T	G	Renault EF4/EF15	John Player Special Team Lotus	1m 11·837s	—
15	Patrick Tambay	F	Elf RENAULT RE60B	G	Renault EF15	Equipe Renault Elf	1m 12·486s	—
16	Derek Warwick	GB	Elf RENAULT RE60B	G	Renault EF15	Equipe Renault Elf	1m 13·289s	—
17	Gerhard Berger	A	ARROWS A8	G	BMW M12/13	Barclay Arrows BMW	1m 13·680s	1m 34·857s
18	Thierry Boutsen	B	ARROWS A8	G	BMW M12/13	Barclay Arrows BMW	1m 12·746s	—
19	Teo Fabi	I	TOLEMAN TG185	P	Hart 415T	Toleman Group Motorsport	1m 12·310s	—
20	Piercarlo Ghinzani	I	TOLEMAN TG185	P	Hart 415T	Toleman Group Motorsport	1m 13·705s	—
22	Riccardo Patrese	I	Benetton ALFA ROMEO 184T	G	Alfa Romeo 890T	Benetton Team Alfa Romeo	1m 14·240s	—
23	Eddie Cheever	USA	Benetton ALFA ROMEO 184T	G	Alfa Romeo 890T	Benetton Team Alfa Romeo	1m 14·912s	1m 32·572s
24	Huub Rothengatter	NL	Kelemata OSELLA FA1G	P	Alfa Romeo 890T	Osella Squadra Corse	1m 19·410s	1m 38·149s
25	Andrea de Cesaris	I	Gitanes LIGIER JS25	P	Renault EF4/EF15	Equipe Ligier Gitanes	1m 13·797s	1m 34·638s
26	Jacques Laffite	F	Gitanes LIGIER JS25	P	Renault EF4/EF15	Equipe Ligier Gitanes	1m 13·435s	1m 28·393s
27	Michele Alboreto	I	Fiat FERRARI 156/85	G	Ferrari 126C	Scuderia Ferrari SpA	1m 13·725s	—
28	Stefan Johansson	S	Fiat FERRARI 156/85	G	Ferrari 126C	Scuderia Ferrari SpA	1m 13·768s	1m 32·544s
29	Pierluigi Martini	I	Simod MINARDI M/85	P	Motori Moderni	Minardi Team	1m 17·919s	1m 38·227s
30	Jonathan Palmer	GB	West ZAKSPEED ZAK 841	G	Zakspeed	West Zakspeed Racing	1m 16·257s	1m 34·316s

Friday morning and Saturday morning practice sessions not officially recorded.

Fri p.m. Warm, dry

Sat p.m. Wet, cool

G – Goodyear, P – Pirelli.

Starting grid

7 PIQUET (1m 11·074s)
Brabham

6 ROSBERG (1m 11·647s)
Williams

2 PROST (1m 11·801s)
McLaren

12 SENNA (1m 11·837s)
Lotus

19 FABI (1m 12·310s)
Toleman

*15 TAMBAY (1m 12·486s)
Renault

5 MANSELL (1m 12·614s)
Williams

18 BOUTSEN (1m 12·746s)
Arrows

8 SURER (1m 12·856s)
Brabham

1 LAUDA (1m 13·059s)
McLaren

11 DE ANGELIS (1m 13·078s)
Lotus

16 WARWICK (1m 13·289s)
Renault

26 LAFFITE (1m 13·435s)
Ligier

17 BERGER (1m 13·680s)
Arrows

20 GHINZANI (1m 13·705s)
Toleman

27 ALBORETO (1m 13·725s)
Ferrari

28 JOHANSSON (1m 13·768s)
Ferrari

25 DE CESARIS (1m 13·797s)
Ligier

22 PATRESE (1m 14·240s)
Alfa Romeo

23 CHEEVER (1m 14·912s)
Alfa Romeo

3 BRUNDLE (1m 14·920s)
Tyrrell

4 BELLOF (1m 15·236s)
Tyrrell

30 PALMER (1m 16·257s)
Zakspeed

29 MARTINI (1m 17·919s)
Minardi

9 ALLIOT (1m 18·525s)
RAM

24 ROTHENGATTER (1m 19·410s)
Osella

* Started from pit lane.
Did not start:
10 Acheson (RAM-Hart), 1m 20·429s, did not qualify.

Results and retirements

Place	Driver	Car	Laps	Time and Speed (mph/km/h)/Retirement	
1	Niki Lauda	McLaren-TAG t/c V6	70	1h 32m 29·263s	119·979/193·089
2	Alain Prost	McLaren-TAG t/c V6	70	1h 32m 29·495s	119·975/193·081
3	Ayrton Senna	Lotus-Renault t/c V6	70	1h 33m 17·754s	118·941/191·417
4	Michele Alboreto	Ferrari t/c V6	70	1h 33m 18·100s	118·933/191·405
5	Elio de Angelis	Lotus-Renault t/c V6	69		
6	Nigel Mansell	Williams-Honda t/c V6	69		
7	Martin Brundle	Tyrrell-Renault t/c V6	69		
8	Nelson Piquet	Brabham-BMW t/c 4	69		
9	Gerhard Berger	Arrows-BMW t/c 4	68		
10	Marc Surer	Brabham-BMW t/c 4	65	Exhaust	
	Huub Rothengatter	Osella-Alfa Romeo t/c V8	46	Running, not classified	
	Thierry Boutsen	Arrows-BMW t/c 4	44	Suspension	
	Philippe Alliot	RAM-Hart t/c 4	42	Engine	
	Stefan Bellof	Tyrrell-Renault t/c V6	39	Engine	
	Derek Warwick	Renault t/c V6	37	Gearbox	
	Andrea de Cesaris	Ligier-Renault t/c V6	35	Turbo	
	Patrick Tambay	Renault t/c V6	32	Transmission	
	Keke Rosberg	Williams-Honda t/c V6	20	Engine	
	Teo Fabi	Toleman-Hart t/c 4	18	Wheel bearing	
	Jacques Laffite	Ligier-Renault t/c V6	17	Electrics	
	Jonathan Palmer	Zakspeed t/c 4	13	Oil pressure	
	Piercarlo Ghinzani	Toleman-Hart t/c 4	12	Engine	
	Stefan Johansson	Ferrari t/c V6	9	Engine	
	Pierluigi Martini	Minardi-MM t/c V6	1	Accident	
	Eddie Cheever	Alfa Romeo t/c V8	1	Turbo	
	Riccardo Patrese	Alfa Romeo t/c V8	1	Turbo	

Fastest lap: Prost, on lap 57, 1m 16·538s, 124·270 mph/199·995 km/h (record).
Previous lap record: René Arnoux (F1 Renault RE t/c V6), 1m 19·35s, 119·867 mph/192·907 km/h (1980).

Past winners

Year	Driver	Nat	Car	Circuit	Distance miles/km	Speed mph/km/h
1949*	Luigi Villoresi	I	1·5 Ferrari 125 GP s/c	Zandvoort	104·22/167·72	77·09/124·06
1950*	Louis Rosier	F	4·5 Lago-Talbot	Zandvoort	234·49/377·37	76·63/123·32
1951*	Louis Rosier	F	4·5 Lago-Talbot	Zandvoort	234·49/377·37	78·45/126·26
1952	Alberto Ascari	I	2·0 Ferrari 500	Zandvoort	234·49/377·37	81·13/130·53
1953	Alberto Ascari	I	2·0 Ferrari 500	Zandvoort	234·49/377·37	81·05/130·43
1955	Juan Manuel Fangio	RA	2·5 Mercedes-Benz W196	Zandvoort	260·54/419·30	89·65/144·27
1958	Stirling Moss	GB	2·5 Vanwall	Zandvoort	195·41/314·48	93·93/151·17
1959	Jo Bonnier	S	2·5 BRM P25	Zandvoort	195·41/314·48	93·46/150·42
1960	Jack Brabham	AUS	2·5 Cooper T53 Climax	Zandvoort	195·41/314·48	96·27/154·93
1961	Wolfgang von Trips	D	1·5 Ferrari Dino 156	Zandvoort	195·41/314·48	96·23/154·83
1962	Graham Hill	GB	1·5 BRM P57	Zandvoort	208·43/335·44	95·44/153·60
1963	Jim Clark	GB	1·5 Lotus 25-Climax	Zandvoort	208·43/335·44	97·53/156·96
1964	Jim Clark	GB	1·5 Lotus 25-Climax	Zandvoort	208·43/335·44	98·02/157·74
1965	Jim Clark	GB	1·5 Lotus 33-Climax	Zandvoort	208·43/335·44	100·87/162·33
1966	Jack Brabham	AUS	3·0 Brabham BT19-Repco	Zandvoort	234·49/377·37	100·10/161·11
1967	Jim Clark	GB	3·0 Lotus 49-Ford	Zandvoort	234·49/377·37	104·45/168·09
1968	Jackie Stewart	GB	3·0 Matra MS10-Ford	Zandvoort	234·49/377·37	84·66/136·25
1969	Jackie Stewart	GB	3·0 Matra MS80-Ford	Zandvoort	234·49/377·37	111·04/178·71
1970	Jochen Rindt	A	3·0 Lotus 72-Ford	Zandvoort	208·43/335·44	112·96/181·78
1971	Jacky Ickx	B	3·0 Ferrari 312B-2/71	Zandvoort	182·38/293·51	94·06/151·38
1973	Jackie Stewart	GB	3·0 Tyrrell 006-Ford	Zandvoort	189·07/304·27	114·35/184·02
1974	Niki Lauda	A	3·0 Ferrari 312B-3/74	Zandvoort	196·94/316·95	114·72/184·62
1975	James Hunt	GB	3·0 Hesketh 308-Ford	Zandvoort	196·94/316·95	100·48/177·80
1976	James Hunt	GB	3·0 McLaren M23-Ford	Zandvoort	196·94/316·95	112·68/181·35
1977	Niki Lauda	A	3·0 Ferrari 312T-2/77	Zandvoort	196·94/316·95	116·12/186·87
1978	Mario Andretti	USA	3·0 JPS/Lotus 79-Ford	Zandvoort	196·94/316·95	116·92/188·16
1979	Alan Jones	AUS	3·0 Williams FW07-Ford	Zandvoort	196·62/187·67	116·62/187·67
1980	Nelson Piquet	BR	3·0 Brabham BT49-Ford	Zandvoort	190·23/306·14	116·19/186·99
1981	Alain Prost	F	1·5 Renault RE t/c	Zandvoort	190·23/306·14	113·71/183·00
1982	Didier Pironi	F	1·5 Ferrari 126C2 t/c	Zandvoort	190·23/306·14	116·38/187·30
1983	René Arnoux	F	1·5 Ferrari 126C3 t/c	Zandvoort	190·23/306·14	115·64/186·10
1984	Alain Prost	F	1·5 McLaren MP4/2-TAG t/c	Zandvoort	187·59/301·89	115·60/186·05
1985	Niki Lauda	A	1·5 McLaren MP4/2B-TAG t/c	Zandvoort	184·94/297·64	119·98/193·09

* Non-championship

Lap chart

1st LAP ORDER		1 2 3 4 5 6 7 8 9 10 11 12 13 14 15 16 17 18 19 20 21 22 23 24 25 26 27 28 29 30 31 32 33 34 35 36 37 38 39 40 41 42 43 44 45 46 47 48 49 50 51 52 53 54 55 56 57 58 59 60 61 62 63 64 65 66 67 68 69 70
6	K. Rosberg	6 6 6 6 6 6 6 6 6 6 6 6 6 6 6 6 6 6 6 6 2 2 2 2 2 2 2 2 2 2 2 2 1 1 1 1 1 1 1 1 1 1 1 1 1 1 1 1 1 1 1 1 1 1 1 1 1 1 1 1 1 1 1 1 1 1 1 1 1 1
12	A. Senna	12 12 12 12 12 12 12 12 12 12 12 2 2 2 2 2 2 12 12 12 12 12 12 27 27 27 27 1 1 12 12 12 12 12 12 12 12 12 12 12 12 2 2 2 2 2 2 2 2 2 2 2 2 2 2 2 2 2 2 2 2 2 2 2 2 2 2 2 2 2
19	T. Fabi	19 2 2 2 2 2 2 2 2 2 2 2 1 1 1 1 1 1 16 16 16 16 16 16 16 1 1 1 12 12 2 2 2 2 2 2 2 2 2 2 2 2 12 12 12 12 12 12 12 12 12 12 12 12 12 12 12 12 12 12 12 12 12 12 12 12 12 12 12 12
2	A. Prost	2 10 10 10 10 1 1 1 1 1 1 12 12 12 12 12 10 10 10 27 27 27 0 0 0 12 12 27 0 0 0 11 11 11 11 11 11 11 11 11 27 27 27 27 27 27 27 27 27 27 27 27 27 27 27 27 27 27 27 27 27 27 27 27 27 27 27 27 27 27
1	N. Lauda	1 1 1 1 1 19 19 19 19 19 19 19 19 19 19 19 5 5 5 5 5 5 5 8 8 8 1 12 12 8 8 8 11 11 11 11 8 8 8 27 27 27 27 11 11 11 11 11 11 11 11 11 11 11 11 11 11 11 11 11 11 11 11 11 11 11 11 11 11 11
5	N. Mansell	5 5 5 5 5 5 5 5 5 5 5 5 5 5 5 5 16 16 15 27 27 8 5 1 1 12 17 11 11 11 11 11 17 17 27 27 27 27 8 8 8 8 8 5 5 5 5 5 5 5 5 5 5 5 5 6 6 6 6 6 6 6 6 6 6 6 6 6 6 6
16	D. Warwick	16 16 16 16 16 16 16 16 16 16 16 16 16 16 16 16 16 11 15 27 8 8 1 1 17 17 17 17 17 17 17 5 5 17 17 5 5 5 3 3 3 3 3 5 8 3 3 3 3 3 3 3 3 3 3 3 3 3 3 3 3 3 3 3 3 3 3 3 3 3
0	M. Surer	0 0 11 11 11 11 11 11 11 11 11 11 11 11 11 11 15 27 8 1 1 17 17 3 3 3 3 3 3 5 27 27 5 5 17 17 17 5 5 5 5 3 3 8 17 17 17 17 17 17 17 17 17 17 17 17 17 17 17 17 17 17 17 17 17 17 17 17
11	E. de Angelis	11 11 8 8 8 27 27 27 27 27 27 27 27 27 27 15 27 11 17 17 17 3 3 11 11 11 5 5 5 3 18 18 3 3 3 3 3 5 17 17 17 17 18 8 8 18 18 18 7 7 7 7 7 7 7 17 17 17 17 17 17 17 17 17 17 17 17 17
27	M. Alboreto	27 27 27 27 27 8 8 8 8 8 8 8 8 8 15 27 8 8 3 3 3 25 25 5 5 5 7 7 7 7 3 18 18 9 9 9 9 18 18 18 18 18 18 18 18 18 18 8 7 7 18 8 8 8 8 8 8 8 8 8 8 8 8 8 8
28	S. Johansson	28 28 28 28 28 28 28 28 4 4 4 15 15 8 8 8 4 4 25 25 25 11 11 25 7 7 18 18 18 18 7 9 9 9 18 18 18 18 9 9 9 9 7 7 7 7 7 7 7 8 8 8 24 24
26	J. Laffite	26 26 26 26 26 26 4 4 26 26 15 4 4 4 4 4 17 17 4 4 11 9 7 18 18 9 9 9 9 9 4 4 4 4 4 7 7 7 7 7 7 9 9 9 9 9 9 9 9 24 24
4	S. Bellof	4 4 4 4 4 26 26 17 17 15 26 26 26 26 26 26 3 3 11 11 4 7 18 18 9 9 4 4 4 4 4 7 7 7 7 7 24 24 24 24 24 24 24 24 24 24 24 24 24 24
17	G. Berger	17 17 17 17 17 17 17 17 17 17 17 17 17 17 17 25 25 9 9 9 18 9 4 4 4 24 24 24 24 24 24 24 24 24 24 24
3	M. Brundle	3 3 3 3 3 3 3 3 3 3 3 3 3 3 3 3 9 9 7 7 7 4 4 4 24 24
20	P. Ghinzani	20 20 20 20 25 15 15 15 25 25 25 25 25 25 25 19 7 18 18 18 24 24 24
30	J. Palmer	30 30 30 30 15 25 25 25 18 18 18 18 18 18 9 9 9 7 18 24 24 24
25	A. de Cesaris	25 25 25 25 20 20 20 18 30 30 30 30 30 9 7 7 7 18 24
15	P. Tambay	15 15 15 15 30 30 18 20 20 20 20 20 9 7 18 18 18 24
9	P. Alliot	9 18 18 18 18 18 30 30 28 9 9 9 7 24 24 24 24
24	H. Rothengatter	24 9 9 9 9 9 9 9 9 7 7 7 24
29	P. Martini	29 24 24 24 7 7 7 7 7 24 24 24
18	T. Boutsen	18 7 7 7 24 24 24 24 24
23	E. Cheever	23
22	R. Patrese	22
7	N. Piquet	7

Circuit data

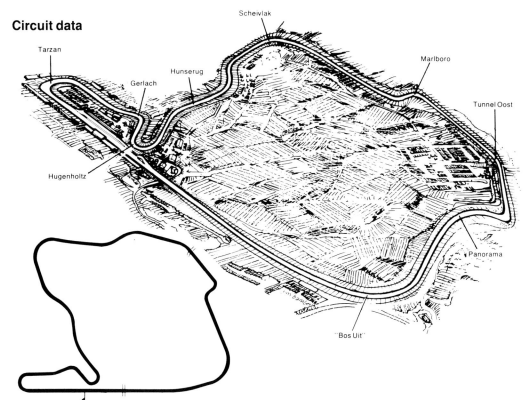

Circuit van Zandvoort, near Haarlem
Circuit length: 2·642 miles/4·252 km
Race distance: 70 laps, 184·944 miles/297·640 km
Race weather: Cool, dry

Labels on map: Scheivlak, Tarzan, Hunserug, Gerlach, Marlboro, Hugenholtz, Tunnel Oost, "Bos Uit", Panorama

Fastest laps

Driver	Time	Lap
Alain Prost	1m 16·538s	57
Niki Lauda	1m 17·054s	60
Nigel Mansell	1m 17·286s	44
Patrick Tambay	1m 17·335s	16
Nelson Piquet	1m 17·577s	51
Michele Alboreto	1m 17·710s	43
Ayrton Senna	1m 17·835s	31
Elio de Angelis	1m 18·229s	39
Derek Warwick	1m 18·230s	4
Keke Rosberg	1m 18·369s	3
Thierry Boutsen	1m 18·730s	47
Stefan Bellof	1m 18·878s	31
Teo Fabi	1m 19·043s	16
Martin Brundle	1m 19·259s	47
Gerhard Berger	1m 19·294s	45
Stefan Johansson	1m 19·385s	5
Marc Surer	1m 19·400s	9
Jacques Laffite	1m 19·549s	5
Andrea de Cesaris	1m 19·980s	14
Jonathan Palmer	1m 20·505s	12
Piercarlo Ghinzani	1m 20·920s	4
Philippe Alliot	1m 20·928s	19
Huub Rothengatter	1m 23·102s	51
Pierluigi Martini	1m 41·482s	1
Eddie Cheever	1m 50·408s	1
Riccardo Patrese	2m 11·271s	1

Points

WORLD CHAMPIONSHIP OF DRIVERS
1	Alain Prost	56 pts
2	Michele Alboreto	53
3	Elio de Angelis	30
4=	Stefan Johansson	19
4=	Ayrton Senna	19
6	Keke Rosberg	18
7	Niki Lauda	14
8	Nelson Piquet	13
9	Patrick Tambay	11
10	Jacques Laffite	10
11	Thierry Boutsen	9
12	Nigel Mansell	7
13=	Stefan Bellof	4
13=	Derek Warwick	4
15=	René Arnoux	3
15=	Andrea de Cesaris	3
17	Marc Surer	2

CONSTRUCTORS' CUP
1	Ferrari	75 pts
2	McLaren	70
3	Lotus	49
4	Williams	25
5=	Renault	15
5=	Brabham	15
7	Ligier	13
8	Arrows	9
9	Tyrrell	4

Gran Premio d'Italia, 8 September/statistics

Entries and practice times

No.	Driver	Nat.	Car	Tyre	Engine	Entrant	Practice 1	Practice 2
1	Niki Lauda	A	Marlboro McLAREN MP4/2B	G	TAG P01 (TTE P01)	Marlboro McLaren International	**1m 28·472s**	1m 28·949s
2	Alain Prost	F	Marlboro McLAREN MP4/2B	G	TAG P01 (TTE P01)	Marlboro McLaren International	1m 27·576s	**1m 25·790s**
3	Martin Brundle	GB	TYRRELL 014	G	Renault EF4	Tyrrell Racing Organisation	1m 33·503s	**1m 28·793s**
5	Nigel Mansell	GB	WILLIAMS FW10	G	Honda RA163–E	Canon Williams Honda Team	1m 26·960s	**1m 25·486s**
6	Keke Rosberg	SF	WILLIAMS FW10	G	Honda RA163–E	Canon Williams Honda Team	1m 26·161s	**1m 25·230s**
7	Nelson Piquet	BR	Olivetti BRABHAM BT54	P	BMW M12/13	Motor Racing Developments Ltd	1m 25·679s	**1m 25·584s**
8	Marc Surer	CH	Olivetti BRABHAM BT54	P	BMW M12/13	Motor Racing Developments Ltd	1m 27·799s	**1m 27·153s**
9	Philippe Alliot	F	RAM 03	P	Hart 415T	Skoal Bandit Formula 1 Team	**1m 36·221s**	1m 37·664s
10	Kenny Acheson	GB	RAM 03	P	Hart 415T	Skoal Bandit Formula 1 Team	**1m 34·919s**	1m 38·325s
11	Elio de Angelis	I	John Player Special LOTUS 97T	G	Renault EF4/EF15	John Player Special Team Lotus	1m 27·098s	**1m 26·044s**
12	Ayrton Senna	BR	John Player Special LOTUS 97T	G	Renault EF4/EF15	John Player Special Team Lotus	1m 27·009s	**1m 25·084s**
15	Patrick Tambay	F	Elf RENAULT RE60B	G	Renault EF15	Equipe Renault Elf	1m 28·578s	**1m 27·020s**
16	Derek Warwick	GB	Elf RENAULT RE60B	G	Renault EF15	Equipe Renault Elf	1m 28·119s	**1m 28·112s**
17	Gerhard Berger	A	ARROWS A8	G	BMW M12/13	Barclay Arrows BMW	1m 27·746s	**1m 27·723s**
18	Thierry Boutsen	B	ARROWS A8	G	BMW M12/13	Barclay Arrows BMW	1m 28·760s	**1m 28·369s**
19	Teo Fabi	I	TOLEMAN TG185	P	Hart 415T	Toleman Group Motorsport	**1m 28·369s**	1m 28·386s
20	Piercarlo Ghinzani	I	TOLEMAN TG185	P	Hart 415T	Toleman Group Motorsport	1m 29·050s	**1m 28·386s**
22	Riccardo Patrese	I	Benetton ALFA ROMEO 184T	G	Alfa Romeo 890T	Benetton Team Alfa Romeo	**1m 30·271s**	1m 31·449s
23	Eddie Cheever	USA	Benetton ALFA ROMEO 184T	G	Alfa Romeo 890T	Benetton Team Alfa Romeo	1m 29·068s	**1m 28·340s**
24	Huub Rothengatter	NL	Kelemata OSELLA FA1G	P	Alfa Romeo 890T	Osella Squadra Corse	1m 33·529s	**1m 37·664s**
25	Philippe Streiff	F	Gitanes LIGIER JS25	P	Renault EF4/EF15	Equipe Ligier Gitanes	1m 31·727s	**1m 29·839s**
26	Jacques Laffite	F	Gitanes LIGIER JS25	P	Renault EF4/EF15	Equipe Ligier Gitanes	**1m 30·186s**	1m 30·376s
27	Michele Alboreto	I	Fiat FERRARI 156/85	G	Ferrari 126C	Scuderia Ferrari SpA	1m 27·552s	**1m 26·468s**
28	Stefan Johansson	S	Fiat FERRARI 156/85	G	Ferrari 126C	Scuderia Ferrari SpA	1m 29·011s	**1m 27·473s**
29	Pierluigi Martini	I	Simod MINARDI M/85	P	Motori Moderni	Minardi Team	1m 35·770s	**1m 33·981s**
33	Alan Jones	AUS	BEATRICE-LOLA THL-1	G	Hart 415T	Team Haas (USA) Ltd	**1m 34·943s**	1m 45·823s

Friday morning and Saturday morning practice sessions not officially recorded.

G – Goodyear, P – Pirelli.

Fri p.m.	Sat p.m.
Hot, dry	Hot, dry

Starting grid

12 SENNA (1m 25·084s)
Lotus

　　　　6 ROSBERG (1m 25·230s)
　　　　Williams

5 MANSELL (1m 25·486s)
Williams

　　　　7 PIQUET (1m 25·584s)
　　　　Brabham

2 PROST (1m 25·790s)
McLaren

　　　　11 DE ANGELIS (1m 26·044s)
　　　　Lotus

27 ALBORETO (1m 26·468s)
Ferrari

　　　　15 TAMBAY (1m 27·020s)
　　　　Renault

8 SURER (1m 27·153s)
Brabham

　　　　28 JOHANSSON (1m 27·473s)
　　　　Ferrari

17 BERGER (1m 27·723s)
Arrows

　　　　16 WARWICK (1m 28·112s)
　　　　Renault

22 PATRESE (1m 28·340s)
Alfa Romeo

　　　　18 BOUTSEN (1m 28·369s)
　　　　Arrows

19 FABI (1m 28·386s)
Toleman

　　　　1 LAUDA (1m 28·472s)
　　　　McLaren

23 CHEEVER (1m 28·629s)
Alfa Romeo

　　　　3 BRUNDLE (1m 28·793s)
　　　　Tyrrell

25 STREIFF (1m 29·839s)
Ligier

　　　　26 LAFFITE (1m 30·186s)
　　　　Ligier

20 GHINZANI (1m 30·271s)
Toleman

　　　　24 ROTHENGATTER (1m 33·529s)
　　　　Osella

29 MARTINI (1m 33·981s)
Minardi

　　　　10 ACHESON (1m 34·919s)
　　　　RAM

33 JONES (1m 34·943s)
Beatrice

　　　　9 ALLIOT (1m 36·221s)
　　　　RAM

Results and retirements

Place	Driver	Car	Laps	Time and Speed (mph/km/h)/Retirement	
1	Alain Prost	McLaren-TAG t/c V6	51	1h 17m 59·451s	141·402/227·565
2	Nelson Piquet	Brabham-BMW t/c 4	51	1h 18m 51·086s	139·859/225·082
3	Ayrton Senna	Lotus-Renault t/c V6	51	1h 18m 59·841s	139·601/224·666
4	Marc Surer	Brabham-BMW t/c 4	51	1h 19m 00·060s	139·594/224·655
5	Stefan Johansson	Ferrari t/c V6	50		
6	Elio de Angelis	Lotus-Renault t/c V6	50		
7	Patrick Tambay	Renault t/c V6	50		
8	Martin Brundle	Tyrrell-Renault t/c V6	50		
9	Thierry Boutsen	Arrows-BMW t/c 4	50		
10	Philippe Streiff	Ligier-Renault t/c V6	49		
11	Nigel Mansell	Williams-Honda t/c V6	47	Engine	
12	Teo Fabi	Toleman-Hart t/c 4	47		
13	Michele Alboreto	Ferrari t/c V6	45	Engine	
	Keke Rosberg	Williams-Honda t/c V6	44	Engine	
	Jacques Laffite	Ligier-Renault t/c V6	40	Engine	
	Niki Lauda	McLaren-TAG t/c V6	33	Transmission	
	Riccardo Patrese	Alfa Romeo t/c V8	31	Exhaust	
	Huub Rothengatter	Osella-Alfa Romeo t/c V8	26	Engine	
	Philippe Alliot	RAM-Hart t/c 4	19	Turbo	
	Gerhard Berger	Arrows-BMW t/c 4	13	Engine	
	Derek Warwick	Renault t/c V6	9	Transmission	
	Alan Jones	Beatrice-Hart t/c 4	6	Distributor	
	Eddie Cheever	Alfa Romeo t/c V8	3	Engine	
	Kenny Acheson	RAM-Hart t/c 4	2	Clutch	
	Pierluigi Martini	Minardi-MM t/c V6	0	Fuel pump	
	Piercarlo Ghinzani	Toleman-Hart t/c 4	0	Stalled at start	

Fastest lap: Mansell, on lap 38, 1m 28·283s, 146·961 mph/236·512 km/h (record).
Previous lap record: Niki Lauda (F1 McLaren MP4/2-TAG t/c), 1m 31·912s, 141·158 mph/227·173 km/h (1984).

Past winners

Year	Driver	Nat.	Car	Circuit	Distance miles/km	Speed mph/km/h
1950	Giuseppe Farina	I	1·5 Alfa Romeo 158 s/c	Monza	313·17/504·00	109·70/176·54
1951	Alberto Ascari	I	4·5 Ferrari 375	Monza	313·17/504·00	115·52/185·92
1952	Alberto Ascari	I	2·0 Ferrari 500	Monza	313·17/504·00	110·04/177·09
1953	Juan Manuel Fangio	RA	2·0 Maserati A6SSG	Monza	313·17/504·00	110·68/178·13
1954	Juan Manuel Fangio	RA	2·5 Mercedes-Benz W196	Monza	313·17/504·00	111·98/180·22
1955	Juan Manuel Fangio	RA	2·0 Mercedes-Benz W196	Monza	310·69/500·00	128·49/206·79
1956	Stirling Moss	GB	2·5 Maserati 250F	Monza	310·69/500·00	129·73/208·79
1957	Stirling Moss	GB	2·5 Vanwall	Monza	310·84/500·25	129·73/208·79
1958	Tony Brooks	GB	2·5 Vanwall	Monza	250·10/402·50	121·21/195·08
1959	Stirling Moss	GB	2·5 Cooper T45-Climax	Monza	257·25/414·00	124·38/200·18
1960	Phil Hill	USA	2·4 Ferrari Dino 246	Monza	310·69/500·00	132·06/212·53
1961	Phil Hill	USA	1·5 Ferrari Dino 156	Monza	267·19/430·00	130·11/209·39
1962	Graham Hill	GB	1·5 BRM P57	Monza	307·27/494·50	123·62/197·94
1963	Jim Clark	GB	1·5 Lotus 25-Climax	Monza	302·27/494·50	127·74/205·58
1964	John Surtees	GB	1·5 Ferrari 158	Monza	278·68/448·50	127·77/205·63
1965	Jackie Stewart	GB	1·5 BRM P261	Monza	271·54/437·00	130·46/209·96
1966	Ludovico Scarfiotti	I	3·0 Ferrari 312/66	Monza	242·96/391·00	135·92/218·75
1967	John Surtees	GB	3·9 Honda RA300	Monza	242·96/391·00	140·50/226·12
1968	Denny Hulme	NZ	3·0 McLaren M7A-Ford	Monza	242·96/391·00	145·41/234·02
1969	Jackie Stewart	GB	3·0 Matra MS80-Ford	Monza	242·96/391·00	146·97/236·52
1970	Clay Regazzoni	CH	3·0 Ferrari 312B-1/70	Monza	242·96/391·00	147·08/236·67
1971	Peter Gethin	GB	3·0 BRM P160	Monza	196·51/316·25	150·75/242·62
1972	Emerson Fittipaldi	BR	3·0 JPS/Lotus 72-Ford	Monza	197·36/317·63	131·61/211·81
1973	Ronnie Peterson	S	3·0 JPS/Lotus 72-Ford	Monza	197·36/317·63	132·63/213·45
1974	Ronnie Peterson	S	3·0 JPS/Lotus 72-Ford	Monza	186·76/300·56	135·10/217·42
1975	Clay Regazzoni	CH	3·0 Ferrari 312T/75	Monza	186·76/300·56	135·48/218·03
1976	Ronnie Peterson	S	3·0 March 761-Ford	Monza	187·41/301·60	124·12/199·75
1977	Mario Andretti	USA	3·0 JPS/Lotus 78-Ford	Monza	187·41/301·60	128·01/206·02
1978	Niki Lauda	A	3·0 Brabham BT46-Alfa Romeo	Monza	144·16/232·00	128·95/207·53
1979	Jody Scheckter	ZA	3·0 Ferrari 312T-4	Monza	180·20/290·00	131·85/212·18
1980	Nelson Piquet	BR	3·0 Brabham BT49-Ford	Imola	186·41/300·00	113·98/183·44
1981	Alain Prost	F	1·5 Renault RE30 t/c	Monza	187·40/301·60	129·87/209·00
1982	René Arnoux	F	1·5 Renault RE30B t/c	Monza	187·40/301·60	136·39/219·50
1983	Nelson Piquet	BR	1·5 Brabham BT52B-BMW t/c	Monza	187·40/301·60	136·18/217·55
1984	Niki Lauda	A	1·5 McLaren MP4/2-TAG t/c	Monza	183·80/295·80	137·02/220·51
1985	Alain Prost	F	1·5 McLaren MP4/2B-TAG t/c	Monza	183·80/295·80	141·40/227·56

Lap chart

1ST LAP ORDER	Lap order (laps 1–51)
6 K. Rosberg	6 6 6 6 6 6 6 6 6 6 6 6 6 6 6 6 6 6 6 6 6 6 6 6 6 6 ? ? ? ? ? ? ? ? 2 2 2 2 2 6 6 6 6 6 2 2 2 2 2 2 2
5 N. Mansell	5 5 5 2 2 2 2 2 2 2 2 ? ? ? ? ? ? ? ? ? ? ? ? ? ? ? 6 6 6 6 6 6 6 6 6 6 6 2 2 2 2 7 7 7 7 7 7 7
2 A. Prost	? 12 ? 12 11 11 11 11 11 11 11 11 11 11 11 11 11 11 11 1 1 1 1 1 11 11 11 11 11 10 10 10 10 10 10 ? ? ? ? 12 12 12 12 12 12 12 12
12 A. Senna	12 2 12 11 12 12 12 12 12 12 12 12 12 1 1 11 11 11 11 11 11 11 11 11 11 11 12 12 12 12 12 12 11 11 11 11 11 11 7 7 7 12 12 12 12 8 8 8 8 8 8
11 E. de Angelis	11 11 11 27 27 27 7 7 7 7 7 1 1 1 12 12 12 12 12 12 12 12 12 12 1 28 28 28 28 28 28 7 7 7 11 11 8 8 8 8 8 27 28 28 28 28 28
27 M. Alboreto	27 27 27 7 7 27 27 27 27 27 27 27 27 27 27 27 27 27 27 27 27 27 8 8 8 8 7 7 28 20 0 0 0 11 11 11 27 11 11 11 11 11 11 11
7 N. Piquet	7 7 7 15 15 15 15 1 1 1 1 15 15 28 28 28 28 28 28 28 28 28 28 28 27 7 7 7 7 8 8 8 28 27 27 27 27 27 11 28 15 15 15 15 15
15 P. Tambay	15 15 15 28 28 28 1 15 15 15 28 28 28 15 8 8 8 8 8 8 8 8 8 8 7 27 27 27 27 27 27 27 27 28 28 28 28 28 28 15 3 3 3 3 3
28 S. Johansson	28 28 28 16 16 1 28 28 28 28 28 8 8 8 15 15 15 15 15 7 7 7 7 7 15 15 1 1 1 1 1 26 26 26 26 26 26 15 15 15 3 18 5 18 18 18
16 D. Warwick	16 16 16 8 8 16 16 8 8 8 8 18 18 18 18 7 7 7 15 15 15 15 15 1 1 15 26 26 26 26 3 3 3 3 3 3 3 3 18 5 18 25 25
8 M. Surer	8 8 8 1 1 8 8 16 16 18 18 7 7 7 7 7 18 18 18 18 26 26 26 26 26 26 26 3 3 3 3 15 15 15 15 15 15 18 18 18 18 5 25 25
22 R. Patrese	22 22 18 18 18 18 18 18 18 3 3 3 26 26 26 26 26 26 26 26 3 3 3 3 3 3 15 15 15 15 18 18 18 18 18 25 25 25 5 25 19 19
18 T. Boutsen	18 18 1 22 22 22 22 22 3 26 26 26 3 3 3 3 3 3 3 25 25 25 25 25 25 25 18 18 18 18 25 25 25 25 25 5 5 5 25 19
23 L. Cheever	23 23 23 19 19 3 3 3 26 25 25 25 25 25 25 25 25 25 25 25 18 18 18 18 18 18 25 25 25 25 5 5 5 5 5 19 19 19 19
3 M. Brundle	3 1 22 3 3 19 19 20 19 9 9 9 9 9 9 9 9 9 24 24 5 5 5 5 5 5 5 5 5 5 5 19 19 19 19 19
19 T. Fabi	19 3 19 25 26 26 19 25 24 24 24 24 24 24 24 24 5 5 24 24 24 22 22 22 22 22 22 19 19 19
1 N. Lauda	1 19 3 26 25 25 25 25 9 19 17 17 17 5 5 5 5 5 5 22 22 22 22 22 22 19 19 19 19 19 19
9 P. Alliot	9 25 25 9 9 9 9 24 17 5 5 5 22 22 22 22 22 22 19 19 19 19 19 19 24
25 P. Streiff	25 26 26 24 24 24 24 24 17 22 22 22 22 19 19 19 19 19
26 J. Laffite	26 9 9 17 17 17 17 22 5 19 19 19
20 P. Ghinzani	20 24 24 33 33 33 5 5 5
24 H. Rothengatter	24 17 17 5 5 5
17 G. Berger	17 33 33
33 A. Jones	33 10
10 K. Acheson	10

Circuit data

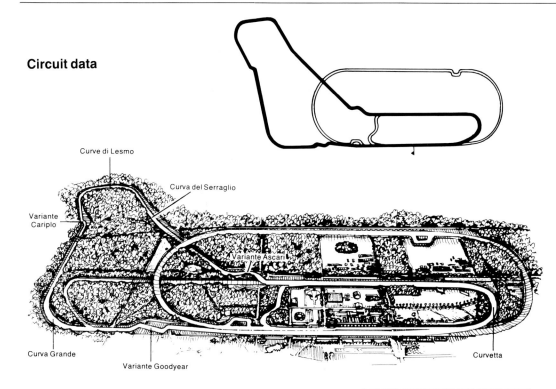

Curve di Lesmo
Curva del Serraglio
Variante Cariplo
Variante Ascari
Curva Grande
Variante Goodyear
Curvetta

Autodromo Nazionale di Monza, near Milan

Circuit length: 3.6039 miles/5.80 km
Race distance: 51 laps, 183.801 miles/295.800 km
Race weather: Hot, dry

Fastest laps

Driver	Time	Lap
Nigel Mansell	1m 28.283s	38
Keke Rosberg	1m 28.421s	39
Alain Prost	1m 29.714s	27
Niki Lauda	1m 29.998s	30
Michele Alboreto	1m 30.163s	45
Nelson Piquet	1m 30.436s	36
Stefan Johansson	1m 30.795s	48
Marc Surer	1m 30.935s	48
Ayrton Senna	1m 31.703s	43
Patrick Tambay	1m 31.745s	43
Elio de Angelis	1m 31.896s	10
Jacques Laffite	1m 32.448s	27
Thierry Boutsen	1m 32.820s	29
Derek Warwick	1m 33.330s	5
Martin Brundle	1m 33.418s	20
Philippe Streiff	1m 33.575s	35
Teo Fabi	1m 33.864s	24
Riccardo Patrese	1m 34.784s	24
Philippe Alliot	1m 35.308s	18
Eddie Cheever	1m 36.311s	3
Gerhard Berger	1m 36.425s	6
Alan Jones	1m 36.536s	6
Huub Rothengatter	1m 37.585s	18
Kenny Acheson	2m 14.092s	1

Points

WORLD CHAMPIONSHIP OF DRIVERS

1	Alain Prost	65 pts
2	Michele Alboreto	53
3	Elio de Angelis	31
4	Ayrton Senna	23
5	Stefan Johansson	21
6	Nelson Piquet	19
7	Keke Rosberg	18
8	Niki Lauda	14
9	Patrick Tambay	11
10	Jacques Laffite	10
11	Thierry Boutsen	9
12	Nigel Mansell	7
13	Marc Surer	5
14=	Stefan Bellof	4
14=	Derek Warwick	4
16=	René Arnoux	3
16=	Andrea de Cesaris	3

CONSTRUCTORS' CUP

1	McLaren	79 pts
2	Ferrari	77
3	Lotus	54
4	Williams	25
5	Brabham	24
6	Renault	15
7	Ligier	13
8	Arrows	9
9	Tyrrell	4

Grand Prix of Belgium, 15 September/statistics

Entries and practice times

No.	Driver	Nat.	Car	Tyre	Engine	Entrant	Practice 1	Practice 2
1	Niki Lauda	A	Marlboro McLAREN MP4/2B	G	TAG P01 (TTE P01)	Marlboro McLaren International	—	—
2	Alain Prost	F	Marlboro McLAREN MP4/2B	G	TAG P01 (TTE P01)	Marlboro McLaren International	1m 56·563s	**1m 55·306s**
3	Martin Brundle	GB	TYRRELL 014	G	Renault EF4	Tyrrell Racing Organisation	**2m 00·950s**	2m 01·364s
5	Nigel Mansell	GB	WILLIAMS FW10	G	Honda RA163–E	Canon Williams Honda Team	**1m 56·727s**	1m 56·996s
6	Keke Rosberg	SF	WILLIAMS FW10	G	Honda RA163–E	Canon Williams Honda Team	1m 57·582s	**1m 57·465s**
7	Nelson Piquet	BR	Olivetti BRABHAM BT54	P	BMW M12/13	Motor Racing Developments Ltd	1m 56·643s	**1m 55·648s**
8	Marc Surer	CH	Olivetti BRABHAM BT54	P	BMW M12/13	Motor Racing Developments Ltd	2m 00·154s	**1m 57·729s**
9	Philippe Alliot	F	RAM 03	P	Hart 415T	Skoal Bandit Formula 1 Team	**1m 59·626s**	1m 59·755s
11	Elio de Angelis	I	John Player Special LOTUS 97T	G	Renault EF4/EF15	John Player Special Team Lotus	1m 58·852s	**1m 57·322s**
12	Ayrton Senna	BR	John Player Special LOTUS 97T	G	Renault EF4/EF15	John Player Special Team Lotus	2m 00·710s	**1m 55·403s**
15	Patrick Tambay	F	Elf RENAULT RE60B	G	Renault EF15	Equipe Renault Elf	**1m 58·105s**	1m 59·335s
16	Derek Warwick	GB	Elf RENAULT RE60B	G	Renault EF15	Equipe Renault Elf	1m 59·761s	**1m 58·407s**
17	Gerhard Berger	A	ARROWS A8	G	BMW M12/13	Barclay Arrows BMW	**1m 56·770s**	—
18	Thierry Boutsen	B	ARROWS A8	G	BMW M12/13	Barclay Arrows BMW	1m 59·046s	**1m 56·697s**
19	Teo Fabi	I	TOLEMAN TG185	P	Hart 415T	Toleman Group Motorsport	**1m 57·588s**	1m 57·857s
20	Piercarlo Ghinzani	I	TOLEMAN TG185	P	Hart 415T	Toleman Group Motorsport	1m 58·820s	**1m 58·706s**
22	Riccardo Patrese	I	Benetton ALFA ROMEO 184T	G	Alfa Romeo 890T	Benetton Team Alfa Romeo	1m 59·703s	**1m 58·414s**
23	Eddie Cheever	USA	Benetton ALFA ROMEO 184T	G	Alfa Romeo 890T	Benetton Team Alfa Romeo	2m 00·861s	**1m 59·370s**
24	Huub Rothengatter	NL	Kelemata OSELLA FA1G	P	Alfa Romeo 890T	Osella Squadra Corse	2m 06·083s	**2m 05·776s**
25	Philippe Streiff	F	Gitanes LIGIER JS25	P	Renault EF4/EF15	Equipe Ligier Gitanes	2m 00·599s	**1m 59·245s**
26	Jacques Laffite	F	Gitanes LIGIER JS25	P	Renault EF4/EF15	Equipe Ligier Gitanes	2m 01·345s	**1m 58·933s**
27	Michele Alboreto	I	Fiat FERRARI 156/85	G	Ferrari 126C	Scuderia Ferrari SpA	1m 56·999s	**1m 56·021s**
28	Stefan Johansson	S	Fiat FERRARI 156/85	G	Ferrari 126C	Scuderia Ferrari SpA	**1m 56·585s**	1m 56·746s
29	Pierluigi Martini	I	Simod MINARDI M/85	P	Motori Moderni	Minardi Team	**2m 06·007s**	2m 06·606s
30	Christian Danner	D	West ZAKSPEED ZAK 841	G	Zakspeed	West Zakspeed Racing	**2m 05·059s**	2m 07·046s

Friday morning and Saturday morning practice sessions not officially recorded.

G – Goodyear, P – Pirelli.

Fri p.m.
Cool, dry

Sat p.m.
Warm, dry

Starting grid

2 PROST (1m 55·306s)
McLaren

12 SENNA (1m 55·403s)
Lotus

7 PIQUET (1m 55·648s)
Brabham

27 ALBORETO (1m 56·021s)
Ferrari

28 JOHANSSON (1m 56·585s)
Ferrari

18 BOUTSEN (1m 56·697s)
Arrows

5 MANSELL (1m 56·727s)
Williams

17 BERGER (1m 56·770s)
Arrows

11 DE ANGELIS (1m 57·322s)
Lotus

6 ROSBERG (1m 57·465s)
Williams

19 FABI (1m 57·588s)
Toleman

8 SURER (1m 57·729s)
Brabham

15 TAMBAY (1m 58·105s)
Renault

16 WARWICK (1m 58·407s)
Renault

22 PATRESE (1m 58·414s)
Alfa Romeo

20 GHINZANI (1m 58·706s)
Toleman

26 LAFFITE (1m 58·933s)
Ligier

25 STREIFF (1m 59·245s)
Ligier

23 CHEEVER (1m 59·370s)
Alfa Romeo

9 ALLIOT (1m 59·626s)
RAM

3 BRUNDLE (2m 00·950s)
Tyrrell

30 DANNER (2m 05·059s)
Zakspeed

24 ROTHENGATTER (2m 05·776s)
Osella

29 MARTINI (2m 06·007s)
Minardi

Did not start:
1 Lauda (McLaren); wrist injury sustained during unofficial practice on Friday. Entry withdrawn.

Results and retirements

Place	Driver	Car	Laps	Time and Speed (mph/km/h)/Retirement	
1	Ayrton Senna	Lotus-Renault t/c V6	43	1h 34m 19·893s	117·943/189·811
2	Nigel Mansell	Williams-Honda t/c V6	43	1h 34m 48·315s	117·354/188·863
3	Alain Prost	McLaren-TAG t/c V6	43	1h 35m 15·002s	116·806/187·981
4	Keke Rosberg	Williams-Honda t/c V6	43	1h 35m 35·183s	116·395/187·320
5	Nelson Piquet	Brabham-BMW t/c 4	42		
6	Derek Warwick	Renault t/c V6	42		
7	Gerhard Berger	Arrows-BMW t/c 4	42		
8	Marc Surer	Brabham-BMW t/c 4	42		
9	Philippe Streiff	Ligier-Renault t/c V6	42		
10	Thierry Boutsen	Arrows-BMW t/c 4	40		
11	Jacques Laffite	Ligier-Renault t/c V6	38	Accident	
12	Pierluigi Martini	Minardi-MM t/c V6	38		
13	Martin Brundle	Tyrrell-Renault t/c V6	38		
	Huub Rothengatter	Osella-Alfa Romeo t/c V8	37	Running, not classified	
	Riccardo Patrese	Alfa Romeo t/c V8	31	Engine	
	Eddie Cheever	Alfa Romeo t/c V8	26	Gearbox	
	Patrick Tambay	Renault t/c V6	24	Gearbox	
	Teo Fabi	Toleman-Hart t/c 4	23	Throttle linkage	
	Elio de Angelis	Lotus-Renault t/c V6	19	Turbo	
	Christian Danner	Zakspeed t/c 4	16	Gearbox	
	Philippe Alliot	RAM-Hart t/c 4	10	Accident	
	Stefan Johansson	Ferrari t/c V6	7	Engine/spun off	
	Piercarlo Ghinzani	Toleman-Hart t/c 4	7	Accident	
	Michele Alboreto	Ferrari t/c V6	3	Clutch	

Fastest lap: Prost, on lap 38, 2m 01·730s, 127·531 mph/205·241 km/h (record).
Previous lap record: Andrea de Cesaris (F1 Alfa Romeo 183T), 2m 07·493s, 121·923 mph/196·217 km/h (1983).

Past winners

Year	Driver	Nat	Car	Circuit	Distance miles/km	Speed mph/km/h
1950	Juan Manuel Fangio	RA	1·5 Alfa Romeo 158 s/c	Francorchamps	307·08/494·20	110·04/177·09
1951	Giuseppe Farina	I	1·5 Alfa Romeo 159 s/c	Francorchamps	315·85/508·31	114·32/183·99
1952	Alberto Ascari	I	2·0 Ferrari 500	Francorchamps	315·85/508·31	103·13/165·96
1953	Alberto Ascari	I	2·0 Ferrari 500	Francorchamps	315·85/508·31	112·47/181·00
1954	Juan Manuel Fangio	RA	2·5 Maserati 250F	Francorchamps	315·85/508·31	115·06/185·17
1955	Juan Manuel Fangio	RA	2·5 Mercedes-Benz W196	Francorchamps	315·85/508·31	118·83/191·24
1956	Peter Collins	GB	2·5 Lancia-Ferrari D50	Francorchamps	315·85/508·31	118·44/190·61
1958	Tony Brooks	GB	2·5 Vanwall	Francorchamps	210·27/338·40	129·92/209·09
1960	Jack Brabham	AUS	2·5 Cooper T53-Climax	Francorchamps	315·41/507·60	133·63/215·06
1961	Phil Hill	USA	1·5 Ferrari Dino 156	Francorchamps	262·84/423·00	128·15/206·24
1962	Jim Clark	GB	1·5 Lotus 25-Climax	Francorchamps	280·36/451·19	131·90/212·27
1963	Jim Clark	GB	1·5 Lotus 25-Climax	Francorchamps	280·36/451·19	114·10/183·63
1964	Jim Clark	GB	1·5 Lotus 25-Climax	Francorchamps	280·36/451·19	132·79/213·71
1965	Jim Clark	GB	1·5 Lotus 33-Climax	Francorchamps	280·36/451·19	117·16/188·55
1966	John Surtees	GB	3·0 Ferrari 312/66	Francorchamps	245·32/394·80	113·93/183·36
1967	Dan Gurney	USA	3·0 Eagle T1G-Gurney-Weslake	Francorchamps	245·32/394·80	145·99/234·95
1968	Bruce McLaren	NZ	3·0 McLaren M7A-Ford	Francorchamps	245·32/394·80	147·14/236·80
1970	Pedro Rodriguez	MEX	3·0 BRM P153	Francorchamps	245·32/394·80	149·97/241·36
1972	Emerson Fittipaldi	BR	3·0 JPS/Lotus 72-Ford	Nivelles-Baulers	196·69/316·54	113·35/182·42
1973	Jackie Stewart	GB	3·0 Tyrrell 006-Ford	Zolder	183·55/295·39	107·74/173·38
1974	Emerson Fittipaldi	BR	3·0 McLaren M23-Ford	Nivelles-Baulers	196·69/316·54	113·10/182·02
1975	Niki Lauda	A	3·0 Ferrari 312T/75	Zolder	185·38/298·34	107·05/172·28
1976	Niki Lauda	A	3·0 Ferrari 312T/76	Zolder	185·38/298·34	108·11/173·98
1977	Gunnar Nilsson	S	3·0 JPS/Lotus 78-Ford	Zolder	185·38/298·34	96·64/155·53
1978	Mario Andretti	USA	3·0 JPS/Lotus 79-Ford	Zolder	185·38/298·34	111·38/179·24
1979	Jody Scheckter	ZA	3·0 Ferrari 312T-4	Zolder	185·38/298·34	111·24/179·02
1980	Didier Pironi	F	3·0 Ligier JS11/15-Ford	Zolder	190·66/306·86	115·82/186·40
1981	Carlos Reutemann	RA	3·0 Williams FW07C-Ford	Zolder	143·01/230·15	112·12/180·44
1982	John Watson	GB	3·0 McLaren MP4B-Ford	Zolder	185·38/298·34	116·19/187·00
1983	Alain Prost	F	1·5 Renault RE40 t/c	Francorchamps	173·13/278·62	119·14/191·73
1984	Michele Alboreto	I	1·5 Ferrari 126C4 t/c	Zolder	185·38/298·34	115·22/185·43
1985	Ayrton Senna	BR	1·5 Lotus 97T-Renault t/c	Francorchamps	185·67/298·81	117·94/189·81

Lap chart

1st LAP ORDER	1 2 3 4 5 6 7 8 9 10 11 12 13 14 15 16 17 18 19 20 21 22 23 24 25 26 27 28 29 30 31 32 33 34 35 36 37 38 39 40 41 42 43
12 A. Senna	12 12 12 12 12 12 12 12 11 12 12 12 12 12 12 12 12 12 12 12 12 12 12 12 12 12 12 12 12 12 12 12 12 12 12 12 12 12 12 12 12 12 12
2 A. Prost	2 2 2 6 6 6 6 6 12 6 6 6 6 6 6 6 6 6 6 6 6 6 6 6 6 6 6 6 6 6 6 6 6 6 6 6 6 6 6 5 5 5 5
5 N. Mansell	5 5 5 2 2 2 2 2 5 11 6 6 6 6 6 6 6 6 6 6 6 6 6 6 6 6 6 6 6 6 6 6 6 2 2 2 2 2 2 2 2 2 2
27 M. Alboreto	27 28 28 28 28 28 18 18 18 6 2 2 2 2 2 2 2 2 2 2 2 2 2 2 2 2 2 2 2 2 2 2 2 6 6 6 6 6 6 6 6 6 6
28 S. Johansson	28 18 18 18 18 18 11 11 2 2 18 18 18 18 18 18 18 18 18 18 18 18 18 18 18 18 18 18 18 18 18 18 18 16 7 7 7 7
18 T. Boutsen	18 6 11 11 11 11 11 17 17 17 17 17 15 15 15 15 15 15 15 15 16 16 16 16 16 16 16 16 16 16 16 16 16 16 7 16 16 16 16
6 K. Rosberg	6 11 17 17 17 17 15 16 6 18 15 11 11 11 11 11 11 16 16 16 16 15 15 23 23 23 7 7 7 7 7 7 7 7 7 18 18 18 17 17
11 E. de Angelis	11 27 27 16 16 15 16 3 9 15 11 16 16 16 16 16 16 23 23 23 23 23 23 7 7 26 26 26 26 26 26 26 26 26 17 17 8 8
17 G. Berger	17 17 16 15 15 16 3 9 15 9 16 23 23 23 23 19 19 7 7 7 7 7 15 26 26 17 17 17 17 17 17 17 17 17 17 8 8 25 25
16 D. Warwick	16 16 15 25 3 3 9 6 16 16 23 17 17 17 17 17 19 19 19 19 17 17 17 25 25 25 25 8 8 8 8 8 8 8 8 8 25 25
19 T. Fabi	19 19 19 8 19 9 28 15 23 23 19 19 19 19 19 7 17 17 17 17 19 26 26 25 25 8 8 8 25 25 25 25 25 25 25 25 25
20 P. Ghinzani	20 15 25 19 20 19 6 22 3 19 22 7 7 7 7 7 26 8 26 26 26 26 19 8 8 8 29 29 29 29 29 29 29 29 29 29
15 P. Tambay	15 20 20 20 9 20 22 29 29 7 22 22 22 26 8 26 8 8 8 8 25 22 22 22 22 22 3 3 3 3 3 3 3 3 3 3
25 P. Streiff	25 25 8 3 23 22 20 23 22 22 26 26 26 26 22 8 25 25 25 25 25 22 29 29 24 3 3 24 24 24 24 24 24 24
8 M. Surer	8 8 7 23 22 23 29 19 19 26 8 8 8 8 25 22 22 22 22 22 29 24 24 3 24 24 22
7 N. Piquet	7 7 23 9 26 6 23 26 26 8 29 25 25 22 11 29 29 29 29 29 24 3 3
22 R. Patrese	22 23 3 26 8 29 19 8 8 25 29 29 29 29 29 24 24 24 24 24 3
23 E. Cheever	23 22 26 22 29 24 24 25 25 3 3 24 30 30 30 24 3 3 3 3 3 3
26 J. Laffite	26 3 9 29 6 26 26 24 24 24 24 30 24 24 24 3
3 M. Brundle	3 26 24 24 24 8 8 7 7 7 30 30 3 3 3 3
9 P. Alliot	9 9 6 25 25 25 30 30 30
24 H. Rothengatter	24 29 29 30 30 30 30
29 P. Martini	29 24 24 7 7 7 7
30 C. Danner	30 30 30

Circuit data

Circuit de Spa-Francorchamps, Francorchamps
Circuit length: 4·3179 miles/6·949 km
Race distance: 43 laps, 185·669 miles/298·807 km
Race weather: Cool, wet, then damp/dry.

Fastest laps

Driver	Time	Lap
Alain Prost	2m 01·730s	38
Marc Surer	2m 02·266s	42
Nelson Piquet	2m 02·655s	35
Keke Rosberg	2m 03·363s	40
Nigel Mansell	2m 03·479s	37
Ayrton Senna	2m 03·700s	40
Gerhard Berger	2m 04·142s	41
Philippe Streiff	2m 04·685s	38
Jacques Laffite	2m 04·835s	35
Teo Fabi	2m 06·350s	18
Martin Brundle	2m 06·557s	37
Eddie Cheever	2m 06·658s	20
Derek Warwick	2m 06·697s	20
Thierry Boutsen	2m 07·488s	30
Patrick Tambay	2m 07·582s	20
Riccardo Patrese	2m 08·113s	18
Elio de Angelis	2m 09·675s	16
Christian Danner	2m 11·835s	16
Pierluigi Martini	2m 15·557s	38
Huub Rothengatter	2m 19·005s	32
Philippe Alliot	2m 22·744s	7
Stefan Johansson	2m 24·045s	3
Piercarlo Ghinzani	2m 29·896s	3
Michele Alboreto	2m 30·110s	3

Grand Prix of Belgium, 2 June

Entries and practice times

No.	Driver	Nat	Car	Tyre	Engine	Practice 1
1	Niki Lauda	A	Marlboro McLAREN MP4/2B	G	TAG P01 (TTE P01)	1m 58·374s
2	Alain Prost	F	Marlboro McLAREN MP4/2B	G	TAG P01 (TTE P01)	—
3	Martin Brundle	GB	TYRRELL 012	G	Ford-Cosworth DFY/DFV	2m 05·782s
4	Stefan Bellof	D	TYRRELL 012	G	Ford-Cosworth DFY	2m 05·070s
5	Nigel Mansell	GB	WILLIAMS FW10	G	Honda RA163–E	1m 58·658s
6	Keke Rosberg	SF	WILLIAMS FW10	G	Honda RA163–E	1m 57·705s
7	Nelson Piquet	BR	Olivetti BRABHAM BT54	P	BMW M12/13	1m 58·122s
8	Marc Surer	CH	Olivetti BRABHAM BT54	P	BMW M12/13	2m 01·555s
9	Manfred Winkelhock	D	RAM 03	P	Hart 415T	2m 06·771s
10	Philippe Alliot	F	RAM 03	P	Hart 415T	—
11	Elio de Angelis	I	John Player Special LOTUS 97T	G	Renault EF4/EF15	1m 56·277s
12	Ayrton Senna	BR	John Player Special LOTUS 97T	G	Renault EF4	1m 56·473s
15	Patrick Tambay	F	Elf RENAULT RE60	G	Renault EF4/EF15	1m 56·586s
16	Derek Warwick	GB	Elf RENAULT RE60	G	Renault EF4/EF15	1m 59·129s
17	Gerhard Berger	A	ARROWS A8	G	BMW M12/13	1m 58·343s
18	Thierry Boutsen	B	ARROWS A8	G	BMW M12/13	1m 58·874s
19	Teo Fabi	I	TOLEMAN TG185	P	Hart 415T	2m 00·592s
22	Riccardo Patrese	I	Benetton ALFA ROMEO 185T	G	Alfa Romeo 890T	2m 01·396s
23	Eddie Cheever	USA	Benetton ALFA ROMEO 185T	G	Alfa Romeo 890T	2m 00·782s
24	Piercarlo Ghinzani	I	Kelemata OSELLA FA1G	P	Alfa Romeo 183T	2m 05·088s
25	Andrea de Cesaris	I	LIGIER JS25	P	Renault EF4/EF15	1m 58·302s
26	Jacques Laffite	F	LIGIER JS25	P	Renault EF4	2m 00·729s
27	Michele Alboreto	I	Fiat FERRARI 156/85	G	Ferrari 126C	1m 56·046s
28	Stefan Johansson	S	Fiat FERRARI 156/85	G	Ferrari 126C	1m 57·506s
29	Pierluigi Martini	I	Simod MINARDI M/85	P	Motori Moderni	2m 12·279s
30	Jonathan Palmer	GB	West ZAKSPEED ZAK 841	G	Zakspeed	2m 04·990s

Friday morning practice session not officially recorded. Practice on Saturday abandoned during unofficial session.   *Fri p.m. Hot, dry*

G – Goodyear, P – Pirelli.

Points

WORLD CHAMPIONSHIP OF DRIVERS

1	Alain Prost	69 pts
2	Michele Alboreto	53
3	Ayrton Senna	32
4	Elio de Angelis	31
5 =	Stefan Johansson	21
5 =	Nelson Piquet	21
5 =	Keke Rosberg	21
8	Niki Lauda	14
9	Nigel Mansell	13
10	Patrick Tambay	11
11	Jacques Laffite	10
12	Thierry Boutsen	9
13 =	Marc Surer	5
13 =	Derek Warwick	5
15	Stefan Bellof	4
16 =	René Arnoux	3
16 =	Andrea de Cesaris	3

CONSTRUCTORS' CUP

1	McLaren	83 pts
2	Ferrari	77
3	Lotus	63
4	Williams	34
5	Brabham	26
6	Renault	16
7	Ligier	13
8	Arrows	9
9	Tyrrell	4

Entries and practice times

No.	Driver	Nat.	Car	Tyre	Engine	Entrant	Practice 1	Practice 2
1	John Watson	GB	Marlboro McLAREN MP4/2B	G	TAG P01 (TTE P01)	Marlboro McLaren International	**1m 12·496s**	1m 12·516s
2	Alain Prost	F	Marlboro McLAREN MP4/2B	G	TAG P01 (TTE P01)	Marlboro McLaren International	1m 10·345s	**1m 09·429s**
3	Martin Brundle	GB	TYRRELL 014	G	Renault EF4	Tyrrell Racing Organisation	1m 11·296s	**1m 10·731s**
4	Ivan Capelli	I	TYRRELL 014	G	Renault EF4	Tyrrell Racing Organisation	1m 16·879s	**1m 13·721s**
5	Nigel Mansell	GB	WILLIAMS FW10	G	Honda RA163–E	Canon Williams Honda Team	1m 10·537s	**1m 08·059s**
6	Keke Rosberg	SF	WILLIAMS FW10	G	Honda RA163–E	Canon Williams Honda Team	1m 09·277s	**1m 08·197s**
7	Nelson Piquet	BR	Olivetti BRABHAM BT54	P	BMW M12/13	Motor Racing Developments Ltd	1m 09·204s	**1m 07·482s**
8	Marc Surer	CH	Olivetti BRABHAM BT54	P	BMW M12/13	Motor Racing Developments Ltd	**1m 09·762s**	1m 09·913s
9	Philippe Alliot	F	RAM 03	P	Hart 415T	Skoal Bandit Formula 1 Team	1m 14·355s	**1m 13·537s**
11	Elio de Angelis	I	John Player Special LOTUS 97T	G	Renault EF4/EF15	John Player Special Team Lotus	1m 11·530s	**1m 10·014s**
12	Ayrton Senna	BR	John Player Special LOTUS 97T	G	Renault EF4/EF15	John Player Special Team Lotus	1m 08·020s	**1m 07·169s**
15	Patrick Tambay	F	Elf RENAULT RE60B	G	Renault EF15	Equipe Renault Elf	1m 13·048s	**1m 10·934s**
16	Derek Warwick	GB	Elf RENAULT RE60B	G	Renault EF15	Equipe Renault Elf	1m 11·014s	**1m 09·904s**
17	Gerhard Berger	A	ARROWS A8	G	BMW M12/13	Barclay Arrows BMW	**1m 11·608s**	1m 11·638s
18	Thierry Boutsen	B	ARROWS A8	G	BMW M12/13	Barclay Arrows BMW	1m 10·918s	**1m 10·323s**
19	Teo Fabi	I	TOLEMAN TG185	P	Hart 415T	Toleman Group Motorsport	1m 13·024s	**1m 12·090s**
20	Piercarlo Ghinzani	I	TOLEMAN TG185	P	Hart 415T	Toleman Group Motorsport	1m 13·517s	**1m 10·570s**
22	Riccardo Patrese	I	Benetton ALFA ROMEO 184T	G	Alfa Romeo 890T	Benetton Team Alfa Romeo	1m 10·963s	**1m 10·251s**
23	Eddie Cheever	USA	Benetton ALFA ROMEO 184T	G	Alfa Romeo 890T	Benetton Team Alfa Romeo	1m 12·766s	**1m 11·500s**
24	Huub Rothengatter	NL	Kelemata OSELLA FA1G	P	Alfa Romeo 890T	Osella Squadra Corse	**1m 16·994s**	1m 18·022s
25	Philippe Streiff	F	Gitanes LIGIER JS25	P	Renault EF4/EF15	Equipe Ligier Gitanes	1m 10·396s	**1m 09·080s**
26	Jacques Laffite	F	Gitanes LIGIER JS25	P	Renault EF4/EF15	Equipe Ligier Gitanes	1m 11·312s	**1m 10·081s**
27	Michele Alboreto	I	Fiat FERRARI 156/85	G	Ferrari 126C	Scuderia Ferrari SpA	1m 10·877s	**1m 10·659s**
28	Stefan Johansson	S	Fiat FERRARI 156/85	G	Ferrari 126C	Scuderia Ferrari SpA	1m 11·309s	**1m 10·517s**
29	Pierluigi Martini	I	Simod MINARDI M/85	P	Motori Moderni	Minardi Team	1m 16·842s	**1m 15·127s**
30	Christian Danner	D	West ZAKSPEED ZAK 841	G	Zakspeed	West Zakspeed Racing	1m 15·947s	**1m 15·054s**
33	Alan Jones	AUS	BEATRICE-LOLA THL-1	G	Hart 415T	Team Haas (USA) Ltd	1m 14·050s	**1m 13·084s**

Friday morning and Saturday morning practice sessions not officially recorded.

G – Goodyear, P – Pirelli.

Fri p.m.
Warm, dry

Sat p.m.
Warm, dry

Starting grid

12 SENNA (1m 07·169s)
Lotus

7 PIQUET (1m 07·482s)
Brabham

5 MANSELL (1m 08·059s)
Williams

6 ROSBERG (1m 08·197s)
Williams

25 STREIFF (1m 09·080s)
Ligier

2 PROST (1m 09·429s)
McLaren

8 SURER (1m 09·762s)
Brabham

16 WARWICK (1m 09·904s)
Renault

11 DE ANGELIS (1m 10·014s)
Lotus

26 LAFFITE (1m 10·081s)
Ligier

22 PATRESE (1m 10·251s)
Alfa Romeo

18 BOUTSEN (1m 10·323s)
Arrows

28 JOHANSSON (1m 10·517s)
Ferrari

20 GHINZANI (1m 10·570s)
Toleman

27 ALBORETO (1m 10·659s)
Ferrari

3 BRUNDLE (1m 10·731s)
Tyrrell

15 TAMBAY (1m 10·934s)
Renault

23 CHEEVER (1m 11·500s)
Alfa Romeo

17 BERGER (1m 11·608s)
Arrows

19 FABI (1m 12·090s)
Toleman

1 WATSON (1m 12·496s)
McLaren

33 JONES (1m 13·084s)
Beatrice

9 ALLIOT (1m 13·537s)
RAM

4 CAPELLI (1m 13·721s)
Tyrrell

30 DANNER (1m 15·054s)
Zakspeed

29 MARTINI (1m 15·127s)
Minardi

Did not start:
24 Rothengatter (Osella), 1m 16·994s, did not qualify.

Results and retirements

Place	Driver	Car	Laps	Time and Speed (mph/km/h)/Retirement	
1	Nigel Mansell	Williams-Honda t/c V6	75	1h 32m 58·109s	126·527/203·625
2	Ayrton Senna	Lotus-Renault t/c V6	75	1h 33m 19·505s	126·043/202·846
3	Keke Rosberg	Williams-Honda t/c V6	75	1h 33m 56·642s	125·213/201·510
4	Alain Prost	McLaren-TAG t/c V6	75	1h 34m 04·230s	125·045/201·239
5	Elio de Angelis	Lotus-Renault t/c V6	74		
6	Thierry Boutsen	Arrows-BMW t/c 4	73		
7	John Watson	McLaren-TAG t/c V6	73		
8	Philippe Streiff	Ligier-Renault t/c V6	73		
9	Riccardo Patrese	Alfa Romeo t/c V8	73		
10	Gerhard Berger	Arrows-BMW t/c 4	73		
11	Eddie Cheever	Alfa Romeo t/c V8	73		
12	Patrick Tambay	Renault t/c V6	72		
	Marc Surer	Brabham-BMW t/c 4	62	Turbo	
	Stefan Johansson	Ferrari t/c V6	59	Electrics	
	Jacques Laffite	Ligier-Renault t/c V6	58	Engine	
	Christian Danner	Zakspeed t/c 4	50	Engine	
	Ivan Capelli	Tyrrell-Renault t/c V6	44	Accident	
	Martin Brundle	Tyrrell-Renault t/c V6	40	Water pipe	
	Teo Fabi	Toleman-Hart t/c 4	33	Engine	
	Philippe Alliot	RAM-Hart t/c 4	31	Engine	
	Piercarlo Ghinzani	Toleman-Hart t/c 4	16	Engine	
	Alan Jones	Beatrice-Hart t/c 4	13	Holed water radiator	
	Michele Alboreto	Ferrari t/c V6	13	Turbo	
	Nelson Piquet	Brabham-BMW t/c 4	6	Accident	
	Derek Warwick	Renault t/c V6	4	Fuel injection	
	Pierluigi Martini	Minardi-MM t/c V6	3	Accident	

Fastest lap: Laffite, on lap 55, 1m 11·526s, 131·566 mph/211·734 km/h (record).
Previous lap record: Didier Pironi (F1 Ligier JS11/15 Cosworth DFV), 1m 12·368s, 130·015 mph/209·239 km/h (1980).

Past winners

Year	Driver	Nat.	Car	Circuit	Distance miles/km	Speed mph/km/h
1983	Nelson Piquet	BR	1·5 Brabham BT52B-BMW t/c	Brands Hatch	198·63/319·67	123·16/198·21
1984	Alain Prost	F	1·5 McLaren MP4/2-TAG t/c	Nürburgring	189·09/304·31	119·15/191·75
1985	Nigel Mansell	GB	1·5 Williams FW10-Honda t/c	Brands Hatch	196·05/315·51	126·53/203·62

Lap chart

1st LAP ORDER	Lap positions 1 → 75
12 A. Senna	12 12 12 12 12 12 12 12 5 5 5 5 5 5 5 5 5 5 5 5 5 5 5 5 5 5 5 5 5 5 5 5 5 5 5 5 5 5 5 5 5 5 5 5 5 5 5 5 5 5 5 5 5 5 5 5 5 5 5 5 5 5 5 5 5 5 5 5 5 5 5 5 5 5 5
0 K. Rosberg	0 0 0 0 0 0 0 0 1E 1E 1E 1E 1E 1E 1E 1E 1E 1E 1E 1E 1E 1E 1E 1A 1A 1A 1A 1 1 1 1 1 1 1 1 1 1 1 1 1 1 1 1 1 1 1 1 1 1 1 1 1 1 1 1 1 1 1 1 1 1 1 1 1 1 10 10 10 10 10 10 10 10 10 10 10
7 N. Piquet	7 7 7 7 7 7 7 11 11 11 11 11 11 11 11 11 11 11 11 11 8 8 8 8 8 8 8 8 8 8 8 12 26 26 26 26 26 26 26 26 26 26 26 26 26 26 26 12 12 12 12 12 12 12 12 12 12 2 2 6 6 6 6 6 6 6 6 6 6 6 6
5 N. Mansell	5 5 5 5 5 28 28 28 28 28 28 28 8 8 8 8 8 8 8 8 11 26 26 26 26 26 26 26 26 26 26 26 12 12 12 12 12 12 12 12 12 12 12 12 12 12 12 26 28 28 28 28 2 2 2 2 2 11 6 2 2 2 2 2 2 2 2 2 2 2 2 2 2
11 E. de Angelis	11 11 11 11 11 11 8 8 8 8 8 8 28 28 28 28 28 26 26 26 11 11 11 11 11 11 11 11 11 11 11 11 11 11 11 11 11 11 11 11 11 11 11 11 11 28 28 28 28 28 28 28 28 28 28 11 11 11 11 2 11 11 11 11 11 6 11 11 11 11 11 11 11 11 11
8 M. Surer	8 8 8 8 8 8 27 27 2 2 2 2 2 2 2 2 26 28 28 28 28 28 28 28 28 28 28 28 28 28 28 28 28 28 28 28 28 28 28 28 28 28 28 28 28 28 28 28 11 11 11 11 11 11 11 11 11 2 2 2 2 2 11 6 6 6 6 6 25 25 25 25 25 18 18 18 18 18
16 D. Warwick	16 28 28 28 28 28 2 2 27 26 26 26 26 26 26 26 2 2 2 2 2 2 2 2 2 2 2 2 2 2 3 2 2 2 2 2 2 2 2 2 2 2 6 6 6 6 26 26 25 25 25 25 18 18 18 18 18 1 1 1 1 1 1
28 S. Johansson	28 27 27 27 27 27 26 26 26 27 27 3 3 3 3 3 3 3 3 3 3 3 3 3 3 3 3 3 3 3 3 3 3 3 2 6 6 6 6 6 6 6 6 6 6 26 26 26 25 18 18 18 18 22 22 22 22 1 25 25 25 25 25
27 M. Alboreto	27 26 26 26 2 2 3 3 3 3 27 23 23 23 23 25 25 25 25 25 25 25 25 25 25 25 25 25 25 25 25 25 25 25 25 25 18 18 18 18 18 18 18 18 18 18 18 18 18 18 22 22 1 1 1 1 22 22 22 22 22 22 22
25 P. Streiff	25 3 2 2 26 26 23 23 23 23 23 18 18 18 25 25 23 23 18 18 18 18 18 18 6 6 6 6 6 6 6 3 18 18 18 18 18 18 18 18 18 18 18 18 18 22 22 1 1 1 1 17 17 17 17 17 17 17 17 17 17 17
26 J. Laffite	26 2 3 3 3 18 18 18 18 18 22 22 25 18 18 18 18 23 23 23 23 23 23 6 18 18 18 18 18 18 18 22 22 22 22 22 22 22 22 22 22 22 1 1 17 17 17 23 23 23 23 23 23 23 23 23
3 M. Brundle	3 25 18 18 23 23 22 22 22 22 22 25 22 22 22 22 22 22 22 22 22 23 23 23 22 22 22 22 22 22 1 1 1 1 1 1 1 1 1 1 1 1 17 23 23 23 15 15 15 15 15 15 15 15 15
18 T. Boutsen	18 18 23 18 18 25 25 25 33 25 25 33 19 19 19 19 19 19 19 19 19 19 19 6 22 22 22 23 23 23 23 23 23 1 17 17 17 17 17 17 17 17 17 17 17 17 23 15 15 15 15
2 A. Prost	2 23 22 22 22 33 33 33 25 33 33 19 20 20 20 17 17 17 17 17 6 19 19 19 19 1 1 1 1 1 23 17 15 15 15 15 15 23 23 23 23 23 23 23 23 15 15 28 28
23 E. Cheever	23 22 33 33 33 19 19 19 19 19 19 20 17 17 17 15 15 15 15 15 6 17 17 17 1 1 1 17 17 17 17 17 17 15 23 23 23 23 23 15 15 15 15 15 15 15 15 28 28
33 A. Jones	33 33 25 25 25 20 20 20 20 20 17 15 15 1 1 1 1 1 1 1 15 1 1 17 17 17 15 15 15 15 15 15 23 4 4 4 30 30 30 30 30 30 30 30 30 30 30
20 P. Ghinzani	20 20 20 20 20 17 17 17 17 17 15 1 1 1 9 9 6 6 6 6 1 15 15 15 15 15 15 15 15 4 4 4 4 4 4 4 30 30 30
22 R. Patrese	22 19 19 19 19 19 15 15 15 15 15 1 9 9 9 4 4 4 9 9 9 9 9 9 9 9 9 9 4 4 4 30 30 30 30 30 30 30
19 T. Fabi	19 15 15 17 17 17 1 1 1 1 1 9 4 4 4 6 6 6 4 4 4 4 4 4 4 9 30 30
15 P. Tambay	15 17 17 17 15 1 1 4 9 9 9 9 4 6 6 6 30 30 30 30 30 30 30 30 30 30 30 30 30
17 G. Berger	17 9 9 1 15 9 9 4 4 4 4 4 27 30 30 30
9 P. Alliot	9 4 4 9 9 4 6 30 30 30 30 6 6 27
4 I. Capelli	4 1 1 4 4 9 30 6 6 6 6 30 30
30 C. Danner	30 30 30 30 30 30
1 N. Lauda	1 29 29 29
29 P. Martini	29 16 16 16

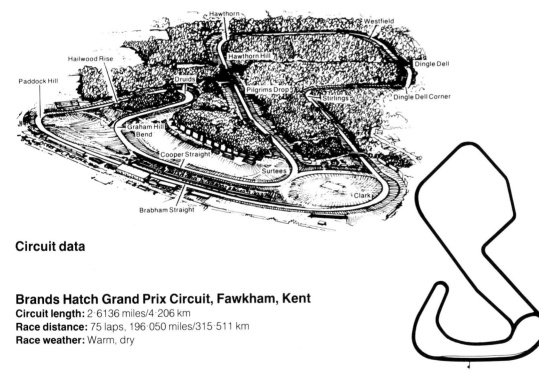

Circuit data

Brands Hatch Grand Prix Circuit, Fawkham, Kent
Circuit length: 2·6136 miles/4·206 km
Race distance: 75 laps, 196·050 miles/315·511 km
Race weather: Warm, dry

Fastest laps

Driver	Time	Lap
Jacques Laffite	1m 11·526s	55
Alain Prost	1m 11·655s	49
Keke Rosberg	1m 12·022s	58
Nigel Mansell	1m 12·583s	60
Ayrton Senna	1m 12·601s	56
Marc Surer	1m 12·862s	38
Stefan Johansson	1m 13·353s	48
Eddie Cheever	1m 13·620s	45
Elio de Angelis	1m 13·793s	50
John Watson	1m 14·007s	52
Riccardo Patrese	1m 14·317s	38
Gerhard Berger	1m 14·391s	54
Martin Brundle	1m 14·462s	35
Philippe Streiff	1m 14·476s	25
Patrick Tambay	1m 14·571s	68
Thierry Boutsen	1m 14·583s	45
Nelson Piquet	1m 14·649s	6
Michele Alboreto	1m 15·224s	6
Ivan Capelli	1m 15·538s	37
Teo Fabi	1m 15·595s	26
Piercarlo Ghinzani	1m 15·946s	15
Philippe Alliot	1m 16·141s	13
Alan Jones	1m 16·390s	9
Christian Danner	1m 19·150s	26
Pierluigi Martini	1m 21·352s	3
Derek Warwick	1m 28·545s	4

Points

WORLD CHAMPIONSHIP OF DRIVERS

1	Alain Prost	72 pts
2	Michele Alboreto	53
3	Ayrton Senna	38
4	Elio de Angelis	33
5	Keke Rosberg	25
6	Nigel Mansell	22
7=	Stefan Johansson	21
7=	Nelson Piquet	21
9	Niki Lauda	14
10	Patrick Tambay	11
11=	Jacques Laffite	10
11=	Thierry Boutsen	10
13=	Marc Surer	5
13=	Derek Warwick	5
15	Stefan Bellof	4
16=	René Arnoux	3
16=	Andrea de Cesaris	3

CONSTRUCTORS' CUP

1	McLaren	86 pts
2	Ferrari	77
3	Lotus	71
4	Williams	47
5	Brabham	26
6	Renault	16
7	Ligier	13
8	Arrows	10
9	Tyrrell	4

Entries and practice times

No.	Driver	Nat.	Car	Tyre	Engine	Entrant	Practice 1	Practice 2
1	Niki Lauda	A	Marlboro McLAREN MP4/2B	G	TAG P01 (TTE P01)	Marlboro McLaren International	1m 05·357s	**1m 04·283s**
2	Alain Prost	F	Marlboro McLAREN MP4/2B	G	TAG P01 (TTE P01)	Marlboro McLaren International	1m 05·757s	**1m 04·376s**
3	Martin Brundle	GB	TYRRELL 014	G	Renault EF4/EF15	Tyrrell Racing Organisation	1m 06·709s	**1m 05·649s**
4	Philippe Streiff	F	TYRRELL 014	G	Renault EF4	Tyrrell Racing Organisation	1m 07·935s	**1m 06·205s**
5	Nigel Mansell	GB	WILLIAMS FW10	G	Honda RA163–E	Canon Williams Honda Team	1m 03·188s	**1m 02·366s**
6	Keke Rosberg	SF	WILLIAMS FW10	G	Honda RA163–E	Canon Williams Honda Team	1m 03·073s	**1m 02·504s**
7	Nelson Piquet	BR	Olivetti BRABHAM BT54	P	BMW M12/13	Motor Racing Developments Ltd	1m 03·844s	**1m 02·490s**
8	Marc Surer	CH	Olivetti BRABHAM BT54	P	BMW M12/13	Motor Racing Developments Ltd	1m 04·611s	**1m 04·088s**
11	Elio de Angelis	I	John Player Special LOTUS 97T	G	Renault EF4/EF15	John Player Special Team Lotus	1m 04·611s	**1m 04·129s**
12	Ayrton Senna	BR	John Player Special LOTUS 97T	G	Renault EF4/EF15	John Player Special Team Lotus	1m 04·517s	**1m 02·825s**
17	Gerhard Berger	A	ARROWS A8	G	BMW M12/13	Barclay Arrows BMW	1m 06·546s	**1m 04·780s**
18	Thierry Boutsen	B	ARROWS A8	G	BMW M12/13	Barclay Arrows BMW	1m 05·079s	**1m 04·518s**
19	Teo Fabi	I	TOLEMAN TG185	P	Hart 415T	Toleman Group Motorsport	1m 06·083s	**1m 04·215s**
20	Piercarlo Ghinzani	I	TOLEMAN TG185	P	Hart 415T	Toleman Group Motorsport	1m 07·800s	**1m 05·114s**
22	Riccardo Patrese	I	Benetton ALFA ROMEO 184T	G	Alfa Romeo 890T	Benetton Team Alfa Romeo	1m 06·386s	**1m 04·948s**
23	Eddie Cheever	USA	Benetton ALFA ROMEO 184T	G	Alfa Romeo 890T	Benetton Team Alfa Romeo	1m 07·159s	**1m 05·260s**
24	Huub Rothengatter	NL	Kelemata OSELLA FA1G	P	Alfa Romeo 890T	Osella Squadra Corse	1m 09·904s	**1m 09·873s**
27	Michele Alboreto	I	Fiat FERRARI 156/85	G	Ferrari 126C	Scuderia Ferrari SpA	**1m 05·268s**	1m 05·757s
28	Stefan Johansson	S	Fiat FERRARI 156/85	G	Ferrari 126C	Scuderia Ferrari SpA	1m 05·406s	**1m 05·388s**
29	Pierluigi Martini	I	Simod MINARDI M/85	P	Motori Moderni	Minardi Team	1m 10·025s	**1m 08·658s**
33	Alan Jones	AUS	BEATRICE-LOLA THL-1	G	Hart 415T	Team Haas (USA) Ltd	1m 07·144s	**1m 05·731s**

Thursday morning and Friday morning practice sessions not officially recorded.

G – Goodyear, P – Pirelli.

Thu p.m.	Fri p.m.
Hot, dry	Hot, dry

Starting grid

5 MANSELL (1m 02·366s)
Williams

7 PIQUET (1m 02·490s)
Brabham

6 ROSBERG (1m 02·504s)
Williams

12 SENNA (1m 02·825s)
Lotus

5 SURER (1m 04·088s)
Brabham

11 DE ANGELIS (1m 04·129s)
Lotus

19 FABI (1m 04·215s)
Toleman

1 LAUDA (1m 04·283s)
McLaren

2 PROST (1m 04·376s)
McLaren

18 BOUTSEN (1m 04·518s)
Arrows

17 BERGER (1m 04·780s)
Arrows

22 PATRESE (1m 04·948s)
Alfa Romeo

20 GHINZANI (1m 05·114s)
Toleman

23 CHEEVER (1m 05·260s)
Alfa Romeo

27 ALBORETO (1m 05·268s)
Ferrari

28 JOHANSSON (1m 05·388s)
Ferrari

3 BRUNDLE (1m 05·649s)
Tyrrell

4 STREIFF (1m 06·205s)
Tyrrell

29 MARTINI (1m 08·658s)
Minardi

24 ROTHENGATTER (1m 09·873s)
Osella

Did not start:
33 Jones (Beatrice), 1m 05·731s, driver unwell.

Results and retirements

Place	Driver	Car	Laps	Time and speed (mph/km/h)/Retirement	
1	Nigel Mansell	Williams-Honda t/c V6	75	1h 28m 22·866s	129·840/208·959
2	Keke Rosberg	Williams-Honda t/c V6	75	1h 28m 30·438s	129·655/208·661
3	Alain Prost	McLaren-TAG t/c V6	75	1h 30m 14·660s	127·159/204·644
4	Stefan Johansson	Ferrari t/c V6	74		
5	Gerhard Berger	Arrows-BMW t/c 4	74		
6	Thierry Boutsen	Arrows-BMW t/c 4	74		
7	Martin Brundle	Tyrrell-Renault t/c V6	73		
	Elio de Angelis	Lotus-Renault t/c V6	52	Engine	
	Pierluigi Martini	Minardi-MM t/c V6	45	Water radiator	
	Niki Lauda	McLaren-TAG t/c V6	37	Turbo	
	Philippe Streiff	Tyrrell-Renault t/c V6	16	Accident	
	Ayrton Senna	Lotus-Renault t/c V6	8	Engine	
	Michele Alboreto	Ferrari t/c V6	8	Turbo	
	Nelson Piquet	Brabham-BMW t/c 4	6	Engine	
	Piercarlo Ghinzani	Toleman-Hart t/c 4	4	Engine	
	Teo Fabi	Toleman-Hart t/c 4	3	Engine	
	Marc Surer	Brabham-BMW t/c 4	3	Engine	
	Huub Rothengatter	Osella-Alfa Romeo t/c V8	1	Electrics	
	Eddie Cheever	Alfa Romeo t/c V8	0	Accident	
	Riccardo Patrese	Alfa Romeo t/c V8	0	Accident	

Fastest lap: Rosberg, on lap 74, 1m 08·149s, 134·710 mph/216·796 km/h (record).
Previous lap record: Alain Prost (F1 Renault RE30B t/c V6), 1m 08·278s, 134·455 mph/216·385 km/h (1982).

Past winners

Year	Driver	Nat.	Car	Circuit	Distance miles/km	Speed mph/km/h
1934	Whitney Straight	GB	2·9 Maserati 8CM s/c	Prince George	91·20/146·77	95·68/153·98
1936	'Mario' Massacurati	I	2·0 Bugatti T35B s/c	Prince George	198·54/319·52	87·43/140·70
1937	Pat Fairfield	ZA	1·0 ERA A-type s/c	Prince Gorge	198·54/319·52	89·17/143·50
1938	Buller Meyer	ZA	1·5 Riley	Prince George	198·54/319·52	86·53/139·26
1939	Luigi Villoresi	I	1·5 Maserati 4CM	Prince George	198·54/319·52	99·67/160·40
1960*	Paul Frère	B	1·5 Cooper T45-Climax	East London	145·80/234·64	84·88/136·60
1960*	Stirling Moss	GB	1·5 Porsche 718	East London	194·40/312·86	89·24/143·62
1961*	Jim Clark	GB	1·5 Lotus 21-Climax	East London	194·40/312·86	92·20/148·38
1962	Graham Hill	GB	1·5 BRM P57	East London	199·26/320·68	93·57/150·59
1963	Jim Clark	GB	1·5 Lotus 25-Climax	East London	206·55/332·41	95·10/153·05
1965	Jim Clark	GB	1·5 Lotus 25-Climax	East London	206·55/332·41	97·97/157·68
1966*	Mike Spence	GB	2·0 Lotus 33-Climax	East London	145·80/234·64	97·75/157·31
1967	Pedro Rodriguez	MEX	3·0 Cooper T81-Maserati	Kyalami	203·52/327·53	97·09/156·25
1968	Jim Clark	GB	3·0 Lotus 49-Ford	Kyalami	204·00/328·31	107·42/172·88
1969	Jackie Stewart	GB	3·0 Matra MS10-Ford	Kyalami	204·00/328·31	110·62/178·03
1970	Jack Brabham	AUS	3·0 Brabham BT33-Ford	Kyalami	204·00/328·31	111·70/179·76
1971	Mario Andretti	USA	3·0 Ferrari 312B-1/71	Kyalami	201·45/324·20	112·36/180·83
1972	Denny Hulme	NZ	3·0 McLaren M19A-Ford	Kyalami	201·41/324·20	114·23/183·83
1973	Jackie Stewart	GB	3·0 Tyrrell 006-Ford	Kyalami	201·45/324·20	117·14/188·52
1974	Carlos Reutemann	RA	3·0 Brabham BT44-Ford	Kyalami	198·90/320·10	116·22/187·04
1975	Jody Scheckter	ZA	3·0 Tyrrell 007-Ford	Kyalami	198·90/320·10	115·55/185·96
1976	Niki Lauda	A	3·0 Ferrari 312T/76	Kyalami	198·90/320·10	116·65/187·73
1977	Niki Lauda	A	3·0 Ferrari 312T-2/77	Kyalami	198·90/320·10	116·59/187·63
1978	Ronnie Peterson	S	3·0 JPS/Lotus 78-Ford	Kyalami	198·90/320·10	116·70/187·81
1979	Gilles Villeneuve	CDN	3·0 Ferrari 312T-4	Kyalami	198·90/320·10	117·19/188·60
1980	René Arnoux	F	1·5 Renault RE t/c	Kyalami	198·90/320·10	123·19/198·25
1981*	Carlos Reutemann	RA	3·0 Williams FWO7B-Ford	Kyalami	196·35/315·99	112·31/180·75
1982	Alain Prost	F	1·5 Renault RE 30B t/c	Kyalami	196·35/315·99	127·82/205·70
1983	Riccardo Patrese	I	1·5 Brabham-BMW BT52B t/c	Kyalami	196·35/315·99	126·10/202·94
1984	Niki Lauda	A	1.5 McLaren-TAG MP4/2 t/c	Kyalami	191·25/307·78	128·37/206·59
1985	Nigel Mansell	GB	1.5 Williams-Honda FW10 t/c	Kyalami	191·25/307·78	129·84/208·96

*Non-championship

Lap chart

1st LAP ORDER — laps 1–75

```
5  N. Mansell        5  5  5  5  5  5  5  5  5  5  5  5  5  5  5  5  5  5  5  5  5  5  5  5  5  5  5  5  5  5  5  5  5  5  5  5  5  5  5  5  5  5  5  5  5  5  5  5  5  5  5  5  5  5  5  5  5  5  5  5  5  5  5  5  5  5  5  5  5  5  5  5  5  5  5
7  N. Piquet         7  7  7  7  6  6  6  5  11 ?  ?  ?  ?  ?  ?  ?  ?  ?  ?  ?  ?  ?  ?  ?  ?  ?  ?  ?  ?  ?  ?  ?  ?  ?  ?  ?  ?  ?  ?  ?  ?  1  ?  ?  ?  ?  ?  ?  ?  ?  ?  ?  ?  ?  ?  ?  ?  ?  ?  ?  ?  ?  ?  ?  ?  ?  ?  ?  ?  ?  6  6  6  6  6
11 E. de Angelis     11 11 11 6  7  11 12 11 2  1  1  1  1  1  1  1  1  1  1  1  1  1  1  1  1  1  1  1  1  1  1  1  1  1  1  1  1  1  1  1  1  1  2  2  6  6  6  6  6  6  6  6  6  6  6  6  6  6  6  6  6  6  6  6  6  6  6  6  6  6  6  2  2  2  2
12 A. Senna          12 12 6  11 11 12 11 2  1  11 11 11 11 11 11 6  6  6  6  6  6  6  6  6  11 11 11 11 6  6  6  6  6  6  1  11 11 11 11 11 11 11 11 11 11 11 11 11 11 11 11 11 28 28 28 28 28 28 28 28 28 28 28 28 28 28 28 28 28 28 28 28 28 28 28
6  K. Rosberg        6  6  12 12 12 2  2  1  6  6  6  6  6  6  6  11 11 11 11 11 11 11 11 11 3  6  6  6  3  3  3  3  3  11 3  3  3  28 28 28 28 28 28 28 28 28 28 18 18 18 18 18 17 17 17 17 17 17 17 17 17 17 17 17 17 17 17 17 17 17 17 17 17 17 17
1  N. Lauda          1  1  1  2  2  1  1  17 17 3  3  3  3  28 28 28 28 28 28 28 28 28 28 28 6  3  3  3  11 11 11 11 11 3  28 28 28 3  18 18 18 18 18 18 18 18 18 17 18 17 17 17 17 17 17 18 18 18 18 18 18 18 18 18 18 18 18 18 18 18 18 18 18 18 18
8  M. Surer          8  2  2  1  1  27 27 3  28 28 28 3  3  3  3  3  3  3  3  3  3  18 17 17 28 28 28 28 28 18 18 18 18 17 17 17 17 17 17 17 17 17 17 17 3  3  3  3  3  3  3  3  3  3  3  3  3  3  3  3  3  3  3  3  3  3  3  3  3  3  3  3  3  3  3
2  A. Prost          2  8  27 27 27 17 17 28 28 18 18 18 18 18 18 18 18 18 18 18 18 18 18 18 18 18 18 18 18 18 18 18 17 17 17 3  3  3  3  3  3  3  3  3
19 T. Fabi           19 27 19 17 17 3  3  18 18 17 17 17 17 17 17 17 17 17 17 17 17 17 17 17 28 28 18 18 17 17 17 17 17 17 29 29 29 29 29 29 29 29
27 M. Alboreto       27 19 17 3  3  28 28 12 4  4  4  4  4  4  4  29 29 29 29 29 29 29 29 29 29 29 29 29 29 29 29 29 29 29 29 29 29 29 29 29
17 G. Berger         17 17 3  28 28 18 18 4  29 29 29 29 29 29 29
3  M. Brundle        3  3  28 18 18 4  4  27
28 S. Johansson      28 28 18 4  4  29 29 29
18 T. Boutsen        18 18 4  29 29 7
4  P. Streiff        4  4  29 20
29 P. Martini        29 29 8
24 H. Rothengatter   24 20 20
20 P. Ghinzani       20
```

Circuit data

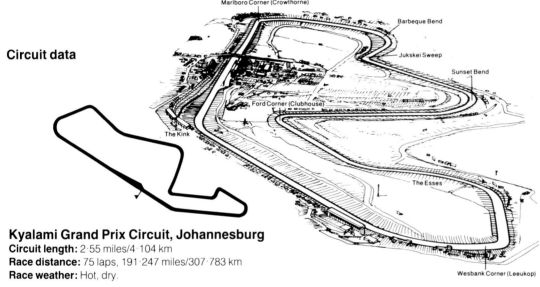

Kyalami Grand Prix Circuit, Johannesburg

Circuit length: 2·55 miles/4·104 km
Race distance: 75 laps, 191·247 miles/307·783 km
Race weather: Hot, dry.

Marlboro Corner (Crowthorne)
Barbeque Bend
Jukskei Sweep
Sunset Bend
Ford Corner (Clubhouse)
The Kink
The Esses
Wesbank Corner (Leeukop)

Fastest laps

Driver	Time	Lap
Keke Rosberg	1m 08·149s	74
Nigel Mansell	1m 08·518s	74
Alain Prost	1m 08·713s	56
Thierry Boutsen	1m 09·230s	63
Niki Lauda	1m 09·500s	35
Elio de Angelis	1m 09·960s	34
Ayrton Senna	1m 10·077s	7
Gerhard Berger	1m 10·258s	33
Martin Brundle	1m 10·339s	45
Stefan Johansson	1m 10·413s	41
Nelson Piquet	1m 10·476s	3
Michele Alboreto	1m 10·850s	5
Philippe Streiff	1m 11·404s	5
Teo Fabi	1m 12·035s	3
Marc Surer	1m 12·100s	2
Pierluigi Martini	1m 14·428s	5
Piercarlo Ghinzani	1m 29·450s	3
Huub Rothengatter	1m 29·792s	1

Points

WORLD CHAMPIONSHIP OF DRIVERS

1	Alain Prost	73 pts
2	Michele Alboreto	53
3	Ayrton Senna	38
4	Elio de Angelis	33
5=	Keke Rosberg	31
5=	Nigel Mansell	31
7	Stefan Johansson	24
8	Nelson Piquet	21
9	Niki Lauda	14
10=	Patrick Tambay	11
10=	Thierry Boutsen	11
12	Jacques Laffite	10
13=	Marc Surer	5
13=	Derek Warwick	5
15	Stefan Bellof	4
16=	René Arnoux	3
16=	Andrea de Cesaris	3
18	Gerhard Berger	2

CONSTRUCTORS' CUP

1	McLaren	90 pts
2	Ferrari	80
3	Lotus	71
4	Williams	62
5	Brabham	26
6	Renault	16
7	Ligier	13
8	Arrows	13
9	Tyrrell	4

Mitsubishi Australian Grand Prix, 3 November/statistics

Entries and practice times

No.	Driver	Nat.	Car	Tyre	Engine	Entrant	Practice 1	Practice 2
1	Niki Lauda	A	Marlboro McLAREN MP4/2B	G	TAG P01 (TTE P01)	Marlboro McLaren International	1m 24·691s	**1m 23·941s**
2	Alain Prost	F	Marlboro McLAREN MP4/2B	G	TAG P01 (TTE P01)	Marlboro McLaren International	1m 23·943s	**1m 21·889s**
3	Martin Brundle	GB	TYRRELL 014	G	Renault EF4/EF15	Tyrrell Racing Organisation	1m 25·646s	**1m 24·241s**
4	Ivan Capelli	I	TYRRELL 014	G	Renault EF4	Tyrrell Racing Organisation	**1m 27·120s**	
5	Nigel Mansell	GB	WILLIAMS FW10	G	Honda RA163–E	Canon Williams Honda Team	1m 22·564s	**1m 20·537s**
6	Keke Rosberg	SF	WILLIAMS FW10	G	Honda RA163–E	Canon Williams Honda Team	1m 22·402s	**1m 21·887s**
7	Nelson Piquet	BR	Olivetti BRABHAM BT54	P	BMW M12/13	Motor Racing Developments Ltd	1m 23·018s	**1m 22·718s**
8	Marc Surer	CH	Olivetti BRABHAM BT54	P	BMW M12/13	Motor Racing Developments Ltd	1m 24·404s	**1m 22·561s**
11	Elio de Angelis	I	John Player Special LOTUS 97T	G	Renault EF4/EF15	John Player Special Team Lotus	1m 24·543s	**1m 23·077s**
12	Ayrton Senna	BR	John Player Special LOTUS 97T	G	Renault EF4/EF15	John Player Special Team Lotus	1m 22·403s	**1m 19·843s**
15	Patrick Tambay	F	Elf RENAULT RE60B	G	Renault EF15	Equipe Renault Elf	1m 25·173s	**1m 22·683s**
16	Derek Warwick	GB	Elf RENAULT RE60B	G	Renault EF15	Equipe Renault Elf	1m 24·372s	**1m 23·426s**
17	Gerhard Berger	A	ARROWS A8	G	BMW M12/13	Barclay Arrows BMW	1m 25·362s	**1m 22·592s**
18	Thierry Boutsen	B	ARROWS A8	G	BMW M12/13	Barclay Arrows BMW	1m 23·960s	**1m 23·196s**
19	Teo Fabi	I	TOLEMAN TG185	P	Hart 415T	Toleman Group Motorsport	1m 28·261s	**1m 28·110s**
20	Piercarlo Ghinzani	I	TOLEMAN TG185	P	Hart 415T	Toleman Group Motorsport	**1m 25·021s**	1m 26·630s
22	Riccardo Patrese	I	Benetton ALFA ROMEO 184T	G	Alfa Romeo 890T	Benetton Team Alfa Romeo	**1m 23·758s**	1m 24·128s
23	Eddie Cheever	USA	Benetton ALFA ROMEO 184T	G	Alfa Romeo 890T	Benetton Team Alfa Romeo	**1m 23·597s**	1m 24·295s
24	Huub Rothengatter	NL	Kelemata OSELLA FA1G	P	Alfa Romeo 890T	Osella Squadra Corse	**1m 30·319s**	
25	Philippe Streiff	F	Gitanes LIGIER JS25	P	Renault EF4/EF15	Equipe Ligier Gitanes	1m 26·618s	**1m 24·286s**
26	Jacques Laffite	F	Gitanes LIGIER JS25	P	Renault EF4/EF15	Equipe Ligier Gitanes	1m 26·972s	**1m 24·830s**
27	Michele Alboreto	I	Fiat FERRARI 156/85	G	Ferrari 126C	Scuderia Ferrari SpA	1m 24·666s	**1m 22·337s**
28	Stefan Johansson	S	Fiat FERRARI 156/85	G	Ferrari 126C	Scuderia Ferrari SpA	1m 24·732s	**1m 23·902s**
29	Pierluigi Martini	I	Simod MINARDI M/85	P	Motori Moderni	Minardi Team	**1m 27·196s**	1m 27·402s
33	Alan Jones	AUS	BEATRICE-LOLA THL-1	G	Hart 415T	Team Haas (USA) Ltd	1m 25·780s	**1m 24·369s**

Thursday afternoon, Friday morning and Saturday morning practice sessions not officially recorded.

G – Goodyear, P – Pirelli.

Fri p.m. — Hot, dry
Sat p.m. — Hot, dry

Starting grid

12 SENNA (1m 19·843s) Lotus
5 MANSELL (1m 20·537s) Williams

6 ROSBERG (1m 21·887s) Williams
2 PROST (1m 21·889s) McLaren

27 ALBORETO (1m 22·337s) Ferrari
8 SURER (1m 22·561s) Brabham

17 BERGER (1m 22·592s) Arrows
15 TAMBAY (1m 22·683s) Renault

7 PIQUET (1m 22·718s) Brabham
11 DE ANGELIS (1m 23·077s) Lotus

18 BOUTSEN (1m 23·196s) Arrows
16 WARWICK (1m 23·426s) Renault

23 CHEEVER (1m 23·597s) Alfa Romeo
22 PATRESE (1m 23·758s) Alfa Romeo

28 JOHANSSON (1m 23·902s) Ferrari
1 LAUDA (1m 23·941s) McLaren

3 BRUNDLE (1m 24·241s) Tyrrell
25 STREIFF (1m 24·286s) Ligier

33 JONES (1m 24·369s) Beatrice
26 LAFFITE (1m 24·830s) Ligier

20 GHINZANI (1m 25·021s) Toleman
4 CAPELLI (1m 27·120s) Tyrrell

29 MARTINI (1m 27·196s) Minardi
19 FABI (1m 28·110s) Toleman

24 ROTHENGATTER (1m 30·319s) Osella

Results and retirements

Place	Driver	Car	Laps	Time and speed (mph/km/h)/Retirement	
1	Keke Rosberg	Williams-Honda t/c V6	82	2h 00m 40·473s	95·71/154·032
2	Jacques Laffite	Ligier-Renault t/c V6	82	2h 01m 26·603s	95·10/153·057
3	Philippe Streiff	Ligier-Renault t/c V6	82	2h 02m 09·009s	94·55/152·171
4	Ivan Capelli	Tyrrell-Renault t/c V6	81		
5	Stefan Johansson	Ferrari t/c V6	81		
6	Gerhard Berger	Arrows-BMW t/c 4	81		
7	Huub Rothengatter	Osella-Alfa Romeo t/c V8	78		
8	Pierluigi Martini	Minardi-MM t/c V6	78		
	Ayrton Senna	Lotus-Renault t/c V6	62	Engine	
	Michele Alboreto	Ferrari t/c V6	61	Gear linkage	
	Niki Lauda	McLaren-TAG t/c V6	57	Accident	
	Derek Warwick	Renault t/c V6	57	Transmission	
	Martin Brundle	Tyrrell-Renault t/c V6	49	Running, not classified	
	Marc Surer	Brabham-BMW t/c 4	42	Engine	
	Riccardo Patrese	Alfa Romeo t/c V8	42	Exhaust	
	Teo Fabi	Toleman-Hart t/c 4	40	Engine	
	Thierry Boutsen	Arrows-BMW t/c 4	37	Oil leak	
	Piercarlo Ghinzani	Toleman-Hart t/c 4	28	Clutch	
	Alain Prost	McLaren-TAG t/c V6	26	Engine	
	Patrick Tambay	Renault t/c V6	20	Transmission	
	Alan Jones	Beatrice-Hart t/c 4	20	Electrics	
	Nelson Piquet	Brabham-BMW t/c 4	14	Electrical fire	
	Eddie Cheever	Alfa Romeo t/c V8	5	Engine	
	Nigel Mansell	Williams-Honda t/c V6	1	Transmission	
	Elio de Angelis	Lotus-Renault t/c V6	—	Excluded	

Fastest lap: Rosberg, on lap 57, 1m 23·758s, 100·899 mph/162·382 km/h (record).

Circuit data

Adelaide Grand Prix Circuit, Adelaide, South Australia

Circuit length: 2·347 miles/3·778 km
Race distance: 82 laps, 192·498 miles/309·796 km
Race weather: Hot, dry

Lap chart

1st LAP ORDER	1 2 3 4 5 6 7 8 9 10 11 12 13 14 15 16 17 18 19 20 21 22 23 24 25 26 27 28 29 30 31 32 33 34 35 36 37 38 39 40 41 42 43 44 45 46 47 48 49 50 51 52 53 54 55 56 57 58 59 60 61 62 63 64 65 66 67 68 69 70 71 72 73 74 75 76 77 78 79 80 81 82
6 K. Rosberg	6 6 6 6 6 6 6 6 6 6 6 6 6 6 6 6 6 6 6 6 6 6 6 6 6 6 6 6 6 6 6 6 6 6 6 6 6 6 6 6 6 6 6 6 6 6 6 6 6 6 6 6 6 6 6 6 6 6 6 6 6 12 12 6 6 6 6 6 6 6 12 1 1 12 12 12 6 6 6 6 6 6 6 6 6 6 6 6 6 6 6 6 6 6 6 6 6 6 6 6 6 6 6
12 A. Senna	12 12 12 12 12 12 12 12 12 12 12 12 12 12 12 12 12 12 12 12 12 12 12 12 12 12 12 12 12 12 12 12 12 12 12 12 12 12 6 1 1 1 1 12 12 12 1 1 12 6 6 6 6 12 26 26 26 26 26 26 26 26 26 26 26 26 26 26 26 26 26 26 26 26 26 26
27 M. Alboreto	27 27 27 27 27 27 27 27 27 27 2 2 2 2 2 2 8 8 8 8 8 2 2 2 8 8 8 8 8 8 8 8 8 8 8 8 8 8 8 1 1 12 12 12 12 1 1 1 6 6 6 6 27 27 27 27 25 25 25 25 25 25 25 25 25 25 25 25 25 25 25 25 25 25 25 25 25
2 A. Prost	2 2 2 2 2 2 17 17 17 2 2 8 8 8 8 8 8 2 2 2 2 2 2 8 8 8 1 1 1 1 1 1 1 1 1 1 1 1 1 27 27 27 27 27 27 27 27 27 27 27 27 27 27 26 26 26 26 4 4 4 4 4 4 4 4 4 4 4 4 4 4 4 4 4 4 4
17 G. Berger	17 17 17 17 17 17 2 2 2 8 8 11 11 11 11 11 11 11 1 1 1 1 1 27 27 27 27 27 27 27 27 27 27 27 16 16 16 16 16 16 16 26 26 26 26 25 25 25 17 17 17 17 17 17 17 17 17 17 28 28 28 28
8 M. Surer	8 8 8 8 8 8 8 8 8 11 11 27 7 7 1 1 1 27 27 27 27 27 25 25 25 25 25 25 25 25 25 26 26 26 26 26 16 16 16 16 16 16 16 4 4 4 28 28 28 28 28 28 28 28 28 28 17 17 17 17
15 P. Tambay	15 15 15 15 11 11 11 11 17 15 18 1 33 33 33 27 15 25 25 25 25 18 18 18 16 16 16 16 16 16 16 4 4 4 4 4 4 25 25 25 17 17 17 17 12 24 24 24 24 24 24 24 24 24 24 24 24
11 E. de Angelis	11 11 11 11 11 15 15 15 7 15 15 7 1 33 27 27 27 33 25 15 18 18 18 18 16 16 16 16 18 4 26 26 26 26 25 25 25 25 25 4 4 4 28 28 28 28 29 29 29 29 29 29 29 29 29 29 29 29
7 N. Piquet	7 7 7 7 7 7 7 15 7 18 16 16 25 15 15 15 18 18 4 4 4 16 16 16 4 4 4 26 4 4 4 4 17 17 17 17 17 17 17 17 17 17 17 17 24 24 24 29
23 E. Cheever	23 23 23 23 23 18 18 18 18 1 33 15 15 25 25 25 4 4 16 16 16 4 4 26 26 26 26 26 18 18 17 17 17 17 28 28 28 28 24 24 24 24 24 24 24 24 29 29 29 29
18 T. Boutsen	18 18 18 18 18 16 16 16 16 16 27 25 18 18 18 18 22 16 17 17 26 17 17 17 17 17 17 17 28 28 28 24 24 24 24 24 24 24 24 24 24
16 D. Warwick	16 16 16 16 16 28 28 28 1 1 33 22 15 22 22 22 22 16 28 28 28 26 19 19 19 28 28 28 28 28 19 19 19 19 24 24 24 29 22 3 3 3 3 3
28 S. Johansson	28 28 28 28 28 1 1 1 28 28 28 25 22 4 4 4 4 17 18 26 26 26 28 17 28 28 28 28 19 19 19 19 24 24 24 29 22 3 3 3 3 3
22 R. Patrese	22 22 22 22 22 22 22 22 33 33 22 15 18 20 20 16 16 16 26 24 19 19 19 24 24 24 24 24 24 24 24 29 29 29 22 3
3 M. Brundle	3 3 1 1 25 25 25 33 22 22 4 4 16 16 17 17 26 24 19 19 24 24 24 29 29 29 29 29 29 29 29 29 29 22 22 22 3
1 N. Lauda	1 1 25 25 25 33 33 19 19 25 4 20 17 17 28 28 28 20 20 29 29 29 29 22 22 22 22 22 22 22 22 22 3 3 3 3
25 P. Streiff	25 25 25 26 26 26 33 19 19 25 25 4 20 17 17 28 24 24 24 19 29 20 20 20 22 20 20 3 3 3 3 3 3 3
26 J. Laffite	26 26 3 19 19 19 4 4 4 4 20 17 19 19 19 20 20 20 19 29 22 22 22 22 22 20 3 3
19 T. Fabi	19 19 19 4 33 4 20 20 20 20 19 19 28 28 24 24 19 19 26 29 22 3 3 3 3 3
4 I. Capelli	4 4 4 33 4 20 20 24 24 24 24 24 24 24 26 26 26 19 33 33
20 P. Ghinzani	20 20 20 20 20 23 24 26 26 26 26 26 26 29 29 29 29 29 3 3
29 P. Martini	29 29 29 33 29 24 24 29 29 29 29 29 29 29 3 3 3 3 3
24 H. Rothengatter	24 24 24 29 24 29 29 3 3 3 3 3 3 3
33 A. Jones	33 33 24 3 3 3
5 N. Mansell	5 5

Fastest laps

Driver	Time	Lap
Keke Rosberg	1m 23·758s	57
Ayrton Senna	1m 24·140s	37
Stefan Johansson	1m 24·337s	74
Niki Lauda	1m 24·498s	54
Michele Alboreto	1m 24·642s	57
Philippe Streiff	1m 25·032s	62
Alain Prost	1m 25·388s	26
Jacques Laffite	1m 25·469s	41
Marc Surer	1m 25·751s	24
Gerhard Berger	1m 26·216s	74
Derek Warwick	1m 26·313s	56
Ivan Capelli	1m 26·497s	47
Thierry Boutsen	1m 26·668s	14
Patrick Tambay	1m 26·819s	20
Elio de Angelis	1m 26·913s	8
Nelson Piquet	1m 27·155s	8
Martin Brundle	1m 27·223s	25
Alan Jones	1m 27·504s	6
Eddie Cheever	1m 27·744s	5
Pierluigi Martini	1m 28·366s	52
Teo Fabi	1m 28·535s	30
Riccardo Patrese	1m 28·675s	8
Piercarlo Ghinzani	1m 28·809s	6
Huub Rothengatter	1m 28·942s	52
Nigel Mansell	2m 23·614s	1

Points

WORLD CHAMPIONSHIP OF DRIVERS

1	Alain Prost	73* (76) pts
2	Michele Alboreto	53
3	Keke Rosberg	40
4	Ayrton Senna	38
5	Elio de Angelis	33
6	Nigel Mansell	31
7	Stefan Johansson	26
8	Nelson Piquet	21
9	Jacques Laffite	16
10	Niki Lauda	14
11=	Patrick Tambay	11
11=	Thierry Boutsen	11
13=	Marc Surer	5
13=	Derek Warwick	5
15=	Stefan Bellof	4
15=	Philippe Streiff	4
17=	René Arnoux	3
17=	Andrea de Cesaris	3
17=	Ivan Capelli	3
17=	Gerhard Berger	3

* Best 11 results in season.

CONSTRUCTORS' CUP

1	McLaren	90 pts
2	Ferrari	82
3	Williams	71
4	Lotus	71
5	Brabham	26
6	Ligier	23
7	Renault	16
8	Arrows	14
9	Tyrrell	7

1985 RESULTS a detailed summary of the season

Formula 3000

MARLBORO/DAILY EXPRESS INTERNATIONAL TROPHY, Silverstone Grand Prix Circuit, Great Britain, 24 March. European Formula 3000 Championship, round 1. 44 laps of the 2·932-mile/4·719-km circuit, 129·01 miles/207·64 km.
1 Mike Thackwell, NZ (Ralt RT20-Cosworth DFV), 1h 07m 41·01s, 114·36 mph/184·04 km/h.
2 John Nielsen, DK (Ralt RT20-Cosworth DFV), 1h 08m 13·35s.
3 Michel Ferté, F (March 85B-Cosworth DFV), 44 laps.
4 Christian Danner, D (March 85B-Cosworth DFV), 43.
5 Gabriele Tarquini, I (March 85B-Cosworth DFV), 42.
6 Roberto Moreno, BR (Tyrrell 012-Cosworth DFV), 42.
7 Emanuele Pirro, I (March 85B-Cosworth DFV), 41; **8** Alain Ferté, F (Lola T950-Cosworth DFV), 41; **9** Mario Hytten, CH (Lola T950-Cosworth DFV) 41; **10** Tomas Kaiser, S (March 85B-Cosworth DFV), 39; **11** Thierry Tassin, B (Williams FW08C-Cosworth DFV), 38 (Running, not classified); **12** Lamberto Leoni, I (Williams FW08C-Cosworth DFV), 38 (Running, not classified); **13** Claudio Langes, I (Tyrrell 012-Cosworth DFV), 33 (DNF, electrics); **14** Philippe Streiff, F (AGS JH20-Cosworth DFV), 7 (DNF, broken rear suspension); **15** Johnny Dumfries, GB (March 85B-Cosworth DFV), 1 (DNF, accident); **16** Alessandro Santin, I (March 85B-Cosworth DFV), 0 (DNF, accident).
Fastest lap: Nielsen, 1m 27·64s, 120·43 mph/193·81 km/h (record).
Did not start: Pierre Chauvet, A (March 85B-Cosworth DFV), accident in warm-up.
Championship points: 1 Thackwell, 9; **2** Nielsen, 6; **3** M. Ferté, 4; **4** Danner, 3; **5** Tarquini, 2; **6** Moreno, 1.

TOWNSEND THORESEN/JOCHEN RINDT TROPHY, Thruxton Circuit, Great Britain, 8 April. European Formula 3000 Championship, round 2. 54 laps of the 2·356-mile/3·792-km circuit, 127·22 miles/204·77 km.
1 Emanuele Pirro, I (March 85B-Cosworth DFV), 1h 05m 00·83s, 117·41 mph/188·95 km/h.
2 Mike Thackwell, NZ (Ralt RT20-Cosworth DFV), 1h 05m 03·31s.
3 Michel Ferté, F (March 85B-Cosworth DFV), 54 laps.
4 Tomas Kaiser, S (March 85B-Cosworth DFV), 54.
5 Gabriele Tarquini, I (March 85B-Cosworth DFV), 53.
6 Christian Danner, D (March 85B-Cosworth DFV), 53.
7 Johnny Dumfries, GB (March 85B-Cosworth DFV), 53; **8** Olivier Grouillard, F (March 85B-Cosworth DFV), 53; **9** Alessandro Santin, I (March 85B-Cosworth DFV), 53; **10** Mario Hytten, CH (Lola T950-Cosworth DFV), 52; **11** Eric Lang, USA (March 85B-Cosworth DFV) 52; **12** Alain Ferté, F (Lola T950-Cosworth DFV) 52; **13** Thierry Tassin, B (Williams FW08C-Cosworth DFV), 52; **14** Roberto del Castello, I (March 85B-Cosworth DFV), 52; **15** Claudio Langes, I (Tyrrell 012-Cosworth DFV), 50; **16** Lamberto Leoni, I (Williams FW08C-Cosworth DFV), 50; **17** John Nielsen, DK (Ralt RT20-Cosworth DFV), 47 (Running, not classified); **18** Juan Manuel Fangio III, RA (Lola T950-Cosworth DFV), 21 (DNF, vibration); **19** Philippe Streiff, F (AGS JH20-Cosworth DFV), 19 (DNF, brakes); **20** Roberto Moreno, BR (Tyrrell 012-Cosworth DFV), 0 (DNF, accident).
Fastest lap: Danner, 1m 09·40s, 122·21 mph/196·68 km/h (record).
Did not start: Slim Borgudd, S (Arrows A6-Cosworth DFV), did not qualify.
Championship points: 1 Thackwell, 15; **2** Pirro, 9; **3** M. Ferté, 8; **4** Nielsen, 6; **5** Danner and Tarquini, 4.

EUROPEAN FORMULA 3000 CHAMPIONSHIP RACE, Autodromo do Estoril, Portugal, 20 April. European Formula 3000 Championship, round 3. 47 laps of the 2·703-mile/4·350-km circuit, 127·04 miles/204·45 km.
1 John Nielsen, DK (Ralt RT20-Cosworth DFV), 1h 12m 44·424s, 104·79 mph/168·64 km/h.
2 Michel Ferté, F (March 85B-Cosworth DFV), 1h 12m 57·792s.
3 Gabriele Tarquini, I (March 85B-Cosworth DFV), 47 laps.
4 Emanuele Pirro, I (March 85B-Cosworth DFV), 47.
5 Roberto Moreno, BR (Tyrrell 012-Cosworth DFV), 46.
6 Olivier Grouillard, F (March 85B-Cosworth DFV), 46.
7 Alain Ferté, F (Lola T950-Cosworth DFV), 46; **8** Roberto del Castello, I (March 85B-Cosworth DFV), 46; **9** Christian Danner, D (March 85B-Cosworth DFV), 46; **10** Philippe Streiff, F (AGS JH20-Cosworth DFV), 45; **11** Juan Manuel Fangio III, RA (Lola T950-Cosworth DFV), 44; **12** Mike Thackwell, NZ (Ralt RT20-Cosworth DFV), 40 (Running, not classified); **13** Thierry Tassin, B (March 85B-Cosworth DFV), 34 (DNF, broken rear wing); **14** Mario Hytten, CH (Lola T950-Cosworth DFV), 29 (DNF, engine problems); **15** Johnny Dumfries, GB (March 85B-Cosworth DFV), 11 (DNF, engine cut out); **16** Tomas Kaiser, S (March 85B-Cosworth DFV), 10 (DNF, disqualified due to start infringement); **17** Alessandro Santin, I (March 85B-Cosworth DFV), 0 (DNF, spun off).
Fastest lap: Thackwell, 1m 30·306s, 107·75 mph/173·41 km/h (record).
Championship points: 1 Thackwell and Nielsen, 15; **3** M. Ferté, 14; **4** Pirro, 12; **5** Tarquini, 8; **6** Danner, 4.

EUROPEAN FORMULA 3000 CHAMPIONSHIP RACE, Autodromo di Vallelunga, Italy, 12 May. European Formula 3000 Championship, round 4. 65 laps of the 1·988-mile/3·200-km circuit, 129·22 miles/208·00 km.
1 Emanuele Pirro, I (March 85B-Cosworth DFV), 1h 15m 14·83s, 103·65 mph/166·81 km/h.
2 John Nielsen, DK (Ralt RT20-Cosworth DFV), 1h 15m 36·66s.
3 Christian Danner, D (March 85B-Cosworth DFV), 65 laps.
4 Olivier Grouillard, F (March 85B-Cosworth DFV), 65.
5 Philippe Streiff, F (AGS JH20-Cosworth DFV), 65.
6 Johnny Dumfries, GB (March 85B-Cosworth DFV), 65.
7 Roberto del Castello, I (March 85B-Cosworth DFV), 65; **8** Tomas Kaiser, S (March 85B-Cosworth DFV), 64; **9** Roberto Moreno, BR (Tyrrell 012-Cosworth DFV), 63; **10** Slim Borgudd, S (Arrows A6-Cosworth DFV), 62; **11** Michel Ferté, F (March 85B-Cosworth DFV), 53 (DNF, electrics); **12** Juan Manuel Fangio III, RA (Lola T950-Cosworth DFV), 45 (DNF, overheating); **13** Mario Hytten, CH (Lola T950-Cosworth DFV), 39 (DNF, accident); **14** Mike Thackwell, NZ (Ralt RT20-Cosworth DFV), 36 (DNF, accident); **15** Alain Ferté, F (Lola T950-Cosworth DFV), 24 (DNF, gear linkage); **16** Gabriele Tarquini, I (March 85B-Cosworth DFV), 16 (DNF, electrics); **17** Alessandro Santin, I (March 85B-Cosworth DFV), 11 (DNF, oil pipe); **18** Lamberto Leoni, I (Williams FW08C-Cosworth DFV), 4 (DNF, accident); **19** Ivan Capelli, I (March 85B-Cosworth DFV), 4 (DNF, accident).
Fastest lap: Pirro, 1m 08·36s, 105·32 mph/169·50 km/h (record).
Championship points: 1 Pirro and Nielsen, 21; **3** Thackwell, 15; **4** M. Ferté, 14; **5** Danner and Tarquini, 8.

45 GRAND PRIX DE PAU, Circuit de Pau, France, 27 May. European Formula 3000 Championship, round 5. 72 laps of the 1·715-mile/2·760-km circuit, 123·48 miles/198·72 km.
1 Christian Danner, D (March 85B-Cosworth DFV), 1h 30m 28·63s, 81·89 mph/131·79 km/h.
2 Emanuele Pirro, I (March 85B-Cosworth DFV), 1h 31m 10·38s.
3 Lamberto Leoni, I (Williams FW08C-Cosworth DFV), 72 laps.
4 Olivier Grouillard, F (March 85B-Cosworth DFV), 72.
5 Philippe Streiff, F (AGS JH20-Cosworth DFV), 71.
6 Juan Manuel Fangio III, RA (Lola T950-Cosworth DFV), 52 (DNF, spin).
7 Alain Ferté, F (March 85B-Cosworth DFV), 31 (DNF, gearbox); **8** Michel Ferté, F (March 85B-Cosworth DFV), 28 (DNF, electrics); **9** John Nielsen, DK (Ralt RT20-Cosworth DFV), 9 (DNF, suspension damage); **10** Mario Hytten, CH (March 85B-Cosworth DFV), 4 (DNF, body damage); **11** Mike Thackwell, NZ (Ralt RT20-Cosworth DFV), 2 (DNF, accident).
Fastest lap: Danner, 1m 13·26s, 84·28 mph/135·64 km/h (record).
Did not start: Jean-Philippe Grand, F (March 85B-Cosworth DFV), fire on warm-up lap; Ivan Capelli, I (March 85B-Cosworth DFV), withdrawn; Gabriele Tarquini, I (March 85B-Cosworth DFV), withdrawn; Guido Dacco, I (March 85B-Cosworth DFV), withdrawn.
Championship points: 1 Pirro, 27; **2** Nielsen, 21; **3** Danner, 17; **4** Thackwell, 15; **5** M. Ferté, 14; **6** Tarquini, 8.

BELGIAN GRAND PRIX, Spa-Francorchamps Circuit, Belgium, 2 June. European Formula 5000 Championship, round 6. 29 laps of the 4·3179-mile/6·9490-km circuit, 125·22 miles/201·52 km.
1 Mike Thackwell, NZ (Ralt RT20-Cosworth DFV), 1h 11m 56·510s, 104·91 mph/168·84 km/h.
2 Alain Ferté, F (March 85B-Cosworth DFV), 1h 12m 46·546s.
3 Christian Danner, D (March 85B-Cosworth DFV), 29 laps.
4 Gabriele Tarquini, I (March 85B-Cosworth DFV), 29.
5 Guido Dacco, I (March 85B-Cosworth DFV), 29.
6 Juan Manuel Fangio III, RA (Lola T950-Cosworth DFV), 29.
7 John Nielsen, DK (Ralt RT20-Cosworth DFV), 25 (DNF, engine); **8** Jean-Philippe Grand, F (March 85B-Cosworth DFV), 22 (DNF, spin); **9** Lamberto Leoni, I (Williams FW08C-Cosworth DFV), 15 (DNF, brakes); **10** Johnny Dumfries, GB (Lola T950-Cosworth DFV), 13 (DNF, spin); **11** Slim Borgudd, S (Arrows A6-Cosworth DFV), 12 (DNF, spin); **12** Mario Hytten, CH (March 85B-Cosworth DFV), 11 (DNF, differential); **13** Thierry Tassin, B (March 85B-Cosworth DFV), 8 (DNF, accident); **14** Olivier Grouillard, F (March 85B-Cosworth DFV), 6 (DNF, spin); **15** Michel Ferté, F (March 85B-Cosworth DFV), 4 (DNF, accident); **16** Ivan Capelli, I (March 85B-Cosworth DFV), 4 (DNF, spin); **17** Philippe Streiff, F (AGS JH20-Cosworth DFV), 4 (DNF, suspension); **18** Emanuele Pirro, I (March 85B-Cosworth DFV), 3 (DNF, suspension).
Fastest lap: Thackwell, 2m 26·769s, 106·39 mph/171·22 km/h (record).
Championship points: 1 Pirro, 27; **2** Thackwell, 24; **3** Danner and Nielsen, 21; **5** M. Ferté, 14; **6** Tarquini, 11.

EUROPEAN FORMULA 3000 CHAMPIONSHIP RACE, Circuit de Dijon-Prenois, France, 30 June. European Formula 3000 Championship, round 7. 55 laps of the 2·361-mile/3·800-km circuit, 129·86 miles/209·00 km.
1 Christian Danner, D (March 85B-Cosworth DFV), 1h 08m 54·10s, 113·75 mph/183·06 km/h.
2 Mike Thackwell, NZ (Ralt RT20-Cosworth DFV), 1h 09m 16·96s.
3 John Nielsen, DK (Ralt RT20-Cosworth DFV), 55 laps.
4 Alain Ferté, F (March 85B-Cosworth DFV), 55.
5 Guido Dacco, I (March 85B-Cosworth DFV), 54.
6 Philippe Alliot, F (March 85B-Cosworth DFV), 54.
7 Olivier Grouillard, F (March 85B-Cosworth DFV), 54; **8** Michel Ferté, F (March 85B-Cosworth DFV), 54; **9** Philippe Streiff, F (AGS JH20-Cosworth DFV), 54; **10** Johnny Dumfries, GB (Lola T950-Cosworth DFV), 54; **11** Aldo Bertuzzi, I (March 85B-Cosworth DFV), 53; **12** Mario Hytten, CH (March 85B-Cosworth DFV), 53; **13** Gabriele Tarquini, I (March 85B-Cosworth DFV), 53; **14** Juan Manuel Fangio III, RA (March 85B-Cosworth DFV), 53; **15** Lamberto Leoni, I (Williams FW08C-Cosworth DFV), 53; **16** Thierry Tassin, B (March 85B-Cosworth DFV), 43 (DNF, accident); **17** Ivan Capelli, I (March 85B-Cosworth DFV), 40 (DNF, lost wheel); **18** Emanuele Pirro, I (March 85B-Cosworth DFV), 19 (DNF, handling).
Fastest lap: Tassin, 1m 13·80s, 115·85 mph/182·22 km/h (record).
Championship points: 1 Thackwell and Danner, 30; **3** Pirro, 27; **4** Nielsen, 25; **5** M. Ferté, 14; **6** Tarquini, 11.

23 GRAN PREMIO del MEDITERRANEO, Ente Autodromo di Pergusa, Sicily, 28 July. European Formula 3000 Championship, round 8. 40 laps of the 3·076-mile/4·950-km circuit, 123·04 miles/198·00 km.
1 Mike Thackwell, NZ (Ralt RT20-Cosworth DFV), 1h 01m 58·99s, 119·09 mph/191·66 km/h.
2 Emanuele Pirro, I (March 85B-Cosworth DFV), 1h 01m 59·62s.
3 Christian Danner, D (March 85B-Cosworth DFV), 40 laps.
4 Gabriele Tarquini, I (March 85B-Cosworth DFV), 40.
5 Mario Hytten, CH (March 85B-Cosworth DFV), 40.
6 Guido Dacco, I (March 85B-Cosworth DFV), 40.
7 Alessandro Santin, I (March 85B-Cosworth DFV), 40; **8** Olivier Grouillard, F (March 85B-Cosworth DFV), 37; **9** Lamberto Leoni, I (March 85B-Cosworth DFV), 31 (DNF, engine); **10** Ivan Capelli, I (March 85B-Cosworth DFV), 18 (DNF, engine); **11** John Nielsen, DK (Ralt RT20-Cosworth DFV), 17 (DNF, overheating); **12** Michel Ferté, F (March 85B-Cosworth DFV), 9 (DNF, accident); **13** Tomas Kaiser, S (March 85B-Cosworth DFV), 9 (DNF, accident); **14** Juan Manuel Fangio III, RA (March 85B-Cosworth DFV), 6 (DNF, suspension damage); **15** Philippe Streiff, F (Lola T950-Cosworth DFV), 6 (DNF, suspension damage).
Fastest lap: Danner, 1m 31·29s, 121·292 mph/195·200 km/h.
Championship points: 1 Thackwell, 39; **2** Danner, 34; **3** Pirro, 33; **4** Nielsen, 25; **5** M. Ferté and Tarquini, 14.

EUROPEAN FORMULA 3000 CHAMPIONSHIP RACE, Österreichring, Austria, 17 August. European Formula 3000 Championship, round 9. 31 laps of the 3·6920-mile/5·9424-km circuit, 114·45 miles/184·21 km.
1 Ivan Capelli, I (March 85B-Cosworth DFV), 53m 56·114s, 127·329 mph/204·916 km/h.
2 John Nielsen, DK (Ralt RT20-Cosworth DFV), 53m 56·698s.
3 Lamberto Leoni, I (March 85B-Cosworth DFV), 31 laps.
4 Emanuele Pirro, I (March 85B-Cosworth DFV), 31.
5 Philippe Streiff, F (AGS JH20-Cosworth DFV), 31.
6 Thierry Tassin, B (March 85B-Cosworth DFV), 31.
7 Alessandro Santin, I (March 85B-Cosworth DFV), 31; **8** Olivier Grouillard, F (March 85B-Cosworth DFV), 31; **9** Mike Thackwell, NZ (Ralt RT20-Cosworth DFV), 31; **10** Mario Hytten, CH (March 85B-Cosworth DFV), 31; **11** Tomas Kaiser, S (March 85B-Cosworth DFV), 31; **12** Guido Dacco, I (March 85B-Cosworth DFV), 31; **13** Gabriele Tarquini, I (March 85B-Cosworth DFV), 30; **14** James Weaver, GB (Lola T950-Cosworth DFV), 30; **15** Max Busslinger, CH (March 85B-Cosworth DFV), 29; **16** Christian Danner, D (March 85B-Cosworth DFV), 29; **17** Michel Ferté, F (March 85B-Cosworth DFV), 27 (DNF, suspension).
Fastest lap: Thackwell, 1m 42·244s, 130·002 mph/209·217 km/h.
Championship points: 1 Thackwell, 39; **2** Pirro, 36; **3** Danner, 34; **4** Nielsen, 31; **5** M. Ferté and Tarquini, 14.

EUROPEAN FORMULA 3000 CHAMPIONSHIP RACE, Circuit van Zandvoort, Holland, 24 August. European Formula 3000 Championship, round 10. 48 laps of the 2·642-mile/4·252-km circuit, 126·82 miles/204·10 km.
1 Christian Danner, D (March 85B-Cosworth DFV), 1h 15m 19·023s, 101·028 mph/162·588 km/h.
2 Mike Thackwell, NZ (Ralt RT20-Cosworth DFV), 1h 15m 23·404s.
3 Philippe Streiff, F (AGS JH20-Cosworth DFV), 48 laps.
4 John Nielsen, DK (Ralt RT20-Cosworth DFV), 48.
5 Emanuele Pirro, I (March 85B-Cosworth DFV), 47.
6 Guido Dacco, I (March 85B-Cosworth DFV), 47.
7 Alessandro Santin, I (March 85B-Cosworth DFV), 47; **8** Thierry Tassin, B (March 85B-Cosworth DFV), 47; **9** Tomas Kaiser, S (March 85B-Cosworth DFV), 47; **10** James Weaver, GB (Lola T950-Cosworth DFV), 46; **11** Lamberto Leoni, I (March 85B-Cosworth DFV), 46; **12** Max Busslinger, CH (March 85B-Cosworth DFV), 43; **13** Gabriele Tarquini, I (March 85B-Cosworth DFV), 28 (DNF, engine); **14** Michel Ferté, F (March 85B-Cosworth DFV), 26 (DNF, electrics); **15** Mario Hytten, CH (March 85B-Cosworth DFV), 22 (DNF, engine); **16** Pierre Chauvet, A (March 85B-Cosworth DFV), 11 (DNF, accident).
Fastest lap: Danner, 1m 23·645s, 113·712 mph/183·001 km/h.
Did not start: Ivan Capelli, I (March 85B-Cosworth DFV), broken diff.
Championship points: 1 Thackwell, 45; **2** Danner, 43; **3** Pirro, 38; **4** Nielsen, 34; **5** M. Ferté and Tarquini, 14.

EUROPEAN FORMULA 3000 CHAMPIONSHIP RACE, Donington Park Circuit, Great Britain, 22 September. European Formula 3000 Championship, round 11. 40 laps of the 2·500-mile/4·023-km circuit, 100·00 miles/160·92 km.
1 Christian Danner, D (March 85B-Cosworth DFV), 59m 17·83s, 101·18 mph/162·83 km/h.
2 Mario Hytten, CH (March 85B-Cosworth DFV), 59m 27·96s.
3 Ivan Capelli, I (March 85B-Cosworth DFV), 40 laps.
4 Michel Ferté, F (March 85B-Cosworth DFV), 40.
5 Philippe Streiff, F (AGS JH20-Cosworth DFV), 40.
6 Alain Ferté, F (March 85B-Cosworth DFV), 40.
7 Guido Dacco, I (March 85B-Cosworth DFV), 40; **8** Tomas Kaiser, S (March 85B-Cosworth DFV), 40; **9** Alessandro Santin, I (March 85B-Cosworth DFV), 40; **10** Pascal Fabre, F (March 85B-Cosworth DFV), 39; **11** Lamberto Leoni, I (March 85B-Cosworth DFV), 39; **12** Eric Lang, USA (March 85B-Cosworth DFV), 39; **13** John Nielsen, DK (Ralt RT20-Cosworth DFV), 39; **14** Fulvio Ballabio, I (Lola T950-Cosworth DFV), 38; **15** Val Musetti, GB (Lola T950-Cosworth DFV), 38; **16** Stefano Livio, I (March 85B-Cosworth DFV), 37; **17** Slim Borgudd, S (Arrows A6-Cosworth DFV), 30 (DNF, gearbox); **18** Thierry Tassin, B (March 85B-Cosworth DFV), 20 (DNF, gearbox); **19** Gabriele Tarquini, I (March 85B-Cosworth DFV), 10 (DNF, accident); **20** Emanuele Pirro, I (March 85B-Cosworth DFV), 0 (DNF, accident); **21** Mike Thackwell, NZ (Ralt RT20-Cosworth DFV), 0 (DNF, accident).
Fastest lap: Capelli, 1m 27·60s, 102·73 mph/165·33 km/h.

Final Championship points

1 Christian Danner, D	51 (52)
2 Mike Thackwell, NZ	45
3 Emanuele Pirro, I	38
4 John Nielsen, DK	34
5 Michel Ferté, F	17
6 Gabriele Tarquini, I	14

7 Ivan Capelli, I, 13; **8** Philippe Streiff, F, 12; **9** Alain Ferté, F, 10; **10** Mario Hytten, CH and Lamberto Leoni, I, 8; **12** Olivier Grouillard, F, 7; **13** Guido Dacco, I, 6; **14** Tomas Kaiser, S and Rober5 Moreno, BR, 3; **16** Philippe Alliot, F, Johnny Dumfries, GB, Juan Manuel Fangio III, RA and Thierry Tassin, B, 1.

CURAÇAO GRAND PRIX, Willemstad Circuit, Curaçao, 13 October. 58 laps of the 2·206-mile/3·550-km circuit, 127·95 miles/205·90 km.
1 John Nielsen, DK (Ralt RT20-Cosworth DFV), 1h 41m 29·572s, 74·33 mph/119·62 km/h.
2 Ivan Capelli, I (March 85B-Cosworth DFV), 1h 41m 50·972s.
3 Claudio Langes, I (March 85B-Cosworth DFV), 58 laps.
4 Christian Danner, D (March 85B-Cosworth DFV), 58.
5 Alain Ferté, F (March 85B-Cosworth DFV), 58.
6 Emanuele Pirro, I (March 85B-Cosworth DFV), 57.
7 Alessandro Santin, I (Lola T950-Cosworth DFV), 56; **8** John Jones, CDN (March 85B-Cosworth DFV), 56; **9** Fulvio Ballabio, I (March 85B-Cosworth DFV), 51; **10** Aldo Bertuzzi, I (March 85B-Cosworth DFV), 51; **11** Gabriele Tarquini, I (Lola T950-Cosworth DFV), 49 (DNF, accident); **12** Michel Ferté, F (March 85B-Cosworth DFV), 47 (DNF, electrics); **13** Lamberto Leoni, I (March 85B-Cosworth DFV), 46 (DNF, brakes); **14** Guido Dacco, I (March 85B-Cosworth DFV), 40 (DNF, gearbox); **15** Eric Lang, USA (March 85B-Cosworth DFV), 38 (DNF, engine); **16** Stefano Livio, I (March 85B-Cosworth DFV), 37 (DNF, accident); **17** Slim Borgudd, S (Arrows A6-Cosworth DFV), 35 (Running, not classified; **18** Johnny Dumfries, GB (March 85B-Cosworth DFV), 32 (DNF, accident); **19** Pierre Chauvet, A (March 85B-Cosworth DFV), 21 (DNF, accident).
Fastest lap: Nielsen, 1m 44·725s, 75·83 mph/122·04 km/h (record).
Did not start: Mike Thackwell, NZ (Ralt RT20-Cosworth DFV), electrics.

Formula 3

MARLBORO CHAMPIONSHIP RACE, Silverstone Short Circuit, Great Britain, 3 March. Marlboro British Formula 3 Championship, round 1. 20 laps of the 1·608-mile/2·588-km circuit, 32·16 miles/51·76 km.
1 Andy Wallace, GB (Reynard 853-VW), 20m 06·32s, 95·97 mph/154·45 km/h (1st class A).
2 Russell Spence, GB (Reynard 853-VW), 20m 15·57s.
3 Mauricio Gugelmin, BR (Ralt RT30-VW), 20 laps.
4 Harald Huysman, N (Ralt RT30-VW), 20.
5 Dave Scott, GB (Ralt RT3-VW), 20.
6 Tim Davies, GB (Reynard 853-VW), 20.
7 Gary Evans, GB (Ralt RT30-VW), 20; **8** Mark Galvin, IRL (Ralt RT30-VW), 20; **9** Steve Harrington, AUS (Ralt RT30-VW), 20; **10** Mike Wright, GB (Ralt RT3-Toyota), 20 (1st class B).

Fastest lap: Gugelmin, 59·54s, 97·22 mph/156·46 km/h.
Marlboro Championship points. Class A: **1** Wallace, 9; **2** Spence, 6; **3** Gugelmin, 5; **4** Huysman, 3; **5** Scott, 2; **6** Davies, 1. **Class B:** **1** Wright, 10; **2** Goddard, 6; **3** Kempton, 4; **4** Tingling, 3; **5** Tolerton, 2.

MARLBORO CHAMPIONSHIP RACE, Thruxton Circuit, Great Britain, 10 March. Marlboro British Formula 3 Championship, round 2. 15 laps of the 2·356-mile/3·792-km circuit, 35·34 miles/56·88 km.
1 Russell Spence, GB (Reynard 853-VW), 18m 50·76s, 112·51 mph/181·07 km/h (1st class A).
2 Tim Davies, GB (Reynard 853-VW), 18m 52·84s.
3 Mauricio Gugelmin, BR (Ralt RT30-VW), 15 laps.
4 Dave Scott, GB (Ralt RT3-VW), 15.
5 Gary Evans, GB (Ralt RT30-VW), 15.
6 Harald Huysman, N (Ralt RT30-VW), 15.
7 Keith Fine, GB (Anson SA6-VW), 15; **8** Cathy Muller, F (Ralt RT3P-VW), 15; **9** Phil Kempe, GB (Ralt RT30-VW), 15; **10** Mark Galvin, IRL (Ralt RT30-VW), 15.
Fastest lap: Gugelmin, 1m 14·43s, 113·95 mph/183·38 km/h.
Class B winner: Carlton Tingling, JA (Ralt RT3-VW), 15.
Marlboro Championship points. Class A: **1** Spence, 15; **2** Gugelmin, 10; **3** Wallace, 9; **4** Davies, 7; **5** Scott, 5; **6** Huysman, 4. **Class B:** **1** Wright, 16; **2** Tingling, 13; **3** Goddard, 10; **4** Kempton, 4; **5** Sobriquet, 3; **6** Tolerton and Coombs, 2.

MARLBORO CHAMPIONSHIP RACE, Silverstone Grand Prix Circuit, Great Britain, 24 March. Marlboro British Formula 3 Championship, round 3. 20 laps of the 2·932-mile/4·719-km circuit, 58·64 miles/94·38 km.
1 Russell Spence, GB (Reynard 853-VW), 29m 44·42s, 118·30 mph/190·38 km/h (1st class A).
2 Andy Wallace, GB (Reynard 853-VW), 30m 01·61s.
3 Mauricio Gugelmin, BR (Ralt RT30-VW), 20 laps.
4 Tim Davies, GB (Reynard 853-VW), 20.
5 Phil Kempe, GB (Ralt RT30-VW), 20.
6 Cathy Muller, F (Ralt RT3P-VW), 20.
7 Maurizio Sandro Sala, BR (Reynard 853-Saab), 20; **8** Graham de Zille, GB (Ralt RT30-VW), 20; **9** Anthony Reid, GB (Reynard 853-Saab), 20; **10** Paul Jackson, GB (Ralt RT3-VW), 20.
Fastest lap: Spence, 1m 27·31s, 120·89 mph/194·55 km/h.
Class B winner: Steve Kempton, GB (Ralt RT3-VW), 20.
Marlboro Championship points. Class A: **1** Spence, 25; **2** Wallace, 15; **3** Gugelmin, 14; **4** Davies, 10; **5** Scott, 5; **6** Huysman, 4. **Class B:** **1** Wright, 22; **2** Tingling, 18; **3** Kempton, 13; **4** Goddard, 10; **5** Coombs, 4; **6** Sobriquet and Stover, 3.

MARLBORO FRENCH FORMULA 3 CHAMPIONSHIP RACE, Circuit Paul Armagnac Nogaro, France, 7 April. Marlboro French Formula 3 Championship, round 1. 25 laps of the 1·939-mile/3·120-km circuit, 48·48 km.
1 Pierre-Henri Raphanel, F (Martini MK45-Alfa Romeo), 32m 20·37s, 89·92 mph/144·71 km/h.
2 Dominique Delestre, F (Ralt RT30-VW), 32m 23·06s.
3 Paul Belmondo, F (Ralt RT3P-VW), 25 laps.
4 Bernard Santal, F (Martini MK45-VW), 25.
5 Michel Trollé, F (Ralt RT30-VW), 25.
6 Eric Bachelart, B (Ralt RT3-VW), 25.
7 Bruno di Gioia, F (Martini MK45-Alfa Romeo), 25; **8** Philippe Pechberty, F (Ralt RT3-Alfa Romeo), 25; **9** Philippe Renault, F (Martini MK45-Alfa Romeo), 25; **10** Jean-Noël Lanctuit, F (Martini MK45-VW), 25.
Fastest lap: Delestre, 1m 16·85s, 90·81 mph/146·14 km/h.
French Championship points: **1** Raphanel, 15; **2** Delestre, 13; **3** Belmondo, 10; **4** Santal, 8; **5** Trollé, 6; **6** di Gioia, 5.

MARLBORO CHAMPIONSHIP RACE, Thruxton Circuit, Great Britain, 8 April. Marlboro British Formula 3 Championship, round 4. 20 laps of the 2·356-mile/3·792-km circuit, 47·12 miles/75·84 km.
1 Russell Spence, GB (Reynard 853-VW), 26m 03·67s, 108·48 mph/174·58 km/h (1st class A).
2 Tim Davies, GB (Reynard 853-VW), 26m 13·46s.
3 Andy Wallace, GB (Reynard 853-VW), 20 laps.
4 Mauricio Gugelmin, BR (Ralt RT30-VW), 20.
5 Anthony Reid, GB (Reynard 853-Saab), 20.
6 Maurizio Sandro Sala, BR (Reynard 853-VW), 20.
7 Harald Huysman, N (Ralt RT30-VW), 20; **8** Cathy Muller, F (Ralt RT3P-VW), 20; **9** Phil Kempe, GB (Ralt RT30-VW), 20; **10** Mark Galvin, IRL (Ralt RT30-VW), 20.
Fastest lap: Davies, 1m 15·05s, 113·01 mph/181·87 km/h.
Class B winner: Carlton Tingling, JA (Ralt RT3-VW), 20.
Marlboro Championship points. Class A: **1** Spence, 34; **2** Wallace, 19; **3** Gugelmin and Davies, 17; **5** Scott, 5; **6** Huysman, 4. **Class B:** **1** Wright and Tingling, 28; **3** Kempton, 13; **4** Goddard, 12; **5** Coombs, 8; **6** Stover, 6.

MARLBORO CHAMPIONSHIP RACE, Donington Park, Great Britain, 14 April. Marlboro British Formula 3 Championship, round 5. 20 laps of the 1·9573-mile/3·1500-km circuit, 39·15 miles/63·00 km.
1 Andy Wallace, GB (Reynard 853-VW), 23m 53·84s, 98·28 mph/158·17 km/h (1st class A).
2 Mauricio Gugelmin, BR (Ralt RT30-VW), 23m 55·61s.
3 Tim Davies, GB (Reynard 853-VW), 20 laps.
4 Maurizio Sandro Sala, BR (Reynard 853-Saab), 20.
5 Anthony Reid, GB (Reynard 853-Saab), 20.
6 Russell Spence, GB (Reynard 853-VW), 20.
7 Gerrit van Kouwen, NL (Ralt RT30-VW), 20; **8** Cathy Muller, F (Ralt RT3P-VW), 20; **9** Mark Galvin, IRL (Ralt RT30-VW), 20; **10** Phil Kempe, GB (Ralt RT30-VW), 20.
Fastest lap: Gugelmin, 1m 10·96s, 99·29 mph/159·79 km/h.
Class B winner: Carlton Tingling, JA (Ralt RT3-VW), 20.
Marlboro Championship points. Class A: **1** Spence, 35; **2** Wallace, 27; **3** Gugelmin, 24; **4** Davies, 21; **5** Scott, 5; **6** Sandro Sala, Reid and Huysman, 4. **Class B:** **1** Tingling, 37; **2** Wright, 28; **3** Goddard and Kempton, 16; **5** Coombs, 9; **6** Hockenhull, 7.

MARLBORO CHAMPIONSHIP RACE, Omloop van Zolder, Belgium, 21 April. Marlboro British Formula 3 Championship, round 6. 22 laps of the 2·648-mile/4·262-km circuit, 58·26 miles/93·76 km.
1 Russell Spence, GB (Reynard 853-VW), 34m 54·65s, 100·13 mph/161·14 km/h (1st class A).
2 Andy Wallace, GB (Reynard 853-VW), 34m 57·62s.
3 Gerrit van Kouwen, NL (Ralt RT30-VW), 22 laps.
4 Mauricio Gugelmin, BR (Ralt RT30-VW), 22.
5 Tim Davies, GB (Reynard 853-VW), 22.
6 Maurizio Sandro Sala, BR (Reynard 853-Saab), 22.
7 Cathy Muller, F (Ralt RT3/84P-VW), 22; **8** Eric Bachelart, B (Ralt RT3/84-VW), 22; **9** Graham de Zille, GB (Ralt RT30-VW), 22; **10** Phil Kempe, GB (Ralt RT30-VW), 22.
Fastest lap: Spence, 1m 34·09s, 101·33 mph/163·07 km/h.
Class B winner: Ray Stover, USA (Ralt RT3/84-VW), 22.
Marlboro Championship points. Class A: **1** Spence, 45; **2** Wallace, 34; **3** Gugelmin, 27; **4** Davies, 23; **5** Scott and Sandro Sala, 5. **Class B:** **1** Tingling, 43; **2** Wright, 28; **3** Goddard, 20; **4** Kempton, 19; **5** Stover, 16; **6** Coombs, 9.

MARLBORO FRENCH FORMULA 3 CHAMPIONSHIP RACE, Circuit de Magny-Cours, France, 28 April. Marlboro French Formula 3 Championship, round 2. 26 laps of the 2·3907-mile/3·8475-km circuit, 62·16 miles/100·04 km.
1 Pierre-Henri Raphanel, F (Martini MK45-Alfa Romeo), 37m 04·02s, 101·41 mph/163·20 km/h.
2 Frédéric Delavallade, F (Martini MK45-Alfa Romeo), 37m 04·62s.
3 Paul Belmondo, F (Ralt RT3P-VW), 26 laps.
4 Eric Bachelart, B (Ralt RT3-VW), 26.
5 Philippe Renault, F (Martini MK45-Alfa Romeo), 26.
6 Dominique Delestre, F (Ralt RT30-VW), 26.
7 Fabien Giroix, F (Reynard 853-VW), 26; **8** Yannick Dalmas, F (Martini MK45-Alfa Romeo), 26; **9** Gilles Duqueine, F (Duqueine DQ4-Alfa Romeo), 26; **10** Jean-Noël Lanctuit, F (Martini MK55-VW), 26.
Fastest lap: Delavallade, 1m 24·61s, 102·52 mph/164·99 km/h.
French Championship points: **1** Raphanel, 30; **2** Belmondo, 20; **3** Delestre, 18; **4** Delavallade, 13; **5** Renault, 9; **6** Bachelart and Santal, 8.

MARLBORO FRENCH FORMULA 3 CHAMPIONSHIP RACE, Circuit de Ledenon, France, 5 May. Marlboro French Formula 3 Championship, round 3. 26 laps of the 1·957-mile/3·150-km circuit, 50·88 miles/81·90 km.
1 Michel Trollé, F (Ralt RT30-VW), 38m 30·10s, 79·31 mph/127·63 km/h.
2 Yannick Dalmas, F (Martini MK45-Alfa Romeo), 38m 31·82s.
3 Philippe Renault, F (Martini MK45-Alfa Romeo), 26 laps.
4 Dominique Delestre, F (Ralt RT30-VW), 26.
5 Gilles Duqueine, F (Duqueine VG4-Alfa Romeo), 26.
6 Eric Bachelart, B (Ralt RT3-VW), 26.
7 Paul Belmondo, F (Ralt RT3P-VW), 26; **8** Jean-Noël Lanctuit, F (Martini MK45-VW), 26; **9** Bruno di Gioia, F (Martini MK45-Alfa Romeo), 26; **10** Gilles Lempereur, F (Ralt RT3-VW), 26.
Fastest lap: Trollé, 1m 27·25s, 80·76 mph/129·97 km/h.
French Championship points: **1** Raphanel, 30; **2** Delestre, 26; **3** Belmondo, 24; **4** Trollé, 22; **5** Renault, 19; **6** Dalmas, 15.

MARLBORO CHAMPIONSHIP RACE, Thruxton Circuit, Great Britain, 6 May. Marlboro British Formula 3 Championship, round 7. 20 laps of the 2·356-mile/3·792-km circuit, 47·12 miles/75·84 km.
1 Gary Evans, GB (Ralt RT30-VW), 25m 28·01s, 111·01 mph/178·65 km/h (1st class A).
2 Andy Wallace, GB (Reynard 853-VW), 25m 29·53s.
3 Tim Davies, GB (Reynard 853-VW), 20 laps.
4 Russell Spence, GB (Reynard 853-VW), 20.
5 Phil Kempe, GB (Ralt RT30-VW), 20.
6 Gerrit van Kouwen, NL (Ralt RT30-VW), 20.
7 Mauricio Gugelmin, BR (Ralt RT30-VW), 20; **8** Maurizio Sandro Sala, BR (Reynard 853-Saab), 20; **9** Harald Huysman, N (Ralt RT30-VW), 20; **10** Steve Harrington, AUS (Ralt RT30-VW), 20.
Fastest lap: Gugelmin, 1m 15·36s, 112·54 mph/181·12 km/h.
Class B winner: Carlton Tingling, JA (Ralt RT3-VW), 20.
Marlboro Championship points. Class A: **1** Spence, 48; **2** Wallace, 40; **3** Gugelmin, 28; **4** Davies, 27; **5** Evans, 11; **6** Scott, Sandro Sala and van Kouwen, 5. **Class B:** **1** Tingling, 53; **2** Wright, 30; **3** Goddard, 24; **4** Stover, 22; **5** Kempton, 19; **6** Coombs, 9.

27 GRAND PRIX DE MONACO FORMULA 3, Monte Carlo, Monaco, 18 May. 24 laps of the 2·058-mile/3·312-km circuit, 49·39 miles/79·49 km.
1 Pierre-Henri Raphanel, F (Martini MK45-Alfa Romeo), 38m 26·553s, 77·05 mph/124·00 km/h.
2 Fabrizio Barbazza, I (Dallara 385-Alfa Romeo), 38m 39·934s.
3 Didier Theys, B (Martini MK45-Alfa Romeo), 24 laps.
4 Dave Scott, GB (Ralt RT30-VW), 24.
5 Philippe Renault, F (Martini MK45-Alfa Romeo), 24.
6 Luis Sala, E (Ralt RT30-Alfa Romeo), 24.
7 Jo Zeller, CH (Ralt RT3/83-Toyota), 23; **8** Gianfranco Tacchino, I (Ralt RT30-Alfa Romeo), 23; **9** Graham de Zille, GB (Ralt RT30-VW), 23; **10** Karl-Christian Lück, D (Ralt RT30-Alfa Romeo), 23.
Fastest lap: Raphanel, 1m [illegible], [illegible] mph/126·37 km/h.

MARLBORO FRENCH FORMULA 3 CHAMPIONSHIP RACE, Circuit de Pau, France, 26 May. Marlboro French Formula 3 Championship, round 4. 25 laps of the 1·715-mile/2·760-km circuit, 42·88 miles/69·00 km.
1 Pierre-Henri Raphanel, F (Martini MK45-Alfa Romeo), 36m 46·40s, 69·96 mph/112·59 km/h.
2 Yannick Dalmas, F (Martini MK45-Alfa Romeo), 36m 56·16s.
3 Denis Morin, F (Martini MK45-Alfa Romeo), 25 laps.
4 Michel Trollé, F (Ralt RT30-VW), 25.
5 Dominique Delestre, F (Ralt RT30-VW), 25.
6 Paul Belmondo, F (Reynard 853-VW), 25.
7 Joe Ris, USA (Martini MK45-Alfa Romeo), 25; **8** Philippe de Henning, F (Martini MK45-Alfa Romeo), 25; **9** James Weaver, GB (Swice 385-VW), 25; **10** Bernard Cognet, F (Martini MK45-Alfa Romeo), 24.
Fastest lap: Raphanel, 1m 18·86s, 78·29 mph/126·00 km/h.
French Championship points: **1** Raphanel, 46; **2** Delestre, 32; **3** Trollé, 30; **4** Belmondo, 29; **5** Dalmas, 27; **6** Renault, 19.

MARLBORO CHAMPIONSHIP RACE, Thruxton Circuit, Great Britain, 27 May. Marlboro British Formula 3 Championship, round 8. 20 laps of the 2·356-mile/3·792-km circuit, 47·12 miles/75·84 km.
1 Andy Wallace, GB (Reynard 853-VW), 25m 50·45s, 109·40 mph/176·06 km/h (1st class A).
2 Tim Davies, GB (Reynard 853-VW), 26m 01·87s.
3 Harald Huysman, N (Ralt RT30-VW), 20 laps.
4 Cathy Muller, F (Reynard 853-VW), 20.
5 Andrew Gilbert-Scott, GB (Ralt RT30-VW), 20.
6 Phil Kempe, GB (Ralt RT30-VW), 20.
7 Gerrit van Kouwen, NL (Ralt RT30-VW), 20; **8** Graham de Zille, GB (Ralt RT30-VW), 20; **9** Joe Foster, USA (Ralt RT30-VW), 20; **10** Mark Goddard, GB (Ralt RT3-Toyota), 20 (1st class B).
Fastest lap: Davies, 1m 15·39s, 112·50 mph/181·05 km/h.
Marlboro Championship points. Class A: **1** Wallace, 49; **2** Spence, 48; **3** Davies, 34; **4** Gugelmin, 28; **5** Evans, 11; **6** Huysmann, 8. **Class B:** **1** Tingling, 53; **2** Goddard, 33; **3** Wright, 31; **4** Stover, 28; **5** Kempton, 19; **6** Coombs, 12.

MARLBORO FRENCH FORMULA 3 CHAMPIONSHIP RACE, Circuit Regional Automobile Mairie de la Châtre, France, 2 June. Marlboro French Formula 3 Championship, round 5. 35 laps of the 1·445-mile/2·325-km circuit, 50·58 miles/81·38 km.
1 Pierre-Henri Raphanel, F (Martini MK45-Alfa Romeo), 38m 56·66s, 77·93 mph/125·42 km/h.
2 Michel Trollé, F (Ralt RT30-VW), 39m 00·68s.
3 Yannick Dalmas, F (Martini MK45-Alfa Romeo), 35 laps.
4 Gilles Lempereur, F (Martini MK45-Alfa Romeo), 35.
* Fabien Giroix, F (Reynard 853-VW), 35.
5 Jean-Noël Lanctuit, F (Martini MK45-Alfa Romeo), 35.
6 Philippe Renault, F (Martini MK45-Alfa Romeo), 35.
7 Joe Ris, USA (Martini MK45-Alfa Romeo), 34; **8** Paul Belmondo, F (Reynard 853-VW), 34; **9** Philippe de Henning, F (Martini MK45-Alfa Romeo), 34; **10** Bruno Ilien, F (Ralt RT3-VW), 34.
Fastest lap: Raphanel, 1m 05·77s, 79·08 mph/127·26 km/h.
French Championship points: **1** Raphanel, 62; **2** Trollé, 42; **3** Dalmas, 37; **4** Delestre and Belmondo, 32; **6** Renault 24.
* Disqualified for passing under yellow flag.

MARLBORO CHAMPIONSHIP RACE, Silverstone Grand Prix Circuit, Great Britain, 9 June. Marlboro British Formula 3 Championship, round 9. 20 laps of the 2·932-mile/4·719-km circuit, 58·64 miles/94·38 km.
1 Mauricio Gugelmin, BR (Ralt RT30-VW), 29m 27·81s, 119·41 mph/192·17 km/h (1st class A).
2 Russell Spence, GB (Reynard 853-VW), 29m 29·26s.
3 Dave Scott, GB (Ralt RT30-VW), 20 laps.
4 Gary Evans, GB (Ralt RT30-VW), 20.
5 Harald Huysman, N (Ralt RT30-VW), 20.
6 Andy Wallace, GB (Reynard 853-VW), 20.
7 Tim Davies, GB (Reynard 853-VW), 20; **8** Cathy Muller, F (Reynard 853-VW), 20; **9** Gerrit van Kouwen, NL (Ralt RT30-VW), 20; **10** Phil Kempe, GB (Ralt RT30-VW), 20.
Fastest lap: Spence, 1m 27·53s, 120·58 mph/194·05 km/h.
Class B winner: Sean Walker, GB (Ralt RT30-VW), 20.
Marlboro Championship points. Class A: **1** Spence, 55; **2** Wallace, 50; **3** Gugelmin, 37; **4** Davies, 34; **5** Evans, 15; **6** Huysman, 10. **Class B:** **1** Tingling, 57; **2** Goddard, 39; **3** Wright, 33; **4** Stover, 27; **5** Kempton, 19; **6** Coombs, 13.

MARLBORO FRENCH FORMULA 3 CHAMPIONSHIP RACE, Circuit Rouen-les-Essarts, France, 23 June. Marlboro French Formula 3 Championship, round 6. 20 laps of the 3·444-mile/5·543-km circuit, 68·88 miles/110·86 km.
1 Yannick Dalmas, F (Martini MK45-Alfa Romeo), 43m 31·59s, 95·57 mph/153·80 km/h.
2 Frédéric Delavallade, F (Martini MK45-VW), 43m 36·20s.
3 Pierre-Henri Raphanel, F (Martini MK45-Alfa Romeo), 20 laps.
4 Michel Trollé, F (Ralt RT30-VW), 20.
5 Denis Morin, F (Martini MK45-Alfa Romeo), 20.
6 Fabien Giroix, F (Reynard 853-VW), 20.
7 Bruno di Gioia, F (Martini MK45-Alfa Romeo), 20; **8** Joe Ris, USA (Martini MK45-Alfa Romeo, 20; **9** Philippe de Henning, F (Martini MK45-Alfa Romeo), 20; **10** Bernard Cognet, F (Martini MK39-Alfa Romeo), 20.
Fastest lap: Raphanel, 2m 08·46s, 97·08 mph/156·23 km/h.
French Championship points: **1** Raphanel, 73; **2** Dalmas, 52; **3** Trollé, 50; **4** Delestre and Belmondo, [illegible].

MARLBORO CHAMPIONSHIP RACE, Brands Hatch Indy Circuit, Great Britain, 23 June. Marlboro British Formula 3 Championship, round 10. 30 laps of the 1·2036-mile/1·9370-km circuit, 36·11 miles/58·11 km.
1 Ross Cheever, USA (Ralt RT30-VW), 22m 22·77s, 96·80 mph/155·78 km/h (1st class A).
2 Dave Scott, GB (Ralt RT30-VW), 22m 24·60s.
3 Mauricio Gugelmin, BR (Ralt RT30-VW), 30 laps.
4 Cathy Muller, F (Reynard 853-VW), 30.
5 Gary Evans, GB (Ralt RT30-VW), 30.
6 Gerrit van Kouwen, NL (Ralt RT30-VW), 30.
7 Maurizio Sandro Sala, BR (Reynard 853-Saab), 30; **8** Harald Huysman, N (Ralt RT30-VW), 30; **9** Andrew Gilbert-Scott, GB (Ralt RT30-VW), 30; **10** Mark Galvin, IRL (Ralt RT30-VW), 30.
Fastest lap: Scott, 44·11s, 98·23 mph/158·09 km/h.
Class B winner: Ross Hockenhull, GB (Ralt RT30-VW), 30.
Marlboro Championship points. Class A: **1** Spence, 55; **2** Wallace, 50; **3** Gugelmin, 41; **4** Davies, 34; **5** Evans and Scott, 16. **Class B:** **1** Tingling, 61; **2** Goddard, 45; **3** Wright, 35; **4** Stover, 31; **5** Kempton, 19; **6** Hockenhull, 17.

MARLBORO FRENCH FORMULA 3 CHAMPIONSHIP RACE, Circuit de Dijon-Prenois, France, 30 June. Marlboro French Formula 3 Championship, round 7. 20 laps of the 2·361-mile/3·800-km circuit, 47·22 miles/76·00 km.
1 Michel Trollé, F (Ralt RT30-VW), 27m 09·88s, 104·92 mph/168·85 km/h.
2 Frédéric Delavallade, F (Martini MK45-VW), 27m 20·50s.
3 Eric Bachelart, B (Ralt RT3-VW), 20 laps.
4 Pierre-Henri Raphanel, F (Martini MK45-Alfa Romeo), 20.
5 Gilles Lempereur, F (Martini MK45-Alfa Romeo), 20.
6 Denis Morin, F (Martini MK45-Alfa Romeo), 20.
7 Gilles Duqueine, F (Duqueine VG4-Alfa Romeo), 20; **8** Fabien Giroix, F (Martini MK45-VW), 20; **9** Paul Belmondo, F (Reynard 853-VW), 20; **10** Bruno di Gioia, F (Martini MK45-Alfa Romeo), 20.
Fastest lap: Yannick Dalmas, F (Martini MK45-Alfa Romeo), 1m 20·32s, 106·45 mph/171·31 km/h.
French Championship points: **1** Raphanel, 81; **2** Trollé, 65; **3** Dalmas, 53; **4** Delavallade, 37; **5** Belmondo, 34; **6** Delestre, 32.

MARLBORO FRENCH FORMULA 3 CHAMPIONSHIP RACE, Circuit Paul Ricard, France, 7 July. Marlboro French Formula 3 Championship, round 8. 17 laps of the 3·610-mile/5·810-km circuit, 61·37 miles/98·77 km.
1 Yannick Dalmas, F (Martini MK45-Alfa Romeo), 34m 27·08s, 106·89 mph/172·02 km/h.
2 Pierre-Henri Raphanel, F (Martini MK45-Alfa Romeo), 34m 27·13s.
3 Frédéric Delavallade, F (Martini MK45-Alfa Romeo), 17 laps.
4 Dominique Delestre, F (Ralt RT30-VW), 17.
5 Gary Evans, GB (Ralt RT30-VW), 17.
6 Gilles Lempereur, F (Martini MK45-Alfa Romeo), 17.
7 Eric Bachelart, B (Ralt RT30-VW), 17; **8** Fabien Giroix, F (Reynard 853-VW), 17; **9** Gilles Duqueine, F (Duqueine VG4-Alfa Romeo), 17; **10** Philippe Renault, F (Martini MK45-Alfa Romeo), 17.
Fastest lap: Dalmas, 2m 00·09s, 108·22 mph/174·16 km/h.
French Championship points: **1** Raphanel, 93; **2** Dalmas, 69; **3** Trollé, 66; **4** Delavallade, 47; **5** Delestre, 40; **6** Belmondo, 34.

MARLBORO CHAMPIONSHIP RACE, Silverstone Grand Prix Circuit, Great Britain, 21 July. Marlboro British Formula 3 Championship, round 11. 15 laps of the 2·932-mile/4·719-km circuit, 43·98 miles/70·79 km.
1 Gerrit van Kouwen, NL (Ralt RT30-VW), 22m 09·50s, 119·08 mph/191·62 km/h (1st class A).
2 Dave Scott, GB (Ralt RT30-VW), 22m 12·78s.
3 Mauricio Gugelmin, BR (Ralt RT30-VW), 15 laps.
4 Ross Cheever, USA (Ralt RT30-VW), 15.
5 Phil Kempe, GB (Ralt RT30-VW), 15.
6 Tim Davies, GB (Reynard 853-Alfa Romeo), 15.
7 Russell Spence, GB (Reynard 853-VW), 15; **8** Keith Fine, GB (Ralt RT30-VW), 15; **9** Graham de Zille, GB (Ralt RT30-VW), 15; **10** Mark Galvin, IRL (Ralt RT30-VW),15.
Fastest lap: Gugelmin, 1m 27·85s, 120·15 mph/193·32 km/h.
Class B winner: Giles Butterfield, GB (Ralt RT3-VW), 15.
Marlboro Championship points. Class A: **1** Spence, 55; **2** Wallace, 50; **3** Gugelmin, 46; **4** Davies, 35; **5** Scott, 22; **6** Evans, 16. **Class B:** **1** Tingling, 62; **2** Goddard, 45; **3** Wright, 35; **4** Stover, 31; **5** Hockenhull, 23; **6** Kempton, 21.

MARLBORO CHAMPIONSHIP RACE, Donington Park Circuit, Great Britain, 28 July. Marlboro British Formula 3 Championship, round 12. 20 laps of the 1·9573-mile/3·1500-km circuit, 39·15 miles/63·00 km.
1 Dave Scott, GB (Ralt RT30-VW), 26m 05·25s, 90·02 mph/144·87 km/h (1st class A).
2 Russell Spence, GB (Reynard 853-VW), 26m 18·87s.
3 Mauricio Gugelmin, BR (Ralt RT30-VW), 20 laps.
4 Andy Wallace, GB (Reynard 853-VW), 20.
5 Rob Wilson, NZ (Ralt RT3-Toyota), 20.
6 Anthony Reid, GB (Reynard 853-Saab), 20.
7 Gary Evans, GB (Ralt RT30-VW), 20; **8** Keith Fine, GB (Ralt RT30-VW), 20; **9** Giles Butterfield, GB (Ralt RT3-Toyota), 20 (1st class B); **10** Godfrey Hall, GB (Ralt RT3-Toyota), 20.

Fastest lap: Tim Davies, GB (Reynard 853-Alfa Romeo), 1m 11·74s, 98·20 mph/158·04 km/h.
Marlboro Championship points. Class A: **1** Spence, 61; **2** Wallace, 53; **3** Gugelmin, 50; **4** Davies, 36; **5** Scott, 31; **6** Evans, 16. **Class B:** **1** Tingling, 64; **2** Goddard, 45; **3** Wright, 35; **4** Stover, 34; **5** Hockenhull, 23; **6** Kempton, 21.

MARLBORO CHAMPIONSHIP RACE, Snetterton Circuit, Great Britain, 11 August. Marlboro British Formula 3 Championship, round 13. 23 laps of the 1·917-mile/3·085-km circuit, 44·09 miles/70·96 km.
1 Gerrit van Kouwen, NL (Ralt RT30-VW), 24m 18·46s, 108·83 mph/175·14 km/h (1st class A).
2 Mauricio Gugelmin, BR (Ralt RT30-VW), 24m 19·82s.
3 Ross Cheever, USA (Ralt RT30-VW), 23 laps.
4 Tim Davies, GB (Reynard 853-Alfa Romeo), 23.
5 Cathy Muller, F (Reynard 853-VW), 23.
6 Andy Wallace, GB (Reynard 853-VW), 23.
7 Keith Fine, GB (Ralt RT30-VW), 23; **8** Graham de Zille, GB (Ralt RT30-VW), 23; **9** Harald Huysman, N (Ralt RT30-VW), 23; **10** Dave Scott, GB (Ralt RT30-VW), 23.
Fastest lap: Gugelmin, 1m 02·71s, 110·04 mph/177·09 km/h. **Class B winner:** Paul Stott, GB (Ralt RT3-VW), 23.
Championship points. Class A: **1** Spence, 61; **2** Gugelmin, 57; **3** Wallace, 54; **4** Davies, 39; **5** Scott, 31; **6** van Kouwen, 24. **Class B: 1** Tingling, 67; **2** Goddard, 45; **3** Stover, 36; **4** Wright, 35; **5** Butterfield, 26; **6** Kempton, 25.

MARLBORO CHAMPIONSHIP RACE, Oulton Park Circuit, Great Britain, 17 August. Marlboro British Formula 3 Championship, round 14. 25 laps of the 2·356-mile/3·792-km circuit, 58·90 miles/94·80 km.
1 Gerrit van Kouwen, NL (Ralt RT30-VW), 32m 34·86s, 108·46 mph/174·55 km/h (1st class A).
2 Mauricio Gugelmin, BR (Ralt RT30-VW), 32m 36·88s.
3 Dave Scott, GB (Ralt RT30-VW), 25 laps.
4 Ross Cheever, USA (Ralt RT30-VW), 25.
5 Gary Evans, GB (Ralt RT30-VW), 25.
6 Dave Coyne, GB (Reynard 853-VW), 25.
7 Cathy Muller, F (Reynard 853-VW), 25; **8** Russell Spence, GB (Ralt RT30-VW), 25; **9** Julian Bailey, GB (Reynard 853-Saab), 25; **10** Keith Fine, GB (Ralt RT30-VW), 25.
Fastest lap: van Kouwen, 1m 17·55s, 109·36 mph/176·00 km/h.
Class B winner: Giles Butterfield, GB (Ralt RT3-Toyota), 25.
Championship points. Class A: 1 Gugelmin, 63; **2** Spence, 61; **3** Wallace, 54; **4** Davies, 39; **5** Scott, 35; **6** van Kouwen, 34.
Class B: 1 Tingling, 71; **2** Goddard, 51; **3** Stover, 38; **4** Butterfield, 36; **5** Wright, 35; **6** Kempton, 28.

MARLBORO CHAMPIONSHIP RACE, Silverstone Short Circuit, Great Britain, 26 August. Marlboro British Formula 3 Championship, round 15. 25 laps of the 1·608-mile/2·588-km circuit, 40·20 miles/64·70 km.
1 Dave Scott, GB (Ralt RT30-VW), 22m 50·06s, 105·63 mph/169·99 km/h (1st class A).
2 Andy Wallace, GB (Reynard 853-VW), 22m 50·43s.
3 Gary Evans, GB (Ralt RT30-VW), 25 laps.
4 Gerrit van Kouwen, NL (Ralt 30-VW), 25.
5 Mauricio Gugelmin, BR (Ralt RT30-VW), 25.
6 Cathy Muller, F (Reynard 853-VW), 25.
7 Russell Spence, GB (Ralt RT30-VW), 25; **8** Keith Fine, GB (Ralt RT30-VW), 25; **9** Graham de Zille, GB (Ralt RT30-VW), 25; **10** Andrew Gilbert-Scott, GB (Ralt RT30-VW), 25.
Fastest lap: Scott, 54·12s, 106·96 mph/172·14 km/h.
Class B winner: Dick Parsons, GB (Ralt RT3P-VW), 25.
Championship points. Class A: 1 Gugelmin, 65; **2** Spence, 61; **3** Wallace, 60; **4** Scott, 45; **5** Davies, 39; **6** van Kouwen, 37.
Class B: 1 Tingling, 71; **2** Goddard, 51; **3** Butterfield, 42; **4** Stover, 41; **5** Wright, 37; **6** Kempton, 31.

MARLBORO CHAMPIONSHIP RACE, Spa-Francorchamps Circuit, Belgium, 1 September. Marlboro British Formula 3 Championship, round 16. 15 laps of the 4·3179-mile/6·9490-km circuit, 64·79 miles/104·24 km.
1 Ross Cheever, USA (Ralt RT30-VW), 36m 21·94s, 106·72 mph/171·75 km/h (1st class A).
2 Gerrit van Kouwen, NL (Ralt RT30-VW), 36m 26·27s.
3 Andy Wallace, GB (Reynard 853-VW), 15 laps.
4 Russell Spence, GB (Ralt RT30-VW), 15.
5 Dave Scott, GB (Ralt RT30-VW), 15.
6 Andrew Gilbert-Scott, GB (Ralt RT30-VW), 15.
7 Mauricio Gugelmin, BR (Ralt RT30-VW), 15; **8** Harald Huysman, N (Ralt RT30-VW), 15; **9** Cathy Muller, F (Reynard 853-VW), 15; **10** Steve Harrington, AUS (Ralt RT30-VW), 15.
Fastest lap: Gugelmin, 2m 24·50s, 107·43 mph/172·89 km/h.
Class B winner: Giles Butterfield, GB (Ralt RT3-Toyota), 15.
Championship points. Class A: 1 Gugelmin, 66; **2** Spence and Wallace, 64; **4** Scott, 47; **5** van Kouwen, 43; **6** Davies, 39.
Class B: 1 Tingling, 71; **2** Goddard and Butterfield, 52; **4** Stover, 41; **5** Wright, 37; **6** Kempton, 35.

MARLBORO FRENCH FORMULA 3 CHAMPIONSHIP RACE, Circuit Automobile Paul Armagnac Nogaro, France, 15 September. Marlboro French Formula 3 Championship, round 9. 25 laps of the 1·939-mile/3·120-km circuit, 48·48 miles/78·00 km.
1 Yannick Dalmas, F (Martini MK45-Alfa Romeo), 32m 15·87s, 90·65 mph/145·89 km/h.
2 Pierre-Henri Raphanel, F (Martini MK45-Alfa Romeo), 32m 19·82s.
3 Denis Morin, F (Martini MK45-Alfa Romeo), 25 laps.
4 Frédéric Delavallade, F (Martini MK45-VW), 25.
5 Dominique Delestre, F (Ralt RT30-VW), 25.
6 Michel Trollé, F (Ralt RT30-VW), 25.
7 Jean-Noël Lanctuit, F (Martini MK45-VW), 25; **8** Paul Belmondo, F (Reynard 853-VW), 25; **9** Gilles Lempereur, F (Martini MK45-VW), 25; **10** Hervé Roger, F (Ralt RT3-VW), 25.
Fastest lap: Dalmas, 1m 16·84s, 91·35 mph/147·01 km/h.
French Championship points: 1 Raphanel, 105; **2** Dalmas, 85; **3** Trollé, 71; **4** Delavallade, 55; **5** Delestre, 46; **6** Belmondo, 37.

MARLBORO CHAMPIONSHIP RACE, Circuit van Zandvoort, Holland, 15 September. Marlboro British Formula 3 Championship, round 17. 20 laps of the 2·642-mile/4·252-km circuit, 52·84 miles/85·04 km.
1 Mauricio Gugelmin, BR (Ralt RT30-VW), 34m 23·58s, 92·18 mph/148·35 km/h (1st class A).
2 Andy Wallace, GB (Reynard 853-VW), 34m 29·55s.
3 Dave Scott, GB (Ralt RT30-VW), 20 laps.
4 Cor Euser, NL (Magnum 853-VW), 20.
5 Gary Evans, GB (Ralt RT30-VW), 20.
6 Keith Fine, GB (Ralt RT30-VW), 20.
7 Andrew Gilbert-Scott, GB (Ralt RT30-VW), 20; **8** Harald Huysman, N (Ralt RT30-VW), 20; **9** Maurizio Sandro Sala, BR (Reynard 853-VW), 20; **10** Graham de Zille, GB (Ralt RT30-VW), 20.
Fastest lap: Gugelmin, 1m 34·13s, 101·04 mph/162·61 km/h.
Class B winner: Dick Parsons, GB (Ralt RT3P-VW), 20.
Championship points. Class A: 1 Gugelmin, 75 (76); **2** Wallace, 70; **3** Spence, 64; **4** Scott, 51; **5** van Kouwen, 43; **6** Davies, 39. **Class B: 1** Tingling, 71; **2** Goddard, 57; **3** Butterfield, 55; **4** Stover, 43; **5** Wright, 37; **6** Kempton, 35.

MARLBORO FRENCH FORMULA 3 CHAMPIONSHIP RACE, Circuit d'Albi, France, 29 September. Marlboro French Formula 3 Championship, round 10. 25 laps of the 2·259-mile/3·636-km circuit, 56·48 miles/90·90 km.
1 Paul Belmondo, F (Reynard 853-VW), 30m 18·93s, 109·65 mph/176·46 km/h.
2 Frédéric Delavallade, F (Martini MK45-VW), 30m 25·13s.
3 Pierre-Henri Raphanel, F (Martini MK45-Alfa Romeo), 25 laps.
4 Denis Morin, F (Martini MK45-Alfa Romeo), 25.
5 Dominique Delestre, F (Ralt RT30-VW), 25.
6 Jean-Noël Lanctuit, F (Martini MK45-VW), 25.
7 Philippe de Henning, F (Martini MK45-Alfa Romeo), 25; **8** Jo Ris, USA (Martini MK45-Alfa Romeo), 25; **9** Bernard Cognet, F (Martini MK42-Alfa Romeo), 24; **10** Hervé Roger, F (Ralt RT3-Toyota), 24.
Fastest lap: Belmondo, 1m 11·88s, 110·99 mph/178·62 km/h.
French Championship points: 1 Raphanel, 115; **2** Dalmas, 85; **3** Trollé, 71; **4** Delavallade, 67; **5** Belmondo, 53; **6** Delestre, 52.

MARLBORO CHAMPIONSHIP RACE, Silverstone Grand Prix Circuit, Great Britain, 13 October. Marlboro British Formula 3 Championship, round 18. 15 laps of the 2·932-mile/4·719-km circuit, 43·98 miles/70·79 km.
1 Mauricio Gugelmin, BR (Ralt RT30-VW), 21m 46·02s, 121·22 mph/195·08 km/h (1st class A).
2 Andy Wallace, GB (Reynard 853-VW), 21m 51·47s.
3 Andrew Gilbert-Scott, GB (Ralt RT30-VW), 15 laps.
4 Gerrit van Kouwen, NL (Ralt RT30-VW), 15.
5 Gary Evans, GB (Ralt 30-VW), 15.
6 Dave Scott, GB (Ralt RT30-VW), 15.
7 Cathy Muller, F (Reynard 853-VW), 15; **8** Maurizio Sandro Sala, BR (Reynard 853-Saab), 15; **9** Cor Euser, NL (Magnum 853-VW), 15; **10** Steve Harrington, AUS (Ralt RT30-VW), 15.
Fastest lap: Gugelmin, 1m 26·25s, 122·37 mph/196·93 km/h.
Class B winner: Giles Butterfield, GB (Ralt RT3-Toyota), 15.

Final Marlboro British Championship points
Class A

1	Mauricio Gugelmin, BR	84 (86)
2	Andy Wallace, GB	76
3	Russell Spence, GB	64
4	Dave Scott, GB	52
5	Gerrit van Kouwen, NL	46
6	Tim Davies, GB	39

7 Ross Cheever, USA, 28; **8** Gary Evans, GB, 26; **9** Harald Huysman, N and Cathy Muller, F, 10; **11** Phil Kempe, GB and Andrew Gilbert-Scott, GB, 7; **13** Maurizio Sandro Sala, BR and Anthony Reid, GB, 7; **15** Cor Euser, NL, 3.
Class B

1	Carlton Tingling, JA	71
2	Giles Butterfield, GB	64
3	Mark Goddard, GB	63
4	Ray Stover, USA	45
5	Mike Wright, GB	37
6	Steve Kempton, GB	35

7 Dick Parsons, GB, 25; **8** Ross Hockenhull, GB, 23; **9** Godfrey Hall, GB, 17; **10** Sean Walker, GB and Hendrik ten Cate, NL, 15.

MARLBORO FRENCH FORMULA 3 Championship Race, Stade Automobile de Croix-en-Ternois, France, 20 October. Marlboro French Formula 3 Championship, round 11. 28 laps of the 1·18-mile/1·90-km circuit, 33·04 miles/53·20 km.
1 Gilles Lempereur, F (Martini MK45-Alfa Romeo), 25m 39·40s, 77·76 mph/125·14 km/h.
2 Frédéric Delavallade, F (Martini MK45-VW), 25m 41·67s.
3 Michel Trollé, F (Ralt RT30-VW), 28 laps.
4 Dominique Dupuy, F (Ralt RT30-VW), 28.
5 Didier Artzet, F (Ralt RT30-VW), 28.
6 Jean-Noël Lanctuit, F (Martini MK45-VW), 28.
7 Eric Bellefroid, F (Martini MK45-Alfa Romeo), 28; **8** Jean-Denis Deletraz, F (Swica 385-Toyota), 28; **9** Dominique Delestre, F (Ralt RT30-VW), 28; **10** Jo Ris, USA (Martini MK45-Alfa Romeo), 28.
Fastest lap: Delavallade, 54·00s, 79·16 mph/127·40 km/h.

Final French Championship points

1	Pierre-Henri Raphanel, F	115
2	Yannick Dalmas, F	85
3	Michel Trollé, F	81
4	Frédéric Delavallade, F	80
5	Dominique Delestre, F	54
6	Paul Belmondo, F	53

7 Denis Morin, F, 39; **8** Gilles Lempereur, F, 38; **9** Eric Bachelart, B, 28; **10** Philippe Renault, F and Jean-Noël Lanctuit, F, 26; **12** Fabien Giroix, F, 17; **13** Gilles Duqueine, F and Jo Ris, USA, 15; **15** Bruno di Gioia, F, 12.

Provisional Final German Championship points (pending appeal against disqualifications at the Österreichring)

1	Volker Weidler, D	192
2	Nils-Kristian Nissen, DK	157
3	Adrian Campos, E	126
4	Manuel Reuter, D	111
5	Jari Nurminen, SF	71
6	Franz Konrad, D	63

7 Altfried Heger, D, 58; **8** Rudi Seher, D, 54; **9** Karl-Christian Lück, D and Wolfgang Kaufmann, D, 45; **11** Eric Bachelart, B, 30; **12** Hans-Peter Kaufmann, CH and Uwe Schafer, D, 28; **14** Alfonso Toledano, MEX, 19; **15** Peter Wisskirchen, D, 18.

Final Italian Championship points

1	Franco Forini, CH	70
2	Alex Caffi, I	53
3	Fabrizio Barbazza, I	52
4	Marco Apicella, I	32
5	Giorgio Montaldo, I	24
6	Nicola Larini, I	22

7 Luis Sala, E, 20; **8** Gianfranco Tacchino, I, 16; **9** Fabio Mancini, I and Enrico Bertaggia, I, 8; **11** Claudio Antonioli, I, 7; **12** Franco Scapini, I, Felice Tedeschi, I and Rinaldo Capello, I, 6; **15** Stefano Modena, I and Giovanni Amati, I, 5.

EUROPEAN FORMULA 3 GRAND PRIX DES NATIONS, ASA Paul Ricard, France, 27 October. 30 laps of the 2·027-mile/3·263-km circuit, 60·81 miles/97·89 km.
1 Alex Caffi, I (Dallara 385-Alfa Romeo), 38m 59·27s, 93·58 mph/150·60 km/h.
2 Thomas Danielsson, S (Reynard 853-VW), 39m 04·56s.
3 Volker Weidner, D (Martini MK45-VW), 30 laps.
4 Nicola Larini, I (Martini MK45-VW), 30.
5 Luis Sala, E (Ralt RT30-VW), 30.
6 Giorgio Montaldo, I (Ralt RT30-VW), 30.
7 Manuel Reuter, D (Ralt RT30-VW), 30; **8** Adrian Campos, E (Dallara 385-VW), 30; **9** Paul Belmondo, F (Reynard 385-VW), 30; **10** Nils-Kristian Nissen, DK (Ralt RT30-VW), 30.
Fastest lap: Caffi, 1m 17·06s, 94·69 mph/152·39 km/h.

World Endurance Championship 1984 results

The final rounds of the 1984 World Endurance Championship were run after *Autocourse 1984/85* went to press

KYALAMI 1000 KMS, Kyalami Grand Prix Circuit, Johannesburg, South Africa, 3 November. World Endurance Championship for Makes, round 8. World Endurance Championship for Drivers, round 10. 244 laps of the 2·550-mile/4·104-km circuit, 622·20 miles/1001·38 km.
1 Riccardo Patrese/Alessandro Nannini, I/I (3.0 t/c Lancia LC2-84), 5h 38m 13·92s, 110·37 mph/177·62 km/h (1st Group C1).
2 Bob Wollek/Paolo Barilla, F/I (3.0 t/c Lancia LC2-84), 242 laps.
3 George Santana/Hanni van der Linde/Errol Shearsby, ZA/ZA/ZA (Modified Nissan Skyline), 202.
4 Ben Morganrood/Johann Coetzee/Willie Hapburn, ZA/ZA/ZA (Modified Mazda RX-7), 201.
5 Nicolo Bianco/Arnold Chatz, ZA/ZA (Modified Alfa Romeo GTV6), 200.
6 Paul Moni/Mick Formato, ZA/ZA (2.6 Alfa Romeo GTV6), 193.
7 Peter Lanz/Geoff Mortimer, ZA/ZA (1.6 VW Golf GTi), 193; **8** William van Zyl/Giovanni Piazza-Musso, ZA/ZA (Modified Alfa Romeo GTV6), 190; **9** Henri Pescarolo/Dieter Schornstein/'Johnny Winter', F/D/D (2.6 t/c Porsche 956), 187; **10** Jannie van Rooyen/Nico van Rensburg, ZA/ZA (Modified Nissan Stanza), 183.
Fastest lap: Patrese/Nannini, 1m 16·18s, 120·79 mph/194·39 km/h.
Championship points. Drivers: 1 Bellof, 119; **2** Mass, 116; **3** Ickx, 89; **4** Pescarolo, 87; **5** Bell, 71; **6** Palmer and Lammers, 63; **8** Hobbs and Stuck, 54; **10** Barilla, 49.
Note: Points revised due to re-instatement of Barilla/Baldi into 3rd place in Monza 1000 Kms.

Final Championship points: manufacturers
Group C1

1	Porsche	120 (140)
2	Lancia	57
3=	Rondeau-Ford/Cosworth	6
3=	Dome-Toyota	6
5	LM-Nissan	2

Group C2

1	Alba-Giannini	82(90)
2	Lola-Mazda	67
3	Tiga-Ford/Cosworth	50
4=	Rondeau-Ford/Cosworth	30
4=	Alba-Ford/Cosworth	30
6	Gebhardt-BMW	22

7 Lotec-BMW, 20; **8** Mazda, 16; **9** Ecosse-Ford/Cosworth and March-Mazda, 15.
Group B

1	BMW	100
2	Porsche	52

SANDOWN PARK 1000 KMS, Sandown Park Circuit, Victoria, Australia, 2 December. World Endurance Championship for Drivers, round 11. 206 laps of the 2·423-mile/3·900-km circuit, 499·14 miles/803·4 km.
1 Stefan Bellof/Derek Bell, D/GB (2.6 t/c Porsche 956-83), 6h 01m 30·3s, 82·84 mph/133·32 km/h (1st Group C1).
2 Jochen Mass/Jacky Ickx, D/B (2.6 t/c Porsche 956-83), 203 laps.
3 Jonathan Palmer/Jan Lammers, GB/NL (2.6 t/c Porsche 956 GTI), 202.
4 Sarel van der Merwe/George Fouche, ZA/ZA (2.6 t/c Porsche 956), 200.
5 Manfred Winkelhock/Rusty French, D/AUS (2.6 t/c Porsche 956B), 200.
6 Colin Bond/Andrew Miedecke, AUS/AUS (2.6 t/c Porsche 962), 198.
7 Klaus Ludwig/Henri Pescarolo, D/F (2.6 t/c Porsche 956B), 197; **8** Alan Jones/Vern Schuppan, AUS/AUS (2.6 t/c Porsche 956-83), 196; **9** Rupert Keegan/Franz Konrad, GB/D (2.6 t/c Porsche 956), 194; **10** Gordon Spice/Neil Crang, GB/AUS (3.0 Tiga GC84-Ford/Cosworth DFV), 189 (1st Group C2).
Fastest lap: Bellof, 1m 34·5s, 92·32 mph/148·57 km/h.

Final Championship points: drivers

1	Stefan Bellof, D	138 (139)
2	Jochen Mass, D	127 (131)
3	Jacky Ickx, B	104
4=	Derek Bell, GB	91
4=	Henri Pescarolo, F	91
6=	Jonathan Palmer, GB	75
6=	Jan Lammers, NL	75

8 David Hobbs, GB and Hans Stuck, D, 54; **10** Paulo Barilla, I, 49; **11** Walter Brun, CH, 47; **12** Rupert Keegan, GB, 44; **13** Klaus Ludwig, D, 39; **14** Dieter Schornstein, D, 38; **15** Harald Grohs, D, 36; **16** Alessandro Nannini, I 35; **17** George Fouche, ZA, 34; **18** 'Johnny Winter', D, 32; **19** Mauro Baldi, I, Massimo Sigala, I and Oscar Larrauri, RA, 28.

1985 results

MUGELLO 6 HOURS, Autodromo Internazionale del Mugello, Italy, 14 April. World Endurance Championship for Teams, round 1. World Endurance Championship for Drivers, round 1. 190 laps of the 3·259-mile/5·245-km circuit, 619·21 miles/996·55 km.
1 Jacky Ickx/Jochen Mass, B/D (2.6 t/c Porsche 962C), 5h 59m 52·21s, 103·24 mph/166·15 km/h (1st Group C).
2 Marc Surer/Manfred Winkelhock, CH/D (2.6 t/c Porsche 962C), 6h 00m 22·05s.
3 Stefan Bellof/Thierry Boutsen, D/B (2.6 t/c Porsche 962C), 189 laps.
4 Mauro Baldi/Bob Wollek, I/F (3.0 t/c Lancia LC2-85), 186.
5 Klaus Ludwig/George Fouche/Gianni Mussati, D/ZA/I (2.6 t/c Porsche 956), 184.
6 Mike Thackwell/Hervé Regout/Jurgen Lässig, NZ/B/D (2.6 t/c Porsche 956), 179.
7 Ray Bellm/Gordon Spice, GB/GB (3.3 Tiga GC85-Ford Cosworth DFL), 174 (1st Group C2); **8** Carlo Facetti/Martino Finotto/Guido Dacco, I/I/I (1.8 t/c Alba 002-Carma), 161; **9** Lars-Viggo Jensen/Jens Winther, DK/DK (3.5 URD C82-BMW), 159; **10** 'Victor'/Aldo Bertuzzi/Gianni Guidici, I/I/I (3.2 t/c Porsche 935), 158.
Fastest lap: Riccardo Patrese, I (3.0 t/c Lancia LC2-85), 1m 45·79s, 110·91 mph/178·49 km/h.
Other class winners. Group B: Helmut Gall/Axel Felder, D/D (3.5 BMW M1), 154.
Disqualified: Derek Bell/Hans Stuck, GB/D (2.6 t/c Porsche 962C) finished 4th on the road but were disqualified for taking too long for their last lap.
Championship points: drivers. Group C: 1 Ickx and Mass, 20; **3** Surer and Winkelhock, 15; **5** Bellof and Boutsen, 12. **Group C2: 1** Spice and Bellm, 20; **3** Facetti, Finotto and Dacco, 15; **6** Jensen and Winther, 12.
Teams. Group C: 1 Rothmans Porsche, 20; **2** Kremer Porsche Racing, 15; **3** Brun Motorsport, 12; **4** Martini Lancia, 10; **5** Obermaier Racing Team, 6; **6** Spice Engineering, 4. **Group C2: 1** Spice Engineering, 20; **2** Carma FF, 15; **3** Jens Winther Denmark, 12; **4** Ark Racing, 10; **5** Roy Baker Promotions, 8.

MONZA 1000 KMS/TROFEO FILIPPO CARACCIOLO, Autodromo Nazionale di Monza, Italy, 28 April. World Endurance Championship for Drivers, round 2. 138 laps of the 3·604-mile/5·800-km circuit, 497·35 miles/800·40 km (Race stopped due to tree falling across the track).
1 Manfred Winkelhock/Marc Surer, D/CH (2.6 t/c Porsche 962C), 4h 04m 41·43s, 121·95 mph/196·26 km/h (1st Group C).
2 Hans Stuck/Derek Bell, D/GB (2.6 t/c Porsche 956-83), 4h 05m 13·07s.
3 Riccardo Patrese/Alessandro Nannini, I/I (3.0 t/c Lancia LC2-85), 138 laps.
4 Jochen Mass/Jacky Ickx, D/B (2.6 t/c Porsche 962C), 138.
5 Jonathan Palmer/Jan Lammers, GB/NL (2.6 t/c Porsche 956 GTI), 132.
6 Oscar Larrauri/Massimo Sigala/Renzo Zorzi, RA/I/I (2.6 t/c Porsche 956B), 129.
7 Gordon Spice/Ray Bellm, GB/GB (3.3 Tiga GC85-Ford Cosworth DFL), 127 (1st Group C2); **8** George Fouche/Sarel van der Merwe/Bruno Giacomelli, ZA/ZA/I (2.6 t/c Porsche 956B), 126; **9** Paolo Barilla/Hans Heyer/Klaus Ludwig, I/D/D (2.6 t/c Porsche 956 B), 125; **10** Ray Mallock/Mike Wilds/David Leslie, GB/GB/GB (3.0 Ecosse C2 85-Ford Cosworth DFV), 124.
Fastest lap: Not given.
Disqualified: Thierry Boutsen/Stefan Bellof, B/D (2.6 t/c Porsche 962C), finished 5th on the road but were disqualified for a refuelling infringement.
Championship points: drivers. Group C: 1 Surer and Winkelhock, 35; **3** Ickx and Mass, 30; **5** Stuck and Bell, 15. **Group C2: 1** Spice and Bellm, 40; **3** Winther, 24; **4** Payne, Ashmore and Andrews, 16.

SILVERSTONE 1000 KMS, Silverstone Grand Prix Circuit, Great Britain, 12 May. World Endurance Championship for Teams, round 2. World Endurance Championship for Drivers, round 3. 212 laps of the 2·932-mile/4·719-km circuit, 621·58 miles/1000·43 km.
1 Jochen Mass/Jacky Ickx, D/B (2.6 t/c Porsche 962C), [illegible] (1st Group C).
2 Derek Bell/Hans Stuck, GB/D (2.6 t/c Porsche 956/962C), 211 laps.
3 Riccardo Patrese/Alessandro Nannini, I/I (3.0 t/c Lancia LC2-85), 210.
4 Manfred Winkelhock/Marc Surer, D/CH (2.6 t/c Porsche 962C), 210.
5 Jonathan Palmer/Jan Lammers, GB/NL (2.6 t/c Porsche 956 GTI), 207.
6 Klaus Ludwig/Paolo Barilla/Paul Belmondo, D/I/F (2.6 t/c Porsche 956B), 206.
7 Hervé Regout/Jurgen Lässig/Jesus Pareja Mayo, B/D/E (2.6 t/c Porsche 956), 204; **8** George Fouche/Sarel van der Merwe/Almo Capelli, ZA/ZA/I (2.6 t/c Porsche 956B), 195; **9** Ray Mallock/Mike Wilds, GB/GB (3.0 Ecosse C2/85-Ford Cosworth DFV), 193 (1st Group C2); **10** Thierry Boutsen/Walter Brun, B/CH (2.6 t/c Porsche 962C), 193.
Fastest lap: Palmer, 1m 15·96s, 138·95 mph/223·62 km/h (record).
Championship points: drivers. Group C: 1 Ickx and Mass, 50; **3** Winkelhock and Surer, 45; **5** Bell and Stuck, 30. **Group C2: 1** Spice and Bellm, 55; **3** Mallock and Wilds, 35; **5** Payne, Ashmore and Winther, 24.
Teams: Group C: 1 Rothmans Porsche, 40; **2** Kremer Porsche Racing, 25; **3** Martini Lancia, 22; **4** Brun Motorsport, 13; **5** Obermaier Racing Team, 10; **6** Richard Lloyd Racing, 8. **Group C2: 1** Spice Engineering, 35; **2** Ecurie Ecosse, 20; **3** Carma FF, 19; **4** Ark Racing, 18; **5** Jens Winther Denmark and Strandell Motors, 12.

Le Mans 24 Hours

53 GRAND PRIX D'ENDURANCE, LES 24 HEURES DU MANS, Circuit de la Sarthe, Le Mans, France 15/16 June. World Endurance Championship for Teams, round 3. World Endurance Championship for Drivers, round 4. 373 laps of the 8·467-mile/13·626-km circuit, 3158·19 miles/5082·50 km.
1 Klaus Ludwig/Paolo Barilla/'Johnny Winter', D/I/D (2.6 t/c Porsche 956B), 373 laps, 131·66 mph/211·89 km/h (1st Group C).
2 Jonathan Palmer/James Weaver/Richard Lloyd, GB/GB/GB (2.6 t/c Porsche 956 GTI), 370 laps.
3 Derek Bell/Hans Stuck, GB/D (2.6 t/c Porsche 962C), 366.
4 David Hobbs/Jo Gartner/Guy Edwards, GB/A/GB (2.6 t/c Porsche 956B), 365.
5 Sarel van der Merwe/George Fouche/Mario Hytten, ZA/ZA/CH (2.6 t/c Porsche 956B), 360.
6 Bob Wollek/Alessandro Nannini/Lucio Cesario, F/I/AUS (3.0 t/c Lancia LC2-85), 359.
7 Henri Pescarolo/Mauro Baldi, F/I (3.0 t/c Lancia LC2-85), 357; **8** Jurgen Lässig/Hervé Regout/Jesus Pareja Mayo, D/B/E (2.6 t/c Porsche 956), 356; **9** Jean-Pierre Jarier/Mike Thackwell/Franz Konrad, F/NZ/D (2.6 t/c Porsche 962C), 347; **11** Tiff Needell/Nick Faure/Steve O'Rourke, GB/GB/GB (5.3 Emka-Aston Martin), 337; **12** Satoru Nakajima/Masanori Sekiya/Kouru Hoshino, J/J/J (2.1 t/c Dome 85C-Toyota), 329; **13** Bob Tullius/Chip Robinson/Claude Ballot-Lena, USA/USA/F (6.0 Jaguar XJR-5), 323 (1st GTP class); **14** Gordon Spice/Ray Bellm/Mark Galvin, GB/GB/IRL (3.3 Tiga GC85-Ford Cosworth DFL), 311 (1st Group C2); **15** Edgar Doren/Martin Birrane/Jean-Paul Libert, D/IRL/B (3.5 BMW M1), 306 (1st Group B); **16** Steve Earle/John Sheldon/Ian Harrower, USA/GB/GB (3.3 Gebhardt 843-Ford Cosworth DFL), 298; **17** Marcel Pignard/Jean-Daniel Raulet/Jean Rondeau, F/F/F (2.6 t/c WM 83B-Peugeot), 298; **18** Jean-Claude Justice/Bruno Soty/Patrick Oudet, F/F/F (3.3 Rondeau M382-Ford Cosworth DFL), 290; **19** David Kennedy/Philippe Martin, IRL/B (2.6 Mazda 737C), 282; **20** Yves Courage/Alain de Cadenet/Jean-François Yvon, F/GB/F (2.6 t/c Cougar C12-Porsche), 278; **21** Paul Smith/Will Hoy/Nick Nicholson, GB/GB/USA (1.7 t/c Tiga C285-Ford), 273; **22** Christian Danner/Graham Duxbury/Almo Copelli, D/ZA/I (2.6 t/c March 85G-Porsche), 269; **23** Dominique Lecaud/Roland Bassaleird/Yvonne Tapy, F/F/F (3.5 Sauber C6-BMW), 267; **24** Yoshimi Katayama/Yojiro Terada/Takashi Yorino, J/J/J (2.6 Mazda 727C), 266.
Disqualified: Pascal Pessiot/Dominique Fornage/'Panic', 2.6 t/c WM 83B-Peugeot), 266.
Running not classified: Neil Crang/Tony Lanfranchi/Tim Lee-Davey, AUS/GB/GB (3.0 Tiga GC84-Ford Cosworth DFV), 225; Frank Jelinski/John Graham/Nick Adams, D/CDN/GB (3.0 Gebhardt 853-Ford Cosworth DFV), 223; François Duret/David Andrews/Duncan Bain, F/GB/GB (1.7 t/c Tiga C284-Ford), 149; Jacques Heuclin/Daniel Hubert/Louis Descartes, F/F/F (3.5 ALD-BMW), 140.
Retired: Oscar Larrauri/Massimo Sigala/Gabriele Tarquini, RA/I/I (2.6 t/c Porsche 956B), 323, engine; Walter Brun/Didier Theys/Joel Gouhier, CH/B/F (2.6 t/c Porsche 962C), 304, accident; Al Holbert/John Watson/Vern Schuppan, USA/GB/AUS (2.6 t/c Porsche 962C), 299, engine; Pierre Yver/Pierre-François Rousselot/François Servanin, F/F/F (3.0 Rondeau M382-Ford Cosworth DFV), 286, engine; Maurizio DeNarvaez/Kenper Miller/Paul Belmondo, COL/USA/F (2.6 t/c Porsche 956), 277, accident; Martino Finotto/Guido Dacco/Aldo Bertuzzi, I/I/I (1.8 t/c Alba AR6-Carma), 228, electrics; Brian Redman/Jim Adams/Hurley Haywood, GB/USA/USA (6.0 Jaguar XJR-5), 151, transmission; Patrick Gonin/Pascal Witmeur/Pierre de Thoisy, F/B/F (3.3 Rondeau M482-Ford Cosworth DFL), 143, engine; Eje Elgh/Geoff Lees/Toshio Suzuki, S/GB/J (2.1 t/c Dome 85C-Toyota), 141, clutch; Jens Winther/David Mercer/Margie Smith-Haas, DK/GB/USA (3.5 URD C83-BMW), 141, engine; Enzo Calderari/Angelo Pallavicini/Marco Vanoli, CH/CH/CH (3.5 BMW M1), 116, engine; Raymond Touroul/Thierry Perrier/Philippe Dermagne, F/F/F (3.0 Porsche 911SC), 107, head gasket; Roger Dorchy/Jean-Claude Andruet/Claude Haldi, (2.6 t/c WM 83B-Peugeot), 73, accident; Michel Dubois/Hubert Striebig/Noel del Bello, F/F/F (3.0 Rondeau M482-Ford Cosworth DFV), 65, suspension; John Cooper/Claude Bourgoignie/Bernard de Dryver, GB/B/B (5.3 Cheetah G604-Aston Martin), 53, accident; Ray Mallock/David Leslie/Mike Wilds, GB/GB/GB (3.0 Ecosse C2-85-Ford Cosworth DFV), 45, oil pump drive; Christian Bussi/Jack Griffith/Marion Speer, F/USA/USA (3.0 Rondeau M482-Ford Cosworth DFV), 36, suspension; Harald Grohs/Altfried Heger/Kurt Koenig, D/D/D (3.5 BMW M1), 32, gearbox; Max Cohen-Olivar/Robin Smith/Richard Jones, MOR/GB/GB (3.3 Chevron B62-Ford Cosworth DFL), 19, engine; Paolo Giangrossi/Pasquale Barberio/Mario Radicella, I/I/I (3.3 Alba AR3-Ford Cosworth DFL), 5, electrics.
Fastest lap: Mass, 3m 25·1s, 148·612 mph/239·167 km/h (record).
Championship points: drivers. Group C: 1 Ickx and Mass, 51; **3** Winkelhock and Surer, 45; **5** Bell and Stuck, 42; **Group C2: 1** Spice and Bellm, 75; **3** Wilds and Mallock, 35; **5** Payne, Ashmore and Winther, 24.
Teams. Group C: 1 Rothmans Porsche, 52; **2** Kremer Porsche Racing, 33; **3** Martini Lancia, 28; **4** New Man Joest Racing, 26; **5** Richard Lloyd Racing, 23; **6** Brun Motorsport and Obermaier Racing Team, 13. **Group C2: 1** Spice Engineering, 55; **2** Ecurie Ecosse, 20; **3** Carma FF, 19; **4** Ark Racing, Roy Baker Promotions and Mazdaspeed Co. Ltd, 18.

DUSCHFRISCH 1000 KMS, Hockenheim-Ring, German Federal Republic, 14 July. World Endurance Championship for Teams, round 4. World Endurance Championship for Drivers, round 5. 147 laps of the 4·2234-mile/6·7970-km circuit, 620·84 miles/999·16 km.
1 Derek Bell/Hans Stuck, GB/D (2.6 t/c Porsche 962C), 5h 23m 00·68s, 115·33 mph/185·61 km/h (1st Group C).
2 Oscar Larrauri/Massimo Sigala, RA/I (2.6 t/c Porsche 956), 5h 23m 40·59s.
3 Klaus Ludwig/Paolo Barilla, D/I (2.6 t/c Porsche 956B), 145 laps.
4 Bob Wollek/Mauro Baldi, F/I (3.0 t/c Lancia LC2-85), 145.
5 Jonathan Palmer/David Hobbs, GB/GB (2.6 t/c Porsche 956 GTI), 143.
6 Gerhard Berger/Walter Brun, A/CH (2.6 t/c Porsche 956), 142.
7 Hervé Regout/Jurgen Lässig/Jesus Pareja Mayo, B/D/E (2.6 t/c Porsche 956), 136; **8** Ray Mallock/David Leslie/Mike Wilds, GB/GB/GB (3.3 Ecosse 285-Cosworth DFL), 134 (1st Group C2); **9** Gordon Spice/Ray Bellm, GB/GB (3.3 Tiga GC85-Cosworth DFL), 132; **10** Carlo Facetti/Martino Finotto/Lucio Cesario, I/I/AUS (2.1 t/c Alba AR6-Carma), 131.
Fastest lap: Stefan Bellof, D (2.6 t/c Porsche 956B), 2m 00·66s, 126·01 mph/202·79 km/h.
Other class winners. Group B: Edgar Doren/Helmut Gall/Uwe Reich, D/D/D (BMW M1), 125.
Championship points: drivers. Group C: 1 Bell and Stuck, 62; **3** Mass and Ickx, 51; **5** Ludwig, 46; **6** Winkelhock and Surer, 45. **Group C2: 1** Spice and Bellm, 90; **3** Mallock and Wilds, 55; **5** Payne, 34; **6** Winther, 32.
Teams. Group C: 1 Rothmans Porsche, 72; **2** New Man Joest Racing and Martini Lancia, 38; **4** Kremer Porsche Racing, 33; **5** Richard Lloyd Racing, 31; **6** Brun Motorsport, 28. **Group C2: 1** Spice Engineering, 70; **2** Ecurie Ecosse, 40; **3** Carma FF, 31; **4** Ark Racing, 28; **5** Jens Winther Denmark, 20; **6** Strandell Motors, 12.

BUDWEISER GT 1000 KMS, Mosport Park Circuit, Ontario, Canada, 11 August. World Endurance Championship for Teams, round 5. World Endurance Championship for Drivers, round 6. 253 laps of the 2·459-mile/3·957-km circuit, 622·13 miles/1001·12 km.
1 Derek Bell/Hans Stuck, GB/D (2.6 t/c Porsche 962C), 5h 55m 41·988s, 104·94 mph/168·88 km/h (1st Group C).
2 Jochen Mass/Jacky Ickx, D/B (2.6 t/c Porsche 962C), 5h 57m 06·848s.
3 Martin Brundle/Mike Thackwell/Jean-Louis Schlesser, GB/NZ/F (5.3 Jaguar XJR-6), 234 laps.
4 Ludwig Heimrath Snr/Ludwig Heimrath Jnr/Kees Kroesemeijer, CDN/CDN/NL (2.6 t/c Porsche 956B), 234.
5 Gordon Spice/Ray Bellm, GB/GB (3.3 Tiga GC85-Cosworth DFL), 231 (1st Group C2).
6 Frank Jelinski/John Graham, D/CDN (3.3 Gebhardt 853-Cosworth DFL), 225.
7 'Fomfor'/Uli Bieri/Matt Gysler, ES/CDN/CDN (6.0 Sauber C9-Chevrolet), 211; **8** David Andrews/Max Payne, GB/GB (2.0 Cheeker-Ford), 203; **9** Jerry Thompson/Gary English, USA/USA (6.0 Chevrolet Camaro), 199 (1st GTO class); **10** Steve Zwiren/Rob Peters/Peter Dawe, USA/CDN/USA (2.6 Mazda RX-7) 184 (1st GTU class).
Fastest lap: Stuck, 1m 12·915s, 121·41 mph/195·39 km/h (record).
Championship points: drivers. Group C: 1 Bell and Stuck, 82; **3** Ickx and Mass, 66; **5** Ludwig, 46; **6** Winkelhock and Surer, 45. **Group C2: 1** Spice and Bellm, 110; **3** Mallock and Wilds, 55; **5** Payne, 44; **6** Winther, 32.
Teams. Group C: 1 Rothmans Porsche, 92; **2** Kremer Porsche Racing, 43; **3** Martini Lancia and New Man Joest Racing, 38; **5** Richard Lloyd Racing, 31; **6** Brun Motorsport, 28. **Group C2: 1** Spice Engineering, 90; **2** Carma FF, 41; **3** Ecurie Ecosse and Ark Racing, 40; **5** Gebhardt Engineering, 25; **6** Jens Winther Denmark, 20.

SPA 1000 KMS, Spa-Francorchamps Circuit, Belgium, 1 September. World Endurance Championship for Teams, round 6. World Endurance Championship for Drivers, round 7. 122 laps of the 4·3179-mile/6·9490-km circuit, 526·78 miles/847·78 km (race stopped at 122 laps due to fatal accident).
1 Bob Wollek/Mauro Baldi/Riccardo Patrese, F/I/I (3.0 t/c Lancia LC2-85), 5h 00m 23·42s, 105·09 mph/169·13 km/h (1st Group C).
2 Hans Stuck/Derek Bell, D/GB (2.6 t/c Porsche 962C), 5h 02m 37·86s.
3 Klaus Ludwig/Paolo Barilla, D/I (2.6 t/c Porsche 956B), 121 laps.
4 Alessandro Nannini/Riccardo Patrese/Mauro Baldi, I/I/I (3.0 t/c Lancia LC2-85), 121.
5 Martin Brundle/Mike Thackwell, GB/NZ (6.0 Jaguar XJR-6), 120.
6 Marc Duez/Johnny Winter/Volker Weidler, B/D/D (2.6 t/c Porsche 956), 120.
7 Christian Danner/Costas Los/Pascal Witmeur, D/GR/B (2.6 t/c March 84G-Porsche), 114; **8** Jurgen Lässig/Hervé Regout/Jesus Pareja Mayo, D/B/E (2.6 t/c Porsche 956), 113; **9** Gordon Spice/Ray Bellm, GB/GB (3.3 Tiga GC85-Cosworth DFL), 112 (1st Group C2); **10** Bernard de Dryver/Pierre Dieudonné/Claude Bourgoignie, B/B/B (5.4 Cheetah-Aston Martin), 110.
Fastest lap: Jochen Mass, D (2.6 t/c Porsche 962C), 2m 10·73s, 118·76 mph/191·13 km/h.
Championship points: drivers. Group C: 1 Bell and Stuck, 97; **2** Mass and Ickx, 66; **5** Ludwig, 58; **6** Barilla, 52.
Group C2: 1 Spice and Bellm, 130; **3** Mallock, 65; **4** Wilds, 55; **5** Payne, 52; **6** Winther, 47.
Teams. Group C: 1 Rothmans Porsche, 107; **2** Martini Lancia, 58; **3** New Man Joest Racing, 50; **4** Kremer Porsche Racing, 43; **5** Richard Lloyd Racing, 31; **6** Brun Motorsport, 28. **Group C2: 1** Spice Engineering, 110; **2** Ecurie Ecosse, 50; **3** Ark Racing, 46; **4** Carma FF, 41; **5** Gebhardt Engineering, 40; **6** Jens Winther Denmark, 32.

SHELL GEMINI 1000, Brands Hatch Grand Prix Circuit, Great Britain, 22 September. World Endurance Championship for Drivers, round 8. 238 laps of the 2·6136-mile/4·2060-km circuit, 622·04 miles/1001·03 km.
1 Derek Bell/Hans Stuck, GB/D (2.6 t/c Porsche 962C), 5h 34m 26·02s, 111·59 mph/179·59 km/h (1st Group C).
2 Jochen Mass/Jacky Ickx, D/B (2.6 t/c Porsche 962C), 5h 34m 38·01s.
3 Bob Wollek/Andrea de Cesaris/Mauro Baldi, F/I/I (3.0 t/c Lancia LC2-85), 237 laps.
4 Riccardo Patrese/Alessandro Nannini, I/I (3.0 t/c Lancia LC2-85), 233.
5 Vern Schuppan/Al Holbert, AUS/USA (2.6 t/c Porsche 956/962C), 224.
6 Ray Mallock/Mike Wilds, GB/GB (3.3 Ecosse C285-Cosworth DFL), 219 (1st Group C2).
7 Anders Olofsson/Costas Los/Divina Galica, S/GR/GB (2.6 t/c March 84G-Porsche), 211; **8** Martino Finotto/Carlo Facetti/Almo Copelli, I/I/I (1.8 t/c Alba AR6-Carma), 208; **9** Louis Descartes/Jacques Heuclin, F/F (2.0 ALD-BMW), 193; **10** Ian Taylor/Ian Harrower/Nick Adams, GB/GB/GB (3.3 Gebhardt 843-Cosworth DFL), 192.
Fastest lap: de Cesaris, 1m 19·11s, 118·93 mph/191·40 km/h (record).
Other class winners. Group B: Helmut Gall/Edgar Doren, D/D (3.5 BMW M1), 191.
Championship points: drivers. Group C: 1 Bell and Stuck, 117; **3** Mass and Ickx, 81; **5** Wollek and Ludwig, 58. **Group C2: 1** Spice and Bellm, 130; **3** Mallock, 75; **4** Wilds, 65; **5** Payne, 52; **6** Jelinski, 50.

FUJI 1000 KMS, Fuji International Speedway, Japan, 6 October. World Endurance Championship for Teams, round 7. World Endurance Championship for Drivers, round 9. 62 laps of the 2·7404-mile/4·4102-mile circuit, 169·90 miles/273·43 km (race stopped due heavy rain).
1 Kazuyoshi Hoshino, J (3.0 t/c March 85G-Nissan), 2h 01m 10·79s, 84·12 mph/135·38 km/h (1st Group C).
2 Osamu Nakako, J (2.6 t/c LM 05C-Nissan), 61 laps.
3 Satoru Nakajima, J (2.1 t/c Dome 85C-Toyota), 61.
4 Naoki Nagasaki, J (2.1 t/c Dome 85C-Toyota), 61.
5 Masahiro Hasemi, J (3.0 t/c March 85G-Nissan), 60.
6 Vern Schuppan, AUS (2.6 t/c Porsche 956), 60.
7 Kaoru Hoshino, J (2.1 t/c Dome 85C-Toyota), 59; **8** Haruhito Yanagida, J (3.0 t/c Lola T810-Nissan), 59; **9** Geoff Lees/Eje Elgh, GB/S (2.1 t/c Dome 85C-Toyota), 58; **10** Tiff Needell, GB (2.1 t/c Dome 85C-Toyota), 57.
Fastest lap: Not given.
Other class winners. Group C2: Kazuo Mogi/Toshio Motohashi, J/J (3.5 Lotec M1C-BMW), 55.

Championship points (prior to the final round of the Drivers' Championship in December).
Drivers: Group C

1=	Derek Bell, GB	117
1=	Hans Stuck, D	117
3=	Jochen Mass, D	81
3=	Jacky Ickx, B	81
5=	Bob Wollek, F	58
5=	Klaus Ludwig, D	58

7 Paolo Barilla, I, 52; **8** Alessandro Nannini, I, 50; **9** Marc Surer, CH, 45; **10** Jonathan Palmer, GB, 36.

Group C2

1=	Gordon Spice, GB	130
1=	Ray Bellm, GB	130
3	Ray Mallock, GB	75
4	Mike Wilds, GB	65
5	Max Payne, GB	52
6	Frank Jelinski, D	50

Teams: Group C (Final points)

1	Rothmans Porsche	107
2	Martini Lancia	58
3	New Man Joest Racing	50
4	Kremer Porsche Racing	43
5	Richard Lloyd Racing	31
6	Brun Motorsports	28

Group C2 (Final points)

1	Spice Engineering	110
2	Ecurie Ecosse	50
3	Ark Racing	46
4	Carma FF	41
5	Gebhardt Engineering	40
6	Jens Winther Denmark	32

Note: Final results will be given in *Autocourse 1986/87.*

European Touring Car Championship

500 KM di MONZA – TROFEO MARIO ANGIOLINI, Autodromo Nazionale di Monza, Italy, 31 March. European Touring Car Championship, round 1. 87 laps of the 3·604-mile/5·800-km circuit, 313·55 miles/504·60 km.
1 Tom Walkinshaw/Win Percy, GB/GB (3.5 Rover Vitesse), 3h 02m 59·64s, 102·08 mph/165·44 km/h (1st over-2500 cc class).
2 Jean-Louis Schlesser/Jeff Allam, F/GB (3.5 Rover Vitesse), 3h 03m 18·57s.
3 Armin Hahne/Eddy Joosen, D/B (3.5 Rover Vitesse), 87 laps.
4 Maurizio Micangeli/Georges Bosshard, I/CH (3.5 BMW 635 CSi), 86.
5 Giancarlo Naddeo/Umberto Grano, I/I (3.5 BMW 635 CSi), 85.
6 Lella Lombardi/Rinaldo Drovandi, I/I (2.5 Alfa Romeo GTV6), 84 (1st 1601cc-2500cc class).
7 Winni Vogt/Walter Nussbaumer, D/D (2.3 BMW 323i), 83; **8** Karl Oppitzhauser/Georg Pacher, A/A (3.5 BMW 635 CSi), 83; **9** Giorgio Francia/Georges Cremer, I/B (2.5 Alfa Romeo GTV6), 83; **10** Marcello Cipriani/Massimo Siena, I/I (2.5 Alfa Romeo GTV6), 82.
Fastest lap: Schlesser, 2m 02·23s, 106·15 mph/170·83 km/h.
Other class winners. Up to 1600cc: Miguel Arias/Santiago Cantero, E/E (1.6 VW Golf GTi), 79.
Championship points. Drivers: 1 Walkinshaw and Percy, 39; **3** Schlesser, Allam, Lombardi and Drovandi, 21.
Manufacturers: 1 Rover, Alfa Romeo and VW, 20; **4** BMW and Audi, 15; **6** BMW and Toyota, 10.

500 KM di VALLELUNGA, Autodromo di Vallelunga, Italy, 21 April. European Touring Car Championship, round 2. 157 laps of the 1·988-mile/3·200-km circuit, 312·12 miles/502·40 km.
1 Tom Walkinshaw/Win Percy, GB/GB (3.5 Rover Vitesse), 3h 44m 28·26s, 83·44 mph/134·28 km/h (1st over-2500 cc class).
2 Gianfranco Brancatelli/Thomas Lindström, I/S (2.0 t/c Volvo 240 Turbo), 3h 45m 06·05s.
3 Armin Hahne/Jeff Allam, D/GB (3.5 Rover Vitesse), 157 laps.
4 Jean-Louis Schlesser/Pierre-Alain Thibault, F/B (3.5 Rover Vitesse), 156.
5 Roberto Ravaglia/Harald Grohs, I/D (3.5 BMW 635 CSi), 154.
6 Georges Bosshard/Maurizio Micangeli, CH/I (3.5 BMW 635 CSi), 154.
7 Claude Ballot-Lena/Alexandre Guyaux, F/F (3.5 BMW 635 CSi), 152; **8** Carlo Rossi/Luigi Taverna, I/I (3.5 BMW 635 CSi), 149; **9** Georges Cremer/Xavier Boucher, B/B (2.5 Alfa Romeo GTV6), 148 (1st 1601 cc-2500 cc class); **10** Pedro Meireles/Christian Melville, P/P (2.5 Alfa Romeo GTV6), 148.
Fastest lap: Walkinshaw, 1m 23·50s, 85·73 mph/137·97 km/h.
Other class winners. Up to 1600 cc: Philippe Müller/Franz Bollinger, D/D (1.6 Toyota Corolla), 142.
Championship points. Drivers: 1 Walkinshaw and Percy, 58; **3** Allam, 37; **4** Schlesser, 34; **5** Lombardi and Drovandi, 33.
Manufacturers: 1 Rover and Alfa Romeo, 40; **3** VW, 35; **4** Toyota, 30; **5** Audi, 23; **6** BMW, 18.

DONINGTON 500, Donington Park Circuit, Great Britain, 5 May. European Touring Car Championship, round 3. 160 laps of the 1·9573-mile/3·1500-km circuit, 313·17 miles/504·00 km.
1 Tom Walkinshaw/Win Percy, GB/GB (3.5 Rover Vitesse), 3h 41m 22·88s, 84·87 mph/136·58 km/h (1st over 2500 cc class).
2 Armin Hahne/Jean-Louis Schlesser, D/F (3.5 Rover Vitesse), 159 laps.
3 Jeff Allam/Pierre-Alain Thibault, GB/B (3.5 Rover Vitesse), 159.
4 Gianfranco Brancatelli/Thomas Lindström, I/S (2.0 t/c Volvo 240 Turbo), 158.
5 Ulf Granberg/Ingvar Carlsson, S/S (2.0 t/c Volvo 240 Turbo), 157.
6 Michel Delcourt/Frank Sytner, B/GB (3.5 BMW 635 CSi), 156.
7 Giancarlo Naddeo/Toni Palma, I/I (3.5 BMW 635 CSi), 154; **8** Slim Borgudd/Sune Ohlsson/Mikael Strauch, S/S/S (2.0 t/c Volvo 240 Turbo), 151; **9** Lella Lombardi/Rinaldo Drovandi, I/I (2.5 Alfa Romeo GTV6), 151 (1st 1601cc-2500cc class); **10** Pedro Meireles/Giorgio Francia, P/I (2.5 Alfa Romeo GTV6), 151.
Fastest lap: Schlesser, 1m 19·58s, 88·54 mph/142·49 km/h.
Other class winners. Up to 1600 cc: Jordi Ripolles/Javier de Castro, E/E (1.6 VW Golf GTi), 143.
Championship points. Drivers: 1 Walkinshaw and Percy, 87; **3** Schlesser, 55; **4** Allam, Hahne, Lombardi and Drovandi, 53.
Manufacturers: 1 Rover and Alfa Romeo, 60; **3** VW, 55; **4** Toyota, 42; **5** Volvo, 25; **6** BMW, 24.

EUROPEAN TOURING CAR CHAMPIONSHIP RACE, Scandinavian Raceway, Anderstorp, Sweden, 12 May. European Touring Car Championship, round 4. 117 laps of the 2·505-mile/4·031-km circuit, 293·09 miles/471·63 km.
1 Gianfranco Brancatelli/Thomas Lindström, I/S (2.0 t/c Volvo 240 Turbo), 3h 31m 44·83s, 83·02 mph/133·61 km/h (1st over 2500 cc class).
2 Ulf Granberg/Anders Olofsson, S/S (2.0 t/c Volvo 240 Turbo), 3h 32m 27·39s.
3 Armin Hahne/Jeff Allam, D/GB (3.5 Rover Vitesse), 117 laps.
4 Georges Bosshard/Maurizio Micangeli, CH/I (3.5 BMW 635 CSi), 114.
5 Giuseppe Briozzi/Gianpiero Moretti, I/I (3.5 BMW 635 CSi), 114.
6 Toni Palma/Carlo Rossi, I/I (3.5 BMW 635 CSi), 114.
7 Lella Lombardi/Rinaldo Drovandi, I/I (2.5 Alfa Romeo GTV6), 113 (1st 1601cc-2500cc class); **8** Marcello Cipriani/Jari Pekkala, I/S (2.5 Alfa

Romeo GTV6), 112; **9** Greger Peterssen/Bertil Engström, S/S (2.0 t/c Volvo 240 Turbo), 111; **10** Romeo Camathias/Jari Pekkala, I/S (Alfa Romeo GTV6), 111.
Fastest lap: Not given.
Other class winners. Up to 1600 cc: John Nielsen/Eric Hoyer, DK/DK (1.6 Toyota Corolla), 106.
Championship points. Drivers: 1 Walkinshaw and Percy, 87; **3** Lombardi and Drovandi, 73; **5** Allam and Hahne, 69.
Manufacturers: 1 Alfa Romeo, 80; **2** Rover, 72; **3** VW and Toyota, 67; **5** Volvo, 45; **6** BMW, 34.

EUROPEAN TOURING CAR CHAMPIONSHIP RACE, Brno, Czechoslovakia, 9 June. European Touring Car Championship, round 5. 57 laps of the 6·788-mile/10·925-km circuit, 386·92 miles/622·73 km.
1 Ulf Granberg/Anders Olofsson, S/S (2.0 t/c Volvo 240 Turbo), 3h 30m 51·89s, 110·69 mph/176·53 km/h (1st over 2500 cc class).
2 Gianfranco Brancatelli/Thomas Lindström, I/S (2.0 t/c Volvo 240 Turbo), 3h 32m 52·06s.
3 Gerhard Berger/Roberto Ravaglia, A/I (3.5 BMW 635 CSi), 57 laps.
4 Umberto Grano/Marco Micangeli, I/I (3.5 BMW CSi), 56.
5 René Metge/Philippe Haezebrouck, F/B (3.5 BMW 635 CSi), 56.
6 Mauricio Micangeli/Georges Bosshard, I/CH (3.5 BMW 635 CSi), 55.
7 Zdenek Vojtech/Bratislav Enge, CS/CS (3.5 BMW 635 CSi), 55; **8** Tom Walkinshaw/Win Percy, GB/GB (3.5 Rover Vitesse), 55; **9** Jeff Allam/Armin Hahne, GB/D (3.5 Rover Vitesse), 54; **10** Lella Lombardi/Rinaldo Drovandi, I/I (2.5 Alfa Romeo GTV6), 54 (1st 1601cc-2500cc class).
Fastest lap: Not given.
Other class winners. Up to 1600cc: Jordi Ripolles/Javier de Castro, E/E (1.6 VW Golf GTi), 51.
Championship points. Drivers: 1 Lombardi and Drovandi, 93; **3** Walkinshaw and Percy, 90; **5** Brancatelli and Lindström, 84.
Manufacturers: 1 Alfa Romeo, 100; **2** VW, 87; **3** Rover, 75; **4** Toyota, 72; **5** Volvo, 65; **6** BMW, 46.

EUROPEAN TOURING CAR CHAMPIONSHIP RACE, Österreichring, Austria, 16 June. European Touring Car Championship, round 6. 99 laps of the 3·692-mile/5·942-km circuit, 365·51 miles/588·26 km.
1 Gianfranco Brancatelli/Thomas Lindström, I/S (2.0 t/c Volvo 240 Turbo), 3h 30m 33·73s, 104·09 mph/167·52 km/h (1st over-2500 cc class).
2 Sigi Müller Jnr/Pierre Dieudonné, D/B (2.0 t/c Volvo 240 Turbo), 98 laps.
3 Marco Micangeli/Emilio Zapico, I/E (3.5 BMW 635 CSi), 97.
4 Georges Bosshard/Mauricio Micangeli, CH/I (3.5 BMW 635 CSi), 96.
5 Winni Vogt/Markus Oestreich, D/D (2.3 BMW 323i), 95 (1st 1601cc-2500cc class).
6 Lella Lombardi/Rinaldo Drovandi, I/I (2.5 Alfa Romeo GTV6), 94.
7 Johnny Reind/Hans Weitgasser, A/A (2.3 BMW 323i), 93; **8** Romeo Camathias/'Spiffero', CH/I (2.5 Alfa Romeo GTV6), 93; **9** Marcello Cipriani/Massimo Siena/Anna Cambiaghi, I/I/I (2.5 Alfa Romeo GTV6), 93; **10** Johannes Wollstadt/Peter Haas, D/D (2.3 BMW 323i), 91.
Fastest lap: Not given.
Other class winners. Up to 1600 cc: Wolfgang Kudrass/Heinz Putz, D/D (1.6 VW Golf GTi), 90.
Championship points. Drivers: 1 Brancatelli and Lindström, 113; **3** Lombardi and Drovandi, 111; **5** Walkinshaw and Percy, 90.
Manufacturers: 1 Alfa Romeo, 115; **2** VW, 107; **3** Toyota, 87; **4** Volvo, 85; **5** Rover, 75; **6** BMW, 58.

EUROPEAN TOURING CAR CHAMPIONSHIP RACE, Salzburgring, Austria, 30 June. European Touring Car Championship, round 7. 141 laps of the 2·635-mile/4·241-km circuit, 371·54 miles/597·98 km.
1 Gianfranco Brancatelli/Thomas Lindström, I/S (2.0 t/c Volvo 240 Turbo), 3h 31m 04·46s, 106·18 mph/170·88 km/h (1st over 2500 cc class).
2 Tom Walkinshaw/Win Percy, GB/GB (3.5 Rover Vitesse), 3h 32m 02·08s.
3 Steve Soper/Eddy Joosen, GB/B (3.5 Rover Vitesse), 140 laps.
4 Pierre Dieudonné/Sigi Müller, Jnr, B/D (2.0 t/c Volvo 240 Turbo), 140.
5 Armin Hahne/Jeff Allam, D/GB (3.5 Rover Vitesse), 140.
6 Marco Micangeli/Umberto Grano, I/I (3.5 BMW 635 CSi), 138.
7 Dieter Quester/Johnny Cecotto, A/YV (3.5 BMW 635 CSi), 137; **8** Gerhard Berger/Roberto Ravaglia, A/I (3.5 BMW 635 CSi), 136; **9** Philippe Martin/Hervé Regout, B/B (3.5 BMW 635 CSi), 136; **10** Lella Lombardi/Rinaldo Drovandi, I/I (2.5 Alfa Romeo GTV6), 134 (1st 1601cc-2500cc class).
Fastest lap: Not given.
Other class winners. Up to 1600 cc: Philippe Müller/Franz Bollinger, CH/CH (1.6 Toyota Corolla), 127.
Championship points. Drivers: 1 Brancatelli and Lindström, 142; **3** Lombardi and Drovandi, 129; **5** Walkinshaw and Percy, 111.
Manufacturers: 1 Alfa Romeo, 135; **2** VW, 111; **3** Toyota, 107; **4** Volvo, 105; **5** Rover, 90; **6** BMW, 64.

GROSSER PREIS der TOURENWAGEN, Nürburgring, German Federal Republic, 7 July. European Touring Car Championship, round 8. 111 laps of the 2·822-mile/4·542-km circuit, 313·24 miles/504·16 km.
1 Gianfranco Brancatelli/Thomas Lindström, I/S (2.0 t/c Volvo 240 Turbo), 3h 42m 34·61s, 84·94 mph/136·70 km/h (1st over-2500 cc class).
2 Steve Soper/Eddy Joosen, GB/B (3.5 Rover Vitesse), 3h 43m 04·69s.
3 Sigi Müller Jnr/Pierre Dieudonné, D/B (2.0 t/c Volvo 240 Turbo), 111 laps.
4 Roberto Ravaglia/Emanuele Pirro, I/I (3.5 BMW 635 CSi), 110.
5 Harald Grohs/Walter Brun, D/CH (3.5 BMW 635 CSi), 110.
6 Dieter Quester/Markus Oestreich, A/D (3.5 BMW 635 CSi), 110.
7 Winni Vogt/Harald Becker, D/D (2.3 BMW 323i), 109 (1st 1601cc–2500cc class); **8** Jean-Michel Martin/Gordon Spice, B/GB (3.5 BMW 635 CSi), 108; **9** Marco Micangeli/Emilio Zapico, I/E (3.5 BMW 635 CSi), 108; **10** Johnny Reindl/Winni Vogt, D/D (2.3 BMW 323i), 108.
Fastest lap: Soper, 1m 52·98s, 89·93 mph/144·73 km/h.
Other class winners. Up to 1600 cc: Robert Schumacher/Hermann Tilke, D/D (1.6 Toyota Corolla), 101.
Championship points. Drivers: 1 Brancatelli and Lindström, 171; **3** Lombardi and Drovandi, 141; **5** Walkinshaw and Percy, 111.
Manufacturers: 1 Alfa Romeo, 147; **2** Toyota, 127; **3** VW, 126; **4** Volvo, 125; **5** Rover, 105; **6** BMW, 74.

SPA 24 HOURS, Spa-Francorchamps, Belgium, 27/28 July. European Touring Car Championship, round 9. 500 laps of the 4·3179-mile/6·9490-km circuit, 2158·95 miles/3474·50 km.
1 Roberto Ravaglia/Gerhard Berger/Marc Surer, I/A/CH (3.5 BMW 635 CSi), 24h 02m 23·24s, 89·81 mph/144·53 km/h (1st over 2500 cc class).
2 Dieter Quester/Johnny Cecotto/Markus Oestreich, A/YV/A (3.5 BMW 635 CSi), 496 laps.
3 Thomas Lindström/Gianfranco Brancatelli/Sigi Müller Jnr, S/I/D (2.0 t/c Volvo 240 Turbo), 491.
4 Pierre Dieudonné/Carlo Rossi/Didier Theys, B/I/B (2.0 t/c Volvo 240 Turbo), 489.
5 Axel Felder/Jurgen Hamelmann/Robert Walterscheid-Müller, D/D/D (3.5 BMW 635 CSi), 485.
6 Umberto Grano/Marco Micangeli/Maurizio Micangeli, I/I/I (3.5 BMW 635 CSi), 485.
7 Paul Belmondo/François Hesnault/Robert Feitler, F/F/L (3.5 BMW 635 CSi), 481; **8** Claude Ballot-Lena/René Metge/Jean-Claude Andruet, F/F/F (3.5 BMW 635 CSi), 473; **9** Giorgio Francia/Georges Cremer/Guy Pirenne, I/B/B (2.5 Alfa Romeo GTV6), 470 (1st 1601cc-2500cc class); **10** Marcello Cipriani/.Massimo Siena/Giuseppe Cipolli, I/I/I (2.5 Alfa Romeo GTV6), 462.
Fastest lap: Berger, 2m 41·67s, 96·15 mph/154·74 km/h.
Other class winners. Up to 1600cc: Jordi Ripolles/Paco Romero/Robert Rutten, E/E/B (1.6 VW Golf GTi), 440.
Championship points. Drivers: 1 Brancatelli and Lindstrom, 187; **3** Lombardi and Drovandi, 141; **5** Walkinshaw and Percy, 111.
Manufacturers: 1 Alfa Romeo, 167; **2** VW, 146; **3** Toyota, 142; **4** Volvo, 137; **5** Rover, 105; **6** BMW, 94.

ISTEL TOURIST TROPHY, Silverstone Grand Prix Circuit, Great Britain, 8 September. European Touring Car Championship, round 10. 107 laps of the 2·932-mile/4·719-km circuit, 313·72 miles/504·93 km.
1 Tom Walkinshaw/Win Percy, GB/GB (3.5 Rover Vitesse), 3h 01m 12·21s, 103·88 mph/167·18 km/h (1st over 2500 cc class).
2 Steve Soper/Jean-Louis Schlesser, GB/F (3.5 Rover Vitesse), 3h 01m 17·87s.
3 Gianfranco Brancatelli/Thomas Lindström, I/S (2.0 t/c Volvo 240 Turbo), 107 laps.
4 Pierre Dieudonné/Sigi Müller Jnr, B/D (2.0 t/c Volvo 240 Turbo), 106.
5 Dave Brodie/Vern Schuppan, GB/AUS (2.0 t/c Colt Starion Turbo), 106.
6 Georges Bosshard/Maurizio Micangeli, CH/I (3.5 BMW 635 CSi), 104.
7 Frank Sytner/John Clark, GB/GB (3.5 BMW 635 CSi), 103; **8** Tony Viana/Nicolo Bianco, ZA/ZA (3.5 BMW 635 CSi), 103; **9** Mike Newman/Robert Speak, GB/GB (3.5 BMW 635 CSi), 103; **10** Lella Lombardi/Rinaldo Drovandi, I/I (2.5 Alfa Romeo), 102 (1st 1601 cc-2500cc class).
Fastest lap: Walkinshaw, 1m 38·78s, 106·85 mph/171·96 km/h (record).
Other class winners. Up to 1600 cc: Wolfgang Kudrass/Heinz Putz, D/D (1.6 VW Golf GTi), 98.
Championship points. Drivers: 1 Brancatelli and Lindström, 203; **3** Lombardi and Drovandi, 161; **3** Walkinshaw and Percy, 140.
Manufacturers: 1 Alfa Romeo, 187; **2** VW, 166; **3** Toyota, 154; **4** Volvo, 149; **5** Rover, 125; **6** BMW, 100.

EUROPEAN TOURING CAR CHAMPIONSHIP RACE, Circuit Automobile Paul Armagnac Nogaro, France, 15 September. European Touring Car Championship, round 11. 142 laps of the 1·939-mile/3·120-km circuit, 275·34 miles/443·04 km.
1 Tom Walkinshaw/Win Percy, GB/GB (3.5 Rover Vitesse), 3h 28m 16·07s, 79·32 mph/127·65 km/h (1st over 2500 cc class).
2 Jean-Louis Schlesser/Steve Soper, F/GB (3.5 Rover Vitesse), 142 laps.
3 Armin Hahne/Jeff Allam, D/GB (3.5 Rover Vitesse), 141.
4 Fabien Giroix/Maurizio Micangeli, F/I (3.5 BMW 635 CSi), 139.
5 Bernard Salam/Pierre Destic, F/F (3.5 BMW 635 CSi), 138.
6 Gianfranco Brancatelli/Thomas Lindström, I/S (2.0 t/c Volvo 240 Turbo), 137.
7 Giorgio Francia/Georges Cremer, I/B (2.5 Alfa Romeo GTV6), 137 (1st 1601 cc-2500 cc class); **8** 'Spiffero'/Rinaldo Drovandi, I/I (2.5 Alfa Romeo GTV6), 136; **9** Pedro Meireles/Christian Melville, P/P (2.5 Alfa Romeo GTV6), 136; **10** Bernard de Dryver/François-Xavier Boucher, B/B (2.5 Alfa Romeo GTV6), 136.
Fastest lap: Brancatelli, 1m 26·24s, 81·40 mph/131·00 km/h.
Other class winners. Up to 1600 cc: Robert Schumacher/Hermann Tilke, CH/CH (Toyota Corolla), 132.
Championship points. Drivers: 1 Brancatelli and Lindström, 210; **3** Drovandi, 176; **4** Walkinshaw and Percy, 169; **6** Lombardi, 161.
Manufacturers: 1 Alfa Romeo, 207; **2** VW, 181; **3** Toyota, 174; **4** Volvo, 155; **5** Rover, 145; **6** BMW, 110.

EUROPEAN TOURING CAR CHAMPIONSHIP RACE, Omloop van Zolder, Belgium, 29 September. European Touring Car Championship, round 12. 113 laps of the 2·648-mile/4·262-km circuit, 299·22 miles/481·61 km.
1 Gianfranco Brancatelli/Thomas Lindström, I/S (2.0 t/c Volvo 240 Turbo), 3h 30m 20·50s, 85·86 mph/138·18 km/h (1st over 2500 cc class).
2 Sigi Müller Jnr/Pierre Dieudonné, D/B (2.0 t/c Volvo 240 Turbo), 3h 32m 04·03s.
3 Armin Hahrne/Jeff Allam, D/GB (3.5 Rover Vitesse), 112 laps.
4 Roberto Ravaglia/Gerhard Berger, I/A (3.5 BMW 635 CSi), 111.
5 Dieter Quester/Markus Oestreich, A/D (3.5 BMW 635 CSi), 110.
6 Maurizio Micangeli/Umberto Grano, I/I (3.5 BMW 635 CSi), 109.
7 Winni Vogt/Franz Dufter, D/D (2.3 BMW 323i), 109 (1st 1601 cc-2500 cc class); **8** Giorgio Francia/Georges Cremer, I/B (2.5 Alfa Romeo GTV6), 108; **9** Marcello Cipriani/Rinaldo Drovandi, I/I (2.5 Alfa Romeo GTV6), 108; **10** Jean-Pierre Castel/Lucien Guitteny, F/B (3.5 BMW 635 CSi), 108.
Fastest lap: Brancatelli, 1m 46·53s, 90·01 mph/144·86 km/h.
Other class winners. Up to 1600 cc: Philippe Müller/Franz Bollinger, CH/CH (1.6 Toyota Corolla), 104.
Championship points. Drivers: 1 Brancatelli and Lindström, 239; **3** Drovandi, 188; **4** Walkinshaw and Percy, 169; **6** Lombardi, 161.
Manufacturers: 1 Alfa Romeo, 210 (222); **2** VW, 196; Toyota, 184 (194); **4** Volvo, 175; **5** Rover, 157; **6** BMW, 114 (120).

EUROPEAN TOURING CAR CHAMPIONSHIP RACE, Autodromo do Estoril, Portugal, 13 October. European Touring Car Championship, round 13. 115 laps of the 2·703-mile/4·350-km circuit, 310·85 miles/500·25 km.
1 Gianfranco Brancatelli/Thomas Lindström, I/S (2.0 t/c Volvo 240 Turbo), 3h 37m 42·25s, 85·67 mph/137·87 km/h (1st over 2500 cc class).
2 Sigi Müller Jnr/Pierre Dieudonné, D/B (2.0 t/c Volvo 240 Turbo), 3h 38m 12·40s.
3 Gerhard Berger/Roberto Ravaglia, A/I (3.5 BMW 635 CSi), 115 laps.
4 Jeff Allam/Armin Hahrne, GB/D (3.5 Rover Vitesse), 114.
5 Maurizio Micangeli/Emilio Zapico, I/E (3.5 BMW 635 CSi), 112.
6 Antonio Rodrigues/Ferreira da Silva, P/P (2.0 t/c Volvo 240 Turbo), 112.
7 José Perez/Joaquim Moutinho, P/P (3.5 BMW 635 CSi), 111; **8** Umberto Grano/Georges Bosshard, I/CH (3.5 BMW 635 CSi), 111; **9** Marcello Cipriani/Rinaldo Drovandi, I/I (2.5 Alfa Romeo GTV6), 109 (1st 1601 cc-2500 cc class); **10** Rufino Contes/Bernardo San Nogueira, P/P (2.5 Alfa Romeo GTV6), 108.
Fastest lap: Brancatelli, 1m 50·12s, 88·37 mph/142·22 km/h.
Other class winners: Up to 1600 cc: Paco Romero/Xavier Miranda, E/E (1.6 VW Golf GTi), 108.
Championship points. Drivers: 1 Brancatelli and Lindström, 261 (268); **3** Drovandi, 188 (200); **4** Walkinshaw and Percy, 169; **6** Lombardi, 161.
Manufacturers: 1 Alfa Romeo, 215 (242); **2** VW, 212 (216); **3** Toyota, 197 (209); **4** Volvo, 189 (195); **5** Rover, 167; **6** BMW, 120 (132).

EUROPEAN TOURING CAR CHAMPIONSHIP RACE, Circuito Permanente del Jarama, Spain, 20 October. European Touring Car Championship, round 14. 152 laps of the 2·058-mile/3·312-km circuit, 312·82 miles/ 503·42 km.
1 Tom Walkinshaw/Win Percy, GB/GB (3.5 Rover Vitesse), 4h 09m 43·42s, 75·59 mph/121·65 km/h (1st over 2500 cc class).
2 Gianfranco Brancatelli/Thomas Lindström, I/S (2.0 t/c Volvo 240 Turbo), 4h 10m 12·27s.
3 Sigi Müller Jnr/Pierre Dieudonné, D/B (2.0 t/c Volvo 240 Turbo), 152 laps.
4 Jeff Allam/Armin Hahrne, GB/D (3.5 Rover Vitesse), 151.
5 Luis Sala/Dieter Quester, E/A (3.5 BMW 635 CSi), 150.
6 Christian Danner/Leopold von Bayern, D/D (2.0 t/c Volvo 240 Turbo), 150.
7 Roberto Ravaglia/Johnny Cecotto, I/YV (3.5 BMW 635 CSi), 150; **8** Umberto Grano/Georges Bosshard, I/CH (3.5 BMW 635 CSi), 147; **9** Winni Vogt/Markus Oestreich, D/D (2.3 BMW 323i), 147 (1st 1601 cc-2500 cc class); **10** Claude Ballot-Lena/René Metge, F/F (3.5 BMW 635 CSi), 147.
Fastest lap: Brancatelli, 1m 35·25s, 78·23 mph/125·90 km/h.
Other class winners: Up to 1600 cc: Milos Bychi/Massimo Micangeli, CZ/I (1.6 Toyota Corolla), 139.

Provisional final points (due to possible disqualification of Volvo at Salzburgring and problems concerning homologation of Volvo 240 Turbo).

Drivers

1=	Gianfranco Brancatelli, I	269 (289)
1=	Thomas Lindström, S	269 (289)
3	Rinaldo Drovandi, I	188 (200)
4=	Tom Walkinshaw, GB	198
4=	Win Percy, GB	198
6	Lella Lombardi, I	161

Manufacturers

1	Alfa Romeo	215 (257)
2	VW	212 (231)
3	Toyota	199 (229)
4	Volvo	192 (210)
5	Rover	184 (187)
6	BMW	122 (140)

CART PPG Indy Car World Series

1984 results

The final round of the 1984 CART PPG Indy Car World Series was run after *Autocourse 1984/85* went to press.

CAESARS PALACE GRAND PRIX IV, Caesars Palace Indy Circuit, Las Vegas, Nevada, United States of America, 11 November. CART PPG Indy Car World Series, round 16. 178 laps of the 1·125-mile/1·811-km circuit, 200·25 miles/322·36 km.
1 Tom Sneva, USA (March 84C-Cosworth DFX), 2h 08m 13·55s, 93·701 mph/150·797 km/h.
2 Mario Andretti, USA (Lola T800-Cosworth DFX), 2h 08m 20·42s.
3 John Paul Jnr, USA (March 84C-Cosworth DFX), 178 laps.
4 Al Unser Jnr, USA (March 84C-Cosworth DFX), 177.
5 Geoff Brabham, AUS (March 84C-Cosworth DFX), 177.
6 Roberto Guerrero, COL (March 84C-Cosworth DFX), 176.
7 Bobby Rahal, USA (March 84C-Cosworth DFX), 176; **8** Scott Brayton, USA (March 84C-Cosworth DFX), 172; **9** Pete Halsmer, USA (Arciero MP10-Cosworth DFX), 172; **10** Josele Garza, MEX (March 84C-Cosworth DFX), 171 (DNF, gearbox); **11** Pancho Carter, USA (March 84C-Cosworth DFX), 162 (DNF, accident); **12** John Morton, USA (March 83C-Cosworth DFX), 162.
Fastest qualifier: Danny Sullivan, USA (Lola T800-Cosworth DFX), 32·952s, 122·906 mph/197·798 km/h.

Final Championship points

1	Mario Andretti, USA	176
2	Tom Sneva, USA	163
3	Bobby Rahal, USA	137
4=	Danny Sullivan, USA	110
4=	Rick Mears, USA	110
6	Al Unser Jnr, USA	103

7 Mike Andretti, USA, 102; **8** Geoff Brabham, AUS, 87; **9** Al Unser Snr, USA, 76; **10** Danny Ongais, USA, 53; **11** Roberto Guerrero, COL 52; **12** Howdy Holmes, USA, 44; **13** Josele Garza, MEX, 42; **14** Gordon Johncock, USA, 39; **15** Emerson Fittipaldi, BR and Jacques Villeneuve, CDN, 30; **17** John Paul Jnr, USA and Al Holbert, USA, 28; **19** Derek Daly, IRL, 26; **20** Chip Ganassi, USA, 24.

1985 results

TOYOTA GRAND PRIX OF LONG BEACH, Long Beach Circuit, Long Beach, California, United States of America, 14 April. CART PPG Indy Car World Series, round 1. 90 laps of the 1·67-mile/2·69-km circuit, 150·30 miles/241·88 km.
1 Mario Andretti, USA (Lola T900-Cosworth DFX), 1h 42m 50·07s, 87·694 mph/141·129 km/h.
2 Emerson Fittipaldi, BR (March 85C-Cosworth DFX), 1h 43m 40·20s.
3 Danny Sullivan, USA (March 85C-Cosworth DFX), 89 laps (DNF, out of fuel).
4 Jim Crawford, GB (Lola T900-Cosworth DFX), 89.
5 Al Unser Snr, USA (March 85C-Cosworth DFX), 89.
6 Geoff Brabham, AUS (March 85C-Cosworth DFX), 88.
7 Jacques Villeneuve, CDN (March 85C-Cosworth DFX), 88; **8** Tom Sneva, USA (Eagle 85C-Cosworth DFX), 87; **9** Al Unser Jnr, USA (Lola T900-Cosworth DFX), 86 (DNF, car on fire); **10** Johnny Rutherford, USA (March 85C-Cosworth DFX), 86; **11** Scott Brayton, USA (March 85C-Cosworth DFX), 85; **12** Ed Pimm, USA (Eagle 85C-Cosworth DFX), 85.
Fastest qualifier: Andretti, 1m 05·21s, 92·194 mph/148·371 km/h.
Championship points: 1 Andretti, 22; **2** Fittipaldi, 16; **3** Sullivan, 14; **4** Crawford, 12; **5** Unser Snr, 10; **6** Brabham, 8.

Indianapolis 500

INDIANAPOLIS 500, Indianapolis Motor Speedway, Indiana, United States of America, 26 May. CART PPG Indy Car World Series, round 2. 200 laps of the 2·500-mile/4·023-km circuit, 500·00 miles/804·57 km.
1 Danny Sullivan, USA (March 85C-Cosworth DFX), 3h 16m 06·069s, 152·982 mph/246·200 km/h.
2 Mario Andretti, USA (Lola T900-Cosworth DFX), 3h 16m 08·546s.
3 Roberto Guerrero, COL (March 85C-Cosworth DFX), 200 laps.
4 Al Unser Snr, USA (March 85C-Cosworth DFX), 199 (1 lap penalty).
5 Johnny Parsons, USA (March 85C-Cosworth DFX), 198.
6 Johnny Rutherford, USA (March 85C-Cosworth DFX), 198 (1 lap penalty).
7 Arie Luyendyk, NL (Lola T900-Cosworth DFX), 198; **8** Mike Andretti, USA (March 85C-Cosworth DFX), 196; **9** Ed Pimm, USA (Eagle 85C-Cosworth DFX), 195; **10** Howdy Holmes, USA (Lola T900-Cosworth DFX), 194; **11** Kevin Cogan, USA (March 85C-Cosworth DFX), 191; **12** Derek Daly, IRL (Lola T900-Cosworth DFX), 189; **13** Emerson Fittipaldi, BR (March 85C Cosworth DFX), 188 (DNF, engine); **14** Bill Whittington, USA (March 85C-Cosworth DFX), 183 (DNF, accident); **15** John Paul Jnr, USA (March 85C-Cosworth DFX), 164 (DNF, accident); **16** Jim Crawford, GB (Lola T900-Cosworth DFX), 142 (DNF, engine); **17** Danny

Ongais, USA (March 85C-Cosworth DFX), 141 (DNF, engine); **18** Raoul Boesel, BR (March 85C-Cosworth DFX), 134 (DNF, engine); **19** Geoff Brabham, AUS (March 85C-Cosworth DFX), 130 (DNF, engine); **20** Tom Sneva, USA (Eagle 85C-Cosworth DFX), 120 (DNF, accident); **21** [illegible], USA (March 85C-Cosworth DFX), 122 (DNF, gear linkage); **22** Chip Ganassi, USA (March 85C-Cosworth DFX), 121 (DNF, engine); **23** Rich Vogler, USA (March 85C-Cosworth DFX), 119 (DNF, accident); **24** Don Whittington, USA (March 85C-Cosworth DFX), 97 (DNF, engine); **25** Al Unser Jnr, USA (Lola T900-Cosworth DFX), 91 (DNF, engine); **26** Dick Simon, USA (March 85C-Cosworth DFX), 86 (DNF, engine); **27** Bobby Rahal, USA (March 85C-Cosworth DFX), 84 (DNF, engine); **28** A. J. Foyt, USA (March 85C-Cosworth DFX), 62 (DNF, fire in pits); **29** Tony Bettenhausen, USA (Lola T900-Cosworth DFX), 31 (DNF, engine); **30** Scott Brayton, USA (March 85C-Buick), 19 (DNF, engine); **31** Josele Garza, MEX (March 85C-Cosworth DFX), 15 (DNF, engine); **32** George Snider, USA (March 85C-Chevrolet), 13 (DNF, engine); **33** Pancho Carter, USA (March 85C-Buick), 6 (DNF, oil pump).
Fastest qualifier; Carter, 2m 49·346s, 212·583 mph/342·118 km/h (4 laps).
Fastest lap: Not given.
Championship points: 1 Andretti, 39; **2** Sullivan, 34; **3** Unser Snr, 22; **4** Fittipaldi, 16; **5** Guerrero, 14; **6** Crawford, 12.

MILLER AMERICAN/REX MAYS 200, Wisconsin State Fair Park Speedway, Wisconsin, United States of America, 2 June. CART PPG Indy Car World Series, round 3. 200 laps of the 1·000-mile/1·609-km circuit, 200·00 miles/321·80 km.
1 Mario Andretti, USA (Lola T900-Cosworth DFX), 1h 36m 38·89s, 124·162 mph/192·819 km/h.
2 Tom Sneva, USA (Eagle 85C-Cosworth DFX), 1h 36m 51·61s.
3 Rick Mears, USA (March 85C-Cosworth DFX), 200 laps.
4 Danny Sullivan, USA (March 85C-Cosworth DFX), 199.
5 Pancho Carter, USA (March 85C-Cosworth DFX), 196.
6 Roberto Guerrero, COL (March 85C-Cosworth DFX), 196.
7 Josele Garza, MEX (March 85C-Cosworth DFX), 195; **8** Emerson Fittipaldi, BR (March 85C-Cosworth DFX), 195; **9** Bobby Rahal, USA (March 85C-Cosworth DFX), 195; **10** Chet Fillip, USA (Lola T900-Cosworth DFX), 192; **11** Howdy Holmes, USA (Lola T900-Cosworth DFX), 191; **12** Geoff Brabham, AUS (March 85C-Cosworth DFX), 191.
Fastest qualifier: Andretti, 24·39s, 147·601 mph/237·540 km/h.
Championship points: 1 Andretti, 61; **2** Sullivan, 46; **3** Unser Snr and Guerrero, 22; **5** Fittipaldi and Sneva, 21.

STROH'S/G.I. JOE'S 200, Portland International Raceway, Portland, Oregon, United States of America, 16 June. CART PPG Indy Car World Series, round 4. 104 laps of the 1·915-mile/3·082-km circuit, 199·16 miles/320·53 km.
1 Mario Andretti, USA (Lola T900-Cosworth DFX), 1h 51m 35·524s, 107·083 mph/172·333 km/h.
2 Al Unser Jnr, USA (Lola T900-Cosworth DFX), 1h 52m 00·700s.
3 Emerson Fittipaldi, BR (March 85C-Cosworth DFX), 104 laps.
4 Al Unser, USA (March 85C-Cosworth DFX), 103.
5 Kevin Cogan, USA (March 85C-Cosworth DFX), 102.
6 Scott Brayton, USA (March 85C-Cosworth DFX), 102.
7 Michael Roe, IRL (March 85C-Cosworth DFX), 102; **8** Pete Halsmer, USA (March 85C-Cosworth DFX), 102; **9** Johnny Rutherford, USA (March 85C-Cosworth DFX), 100; **10** Bruno Giacomelli, I (March 85C-Cosworth DFX), 99; **11** Raoul Boesel, BR (March 85C-Cosworth DFX), 97; **12** Josele Garza, MEX (March 85C-Cosworth DFX), 96.
Fastest qualifier: Danny Sullivan, USA (March 85C-Cosworth DFX), 59·932s, 115·030 mph/185·122 km/h.
Championship points: 1 Andretti, 81; **2** Sullivan, 47; **3** Fittipaldi, 35; **4** Unser Snr, 34; **5** Guerrero, 22; **6** Sneva and Unser Jnr, 21.

MEADOWLANDS GRAND PRIX, Meadowlands Grand Prix Circuit, New York, United States of America, 30 June. CART PPG Indy Car World Series, round 5. 100 laps of the 1·682-mile/2·707-km circuit, 168·20 miles/270·70 km.
1 Al Unser Jnr, USA (Lola T900-Cosworth DFX), 1h 51m 55·51s, 90·167 mph/145·109 km/h.
2 Emerson Fittipaldi, BR (March 85C-Cosworth DFX), 1h 52m 32·08s.
3 Al Unser Snr, USA (March 85C-Cosworth DFX), 100 laps.
4 Mike Andretti, USA (March 85C-Cosworth DFX), 100.
5 Bruno Giacomelli, I (March 85C-Cosworth DFX), 99.
6 Tom Sneva, USA (Eagle 85C-Cosworth DFX), 99.
7 Kevin Cogan, USA (March 85C-Cosworth DFX), 98; **8** Michael Roe, IRL (Lola T900-Cosworth DFX), 98; **9** Jim Crawford, GB (Lola T900-Cosworth DFX), 98; **10** Arie Luyendyk, NL (Lola T900-Cosworth DFX), 97; **11** Raoul Boesel, BR (March 85C-Cosworth DFX), 97; **12** Jan Lammers, NL (March 85C-Cosworth DFX), 97.
Fastest qualifier: Mario Andretti, USA (Lola T900-Cosworth DFX), 1m 01·504s, 98·452 mph/158·443 km/h.
Championship points: 1 Andretti, 82; **2** Fittipaldi, 51; **3** Unser Snr, 48; **4** Sullivan, 47; **5** Unser Jnr, 42; **6** Sneva, 29.

BUDWEISER CLEVELAND GRAND PRIX, Burke Lakefront Airport Circuit, Cleveland, Ohio, United States of America, 7 July. CART PPG Indy Car World Series, round 6. 88 laps of the 2·485-mile/3·999-km circuit, 218·68 miles/351·91 km.
1 Al Unser Jnr, USA (Lola T900-Cosworth DFX), 1h 45m 31·85s, 124·08 mph/199·687 km/h.
2 Geoff Braham, AUS (March 85C-Cosworth DFX), 1h 45m 47·00s.
3 Al Unser Snr, USA (March 85C-Cosworth DFX), 88 laps.
4 Jacques Villeneuve, CDN (March 85C-Cosworth DFX), 88.
5 Arie Luyendyk, NL (Lola T900-Cosworth DFX), 88.
6 Josele Garza, MEX (March 85C-Cosworth DFX), 88.
7 Mike Andretti, USA (March 85C-Cosworth DFX), 87; **8** Emerson Fittipaldi, BR (March 85C-Cosworth DFX), 87; **9** Kevin Cogan, USA (March 85C-Cosworth DFX), 86; **10** Bruno Giacomelli, I (March 85C-Cosworth DFX), 86; **11** Tom Sneva, USA (Eagle 85C-Cosworth DFX), 86; **12** Raoul Boesel, BR (March 85C-Cosworth DFX), 86.
Fastest qualifier: Bobby Rahal, USA (March 85C-Cosworth DFX), 1m 07·79s, 131·966 mph/212·378 km/h (record).
Championship points: 1 Andretti, 83; **2** Unser Snr and Unser Jnr, 62; **4** Fittipaldi, 56; **5** Sullivan, 47; **6** Sneva, 31.

MICHIGAN 500, Michigan International Speedway, Brooklyn, Michigan, United States of America, 28 July. CART PPG Indy Car World Series, round 7. 250 laps of the 2·000-mile/3·219-km circuit, 500·00 miles/804·75 km.
1 Emerson Fittipaldi, BR (March 85C-Cosworth DFX), 3h 53m 58·33s, 128·220 mph/206·350 km/h.
2 Al Unser Snr, USA (March 85C-Cosworth DFX), 3h 53m 58·43s.
3 Tom Sneva, USA (Eagle 85C-Cosworth DFX), 249 laps.
4 Johnny Rutherford, USA (March 85C-Cosworth DFX), 248.
5 Ed Pimm, USA (Eagle 85C-Cosworth DFX), 248.
6 Bobby Rahal, USA (March 85C-Cosworth DFX), 247.
7 Kevin Cogan, USA (March 85C-Cosworth DFX), 247; **8** Scott Brayton, USA (March 85C-Buick), 245; **9** Howdy Holmes, USA (Lola T900-Cosworth DFX), 244; **10** Mario Andretti, USA (Lola T900-Cosworth DFX), 241 (DNF, accident); **11** Dennis Firestone, USA (Lola T900-Cosworth DFX), 231; **12** Steve Chassey, USA (March 85C-Chevrolet), 228 (DNF, engine).
Fastest qualifier: Rick Mears, USA (March 85C-Cosworth DFX), 33·689s, 213·719 mph/343·947 km/h.
Championship points: 1 Andretti, 86; **2** Unser Snr, 79; **3** Fittipaldi, 76; **4** Unser Jnr, 62; **5** Sullivan, 47; **6** Sneva, 45.

PROVIMI VEAL 200, Road America, Elkhart Lake, Wisconsin, United States of America, 4 August. CART PPG Indy Car World Series, round 8. 50 laps of the 4·000-mile/6·437-km circuit, 200·00 miles/257·48 km.
1 Jacques Villeneuve, CDN (March 85C-Cosworth DFX), 1h 45m 12·15s, 114·066 mph/183·571 km/h.
2 Mike Andretti, USA (March 85C-Cosworth DFX), 1h 45m 22·20s.
3 Alan Jones, AUS (Lola T900-Cosworth DFX), 50 laps.
4 Bobby Rahal, USA (March 85C-Cosworth DFX), 50.
5 Emerson Fittipaldi, BR (March 85C-Cosworth DFX), 50.
6 Arie Luyendyk, NL (Lola T900-Cosworth DFX), 50.
7 Al Unser Snr, USA (March 85C-Cosworth DFX), 50; **8** Raoul Boesel, BR (March 85C-Cosworth DFX), 49; **9** Enrique Mansilla, RA (Lola T900-Cosworth DFX), 48; **10** Howdy Holmes, USA (Lola T900-Cosworth DFX), 48; **11** Ed Pimm, USA (Eagle 85C-Cosworth DFX), 48; **12** Herm Johnson, USA (March 85C-Cosworth DFX), 47.
Fastest qualifier: Danny Sullivan, USA (March 85C-Cosworth DFX), 1m 52·029s, 128·538 mph/206·861 km/h (record).
Championship points: 1 Andretti and Fittipaldi, 86; **3** Unser Snr, 85; **4** Unser Jnr, 63; **5** Sullivan, 48; **6** Sneva, 45.

DOMINO'S PIZZA 500, Pocono International Raceway, Pennsylvania, United States of America, 18 August. CART PPG Indy Car World Series, round 9. 200 laps of the 2·500-mile/4·023-km circuit, 500·00 miles/804·60 km.
1 Rick Mears, USA (March 85C-Cosworth DFX), 3h 17m 47·44s, 151·676 mph/244·098 km/h.
2 Al Unser Jnr, USA (Lola T900-Cosworth DFX), 3h 17m 49·62s.
3 Al Unser Snr, USA (March 85C-Cosworth DFX), 200 laps.
4 Bobby Rahal, USA (March 85C-Cosworth DFX), 200.
5 Danny Sullivan, USA (March 85C-Cosworth DFX), 199.
6 Emerson Fittipaldi, BR (March 85C-Cosworth DFX), 198.
7 Mario Andretti, USA (Lola T900-Cosworth DFX), 198; **8** Tom Sneva, USA (Eagle 85C-Cosworth DFX), 195; **9** Dennis Firestone, USA (Lola T900-Cosworth DFX), 193; **10** Dick Simon, USA (March 85C-Cosworth DFX), 191; **11** Steve Chassey, USA (March 85C-Chevrolet), 189; **12** Pancho Carter, USA (March 85C-Cosworth DFX), 188.
Fastest qualifier: Mears, 44·219s, 203·532 mph/327·552 km/h.
Championship points: 1 Unser Snr, 99; **2** Fittipaldi, 94; **3** Andretti, 92; **4** Unser Jnr, 80; **5** Sullivan, 58; **6** Sneva, 50.

ESCORT RADAR WARNING 200, Mid-Ohio Sports Car Course, Lexington, Ohio, United States of America, 1 September. CART PPG Indy Car World Series, round 10. 84 laps of the 2·400-mile/3·863-km circuit, 201·60 miles/324·41 km.
1 Bobby Rahal, USA (March 85C-Cosworth DFX), 1h 52m 23·20s, 107·041 mph/172·265 km/h.
2 Danny Sullivan, USA (March 85C-Cosworth DFX), 1h 53m 19·33s.
3 Jacques Villeneuve, CDN (March 85C-Cosworth DFX), 84 laps.
4 Al Unser Jnr, USA (Lola T900-Cosworth DFX), 83.
5 Bill Whittington, USA (Lola T900-Cosworth DFX), 83.
6 Bruno Giacomelli, I (March 85C-Cosworth DFX), 83.
7 Mario Andretti, USA (Lola T900-Cosworth DFX), 82 (DNF, [illegible]); **8** Emerson Fittipaldi, BR (March 85C-Cosworth DFX), 82; **9** Ed Pimm, USA (Eagle 85C-Cosworth DFX), 81; **10** Enrique Mansilla, RA (Lola T900-Cosworth DFX), 80; **11** Josele Garza, MEX (March 85C-Cosworth DFX), 79; **12** Steve Chassey, USA (March 85C-Chevrolet), 79.
Fastest qualifier: Rahal, 1m 15·26s, 114·802 mph/184·755 km/h.
Championship points: 1 Unser Snr and Fittipaldi, 99; **3** Andretti, 98; **4** Unser Jnr, 92; **5** Sullivan, 74; **6** Rahal, 60.

GRAND PRIX MOLSON INDY, Sanair Super-speedway, Quebec, Canada, 8 September. CART PPG Indy Car World Series, round 11. 225 laps of the 0·826-mile/1·329-km circuit, 185·85 miles/299·03 km.
1 Johnny Rutherford, USA (March 85C-Cosworth DFX), 2h 03m 54·37s, 89·993 mph/144·829 km/h.
2 Pancho Carter, USA (March 85C-Cosworth DFX), 2h 03m 54·27s (Rutherford adjudged the winner after last-lap yellow flag/green flag incident).
3 Al Unser Jnr, USA (Lola T900-Cosworth DFX), 225 laps.
4 Geoff Brabham, AUS (March 85C-Cosworth DFX), 225.
5 Danny Sullivan, USA (March 85C-Cosworth DFX), 224.
6 Josele Garza, MEX (March 85C-Cosworth DFX), 223.
7 Tom Sneva, USA (Lola T900-Cosworth DFX), 223; **8** Ed Pimm, USA (Eagle 85C-Cosworth DFX), 223; **9** Kevin Cogan, USA (March 85C-Cosworth DFX), 218; **10** Bobby Rahal, USA (March 85C-Cosworth DFX), 208 (DNF, accident); **11** Jacques Villeneuve, CDN (March 85C-Cosworth DFX), 208 (DNF, accident); **12** Enrique Mansilla, RA (Lola T900-Cosworth DFX), 201 (DNF, accident).
Fastest qualifier: Rahal, 20·252s, 146·830 mph/236·299 km/h.
Championship points: 1 Unser Jnr, 106; **2** Unser Snr, 100; **3** Fittipaldi, 99; **4** Andretti, 98; **5** Sullivan, 84; **6** Rahal, 64.

DETROIT NEWS GRAND PRIX 200, Michigan International Speedway, Michigan, United States of America, 22 September. CART PPG Indy Car World Series, round 12. 100 laps of the 2·000-mile/3·219-km circuit, 200·00 miles/321·90 km.
1 Bobby Rahal, USA (March 85C-Cosworth DFX), 1h 13m 19·45s, 163·647 mph/263·364 km/h.
2 Rick Mears, USA (March 85C-Cosworth DFX), 1h 13m 20·16s.
3 Ed Pimm, USA (Eagle 85C-Cosworth DFX), 100 laps.
4 Kevin Cogan, USA (March 85C-Cosworth DFX), 99.
5 Tom Sneva, USA (Eagle 85C-Cosworth DFX), 99.
6 Josele Garza, MEX (March 85C-Cosworth DFX), 99.
7 Danny Ongais, USA (March 85C-Cosworth DFX), 99; **8** Danny Sullivan, USA (March 85C-Cosworth DFX), 98; **9** Johnny Rutherford, USA (March 85C-Cosworth DFX), 98; **10** Pancho Carter, USA (March 85C-Cosworth DFX), 98; **11** Pete Halsmer, USA (March 85C-Cosworth DFX), 98; **12** Al Unser Snr, USA (March 85C-Cosworth DFX), 98.
Fastest qualifier: Rahal, 33·605s, 214·254 mph/344·808 km/h.
Championship points: 1 Unser Jnr, 106; **2** Unser Snr, 101; **3** Fittipaldi, 99; **4** Andretti, 98; **5** Sullivan, 89; **6** Rahal, 86.

STROH'S 300, Laguna Seca Raceway, California, United States of America, 6 October. CART PPG Indy Car World Series, round 13. 98 laps of the 1·900-mile/3·056-km circuit, 186·20 miles/299·49 km.
1 Bobby Rahal, USA (March 85C-Cosworth DFX), 1h 38m 56·09s, 112·923 mph/181·732 km/h.
2 Al Unser Snr, USA (March 85C-Cosworth DFX), 1h 39m 08·81s.
3 Al Unser Jnr, USA (Lola T900-Cosworth DFX), 98 laps.
4 Roberto Guerrero, COL (March 85C-Cosworth DFX), 98.
5 Jan Lammers, NL (Lola T900-Cosworth DFX), 97.
6 Bruno Giacomelli, I (March 85C-Cosworth DFX), 97.
7 Josele Garza, MEX (March 85C-Cosworth DFX), 96; **8** Danny Sullivan, USA (March 85C-Cosworth DFX), 96 (1 lap penalty); **9** Mike Andretti, USA (March 85C-Cosworth DFX), 96; **10** Geoff Brabham, AUS (March 85C-Cosworth DFX), 95 (DNF, oil leak); **11** Mario Andretti, USA (Lola T900-Cosworth DFX), 94 (DNF, engine fire); **12** Rupert Keegan, GB (March 85C-Cosworth DFX), 85.
Fastest qualifier: Rahal, 54·164s, 126·283 mph/203·232 km/h.
Championship points: 1 Unser Jnr, 120; **2** Unser Snr, 117; **3** Rahal, 108; **4** Andretti, 100; **5** Fittipaldi, 99; **6** Sullivan, 94.

DANA-JIMMY BRYAN 150, Phoenix International Raceway, Arizona, United States of America, 13 October. CART PPG Indy Car World Series, round 14. 150 laps of the 1·000-mile/1·609-km circuit, 150·00 miles/241·35 km.
1 Al Unser Snr, USA (March 85C-Cosworth DFX), 1h 14m 35·99s, 120·644 mph/194·157 km/h.
2 Al Unser Jnr, USA (Lola T900-Cosworth DFX), 149 laps.
3 Mario Andretti, USA (Lola T900-Cosworth DFX), 149.
4 Danny Sullivan, USA (March 85C-Cosworth DFX), 149.
5 Mike Andretti, USA (March 85C-Cosworth DFX), 149.
6 Bobby Rahal, USA (March 85C-Cosworth DFX), 149.
7 Pancho Carter, USA (March 85C-Cosworth DFX), 148; **8** Emerson Fittipaldi, BR (March 85C-Cosworth DFX), 146; **9** Ed Pimm, USA (Eagle 85C-Cosworth DFX), 145; **10** Josele Garza, MEX (March 85C-Cosworth DFX), 145; **11** Steve Chassey, USA (March 85C-Chevrolet), 144; **12** Geoff Brabham, AUS (March 85C-Cosworth DFX), 144.
Fastest qualifier: Unser Snr, 22·238s, 161·885 mph/260·528 km/h.

Championship points (prior to final round in November)

1	Al Unser Snr, USA	139
2	Al Unser Jnr, USA	136
3	Bobby Rahal, USA	116
4	Mario Andretti, USA	114
5	Danny Sullivan, USA	106
6	Emerson Fittipaldi, BR	104

7 Tom Sneva, USA, 66; **8** Jacques Villeneuve, CDN, 54; **9** Mike Andretti, USA, 53; **10** Rick Mears, USA, 51; **11** Johnny Rutherford, USA, 47; **12** Ed Pimm, USA, 43; **13** Geoff Brabham, AUS and Pancho Carter, USA, 41; **15** Josele Garza, MEX, 39.
Note: Final results will be given in *Autocourse 1986/87*.

IMSA CAMEL GT Championship

1984 results

The final round of the 1984 IMSA CAMEL GT Championship was run after *Autocourse 1984/85* went to press.

EASTERN AIRLINES 3 HOUR CAMEL GT, Daytona International Speedway, Florida, United States of America, 25 November. IMSA CAMEL GT Championship, round 17. 91 laps of the 3·560-mile/5·729-km circuit, 232·96 miles/521·34 km.
1 Al Holbert/Derek Bell, USA/GB (2.6 t/c Porsche 962), 3h 00m 59·610s, 107·39 mph/172·83 km/h.
2 Brian Redman/Hurley Haywood, GB/USA (6.0 Jaguar XJR-5), 3h 01m 30·120s.
3 Bob Wollek/Al Holbert, F/USA (2.6 t/c Porsche 962), 88 laps.
4 Bruce Leven/David Hobbs, USA/GB (2.6 t/c Porsche 962), 88.
5 Klaus Ludwig/Tom Gloy, D/USA 2.1 t/c Ford Mustang GTP), 86.
6 Sarel van der Merwe/Ian Scheckter, ZA/ZA (3.1 t/c March 84G-Porsche), 86.
7 Lyn St James/Jim Trueman, USA/USA (3.0 Argo JM16-Cosworth DFV), 86; **8** Willy T. Ribbs/Wally Dallenbach, Jnr, USA/USA (5.0 Ford Mustang), 85 (1st over 2500 cc GT class); **9** Walt Bohren, USA (5.9 Chevrolet Corvette), 85; **10** Terry Labonte, USA (5.9 Chevrolet Camaro), 84.
1st up to 2500cc GT class: John Schneider/Elliott Forbes-Robinson, USA/USA (2.0 Porsche 924 Carrera), 80.
Fastest qualifier: Bell, 1m 41·508s, 126·26 mph/203·20 km/h (record).
Fastest lap: Bell, 1m 45·209s, 121·82 mph/196·05 km/h (record).

Final Championship points: overall

1	Randy Lanier, USA	189
2	Bill Whittington, USA	168
3	Derek Bell, GB	164
4	Al Holbert, USA	136
5	Sarel van der Merwe, ZA	105
6	Brian Redman, GB	97

7 Doc Bundy, USA, 94; **8** Bob Tullius, USA, 74; **9** Kenper Miller, USA, 70; **10** Hurley Haywood, USA, 68.

Over 2500cc GT class

1	Roger Mandeville, USA	200
2	Gene Felton, USA	163
3	Amos Johnson, USA	152
4	Billy Hagen, USA	143
5	Chester Vincentz, USA	139
6	Jim Mullen, USA	95

Up to 2500cc GT class

1	Jack Baldwin, USA	225
2	Jack Dunham, USA	154
3	Jeff Kline, USA	129
4	John Schneider, USA	124
5	Elliott Forbes-Robinson, USA	111
6	Chris Cord, USA	106

1985 results

24 SUNBANK DAYTONA 24 HOURS, Daytona International Speedway, Florida, United States of America, 2/3 February. IMSA CAMEL GT Championship, round 1. 703 laps of the 3·56-mile/5·73-km circuit. 2502·68 miles/4028·19 km.
1 A. J. Foyt/Bob Wollek/Al Unser/Thierry Boutsen, USA/USA/F/B (t/c Porsche 962), 24h 01m 36·240s, 104·162 mph/167·632 km/h (1st GTP class).
2 Al Holbert/Derek Bell/Al Unser Jnr, USA/GB/USA (t/c Porsche 962), 686 laps.
3 Jim Busby/Rick Knoop/Jochen Mass, USA/USA/D (t/c Porsche 962), 674.
4 Bob Akin/Hans Stuck/Paul Miller, USA/D/USA (t/c Porsche 962), 670.
5 Jim Mullen/Ray McIntyre/Kees Nierop, USA/USA/CDN (t/c Porsche 935), 668.
6 Art Leon/Skeeter McKitterick/Terry Wolters, USA/USA/USA (March 84G-Chevrolet), 654.
7 Al Leon/Randy Lanier/Bill Whittington, USA/USA/USA (t/c March 84G-Porsche), 652; **8** John

Jones/Wally Dallenbach Jnr/Doc Bundy, CDN/USA/USA (Ford Mustang), 637 (1st GTO class); **9** Wayne Baker/Jack Newsum/Chip Mead, USA/USA/USA (t/c Porsche 934/935), 624; **10** Kelly Marsh/Ron Pawley/Don Marsh, USA/USA/USA (Argo JM16-Mazda), 602 (1st 700 kg class).
Fastest qualifier: John Paul Jnr, USA (t/c March 84G-Buick), 1m 41·490s, 126·278 mph/203·224 km/h (record).
Fastest lap: Holbert, 1m 48·435s, 118·191 mph/190·210 km/h.
Other class winners. GTU: Amos Johnson/Jack Dunham/Yojiro Terada, USA/USA/J (Mazda RX-7), 599.
Championship points. GTP: 1 Wollek, 20; **2** Holbert, Bell and Unser Jnr, 15; **5** Busby and Knoop, 12. **GTO: 1** Jones, Dallenbach Jnr and Bundy, 20. **GTU: 1** Johnson, Dunham and Terada, 20; **700 kg: 1** Marsh and Marsh, 20; **3** Downing, Maffucci and Katayama, 15.

LOWENBRAU GRAND PRIX OF MIAMI, Miami Street Circuit, Miami, Florida, United States of America, 24 February. IMSA CAMEL GT Championship, round 2. 111 laps of the 1·85-mile/2·98-km circuit, 205·35 miles/330·78 km.
1 Al Holbert/Derek Bell, USA/GB (t/c Porsche 962), 3h 00m 17·060s, 68·342 mph/109·986 km/h (1st GTP class).
2 David Hobbs/Darin Brassfield, GB /USA (March 85G-Chevrolet), 3h 00m 22·230s.
3 Emerson Fittipaldi/Tony Garcia, BR/USA (March 85G-Chevrolet), 111 laps.
4 Hurley Haywood/Chip Robinson, USA/USA (Jaguar XJR-5), 110.
5 John Kalagian/John Lloyd, USA/USA (March 84G-Chevrolet), 108.
6 Jim Busby/Rick Knoop, USA/USA (t/c Porsche 962), 108.
7 Chip Mead/Carson Baird, USA/USA (Lola T710-Chevrolet), 107; **8** Henri Pescarolo/Claude Ballot-Lena, F/F (t/c Porsche 962), 106; **9** Jan Lammers/Roberto Guerrero, NL/COL (t/c March 84G-Buick), 106; **10** David Cowart/Kenper Miller, USA/USA (March 84G-Chevrolet), 104.
Fastest qualifier: John Paul Jnr, USA (t/c March 85G-Buick), 1m 21·154s, 82·066 mph/132·072 km/h (record).
Fastest lap: Hobbs, 1m 23·987s, 79·298 mph/127·617 km/h (record).
Other class winners. 700 kg: Jim Downing/John Maffucci, USA/USA (Argo JM16-Mazda), 99.

COCA-COLA 12 HOURS OF SEBRING CAMEL GT, Sebring International Raceway, Florida, United States of America, 23 March. IMSA CAMEL GT Championship, round 3. 281 laps of the 4·86-mile/7·82-km circuit, 1365·66 miles/2197·42 km.
1 Bob Wollek/A. J. Foyt, F/USA (t/c Porsche 962), 12h 00m 06·858s, 113·787 mph/183·122 km/h (1st GTP class).
2 Al Holbert/Derek Bell/Al Unser Jnr, USA/GB/USA (t/c Porsche 962), 277 laps.
3 Pete Halsmer/Rick Knoop/Dieter Quester, USA/USA/A (t/c Porsche 962), 268.
4 Bob Tullius/Chip Robinson, USA/USA (Jaguar XJR-5), 259.
5 Jim Downing/John Maffucci, USA/USA (Argo JM16-Mazda), 253 (1st 700 kg class).
6 Wally Dallenbach Jnr/John Jones, USA/CDN (Ford Mustang), 251 (1st GTO class).
7 Al Leon/Art Leon/Skeeter McKitterick, USA/USA/USA (t/c March 85G-Porsche), 250; **8** Chuck Kendall/John Hotchkis/Bob Kirby, USA/USA/USA (t/c Porsche 935), 240; **9** Les Delano/Andy Petery/Patty Moise, USA/USA/USA (Pontiac Firebird), 239; **10** Pete Uria/Mike Schaefer/Larry Figaro, USA/USA/USA (Porsche Carrera), 237.
Fastest qualifier: Hans Stuck, D (t/c Porsche 962), 2m 12·975s, 131·574 mph/211·747 km/h (record).
Fastest lap: Holbert, 2m 15·716s, 128·916 mph/207·470 km/h (record).
Other class winners: GTU: Gary Auberlen/Pete Jauker/Adrian Gang, USA/USA/USA (Porsche 911), 209.
Championship points. GTP: 1 Holbert and Bell, 50; **3** Knoop, 30; **4** Wollek, Foyt and Robinson, 20. **GTO: 1** Jones, 55; **2** Dallenbach Jnr, 40; **3** Smith and Petery, 25. **GTU: 1** Dunham, 32; **2** Johnson and Pruett, 30. **700 kg: 1** Downing and Maffucci, 55; **3** Marsh and Marsh, 44.

LOWENBRAU GTO GRAND PRIX OF MIAMI, Miami Street Circuit, Miami, Florida, United States of America, 27 March. 30 laps of the 1·85-mile/2·98-km circuit, 55·50 miles/89·40 km.
1 Willy T. Ribbs, USA (Ford Mustang), 46m 24·310s, 71·759 mph/115·485 km/h (1st GTO class).
2 John Jones, CDN (Ford Mustang), 46m 58·620s.
3 Walt Bohren, USA (Pontiac Firebird), 30 laps.
4 Kikos Fonseca, USA (t/c Porsche 934), 29.
5 Bruce Jenner, USA (Ford Thunderbird), 29.
6 Roger Mandeville, USA (Mazda RX-7), 29.
7 Danny Smith, USA (Mazda RX-7), 29; **8** Billy Scyphers, USA (Chevrolet Corvette), 29; **9** 'Jamsel', ES (t/c Porsche 934), 29; **10** Ken Murrey, USA (Pontiac Firebird), 29.
Fastest qualifier: Ribbs, 1m 27·548s, 76·073 mph/122·427 km/h (record).
Fastest lap: Ribbs, 1m 29·993s, 74·006 mph/119·101 km/h (record).
GTU race winner: Jack Baldwin, USA (Mazda RX-7), 30 laps, 55·50 miles/89·40 km in 46m 18·340s, 71·913 mph/m115·732 km/h.
Championship points. GTP: 1 Holbert and Bell, 35; **3** Wollek, 20; **4** Busby and Knoop, 18; **6** Hobbs, Brassfield and Unser Jnr, 15. **GTO 1:** Jones, 35; **2** Bundy, Ribbs and Dallenbach Jnr, 20; **GTU: 1** Dunham, 32; **2** Johnson and Pruett, 30. **700 kg: 1** Downing and Maffucci, 35; **3** Marsh and Marsh, 20.

ATLANTA JOURNAL/CONSTITUTION GRAND PRIX, Road Atlanta, Georgia, United States of America, 15. April. IMSA CAMEL GT Championship, round 4. 124 laps of the 2·520-mile/4·055-km circuit, 312·48 miles/502·82 km.
1 Brian Redman/Hurley Haywood, GB/USA (Jaguar XJR-5), 2h 52m 10·614s, 108·893 mph/175·246 km/h (1st GTP class).
2 Bob Tullius/Chip Robinson, USA/USA (Jaguar XJR-5), 123 laps.
3 Bruce Levin/David Hobbs, USA/GB (t/c Porsche 962), 122.
4 Pete Halsmer/John Morton, USA/USA (t/c Porsche 962), 122.
5 Al Holbert, USA (t/c Porsche 962), 120.
6 Steve Shelton/Darin Brassfield, USA/USA (March 82G-Chevrolet), 120.
7 Jim Busby/Rick Knoop, USA/USA (t/c Porsche 962), 117; **8** Art Leon/Don Whittington, USA/USA (March 84G-Chevrolet), 116; **9** Al Leon/Skeeter McKitterick, USA/USA (t/c March 85G-Porsche), 116; **10** Richard Anderson/Bard Boand, USA/USA (Lola T600-Chevrolet), 115.
Fastest qualifier: Holbert, 1m 14·518s, 121·742 mph/195·924 km/h (record).
Fastest lap: John Paul Jnr, USA (t/c March 85G-Buick), 1m 17·576s, 116·943 mph/188·201 km/h (record).
Other class winners. GTO: John Jones/Wally Dallenbach Jnr, CDN/USA (Ford Mustang), 114. **GTU:** Jack Baldwin, USA (Mazda RX-7), 109. **700 kg:** Elliott Forbes-Robinson/Tom Winters, USA/USA (Fabcar-Porsche), 105.
Championship points. GTP: 1 Holbert, 58; **2** Bell, 50; **3** Robinson, 35; **4** Knoop, 34; **5** Hobbs, 27; **6** Busby, 22. **GTO: 1** Jones, 75; **2** Dallenbach Jnr, 60; **3** Smith and Petery, 25. **GTU: 1** Dunham, 44; **2** Johnson, 42; **3** Baldwin, 40. **700 kg: 1** Downing and Maffucci, 70; **3** Marsh, 54.

LOS ANGELES TIMES/NISSAN GRAND PRIX OF ENDURANCE, Riverside International Raceway, California, United States of America, 28 April. IMSA CAMEL GT Championship, round 5. 115 laps of the 3·25-mile/5·23-km circuit, 373·75 miles/601·45 km.
1 Pete Halsmer/John Morton, USA/USA (t/c Porsche 962), 3h 27m 25·673s, 108·110 mph/173·986 km/h (1st GTP class).
2 Jim Busby/Rick Knoop, USA/USA (t/c Porsche 962), 3h 27m 25·811s.
3 Bob Tullius/Chip Robinson, USA/USA (Jaguar XJR-5), 110 laps.
4 Bob Akin/Jim Mullen, USA/USA (t/c Porsche 962), 109.
5 Jim Adams/John Hotchkis, USA/USA (t/c March 84G-Porsche), 109.
6 John Jones/Wally Dallenbach Jnr, CDN/USA (Ford Mustang), 108 (1st GTO class).
7 Jim Downing/John Maffucci, USA/USA (Argo JM16-Mazda), 106 (1st 700 kg class); **8** Kelly Marsh/Ron Pawley, USA/USA (Argo JM16-Mazda), 106; **9** Lyn St James/Bruce Jenner, USA/USA (Ford Mustang), 106; **10** Charles Morgan/Bill Alsup, USA/USA (Royale RP39-Buick), 105.
Fastest qualifier: John Paul Jnr, USA (t/c March 85G-Buick), 1m 32·254s, 126·824 mph/204·103 km/h (record).
Fastest lap: Al Holbert, USA (t/c Porsche 962), 1m 36·776s, 120·898 mph/194·566 km/h.
Other class winners: GTU: Jack Baldwin/Jeff Kline, USA/USA (Mazda RX-7), 103.
Championship points. GTP: 1 Holbert, 64; **2** Bell, 50; **3** Knoop, 49; **4** Robinson, 47; **5** Halsmer, 42; **6** Tullius, 37. **GTP: 1** Jones, 95; **2** Dallenbach Jnr, 80; **3** Uria and Figaro, 30. **GTU: 1** Baldwin, 60; **2** Pruett, 50; **3** Dunham. 45. **700 kg: 1** Downing and Maffucci, 90; **3** Marsh, 59.

NISSAN MONTEREY TRIPLE CROWN CAMEL GT, Laguna Seca Raceway, California, United States of America, 5 May. IMSA CAMEL GT Championship, round 6. 98 laps of the 1·900-mile/3·058-km circuit, 186·20 miles/299·68 km.
1 Al Holbert, USA (t/c Porsche 962), 1h 42m 36·800s, 108·875 mph/175·217 km/h (1st GTP class).
2 Bob Tullius/Chip Robinson, USA/USA (Jaguar XJR-5), 1h 43m 01·387s.
3 Brian Redman/Hurley Haywood, GB/USA (Jaguar XJR-5), 98 laps.
4 Pete Halsmer/John Morton, USA/USA (t/c Porsche 962), 96.
5 Jim Busby/Rick Knoop, USA/USA (t/c Porsche 962), 96.
6 John Kalagian, USA (t/c March 84G-Porsche), 93.
7 Ludwig Heimrath Jnr, CDN (Alba AR3-Ford), 93; **8** Bill Alsup, USA (Royale RP39-Buick), 91 (1st 700 kg class); **9** Jim Downing, USA (Argo JM16-Mazda), 91; **10** Kelly Marsh, USA (Argo JM16-Mazda), 91.
Fastest qualifier: Bob Wollek, F (t/c Porsche 962), 58·331s, 117·262 mph/188·714 km/h (record).
Fastest lap: Holbert, 1m 00·065s, 113·877 mph/183·267 km/h (record).

NISSAN MONTEREY TRIPLE CROWN CAMEL GTU/GTO, Laguna Seca Raceway, California, United States of America, 5 May. 33 laps of the 1·900-mile/3·058-km circuit, 62·70 miles/100·91 km.
1 Dennis Aase, USA (Toyota Celica), 42m 25·279s, 88·682 mph/142·719 km/h (1st GTO class).
2 Billy Scyphers, USA (Chevrolet Corvette), 42m 40·355s.
3 Bob Earl, USA (Pontiac Fiero), 33 laps (1st GTU class).
4 Jack Baldwin, USA (Mazda RX-7), 33.
5 Chris Cord, USA (Toyota Celica), 33.
6 Lee Mueller, USA (Merkur), 33.
7 Clay Young, USA (Pontiac Firebird), 33; **8** Scott Pruett, USA (Mazda RX-7), 32; **9** Les Lindley, USA (Chevrolet Camaro), 32; **10** Roger Mandeville, USA (Mazda RX-7), 32.
Fastest lap: Aase, 1m 06·476s, 102·894 mph/165·591 km/h (record).
Championship points. GTP: 1 Holbert, 84; **2** Robinson, 62; **3** Knoop, 57; **4** Tullius and Halsmer, 52; **6** Bell, 50. **GTO: 1** Jones, 101; **2** Dallenbach Jnr, 80; **3** Smith, 33. **GTU: 1** Baldwin, 75; **2** Pruett, 58; **3** Johnson, 50. **700 kg: 1** Downing, 105; **2** Maffucci, 90; **3** Marsh, 71.

CHARLOTTE 500 KM CAMEL GT, Charlotte Motor Speedway, North Carolina, United States of America, 19 May. IMSA CAMEL GT Championship, round 7. 138 laps of the 2·250-mile/3·621-km circuit, 310·50 miles/499·70 km.
1 Al Holbert/Derek Bell, USA/GB (t/c Porsche 962), 2h 54m 36·950s, 106·691 mph/171·702 km/h (1st GTP class).
2 Brian Redman/Hurley Haywood, GB/USA (Jaguar XJR-5), 2h 55m 42·615s.
3 Jim Busby/Rick Knoop, USA/USA (t/c Porsche 962), 136 laps.
4 Bob Tullius/Chip Robinson, USA/USA (Jaguar XJR-5), 135.
5 Jim Downing/John Maffucci, USA/USA (Argo JM16-Mazda), 131 (1st 700 kg class).
6 Charles Morgan/Bill Alsup, USA/USA (Royale RP39-Buick), 130.
7 Kelly Marsh/Ron Pawley, USA/USA (Argo JM16-Mazda), 126; **8** Peter Greenfield/Robert Herlin, USA/USA (Tiga GC84-Mazda), 126; **9** Gene Felton/Tommy Riggins, USA/USA (Pontiac Firebird), 124; **10** Werner Frank/Dave White, USA/USA (t/c Porsche 935), 124.
Fastest qualifier: Holbert, 1m 04·920s, 124·769 mph/200·796 km/h (record).
Fastest lap: Klaus Ludwig, D (t/c Ford Mustang Probe), 1m 08·568s, 118·131 mph/190·113 km/h.

CHARLOTTE 300 KM CAMEL GTU/GTO, Charlotte Motor Speedway, North Carolina, United States of America, 19 May. 83 laps, of the 2·250-mile/3·621-km circuit, 186·75 miles/300·543 km.
1 Danny Smith, USA (Mazda RX-7), 1h 53m 28·183s, 98·749 mph/158·921 km/h (1st GTO class).
2 Bob Earl, USA (Pontiac Fiero), 1h 54m 23·485s (1st GTU class).
3 Amos Johnson, USA (Mazda RX-7), 83 laps.
4 Billy Scyphers, USA (Chevrolet Corvette), 82.
5 Jack Baldwin, USA (Mazda RX-7), 82.
6 Chris Cord, USA (Toyota Celica), 81.
7 Del Taylor/John Hayes-Harlow, USA/USA (Pontiac Firebird), 81; **8** Ken Bupp/Peter Uria, USA/USA (Chevrolet Camaro), 80; **9** Al Bacon, USA (Mazda RX-7), 80; **10** Helmut Silberberger, USA (Mazda RX-7), 79.
Fastest lap: Dennis Aase, USA (Toyota Celica), 1m 12·756s, 111·331 mph/179·169 km/h (record).
Championship points. GTP: 1 Holbert, 104; **2** Robinson, 72; **3** Bell, 70; **4** Knoop, 69; **5** Tullius, 62; **6** Busby and Haywood, 57. **GTO: 1** Jones, 101; **2** Dallenbach Jnr, 80; **3** Smith, 53. **GTU: 1** Baldwin, 87; **2** Johnson, 65; **3** Pruett, 58. **700 kg: 1** Downing, 125; **2** Maffucci, 110; **3** Marsh, 83.

LIME ROCK 2 HOUR CAMEL GT, Lime Rock Park, Connecticut, United States of America, 27 May. IMSA CAMEL GT Championship, round 8. 137 laps of the 1·53-mile/2·46-km circuit, 209·61 miles/337·02 km.
1 Drake Olson, USA (t/c Porsche 962), 2h 00m 42·858s, 104·185 mph/167·669 km/h (1st GTP class).
2 Brian Redman/Hurley Haywood, GB/USA (Jaguar XJR-5), 2h 01m 41·153s.
3 Pete Halsmer/John Morton, USA/USA (t/c Porsche 962), 135 laps.
4 Al Holbert, USA (t/c Porsche 962), 134.
5 Jim Busby/Rick Knoop, USA/USA (t/c Porsche 962), 130.
6 Bob Tullius/Chip Robinson, USA/USA (Jaguar XJR-5), 127.
7 Peter Greenfield/Michael Greenfield, USA/USA (Tiga GC84-Mazda), 127 (1st 700 kg class); **8** Jim Downing/Whitney Ganz, USA/USA (Argo JM16-Mazda), 124; **9** John Jones, CDN (Ford Mustang), 119; **10** Jack Miller, USA (Nimrod-Aston Martin), 112.
Fastest qualifier: Holbert, 47·671s, 114·787
Fastest lap: Redman, 49·310s, 110·971 mph/178·590 km/h (record).

LIME ROCK 2 HOUR CAMEL GTU/GTO, Lime Rock Park, Connecticut, United States of America, 27 May. 121 laps of the 1·53-mile/2·46-km circuit, 185·13 miles/297·66 km.
1 Darin Brassfield, USA (Ford Thunderbird), 2h 00m 02·688s, 92·530 mph/148·912 km/h (1st GTO class).
2 Chris Cord, USA (Toyota Celica), 119 laps (1st GTU class).
3 Roger Mandeville, USA (Mazda RX-7), 118.
4 Jack Baldwin, USA (Mazda RX-7), 118.
5 Danny Smith, USA (Mazda RX-7), 117.
6 John Jones/Wally Dallenbach Jnr, USA/USA (Ford Mustang), 117.
7 Amos Johnson, USA (Mazda RX-7), 116; **8** Andy Petery/Tommy Riggins, USA/USA (Pontiac Firebird), 116; **9** Jerry Kuhn, USA (Chevrolet Camaro), 114; **10** Al Bacon, USA (Mazda RX-7), 114.
Fastest lap: Brassfield, 53·850s, 101·616 mph/163·535 km/h (record).
Championship points. GTP: 1 Holbert, 114; **2** Robinson, 78; **3** Knoop, 77; **4** Haywood, 72; **5** Bell, 70; **6** Tullius, 68. **GTO: 1** Jones, 111; **2** Dallenbach Jnr, 90; **3** Smith, 65. **GTU: 1** Baldwin, 102; **2** Johnson, 77; **3** Pruett, 58. **700 kg: 1** Downing, 140; **2** Maffucci, 110; **3** Marsh, 83.

LUMBERMANS 500 NORTH AMERICAN SPORTS CAR CHAMPIONSHIP, Mid-Ohio Sports Car Course, Lexington, Ohio, United States of America, 9 June. IMSA CAMEL GT Championship, round 9. 129 laps of the 2·400-mile/3·862-km circuit, 309·60 miles/498·20 km.
1 Al Holbert/Derek Bell, USA/GB (t/c Porsche 962), 3h 09m 35·406s, 97·980 mph/157·683 km/h (1st GTP class).
2 Bob Wollek/David Hobbs, F/GB (t/c Porsche 962), 3h 10m 24·787s.
3 Hurley Haywood/Chip Robinson, USA/USA (Jaguar XJR-5), 128 laps.
4 Robert Dyson/Drake Olson, USA/USA (t/c Porsche 962), 125.
5 Pete Halsmer/John Morton/Rick Knoop, USA/USA/USA (t/c Porsche 962), 124.
6 Al Leon/Art Leon, USA/USA (March 84G-Chevrolet), 120.
7 Jeff Kline/Jack Baldwin, USA/USA (Alba AR4-Mazda), 119 (1st 700 kg class); **8** John Kalagian/Tommy Grunnah, USA/USA (t/c March 84G-Porsche), 119; **9** Jim Downing/John Maffucci, USA/USA (Argo JM16-Mazda), 119; **10** Charles Morgan/Bill Alsup, USA/USA (Royale RP39-Buick), 116.
Fastest qualifier: Hobbs, 1m 21·335s, 106·227 mph/170·955 km/h (record).
Fastest lap: Holbert, 1m 24·390s, 102·382 mph/164·767 km/h (record).

MID-OHIO 300 KM CAMEL GTU/GTO, Mid-Ohio Sports Car Course, Lexington, Ohio, United States of America, 9 June. 78 laps of the 2·400-mile/3·862-km circuit, 187·20 miles/301·24 km.
1 John Jones/Wally Dallenbach Jnr, CDN/USA (Ford Mustang), 2h 05m 47·323s, 89·293 mph/143·703 km/h (1st GTO class).
2 Roger Mandeville, USA (Mazda RX-7), 77 laps.
3 Lyn St James/Bruce Jenner, USA/USA (Ford Mustang), 76.
4 Clay Young, USA (Pontiac Fiero), 76 (1st GTU Class).
5 Jack Baldwin, USA (Mazda RX-7), 75.
6 Danny Smith, USA (Mazda RX-7), 75.
7 Chris Cord, USA (Toyota Celica), 75; **8** Bob Bergstrom, USA (Porsche 924 Carrera), 75; **9** Amos Johnson, USA (Mazda RX-7), 74; **10** Dave Heinz/Jerry Thompson, USA/USA (Chevrolet Corvette), 74.
Fastest lap: Darin Brassfield, USA (Ford Thunderbird), 1m 32·006s, 93·907 mph/151·128 km/h (record).
Championship points. GTP: 1 Holbert, 134; **2** Robinson and Bell, 90; **4** Knoop, 85; **5** Haywood, 84; **6** Halsmer, 72. **GTO: 1** Jones, 131; **2** Dallenbach Jnr, 110; **3** Smith, 75. **GTU: 1** Baldwin, 117; **2** Johnson, 85; **3** Cord, 66. **700 kg: 1** Downing, 155; **2** Maffucci, 125; **3** Marsh, 93.

WATKINS GLEN 3 HOUR CAMEL GTO/GTU RACE, Watkins Glen Grand Prix Circuit, New York, United States of America, 6 July. 86 laps of the 3·377-mile/5·435-km circuit, 290·42 miles/467·41 km.
1 Darin Brassfield/Klaus Ludwig, USA/D (Ford Thunderbird), 3h 01m 23·140s, 96·068 mph/154·606 km/h (1st GTO class).
2 John Jones/Doc Bundy, CDN/USA (Ford Mustang), 3h 01m 25·110s.
3 Tommy Riggins, USA (Pontiac Firebird), 86 laps.
4 Lyn St James/Bill Elliott, USA/USA (Ford Mustang), 85.
5 Billy Scyphers/Allan Glick, USA/USA (Chevrolet Corvette), 83.
6 Bob Earl, USA (Pontiac Fiero), 83 (1st GTU class).
7 Chris Cord, USA (Toyota Celica), 83; **8** Ken Bupp/Guy Church, USA/USA (Chevrolet Camaro), 82; **9** Jack Baldwin, USA (Mazda RX-7), 81; **10** Al Bacon/Scott Pruett, USA/USA (Mazda RX-7), 81.
Fastest lap: Elliott, 1m 53·480s, 107·131 mph/172·410 km/h (record).
Championship points. GTP: 1 Holbert, 154; **2** Bell, 110; **3** Haywood, 94; **4** Robinson, 91; **5** Knoop, 88; **6** Halsmer, 78. **GTO: 1** Jones, 146; **2** Dallenbach Jnr, 110; **3** Smith, 81. **GTU: 1** Baldwin, 129; **2** Johnson, 88; **3** Cord, 81 **700 kg: 1** Downing, 167; **2** Maffucci, 137; **3** Marsh, 103.

WATKINS GLEN 3 HOUR CAMEL CONTINENTAL, Watkins Glen Grand Prix Circuit, New York, United States of America, 7 July. IMSA CAMEL GT Championship, round 10. 101 laps of the 3·377-mile/5·435-km circuit, 341·08 miles/548·94 km.
1 Al Holbert/Derek Bell, USA/GB (t/c Porsche 962), 3h 00m 29·450s, 113·383 mph/182·472 km/h (1st GTP class).
2 Klaus Ludwig/Doc Bundy, D/USA (t/c Ford Mustang Probe), 3h 01m 08·163s.
3 Robert Dyson/Drake Olson, USA/USA (t/c Porsche 926), 100 laps.
4 Brian Redman/Hurley Haywood, GB/USA (Jaguar XJR-5), 97.
5 Bruce Leven/Bob Wollek, USA/F (t/c Porsche 962), 97.
6 Pete Halsmer/John Morton, USA/USA (t/c Porsche 962), 97.
7 John Kalagian/Tommy Grunnah, USA/USA (t/c March 85G-Porsche), 96; **8** Jim Busby/Rick Knoop, USA/USA (t/c Porsche 962), 93; **9** Charles Morgan/Bill Alsup, USA/USA (Royale RP39-Buick), 92 (1st 700 kg class); **10** Keff Kline/Jack Baldwin, USA/USA (Alba AR4-Mazda), 91.
Fastest qualifier: Holbert, 1m 38·044s, 123·977 mph/199·521 km/h (record).
Fastest lap: Olson, 1m 40·930s, 120·452 mph/193·848 km/h (record).

G.I. JOE'S GRAN PRIX, Portland International Raceway, Portland, Oregon, United States of America, 28 July. IMSA CAMEL GT Championship, round 11. 97 laps of the 1·915-mile/3·082-km circuit, 185·76 miles/298·95 km.
1 Al Holbert, USA (t/c Porsche 962), 1h 45m 56·621s, 105·200 mph/169·303 km/h (1st GTP class).
2 Bob Tullius/Chip Robinson, USA/USA (Jaguar XJR-5), 1h 46m 07·486s.
3 Drake Olson, USA (t/c Porsche 962), 97 laps.
4 Brian Redman/Hurley Haywood, GB/USA (Jaguar XJR-5), 97.
5 Klaus Ludwig/Doc Bundy, D/USA (t/c Ford Mustang Probe), 95.
6 Pete Halsmer/John Morton, USA/USA (t/c Porsche 962), 95.
7 John Kalagian/Whitney Ganz, USA/USA (t/c March 85G-Porsche), 90; **8** Jim Downing, USA (Argo JM16-Mazda), 89 (1st 700 kg class); **9** Kelly Marsh, USA (Argo JM19-Mazda), 89; **10** Jeff Kline, USA (Alba AR4-Mazda), 88.
Fastest qualifier: Holbert, 1m 00·247s, 114·429 mph/184·155 km/h (record).
Fastest lap: Holbert, 1m 02·440s, 110·410 mph/177·687 km/h (record).

PORTLAND CAMEL GTO/GTU, Portland International Raceway, Portland, Oregon, United States of America, 28 July. 65 laps of the 1·915-mile/3·082-km circuit, 124·48 miles/ 200·33 km.
1 Darin Brassfield, USA (Ford Thunderbird), 1h 17m 18·208s, 96·613 mph/155·483 km/h (1st GTO class).
2 John Jones/Wally Dallenbach Jnr, CDN/USA (Ford Mustang), 1h 17m 27·728s.
3 Dennis Aase, USA (t/c Toyota Celica Turbo), 65.
4 Craig Carter, USA (Chevrolet Camaro), 65.
5 Steve Millen, NZ (Pontiac Firebird), 64.
6 Bill Doyle, USA (Pontiac Firebird), 63.
7 Bob Earl, USA (Pontiac Fiero), 62 (1st GTU class); **8** Danny Smith, USA (Mazda RX-7), 62; **9** Terry Visger, USA (Pontiac Fiero), 62; **10** Monte Sheldon, USA (Porsche Carrera), 62.
Fastest lap: Jones, 1m 08·280s, 100·967 mph/ 162·490 km/h (record).
Championship points. GTP: 1 Holbert, 174; **2** Bell, 110; **3** Robinson, 106; **4** Haywood, 104; **5** Knoop, 88; **6** Halsmer and Tullius, 84. **GTO: 1** Jones, 161; **2** Dallenbach Jnr, 110; **3** Smith, 85. **GTU: 1** Baldwin, 139; **2** Johnson, 96; **3** Cord, 93. **700 kg: 1** Downing, 181; **2** Maffucci, 137; **3** Marsh, 110.

FORD CALIFORNIA CAMEL GT, Sears Point International Raceway, Sonoma, California, United States of America, 4 August. IMSA CAMEL GT Championship, round 12. 75 laps of the 2·523-mile/4·060-km circuit, 189·23 miles/ 304·50 km.
1 Bob Wollek, F (t/c Porsche 962), 1h 55m 48·549s, 98·036 mph/157·77 km/h (1st GTP class).
2 Klaus Ludwig/Doc Bundy, D/USA (t/c Ford Mustang Probe), 1h 56m 19·530s.
3 Robert Dyson/Drake Olson, USA/USA (t/c Porsche 962), 75 laps.
4 Pete Halsmer/John Morton, USA/USA (t/c Porsche 962), 74.
5 Bob Akin/Jim Mullen, USA/USA (t/c Porsche 962), 73.
6 Gianpiero Moretti/Steve Millen, I/NZ (Alba AR3-Cosworth DFL), 73.
7 Al Holbert/Derek Bell, USA/GB (t/c Porsche 962), 72; **8** Jim Busby/Rick Knoop, USA/USA (t/c Porsche 962), 72; **9** Don Devendorf/Tony Adamowicz, USA/USA (t/c Lola T810-Nissan), 72; **10** Jeff Kline, USA (Alba AR4-Mazda), 71 (1st 700 kg class).
Fastest qualifier: Wollek, 1m 25·212s, 106·591 mph/171·541 km/h (record).
Fastest lap: Ludwig, 1m 28·090s, 103·108 mph/ 165·936 km/h (record).

SEARS POINT 100 KM CAMEL GTO/GTU, Sears Point International Raceway, Sonoma, California, United States of America, 4 August. 25 laps of the 2·523-mile/4·060-km circuit, 63·08 miles/ 101·50 km.
1 Darin Brassfield, USA (Ford Thunderbird), 41m 28·899s, 91·233 mph/146·825 km/h (1st GTO class).
2 John Jones, CDN (Ford Mustang), 41m 48·193s.
3 Craig Carter, USA (Chevrolet Camaro), 25 laps.
4 Bruce Jenner, USA (Ford Mustang), 25.
5 Lyn St James, USA (Ford Mustang), 25.
6 Dennis Aase, USA (t/c Toyota Celica Turbo), 25.
7 Tommy Riggins, USA (Pontiac Firebird), 25; **8** Bob Earl, USA (Pontiac Fiero), 25 (1st GTU class); **9** Chris Cord, USA (Toyota Celica), 24; **10** Roger Mandeville, USA (Mazda RX-7), 24.
Fastest lap: Jones, 1m 37·310s, 93·339 mph/ 150·214 km/h (record).
Championship points. GTP: 1 Holbert, 178; **2** Bell, 114; **3** Robinson, 106; **4** Haywood, 104; **5** Halsmer, 94; **6** Knoop, 91. **GTO: 1** Jones, 176; **2** Dallenbach, Jnr, 110; **3** Smith, 85. **GTU: 1** Baldwin, 151; **2** Cord and Earl, 108. **700 kg: 1** Downing, 187; **2** Maffucci, 137; **3** Marsh, 118.

ROAD AMERICA LOWENBRAU CLASSIC, Road America, Elkhart Lake Wisconsin, United States of America, 25 August. IMSA CAMEL GT Championship, round 13. 125 laps of the 4·000-mile/6·437-km circuit, 500·00 miles/ 804·63 km.
1 Drake Olson/Bobby Rahal, USA/USA (t/c Porsche 962), 4h 52m 04·919s, 102·711 mph/165·297 km/h (1st GTP class).
2 Bruce Leven/Bob Wollek, USA/F (t/c Porsche 962), 124 laps.
3 Jim Busby/Jochen Mass, USA/D (t/c Porsche 962), 121.
4 Pete Halsmer/John Morton, USA/USA (t/c Porsche 962), 121.
5 John Kalagian/Steve Shelton, USA/USA (t/c March 85G-Porsche), 119.
6 Al Leon/Randy Lanier, USA/USA (t/c March 84G-Porsche), 119.
7 Jim Trueman/Ludwig Heimrath Jnr, USA/CDN (Alba AR3-Cosworth DFV), 115; **8** Brian Redman/ Hurley Haywood, GB/USA (Jaguar XJR-5), 114; **9** Kelly Marsh/Ron Pawley/Don Marsh, USA/USA/ USA (Argo JM19-Mazda), 112 (1st 700 kg class); **10** Jim Downing/John Maffucci, USA/USA (Argo JM16-Mazda), 112.
Other class winners: GTO: John Jones/Lyn St James, CDN/USA (Ford Mustang), 112. **GTU:** Jack Baldwin/Jeff Kline, USA/USA (Mazda RX-7), 108.
Fastest qualifier: Klaus Ludwig, D (t/c Ford Mustang Probe), 1m 59·881s, 120·119 mph/ 193·312 km/h (record).
Fastest lap: Derek Bell, GB (t/c Porsche 962), 2m 02·660s, 117·398 mph/188·933 km/h (record).
Championship points. GTP: 1 Holbert, 178; **2** Bell, 114; **3** Haywood, 107; **4** Robinson, 106; **5** Halsmer, 104; **6** Knoop, 91. **GTO: 1** Jones, 196; **2** Dallenbach Jnr, 110; **3** Smith, 85. **GTU: 1** Baldwin, 171; **2** Cord, 123; **3** Earl and Johnson, 108. **700 kg: 1** Downing, 202; **2** Maffucci, 152; **3** Marsh, 138.

POCONO CAMEL GT 500, Pocono International Raceway, Pennsylvania, United States of America, 8 September. IMSA CAMEL GT Championship, round 14. 124 laps of the 2·500-mile/ 4·023-km circuit, 310·00 miles/498·85 km.
1 Al Holbert/Derek Bell, USA/GB (t/c Porsche 962), 2h 49m 16·706s, 109·878 mph/176·831 km/h (1st GTP class).
2 Chip Robinson/Hurley Haywood, USA/USA (Jaguar XJR-6), 2h 49m 20·822s.
3 Bob Wollek/Mauro Baldi, F/I (t/c Porsche 962), 122 laps.
4 John Morton/Pete Halsmer, USA/USA (t/c Porsche 962), 122.
5 Whitney Ganz/Bill Adam, USA/USA (March 85G-Buick), 121.
6 Steve Millen/Ludwig Heimrath Jnr, NZ/CDN (Alba AR3-Cosworth DFV), 119.
7 Darin Brassfield/Scott Pruett, USA/USA (Ford Thunderbird), 114 (1st GTO class); **8** Craig Carter/ Billy Scyphers, USA/USA (Chevrolet Camaro), 112; **9** Scott Schubot/Dennis Vitolo, USA/USA (Tiga-Mazda), 110 (1st 700 kg class); **10** Pierre Honegger/David Loring, USA/USA (Mazda GTP), 110.
GTU class winner: Chris Cord/Dennis Aase, USA/USA (Toyota Celica), 107.
Fastest qualifier: Halsmer, 1m 12·055s, 124·905 mph/201·015 km/h (record).
Fastest lap: Holbert, 1m 15·440s, 119·300 mph/ 191·994 km/h (record).
Championship points. GTP: 1 Holbert, 198; **2** Bell, 134; **3** Haywood, 122; **4** Robinson, 121; **5** Halsmer, 114; **6** Knoop, 91. **GTO: 1** Jones, 196; **2** Dallenbach Jnr, 110; **3** Brassfield, 100. **GTU: 1** Baldwin, 186; **2** Cord, 143; **3** Johnson, 120. **700 kg: 1** Downing, 205; **2** Maffucci, 152; **3** Marsh, 150.

SERENGETI DRIVERS NEW YORK 500 KM CAMEL GT, Watkins Glen Grand Prix Circuit, New York, United States of America, 29 September. IMSA CAMEL GT Championship, round 15. 92 laps of the 3·377-mile/5·435-km circuit, 310·68 miles/500·02 km.
1 Al Holbert/Derek Bell, USA/GB (t/c Porsche 962), 2h 48m 19·917s, 110·740 mph/178·218 km/h (1st GTP class).
2 Jochen Mass/Jim Busby, D/USA (t/c Porsche 962), 2h 49m 35·309s.
3 Brian Redman/Hurley Haywood, GB/USA (Jaguar XJR-5), 92 laps.
4 Klaus Ludwig/Doc Bundy, D/USA (t/c Ford Mustang Probe), 91.
5 Al Unser Jnr, USA (t/c Porsche 962), 91.
6 Bob Tullius/Chip Robinson, USA/USA (Jaguar XJR-5), 90.
7 Robert Dyson/Drake Olson/Price Cobb, USA/ USA/USA (t/c Porsche 962), 89; **8** Lew Price/ Carson Baird, USA/USA (t/c Lola T710-Chevrolet), 84; **9** Lyn St James/Whitney Ganz, USA/USA (Ford Mustang), 84 (1st GTO class); **10** Jim Downing/ John Maffucci, USA/USA (Argo JM16-Mazda), 83 (1st 700 kg class).
GTU class winner: Jack Baldwin, USA (Mazda RX-7), 79.
Fastest qualifier: Hans Stuck, D (t/c Porsche 962), 1m 37·738s, 124·386 mph/200·179 km/h (record).
Fastest lap: Ludwig, 1m 40·260s, 121·257 mph/ 195·144 km/h (record).
Championship points. GTP: 1 Holbert, 218; **2** Bell, 154; **3** Haywood, 134; **4** Robinson, 127; **5** Halsmer, 114; **6** Busby, 98. **GTO: 1** Jones, 196; **2** Dallenbach Jnr, 110; **3** Brassfield, 100. **GTU: 1** Baldwin, 206; **2** Cord, 143; **3** Johnson, 132. **700 kg: 1** Downing, 225; **3** Maffucci, 172; **3** Marsh, 165.

COLUMBUS CAMEL GTO/GTU 1 HOUR, Ohio Street Circuit, Columbus, Ohio, United States of America, 5 October. 36 laps of the 2·30-mile/ 3·70-km circuit, 82·80 miles/133·20 km.
1 Steve Millen, NZ (Pontiac Firebird), 1h 01m 11·672s, 81·184 mph/130·653 km/h (1st GTO class).
2 Lyn St James, USA (Ford Mustang), 1h 01m 57·690s.
3 Bruce Jenner, USA (Ford Mustang), 36 laps.
4 Chester Vincentz, USA (t/c Porsche 934), 36.
5 Ken Murrey, USA (Chevrolet Camaro), 36.
6 Roger Mandeville, USA (Mazda RX-7), 35.
7 Bob Earl, USA (Pontiac Fiero), 35 (1st GTU class); **8** Jack Baldwin, USA (Mazda RX-7), 35; **9** Danny Smith, USA (Mazda RX-7), 35; **10** Chris Cord, USA (Toyota Celica), 34.
Fastest lap: Darin Brassfield, USA (Ford Thunderbird), 1m 40·970s, 82·005 mph/131·974 km/h (record).

COLUMBUS FORD DEALERS 500, Ohio Street Circuit, Columbus, Ohio, United States of America, 6 October. IMSA CAMEL GT Championship, round 16. 136 laps of the 2·30-mile/ 3·70-km circuit, 312·80 miles/503·40 km.
1 Drake Olson/Price Cobb, USA/USA (t/c Porsche 962), 3h 46m 08·611s, 82·992 mph/133·562 km/h (1st GTP class).
2 Bob Wollek/Mauro Baldi, F/I (t/c Porsche 962), 3h 46m 23·985s.
3 Pete Halsmer/John Morton, USA/USA (t/c Porsche 962), 136 laps.
4 Jim Trueman/Ludwig Heimrath Jnr, USA/CDN (Alba AR3-Cosworth DFV), 132.
5 Bob Akin/Dennis Aase, USA/USA (t/c Porsche 962), 123.
6 Jim Downing/John Maffucci, USA/USA (Argo JM16-Mazda), 123 (1st 700 kg class).
7 Bill Alsup/Charles Morgan Jnr, USA/USA (Royale RP39-Buick), 123; **8** Don Bell/Mike Brockman, USA/USA (Argo JM 16-Buick), 115; **9** Ken Knott/Mike Carder, USA/USA (Argo JM16-Cosworth DFV), 115; **10** Gianpiero Moretti/Steve Millen, I/NZ (Momo AR3-Cosworth DFV), 107.
Fastest qualifier: Klaus Ludwig, D (t/c Ford Mustang Probe), 1m 30·994s, 90·995 mph/ 146·442 km/h (record).
Fastest lap: Olson, 1m 32·520s, 89·494 mph/ 144·026 km/h (record).

Championship points (prior to final round in December)
GTP

1 Al Holbert, USA	218
2 Derek Bell, GB	154
3 Hurley Haywood, USA	131
4 Chip Robinson, USA	127
5 Pete Halsmer, USA	120
6 Drake Olson, USA	[illegible]

7 Bob Wollek, F, 105; **8** Jim Busby, USA, 98; **9** Brian Redman, GB, 97; **10** John Morton, USA, 96. **GTO: 1** John Jones, CDN, 196; **2** Wally Dallenbach Jnr, USA, 110; **3** Lyn St James, USA, 104; **4** Darin Brassfield, USA, 100; **5** Danny Smith, USA, 99; **6** Roger Mandeville, USA, 69. **GTU: 1** Jack Baldwin, USA, 221; **2** Chris Cord, USA, 155; **3** Amos Johnson, 136; **4** Bob Earl, USA, 130; **5** Scott Pruett, USA and Al Bacon, USA, 72. **700 kg: 1** Jim Downing, USA, 245; **2** John Maffucci, USA, 192; **3** Kelly Marsh, USA, 165; **4** Jeff Kline, USA, 107; **5** Bill Alsup, USA, 94; **6** Don Marsh, USA, 81.
Note: Final results will be given in *Autocourse 1986/87*.

NASCAR Winston Cup Grand National

1984 Results

The final rounds of the 1984 NASCAR Winston Cup Grand National were run after *Autocourse 1984/85* went to press.

ATLANTA JOURNAL 500, Atlanta International Raceway, Georgia, United States of America, 11 November. NASCAR Winston Cup Grand National, round 29. 328 laps of the 1·522-mile/ 2·449-km circuit, 499·22 miles/803·41 km.
1 Dale Earnhardt, USA (Chevrolet), 3h 42m 31s, 134·610 mph/216·633 km/h.
2 Bill Elliott, USA (Ford), 3h 42m 31·56s.
3 Ricky Rudd, USA (Ford), 328 laps.
4 Benny Parsons, USA (Chevrolet), 328.
5 Bobby Allison, USA (Buick), 327.
6 Darrell Waltrip, USA (Chevrolet), 327.
7 Lake Speed, USA (Chevrolet), 327; **8** Richard Petty, USA (Pontiac), 327; **9** Sterling Marlin, USA (Chevrolet), 326; **10** Dave Marcis, USA (Pontiac), 325.
Fastest qualifier: Elliott, 32·193s, 170·198 mph/ 273·906 km/h (record).
Championship points. Drivers: 1 Labonte, 4338; **2** Gant, 4296; **3** Elliott, 4217; **4** Waltrip, 4164; **5** Earnhardt, 4135; **6** Allison, 3938.
Manufacturers: 1 Chevrolet, 232; **2** Ford, 104; **3** Buick, 63; **4** Pontiac, 58.

WINSTON WESTERN 500, Riverside International Raceway, California, United States of America, 18 November. NASCAR Winston Cup Grand National, round 30. 119 laps of the 2·620-mile/4·216-km circuit, 311·78 miles/ 501·76 km.
1 Geoff Bodine, USA (Chevrolet), 3h 10m 01·02s, 98·448 mph/158·436 km/h.
2 Tim Richmond, USA (Pontiac), 119 laps.
3 Terry Labonte, USA (Chevrolet), 119.
4 Bill Elliott, USA (Ford), 119.
5 Benny Parsons, USA (Chevrolet), 119.
6 Neil Bonnett, USA (Chevrolet), 119.
7 Bobby Allison, USA (Buick), 119; **8** Harry Gant, USA (Chevrolet), 119; **9** Herschel McGriff, USA (Pontiac), 119; **10** Joe Ruttman, USA (Chevrolet), 119.
Fastest qualifier: Labonte, 1m 20·813s, 116·714 mph/187·833 km/h.

Final Championship points
Drivers

1 Terry Labonte, USA	4508
2 Harry Gant, USA	4443
3 Bill Elliott, USA	4377
4 Dale Earnhardt, USA	4265
5 Darrell Waltrip, USA	4230
6 Bobby Allison, USA	4094

7 Ricky Rudd, USA, 3918; **8** Neil Bonnett, USA, 3802; **9** Geoff Bodine, USA, 3734; **10** Richard Petty, USA, 3643; **11** Ron Bouchard, USA, 3609; **12** Tim Richmond, USA, 3505; **13** Dave Marcis, USA, 3416; **14** Rusty Wallace, USA, 3316; **15** Dick Brooks, USA, 3265; **16** Kyle Petty, USA, 3159; **17** Trevor Boys, CDN, 3040; **18** Joe Ruttman, USA, 2945; **19** Greg Sacks, USA, 2545; **20** Buddy Arrington, USA, 2504.
Manufacturers

1 Chevrolet	241
2 Ford	107
3 Pontiac	64
4 Buick	63

1985 results

DAYTONA 500, Daytona International Speedway, Florida, United States of America, 17 February. NASCAR Winston Cup Grand National, round 1. 200 laps of the 2·500-mile/ 4·023-km circuit, 500·00 miles/804·67 km.
1 Bill Elliott, USA (Ford), 2h 54m 09s, 172·265 mph/277·233 km/h.
2 Lake Speed, USA (Pontiac), 2h 54m 10s.
3 Darrell Waltrip, USA (Chevrolet), 199 laps.
4 Buddy Baker, USA (Oldsmobile), 199.
5 Ricky Rudd, USA (Ford), 199.
6 Greg Sacks, USA (Chevrolet), 199.
7 Geoff Bodine, USA (Chevrolet), 198; **8** Rusty Wallace, USA (Pontiac), 197; **9** Bobby Hillin Jnr, USA (Chevrolet), 197; **10** Neil Bonnett, USA (Chevrolet), 195.
Fastest qualifier: Elliott, 43·878s, 205·114 mph/ 330·098 km/h (record).
Championship points. Drivers: 1 Elliott, 185; **2** Speed, 170; **3** Waltrip, 165; **4** Baker, 160; **5** Rudd and Sacks, 155.
Manufacturers: 1 Ford, 9; **2** Pontiac, 6; **3** Chevrolet, [illegible]; **4** Oldsmobile, [illegible].

MILLER HIGH LIFE 400, Richmond Fairgrounds Raceway, Virginia, United States of America, 24 February. NASCAR Winston Cup Grand National, round 2. 400 laps of the 0·542-mile/ 0·872-km circuit, 216·80 miles/348·80 km.
1 Dale Earnhardt, USA (Chevrolet), 3h 11m 27s, 67·945 mph/109·347 km/h.
2 Geoff Bodine, USA (Chevrolet), 3h 11m 27·3s.
3 Darrell Waltrip, USA (Chevrolet), 400 laps.
4 Ron Bouchard, USA (Buick), 400.
5 Harry Gant, USA (Chevrolet), 399.
6 Terry Labonte, USA (Chevrolet), 399.
7 Kyle Petty, USA (Ford), 399; **8** Dave Marcis, USA (Oldsmobile), 399; **9** Tim Richmond, USA (Pontiac), 399; **10** Lake Speed, USA (Pontiac), 398.
Fastest qualifier: Waltrip, 20·492s, 95·218 mph/ 153·238 km/h (record).
Championship points. Drivers: 1 Waltrip, 340; **2** Bodine, 316; **3** Speed, 309; **4** Elliott, 282; **5** Hillin Jnr, 268; **6** Schrader, 251.
Manufacturers: 1 Chevrolet, 13; **2** Ford, 9; **3** Pontiac, 6; **4** Oldsmobile and Buick, 3.

CAROLINA 500, North Carolina Motor Speedway, North Carolina, United States of America, 3 March. NASCAR Winston Cup Grand National, round 3. 492 laps of the 1·017-mile/ 1·637-km circuit, 500·36 miles/805·26 km.
1 Neil Bonnett, USA (Chevrolet), 4h 21m 10s, 114·953 mph/184·998 km/h.
2 Harry Gant, USA (Chevrolet), 4h 21m 10s (Bonnett won by 8 inches).
3 Terry Labonte, USA (Chevrolet), 492 laps.
4 Lake Speed, USA (Pontiac), 492.
5 Kyle Petty, USA (Ford), 491.
6 Joe Ruttmann, USA (Chevrolet), 491.
7 Cale Yarborough, USA (Ford), 491; **8** Richard Petty, USA (Pontiac), 491; **9** Rusty Wallace, USA (Pontiac), 491; **10** Dale Earnhardt, USA (Chevrolet), 491.
Fastest qualifier: Labonte, 25·238s, 145·067 mph/233·462 km/h (record).
Championship points. Drivers: 1 Speed, 469; **2** Waltrip, 454; **3** Bodine, 443; **4** Gant, 425; **5** Bonnett, 418; **6** Labonte, 418.
Manufacturers: 1 Chevrolet, 22; **2** Ford, 11; **3** Pontiac, 9; **4** Oldsmobile and Buick, 3.

COCA-COLA 500, Atlanta International Raceway, Georgia, United States of America, 17 March. NASCAR Winston Cup Grand National, round 4. 328 laps of the 1·522-mile/2·449-km circuit, 499·22 miles/803·27 km.
1 Bill Elliott, USA (Ford), 3h 33m 32s, 140·273 mph/225·747 km/h.
2 Geoff Bodine, USA (Chevrolet), 3h 33m 34·64s.
3 Neil Bonnett, USA (Chevrolet), 328 laps.
4 Ricky Rudd, USA (Ford), 327.
5 Bobby Allison, USA (Buick), 327.
6 Terry Labonte, USA (Chevrolet), 327.
7 Ron Bouchard, USA (Buick), 327; **8** Benny Parsons, USA (Chevrolet), 327; **9** Dale Earnhardt, USA (Chevrolet), 326; **10** Greg Sacks, USA (Chevrolet), 325.
Fastest qualifier: Bonnett, 32·178s, 170·278 mph/274·035 km/h.
Championship points. Drivers: 1 Bodine, 618; **2** Bonnett, 588; **3** Labonte, 573; **4** Waltrip, 566; **5** Elliott, 543; **6** Earnhardt, 524.
Manufacturers: 1 Chevrolet, 28; **2** Ford, 20; **3** Pontiac, 9; **4** Buick, 5; **5** Oldsmobile, 3.

VALLEYDALE 500, Bristol International Raceway, Tennessee, United States of America, 6 April. NASCAR Winston Cup Grand National, round 5. 500 laps of the 0·533-mile/0·858-km circuit, 266·50 miles/428·89 km.
1 Dale Earnhardt, USA (Chevrolet), 3h 15m 42s, 81·790 mph/131·628 km/h.
2 Ricky Rudd, USA (Ford), 3h 15m 43s.
3 Terry Labonte, USA (Chevrolet), 498 laps.
4 Buddy Baker, USA (Oldsmobile), 498.
5 Rusty Wallace, USA (Pontiac), 497.
6 Kyle Petty, USA (Ford), 495.
7 Lake Speed, USA (Pontiac), 495; **8** Richard Petty, USA (Pontiac), 495; **9** Bobby Hillin Jnr, USA (Chevrolet), 495; **10** Ken Schrader, USA (Ford), 495.
Fastest qualifier: Harry Gant, USA (Chevrolet), 17·014s, 112·778 mph/181·498 km/h (record).
Championship points. Drivers: 1 Labonte, 738; **2** Bodine, 732; **3** Earnhardt, 709; **4** Bonnett, 694; **5** Elliott, 673; **6** Waltrip, 663
Manufacturers: 1 Chevrolet, 37; **2** Ford, 26; **3** Pontiac, 11; **4** Oldsmobile, 6; **5** Buick, 5.

TRANSOUTH 500, Darlington International Raceway, South Carolina, United States of America, 14 April. NASCAR Winston Cup Grand National, round 6. 367 laps of the 1·366-mile/ 2·198-km circuit, 501·32 miles/806·67 km.
1 Bill Elliott, USA (Ford), 3h 58m 08s, 126·295 mph/203·252 km/h.
2 Darrell Waltrip, USA (Chevrolet), 3h 58m 10·5s.
3 Tim Richmond, USA (Pontiac), 367 laps.
4 Terry Labonte, USA (Chevrolet), 366.
5 Rusty Wallace, USA (Pontiac), 365.
6 Neil Bonnett, USA (Chevrolet), 365.
7 Geoff Bodine, USA (Chevrolet), 365; **8** Phil Parsons, USA (Chevrolet), 364; **9** Lake Speed, USA (Pontiac), 364; **10** Bobby Allison, USA (Buick), 364.
Fastest qualifier: Elliott, 31·232s, 157·454 mph/ 253·397 km/h.
Championship points. Drivers: 1 Labonte, 903; **2** Bodine, 883; **3** Elliott, 858; **4** Bonnett, 849; **5** Waltrip, 838; **6** Earnhardt, 805.
Manufacturers: 1 Chevrolet, 43; **2** Ford, 35; **3** Pontiac, 15; **4** Oldsmobile, 6; **5** Buick, 5.

NORTHWESTERN BANK 400, North Wilksboro Speedway, North Carolina, United States of America, 21 April. NASCAR Winston Cup Grand National, round 7. 400 laps of the 0·625-mile/1·006-km circuit, 250·00 miles/402·34 km.
1 Neil Bonnett, USA (Chevrolet), 2h 39m 53s, 93·818 mph/150·985 km/h.
2 Darrell Waltrip, USA (Chevrolet), 2h 39m 53s (1 car length).
3 Bobby Allison, USA (Buick), 400 laps.
4 Ricky Rudd, USA (Ford), 400.
5 Geoff Bodine, USA (Chevrolet), 400.
6 Bill Elliott, USA (Ford), 399.
7 Terry Labonte, USA (Chevrolet), 399; **8** Dale Earnhardt, USA (Chevrolet), 398; **9** Lake Speed, USA (Pontiac), 398; **10** Harry Gant, USA (Chevrolet), 397.
Fastest qualifier: Waltrip, 20·107s, 111·899 mph/180·084 km/h (2-day average).
Championship points. Drivers: 1 Labonte, 1049; **2** Bodine, 1043; **3** Bonnett, 1034; **4** Waltrip, 1013; **5** Elliott, 1008; **6** Earnhardt, 952.
Manufacturers: 1 Chevrolet, 52; **2** Ford, 38; **3** Pontiac, 15; **4** Buick, 9; **5** Oldsmobile, 6.

SOVRAN BANK 500, Martinsville Speedway, Virginia, United States of America, 28 April. NASCAR Winston Cup Grand National, round 8. 500 laps of the 0·525-mile/0·845-km circuit, 262·50 miles/422·45 km.
1 Harry Gant, USA (Chevrolet), 3h 36m 06s, 73·022 mph/117·517 km/h.
2 Ricky Rudd, USA (Ford), 3h 36m 09s.
3 Geoff Bodine, USA (Chevrolet), 500 laps.
4 Bobby Allison, USA (Buick), 500.
5 Neil Bonnett, USA (Chevrolet), 500.
6 Terry Labonte, USA (Chevrolet), 498.
7 Richard Petty, USA (Pontiac), 498; **8** Lake Speed, USA (Pontiac), 497; **9** Phil Parsons, USA (Chevrolet), 496; **10** Rusty Wallace, USA (Pontiac), 496.
Fastest qualifier: Darrell Waltrip, USA (Chevrolet), 20·975s, 90·279 mph/145·290 km/h (record).
Championship points. Drivers: 1 Bodine, 1213; **2** Labonte, 1204; **3** Bonnett, 1189; **4** Elliott, 1132; **5** Waltrip, 1112; **6** Speed, 1081.
Manufacturers: 1 Chevrolet, 61; **2** Ford, 44; **3** Pontiac, 15; **4** Buick, 12; **5** Oldsmobile, 6.

WINSTON 500, Alabama International Motor Speedway, Talladega, Alabama, United States of America, 5 May. NASCAR Winston Cup Grand National, round 9. 188 laps of the 2·660-mile/4·281-km circuit, 500·08 miles/804·80 km.
1 Bill Elliott, USA (Ford), 2h 41m 04s, 186·288 mph/299·801 km/h.
2 Kyle Petty, USA (Ford), 2h 41m 06s.
3 Cale Yarborough, USA (Ford), 188 laps.
4 Bobby Allison, USA (Buick), 187.
5 Ricky Rudd, USA (Ford), 187.
6 Buddy Baker, USA (Oldsmobile), 185.
7 Terry Labonte, USA (Chevrolet), 185; **8** Dave Marcis, USA (Chevrolet), 185; **9** Bobby Hillin Jnr, USA (Chevrolet), 184; **10** Lake Speed, USA (Pontiac), 184.
Fastest qualifier: Elliott, 45·713s, 209·398 mph/336·993 km/h.
Championship points. Drivers: 1 Labonte, 1355; **2** Bodine, 1343; **3** Elliott, 1312; **4** Bonnett, 1279; **5** Rudd, 1228; **6** Speed, 1215.
Manufacturers: 1 Chevrolet, 61; **2** Ford, 53; **3** Pontiac, 15; **4** Buick, 15; **5** Oldsmobile, 7.

BUDWEISER 500, Dover Downs International Speedway, Delaware, United States of America, 19 May. NASCAR Winston Cup Grand National, round 10. 500 laps of the 1·000-mile/1·609-km circuit, 500·00 miles/804·67 km.
1 Bill Elliott, USA (Ford), 4h 03m 43s, 123·094 mph/198·100 km/h.
2 Harry Gant, USA (Chevrolet), 499 laps.
3 Kyle Petty, USA (Ford), 499.
4 Ricky Rudd, USA (Ford), 498.
5 Darrell Waltrip, USA (Chevrolet), 497.
6 Tim Richmond, USA (Pontiac), 497.
7 Richard Petty, USA (Pontiac), 494; **8** Neil Bonnett, USA (Chevrolet), 494; **9** Dave Marcis, USA (Oldsmobile), 488; **10** Ken Schrader, USA (Ford), 487.
Fastest qualifier: Not given.
Championship points. Drivers: 1 Elliott, 1497; **2** Bodine, 1478; **3** Labonte, 1475; **4** Bonnett, 1426; **5** Rudd, 1388; **6** Waltrip, 1363.
Manufacturers: 1 Chevrolet, 67; **2** Ford, 62; **3** Pontiac, 16; **4** Buick, 15; **5** Oldsmobile, 7.

COCA-COLA WORLD 600, Charlotte Motor Speedway, North Carolina, United States of America, 26 May. NASCAR Winston Cup Grand National, round 11. 400 laps of the 1·500-mile/2·414-km circuit, 600·00 miles/965·80 km.
1 Darrell Waltrip, USA (Chevrolet), 4h 13m 52s, 141·807 mph/228·516 km/h.
2 Harry Gant, USA (Chevrolet), 4h 14m 06s.
3 Bobby Allison, USA (Buick), 400 laps.
4 Dale Earnhardt, USA (Chevrolet), 399.
5 Terry Labonte, USA (Chevrolet), 398.
6 Lake Speed, USA (Pontiac), 397.
7 Joe Ruttmann, USA (Chevrolet), 396; **8** Rusty Wallace, USA (Pontiac), 396; **9** Tim Richmond, USA (Pontiac), 394; **10** Dick Brooks, USA (Chevrolet), 393.
Fastest qualifier: Bill Elliott, USA (Ford), 2m 11·145s, 164·703 mph/265·063 km/h (4 laps).
Championship points. drivers: 1 Labonte, 1630; **2** Elliott, 1611; **3** Bodine, 1598; **4** Bonnett, 1544; **5** Waltrip, 1543; **6** Rudd, 1512.
Manufacturers: 1 Chevrolet, 76; **2** Ford, 62; **3** Buick, 19; **4** Pontiac, 16; **5** Oldsmobile, 7.

BUDWEISER 400, Riverside International Raceway, California, United States of America, 2 June. NASCAR Winston Cup Grand National, round 12. 95 laps of the 2·620-mile/4·126-km circuit, 248·90 miles/400·56 km.
1 Terry Labonte, USA (Chevrolet), 2h 23m 13s, 104·276 mph/167·816 km/h.
2 Harry Gant, USA (Chevrolet), 2h 23m 18s.
3 Bobby Allison, USA (Buick), 95 laps.
4 Ricky Rudd, USA (Ford), 95.
5 Kyle Petty, USA (Ford), 95.
6 Bill Elliott, USA (Ford), 95.
7 Richard Petty, USA (Pontiac), 95; **8** Darrell Waltrip, USA (Chevrolet), 95; **9** Tim Richmond, USA (Pontiac), 95; **10** Ken Schrader, USA (Ford), 94.
Fastest qualifier: Waltrip, 1m 21·639s, 115·533 mph/185·932 km/h.
Championship points. Drivers: 1 Labonte, 1815; **2** Elliott, 1766; **3** Bodine, 1695; **4** Waltrip, 1690; **5** Rudd, 1672; **6** Allison, 1651.
Manufacturers: 1 Chevrolet, 85; **2** Ford, 65; **3** Buick, 23; **4** Pontiac, 16; **5** Oldsmobile, 7.

VAN SCOY DIAMOND MINE 500, Pocono International Raceway, Pennsylvania, United States of America, 9 June. NASCAR Winston Cup Grand National, round 13. 200 laps of the 2·500-mile/4·023-km circuit, 500·00 miles/804·57 km.
1 Bill Elliott, USA (Ford), 3h 35m 48s, 138·974 mph/223·656 km/h.
2 Harry Gant, USA (Chevrolet), 3h 35m 48·02s.
3 Darrell Waltrip, USA (Chevrolet), 200 laps.
4 Geoff Bodine, USA (Chevrolet), 200.
5 Neill Bonnett, USA (Chevrolet), 199.
6 Benny Parsons, USA (Chevrolet), 199.
7 Ricky Rudd, USA (Ford), 198; **8** Buddy Baker, USA (Oldsmobile), 198; **9** Bobby Allison, USA (Buick), 198; **10** Tim Richmond, USA (Pontiac), 198.
Fastest qualifier: Elliott, 58·922s, 152·563 mph/245·526 km/h.
Championship points. Drivers: 1 Elliott, 1946; **2** Labonte, 1894; **3** Bodine, 1865; **4** Waltrip, 1860; **5** Rudd, 1818; **6** Gant, 1813.
Manufacturers: 1 Chevrolet, 91; **2** Ford, 74; **3** Buick, 23; **4** Pontiac, 16; **5** Oldsmobile, 7.

MILLER 400, Michigan International Speedway, Brooklyn, Michigan, United States of America, 16 June. NASCAR Winston Cup Grand National, round 14. 200 laps of the 2·000-mile/3·219-km circuit, 400·00 miles/643·80 km.
1 Bill Elliott, USA (Ford), 2h 45m 48s, 144·724 mph/232·910 km/h.
2 Darrell Waltrip, USA (Chevrolet), 2h 46m 01s.
3 Cale Yarborough, USA (Ford), 299 laps.
4 Tim Richmond, USA (Pontiac), 200.
5 Dale Earnhardt, USA (Chevrolet), 200.
6 Bobby Allison, USA (Buick), 200.
7 Ricky Rudd, USA (Ford), 199; **8** Neil Bonnett, USA (Chevrolet), 199; **9** Dave Marcis, USA (Chevrolet), 199; **10** Benny Parsons, USA (Chevrolet), 198.
Fastest qualifier: Not given.
Championship points. Drivers: 1 Elliott, 2126; **2** Waltrip, 2040; **3** Bodine, 2000; **4** Labonte, 1991; **5** Rudd, 1964; **6** Allison, 1939.
Manufacturers: 1 Chevrolet, 97; **2** Ford, 83; **3** Buick, 24; **4** Pontiac, 19; **5** Oldsmobile, 7.

PEPSI FIRECRACKER 400, Daytona International Speedway, Florida, United States of America, 4 July. NASCAR Winston Cup Grand National, round 15. 160 laps of the 2·500-mile/4·023-km circuit, 400·00 miles/643·68 km.
1 Greg Sacks, USA (Chevrolet), 2h 31m 12s, 158·730 mph/255·451 km/h.
2 Bill Elliott, USA (Ford), 2h 31m 35·5s.
3 Darrell Waltrip, USA (Chevrolet), 160 laps.
4 Ron Bouchard, USA (Buick), 160.
5 Kyle Petty, USA (Ford), 160.
6 Buddy Baker, USA (Oldsmobile), 160.
7 Ricky Rudd, USA (Ford), 160; **8** Terry Labonte, USA (Chevrolet), 159; **9** Dale Earnhardt, USA (Chevrolet), 159; **10** David Pearson, USA (Chevrolet), 159.
Fastest qualifier: Elliott, 44·660s, 201·523 mph/324·319 km/h.
Championship points. Drivers: 1 Elliott, 2306; **2** Waltrip, 2205; **3** Labonte, 2138; **4** Bodine, 2121; **5** Rudd, 2110; **6** Bonnett, 2060.
Manufacturers: 1 Chevrolet, 106; **2** Ford, 89; **3** Buick, 27; **4** Pontiac, 19; **5** Oldsmobile, 8.

SUMMER 500, Pocono International Raceway, Pennsylvania, United States of America, 21 July. NASCAR Winston Cup Grand National, round 16. 200 laps of the 2·500-mile/4·023-km circuit, 500·00 miles/804·57 km.
1 Bill Elliott, USA (Ford), 3h 43m 52s, 134·008 mph/215·664 km/h.
2 Neil Bonnett, USA (Chevrolet), 3h 43m 57s.
3 Darrell Waltrip, USA (Chevrolet), 200 laps.
4 Geoff Bodine, USA (Chevreolet), 200.
5 Harry Gant, USA (Chevrolet), 200.
6 Benny Parsons, USA (Chevrolet), 200.
7 Kyle Petty, USA (Ford), 200; **8** Phil Parsons, USA (Chevrolet), 199; **9** Ron Bouchard, USA (Buick), 199; **10** Buddy Baker, USA (Oldsmobile), 199.
Fastest qualifier: Waltrip, 59·125s, 152·220 mph/249·802 km/h.
Championship points. Drivers: 1 Elliott, 2486; **2** Waltrip, 2375; **3** Bodine, 2286; **4** Bonnett, 2240; **5** Rudd, 2231; **6** Labonte, 2223.
Manfuacturers: 1 Chevrolet, 112; **2** Ford, 98; **3** Buick, 27; **4** Pontiac, 19; **5** Oldsmobile, 8.

TALLADEGA 500, Alabama International Motor Speedway, Talladega, Alabama, United States of America, 28 July. NASCAR Winston Cup Grand National, round 17. 188 laps of the 2·660-mile/4·281-km circuit, 500·08 miles/804·83 km.
1 Cale Yarborough, USA (Ford), 3h 21m 41s, 148·772 mph/239·425 km/h.
2 Neil Bonnett, USA (Chevrolet), 3h 21m 42s.
3 Ron Bouchard, USA (Buick), 188 laps.
4 Bill Elliott, USA (Ford), 188.
5 A. J. Foyt, USA (Oldsmobile), 187.
6 Richard Petty, USA (Pontiac), 187.
7 Harry Gant, USA (Chevrolet), 187; **8** Lake Speed, USA (Pontiac), 187; **9** Darrell Waltrip, USA (Chevrolet), 186; **10** Davy Allison, USA (Chevrolet), 186.
Fastest qualifier: Elliott, 46·132s, 207·578 mph/334·064 km/h.
Championship points. Drivers: 1 Elliott, 2656; **2** Waltrip, 2513; **3** Bonnett, 2415; **4** Bodine, 2385; **5** Rudd, 2340; **6** Gant, 2335.
Manufacturers: 1 Chevrolet, 118; **2** Ford, 107; **3** Buick, 31; **4** Pontiac, 20; **5** Oldsmobile, 10.

CHAMPION SPARK PLUG 400, Michigan International Speedway, Brooklyn, Michigan, United States of America, 11 August. NASCAR Winston Cup Grand National, round 18. 200 laps of the 2·000-mile/3·219-km circuit, 400·00 miles/643·80 km.
1 Bill Elliott, USA (Ford), 2h 54m 38s, 137·430 mph/221·172 km/h.
2 Darrell Waltrip, USA (Chevrolet), 2h 54m 42s.
3 Harry Gant, USA (Chevrolet), 200 laps.
4 Kyle Petty, USA (Ford), 200.
5 Benny Parsons, USA (Chevrolet), 199.
6 Phil Parsons, USA (Chevrolet), 199.
7 Rusty Wallace, USA (Pontiac), 199; **8** Dick Trickle, USA (Chevrolet), 199; **9** Terry Labonte, USA (Chevrolet), 199; **10** Buddy Arrington, USA (Ford), 198.
Fastest qualifier: Elliott, 43·510s, 165·479 mph/266·312 km/h (record).
Championship points. Drivers: 1 Elliott, 2836; **2** Waltrip, 2693; **3** Bonnett, 2550; **4** Gant, 2505; **5** Bodine, 2484; **6** Petty (Kyle), 2450.
Manufacturers: 1 Chevrolet, 124; **2** Ford, 116; **3** Buick, 31; **4** Pontiac, 20; **5** Oldsmobile, 10.

BUSCH 500, Bristol International Raceway, Tennessee, United States of America, 24 August. NASCAR Winston Cup Grand National, round 19. 500 laps of the 0·533-mile/0·858-km circuit, 266·50 miles/429·00 km.
1 Dale Earnhardt, USA (Chevrolet), 3h 27m 44s, 81·388 mph/130·981 km/h.
2 Tim Richmond, USA (Pontiac), 3h 27m 44s (Earnhardt won by three car lengths).
3 Neil Bonnett, USA (Chevrolet), 500 laps.
4 Darrell Waltrip, USA (Chevrolet), 500.
5 Bill Elliott, USA (Ford), 499.
6 Harry Gant, USA (Chevrolet), 498.
7 Ron Bouchard, USA (Buick), 497; **8** Richard Petty, USA (Pontiac), 496; **9** Ricky Rudd, USA (Ford), 495; **10** Lake Speed, USA (Pontiac), 490.
Fastest qualifier: Earnhardt, 16·893s, 113·586 mph/182·798 km/h (record).
Championship points. Drivers: 1 Elliott, 2996; **2** Waltrip, 2858; **3** Bonnett, 2720; **4** Gant, 2620; **5** Bodine, 2572; **6** Petty (Kyle), 2565.
Manufacturers: 1 Chevrolet, 133; **2** Ford, 118; **3** Buick, 31; **4** Pontiac, 26; **5** Oldsmobile, 10.

SOUTHERN 500, Darlington International Raceway, South Carolina, United States of America, 1 September. NASCAR Winston Cup Grand National, round 20. 367 laps of the 1·366-mile/2·198-km circuit, 501·32 miles/806·67 km.
1 Bill Elliott, USA (Ford), 4h 08m 02s, 121·254 mph/195·139 km/h.
2 Cale Yarborough, USA (Ford), 4h 08m 04s.
3 Geoff Bodine, USA (Chevrolet), 367 laps.
4 Neil Bonnett, USA (Chevrolet), 366.
5 Ron Bouchard, USA (Buick), 366.
6 Ricky Rudd, USA (Ford), 366.
7 Terry Labonte, USA (Chevrolet), 365; **8** Benny Parsons, USA (Chevrolet) 365; **9** Joe Ruttman, USA (Chevrolet), 364; **10** Kyle Petty, USA (Ford), 364.
Fastest qualifier: Elliott, 31·394s, 156·641 mph/252·089 km/h.
Championship points. Drivers: 1 Elliott, 3176; **2** Waltrip, 2970; **3** Bonnett, 2880; **4** Bodine, 2742; **5** Gant, 2725; **6** Petty (Kyle), 2699.
Manufacturers: 1 Chevrolet, 137; **2** Ford, 127; **3** Buick, 33; **4** Pontiac, 26; **5** Oldsmobile, 10.

WRANGLER SANFORSET 400, Richmond Fairgrounds Raceway, Virginia, United States of America, 8 September. NASCAR Winston Cup Grand National, round 21. 400 laps of the 0·542-mile/0·972-km circuit, 216·80 miles/348·90 km.
1 Darrell Waltrip, USA (Chevrolet), 2h 58m 54s, 72·508 mph/116·690 km/h.
2 Terry Labonte, USA (Chevrolet), 2h 58m 54s (Waltrip won by one car length).
3 Richard Petty, USA (Pontiac), 400 laps.
4 Dale Earnhardt, USA (Chevrolet), 400.
5 Ricky Rudd, USA (Ford), 400.
6 Harry Gant, USA (Chevrolet), 400.
7 Geoff Bodine, USA (Chevrolet), 399; **8** Kyle Petty, USA (Ford), 399; **9** Neil Bonnett, USA (Chevrolet), 398; **10** Tommy Ellis, USA (Chevrolet), 398.
Fastest qualifier: Bodine, 20·640s, 94·535 mph/152·139 km/h.
Championship points. Drivers: 1 Elliott, 3303; **2** Waltrip, 3150; **3** Bonnett, 3018; **4** Gant, 2915; **5** Bodine, 2893; **6** Rudd, 2858.
Manufacturers: 1 Chevrolet, 146; **2** Ford, 129; **3** Buick, 33; **4** Pontiac, 30; **5** Oldsmobile, 10.

DELAWARE 500, Dover Downs International Speedway, Delaware, United States of America, 15 September. NASCAR Winston Cup Grand National, round 22. 500 laps of the 1·000-mile/1·609-km circuit, 500·00 miles/804·50 km.
1 Harry Gant, USA (Chevrolet), 4h 08m 52s, 120·538 mph/193·987 km/h.
2 Darrell Waltrip, USA (Chevrolet), 4h 09 m 20s.
3 Ricky Rudd, USA (Ford), 499 laps.
4 Bobby Allison, USA (Ford), 496.
5 Neil Bonnett, USA (Chevrolet), 496.
6 Tim Richmond, USA (Pontiac), 496.
7 Dale Earnhardt, USA (Chevrolet), 496; **8** Ron Bouchard, USA (Buick), 494; **9** Richard Petty, USA (Pontiac), 492; **10** Lake Speed, USA (Pontiac), 491.
Fastest qualifier: Bill Elliott, USA (Ford), 25·434s, 141·643 mph/227·952 km/h.
Championship points. Drivers: 1 Elliott, 3411; **2** Waltrip, 3325; **3** Bonnett, 3173; **4** Gant, 3100; **5** Rudd, 3028; **6** Bodine, 2981.
Manufacturers: 1 Chevrolet, 155; **2** Ford, 133; **3** Buick, 33; **4** Pontiac, 31; **5** Oldsmobile, 10.

GOODY's 500, Martinsville Speedway, Virginia, United States of America, 22 September. NASCAR Winston Cup, round 23. 500 laps of the 0·525-mile/0·845-km circuit, 262·50 miles/422·25 km.
1 Dale Earnhardt, USA (Chevrolet), 3h 43m 13s 70·694 mph/113·77 km/h.
2 Darrell Waltrip, USA (Chevrolet), 3h 43m 13s (Earnhardt won by two car lengths).
3 Harry Gant, USA (Chevrolet), 499 laps.
4 Ricky Rudd, USA (Ford), 499.
5 Kyle Petty, USA (Ford), 498.
6 Ron Bouchard, USA (Buick), 498.
7 Tim Richmond, USA (Pontiac), 498; **8** Bobby Hillin Jnr, USA (Chevrolet), 495; **9** Neil Bonnett, USA (Chevrolet), 495; **10** Bobby Allison, USA (Buick), 494.
Fastest qualifier: Geoff Bodine, USA (Chevrolet), 20·919s, 90·521 mph/145·679 km/h (record).
Championship points. Drivers: 1 Elliott, 3523; **2** Waltrip, 3500; **3** Bonnett, 3311; **4** Gant, 3270; **5** Rudd, 3188; **6** Petty, 3119.
Manufacturers: 1 Chevrolet, 164; **2** Ford, 136; **3** Buick, 34; **4** Pontiac, 31; **5** Oldsmobile, 10.

HOLLY FARMS 400, North Wilksboro Speedway, North Carolina, United States of America, 29 September. NASCAR Winston Cup Grand National, round 24. 400 laps of the 0·625-mile/1·006-km circuit, 250·00 miles/402·34 km.
1 Harry Gant, USA (Chevrolet), 2h 37m 44s, 95·077 mph/153·011 km/h.
2 Geoff Bodine, USA (Chevrolet), 2h 37m 58s.
3 Terry Labonte, USA (Chevrolet), 400 laps.
4 Dale Earnhardt, USA (Chevrolet), 400.
5 Ricky Rudd, USA (Ford), 399.
6 Ron Bouchard, USA (Buick), 398.
7 Tim Richmond, USA (Pontiac), 398; **8** Richard Petty, USA (Pontiac), 398; **9** Dave Marcis, USA (Chevrolet), 397; **10** Neil Bonnett, USA (Chevrolet), 397.
Fastest qualifier: Bodine, 39·485s, 113·967 mph/183·412 km/h.
Championship points. Drivers: 1 Waltrip, 3626; **2** Elliott, 3596; **3** Gant, 3455; **4** Bonnett, 3445; **5** Rudd, 3343; **6** Bodine, 3252.
Manufacturers: 1 Chevrolet, 173; **2** Ford, 138; **3** Buick, 35; **4** Pontiac, 31; **5** Oldsmobile, 10.

MILLER 500, Charlotte Motor Speedway, North Carolina, United States of America, 6 October. NASCAR Winston Cup Grand National, round 25. 334 laps of the 1·500-mile/2·414-km circuit, 501·00 miles/806·28 km.
1 Cale Yarborough, USA (Ford), 3h 39m 48s, 136·761 mph/220·095 km/h.
2 Bill Elliott, USA (Ford), 3h 39m 49s.
3 Geoff Bodine, USA (Chevrolet), 334 laps.
4 Darrell Waltrip, USA (Chevrolet), 333.
5 Joe Ruttman, USA (Chevrolet), 333.
6 Tim Richmond, USA (Pontiac), 333.
7 Morgan Shepherd, USA (Chevrolet), 332; **8** Buddy Baker, USA (Oldsmobile), 332; **9** Bobby Hillin Jnr, USA (Chevrolet), 331; **10** Richard Petty, USA (Pontiac), 330.
Fastest qualifier: Harry Gant, USA (Chevrolet), 32·503s, 166·139 mph/267·374 km/h.
Championship points. Drivers: 1 Waltrip, 3791; **2** Elliott, 3771; **3** Gant, 3556; **4** Bonnett, 3482; **5** Rudd, 3461; **6** Bodine, 3417.
Manufacturers: 1 Chevrolet, 177; **2** Ford, 147; **3** Buick, 35; **4** Pontiac, 32; **6** Oldsmobile, 10.

NATIONWISE 500, North Carolina Motor Speedway, Rockingham, North Carolina, United States of America, 20 October. NASCAR Winston Cup Grand National, round 26. 492 laps of the 1·017-mile/1·627-km circuit, 500·36 miles/805·26 km.
1 Darrell Waltrip, USA (Chevrolet), 4h 13m 40s, 118·344 mph/190·456 km/h.
2 Ron Bouchard, USA (Buick), 4h 13m 41s.
3 Harry Gant, USA (Chevrolet), 492 laps.
4 Bill Elliott, USA (Ford), 492.
5 Geoff Bodine, USA (Chevrolet), 492.
6 Tim Richmond, USA (Pontiac), 492.
7 Ricky Rudd, USA (Ford), 492; **8** Dale Earnhardt, USA (Chevrolet), 489; **9** Rusty Wallace, USA (Pontiac), 489; **10** Greg Sacks, USA (Buick), 488.
Fastest qualifier: Terry Labonte, USA (Chevrolet), 25·812s, 141·841 mph/228·270 km/h.
Championship points (prior to final two races in November)

Drivers

1 Darrell Waltrip, USA	3971
2 Bill Elliott, USA	3936
3 Harry Gant, USA	3721
4 Ricky Rudd, USA	3607
5 Neil Bonnett, USA	3605
6 Geoff Bodine, USA	3577

7 Kyle Petty, USA, 3370; **8** Terry Labonte, USA, 3353; **9** Tim Richmond, USA, 3249; **10** Dale Earnhardt, USA, 3241.

Manufacturers

1 Chevrolet	186
2 Ford	150
3 Buick	41
4 Pontiac	33
5 Oldsmobile	10

Note: Final results will be given in *Autocourse 1986/87*.

SCCA Budweiser Trans-Am Championship 1984 results

The final rounds of the 1984 SCCA Budweiser Trans-Am Championship were run after *Autocourse 1984/85* went to press.

SCCA BUDWEISER TRANS-AM CHAM-

PIONSHIP RACE, Green Valley Race City, Texas, United States of America, 28 October. SCCA Budweiser Trans-Am Championship, round 15. 63 laps of the 1·600-mile/2·575-km circuit, 100·80 miles/162·23 km.
1 Willy T. Ribbs, USA (Mercury Capri), 1h 11m 11·60s, 81·30 mph/135·67 km/h.
2 John Jones, CDN (Mercury Capri), 1h 13m 15·57s.
3 Jim Miller, USA (Pontiac Trans-Am), 62 laps.
4 John Brandt, USA (Chevrolet Corvette), 60.
5 Del Taylor, USA (Pontiac Trans-Am), 60.
6 Gary Schons, USA (Pontiac Firebird), 57.
7 P. J. Brallier, USA (Pontiac Firebird), 56; **8** Dave Watson, USA (Chevrolet Camaro), 55; **9** Pancho Weaver, USA (Chevrolet Camaro), 54; **10** Les Lindley, USA (Chevrolet Camaro), 51.
Fastest qualifier: Ribbs, 1m 02·791s, 91·73 mph/147·62 km/h (record).
Fastest lap: Ribbs, 1m 03·639s, 90·51 mph/145·66 km/h (record).
Championship points. Drivers: **1** Gloy, 204; **2** Pickett, 177; **3** Ribbs, 155; **4** Lobenberg, 128; **5** Dallenbach Jnr, 126; **6** Brassfield, 120.
Manufacturers: **1** Mercury, 110; **2** Chevrolet, 60; **3** Pontiac, 54; **4** Porsche, 18; **5** Nissan, 8.

SCCA BUDWEISER TRANS-AM CHAMPIONSHIP RACE, Caesars Palace Indy Circuit, Nevada, United States of America, 11 November. SCCA Budweiser Trans-Am Championship, round 16. 89 laps of the 1·125-mile/1·811-km circuit, 100·13 miles/161·18 km.
1 Tom Gloy, USA (Mercury Capri), 1h 07m 08s, 88·82 mph/142·94 km/h.
2 Wally Dallenbach Jnr, USA (Chevrolet Camaro), 1h 07m 13s.
3 David Hobbs, GB (Chevrolet Corvette), 89 laps.
4 Greg Pickett, USA (Mercury Capri), 89.
5 Craig Carter, USA (Chevrolet Camaro), 88.
6 Bob Lobenberg, USA (Pontiac Trans-Am), 88.
7 John Jones, CDN (Mercury Capri), 87; **8** Andy Porterfield, USA (Chevrolet Camaro), 87; **9** Jerry Brassfield, USA (Chevrolet Corvette), 86; **10** John Brandt, USA (Chevrolet Corvette), 85.
Fastest qualifier: Dave Watson, USA (Chevrolet Camaro), 39·594s, 102·29 mph/164·62 km/h (record).
Fastest lap: Gloy, 38·00s, 106·58 mph/171·52 km/h (record).

Final Championship points
Drivers

1 Tom Gloy, USA	225
2 Greg Pickett, USA	189
3 Willy T. Ribbs, USA	155
4 Wally Dallenbach Jnr, USA	142
5 Bob Lobenberg, USA	138
6 Darin Brassfield, USA	120

7 Jim Miller, USA, 110; **8** David Hobbs, GB, 106; **9** Paul Miller, USA, 76; **10** Jim Derhaag, USA, 59; **11** Eppie Wietzes, CDN, 56; **12** Dave Watson, USA, 44; **13** John Brandt, USA, 43; **14** John Jones, CDN, 40; **15** Paul Newman, USA, 39; **16** Richard Wall, USA, 37; **17** Richard Spenard, CDN, 32; **18** Rob McFarlin, USA, 29; **19** Andy Porterfield, USA, 23; **20** Del Taylor, USA and Doug Mills, USA, 22.

Manufacturers

1 Mercury	119
2 Chevrolet	66
3 Pontiac	55
4 Porsche	18
5 Nissan	8

Bendix Brake Trans-Am Championship 1985 results

BENDIX BRAKE TRANS-AM CHAMPIONSHIP RACE, Firebird International Raceway, Arizona, United States of America, 21 April. Bendix Brake Trans-Am Championship, round 1. 67 laps of the 1·500-mile/2·414-km circuit, 100·50 miles/161·74 km.
1 Willy T. Ribbs, USA (Mercury Capri), 1h 16m 56·91s, 78·36 mph/126·11 km/h.
2 Wally Dallenbach, Jnr, USA (Mercury Capri), 1h 17m 16·47s.
3 Tom Gloy, USA (Mercury Capri), 67 laps.
4 Chris Kniefel, USA (Mercury Capri), 66.
5 Rob McFarlin, USA (Pontiac Trans-Am), 66.
6 Jim Derhaag, USA (Pontiac Trans-Am), 66.
7 Scott Goodyear, CDN (Pontiac Trans-Am), 66; **8** Andy Porterfield, USA (Chevrolet Camaro), 66; **9** Bill Doyle, USA (Pontiac Trans-Am), 65; **10** Bob Hagestad, USA (Porsche 924 Turbo), 65.
Fastest qualifier: Paul Miller, USA (Porsche 924 Turbo), 1m 00·16s, 89·75 mph/144·44 km/h (record).
Fastest lap: Ribbs, 1m 02·19s, 86·83 mph/139·74 km/h (record).
Championship points. Drivers: **1** Ribbs, 21; **2** Dallenbach Jnr, 16; **3** Gloy, 14; **4** Kniefel, 12; **5** McFarlin, 11; **6** Derhaag, 10.
Manufacturers: **1** Mercury, 9; **2** Pontiac, 2.

BENDIX BRAKE TRANS-AM CHAMPIONSHIP RACE, Sears Point International Raceway, Sonoma, California, United States of America, 2 June. Bendix Brake Trans-Am Championship, round 2. 40 laps of the 2·523-mile/4·060-km circuit, 100·92 miles/162·40 km.
1 Willy T. Ribbs, USA (Mercury Capri), 1h 10m 32·300s, 85·843 mph/138·15 km/h.
2 Wally Dallenbach Jnr, USA (Mercury Capri), 1h 10m 41·090s.
3 Tom Gloy, USA (Mercury Capri), 40 laps.
4 Jim Miller, USA (Mercury Capri), 40.
5 Rob McFarlin, USA (Pontiac Trans-Am), 40.
6 Paul Newman, USA (Nissan 300 ZX Turbo), 40.
7 Bill Doyle, USA (Pontiac Trans-Am), 40; **8** Chris Kneifel, USA (Mercury Capri), 39; **9** Andy Porterfield, USA (Chevrolet Camaro), 39; **10** Richard Wall, USA (Chevrolet Camaro), 39.
Fastest qualifier: Paul Miller, USA (Porsche 924 Turbo), 1m 34·234s, 96·386 mph/155·118 km/h (record).
Fastest lap: Miller, 1m 37·850s, 92·834 mph/149·383 km/h (record).
Championship points. Drivers: **1** Ribbs, 42; **2** Dallenbach Jnr, 32; **3** Gloy, 28; **4** McFarlin, 22; **5** Kneifer, 20; **6** Doyle, 16.
Manufacturers: **1** Mercury, 18; **2** Pontiac, 4; **3** Nissan, 1.

BENDIX BRAKE TRANS-AM CHAMPIONSHIP RACE, Portland International Raceway, Oregon, United States of America, 15 June. Bendix Brake Trans-Am Championship, round 3. 53 laps of the 1·915-mile/3·082-km circuit, 101·45 miles/163·65 km.
1 Wally Dallenbach Jnr, USA (Mercury Capri), 1h 05m 24·00s, 93·101 mph/149·831 km/h.
2 Willy T. Ribbs, USA (Mercury Capri), 1h 05m 24·62s.
3 Tom Gloy, USA (Mercury Capri), 53 laps.
4 Elliott Forbes-Robinson, USA (Buick Century Regal), 53.
5 Rob McFarlin, USA (Pontiac Trans-Am), 52.
6 Jim Derhaag, USA (Pontiac Firebird), 51.
7 Paul Miller, USA (Porsche 924 Turbo), 51; **8** Paul Newman, USA (Nissan 300 ZX Turbo), 51; **9** Monte Shelton, USA (Porsche 911SC), 560; **10** Jerry Miller, USA (Buick Century Regal), 50.
Fastest qualifier: Ribbs, 1m 11·190s, 96·839 mph/155·847 km/h.
Fastest lap: Dallenbach Jnr, 1m 11·320s, 96·663 mph/155·564 km/h.
Championship points. Drivers:1 Ribbs, 60; **2** Dallenbach Jnr, 52; **3** Gloy, 42; **4** McFarlin, 33; **5** Doyle, 21; **6** Kneifel, 20.
Manufacturers: **1** Mercury, 27; **2** Pontiac, 6; **3** Buick, 3; **4** Nissan, 1.

BENDIX BRAKE TRANS-AM CHAMPIONSHIP RACE, Detroit Grand Prix Circuit, Michigan, United States of America, 22 June. Bendix Brake Trans-Am Championship, round 4. 40 laps of the 2·500-mile/4·023-km circuit, 100·00 miles/160·92 km.
* Wally Dallenbach Jnr, USA (Mercury Capri), 1h 25m 35·735s, 70·097 mph/112·810 km/h.
1 Elliott Forbes-Robinson, USA (Buick Century Regal), 1h 25m 57·592s, 69·800 mph/112·332 km/h.
2 John Jones, CDN (Mercury Capri), 1h 26m 02·862s.
3 Chris Kneifel, USA (Mercury Capri), 39 laps.
4 Paul Newman, USA (Nissan 300 ZX Turbo), 39.
5 Jim Derhaag, USA (Pontiac Firebird), 39.
6 Jim Miller, USA (Mercury Capri), 38.
7 Ken Murrey, USA (Pontiac Trans-Am), 38; **8** John Schneider, USA (Porsche 924 Turbo), 38; **9** Gary Fautch, USA (Pontiac Trans-Am), 38; **10** David Hobbs, GB (Chevrolet Camaro), 38.
Fastest qualifier: Dallenbach Jnr, 2m 01·530s, 74·055 mph/119·180 km/h.
Fastest lap: Dallenbach Jnr, 2m 05·044s, 71·975 mph/115·832 km/h.
* Dallenbach disqualified due car under weight. He was awarded second-place points plus 1 point for pole position but Mercury received no Manufacturers' points for win.
Championship points. Drivers: **1** Dallenbach Jnr, 69; **2** Ribbs, 60; **3** Gloy, 46; **4** McFarlin, 33; **5** Kneifel, 32; **6** Derhaag, 30.
Manufacturers: **1** Mercury, 33; **2** Buick, 12; **3** Pontiac, 8; **4** Nissan, 4.

BENDIX BRAKE TRANS-AM CHAMPIONSHIP RACE, Summit Point Raceway, West Virginia, United States of America, 7 July. Bendix Brake Trans-Am Championship, round 5. 50 laps of the 2·00-mile/3·22-km circuit, 100·00 miles/161·00 km.
1 Willy T. Ribbs, USA (Mercury Capri), 1h 05m 14·900s, 91·956 mph/147·988 km/h.
2 Wally Dallenbach Jnr, USA (Mercury Capri), 1h 05m 30·440s.
3 Tom Gloy, USA (Mercury Capri), 50 laps.
4 Eppie Wietzes, CDN (Pontiac Firebird), 50.
5 Paul Newman, USA (Nissan 300 ZX Turbo), 48.
6 Peter Dus, USA (Pontiac Trans-Am), 48.
7 Wayne Strout, USA (Chevrolet Camaro), 46; **8** Rick Dittman, USA (Pontiac Firebird), 46; **9** Bruce Jenner, USA (Pontiac Trans-Am), 46; **10** Chris Kneifel, USA (Mercury Capri), 45.
Fastest qualifier: Paul Miller, USA (Porsche 924 Turbo), 1m 13·326s, 98·192 mph/158·024 km/h (record).
Fastest lap: Ribbs, 1m 15·480s, 95·389 mph/153·513 km/h (record).
Championship points. Drivers: **1** Dallenbach Jnr, 85; **2** Ribbs, 80; **3** Gloy, 60; **4** Newman, 40; **5** Kneifel, 38; **6** McFarlin, 33.
Manufacturers: **1** Mercury, 42; **2** Buick, 12; **3** Pontiac, 11; **4** Nissan, 6.

BENDIX BRAKE TRANS-AM CHAMPIONSHIP RACE, Mid-Ohio Sports Car Course, Lexington, Ohio, United States of America, 14 July. Bendix Brake Trans-Am Championship, round 6. 42 laps of the 2·400-mile/3·863-km circuit, 100·80 miles/162·25 km.
1 Wally Dallenbach, Jnr, USA (Mercury Capri), 1h 06m 03·90s, 91·753 mph/147·662 km/h.
2 Elliott Forbes-Robinson, USA (Buick Somerset Regal), 1h 06m 14·60s.
3 Chris Kneifel, USA (Mercury Capri), 42 laps.
4 Willy T. Ribbs, USA (Mercury Capri), 42.
5 Jim Fitzgerald, USA (Nissan 300 ZX Turbo), 42.
6 Jim Miller, USA (Mercury Capri), 42.
7 Rob McFarlin, USA (Pontiac Trans-Am), 41; **8** Tom Gloy, USA (Mercury Capri), 41; **9** Ken Murrey, USA (Pontiac Trans-Am), 40; **10** Craig Shafer, USA (Chevrolet Camaro), 40.
Fastest qualifier: Forbes-Robinson, 1m 30·572s, 95·390 mph/153·51 km/h (record).
Fastest lap: Forbes-Robinson, 1m 31·767s, 94·151 mph/151·52 km/h (record).
Championship points. Drivers: Dallenbach Jnr, 96; **2** Ribbs, 92; **3** Gloy, 68; **4** Kneifel, 52; **5** Forbes-Robinson, 45; **6** McFarlin, 42.
Manufacturers: **1** Mercury, 51; **2** Buick, 18; **3** Pontiac, 11; **4** Nissan, 8.

BENDIX BRAKE TRANS-AM CHAMPIONSHIP RACE, Brainerd International Raceway, Minnesota, United States of America, 21 July. Bendix Brake Trans-Am Championship, round 7. 33 laps of the 3·000-mile/4·828-km circuit, 99·00 miles/159·32 km.
1 Willy T. Ribbs, USA (Mercury Capri), 57m 04·340s, 104·078 mph/167·487 km/h.
2 Elliott Forbes-Robinson, USA (Buick Somerset Regal), 57m 06·980s.
3 Tom Gloy, USA (Mercury Capri), 33 laps.
4 Wally Dallenbach Jnr, USA (Mercury Capri), 33.
5 John Jones, CDN (Mercury Capri), 33.
6 Paul Newman, USA (Nissan 300 ZX Turbo), 33.
7 Rob McFarlin, USA (Pontiac Trans-Am), 33; **8** Les Lindley, USA (Chevrolet Camaro), 32; **9** Bruce Jenner, USA (Pontiac Trans-Am), 32; **10** Wayne Strout, USA (Chevrolet Camaro), 32.
Fastest qualifier: Ribbs, 1m 37·039s, 111·295 mph/179·111 km/h.
Fastest lap: Ribbs, 1m 38·230s, 109·946 mph/176·940 km/h (record).
Championship points. Drivers: **1** Dallenbach Jnr, 118; **2** Ribbs, 114; **3** Gloy, 82; **4** Forbes-Robinson, 61; **5** Kneifel, 52; **6** McFarlin, 51.
Manufacturers: **1** Mercury, 60; **2** Buick, 24; **3** Pontiac, 11; **4** Nissan, 9.

BENDIX BRAKE TRANS-AM CHAMPIONSHIP RACE, Road America, Elkhart Lake, Wisconsin, United States of America, 4 August. Bendix Brake Trans-Am Championship, round 8. 25 laps of the 4·000-mile/6·437-km circuit, 100·00 miles/160·93 km.
1 Willy T. Ribbs, USA (Mercury Capri), 58m 06·31s, 103·261 mph/166·182 km/h.
2 Tom Gloy, USA (Mercury Capri), 58m 11·230s.
3 Chris Kneifel, USA (Mercury Capri), 25 laps.
4 Elliott Forbes-Robinson, USA (Buick Somerset Regal), 25.
5 Wally Dallenbach Jnr, USA (Mercury Capri), 25.
6 Eppie Wietzes, CDN (Pontiac Firebird), 25.
7 Paul DePirro, USA (Chevrolet Camaro), 25; **8** Jim Miller, USA (Mercury Capri), 25; **9** Jerry Clinton, USA (Ford Mustang), 24; **10** Andy Porterfield, USA (Chevrolet Camaro), 24.
Fastest qualifier: Paul Newman, USA (Nissan 300 ZX Turbo), 2m 14·611s, 106·975 mph/172·159 km/h.
Fastest lap: Newman, 2m 17·704s, 104·572 mph/168·29 km/h.
Championship points. Drivers: **1** Ribbs, 134; **2** Dallenbach Jnr, 129; **3** Gloy, 98; **4** Forbes-Robinson, 73; **5** Kneifel, 66; **6** Newman, 51.
Manufacturers: **1** Mercury, 69; **2** Buick, 27; **3** Pontiac, 12; **4** Nissan, 9.

BENDIX BRAKE TRANS-AM CHAMPIONSHIP RACE, Lime Rock Park, Connecticut, United States of America, 10 August. Bendix Brake Trans-Am Championship, round 9. 66 laps of the 1·53-mile/2·46-km circuit, 100·98 miles/162·36 km.
1 Paul Miller, USA (Porsche 924 Turbo), 1h 06m 46·764s, 90·734 mph/146·022 km/h.
2 Elliott Forbes-Robinson, USA (Buick Somerset Regal), 1h 06m 47·674s.
3 Wally Dallenbach Jnr, USA (Mercury Capri), 66 laps.
4 Chris Kneifel, USA (Mercury Capri), 66.
5 Les Lindley, USA (Chevrolet Camaro), 65.
6 Jim Miller, USA (Mercury Capri), 65.
7 Jerry Miller, USA (Buick Century Regal), 64; **8** John Brandt Jnr, USA (Chevrolet Corvette), 64; **9** Bob Hagestad, USA (Porsche 924 Turbo), 63; **10** Murray Edwards, CDN (Chevrolet Corvette), 62.
Fastest qualifier: Paul Newman, USA (Nissan 300 ZX Turbo), 53·69s, 102·595 mph/165·110 km/h.
Fastest lap: Newman, 54·80s, 100·510 mph/161·755 km/h.
Championship points. Drivers: **1** Dallenbach Jnr, 143; **2** Ribbs, 134; **3** Gloy, 98; **4** Forbes-Robinson, 89; **5** Kneifel, 78; **6** Newman, 55.
Manufacturers: **1** Mercury, 73; **2** Buick, 33; **3** Pontiac, 12; **4** Porsche and Nissan, 9; **6** Chevrolet, 2.

BENDIX BRAKE TRANS-AM CHAMPIONSHIP RACE, Watkins Glen Grand Prix Circuit, New York, United States of America, 25 August. Bendix Brake Trans-Am Championship, round 10. 30 laps of the 3·377-mile/5·435-km circuit, 101·31 miles/163·05 km.
1 Wally Dallenbach Jnr, USA (Mercury Capri), 58m 45·661s, 103·446 mph/166·480 km/h.
2 Paul Newman, USA (Nissan 300 ZX Turbo), 59m 02·141s.
3 Paul Miller, USA (Porsche 924 Turbo), 30 laps.
4 Eppie Wietzes, CDN (Pontiac Firebird), 30.
5 Tom Gloy, USA (Mercury Capri), 30.
6 Les Lindley, USA (Chevrolet Camaro), 29.
7 Jim Fitzgerald, USA (Nissan 300 ZX Turbo), 29; **8** Doug Mills, USA (Chevrolet Camaro), 29; **9** Craig Shafer, USA (Chevrolet Camaro), 29; **10** Jerry Simmons, USA (Chevrolet Corvette), 29.
Fastest qualifier: Newman, 1m 52·648s, 107·888 mph/173·628 km/h.
Fastest lap: Willy T. Ribbs, USA (Mercury Capri), 1m 54·610s, 106·075 mph/170·711 km/h.
Championship points. Drivers: **1** Dallenbach Jnr, 169; **2** Ribbs, 134; **3** Gloy, 109; **4** Forbes-Robinson, 89; **5** Kneifel, 78; **6** Newman, 69.
Manufacturers: **1** Mercury, 82; **2** Buick, 33; **3** Pontiac, 15; **4** Nissan, 15; **5** Porsche, 13; **6** Chevrolet, 3.

BENDIX BRAKE TRANS-AM CHAMPIONSHIP RACE, Trois-Rivières, Quebec, Canada, 1 September. Bendix Brake Trans-Am Championship, round 11. 40 laps of the 2·100-mile/3·380-km circuit, 84·00 miles/135·20 km.
1 Willy T. Ribbs, USA (Mercury Capri), 1h 09m 50·948s, 72·156 mph/116·124 km/h.
2 Wally Dallenbach Jnr, USA (Mercury Capri), 1h 09m 56·122s.
3 Elliott Forbes-Robinson, USA (Buick Somerset Regal), 40 laps.
4 Tom Gloy, USA (Mercury Capri), 40.
5 Eppie Wietzes, CDN (Pontiac Firebird), 40.
6 Les Lindley, USA (Chevrolet Camaro), 40.
7 Paul Miller, USA (Porsche 924 Turbo), 40.
8 Bruce Jenner, USA (Pontiac Trans-Am), 39; **9** Peter Deman, USA (Chevrolet Corvette), 39; **10** John Schneider, USA (Porsche 924 Turbo), 39.
Fastest qualifier: Ribbs, 1m 32·440s, 81·783 mph/131·617 km/h.
Fastest lap: Ribbs, 1m 33·583s, 80·784 mph/130·009 km/h.
Championship points. Drivers: **1** Dallenbach Jnr, 180; **2** Ribbs, 156; **3** Gloy, 121; **4** Forbes-Robinson, 103; **5** Kneifel, 78; **6** Newman, 69.
Manufacturers: **1** Mercury, 91; **2** Buick, 37; **3** Pontiac, 17; **4** Nissan, 15; **5** Porsche, 13; **6** Chevrolet, 4.

BENDIX BRAKE TRANS-AM CHAMPIONSHIP RACE, Mosport Park Circuit, Ontario, Canada, 8 September. Bendix Brake Trans-Am Championship, round 12. 40 laps of the 2·459-mile/3·957-km circuit, 98·36 miles/158·28 km.
1 Wally Dallenbach Jnr, USA (Mercury Capri), 1h 07m 16·402s, 87·726 mph/141·181 km/h.
2 Willy T. Ribbs, USA (Mercury Capri), 1h 07m 16·926s.
3 John Jones, CDN (Mercury Capri), 40 laps.
4 Tom Gloy, USA (Mercury Capri), 40.
5 Eppie Wietzes, CDN (Pontiac Firebird), 40.
6 John Brandt Jnr, USA (Chevrolet Camaro), 40.
7 Bruce Jenner, USA (Pontiac Trans-Am), 40; **8** Dave Smith, CDN (Chevrolet Camaro), 39; **9** Rick Dittman, USA (Pontiac Firebird), 39; **10** Murray Edwards, CDN (Chevrolet Corvette), 39.
Fastest qualifier: Dallenbach Jnr, 1m 23·640s, 105·839 mph/170·331 km/h.
Fastest lap: Dallenbach Jnr, 1m 24·205s, 105·129 mph/169·188 km/h.
Championship points. Drivers: **1** Dallenbach Jnr, 201; **2** Ribbs, 174; **3** Gloy, 133; **4** Forbes-Robinson, 103; **5** Kneifel, 78; **6** Newman, 72.
Manufacturers: **1** Mercury, 100; **2** Buick, 37; **3** Pontiac, 19; **4** Nissan, 15; **5** Porsche, 13; **6** Chevrolet, 5.

BENDIX BRAKE TRANS-AM CHAMPIONSHIP RACE, St Louis International Raceway, Fairmont City, Illinois, United States of America, 15 September. Bendix Brake Trans-Am Championship, round 13. 46 laps of the 2·20-mile/3·54 km circuit, 101·209 miles/162·84 km.
1 Wally Dallenbach Jnr, USA (Mercury Capri), 1h 12m 36·34s, 83·63 mph/134·59 km/h.
2 Tom Gloy, USA (Mercury Capri), 1h 12m 38·02s.
3 Jim Miller, USA (Mercury Capri), 46 laps.
4 Chris Kneifel, USA (Mercury Capri), 46.
5 Les Lindley, USA (Chevrolet Camaro), 46.
6 Jim Derhaag, USA (Pontiac Trans-Am), 45.
7 Paul DePirro, USA (Chevrolet Camaro), 45; **8** John Brandt Jnr, USA (Chevrolet Camaro), 45; **9** Jim Sanborn, USA (Pontiac Trans-Am), 45; **10** Bill Doyle, USA (Pontiac Trans-Am), 45.
Fastest qualifier: Gloy, 1m 28·060s, 89·939 mph/144·74 km/h.
Fastest lap: Willy T. Ribbs, USA (Mercury Capri), 1m 30·110s, 87·893 mph/141·45 km/h.
Championship points. Drivers: **1** Dallenbach Jnr, 221; **2** Ribbs, 174; **3** Gloy, 151; **4** Forbes-Robinson, 103; **5** Kneifel, 90; **6** Newman, 72.
Manufacturers: **1** Mercury, 109; **2** Buick, 37; **3** Pontiac, 20; **4** Nissan, 15; **5** Porsche, 13; **6** Chevrolet, 7.

BENDIX BRAKE TRANS-AM CHAMPIONSHIP RACE, Sears Point International Raceway, Sonoma, California, 29 September. Bendix Brake Trans-Am Championship, round 14. 20 laps of the 2·523-mile/4·060-km circuit, 100·92 miles/162·40 km.
1 Elliott Forbes-Robinson, USA (Buick Somerset Regal), 1h 13m 00·310s, 82·942 mph/133·482 km/h.
2 Willy T. Ribbs, USA (Mercury Capri), 1h 13m 02·930s.
3 Tom Gloy, USA (Mercury Capri), 40 laps.
4 Paul Miller, USA (Porsche 924 Turbo), 40.
5 Chris Kneifel, USA (Mercury Capri), 40.
6 Jim Miller, USA (Mercury Capri), 40.
7 Pancho Weaver, USA (Chevrolet Camaro), 40; **8** John Brandt Jnr, USA (Chevrolet Camaro), 40; **9** Larry Park, USA (Chevrolet Corvette), 39; **10** Frank Emmett, USA (Pontiac Trans-Am), 39.
Fastest qualifier: Gloy, 1m 37·777s, 92·893 mph/149·496 km/h.
Fastest lap: Wally Dallenbach Jnr, USA (Mercury Capri), 1m 39·350s, 91·422 mph/147·129 km/h.

Championship points (prior to final round in November)
Drivers

1 Wally Dallenbach Jnr, USA	226
2 Willy T. Ribbs, USA	191
3 Tom Gloy, USA	166
4 Elliott Forbes-Robinson, USA	123
5 Chris Kneifel, USA	101
6 Paul Miller, USA	79

7 Jim Miller, USA, 77; **8** Paul Newman, USA, 72; **9** Eppie Wietzes, CDN, 56; **10** Les Lindley, USA, 55; **11** Rob McFarlin, USA, 51; **12** Jim Derhaag, USA, 44; **13** Bruce Jenner, USA, 40; **14** John Brandt Jnr, USA, 40; **15** John Jones, CDN, 39.

Manufacturers

1 Mercury	115
2 Buick	46
3 Pontiac	20
4 Porsche	16
5 Nissan	15
6 Chevrolet	7

Note: Final results will be given in *Autocourse 1986/87*.

Robert Bosch/VW Super Vee Championship 1984 results

The final round of the 1984 Robert Bosch/VW Super Vee Championship was run after *Autocourse 1984/85* went to press.

ROBERT BOSCH/VW SUPER VEE RACE, Caesars Palace Indy Circuit, Nevada, United States of America, 11 November. Robert Bosch/VW Super Vee Championship, round 12. 55 laps of the 1·125-mile/1·811-km circuit, 61·88 miles/99·61 km.
1 Ludwig Heimrath, Jnr, CDN (Ralt RT5-VW), 54m 06s, 68·60 mph/110·40 km/h.
2 Arie Luyendyk, NL (Ralt RT5-VW), 54m 39s.
3 Roger Penske Jnr, USA (Ralt RT5-VW), 55 laps.
4 Tommy Byrne, IRL (Ralt RT5-VW), 54.
5 Dominic Dobson, USA (Ralt RT5-VW), 54.
6 Jeff MacPherson, USA (Ralt RT5-VW), 54.
7 Mike Groff, USA (Ralt RT5-VW), 54; 8 John Richards, USA (Ralt RT5-VW), 54; 9 Ben Gustafson, USA (Ralt RT5-VW), 54; 10 Chip Robinson, USA (Ralt RT5-VW), 54.
Fastest lap: Heimrath Jnr, 37·00s, 109·459 mph/176·157 km/h (record).

Final Championship points
1	Arie Luyendyk, NL	172
2	Chip Robinson, USA	150
3	Jeff MacPherson, USA	116
4	Ludwig Heimrath Jnr, CDN	111
5	Roger Penske Jnr, USA	104
6	Peter Moodie, JA	86

7 Mike Hooper, USA, 76; 8 Ted Prappas, USA, 66; 9 Dominic Dobson, USA, 59; 10 John Richards, USA, 52; 11 Craig Dummit, USA, 49; 12 Ben Gustafson, USA, 35; 13 Tommy Byrne, IRL and John Fergus, USA, 28; 15 Cary Bren, USA, 26; 16 Steve Millen, NZ, John Gimbel, USA and Justin Revenue, USA, 25; 19 John David Briggs, USA, 24; 20 Ken Johnson, USA and Ken Murrey, USA, 20.

1985 results

ROBERT BOSCH/VW SUPER VEE RACE, Long Beach Circuit, Long Beach, California, United States of America, 13 April. Robert Bosch/VW Super Vee Championship, round 1. 37 laps of the 1·67-mile/2·69-km circuit, 6£·79 miles/99·53 km.
1 Davy Jones, US (Ralt RT5-VW), 45m 52·00s, 80·82 mph/130·07 km/h.
2 Ken Johnson, USA (Ralt RT5-VW), 45m 59·57s.
3 Ted Prappas, USA (Ralt RT5-VW), 37 laps.
4 Mike Groff, USA (Ralt RT5-VW), 37.
5 Cary Bren, USA (Ralt RT5-VW), 37.
6 Hans-Peter Pandur, A (Ralt RT5-VW), 37.
7 Steve Brèn, USA (Ralt RT5-VW), 37; 8 John Stephanus, USA (Ralt RT5-VW), 37; 9 David Kudrave, USA (Ralt RT5-VW), 37; 10 Scott Aitcheson, USA (Ralt RT5-VW), 36.
Fastest lap: Steve Bren, 1m 11·16s, 84·49 mph/135·97 km/h (record).
Championship points: 1 Jones, 20; 2 Johnson, 16; 3 Prappas, 14; 4 Groff, 12; 5 Bren (Cary), 11; 6 Pandur, 10.

ROBERT BOSCH/VW SUPER VEE RACE, Indianapolis Raceway Park, Indianapolis, Indiana, United States of America, 25 May. Robert

Bosch/VW Super Vee Championship, round 2. 80 laps of the 0·686-mile/1·104-km circuit, 54·88 miles/88·32 km.
1 Mike Hooper, USA (Ralt RT5-VW), 38m 45·32s, 79·019 mph/127·168 km/h.
2 Mike Groff, USA (Ralt RT5-VW), 38m 46·42s.
3 Jeff MacPherson, USA (Ralt RT5-VW), 80 laps.
4 Steve Bren, USA (Ralt RT5-VW), 80.
5 Kevin Whitesides, USA (Ralt RT5-VW), 80.
6 Kim Campbell, USA (Ralt RT5-VW), 80.
7 Matt McBride, USA (Ralt RT5-VW), 80; 8 Mike Miller, USA (Ralt RT5-VW), 80; 9 John Stephanus, USA (Ralt RT5-VW), 80; 10 Ken Johnson, USA (Ralt RT5-VW), 79.
Fastest lap: Not given.
Championship points: 1 Groff, 28; 2 Johnson, 22; 3 Bren (Steve), 21; 4 Jones and Hooper, 20; 6 Bren (Cary), 16.

ROBERT BOSCH/VW SUPER VEE RACE, Wisconsin State Fair Park Speedway, Milwaukee, Wisconsin, United States of America, 2 June. Robert Bosch/VW Super Vee Championship, round 3. 62 laps of the 1·000-mile/1·609-km circuit, 62·00 miles/99·76 km.
1 Jeff Andretti, USA (Ralt RT5-VW), 38m 22·05s, 96·957 mp/156·037 km/h.
2 Ted Prappas, USA (Ralt RT5-VW), 38m 30·28s.
3 Ken Johnson, USA (Ralt RT5-VW), 62 laps.
4 Jerrill Rice, USA (Anson SA6-VW), 62.
5 Davy Jones, USA (Ralt RT5-VW), 62.
6 Mike Miller, USA (Ralt RT5-VW), 62.
7 John Stephanus, USA (Ralt RT5-VW), 62; 8 Steve Bren, USA (Ralt RT5-VW), 62; 9 Dave Kudrave, USA (Ralt RT5-VW), 62; 10 Mike Groff, USA (Ralt RT5-VW), 62.
Fastest lap: Not given.
Championship points: 1 Johnson, 36; 2 Groff, 34; 3 Jones, 31; 4 Prappas, 30; 5 Bren (Steve), 29; 6 Stephanus, 24.

ROBERT BOSCH/VW SUPER VEE RACE, Detroit Grand Prix Circuit, Michigan, United States of America, 23 June. Robert Bosch/VW Super Vee Championship, round 4. 24 laps of the 2·500-mile/4·023-km circuit, 60·00 miles/96·55 km.
1 Hans-Peter Pandur, A (Ralt RT5-VW), 44m 14·727s, 71·601 mph/115·230 km/h.
2 Davy Jones, USA (Ralt RT5-VW), 44m 23·354s.
3 Cary Bren, USA (Ralt RT5-VW), 24 laps.
4 Ken Johnson, USA (Ralt RT5-VW), 24.
5 Matt McBride, USA (Ralt RT5-VW), 24.
6 Mike Groff, USA (Ralt RT5-VW), 24.
7 David Diem, USA (Ralt RT5-VW), 23; 8 Rob Stevens, USA (Ralt RT5-VW), 23; 9 Jim Putnam, USA (Ralt RT5-VW), 23; 10 Michael McHugh, USA (Anson SA4-VW), 23.
Fastest lap: Jones, 1m 57·981s, 76·283 mph/122·765 km/h.
Championship points: 1 Johnson, 48; 2 Jones, 47; 3 Groff, 44; 4 Prappas, Pandur and Bren (Cary), 30.

ROBERT BOSCH/VW SUPER VEE RACE, Meadowlands Grand Prix Circuit, New York, United States of America, 30 June. Robert Bosch/VW Super Vee Championship, round 5. 33 laps of the 1·682-mile/2·707-km circuit, 55·51 miles/89·33 km.
1 Ken Johnson, USA (Ralt RT5-VW), 40m 59·73s, 81·243 mph/130·748 km/h.
2 Steve Bren, USA (Ralt RT5-VW), 41m 08·85s.
3 John Stephanus, USA (Ralt RT5-VW), 33 laps.
4 Dave Kudrave, USA (Ralt RT5-VW), 33.
5 Ted Prappas, USA (Ralt RT5-VW), 33.
6 Cary Bren, USA (Ralt RT5-VW), 33.
7 Mike Groff, USA (Ralt RT5-VW), 33; 8 Jeff MacPherson, USA (Ralt RT5-VW), 33; 9 Mike Hooper, USA (Ralt RT5-VW), 33; 10 Didier Theys, B (Martini MK47-VW), 33.
Fastest lap: Johnson, 1m 08·643s, 88·312 mph/142·12 km/h.
Championship points: 1 Johnson, 68; 2 Groff, 53; 3 Jones, 49; 4 Bren (Steve), 45; 5 Prappas, 41; 6 Stephanus, 41.

ROBERT BOSCH/VW SUPER VEE RACE, Burke Lakefront Airport Circuit, Cleveland, Ohio, United States of America, 7 July. Robert Bosch/VW Super Vee Championship, round 6. 25 laps of the 2·485-mile/3·999-km circuit, 62·13 miles/99·98 km.
1 Jeff Andretti, USA (Ralt RT5-VW), 32m 19·01s, 115·11 mph/185·25 km/h.
2 Davy Jones, USA (Ralt RT5-VW), 32m 28·34s.
3 Jeff MacPherson, USA (Ralt RT5-VW), 25 laps.
4 Didier Theys, B (Martini MK47-VW), 25.
5 Cary Bren, USA (Ralt RT5-VW), 25.
6 Ken Johnson, USA (Ralt RT5-VW), 25.
7 Gary Rubio, USA (Ralt RT5-VW), 25; 8 Ted Prappas, USA (Ralt RT5-VW), 25; 9 Matt McBride, USA (Ralt RT5-VW), 25; 10 Kim Campbell, USA (Anson SA6-VW), 25 (penalised 5 places for passing under yellow flag).
Fastest lap: Not given.
Championship points: 1 Johnson, 78; 2 Jones, 67; 3 Groff, 53; 4 Bren (Cary), 51; 5 Prappas, 49; 6 Bren (Steve), 46.

ROBERT BOSCH/VW SUPER VEE RACE, Road America, Elkhart Lake, Wisconsin, United States of America, 4 August. Robert Bosch/VW Super Vee Championship, round 7. 15 laps of the 4·000-mile/6·437-km circuit, 60·00 miles/96·56 km.
1 Davy Jones, USA (Ralt RT5-VW), 32m 43·94s, 109·983 mph/177·000 km/h.
2 Cary Bren, USA (Ralt RT5-VW).
3 Jeff Andretti, USA (Ralt RT5-VW), 15 laps.
4 Jeff MacPherson, USA (Ralt RT5-VW), 15.
5 Ken Johnson, USA (Ralt RT5-VW), 15.
6 John Stephanus, USA (Ralt RT5-VW), 15.
7 Matt McBride, USA (Ralt RT5-VW), 15; 8 Dennis Vitolo, USA (Ralt RT5-VW), 15; 9 Richard Myhre, USA (Ralt RT5-VW), 15; 10 David Diem, USA (Ralt RT5-VW), 15.
Fastest lap: Jones, 2m 10·02s, 110·752 mph/178·238 km/h.
Championship points: 1 Johnson, 89; 2 Jones, 87; 3 Bren (Cary), 67; 4 Andretti, 59; 5 Prappas, 53; 6 Groff, 53.

ROBERT BOSCH/VW SUPER VEE RACE, Watkins Glen Grand Prix Circuit, New York, United States of America, 25 August. Robert Bosch/VW Super Vee Championship, round 8. 17 laps of the 3·377-mile/5·435-km circuit, 57·41 miles/92·40 km.
1 Didier Theys, B (Martini MK47-VW), 31m 14·378s, 110·262 mph/177·449 km/h.
2 Cary Bren, USA (Ralt RT5-VW), 31m 29·851s.
3 Mike Groff, USA (Ralt RT5-VW), 17 laps.
4 Ken Johnson, USA (Ralt RT5-VW), 17.
5 Steve Bren, USA (Ralt RT5-VW), 17.
6 Ted Prappas, USA (Ralt RT5-VW), 17.
7 Richard Myhre, USA (Ralt RT5-VW), 17; 8 Kim Campbell, USA (Anson SA6-VW), 17; 9 Gary Rubio, USA (Ralt RT5-VW), 17; 10 Dennis Vitolo, USA (Ralt RT5-VW), 17.
Fastest lap: Theys, 1m 49·220s, 111·309 mph/179·134 km/h.
Championship points: 1 Johnson, 101; 2 Jones, 87; 3 Bren (Cary), 83; 4 Groff, 67; 5 Prappas, 63; 6 Andretti, 59.

ROBERT BOSCH/VW SUPER VEE RACE, Mid-Ohio Sports Car Course, Lexington, Ohio, United States of America, 1 September. Robert Bosch/VW Super Vee Championship, round 9. 25 laps of the 2·400-mile/3·863-km circuit, 60·00 miles/96·58 km.
1 Mike Groff, USA (Ralt RT5-VW), 36m 09·430s, 99·565 mph/160·234 km/h.
2 Jeff MacPherson, USA (Ralt RT5-VW), 36m 15·310s.
3 Didier Theys, B (Martini MK47-VW), 25 laps.
4 Jeff Andretti, USA (Ralt RT5-VW), 25.
5 Ken Johnson, USA (Ralt RT5-VW), 25.
6 Ted Prappas, USA (Ralt RT5-VW), 25.
7 Cary Bren, USA (Ralt RT5-VW), 25; 8 Matt McBride, USA (Ralt RT5-VW), 25; 9 Mike Hooper,

USA (Ralt RT5-VW), 25; 10 Dave Kudrave, USA (Ralt RT5-VW), 25.
Fastest lap: Davy Jones, USA (Ralt RT5-VW), 1m 25·570s, 100·970 mph/162·495 km/h (record).
Championship points: 1 Johnson, 112; 2 Bren (Cary), 92; 3 Jones and Groff, 87; 5 Prappas, 73; 6 Andretti, 71.

ROBERT BOSCH/VW SUPER VEE RACE, Sanair Superspeedway, Quebec, Canada, 8 September. Robert Bosch/VW Super Vee Championship, round 10. 72 laps of the 0·826-mile/1·329-km circuit, 59·47 miles/95·69 km.
1 Mike Groff, USA (Ralt RT5-VW), 29m 42·102s, 119·92 mph/192·99 km/h.
2 Davy Jones, USA (Ralt RT5-VW), 29m 42·302s.
3 Ken Johnson, USA (Ralt RT5-VW), 72 laps.
4 Cary Bren, USA (Ralt RT5-VW), 71.
5 Steve Bren, USA (Ralt RT5-VW), 71.
6 Jeff Andretti, USA (Ralt RT5-VW), 71.
7 Didier Theys, B (Martini MK47-VW), 71; 8 Ted Prappas, USA (Ralt RT5-VW), 71; 9 Matt McBride, USA (Ralt RT5-VW), 71; 10 Richard Myhre, USA (Ralt RT5-VW), 70.
Fastest lap: Jones, 23·925s, 124·063 mph/199·660 km/h.
Championship points: 1 Johnson, 126; 2 Groff, 107; 3 Bren (Cary), 104; 4 Jones, 103; 5 Andretti and Prappas, 81.

ROBERT BOSCH/VW SUPER VEE RACE, Laguna Seca Raceway, California, United States of America, 6 October. Robert Bosch/VW Super Vee Championship, round 11. 33 laps of the 1·900-mile/3·056 km circuit, 62·70 miles/100·85 km.
1 Davy Jones, USA (Ralt RT5-VW), 34m 07·140s, 110·261 mph/177·447 km/h.
2 Didier Theys, B (Martini MK47-VW), 34m 09·790s.
3 Cary Bren, USA (Ralt RT5-VW), 33 laps.
4 Jeff MacPherson, USA (Ralt RT5-VW), 33.
5 Jeff Andretti, USA (Ralt RT5-VW), 33.
6 Mike Groff, USA (Ralt RT5-VW), 33.
7 Steve Bren, USA (Ralt RT5-VW), 33; 8 Hans-Peter Pandur, A (Ralt RT5-VW), 33; 9 Matt McBride, USA (Ralt RT5-VW), 33; 10 Ken Johnson, USA (Ralt RT5-VW), 33.
Fastest lap: Theys, 1m 01·360s, 111·473 mph/179·398 km/h.
Championship points: 1 Johnson, 132; 2 Jones, 123; 3 Bren (Cary), 118; 4 Groff, 117; 5 Andretti, 92; 6 Prappas, 86.

ROBERT BOSCH/VW SUPER VEE RACE, Phoenix International Raceway, Arizona, United States of America, 13 October. Robert Bosch/VW Super Vee Championship, round 12. 60 laps of the 1·000-mile/1·609-km circuit, 60·00 miles/96·54 km.
1 Jeff Andretti, USA (Ralt RT5-VW), 35m 31·560s, 101·334 mph/163·081 km/h.
2 Davy Jones, USA (Ralt RT3-VW), 35m 31·600s.
3 Mike Groff, USA (Ralt RT5-VW), 60 laps.
4 Ken Johnson, USA (Ralt RT5-VW), 60.
5 Jeff MacPherson, USA (Ralt RT5-VW), 60.
6 Steve Bren, USA (Ralt RT5-VW), 60.
7 John Stephanus, USA (Ralt RT5-VW), 60; 8 Mike Hooper, USA (Ralt RT5-VW), 60; 9 Gary Rubio, USA (Ralt RT5-VW), 60; 10 Didier Theys, B (Martini MK47-VW), 60.
Fastest lap: Jones, 26·18s, 137·878 mph/221·893 km/h.

Final Championship points
1	Ken Johnson, USA	144
2	Davy Jones, USA	139
3	Mike Groff, USA	131
4	Cary Bren, USA	118
5	Jeff Andretti, USA	112
6	Jeff MacPherson, USA	91

7 Steve Bren, USA, 87; 8 Didier Theys, B, 86; 9 Ted Prappas, USA, 86; 10 Matt McBride, USA, 70; 11 John Stephanus, USA, 60; 12 Mike Hooper, USA, 44; 13 Gary Rubio, USA, 44; 14 Hans-Peter Pandur, A, 41; 15 Dave Kudrave, USA, 32.